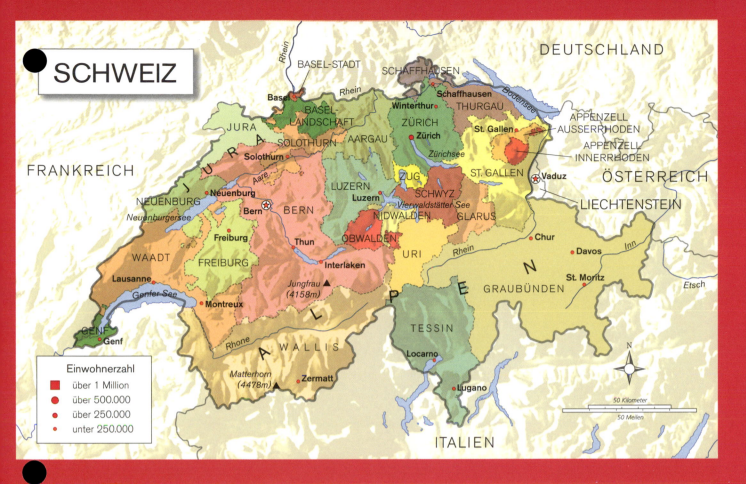

SCHWEIZ

Einwohnerzahl
- ■ über 1 Million
- ● über 500.000
- ● über 250.000
- • unter 250.000

DEUTSCHLAND
FRANKREICH
ÖSTERREICH
LIECHTENSTEIN
ITALIEN

BASEL-STADT
Basel
BASEL-LANDSCHAFT
JURA
SOLOTHURN
Solothurn
NEUENBURG
Neuenburg
Bern
BERN
AARGAU
LUZERN
Luzern
ZUG
SCHWYZ
NIDWALDEN
OBWALDEN
URI
GLARUS
SCHAFFHAUSEN
Schaffhausen
Winterthur
THURGAU
ZÜRICH
Zürich
Zürichsee
ST. GALLEN
St. Gallen
APPENZELL AUSSERRHODEN
APPENZELL INNERRHODEN
Vaduz
Chur
Davos
St. Moritz
GRAUBÜNDEN
A L P E N
WAADT
Lausanne
FREIBURG
Freiburg
Thun
Interlaken
Jungfrau (4158m)
Montreux
Genf
GENF
Genfer See
Neuenburgersee
Rhone
WALLIS
Matterhorn (4478m)
Zermatt
TESSIN
Locarno
Lugano
Rhein
Rhein
Aare
Vierwaldstätter See
Rhein
Inn
Etsch

50 Kilometer
50 Meilen
N

ÖSTERREICH

Einwohnerzahl
- ■ über 1 Million
- ● über 500.000
- ● über 250.000
- • unter 250.000

TSCHECHIEN
DEUTSCHLAND
SLOWAKEI
NIEDERÖSTERREICH
Krems
WIEN
Wien
St. Pölten
Linz
Wels
Steyr
Eisenstadt
Neusiedler See
OBERÖSTERREICH
Attersee
Traunsee
Salzburg
Wolfgangsee
St. Wolfgang
STEIERMARK
BURGENLAND
Graz
UNGARN
Bregenz
VORARLBERG
Kitzbühel
Innsbruck
TIROL
A L P E N
SALZBURG
Salzach
Badgastein
Mur
Enns
Donau
Donau
Großglockner (3797m)
Lienz
TIROL
Alto Adige (Südtirol)
Drau
KÄRNTEN
Wörther See
Villach
Klagenfurt
Bodensee
LIECHTENSTEIN
SCHWEIZ
Etsch
Inn
ITALIEN
SLOWENIEN
KROATIEN
Drau
N

50 Kilometer
50 Meilen

mygermanlab *Hallo!*

Part of the award-winning MyLanguageLabs suite of online learning and assessment systems for basic language courses, MyGermanLab brings together – in one convenient, easily navigable site – a wide array of language-learning tools and resources, including an interactive version of the *Treffpunkt Deutsch* student text, an online Student Activities Manual, and all materials from the audio and video programs. Chapter Practice Tests, tutorials, and English grammar Readiness Checks personalize instruction to meet the unique needs of individual students. Instructors can use the system to make assignments, set grading parameters, listen to student-created audio recordings, and provide feedback on student work. MyGermanLab can be packaged with the text at a substantial savings. For more information, visit us online at http://www.mylanguagelabs.com/books.html

A GUIDE TO *TREFFPUNKT DEUTSCH* ICONS

Hallo!	MyGermanLab	This icon indicates that additional activities for speaking and pronunciation, and additional resources for culture are available in MyGermanLab.
	Text Audio Program	This icon indicates that recorded material to accompany *Treffpunkt Deutsch* is available in MyGermanLab (www.mylanguagelabs.com), on audio CD, or on the Companion Website (www.pearsonhighered.com/treffpunkt)
	Pair Activity	This icon indicates that the activity is designed to be done by students working in pairs.
	Group Activity	This icon indicates that the activity is designed to be done by students working in small groups or as a whole class.
	Video icon	This icon indicates that a video episode is available for the video that accompanies the *Treffpunkt Deutsch* program. The video is available on DVD and in MyGermanLab.
	Student Activities Manual	This icon indicates that there are practice activities available in the *Treffpunkt Deutsch* Student Activities Manual. The activities may be found either in the printed version of the manual or in the interactive version available through MyGermanLab. Activity numbers are indicated in the text for ease of reference.

Treffpunkt Deutsch
GRUNDSTUFE

SIXTH EDITION

Margaret Gonglewski

The George Washington University

Beverly Moser

Appalachian State University

Cornelius Partsch

Western Washington University

E. Rosemarie Widmaier

Fritz T. Widmaier

PEARSON

Boston   Columbus   Indianapolis   New York   San Francisco   Upper Saddle River
Amsterdam   Cape Town   Dubai   London   Madrid   Milan   Munich   Paris   Montreal   Toronto
Delhi   Mexico City   Sao Paulo   Sydney   Hong Kong   Seoul   Singapore   Taipei   Tokyo

Executive Acquisitions Editor: *Rachel McCoy*
Editorial Assistant: *Lindsay Miglionica*
Publishing Coordinator: *Regina Rivera*
Executive Marketing Manager: *Kris Ellis-Levy*
Marketing Assistant: *Michele Marchese*
Senior Managing Editor for Product Development:
  Mary Rottino
Associate Managing Editor: *Janice Stangel*
Production Project Manager: *Manuel Echevarria*
Executive Editor, MyLanguageLabs: *Bob Hemmer*
Senior Media Editor: *Samantha Alducin*
MyLanguageLabs Development Editor: *Bill Bliss*

Development Editor: *Karen Storz*
Procurement Manager: *Mary Fischer*
Senior Operations Specialist: *Alan Fisher*
Senior Art Director: *Maria Lange*
Cover Designer: *DePinho Design*
Interior Designer: *PreMediaGlobal USA, Inc.*
Composition: *PreMediaGlobal USA, Inc.*
Printer/Binder: *RR Donnelley/Willard*
Cover Printer: *Lehigh/Phoenix Color*
Publisher: *Phil Miller*
This book was set in 10.5/13 Bembo.

Library of Congress Cataloging-in-Publication Data
Gonglewski, Margaret.
  Treffpunkt Deutsch: Grundstufe/Margaret Gonglewski, Beverly Moser, Cornelius Partsch. — 6th ed.
    p. cm.
  Text in English and German.
  Includes bibliographical references and index.
  ISBN-13: 978-0-205-78278-9 (alk. paper)
  ISBN-10: 0-205-78278-7 (alk. paper)
  1. German language—Grammar.   2. German language—Textbooks for foreign speakers—English.
I. Partsch, Cornelius, 1967–   II. Moser, Beverly.   III. Title.
  PF3112.W5 2012
  438.2'421—dc23

2011049065

Printed in the United States of America
10 9 8 7 6 5 4 3 2

ISBN 10: 0-205-78278-7
ISBN 13: 978-0-205-78278-9

Brief Contents //////////////////

PREFACE   xxi

ERSTE KONTAKTE   1

KAPITEL 1   Jahraus, jahrein   16

KAPITEL 2   Freunde   54

KAPITEL 3   Familie   84

KAPITEL 4   Alltagsleben   120

KAPITEL 5   Freizeit – Ferienzeit   154

KAPITEL 6   Ein Blick zurück   190

KAPITEL 7   Feste und Feiertage   224

KAPITEL 8   Wohnen   258

KAPITEL 9   Andere Länder, andere Sitten   290

KAPITEL 10   Lust auf Lesen   322

KAPITEL 11   Geschichte und Gegenwart   354

KAPITEL 12   So ist das Leben   382

ANHANG

- Information Gap Activities   A1
- Expressions for the Classroom   A12
- German Grammatical Terms   A13
- Useful Word Sets   A14
- Grammatical Tables   A21
- Principal Parts of Irregular and Mixed Verbs   A28
- German-English Vocabulary   A32
- English-German Vocabulary   A68
- Index   A91

Scope & Sequence ///////////////

Kommunikationsziele und Kultur	Sprache im Kontext
ERSTE KONTAKTE xxxii • Greeting someone and responding to greetings • Introducing yourself • Making phone calls • Addressing letters • Saying good-bye **KULTUR** • Affordable education at German universities 2 • Social implications of **du, ihr,** and **Sie** 4 • A first look at the German-speaking cultures 6 • German words used in English 13	• Semesterticket 1 • Beim Studentenwerk 1 • Im Hörsaal 2 • Im Konferenzsaal 4

KAPITEL 1
 	
JAHRAUS, JAHREIN 16
• Talking about . . .
  • the weather and the seasons
  • student life
  • everyday activities and objects
  • colors
  • nationality
 	
KULTUR
• Welcome to the German-speaking countries 20
• Studying at the university 27
• About university life 34
• Why German and English are similar: The Angles and Saxons 48
	Vorschau
	• Eine Wetterkarte 17
	• Der Tag beginnt 17
	• Semesterbeginn 18
	
	Video-Treff
	• Das bin ich 36
	
	Zusammenschau
	• Hören: Beim Auslandsamt 44
	• Schreiben und Sprechen:
	  • Das bin ich 45
	  • Wer ist das? 45
	• Lesen: Eine Schweizerin, eine deutsche Familie und zwei Österreicher 46

Strukturen im Kontext	Wörter: Bedeutung, Form, Aussprache
• **Du, ihr,** and **Sie** 4 • The alphabet 8 • The numbers from 0 to 1000 9	**Zur Aussprache** • **ä, ö, ü** 12 • **ß, ch, v, w, z** 12 **Sprachnotizen** • Some distinctive features of written German 3 • Saying e-mail and Web addresses 10 **Wortschatz** 14
• Nouns: gender and definite articles 24 • Plural forms: definite articles and nouns 25 • The indefinite articles **ein** and **kein** 27 • Personal pronouns: subject forms 38 • The present tense of **sein** 40 • The verb: infinitive and present tense 41 **Word order** • Position of the verb in yes/no questions 28 • Position of the verb in information questions 29 • Position of the verb in statements 30 • Expressions of time and place 33 • Position of **nicht** 34	**Wörter unter der Lupe** • Cognates 48 **Zur Aussprache** • German **ei** and **ie** 49 **Sprachnotizen** • Verb forms in English and German 31 • The present tense to express future time 43 • **lernen** vs. **studieren** 52 **Wortschatz 1** 22 **Wortschatz 2** 50

Kommunikationsziele und Kultur	Sprache im Kontext
KAPITEL 2 **FREUNDE 54** • Talking about . . . • friends • hobbies and leisure activities • clothing and possessions • Expressing likes, dislikes, and preferences • Telling time • Describing people, places, and things **KULTUR** • English loan words in German 57 • The Black Forest and the cuckoo clock 64 • Liechtenstein 71	**Vorschau** • Uni-Sport 55 • Freunde 56 **Video-Treff** • Freundschaften 69 **Zusammenschau** • Hören: Freundinnen 76 • Schreiben und Sprechen: • Meine beste Freundin/ mein bester Freund 77 • Deine beste Freundin/ dein bester Freund 77 • Lesen: Eine Website für soziales Netzwerken 78
KAPITEL 3 **FAMILIE 84** • Talking about . . . • family • shopping and other activities • useful everyday objects • occupations • Expressing preferences and favorites • Describing people, places, and things **KULTUR** • Austria 88 • Family policies in Germany and Austria 110	**Vorschau** • Ein Familienauto? 85 • Verwandte 85 **Video-Treff** • Meine Familie 100 **Zusammenschau** • Hören: Wie erkennen wir einander? 110 • Schreiben und Sprechen: • Wer ist das? 111 • Meine Familie 112 • Lesen: Mozart, das musikalische Wunderkind Österreichs 113

Strukturen im Kontext

- The verb **haben** 60
- Verb + **gern** 61
- Verb + **lieber** 62
- Telling time 62
- Expressions of time 65
- The subject 67
- The nominative case 68
- The interrogative pronouns **wer** and **was** 68
- **Der-**words in the nominative case 70
- **Ein-**words in the nominative case 71
- Nominative endings of adjectives
  - preceded by **der-**words 73
  - preceded by **ein-**words 74
  - unpreceded 75

Wörter: Bedeutung, Form, Aussprache

Wörter unter der Lupe
- More on cognates 80

Zur Aussprache
- The vowels **a, e, i, o,** and **u** 80

Sprachnotizen
- **gern haben** 61
- More on colloquial time expressions 65
- The subject completion 74

Wortschatz 1 58

Wortschatz 2 82

- The direct object 94
- The accusative case 94
- The interrogative pronoun **wen** 96
- **Der-**words in the accusative case 97
- **Ein-**words in the accusative case 98
- Adjective endings in the accusative case 101
- Verbs with stem-vowel changes in the present tense 105

Word order
- More on the position of **nicht** 104

Wörter unter der Lupe
- More cognates 115
- Words as chameleons: **wie** 115

Zur Aussprache
- The diphthongs 116

Sprachnotizen
- Expressing *favorite* 87
- Expressing time with the accusative case 98
- Omission of the indefinite article 100
- The expression **es gibt** 106

Wortschatz 1 92

Wortschatz 2 117

Kommunikationsziele und Kultur	Sprache im Kontext

KAPITEL 4
 	
ALLTAGSLEBEN 120
• Talking about . . .
  • daily routines
  • food and meals
  • abilities, necessities, and obligations
• Expressing permission, wishes, and likes
• Telling someone what to do
• Making requests and giving advice
• Giving reasons and conditions
 	
KULTUR
• Meal traditions in the German-speaking countries
  • Breakfast 122
  • Other meals 146
• Switzerland 124
• Railways in the German-speaking countries 137
	Vorschau
	• Wie frühstückt man? 121
	• So bin ich eben 122
	
	Video-Treff
	• Ein typischer Tag 139
	
	Zusammenschau
	• Hören: Ein typischer Tag in Lisas Leben 147
	• Schreiben und Sprechen:
	  • Ein Interview 147
	  • Das ist mein Tag 148
	• Lesen: Schweizer Innovation: Die Firma Victorinox 149

KAPITEL 5
 	
FREIZEIT – FERIENZEIT 154
• Making plans . . .
  • for a vacation
  • for a day off
• Expressing personal opinions and tastes
• Comparing qualities and characteristics
• Talking about . . .
  • whom and what you know
  • events in the past
 	
KULTUR
• Affordable travel 158
• Soccer 166
• Paid vacations in North America and Europe 172
• Munich 176
• South Tyrol 181
	Vorschau
	• Am Grundlsee 155
	• Ferienpläne 156
	
	Video-Treff
	• Ferienzeit 173
	
	Zusammenschau
	• Hören: Morgen haben wir keine Vorlesungen 182
	• Schreiben und Sprechen:
	  • Mein Kalender 182
	  • Gehst du mit? 183
	• Lesen: Ludwig II. von Bayern und seine Märchenschlösser 184

Strukturen im Kontext

- Modal verbs 128
- **Können, müssen,** and **wollen** 128
- **Dürfen, sollen,** and **mögen** 129
- **Möchte** versus **mögen** 130
- Omission of the infinitive after modal verbs 131
- Separable-prefix verbs 132
- Verb-noun and verb-verb combinations 136
- **Sie-, ihr-,** and **du-**imperatives 140

Word order
- Position of **nicht** with modal verbs 131
- Position of separable-prefix verbs with modals 134
- Position of the verb in independent and dependent clauses 144

Wörter: Bedeutung, Form, Aussprache

Wörter unter der Lupe
- **denn** versus **dann** 150

Zur Aussprache
- The vowels **ä, ö,** and **ü** 151

Sprachnotizen
- The pronoun **man** 122
- More about separable prefixes 132
- Position of **nicht** with separable-prefix verbs 134
- Flavoring particles and **bitte** in imperative sentences 141
- Word order when the dependent clause comes first 145

Wortschatz 1 126

Wortschatz 2 152

- Personal pronouns in the accusative case 162
- Accusative prepositions 164
- The comparative 167
- Comparative adjectives before nouns 168
- The superlative 170
- Superlative adjectives before nouns 170
- **Wissen** 177
- The simple past of **sein, haben,** and the modal verbs 178

Word order
- Object clauses introduced by **dass** 174
- Information questions as object clauses 175
- Yes/no questions as object clauses 175

Wörter unter der Lupe
- Predicting gender: the suffixes **-or, -ent, -er, -in, -ur, -ment, -(i)um, -chen, -lein** 186

Zur Aussprache
- German **ch** 187

Sprachnotizen
- Accusative prepositions in contractions 164
- **Dafür** and **dagegen** 166
- **Wissen** vs. **kennen** 178

Wortschatz 1 160

Wortschatz 2 188

Kommunikationsziele und Kultur	Sprache im Kontext

KAPITEL 6
 	
EIN BLICK ZURÜCK 190
• Describing past events . . .
  • in conversational situations
  • in personal narratives
• Talking about . . .
  • one's ancestors
  • education and job qualifications
• Describing someone's appearance
 	
KULTUR
• German roots in North America 194
• The German language in North America 206
	Vorschau
	• Ein deutscher Auswanderer 191
	• Ein deutscher Einwanderer sucht Arbeit 192
	
	Video-Treff
	• Mein erster Job 208
	
	Zusammenschau
	• Hören: Martin sucht einen Ferienjob 216
	• Sprechen: Was für Arbeitserfahrung haben Sie? 217
	• Lesen: Aus Christian Köchlings Tagebuch 218
	• Schreiben: Aus meinem Tagebuch 219

KAPITEL 7
 	
FESTE UND FEIERTAGE 224
• Talking about . . .
  • birthdays and holidays
  • buying and giving gifts
  • personal tastes and opinions
• Expressing congratulations, best wishes, and thanks
 	
KULTUR
• KaDeWe in Berlin 226
• Feste und Feiertage 228
• Parties and presents 236
	Vorschau
	• Eine Geburtstagskarte 225
	• Das Geburtstagsgeschenk 225
	• Beim KaDeWe 226
	
	Video-Treff
	• Mein bestes Geschenk 239
	
	Zusammenschau
	• Hören: Blumen zum Geburtstag 249
	• Sprechen: Im Blumengeschäft 250
	• Lesen: Glückwunschanzeigen 251
	• Schreiben: Die besten Glückwünsche 253

Strukturen im Kontext

- The perfect tense 198
  - Regular verbs 199
  - Irregular verbs 201
  - **Sein** as auxiliary 204
  - Verbs with separable prefixes 209
  - Verbs with inseparable prefixes 211
  - Mixed verbs 211
- Ordinal numbers 212
- Dates 213
- **Hin** and **her** 214

Word order
- Position of auxiliary verb and past participle 198
- Position of auxiliary verb and past participle in a dependent clause 199
- Position of **nicht** in the perfect 200

Wörter: Bedeutung, Form, Aussprache

Wörter unter der Lupe
- Predicting gender: the suffix **-ung** 220
- Giving language color: expressions using names of parts of the body 220

Zur Aussprache
- German **l** 221

Sprachnotizen
- The perfect tense of **sein** and **haben** 205
- *Away from* and *toward* in colloquial German 215
- The expression **Bitte schön!** 216

Wortschatz 1 196

Wortschatz 2 222

- The dative case: the indirect object 232
- The interrogative pronoun in the dative case 233
- Personal pronouns in the dative case 234
- Dative verbs 237
- The dative case with adjectives 237
- The dative case in idioms 238
- The dative prepositions 241
- Dative prepositions in contractions 243
- **Da**-compounds 244
- **Nach** versus **zu; aus** versus **von** 244
- The preposition **seit** 246
- Adjective endings in the dative case 248

Word order
- Sequence of objects 236

Wörter unter der Lupe
- Predicting gender: infinitives used as nouns 254
- Giving language color: expressions using food vocabulary 255

Zur Aussprache
- German **r** 255

Sprachnotizen
- Word order: time/manner/place 240
- Expressing congratulations, best wishes, or toasts with **zu** 253
- **Derselbe, dasselbe, dieselbe** 257

Wortschatz 1 230

Wortschatz 2 256

Kommunikationsziele und Kultur	Sprache im Kontext
KAPITEL 8	**Vorschau**
WOHNEN 258	• Mitbewohner gesucht! 259
• Talking about . . .	• Zimmersuche 260
• how and where you live	
• destination and location	**Video-Treff**
• possessions and relationships	• Mein Zuhause 273
• Finding a roommate	
• Finding a place to live	**Zusammenschau**
• Discussing the pros and cons of where you live	• Hören: Privathaus oder WG? 282
• Describing people, places, and things	• Schreiben und Sprechen:
	• Vorteile und Nachteile meiner Wohnsituation 282
KULTUR	• Verschiedene Wohnsituationen 283
• Student housing 262	• Lesen: Das Bauhaus 284
• Green living: **Recyceln** 271	
• Green living: **Regenerative Energien** 278	
KAPITEL 9	**Vorschau**
ANDERE LÄNDER, ANDERE SITTEN 290	• Vor dem Restaurant 291
• Talking about . . .	• Im Gasthaus 292
• cultural differences	
• personal grooming	**Video-Treff**
• Ordering a meal in a restaurant	• Was ich gern esse und trinke 306
• Describing people, places, and things	
	Zusammenschau
KULTUR	• Hören: Wandern macht hungrig 313
• Im Gasthaus 294	• Schreiben und Sprechen:
• Beim Schnellimbiss 307	• Ein Abendessen im Gasthof Fraundorfer 314
• Einkaufsgewohnheiten 312	• Wie war's? 315
	• Lesen: Robert Kalina und der Euro 316

Strukturen im Kontext

- A review of **wohin** and **wo** 266
- Two-case prepositions 267
- **Stellen, legen,** and **hängen** 268
- **Stehen, liegen,** and **hängen** 269
- More **da-**compounds 270
- German **an, auf, in,** and English *to* 272
- Two-case prepositions in time phrases 274
- The genitive case 278
- The interrogative pronoun **wessen** 279
- Adjective endings with the genitive case 281

Word order
- Infinitive phrases 275
- Infinitive phrases introduced by **um** 277

Wörter: Bedeutung, Form, Aussprache

Wörter unter der Lupe
- Compound nouns 286
- Giving language color: expressions using house and furniture vocabulary 287

Zur Aussprache
- German **s**-sounds: **st** and **sp** 287

Sprachnotizen
- Using **von** + dative instead of the genitive 281

Wortschatz 1 264

Wortschatz 2 288

- Reflexive pronouns in the accusative case 298
- Reflexive pronouns in the dative case 301
- Reflexive pronouns used to express *each other* 304
- Reflexive verbs 304
- Relative clauses and relative pronouns 308
- **N-**nouns 312

Wörter unter der Lupe
- Predicting gender: agent nouns 318
- Giving language color: more expressions using names of parts of the body 318

Zur Aussprache
- German **s**-sounds: voiced and voiceless **s** 319
- Contrasting German **s**-sounds 319

Sprachnotizen
- Using modal verbs in reflexive constructions 300

Wortschatz 1 296

Wortschatz 2 320

Kommunikationsziele und Kultur	Sprache im Kontext

KAPITEL 10
 	
LUST AUF LESEN 322
• Telling stories
• Talking about...
  • history
  • your own past experiences
• Describing people, places, and things
 	
KULTUR
• Vom Buch zum E-Buch 326
• Zeitungen und Zeitschriften 337
• Die Brüder Grimm 349
	Vorschau
	• Der schlaue Student vom Paradies 323
	
	Video-Treff
	• Meine Lieblingslektüre 338
	
	Zusammenschau
	• Hören: Es allen recht machen 344
	• Schreiben und Sprechen:
	  • Ein neues Ende 346
	  • Wir erzählen eine neue Fabel 346
	• Lesen: Der Hase und der Igel 347

KAPITEL 11
 	
GESCHICHTE UND GEGENWART 354
• Talking about recent German history and current events
• Making resolutions
• Describing people, places, and things
• Expressing feelings and emotions
 	
KULTUR
• Die Berliner Mauer 357
• Kleine deutsche Chronik: 1918 bis heute 358
• Ethnische Gruppen und Nationalitäten in Deutschland 374
	Vorschau
	• Extrablatt: *Berliner Morgenpost* 355
	• 13. August 1961 355
	
	Video-Treff
	• So war's in der DDR 367
	
	Zusammenschau
	• Hören: Eine Radtour in den neuen Bundesländern 372
	• Schreiben und Sprechen:
	  • Ferienerlebnisse 373
	  • Besuch in Berlin, der Hauptstadt Deutschlands 373
	• Lesen: Go West! (aus *Zonenkinder*) 376

Strukturen im Kontext	Wörter: Bedeutung, Form, Aussprache

• The simple past tense 330
  • Regular verbs 330
  • Irregular verbs 332
  • Mixed verbs 333
• **Wann, als,** and **wenn** 336
• The relative pronoun as object of a preposition 340
• A review of adjective endings 342
  • Adjectives preceded by **der**-words 342
  • Adjectives preceded by **ein**-words 343
  • Unpreceded adjectives 344
	Wörter unter der Lupe
	• Words as chameleons: **als** 349
	• Giving language color: expressions using names of animals 350
	
	Zur Aussprache
	• German **f, v,** and **w** 351
	
	Sprachnotizen
	• The past perfect tense 324
	• The simple past of separable-prefix verbs 332
	• Principal parts of verbs 335
	• Contradicting negative statements or questions 348
	
	Wortschatz 1 328
	
	Wortschatz 2 352

• The passive voice 362 • Mentioning the agent in a passive sentence 365 • The past participle used as an adjective 366 • Special verb-preposition combinations 368 • **Wo-**compounds 371	**Wörter unter der Lupe** • Words as chameleons: **gleich** 378 • Predicting gender: the suffixes **-heit** and **-keit** 378 **Zur Aussprache** • The consonant clusters **pf** and **kn** 379 **Sprachnotizen** • Using **eigentlich** and **überhaupt** to intensify expressions 356 • The future tense 361 **Wortschatz 1** 360 **Wortschatz 2** 380

Kommunikationsziele und Kultur	Sprache im Kontext

KAPITEL 12
 	
SO IST DAS LEBEN 382
• Talking about . . .
  • relationships
  • equal rights for women and men
  • careers and family obligations
  • your dreams for the future
• Expressing feelings
• Expressing wishes, regrets, and polite requests and questions
• Asking for and giving advice
 	
KULTUR
• Frauen im 21. Jahrhundert 386
• Luxemburg 402
	Vorschau
	• Eve 383
	
	Video-Treff
	• Wenn ich im Lotto gewinnen würde 396
	
	Zusammenschau
	• Lesen: Meine Zukunft 403
	• Schreiben: Meine Zukunft 405
	• Hören: Karrieren 405
	• Sprechen
	  • Traumberufe der deutschen Jugend 406
	  • Unsere Traumberufe 407

ANHANG

Information Gap Activities A1
Expressions for the Classroom A12
German Grammatical Terms A13
Useful Word Sets A14
• Studienfächer A14
• Jobs und Berufe A14
• Hobbys und Sport A15
• Musikinstrumente A16
• Kleidungsstücke A16
• Accessoires A17
• Essen und Trinken A17
• Länder und Sprachen A18
• Persönliche Merkmale A19
• Höfliche Ausdrücke A20

Grammatical Tables A21
Principal Parts of Irregular and
  Mixed Verbs A28
German-English Vocabulary A32
English-German Vocabulary A68
Index A91

Strukturen im Kontext

- Present-time subjunctive 390
- **Würde** + infinitive 392
- The subjunctive in wishes and polite requests 394
- The subjunctive in polite questions 395
- Past-time subjunctive 397
- **Haben** and **sein** in past-time subjunctive 399
- Genitive prepositions 401

Wörter: Bedeutung, Form, Aussprache

Wörter unter der Lupe
- The adjective suffix **-los** 408
- The adjective suffix **-bar** 408

Zur Aussprache
- The glottal stop 409

Sprachnotizen
- **Kommen** and **gehen** in present-time subjunctive 395
- The relative pronoun in the genitive case 402

Wortschatz 1 388

Wortschatz 2 410

Preface //////////////////////////////

We are pleased to present you with the sixth edition of *Treffpunkt Deutsch,* an introductory program that takes a student-centered, communicative approach to teaching German. Since the first edition, *Treffpunkt Deutsch* has been carefully designed to enable students to use the language actively and successfully. The title itself reflects a major objective of the program: to transform the classroom into a **Treffpunkt,** a *meeting place,* where students get to know one another, as well as the German-speaking countries, by using German.

We are indebted to our loyal following of instructors and students from the previous five editions. The changes to the sixth edition stem from valuable feedback they provided and from the authors' commitment to provide an up-to-date view of the German-speaking world and a compelling way to reach today's students. We hope that new users of this program will become equally committed to the pedagogy of *Treffpunkt Deutsch*.

What's New in This Edition?

- The book's **new design** provides a contemporary look and feel, including easy-to-use grammar charts and eye-catching treatment for Student Notes and *Lerntipps.*

- **All chapters now open with realia** (ads, menus, campus posters, and more) with accompanying tasks to capture students' interest up front. The authentic materials of the new *Vorschau* sections are graphically stimulating and provide a fun and culturally relevant way to start each chapter and introduce chapter themes.

- **A brand new *Kultur* section in the opening chapter, *Erste Kontakte,*** highlights people, places, and products of the German-speaking cultures to whet students' appetite for learning more about these cultures and their language.

- **All *Kultur* sections have been extensively revised** to include up-to-date views of a changing Europe. New culture topics include the use of English words in German, green living in the German-speaking countries, German inventions in communication technology, and young women in today's society. New activities encourage students to interact more fully with the cultural material in each chapter.

- **The culture-focused *Infobox* sections have been revised and updated.** New information on everyday life was added to encourage students to consider studying abroad in a German-speaking country.

- **New readings expose students to an even wider variety of genres** popular among college students, such as song lyrics and a social-networking page. These readings grab students' attention while exposing them to language and culture in the modern context they are looking for.

- Approximately **25% of the photographs in the book are new,** providing fresh views of contemporary scenes from the German-speaking countries. New exercises have also been added to encourage students to engage actively with the language that appears in photos throughout the text.

- The authentic *Treffpunkt Deutsch* **video plays a more central role** in the sixth edition and is integrated earlier in each chapter. The viewing activities provide brief, manageable encounters with authentic speech from the target culture.

- **Grammar explanations are even more concise and accessible,** and some non-essential elements of grammar for the introductory level have been de-emphasized.

- The **grammar in some chapters has been re-sequenced** for optimal teaching, moving from easier to more challenging concepts (e.g., presentation of the imperative forms, negation, etc.).

- Many **grammar exercises have been streamlined** to focus students' attention on fewer new forms at once. This facilitates comprehension and leads to a greater level of accuracy and comfort in communication.

- **Vocabulary sections have been updated** to reflect new chapter content and a more contemporary focus.

These important changes encourage students to interact more intensively with material in German and begin making meaning from the first day of instruction. This develops strong language-learning strategies that students can transfer to new contexts and interactions.

Hallmark Features of *Treffpunkt Deutsch*

Treffpunkt Deutsch builds students' ability to communicate in German in many ways: to listen to and understand spoken German and read short texts, to interact with others in brief interchanges (including with native speakers), and to write simple texts that convey an individual point of view.

- In **speaking and writing activities,** students are guided from contextualized, form-focused exercises to more open-ended activities in which they express individual preferences and viewpoints. Speaking and writing tasks synthesize material, add depth to chapter content, and provide opportunities to communicate in real-life contexts.

- **Listening practice** is also provided in stages, ranging from highly structured to completely unscripted excerpts of spoken language. The *Treffpunkt Deutsch* video puts students face-to-face with real speakers from the target culture, adding both visual and cultural interest to listening comprehension activities.

- **Reading practice** encourages students to negotiate meaning in the target language in realia and informational texts, as well as short literary excerpts, including poetry and fairy tales. These varied genres respond to multiple learning styles and interests and expose students to a broad range of models of the target language.

- **Vocabulary development** is crucial to this communication-focused program. *Treffpunkt Deutsch* provides two vocabulary lists in each chapter, organized according to parts of speech. Within these sections, words are grouped semantically. The lists are followed by exercises *(Wörter im Kontext)* that reinforce the new lexical items and support growing communication abilities even at the very beginning level.

- **Engagement with culture** is a cornerstone of *Treffpunkt Deutsch.* The program highlights significant events and accomplishments as well as the daily life of those living in the German-speaking countries today. *Kultur* and *Infobox* sections provide insights into the ways our cultures are similar yet different, and examine differences between German, Austrian, and Swiss cultures.

- **Pronunciation practice** is linked with vocabulary learning in the unique *Wort, Sinn und Klang* section at the end of each chapter. The fun activities help students develop strong pronunciation skills that enhance their ability to communicate effectively. Direct comparisons to English help students build on what they know.

The process-oriented, student-centered approach in *Treffpunkt Deutsch* is not merely aligned with The National Standards for Foreign Language Education (*Standards for Foreign Language Learning; Preparing for the 21st Century*). The "Five C's" of the National Standards – Communication, Culture, Connections, Comparisons, and Communities – have guided our work, and the three modes of communication (interpersonal, interpretive, presentational) provide a framework for activities throughout *Treffpunkt Deutsch.* Through the various authentic materials, students encounter the cultures of the German-speaking countries and learn to communicate in meaningful, real-life contexts. They are encouraged to draw cross-cultural comparisons and to connect their study of German language and culture with other disciplines and experiences. Opportunities for students to interact with German-speaking communities are suggested in annotations to instructors, and students gain practice with these in new Internet-based tasks and realia incorporated throughout.

Organization of *Treffpunkt Deutsch*

Treffpunkt Deutsch consists of an introduction (*Erste Kontakte*) and twelve full-length chapters. *Erste Kontakte* is the warm-up for the course. Each of the twelve subsequent chapters focuses on a theme. Each chapter follows a consistent structure with four main sections, *Vorschau, Kommunikation und Formen, Zusammenschau*, and *Wort, Sinn und Klang*, with additional cultural information integrated throughout to promote enjoyable and engaging language learning.

- **Vorschau.** Each chapter opens with engaging realia (such as a poster or an ad), followed by language models (such as dialogues), to introduce vocabulary and structures connected to the chapter theme in natural, idiomatic German. Follow-up activities check comprehension and encourage immediate use of new vocabulary and forms.

- **Kultur.** These sections present a cultural reading related to the chapter theme along with an activity that encourages students to engage with the topic. Many activities are based on authentic materials, ranging from recipes to short literary texts. *Kultur* sections are presented entirely in German in the last four chapters.

- **Kommunikation und Formen.** Clear, concise, and directed to the student, grammar explanations focus on basic structures essential to communication. The accompanying exercises, often based on photos or colorful line drawings, move from guided, contextualized practice to open-ended, personalized expression.

- **Video-Treff.** The *Treffpunkt Deutsch* video, now positioned at the midpoint in all chapters, presents dynamic, on-the-scene interviews with young Germans. The video provides ample visual context to support comprehension of the un-scripted language. This offers a direct window into German-speaking cultures at a level manageable to introductory students.

- **Infoboxen.** Strategically placed throughout the text, *Infoboxen* highlight additional cultural information. They enrich students' understanding of daily life and cultural practices of the German-speaking countries.

- **Zusammenschau.** Activities in this section synthesize the development of students' communication in all modes. The four skills and the vocabulary and grammar of the chapter are practiced in a unified, content-rich communicative context. *Hören* hones listening skills for global and detailed understanding. The *Schreiben* and *Sprechen* sections further contextualize the chapter theme in guided activities to develop solid writing and speaking skills. *Lesen* spotlights some famous and some ordinary people in the German-speaking countries through a variety of genres, including a social-networking site, while the last three chapters feature literary texts.

- **Sprachnotizen.** These brief sections help students express themselves better in German by providing discourse strategies, idiomatic features of colloquial German, and short grammar points relevant to the chapter's communicative goals.

- **Wort, Sinn und Klang.** With an eye to enhancing vocabulary learning, *Wörter unter der Lupe* takes a closer look at words by discussing cognates, words that change their meaning in different contexts, word families, compound words, suffixes that signal gender, and idiomatic expressions. *Zur Aussprache* rounds off this section with engaging pronunciation activities.

- **Wortschatz 1** and **Wortschatz 2.** Chapter vocabulary appears in two lists containing useful, high-frequency words related to the chapter theme. The lists are followed by *Wörter im Kontext* exercises that encourage students to use the new words in a variety of contexts.

Other Program Components

Student Resources

Student Activities Manual (SAM). The Student Activities Manual provides meaningful and communicative writing, listening, and speaking practice, incorporating the vocabulary and structures introduced in each chapter and offering additional skill-building activities. The SAM is available in the traditional paper format and in an electronic format via **MyGermanLab™**.

Answer Key for the Student Activities Manual. This Answer Key is available for optional inclusion in course packages; it includes answers for all discrete and short answer exercises in the SAM.

Audio for the Student Activities Manual. Students and instructors have access to the audio recordings for the SAM on audio CD, on the Companion Website, and on **MyGermanLab™**.

Treffpunkt Deutsch Video. The well loved _Treffpunkt Deutsch_ **Video,** featuring unscripted interviews with young native speakers in the places where they live, work and play, can be accessed on DVD or online through **MyGermanLab™**.

Audio for the Text. All audio materials from the text, including materials from the **Vorschau, Wortschatz, Zusammenschau,** and **Zur Aussprache** sections, are available on the **MyGermanLab™,** and much of the audio is available on CD and on the Companion Website.

Instructor Resources

Annotated Instructor's Edition (AIE). The extensive, insightful marginal notes make the AIE an indispensible resource for the novice and experienced instructor alike. They offer warm-up activities, cultural information, and suggestions for using and expanding activities and materials in the textbook. Instructor's annotations also include the scripts and answer keys for listening sections for ease in teaching.

Instructor's Resource Manual. The IRM provides _Treffpunkt Deutsch_ instructors with an extensive array of resources, including sample syllabi for one-, two- and three-term course sequences, along with numerous sample lesson plans. The IRM is available in downloadable format via the **Instructor's Resource Center** and **MyGermanLab™**.

Testing Program. A highly flexible testing program allows instructors to customize tests by selecting the modules they wish to use or changing individual items. This complete testing program, available in a downloadable electronic format via the **Instructor's Resource Center** and **MyGermanLab™**, includes quizzes, chapter tests, and comprehensive examinations that test listening, reading, and writing skills as well as cultural knowledge.

Audio for the Testing Program. All listening tests are recorded for the instructor's use in a classroom or laboratory setting on **MyGermanLab™** and on CD.

Online Resources

Instructor's Resource Center. The IRC can be found at http://www.pearsonhighered.com and provides password-protected instructor access to the Instructor's Resource Manual and Testing Program, available in a downloadable format.

MyGermanLab™. The moment you know. Educators know it. Students know it. It's that inspired moment when something that was difficult to understand suddenly makes perfect sense. Pearson's MyLab products have been designed and refined with a single purpose in mind—to help educators create that moment of understanding for their students.

MyLanguageLabs deliver proven results in helping individual students succeed. They provide engaging experiences that personalize, stimulate, and measure learning for each student. And, they come from a trusted partner with educational expertise and an eye on the future.

MyLanguageLabs can be linked out to any learning management system. To learn more about how the MyLanguageLabs combine proven learning applications with powerful assessment, visit http://www.mylanguagelabs.com .

MyLanguageLabs—the moment you know.

Companion Website. The Companion Website contains some of the text audio recordings and all of the SAM audio recordings.

www.pearsonhighered.com/treffpunkt

Acknowledgments ////////////

We would like to express our gratitude to the many instructors and coordinators who took time from their busy schedules to assist us with comments and suggestions over the course of the development of all six editions of *Treffpunkt Deutsch*.

Rita Abercrombie, *Baylor University;* Tim Altanero, *Austin Community College;* Keith Anderson, *St. Olaf College;* Reinhard Andress, *St. Louis University;* William Anthony, *Northwestern University;* John Austin, *Georgia State University;* Linda Austin, *Glendale Community College;* Thomas Bacon, *Texas Tech University;* Linda Daves Baldwin, *Washington College;* Katharina Barbe, *Northern Illinois University;* Gamin Bartle, *University of Alabama;* Gary Bartlett, *Normandale Community College;* Claudia A. Becker, *Loyola University;* Christel Bell, *University of Alabama;* Helga Bister-Broosen, *University of North Carolina;* John M. Brawner, *University of California, Irvine;* Brigitte Breitenbücher, *Elgin Community College;* Johannes Bruestle, *Grossmont College;* Joan Keck Campbell, *Dartmouth College;* Belinda Carstens-Wickham, *Southern Illinois University:* Heidi Crabbs, *Fullerton College;* Rudolph Debernitz, *Golden West College;* Sharon M. DiFino, *University of Florida;* Thomas John DiNapoli, *Louisiana State University;* Christopher Dolmetsch, *Marshall University*; Esther Enns-Connolly, *University of Calgary;* Nikolaus Euba, *University of California, Berkeley;* Judith Fogle, *Pasadena City College*; Catherine C. Fraser, *Indiana University, Bloomington;* Juergen Froehlich, *Pomona College;* Harold P. Fry, *Kent State University;* Henry Fullenwider, *University of Kansas;* Anna Glapa-Grossklag, *College of the Canyons;* Andrea Golato, *University of Illinois at Urbana-Champaign;* Peter Gölz, *University of Victoria;* Anne-Katrin Gramberg, *Auburn University;* Christian Hallstein, *Carnegie Mellon University;* Barbara Harding, *Georgetown University;* Beverly Harris-Schenz, *University of Pittsburgh;* Frauke A. Harvey, *Baylor University;* Elizabeth Hasler, *Xavier University;* Gisela Hoecherl-Alden, *University of Maine;* Robert G. Hoeing, *SUNY Buffalo;* Bradley A. Holtman, *Mansfield University:* Deborah L. Horzen, *University of Central Florida;* Carrie N. Jackson, *Pennsylvania State University;* Charles James, *University of Wisconsin, Madison;* William Keel, *University of Kansas;* George Koenig, *SUNY Oswego;* Richard Alan Korb, *Columbia University,* Arndt A. Krüger, *Trent University;* John A. Lalande II, *University of Illinois, Chicago;* Alan H. Lareau, *University of Wisconsin, Oshkosh;* Martina Lindseth, *University of Wisconsin-Eau Claire;* Betty Mason, *Valencia Community College;* Dennis R. McCormick, *University of Montana;* Dr. Laura McGee, *Western Kentucky University;* Robert Mollenauer, *University of Texas;* Juan Carlos Morales, *Miami Palmetto Sr. High School;* Kamakshi P. Murti, *Middlebury College;* Eva Margareta Norling, *Bellevue College;* Margaret Peischl, *Virginia Commonwealth University;* Manfred Prokop, *University of Alberta;* Robert C. Reimer, *University of North Carolina, Charlotte;* Richard C. Reinholdt, *Orange Coast College;* Michael D. Richardson, *Ithaca College;* Veronica Richel, *University of Vermont;* Roger Russi, *Middlebury College;* Gerd Schneider, *Syracuse University;* Carolyn Wolf Spanier, *Mt. San Antonio College;* Bruce H. Spencer, *University of Iowa;* Christine Spreizer, *Queens College CUNY;* Gerhard Strasser, *Pennsylvania State University;* Michael L. Thompson,

University of Pennsylvania; Suzanne Toliver, *University of Cincinnati;* Walter Tschacher, *Chapman University,* Hulya Unlu, *Penn State University,* Helga Van Iten, *Iowa State University;* Janet Van Valkenburg, *University of Michigan;* Wilfried Voge, *University of California, Los Angeles;* Morris Vos, *Western Illinois University;* Elizabeth I. Wade, *University of Wisconsin, Oshkosh;* Susan Wansink, *Virginia Wesleyan College;* William Garrett Welch, *West Texas A&M University,* Hendrik H. Winterstein, *University of Houston,* Margrit V. Zinggeler, *Eastern Michigan University.*

We gratefully acknowledge the many people at Pearson Eduction who participated in the development of the sixth edition of **Treffpunkt Deutsch.** A special *Danke schön* goes to Phil Miller, former publisher of World Languages, for his genuine dedication to this project. We have considered ourselves fortunate to work with a publisher proficient in German for so many years, through multiple editions, and we congratulate Phil on his well-deserved retirement! We are grateful to Rachel McCoy, Executive Acquisitions Editor, for her enthusiasm and commitment to the success of this project and her encouragement throughout all stages. We are also deeply indebted to Karen Storz, our Developmental Editor, an indispensible member of our team, for her insightful editorial comments, attention to detail, not to mention unlimited patience and good humor. We are grateful also to Lieselotte Betz for her careful and thorough copyediting of the manuscript. Enormous thanks to Mary Rottino, Senior Managing Editor, Janice Stangel, Associate Managing Editor, and Manuel Echevarria, our Production Project Manager, for their eager and competent assistance throughout the revision process. We also thank Bob Hemmer, Executive Editor for MyLanguageLabs, and Samantha Alducin, Senior Media Editor, for their work in making the first MyGermanLab an exciting reality, and Bill Bliss, MyLanguageLabs Developmental Editor, for his approachability, as well as his constant guidance in ensuring the effectiveness of the activities developed for this book's first MyGermanLab.

Lindsay Miglionica, Editorial Assistant, has our thanks for diligently managing the turnover of all materials, helping to keep us organized. For the new interior design we sincerely thank PreMediaGlobal. It has been an absolute pleasure working with Stacy Drew and Harriet Dishman, also of PreMediaGlobal. We thank the marketing team, Kris Ellis-Levy, Executive Marketing Manager, and Michele Marchese, for their enthusiasm in promoting the book!

We gratefully dedicate **Treffpunkt Deutsch** to our students and fellow German teachers and also to our families. Their unconditional support for us made our work on this edition possible, and their enthusiasm for the final product made this work enjoyable, too.

About the Authors ////////////

Margaret Gonglewski

Margaret Gonglewski is Associate Professor of German and International Affairs at the George Washington University in Washington, DC, where she directs the German language program. She received her PhD from Georgetown University. She has published articles on topics such as effective uses of technology in language teaching and learning, business language teaching methodology, and critical issues in materials selection and creation. From 2004 to 2008, she served as the first Director of the George Washington University Language Center, initiating innovative programming as well as support and recognition for language faculty. She has been awarded several grants for developing materials to assist faculty in teaching business languages, and she is currently Business Languages Coordinator for the University's Center for Business Education and Research, funded by a grant for the U.S. Department of Education. She has received university awards for innovations in teaching and excellence in undergraduate advising.

Beverly Moser

Beverly Moser is Associate Professor of German and the Director of the MA program with a language teaching focus at Appalachian State University in Boone, North Carolina. She received her PhD from Georgetown University, where her dissertation received the Emma Marie Birkmaier award from ACTFL and the Modern Language Journal for its contribution to foreign language education. A specialist in reading and writing pedagogy for German as a foreign language, she publishes teaching materials that develop students' literacy skills. Her most recent work adapts authentic youth literature for the college classroom. Dr. Moser serves as Principal and Co-Principal Investigator on three grants funded by the U.S. Department of Education for projects directed at improving the quality and scope of foreign language teaching, in the K–12 or college setting, on strengthening interdisciplinary connections for all foreign languages, and on teacher development. She has served as the Director of a large-scale German program, helping graduate students through their first few semesters teaching college level German, and she regularly conducts methodology workshops for pre-collegiate and postsecondary instructors of German, French, Spanish and English as a Second Language.

Cornelius Partsch

Cornelius Partsch is a native of Landstuhl and grew up in the nearby Saarland in southwestern Germany. He is Professor of German at Western Washington University in Bellingham, Washington. He received his PhD from Brown University. He previously taught German at Hamilton College, Colby College, Smith College, and Mount Holyoke College, as well as at the German summer schools at the University of Rhode Island, Middlebury College, and Portland State University. He is the author of *Schräge Töne. Jazz und Unterhaltungsmusik in der Kultur der Weimarer Republik* (Stuttgart: J. B. Metzler) and has written widely on various aspects of 20th- and 21st-century German popular culture. His particular interest in language pedagogy lies in the construction of foreign language curricula and the teaching of culture using film, music, and fiction. He served as a teacher/trainer in the Goethe Institute's trainer network for the western United States from 2007–2011.

Erste Kontakte

Studenten in Berlin

Kommunikationsziele

Greeting someone and responding
   to greetings
Introducing yourself
Making phone calls
Addressing letters
Saying good-bye

Strukturen

Du, ihr, and **Sie**
The alphabet
The numbers from 0–1000

Kultur

Affordable education at German universities
Social implications of **du, ihr,** and **Sie**
A first look at the German-speaking cultures
German words used in English

SemesterTicket
Verkehrsverbund
Bremen/Niedersachsen GmbH VBN

Dexter, Andrew
Name, Vorname

12.11.1992
Geburtsdatum

01.04.2011 – 30.09.2011
Gültigkeitszeitraum

2280588
Matrikelnummer

Universität Bremen
Hochschule

VBN

Semesters at German universities usually run from mid-October to mid-February (**Wintersemester**) and from mid-April through mid-July (**Sommersemester**).

E-1 **Semesterticket.** Look at this public transportation pass from an exchange student living in Germany. What can you learn about him by looking carefully at his pass?

1. The student's name is: _____
2. He's studying at: _____
3. His ticket is valid for the months of: _____
4. His birthday is: _____

Beim Studentenwerk

*Christian Lohner and Asha Singh meet at the student center at the **Humboldt-Universität** in Berlin.*

— Hallo, ich heiße Christian, Christian Lohner.
— Und ich bin Asha Singh. Woher kommst du, Christian?
— Ich komme aus Hamburg. Und du, woher bist du?
— Ich bin aus Mumbai.

STUDENTENWERK

E-2 **Wir lernen einander kennen.** *(Getting to know each other.)* Walk around the classroom and get to know as many classmates as possible. In the German-speaking countries, people often shake hands when greeting each other.

Student 1: Hallo, ich heiße _____.
Wie heißt du?

Student 2: Ich heiße _____.

Student 1: Ich komme aus _____.
Woher bist du?

Student 2: Ich bin aus _____.
(Ich bin auch° aus _____.)   *too*

Infobox

Affordable education at German universities

Studying at the **Universität** (or **Uni**) is much less expensive in Germany than in North America. Tuition did not exist at German public universities until recently. Since 2005, each of Germany's 16 states can decide whether to charge tuition; by 2010 only five states had introduced a tuition fee. Even a tuition fee of 500 euros per semester caused an outcry. Opponents argue that such fees are unfair because they deny less affluent students access to higher education.

Students can also live very cheaply because the government subsidizes dormitory rooms and meals in the **Mensa** and in smaller cafeterias and pubs on campus. Another benefit for students is the **Semesterticket,** a low-cost pass valid on public transportation in the area where they study.

Im Hörsaal

Peter knows Martin and Claudia, but he hasn't met Claudia's roommate Stephanie yet. Claudia introduces them after class in the lecture hall.

MARTIN:	(*to Claudia and Stephanie*) Hallo, ihr zwei! Wie geht's?
CLAUDIA:	Super. Du, Peter, das ist Stephanie, meine Mitbewohnerin.
PETER:	Grüß dich, Stephanie.
STEPHANIE:	Hallo, Peter.
now MARTIN:	Geht ihr jetzt° auch in die Mensa?
CLAUDIA:	Nein, noch nicht.
MARTIN:	Na, dann tschüss, ihr zwei.
STEPHANIE:	Ciao!

- In German all nouns (people, places, and things) are capitalized: **Student, Mensa, Telefon.**
- In addition to the letter **s,** German also uses **ß** (called **Eszett**) to represent the **s**-sound: **Grüß dich!**
- The letter **ä** in **Universität** is called **a–Umlaut.** The letters **o** and **u** can also be umlauted: **Hörsaal, tschüss.**
- German verbs have endings that change, depending on the subject, e.g., **ich komm*e*, du komm*st*.**

E-3 Grüß dich! Walk up to two classmates and greet one by name. She/He will then introduce the other classmate to you.

S1: Grüß dich, _____, wie geht's?

S2: Super. Du, _____ *(name of S1)*, das ist _____ *(name of S3)*.

S1: *(to S3)* Grüß dich, _____.

S3: *(to S1)* Hallo, _____.

S1: Woher kommst du, _____?

S3: Ich bin aus _____. Und du?

S1: Ich komme aus _____.

S1: *(to S2 and S3)* Geht ihr jetzt auch in die Mensa?

S2: Nein, noch nicht.

S1: Na, dann tschüss, ihr zwei.

S3: Tschüss.

S2: Ciao!

How to say you in German

E-1 to E-3

German has more than one way of saying *you.* The familiar **du** is used to address family members, close friends, children, and teenagers up to about age sixteen. It is also used among students, even if they are not close friends. The plural form of **du** is **ihr.**

The formal **Sie** is used for addressing adults who are not close friends. **Sie** is always capitalized and does not change in the plural.

	singular	plural
FAMILIAR	du	ihr
FORMAL	Sie	Sie

E-4 *Du, ihr oder Sie?* Indicate how you would address the following people in a German–speaking setting.

	du	ihr	Sie
1. your professor	____	____	____
2. your roommate	____	____	____
3. your roommate's parents	____	____	____
4. two classmates	____	____	____
5. your doctor	____	____	____
6. your dog	____	____	____
7. a store clerk	____	____	____
8. a kindergarten class	____	____	____

Im Konferenzsaal

Ms. Ziegler and Mr. O'Brien are business associates who have frequently corresponded, but are meeting for the first time at a conference.

— Entschuldigung, mein Name ist O'Brien. Sind Sie Frau Ziegler aus Göttingen?
— Ja. – Ach, Herr O'Brien aus Dublin! Guten Tag! Wie geht es Ihnen?
— Danke, gut.

 E-5 Guten Tag! You are meeting a German business associate with whom you have been corresponding. Introduce yourself, using your last name. Address your partner with **Frau** or **Herr** and don't forget to shake hands!

S1: Entschuldigung, mein Name ist _____ *(your last name)*. Sind Sie Frau/Herr _____ aus _____?

S2: Ja. – Ach, Frau/Herr _____ aus _____! Guten Tag! Wie geht es Ihnen?

S1: Danke, gut.

Greetings and farewells

In the German-speaking countries, there are various ways of saying hello and good-bye. In North America it is customary for people to shake hands when they first meet each other. In the German-speaking countries, people often shake hands whenever they meet or say good-bye.

	FORMAL	LESS FORMAL	
GREETINGS	**Guten Tag!**	**Tag!**	*Hello!*
	Guten Morgen!	**Morgen!**	*Good morning!*
	Guten Abend!	**'n Abend!**	*Good evening!*
		Hallo!	
		Grüß dich!	
		Grüß Gott! *(S. German)*	*Hello! Hi!*
		Grüezi! *(Swiss)*	
		Servus! *(Austrian)*	
FAREWELLS	**Auf Wiedersehen!**	**Wiedersehen!**	*Good-bye!*
		Tschüss!	
		Ciao!	*Bye! So long!*
		Servus! *(Austrian)*	
	Gute Nacht!		*Good night!*

E-6 Grußformeln. Find greetings that are used in the German-speaking countries. If you recognize any other non-English greetings, identify them and say them for your classmates.

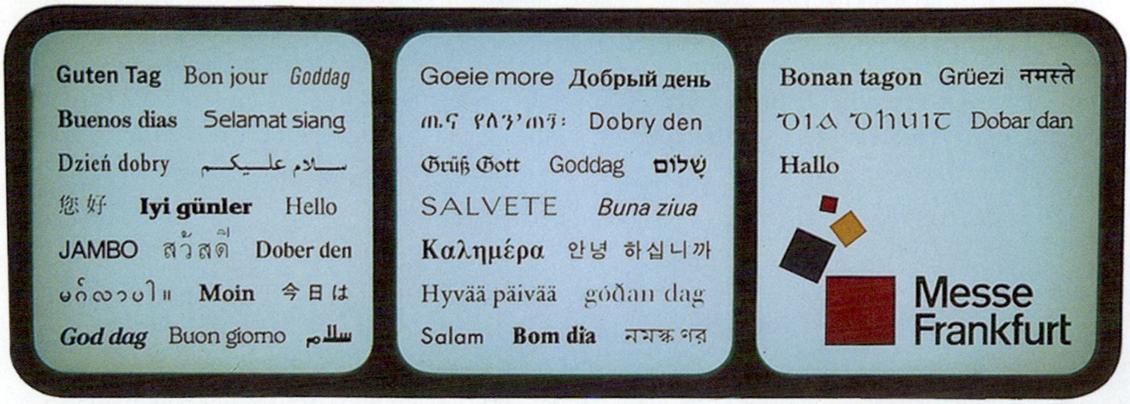

Guten Tag Bon jour *Goddag*
Buenos dias Selamat siang
Dzień dobry سلام عليكم
您好 **Iyi günler** Hello
JAMBO สวัสดี Dober den
ဗၟာစၠ Moin 今日は
God dag Buon giorno سلام

Goeie more Добрый день
ௗ.௭ ௲௮௱'௩: Dobry den
Grüß Gott Goddag שלום
SALVETE *Buna ziua*
Καλημέρα 안녕 하십니까
Hyvää päivää *gódan dag*
Salam **Bom dia** নমস্কার

Bonan tagon Grüezi नमस्ते
םולש םולש Dobar dan
Hallo

Messe Frankfurt

Kultur / A first look at the German-speaking cultures

Studying German involves not only becoming proficient in the language but also acquiring cultural literacy — learning about the various peoples, practices, products, and perspectives of the German-speaking countries. An integral part of your learning will be to reflect on the similarities and the differences between your own familiar culture and another culture, which may be unfamiliar and full of surprises. Here is a first look at the cultural variety of the German-speaking countries.

1. Sächsische Schweiz

2. Windenergie

Switzerland in Germany? This national park gets its name from its alpine look. A unique blend of craggy sandstone formations, deep ravines, pristine streams, and primeval forests make it a favorite destination for climbers, hikers, and bikers. The Elbe river winds its way through this dramatic landscape, known as Saxon Switzerland.

Wind energy is valued as an alternative to fossil fuels because it is plentiful, renewable, clean, and produces no greenhouse gas emissions as it generates electricity. Large-scale wind farms, such as this one in the Tauern mountain range in the Austrian state of Styria **(Steiermark)**, can also be found in the waters of the North and Baltic Seas. At an elevation of 6,234 feet, the Tauern Wind Park is the highest in Europe. Austria ranked as the world's seventeenth largest producer of wind power in 2008.

3. Land der Ideen

For the 2006 Soccer World Cup **(Fußball-Weltmeisterschaft)**, this giant sculpture of soccer shoes was placed in front of Berlin's central train station to commemorate an influential idea the family of Adi Dassler had in 1953. Can you guess which company was the first to mass-produce this type of shoe?

In the **Autostadt** in Wolfsburg there are two of these glass silos—high-tech storage facilities for new Volkswagens. When purchasing a car, a customer may opt to travel to the **Autostadt** to pick it up. There, the customer can watch how a robotic arm plucks the new car out of the silo compartment and moves it onto an automatic elevator. The car is then transported through a tunnel to the customer service center without having been driven a single yard and with the odometer showing "0."

4. Volkswagen in Wolfsburg

Techno, Rave, and House music are hugely popular in the German-speaking countries. The award-winning Cocoon Club in Frankfurt was opened in July 2004 and is known for its innovative design and state-of-the-art sound system. Co-owner Sven Väth is also one of Germany's legendary DJs and the driving force behind the label Cocoon Recordings.

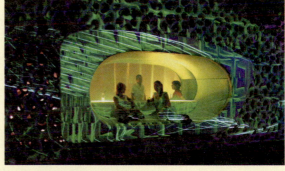

5. Cocoon Club in Frankfurt

The "Swiss Maestro" is, by some accounts, the greatest tennis player of all time. He held the number-one position in the world rankings for a record 237 consecutive weeks and has won more Grand Slam singles titles than any other male player. He also won an Olympic Gold Medal in doubles with his compatriot Stanislas Wawrinka at the 2008 Summer Games in Beijing. A native of Basel, Federer is the first living individual to be honored on a Swiss stamp.

6. Roger Federer

E-7 **Was ist das?** Each German term below relates to one of the themes of this **Kultur** section. Match each word to the number of the appropriate **Kultur** reading.

Windpark _____

Fußballschuh _____

Autosilo _____

Tanzrhythmus _____

Vorhand _____

Sandstein _____

Spelling

E-4 to E-8

The alphabet

The name of almost every letter in the German alphabet contains the sound represented by that letter. Learning the alphabet is therefore useful not only for spelling, but also for your pronunciation. Listen carefully to the recording and to your instructor. Repeat what you hear.

E-8 Hören Sie gut zu und wiederholen Sie! *(Listen carefully and repeat!)*

a	ah	**g**	geh	**m**	emm	**s**	ess	**y**	üppsilon
b	beh	**h**	hah	**n**	enn	**t**	teh	**z**	tsett
c	tseh	**i**	ee	**o**	oh	**u**	oo		
d	deh	**j**	yott	**p**	peh	**v**	fow		
e	eh	**k**	kah	**q**	coo	**w**	veh		
f	eff	**l**	ell	**r**	airr	**x**	iks		

E-9 Wie schreibt man das? *(How do you spell that?)* As you hear some German words spelled, find the beginning of the word and fill in the rest of the word according to what you hear. Can you guess the meaning of each word in English?

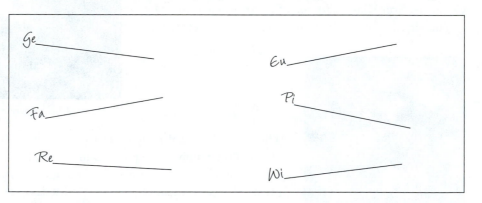

Ge_____

Fa_____

Re_____

Eu_____

Pi_____

Wi_____

E-10 Abkürzungen. Your instructor will read the names below. For each name, find the appropriate abbreviation in the illustrations and spell it aloud.

Bundesrepublik Deutschland

Vereinigte Staaten von Amerika

Bayerische Motorenwerke

Volkswagen

Allgemeiner Deutscher Automobilclub

Deutsches Jugendherbergswerk

Christlich-Demokratische Union

Counting

The numbers from 0 to 1000

0	null						
1	ei**ns**	11	elf	21	ei**nu**ndzwanzig	10	zehn
2	zwei	12	zwölf	22	zweiundzwanzig	20	zwanzig
3	drei	13	dreizehn	23	dreiundzwanzig	30	drei**ß**ig
4	vier	14	vierzehn	24	vierundzwanzig	40	vierzig
5	fünf	15	fünfzehn	25	fünfundzwanzig	50	fünfzig
6	sech**s**	16	se**chz**ehn	26	sech**s**undzwanzig	60	se**chz**ig
7	sieb**en**	17	sie**bz**ehn	27	sieb**en**undzwanzig	70	sie**bz**ig
8	acht	18	achtzehn	28	achtundzwanzig	80	achtzig
9	neun	19	neunzehn	29	neunundzwanzig	90	neunzig
10	zehn	20	zwanzig	30	drei**ß**ig	100	hundert

101	(ein)hunderteins	200	zweihundert	1000	(ein)tausend
102	(ein)hundertzwei	300	dreihundert		
usw.° (und so weiter)		usw.		*etc.*	

Note the following:

1. The **–s** in **eins** is dropped in combination with **zwanzig, dreißig,** etc.: **einundzwanzig, einunddreißig,** etc.
2. The numbers from the twenties through the nineties are "turned around": **vierundzwanzig** (four and twenty), **achtundsechzig** (eight and sixty), etc.
3. **Dreißig** is the only one of the tens that ends in **–ßig** instead of **–zig.**
4. The final **–s** in **sechs** is dropped in **sechzehn** and **sechzig.**
5. The **–en** of **sieben** is dropped in **siebzehn** and **siebzig.**

E-11 Mathematik.

▶ 2 + 2

S1: Was ist zwei plus zwei?　　**S2:** Zwei plus zwei ist vier.

▶ 4 − 2

S1: Wie viel ist vier minus zwei?　　**S2:** Vier minus zwei ist zwei.

1. 2 + 1	3. 5 + 0	5. 9 + 1
2. 4 − 3	4. 8 − 6	6. 7 − 5

> Just as in English, you can say either **"Was ist…"** *(What is)* or **"Wie viel ist…"** *(How much is)* for math problems.

> In the Celsius scale, 0° represents the freezing point of water and 100° the boiling point. In the Fahrenheit scale, 32° represents the freezing point and 212° the boiling point.

E-12 Celsius und Fahrenheit. When traveling in Europe, it is helpful to be familiar with the Celsius scale. With a partner, work on converting Celsius to Fahrenheit.

S1: Was ist zwanzig Grad Celsius in Fahrenheit?　　**S2:** Zwanzig Grad Celsius ist etwa° achtundsechzig Grad Fahrenheit.

approximately

-40　-30　-20　-10　0　10　20　30　40　Grad Celsius

-40 -30 -20 -10　0　10 20 30 40 50 60 70 80 90 100　Grad Fahrenheit

Making Phone Calls

Most German telephone numbers are written as pairs of digits.

The telephone number **25 13 84** can be said either as individual numbers **"zwei, fünf, eins, drei, acht, vier,"** or in pairs **"fünfundzwanzig, dreizehn, vierundachtzig."** The area code is called **die Vorwahl.**

E-13 **Was ist die Telefonnummer?** Listen to the snippets from radio ads and match the numbers with the businesses listed below.

1.	Pizzeria Roma	a.	4 30 24
2.	Tai Chi Studio	b.	3 08 65
3.	Amendt Computersysteme	c.	4 51 13
4.	Cinema Metropolis	d.	3 77 10

E-14 **Telefonnummer.** You **(S1)** and a friend **(S2)** are students in Heidelberg and are updating your phone contact lists. The information for **S1** is on this page; the information for **S2** is in the *Anhang* on page A1.

S1: Was ist Daniels Telefonnummer?   **S2:** Daniels Nummer ist 2 10 72.

> Telephone etiquette requires that both the person answering the phone and the caller give their names. To say good-bye on the phone, you use **auf Wiederhören** (a variant of **auf Wiedersehen**) in formal situations. In colloquial German most people say **tschüss.**

NAME	TELEFON
Daniel	
Justin	1 63 45
Heather	
Lilli	80 27 16

Sprachnotiz **Saying e-mail and Web addresses**

German speakers typically use English when saying the @ sign in e-mail addresses. The English term *dot* is used for the period in e-mail and Web addresses, although it is also common to hear **Punkt.** All other words and numbers are simply spoken as words, unless it is necessary to clarify spelling.

Written: claudia.berger1@yahoo.de
Spoken: **Claudia Punkt Berger eins at yahoo Punkt deh eh**

Other common symbols in email and web addresses are **- (Strich)** and / **(Querstrich).**

Addressing Letters

In the German-speaking countries, letters are addressed a bit differently than in North America. The house number follows the name of the street (e.g., **Lindenstraße 29**). The postal code **(die Postleitzahl)** precedes the name of the city. It has five digits in Germany and four in Austria and Switzerland.

E-15 Ein Brief von Mutter. Peter has just received a letter from his mother.

1. Peters Familienname ist _____.
2. Peters Hausnummer ist _____.
3. Die Hausnummer von Peters Mutter ist _____.
4. Peters Postleitzahl ist _____.
5. Die Postleitzahl von Peters Mutter ist _____.
6. Ein Brief von Berlin nach München kostet _____ Cent.

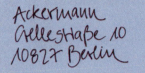

E-16 Wir lernen einander besser kennen. Find out the last name, address, and telephone number of two of your classmates.

S1: Was ist dein Familienname?	**S2:** Mein Familienname ist _____.
Wie bitte?° Wie schreibt man das?	…
Was ist deine Adresse?	Meine Adresse ist …
Was ist deine Telefonnummer?	Meine Telefonnummer ist _____.

Pardon?

E-17 Eine SMS an Stephanie. Read Peter's text message to Stephanie on the display of his **Handy** and then mark the correct answers to the questions below.

1. Where will Stephanie be able to find Peter at 10 a.m.?
   a. in lecture hall 9   b. in lecture hall 12   c. in the cafeteria
2. Where will Stephanie be able to find Peter at 12 noon?
   a. in lecture hall 9   b. in lecture hall 10   c. in the cafeteria
3. When did Peter send this text message to Stephanie?
   a. at 8 a.m.   b. at night   c. in the afternoon

E-18 **Eine Jugendherberge.** For young people traveling in Europe, youth hostels are a popular and inexpensive place to stay. Find out more about one German hostel by reading the sign and answering the questions.

1. What is the **Postleitzahl** of Sellin?
2. What do you think the **D** preceding the **Postleitzahl** stands for?
3. The **Seebad** in **Ostseebad** means *seaside resort*. Look at the map **Deutschland Bundesländer** on the third page at the very front of your textbook, find the **Ostsee,** and give the English equivalent.
4. Look at the same map to find out what the **mv** in the e-mail and website addresses stands for. Visit the website to see what this hostel looks like!

 ## Zur Aussprache

Some sounds and letters that are quite different from those found in English are discussed here. Listen carefully and imitate the sounds you hear.

The umlauted vowels *ä, ö,* and *ü*

The sound represented by the letter **ä** is close to the sound represented by the letter *e* in English *let*.

short *ä*		long *ä*	
Bäcker	Gärtner	Käse	Universität

The sound represented by the letter **ö** has no equivalent in English. To produce this sound, pucker your lips as if to whistle, hold them in this position, and say *eh*.

short *ö*		long *ö*	
zwölf	Göttingen	schön	hören

The sound represented by the letter **ü** also has no equivalent in English. To produce this sound, pucker your lips as if to whistle, hold them in this position, and say *ee*.

short *ü*		long *ü*	
fünf	Tschüss!	grün	Grüß dich!

The *Eszett*

The letter **ß,** which is called **Eszett,** is pronounced like an *s*.

heiß	heißen	dreißig

German *ch*

After **a, o,** and **u,** the sound represented by **ch** resembles a gentle gargling.

acht	noch	auch

After **i** and **e,** the sound represented by **ch** is pronounced like a loudly whispered *h* in *huge.*

          ich   nicht   sechzehn

The suffix **–ig** is pronounced as if it were spelled **–ich.**

          windig   zwanzig   dreißig

German *v*

The sound represented by the letter **v** is generally pronounced like English *f.*

          vier   viel   Volkswagen

German *w*

The sound represented by the letter **w** is always pronounced like English *v.*

          woher   Wie geht's?   Wiedersehen!

German *z*

The sound represented by the letter **z** is pronounced like English *ts* in *hits*.

          zwei   zehn   zwanzig

Infobox

German words used in English

Of the many words you will encounter as you learn German, some will already be familiar to you. This is because languages borrow words from one another. Some German words used in English are specific to the jargon of a particular field, such as *doppelgänger* in psychology. Others have become so commonplace that their German origin has been largely forgotten, such as *kitsch* and *hamburger.*

German also borrows many words from English, as you will see throughout this book. Check out the **Kultur** section of chapter 2 on p. 57 to learn about English loan words in German.

Kind mit Rucksack und Knackwurst

E-19 **Deutsch in Englisch.** By matching appropriately in each of the two sets below, you can reconstruct some German words commonly used in English.

1. kinder–   a. sack
2. wunder–   b. garten
3. knack–   c. geist
4. polter–   d. kind
5. ruck–   e. wurst

6. sauer–   f. land
7. leit–   g. lust
8. hinter–   h. heit
9. gesund– i. motiv
10. wander– j. kraut

Be sure to learn the numbers listed on page 9.

Informelle Situationen

Morgen!	Good morning!
Tag!	Hello!
'n Abend!	Good evening!
Grüß dich!	Hi! *(to greet one person)*
Hallo!	Hi!
Tschüss! } **Ciao!** }	Bye!
Entschuldigung!★	Excuse me!
Wie heißt du?	What's your name?
Ich heiße …	My name is …
Ich bin …	I'm …
Woher kommst (bist) du?	Where are you from?
Ich komme (bin) aus …	I'm from …
Wie geht's?	How are you?
Danke, gut.★	Fine, thanks.
Super.	Super.

Formelle Situationen

Guten Morgen!	Good morning!
Guten Tag!	Hello!
Guten Abend!	Good evening!
Auf Wiedersehen!	Good-bye!
Auf Wiederhören!	Good-bye! *(on phone)*
Wie heißen Sie?	What is your name?
Ich heiße … } **Mein Name ist …** }	My name is …
Woher kommen (sind) Sie?	Where are you from?
Wie geht es Ihnen?	How are you?
Wie bitte?	Pardon?
Frau	Mrs., Ms.
Herr	Mr.
ja ≠ nein	yes ≠ no

★ *The phrases marked with an asterisk can be used formally and informally.*

Wörter im Kontext

E-20 **Formell oder informell?** How could you greet the following people at the times given?

	YOUR PROFESSOR	YOUR FELLOW STUDENTS
9 a.m.	_____	_____
3 p.m.	_____	_____
7 p.m.	_____	_____

E-21 **Wie viel ist das?** Match each problem with its correct solution.

1. Wie viel ist zwei plus fünf?
2. Was ist elf minus eins?
3. Wie viel ist dreizehn plus vier?
4. Was ist siebzig minus zehn?

a. Das ist zehn.
b. Das ist sechzig.
c. Das ist sieben.
d. Das ist siebzehn.

E-22 **Was passt wo?** *(What goes where?)* Complete with the appropriate word or expression.

Wie geht's / Name / Nein / Entschuldigung /
Wie geht es Ihnen / Super / Wie bitte

1. MARTIN: Grüß dich, Claudia. _____?
   CLAUDIA: _____.
2. PETER: _____, bist du Asha Singh?
   YVONNE: _____, ich bin Yvonne Harris.
3. HERR PEERY: Guten Tag. Mein _____ ist Peery.
   FRAU BORG: _____? Wie heißen Sie?
   HERR PEERY: Ich bin Frank Peery.
   FRAU BORG: Oh, Herr Peery aus Iowa! _____?
   HERR PEERY: Danke, gut.

> In this course you'll want to communicate in German with your instructor and your classmates as much as possible. On p. A12 in the *Anhang* at the back of this book, you'll find some useful classroom expressions to help you do this.

Jahraus, jahrein

Universitätsstadt Tübingen: Stocherkähne auf dem Neckar

Kommunikationsziele

Talking about …
- the weather and the seasons
- student life
- everyday activities and objects
- colors
- nationality

Strukturen

Gender and number of nouns

Ein and **kein**

Word order:
- Position of the verb in questions and statements
- Expressions of time and place
- Position of **nicht**

Personal pronouns

Present tense of **sein**

The verb: infinitive and present tense

Kultur

Welcome to the German-speaking countries

Studying at the university

About university life

Why German and English are similar

Video-Treff: **Das bin ich**

Lesen: **Eine Schweizerin, eine deutsche Familie und zwei Österreicher**

Vorschau

Eine Wetterkarte

1-1 Wie ist das Wetter? Match each city with the appropriate weather description based on the information on the weather map.

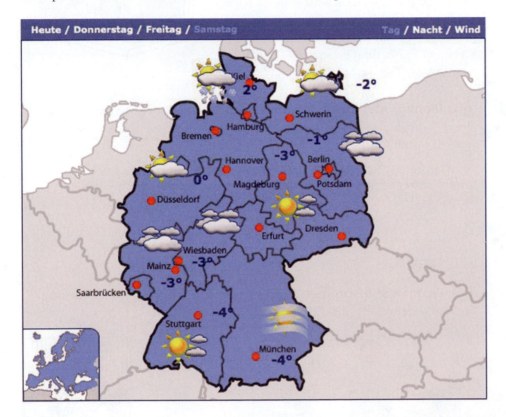

In Hannover …	ist es sonnig!
In Stuttgart …	scheint die Sonne gar nicht.
In Kiel …	ist es sonnig aber windig.
In Wiesbaden …	zeigt das Thermometer 0 Grad.
In München …	ist Schneeregen.

Der Tag beginnt

Frau Ziegler steht am Fenster. Herr Ziegler ist noch im Bett.

HERR ZIEGLER: Wie ist das Wetter?

FRAU ZIEGLER: Gar nicht schön. Der Himmel ist grau und es regnet.

HERR ZIEGLER: Ist es kalt?

FRAU ZIEGLER: Das Thermometer zeigt zehn Grad.

HERR ZIEGLER: Nur zehn Grad! Was für ein Hundewetter!

Semesterbeginn

Stephanie und Claudia sitzen zusammen beim Frühstück.

CLAUDIA: Gehst du jetzt in die Vorlesung, Stephanie?

STEPHANIE: Ja, und dann zum Auslandsamt.

CLAUDIA: Meine Vorlesungen beginnen erst morgen.

STEPHANIE: Und was machst du heute?

CLAUDIA: Nicht viel. Zuerst schreibe ich ein paar Karten und heute Nachmittag kaufe ich meine Bücher.

STEPHANIE: Na, dann bis später.

CLAUDIA: Tschüss, Stephanie.

 1-2 Richtig oder falsch? You will hear the conversations on page 17 and above. Indicate whether the statements that follow each conversation are **richtig** *(true)* or **falsch** *(false).*

	DER TAG BEGINNT		SEMESTERBEGINN	
	RICHTIG	FALSCH	RICHTIG	FALSCH
1.	_____	_____	_____	_____
2.	_____	_____	_____	_____
3.	_____	_____	_____	_____

1-3 Was passt zusammen? *(What goes together?)* Working with a partner, find the sentences that describe each illustration.

Heute ist es gar nicht schön.

Heute ist es schön.

Die Sonne scheint.

Es regnet.

Der Himmel ist grau.

Der Himmel ist blau.

Es ist windig.

Es ist windstill.

Was für ein Hundewetter!

1-4 Drei kleine Gespräche. With a partner, unscramble the exchanges in the following three mini-conversations by numbering appropriately. Then read the conversations for your classmates.

S1:

_____ Toll°! Gehst du heute schwimmen?

_____ Na, dann bis später.

__1__ Wie ist das Wetter?

S2:

_____ Ja, klar!   *super*

_____ Sehr schön! Das Thermometer zeigt fast dreißig Grad.

_____ Ciao!

S1:

__1__ Hallo!

_____ Und wann kaufst du deine Bücher?

_____ Was machst du jetzt?

S2:

_____ Das mache ich heute Nachmittag.

_____ Ich gehe in die Vorlesung.

_____ Grüß dich!

S1:

_____ Was für ein Hundewetter!

__1__ Regnet es noch?

_____ Nein, meine Vorlesungen beginnen erst morgen.

S2:

_____ Ja, und das Thermometer zeigt fünf Grad.

_____ Gehst du heute in die Vorlesung?

_____ Na, dann tschüss!

30 Grad Celsius ist *fast* 90 Grad Fahrenheit.

Kultur / Welcome to the German-speaking countries

Located in the center of Europe, the German-speaking countries together are only about two-thirds the size of Texas. And yet, the topography and climate of **Deutschland, Österreich,** and **die Schweiz** are enormously varied.

👥 **1-5** With a partner, take turns reading aloud about the German-speaking countries and finding the places mentioned on the map inside the front cover.

Landscapes

It is about a day's journey from the coast of the **Nordsee** to the peaks of the German, Swiss, and Austrian **Alpen** in the south. The Lowlands of Northern Germany extend from the Dutch border in the west to the border of Poland in the east. Just south of the **Lüneburger Heide,** where you can hike through thousands of acres of purple heather, the Lowlands give way to the mountain ranges of Central Germany. The most famous of these are the **Harz** mountains. To the southwest lies the **Rheintal,** and following the Rhine south, you reach the densely forested mountains of the **Schwarzwald.** From its highest point, you can see the snow-covered peaks of the Swiss **Alpen** to the southwest.

An der Nordsee ist es oft sehr windig.

On the beaches of the North Sea and the Baltic Sea there is often a cool onshore wind. **Strandkörbe** (literally: *beach baskets*) can be rented as shelter from the wind.

It also takes about a day to drive from **Freiburg,** at the western edge of Southern Germany, to the eastern border of Austria. You can follow the **Donau,** as it flows through a succession of culturally significant towns like **Regensburg, Passau,** and **Linz,** until you reach **Wien,** the capital of Austria.

Climate

The German-speaking countries show considerable climatic variation. In the north, the weather is influenced by the cool air currents off the **Nordsee** and the **Ostsee.** The summers are only moderately warm and the winters are mild, but often stormy and very wet.

In the central region, between the Northern Lowlands and the **Alpen** in the south, the summers are usually much warmer and the winters much colder than in the north. The highest summer temperatures occur in the protected valleys of the **Rhein** and **Mosel** rivers, providing perfect growing conditions for the thousands of acres of vineyards that produce the famous white wines of Germany.

To the south, the climate of the Swiss and Austrian **Alpen** is characterized by high precipitation, shorter summers, and longer winters. But even in these small

Weinberge in Süddeutschland

countries, the variation in climate from one area to the next is quite striking. In Switzerland, which is about half the size of the state of Maine, the climate is so varied that you can go windsurfing and skiing in a single summer's day!

1-6 Ein bisschen Geographie. First supply the two missing letters in each geographical name, then identify the appropriate category for each. Can you give the English names as well?

	REGION OR COUNTRY	CITY	RIVER OR SEA
1. Alp___	___	___	___
2. S___warzwald	___	___	___
3. W___n	___	___	___
4. Schw___z	___	___	___
5. N___dsee	___	___	___
6. Rh___ntal	___	___	___
7. Osts___	___	___	___
8. Mos___	___	___	___
9. ___terreich	___	___	___
10. Don___	___	___	___

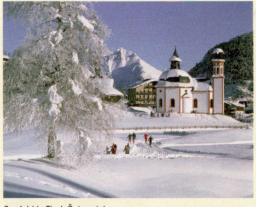
Seefeld in Tirol, Österreich

Bauernhäuser im Schwarzwald

In den Schweizer Alpen

There are two vocabulary lists per chapter. Organized according to parts of speech, items are also grouped alphabetically by theme wherever possible.

Nomen (Nouns)

der Himmel	sky; heaven
die Sonne	sun
das Wetter	weather
das Auslandsamt	foreign students office
das Buch, die Bücher	book
die Karte, die Karten	card; postcard; map
die Mensa	university cafeteria
die Vorlesung, die Vorlesungen	lecture; class

Verben

beginnen	to begin
gehen	to go
kaufen	to buy
kommen	to come
machen	to do; to make
regnen	to rain
scheinen	to shine
schreiben	to write
studieren	to study; to major in

Andere Wörter (Other words)

auch	also
dann	then
ein paar	a few
fast	almost
gar nicht	not at all
heute	today
heute Nachmittag	this afternoon
jetzt	now
morgen	tomorrow

nicht	not
noch	still
noch nicht	not yet
nur	only
oft	often
schön	nice; beautiful
viel	much; a lot
windig	windy
zuerst	first

Ausdrücke (Expressions)

Bis später!	See you later!
Klar!	Of course!
Toll!	Super!

Das Thermometer
   zeigt zehn Grad.
	The thermometer
	   reads (shows) ten degrees.

Die Vorlesungen
   beginnen
   erst morgen.
	(The) lectures don't
	   begin until tomorrow.

Das Gegenteil (Opposites)

bitte ≠ danke	please ≠ thank you
heiß ≠ kalt	hot ≠ cold
richtig ≠ falsch	true; right ≠ false; wrong

Die Farben

blau		blue
braun		brown
gelb		yellow
grau		gray
grün		green
rosarot		pink
rot		red
schwarz		black
violett		purple
weiß		white

Leicht zu verstehen (Easy to understand)

das Semester, die Semester
der Student, die Studenten
die Studentin, die Studentinnen
die Universität, die Universitäten
   (die Uni, die Unis)

Lerntipp: Some helpful strategies for learning vocabulary include writing out words, quizzing a partner, and creating your own sentences. You should also listen to and repeat aloud the recorded vocabulary items.

Ländernamen

die Bundesrepublik Deutschland (die BRD)	the Federal Republic of Germany (the FRG)
Österreich	Austria
die Schweiz	Switzerland
die Vereinigten Staaten (die USA)	the United States (the U.S.)
Kanada	Canada

> The names of most countries are neuter and are not normally preceded by an article (e.g., **England, Dänemark**). When the name of a country is masculine, feminine, or plural, the article must be used (e.g., **der Libanon, die Türkei, die USA**).

Die Nationalität

Er ist Deutscher.	He's a German.
Sie ist Deutsche.	She's a German.
Er ist Österreicher.	He's an Austrian.
Sie ist Österreicherin.	She's an Austrian.
Er ist Schweizer.	He's Swiss.
Sie ist Schweizerin.	She's Swiss.
Er ist Amerikaner.	He's an American.
Sie ist Amerikanerin.	She's an American.
Er ist Kanadier.	He's a Canadian.
Sie ist Kanadierin.	She's a Canadian.

Wörter im Kontext

1-7 Fragen und Antworten. Choose the appropriate response to your partner's questions or statements.

S1:	S2:
1. Woher kommst du?	a. Biologie und Chemie.
2. Was studierst du?	b. Ich auch nicht.
3. Beginnen die Vorlesungen heute?	c. Nicht viel.
4. Gehst du in die Mensa?	d. Nein, erst morgen.
5. Was machst du heute Nachmittag?	e. Aus Österreich.
6. Ich gehe nicht oft in die Disco.	f. Nein, noch nicht.

> Signs similar to the one depicted here can be found at border points of the European Union member countries (27 as of 2011).

1-8 Fragen und Antworten. Choose the appropriate response to your partner's questions.

S1:	S2:
1. Wie ist das Wetter?	a. Ja, fast dreißig Grad.
2. Regnet es noch?	b. Nur zehn Grad.
3. Was zeigt das Thermometer?	c. Nein, jetzt scheint die Sonne.
4. Ist es heiß?	d. Gar nicht schön.
5. Was machst du morgen?	e. Nein, ich komme erst morgen.
6. Kommst du heute?	f. Zuerst schreibe ich ein paar Karten und dann gehe ich schwimmen.

1-9 Was sind die Farben?

1. Schokolade ist _____.
2. Gras ist _____.
3. Milch ist _____.
4. Butter ist _____.
5. Ein Panther ist _____.
6. Blut ist _____.
7. Die Sonne scheint und der Himmel ist _____.
8. Der Himmel ist _____ und es regnet.

1-10 Die Nationalität, bitte!

1. Frau Bürgli ist aus Zürich. Sie ist _____.
2. Herr Karlhuber kommt aus Salzburg. Er ist _____.
3. Frau Kröger ist aus Hamburg. Sie ist _____.
4. Herr Chang ist aus San Francisco. Er ist _____.
5. Frau Thomson kommt aus Vancouver. Sie ist _____.

Kommunikation und Formen

1 Identifying people and things

1-1 to 1-4

Nouns: gender and definite articles

Nouns are the words used to name people and things. In English all nouns have the definite article *the*. In German every noun has *grammatical gender*, i.e., it is either masculine, neuter, or feminine. Nouns that are masculine have the definite article **der,** nouns that are neuter have the definite article **das,** and nouns that are feminine have the definite article **die.**

masculine	neuter	feminine
der	das	die
the	*the*	*the*

Although nouns referring to males are usually masculine (*der* Mann, *der* Vater) and nouns referring to females are usually feminine (*die* Frau, *die* Mutter), the gender of German nouns is not always logical.

der Himmel	**das** Wetter	**die** Sonne
der Computer	**das** Buch	**die** Vorlesung

You should learn each noun with its definite article as *one unit*.

Lerntipp: When you learn the vocabulary listed in the *Wortschatz* sections, you may find it helpful to highlight the nouns and their articles in three different colors according to gender.

1-11 **Wer ist das?** Identify the members of the Ziegler family.

1. Das ist …
2. Das ist …
3. Das ist …
4. Das ist …

die Mutter	der Vater	die Tochter	der Sohn

1-12 Verwandte Wörter. *(Related words.)* The names of the objects below are very close in form and meaning to their English equivalents. With a partner, read the names of the objects listed in the box, find each one in the illustration, and read the corresponding number.

S1: Der Computer ist Nummer vierzehn. Und der Fußball?
…

S2: Der Fußball ist Nummer siebzehn. Und der Hammer?
…

Words in different languages that are similar or identical in form and meaning are called cognates.

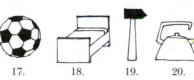

MASCULINE	NEUTER	FEMININE
der Computer	das Auto	die Bluse
der Fußball	das Boot	die Jacke
der Hammer	das Bett	die Karotte
der Mond	das Buch	die Maus
der Ring	das Weinglas	die Lampe
der Schuh	das Haus	die Rose
der Teekessel	das Telefon	die Vase

Most nouns that end in **-e** are feminine.

Plural forms: definite articles and nouns

1-5 to 1-7

All three definite articles **(der, das, die)** have the same plural form: **die.**

singular	plural
der	
das	die
die	

Although a few English nouns have irregular plural forms (e.g., woman, wom*e*n; child, child*ren*; mouse, m*ice*), most English nouns form the plural by adding *-s* or *-es* (e.g., student, student*s*; class, class*es*).

The table below shows the five basic plural forms for German nouns. The column *dictionary entry* shows how nouns are presented in vocabulary lists with the abbreviated plural forms. The column *you should learn* shows how a German noun must be learned, i.e., with its definite article and its plural form.

	abbreviation of plural form	dictionary entry	you should learn
1	-	der Finger, -	der Finger, die Finger
	¨	die Mutter, ¨	die Mutter, die M**ü**tter
2	-**e**	der Freund, -**e**	der Freund, die Freund**e**
	¨**e**	die Maus, ¨**e**	die Maus, die M**ä**use*
3	-**er**	das Kind, -**er**	das Kind, die Kind**er**
	¨**er**	das Buch, ¨**er**	das Buch, die B**ü**ch**er**
4	-**n**	die Karte, -**n**	die Karte, die Karte**n**
	-**en**	die Vorlesung, -**en**	die Vorlesung, die Vorlesung**en**
	-**nen**	die Freundin, -**nen**	die Freundin, die Freundin**nen*** *
5	-**s**	das Auto, -**s**	das Auto, die Auto**s**

* In the diphthong (vowel combination) **au**, it is always the **a** that receives the umlaut in the plural.
** All nouns with the plural ending **-nen** are derived from masculine nouns, e.g., **der Student, die Student*in*, die Student*innen*.**

1-13 Was sind die Farben? The nouns beneath the illustrations are listed as you would find them in a dictionary. Using the plural forms, say what colors the objects or animals are.

S1: Die Tennisbälle sind gelb.
   Und die Schuhe?
   …

S2: Die Schuhe sind braun.
   Und die Äpfel?
   …

1.
der Tennisball, ¨e

2.
der Schuh, -e

3.
der Apfel, ¨

4.
der Pullover, -

5.
das Auto, -s

6.
das Haus, ¨er

7.
das Bett, -en

8.
das Buch, ¨er

9.
die Banane, -n

10.
die Blume, -n

11.
die Katze, -n

12.
die Maus, ¨e

1-8 to 1-11

The indefinite articles *ein* and *kein*

The forms of the indefinite article *(a, an)* are **ein** (masculine and neuter) and **eine** (feminine). Just like *a* and *an,* **ein** and **eine** have no plural form.

Das ist **ein** Buch über die EU und hier ist **eine** Karte von Europa.

*This is **a** book about the EU and here is **a** map of Europe.*

	masculine	neuter	feminine
DEFINITE	**der** Student	**das** Buch	**die** Studentin
INDEFINITE	**ein** Student	**ein** Buch	**eine** Studentin

If the numeral *one* **(eins)** precedes a noun, German uses the indefinite article instead.

Jen hat heute nur **eine** Vorlesung.

*Jen has only **one** lecture today.*

The negative forms of the indefinite article *(not a, not any, not, no)* are **kein** (masculine and neuter) and **keine** (feminine). Note that **kein** does have a plural form: **keine.**

Das ist **kein** Restaurant, das ist eine Mensa.
Das sind **keine** Amerikaner, das sind Kanadier.

*That's **not a** restaurant, that's a cafeteria.*
*Those are**n't** Americans, they're Canadians.*

Infobox

Studying at the university

In Germany a smaller percentage of the population than in North America attends the **Universität**, but those who do are more likely than their North American counterparts to complete a master's degree. In order to be considered for admission, students must successfully complete the **Abitur,** a series of exams given in the last year of a **Gymnasium,** a college preparatory high school.

Students choose their area of study right away and take courses in that field from the beginning; there are no general education requirements. There are also no semester finals in the North American sense. Usually the first set of major exams is taken after the fourth semester. To qualify for these exams **(Zwischenprüfungen)**, students must acquire a certain number of **Scheine** *(certificates)*. To document their studies and areas of concentration, students collect the **Scheine** they earn in a **Studienbuch** (often electronic), similar to the North American transcript. The grading system uses numbers rather than letters: An A is a **1 (eine Eins)**, a B is a **2 (eine Zwei)**, etc.

Leipzig: Universitätsbibliothek

1-14 Was für dumme Fragen! Correct your partner.

▶ Glas (n)

S1: Ist das ein Glas?

S2: Nein, das ist kein Glas. Das ist eine Vase.

▶ Lilien (pl)

S1: Sind das Lilien?

S2: Nein, das sind keine Lilien. Das sind Tulpen.

1. Mikroskop (n)

2. Tennisball (m)

3. Jacke (f)

4. Biergläser (pl)

5. Pullover (m)

6. Mäuse (pl)

| Sweatshirt (n) | Ratten (pl) | Fußball (m) |
| Teleskop (n) | Bluse (f) | Weingläser (pl) |

2 Word Order

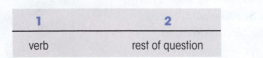

Position of the verb in yes/no questions

In yes/no questions the verb is always the *first element*.

Regnet es noch?   *Is it still **raining?***
Scheint die Sonne heute?   *Is the sun **shining** today?*

1	2
verb	rest of question

Position of the verb in information questions

In information questions the verb immediately follows a question word or phrase.

Wie **ist** das Wetter heute?   *How **is** the weather today?*
Was **zeigt** das Thermometer?   *What **does** the thermometer **read?***
Wie kalt **ist** es heute?   *How cold **is** it today?*

1	2	3
question word or phrase	verb	rest of question
Was	**machst**	**du heute?**

In German all question words begin with the letter **w** (pronounced like English *v*).

wann?	*when?*	**wie viel?**	*how much?*
warum?	*why?*	**wie viele?**	*how many?*
was?	*what?*	**wo?**	*where? (in what place?)*
wer?	*who?*	**woher?**	*where … from? (from what place?)*
wie?	*how?*	**wohin?**	*where? (to what place?)*

Be careful to distinguish between **wo** *(where)* and **wer** *(who)*. Don't let the similarities with English confuse you!

Note that German uses three words for the word *where*, according to whether it means *in what place, from what place,* or *to what place.*

Wo ist Graz?   ***Where** is Graz?*
Woher ist Martin?   ***Where** is Martin **from?***
Wohin gehst du heute Abend?   ***Where** are you going tonight?*

1-15 Fragen und Antworten. Choose the appropriate response to your partner's questions.

S1:
1. Wann beginnt der Winter?
2. Was kostet die Winterjacke?
3. Warum gehst du nicht schwimmen?
4. Was macht ihr heute Abend?

5. Woher kommt Stephanie?
6. Wo ist Chicago?
7. Wer ist Stephanie?
8. Wohin geht Stephanie?

9. Wann ist die Party?
10. Wie alt ist Karl?
11. Wie viele Studenten studieren hier?
12. Wie viel ist 32 Grad Fahrenheit in Celsius?

S2:
a. Ich finde es zu kalt.
b. Hundert Euro.
c. Im Dezember.
d. Wir gehen ins Kino.

a. In die Mensa.
b. In Illinois.
c. Aus Chicago.
d. Amerikanische Studentin.

a. Null Grad.
b. Zweitausend.
c. Im Sommer.
d. Er ist 18.

Wann und wo ist die Party?

1-16 So viele Fragen! Introduce the following questions with a question word. Your partner should know the answers.

▶ _____ kommt Heidi Klum?

S1: Woher kommt Heidi Klum?   **S2:** Heidi Klum ist aus Deutschland.

1. _____ ist das Wetter heute?
2. _____ beginnt der Sommer, im Juni oder im Juli?
3. _____ ist Innsbruck, in Deutschland oder in Österreich?
4. _____ kommt Neil Young, aus England oder aus Kanada?
5. _____ singt besser, Rihanna oder Beyoncé?
6. _____ Meter hat ein Kilometer?
7. _____ ist einunddreißig plus sechs?
8. _____ sind im Winter so viele Deutsche in Florida?

1-17 Smalltalk. Answer your partner's questions appropriately.

S1:	**S2:**
1. Wie heißt du?	Ich heiße …
2. Woher bist du?	Ich bin aus …
3. Wo ist das?	Das ist in …
4. Was ist deine Telefonnummer?	Meine Telefonnummer ist …
5. Wie viele Vorlesungen hast du heute?	Heute habe ich …

Position of the verb in statements

In English statements the verb usually follows the subject. This holds true whether the statement begins with the subject or with another element (e.g., an expression of time or place).

	The thermometer	**reads**	*only ten degrees.*
Today	*the thermometer*	*reads*	*only ten degrees.*

In German statements the verb is *always the second element*. If the statement begins with an element other than the subject, the subject follows the verb.

1	**2**	**3**	
subject	verb	rest of statement	
Das Thermometer	**zeigt**	nur zehn Grad.	

1	**2**	**3**	**4**
other element	verb	subject	rest of statement
Heute	**zeigt**	**das Thermometer**	nur zehn Grad.

1-18 Schönes Wetter. Read the following sentences, beginning each one with the expression of place or time given in parentheses.

1. Das Wetter ist heute sehr schön. (in München)
2. Das Thermometer zeigt fast dreißig Grad. (im Moment)
3. Stephanie hat keine Vorlesungen. (heute Nachmittag)
4. Sie geht mit Claudia, Peter und Martin schwimmen. (später)

Ja, nein, and the conjunctions in the table below do not count as elements in a sentence.

und	*and*	**aber**	*but*
oder	*or*	**denn**	*because*

Ist das Wetter schön?	*Is the weather nice?*
Ja, die Sonne **scheint**	*Yes, the sun is shining*
und der Himmel **ist** blau,	*and the sky is blue,*
aber es **ist** sehr windig.	*but it's very windy.*

Heute ist das Wetter in München sehr schön.

1-19 Und, oder, denn, aber?

1. Regnet es _____ scheint die Sonne?
2. Der Himmel ist grau, _____ es regnet nicht.
3. Ich gehe heute nicht schwimmen, _____ es ist kalt _____ es regnet.
4. Fünfzehn Grad ist nicht sehr warm, _____ es ist auch nicht sehr kalt.
5. Der Himmel ist blau, _____ es regnet nicht mehr.

Sprachnotiz **Verb forms in English and German**

The three forms of the English present tense have only one equivalent in German, i.e., forms like *it is raining* and *it does rain* do not exist in German.

it rains	
it is raining	**es regnet**
it does rain	

*How often **does** it **rain** in Hamburg?*   Wie oft **regnet** es in Hamburg?
*In Hamburg it **rains** very often.*   In Hamburg **regnet** es sehr oft.
*It's **raining** today.*   Es **regnet** heute.

Signal kommt: How would you say this in English?

1-20 Auf Englisch, bitte!

1. PETER: Kommt Stephanie heute oder kommt sie morgen?
   CLAUDIA: Sie kommt erst morgen.
2. MARTIN: Beginnen die Vorlesungen morgen?
   PETER: Nein, die Vorlesungen beginnen heute.
3. MARTIN: Wie viele Vorlesungen hast du heute?
   PETER: Heute habe ich keine Vorlesungen, aber morgen habe ich fünf.

1-21 Wie ist das Wetter? Answer your partner's questions according to the illustration.

S1: Ist der Himmel blau oder grau?   S2: Der Himmel ist grau.

1. Regnet es oder scheint die Sonne?
2. Ist es heiß oder kalt?
3. Ist es windig oder windstill?
4. Zeigt das Thermometer fünf Grad oder zehn Grad?

1-22 Wie ist das Wetter heute? Again, answer your partner's questions according to the illustration. Begin each answer with heute.

S1: Ist der Himmel heute grau   S2: Heute ist der Himmel blau.
oder blau?

1. Ist es heute kalt oder heiß?
2. Zeigt das Thermometer heute zwanzig Grad oder dreißig Grad?
3. Ist es heute windig oder windstill?
4. Scheint die Sonne heute oder regnet es?

1-23 So ist das Wetter heute. Look out the window and write a few lines describing what the weather is like today. Use the questions from the previous exercise and the additional vocabulary below as a guide. Begin your description with Heute ... Read your weather report to the class.

es nieselt	*it's drizzling*
es schneit	*it's snowing*
es donnert und blitzt	*it's thundering and lightning*
es ist neblig	*it's foggy*
es ist schwül	*it's humid*
es ist heiter	*it's sunny with some clouds*

Expressions of time and place

1-17

In German, expressions of time precede expressions of place. In English it is the reverse.

	TIME	PLACE		PLACE	TIME
Gehst du	**jetzt**	**in die Bibliothek?**	*Are you going*	*to the library*	*now?*
Nein, ich gehe	**jetzt**	**in die Kneipe.**	*No, I'm going*	*to the pub*	*now.*

> GERMAN: **time**   before   **place**

1-24 **Wohin gehst du jetzt?** Your partner isn't going where you expect. Use the expressions of place from the box below.

► jetzt

 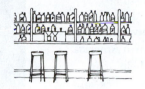

S1: Gehst du jetzt in die Bibliothek?   **S2:** Nein, ich gehe jetzt in die Kneipe.

1. jetzt

2. heute Abend

 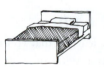

3. morgen Abend

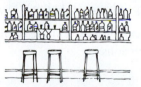 

4. am Sonntagabend

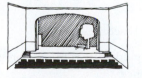 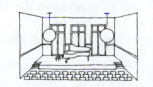

ins Theater	in die Mensa	in die Kneipe	ins Bett
in die Disco	in die Bibliothek	ins Konzert	in die Vorlesung

1-25 **Was machst du heute Abend?** Walk around the classroom, ask two of your classmates where they are going tonight, and respond to their questions.

Additional places you might be going: **ins Fitnesscenter, ins Cafe, auf eine Party, nach Hause** *(home).*

S1: Hallo, _____. Wohin gehst du heute Abend?

S2: Ich gehe heute Abend … Und du? Wohin gehst du?

S1: Ich gehe …

Continue by asking two other classmates where they are going **morgen Abend** and **am Sonntagabend.**

Infobox

About university life

In the German-speaking countries, university students receive much less guidance than in North America. They select their courses without the help of an advisor. Classes often meet just once per week, and no attendance is taken. Students' schedules are flexible, as is the number of semesters they spend at the university. For this reason, students talk about where they are in their studies according to semesters (e.g., **Ich bin im vierten Semester**), instead of using terms like "sophomore" or "junior."

Ich bin noch im ersten Semester.

1-18 to 1-19

Position of *nicht*

You have already learned that you use **kein/keine** to negate a noun preceded by **ein/eine** or a noun without an article.

Ist das ein Restaurant oder eine Kneipe?

Das ist **kein** Restaurant und auch **keine** Kneipe. Das ist ein Bistro.

Hast du morgen Vorlesungen?

Nein, morgen habe ich **keine** Vorlesungen.

When you want to negate any other words or expressions, you use **nicht** and place it directly in front of those words or expressions.

Es ist **nicht kalt.**
Es ist **nicht sehr** windig.
Ich gehe **nicht in die Disco.**
Ich gehe **nicht oft** in die Disco.
Ich gehe **nicht mit Bernd** in die Disco.

When you don't want to negate a particular word or expression, you place **nicht** at the end of the sentence.

Claudia kommt heute Abend **nicht.**
Martin kommt auch **nicht.**
Heute scheint die Sonne **nicht.**

1-26 Was für dumme Fragen! Your partner doesn't seem to be very knowledgeable. Use **nicht** to answer her/his questions.

S1: Ist fünf plus sechs zwölf?   **S2:** Nein, fünf plus sechs ist nicht zwölf.

1. Regnet es in Israel viel?   Nein, in Israel …
2. Beginnt der Winter im Januar?   Nein, der Winter …
3. Ist der Winter in Italien sehr kalt? Nein, in Italien …
4. Beginnt der Sommer im Juli?   Nein, der Sommer …
5. Donnert und blitzt es am Nordpol?   Nein, am Nordpol …
6. Regnet es am Südpol?   Nein, am Südpol …
7. Schneit es oft in Houston?   Nein, es schneit …

1-27 Was zeigt die Wetterkarte? With a partner look at the weather map. Using the weather symbols on the right and the description of the weather in Hamburg as a model, make up a weather report for another city. Read your reports to the class.

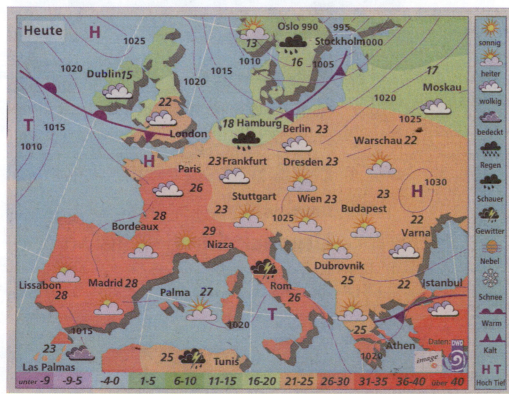

DAS WETTER IN HAMBURG

Heute ist das Wetter in Hamburg nicht sehr schön. Der Himmel ist grau und es regnet. Das Thermometer zeigt 18 Grad. Das ist nicht kalt, aber es ist auch nicht *sehr* warm.

1-28 Hauptstadtwetter. The electronic billboard on the **Kurfürstendamm** in Berlin shows the temperatures and weather conditions of four European **Hauptstädte.**

1. What do you think the word **Hauptstadt** means?
2. Referring to the key in the weather map above, describe in English the weather for each city on the billboard. (Note: **bewölkt = bedeckt**).

Video-Treff

Das bin ich

In the *Treffpunkt Deutsch* video, you will get to know some Germans – where they live, study, work, and have fun. Each of the 12 segments contains clips from informal, unscripted interviews with native speakers on topics relating to the chapter theme. In this segment the interviewees introduce themselves.

1-29 Was ist das auf Englisch? Find the English equivalents for the German words in boldface.

1. Ich **arbeite als** Radiomoderator.
2. Das **buchstabiert sich** S-o-w-a-d-e.
3. Homburg ist **eine Kleinstadt** nahe der französischen Grenze.
4. Nicolai **ist bald** drei Jahre alt.
5. Brandenburg ist **im Osten von Deutschland.**
6. Ich studiere **an der** Humboldt-Universität.
7. Ich studiere hier **Germanistik** und Sport.
8. Ich **bin** in Mainz **geboren.**
9. Ich **lebe** in Berlin und arbeite auch hier.

a. live
b. at the
c. work as
d. was born
e. is spelled
f. will soon be
g. a small town
h. German Studies
i. in Eastern Germany

Der Löwe ist das Symbol von Leipzig.

Always complete the **Was ist das auf Englisch?** exercise *before* watching the video in every chapter. This pre-viewing activity introduces you to some words and expressions you'll encounter in the video.

Before you watch the video, read through the exercises below. This will give you some additional information and let you know what you should be watching and listening for. Then watch the video and complete the exercises.

Lerntipps: Look for visual cues in the video for more information about the speakers and what they're saying.

Watch the entire video first, then watch again and pause and replay as needed to complete the tasks. Keep in mind that it's not necessary to understand every single word!

 1-30 **Was passt?** Choose the appropriate information to complete the sentences below.

1. Stefan Kuhlmann ist _____ und Radiomoderator in Berlin.
   ☐ Student   ☐ DJ

2. Ursula Klein-Turak ist 36 und kommt aus _____.
   ☐ Homburg   ☐ Leipzig

3. Thomas Scheier ist Student und ist _____ Jahre alt.
   ☐ 24   ☐ 23

4. Thomas studiert in Berlin _____.
   ☐ Finanzwirtschaft   ☐ Volkswirtschaft

5. Maiga Reitzenstein studiert an der _____ in Berlin.
   ☐ Humboldt-Universität   ☐ Freien Universität

6. Maiga Reitzenstein ist aus Göttingen und studiert _____.
   ☐ Englisch und Japanisch   ☐ Englisch und Spanisch

7. _____ Brieger ist 35 Jahre alt und ist aus Bocholt.
   ☐ Christoph   ☐ Christina

8. _____ Brieger ist 37 Jahre alt und kommt aus Mainz.
   ☐ Christoph   ☐ Christina

9. Nicolai Brieger ist fast 3 Jahre alt und kommt aus _____.
   ☐ Wiesbaden   ☐ Mainz

1-31 **Richtig oder falsch?** Decide whether the following statements are **richtig** or **falsch**. If the statement is **falsch**, provide a corrected version.

	RICHTIG	FALSCH
1. André Sowade kommt aus Ostdeutschland.	☐	☐
2. André ist 21 Jahre alt.	☐	☐
3. Anja Peter ist 23 und ist aus Brandenburg im Osten von Deutschland.	☐	☐
4. Susann arbeitet in Dresden, aber sie kommt aus Berlin.	☐	☐
5. Karen studiert Politik, Philosophie und Kunstgeschichte.	☐	☐
6. Stefan Meister ist 31.	☐	☐
7. Stefan Meister ist Student.	☐	☐
8. Anja Szustak kommt aus Leipzig und studiert auch dort.	☐	☐
9. Der Löwe ist das Symbol von Berlin.	☐	☐

3 Talking about people and things without naming them

What facility does this sign point to?

Personal pronouns: subject forms

When you want to talk about people without repeating their names, you use personal pronouns. The personal pronouns are categorized under three "persons."

1st person:	I / we *(to talk about oneself)*
2nd person:	you / you *(pl)* *(to talk to a second party)*
3rd person:	he, it, she / they *(to talk about a third party)*

		singular		**plural**
1ST PERSON	ich	*I*	wir	*we*
2ND PERSON	du	*you (familiar)*	ihr	*you (familiar)*
	Sie	*you (formal)*	Sie	*you (formal)*
3RD PERSON	er	*he, it*		
	es	*it*	sie	*they*
	sie	*she, it*		

As you have already learned, German nouns are either masculine, neuter, or feminine. The pronouns in the 3rd person singular (**er, es, sie**) are chosen according to the principle of *grammatical gender*, i.e., **er** for all nouns with the article **der, es** for all nouns with the article **das,** and **sie** for all nouns with the article **die.**

Ist **der** Student intelligent? Ja, **er** ist sehr intelligent.
Ist **der** Film lang? Ja, **er** ist sehr lang.

Ist **das** Kind intelligent? Ja, **es** ist sehr intelligent.
big Ist **das** Studentenheim groß°? Ja, **es** ist sehr groß.

Ist **die** Professorin fair? Ja, **sie** ist sehr fair.
Ist **die** Vorlesung interessant? Ja, **sie** ist sehr interessant.

In the 3rd person plural, the personal pronoun for all three genders is **sie** *(they).*

Sind **die** Studenten intelligent? Ja, **sie** sind sehr intelligent.
Sind **die** Vorlesungen gut? Ja, **sie** sind sehr gut.

singular	**plural**
der → er	
das → es	die → sie
die → sie	

1-32 Wie ist die Uni? You and your partner know different things about a university you've visited. Find out what your partner knows, and tell what you know. The questions and information for **S2** are in the *Anhang* on page A1.

S1: Ist die Uni gut?   **S2:** Ja, sie ist sehr gut.
S2: Sind die Computer up to date?   **S1:** Nein, sie sind nicht alle up to date.

…   …

Ist die Uni gut?	
	Nein, _____ sind nicht alle up to date.
Ist der Campus groß?	
Sind die Vorlesungen interessant?	
	Ja, _____ ist sehr gut.
	Ja, _____ ist gut, aber _____ ist noch nicht sehr gut.
Sind die Professoren fair?	
Ist der Präsident populär?	
	Ja, _____ sind fast alle sehr intelligent.
Ist die Bibliothek groß?	
	Nein, _____ sind nicht sehr modern, aber _____ sind sehr schön.
Ist die Mensa gut?	

1-33 Meine Uni. Using the previous activity as a guide, write a short description of your own university or college.

1-34 Welche Farbe hat Lisas Bluse? Your instructor will ask you the colors of your classmates' clothes. Sometimes you may want to add **hell** or **dunkel** to the basic color, e.g., **hellblau** *(light blue)*, **dunkelblau** *(dark blue)*.

LEHRER(IN):   Welche Farbe hat   STUDENT(IN):   Sie ist rot.
Lisas Bluse?

1. die Jacke   2. der Pullover   3. die Bluse   4. das Hemd

5. die Hose   6. der Rock   7. das Sweatshirt   8. die Jeans

4 Expressing states and actions

1-22

The present tense of *sein*

The present-tense forms of **sein** *(to be)* are as frequently used and as irregular as their English counterparts. Be sure to learn them well.

	singular			plural	
ich	bin	*I am*	wir	sind	*we are*
du	bist	*you are*	ihr	seid	*you are*
er/es/sie	ist	*he/it/she is*	sie	sind	*they are*
			Sie sind		*you are*

1-35 Ergänzen Sie! *(Complete!)* With a partner, take on the roles of the people below. Read the conversations, using the appropriate forms of **sein.**

1. Hallo!

   MARTIN: Hallo! Ich _____ Martin und das _____ Peter.
   HELGA: _____ ihr Brüder°?   *brothers*
   MARTIN: Nein, wir _____ Freunde.
   HELGA: Woher _____ ihr?
   MARTIN: Ich _____ aus Mannheim und Peter _____ aus Berlin.

2. Woher sind Stephanie und Tom?

   DAVID: _____ Stephanie Amerikanerin?
   MARTIN: Ja, sie _____ aus Chicago.
   DAVID: Und woher _____ Tom?
   MARTIN: Ich glaube, er _____ aus Kanada.

3. Wo sind Herr und Frau Ziegler?

   FRAU HOLZ: Entschuldigung, _____ Sie Herr und Frau Ziegler aus Göttingen?
   FRAU NAGLER: Nein, wir _____ nicht Herr und Frau Ziegler.
   FRAU HOLZ: Aber wer _____ Sie dann?
   FRAU NAGLER: Ich _____ Beate Nagler aus Kassel und das _____ Herr Müger aus Frankfurt.

1-36 Kleine Gespräche. In groups of three, take on the roles of the people below. Read the conversations, supplying the correct forms of **sein**.

1.
LUKAS: Hier ist ein Foto von Stephanie und Peter.
Sie _____ gute Freunde.
JULIA: Wie alt _____ Stephanie?
LUKAS: Sie _____ neunzehn.
ERGEM: Und wie alt _____ Peter?
LUKAS: Er _____ einundzwanzig.

2.
FRAU ERB: Wie alt _____ du, Brigitte?
BRIGITTE: Ich _____ fünf.
FRAU ERB: Und du, Holger, wie alt _____ du?
HOLGER: Ich _____ drei.
FRAU ERB: Und woher _____ ihr zwei?
BRIGITTE
UND HOLGER: Wir _____ aus Stuttgart.

3.
REPORTER: _____ Sie Amerikaner, Herr Smith?
HERR SMITH: Nein, ich _____ Kanadier.
REPORTER: Und Sie, Frau Jones, _____ Sie auch Kanadierin?
FRAU JONES: Nein, ich _____ Amerikanerin.

The verb: infinitive and present tense

1-23 to 1-29

The infinitive In English the infinitive form of the verb is usually signaled by *to: to ask, to answer, to travel, to do.* German infinitives consist of a *verb stem* plus the ending **–en** or **–n.**

infinitive	stem	ending
fragen *(to ask)*	**frag**	-en
antworten *(to answer)*	**antwort**	-en
reisen *(to travel)*	**reis**	-en
tun *(to do)*	**tu**	-n

The present tense In English only the 3rd person singular has an ending in the present tense: he ask*s*, she answer*s*, she do*es*, it work*s*. In German *all* the forms of the present tense have endings. These endings are attached to the verb stem.

singular		plural	
ich	frag**e**	wir	frag**en**
du	frag**st**	ihr	frag**t**
er/es/sie	frag**t**	sie	frag**en**
		Sie	frag**en**

1-37 Semesterbeginn. On their way to the cafeteria, Claudia and Martin meet Peter and Christo. Supply the appropriate verb endings.

PETER:	Grüß dich, Claudia! Tag, Martin! Das ist mein Freund Christo aus Italien.
CLAUDIA:	Tag, Christo. Woher in Italien komm__ du?
CHRISTO:	Ich komm__ aus Rom. Und ihr, woher komm__ ihr?
CLAUDIA:	Ich bin aus Hamburg und Martin komm__ aus Mannheim.
MARTIN:	Was studier__ du, Christo?
CHRISTO:	Ich studier__ Linguistik.
CLAUDIA:	Was mach__ ihr jetzt? Geh__ ihr auch in die Mensa?
PETER:	Nein, wir kauf__ jetzt unsere° Bücher, denn morgen beginn__ die Vorlesungen.

our

If a verb stem ends in **-t** or **-d** (**antwort-en, arbeit-en, find-en**) or in certain consonant combinations like the **-gn** in **regnen,** an **-e-** is inserted before the personal endings **-st** and **-t** (**du arbeit*e*st, er find*e*t, es regn*e*t**).

singular		plural	
ich	antwort**e**	wir	antwort**en**
du	antwort**est**	ihr	antwort**et**
er/es/sie	antwort**et**	sie	antwort**en**
	Sie antwort**en**		

If a verb stem ends in **-s, -ß,** or **-z,** the personal ending in the 2nd person singular is only a **-t** (not an **-st**): **du reis*t*, du heiß*t*, du sitz*t*.**

singular		plural	
ich	reis**e**	wir	reis**en**
du	reis**t**	ihr	reis**t**
er/es/sie	reis**t**	sie	reis**en**
	Sie reis**en**		

Verbs with the infinitive ending **-n** (as opposed to **-en**) also have the ending **-n** in the 1st and 3rd person plural and in the **Sie-**form: **wir tu*n*, sie tu*n*, Sie tu*n*.**

1-38 Wer macht das? Supply the verb ending that agrees with the subject given.

1. Warum antwort__ du nicht?
2. Sitz__ Frau Vogel oft im Park?
3. Maria find__ die Musik toll.
4. Warum tanz__ ihr nicht?
5. Jessica arbeit__ zu viel.
6. Was tu__ ihr im Moment?
7. Wann reis__ du nach° Spanien?

to

1-39 Kleine Gespräche. Complete the following conversations with the correct forms of the verbs given in parentheses.

Im Garten

FRAU ZIEGLER: Du, Robert, warum _____ du hier und _____ nichts? (stehen, tun)

ROBERT: Warum _____ du? (fragen)

FRAU ZIEGLER: Vater und ich _____ im Garten. (arbeiten)

ROBERT: Ich _____, ihr _____ zu viel. (glauben, arbeiten)

FRAU ZIEGLER: Und du, du _____ zu wenig°. (arbeiten)   *little*

Beim Rockfest

SABINE: Ich _____ Sabine. Wie _____ du? (heißen, heißen)

THOMAS: Ich _____ Thomas. Wie _____ du die Band? (heißen, finden)

SABINE: Die Band _____ sehr gut. Sag mal, _____ du? (spielen°, tanzen)   *to play*

THOMAS: Klar! Komm, wir _____. (tanzen)

Im Winter

FRAU ZIEGLER: Tag, Frau Berg. Das _____ ja kalt! (sein)

FRAU BERG: Ja, das Thermometer _____ minus zehn! (zeigen)

FRAU ZIEGLER: Wann _____ Sie nach Spanien, Ende Dezember? (reisen)

FRAU BERG: Nein, wir _____ erst im Januar, da° _____ es nicht so viel. (reisen, kosten)   *then*

Sprachnotiz **The present tense to express future time**

German uses the present tense to express future time more frequently than English. However, the context must show that one is referring to the future.

Nächstes Jahr **fliege** ich nach Leipzig.	*Next year I'm **flying** to Leipzig.*
	*Next year I'll **be flying** to Leipzig.*
Was **machst** du dort?	*What **will** you **be doing** there?*
	*What **are** you **going to do** there?*
Ich **arbeite** bei DHL.	*I'll **be working** for DHL.*
	*I'm **going to be working** for DHL.*

The international courier firm DHL is a subsidiary of Deutsche Post World Net. In 2005 the company decided to move its European Logistics center from Brussels to Leipzig, creating about 10,000 new jobs in the area. DHL stands for the first letter of the last names of Adrian Dalsey, Larry Hillblom, and Robert Lynn, the American founders of the company.

1-40 **Klischees.** With a partner, match the cities and activities according to the map.

Städte	Aktivitäten
Berlin	segeln gehen
Innsbruck	zum Karneval gehen
trade fair Kiel	auf die Messe° gehen
Köln	Walzer tanzen
money Leipzig	viel Geld° investieren
München	ins Daimler-Benz-Museum gehen
Norderney	Skilaufen gehen
Stuttgart	in die Philharmonie gehen
Wien	aufs Oktoberfest gehen
beach Zürich	am Strand° sitzen

1-41 **Reisepläne.** You **(S2)** and your friends are going to travel in the German-speaking countries during a year abroad. Your roommate **(S1)** wants to know what you are going to do in the cities you visit.

▶ August   Kiel / segeln gehen

S1: Wo seid ihr im August?   **S2:** Im August sind wir in Kiel.
S1: Was macht ihr dort?   **S2:** Wir gehen segeln.

1. September   München / aufs Oktoberfest gehen
2. Oktober   Stuttgart / ins Daimler-Benz-Museum gehen
3. Dezember   Wien / Walzer tanzen
4. Januar   Innsbruck / Skilaufen gehen
5. Februar   Köln / zum Karneval gehen

 1-42 **Hast du Reisepläne?** Interview your partner about her or his travel plans and report your findings to the class.

Hast du Reisepläne? Reist du im Sommer oder im Winter? Wohin reist du? Was *particularly* ist dort besonders° interessant? Wie ist das Wetter dort? Und was machst du dort?

Zusammenschau

🔊 Hören

Beim Auslandsamt

Claudia has accompanied Stephanie to a reception organized by the **Auslandsamt** of the **Ludwig-Maximilians-Universität** in **München.**

1-43 **Erstes Verstehen.** Listen to the conversation and choose the correct responses.

1. How many people are speaking?
   1   2   3   4

2. Which names do you hear?
   Tom   Martin   Stephanie   Claudia

3. Which of the following cities are mentioned in the conversation?
   Hamburg   Toronto   Frankfurt   Chicago

4. How many Americans are among the speakers?
   0   1   2   3

5. How many Canadians are among the speakers?
   0   1   2   3

1-44 **Detailverstehen.** Listen to the conversation again. Then write the answers to the following questions in German. Note the German spellings of physics and biology: **Physik, Biologie.**

1. Woher kommt Claudia?
2. Was ist Toms Nationalität? Ist er Amerikaner?
3. Kommt Tom aus Vancouver?
4. Was ist Stephanies Nationalität und woher kommt sie?
5. Was studiert Stephanie?
6. Was studiert Tom?

Schreiben und Sprechen

1-45 **Das bin ich.** Write about yourself, using the following questions as a guide.

Wie heißt du und wie alt bist du?

Was studierst du?

Was ist deine Nationalität? (*Ich bin …*)

Woher kommst du?

Ist das weit° von hier?   *far*

Ist es dort schön oder nicht sehr schön?

Wie groß° bist du?   *tall*

Welche Farbe haben deine Haare? (*Meine Haare sind …*)

1-46 **Wer ist das?** Your instructor will collect and randomly distribute the profiles you and your classmates wrote in the activity above. Read the profile you receive, omitting the name of the writer. The class will guess who the author is.

> Write your height in meters and centimeters. A height of **ein Meter und siebzig Zentimeter**, for example, is written **1,70** (spoken as **"eins siebzig"**).
>
> *Blonde* in German is **blond.**
>
> There are lists for fields of study in the *Anhang* on p. A14.

ft	cm
7	210
	200
	190
6	180
	170
	160
5	150
	140
	130
4	120
	110
	100
3	90

Lesen

Zum besseren Verstehen

1-47 **Ein paar Fragen.** Look at the title of the reading and the accompanying photos as you answer the following questions.

1. What is Kathrin Spyri's nationality? Approximately how old is she? Name one sport she likes to do.
2. In which country do the Schürers live? What is Mr. Schürer's profession? How old do you judge the children to be?
3. The man in the red jacket in the photo of the skiers is Arnold Karlhuber. What is his nationality? What is his winter occupation? Where do you think this picture was taken?

Eine Schweizerin, eine deutsche Familie und zwei Österreicher

Kathrin Spyri ist Schweizerin. Sie kommt aus Bern und studiert in Zürich Architektur. Sie ist im zehnten Semester und nächsten Sommer macht sie ihr Diplom. Kathrin jobbt oft für ein Züricher Architekturbüro, denn ihr Vater und ihre Mutter haben nicht viel Geld. Kathrin ist nicht sehr sportlich, aber sie spielt oft Federball, und im Sommer geht sie in die Alpen und wandert.

Kathrin Spyri

fun Familie Schürer

Das sind Sybille und Stefan Schürer aus Dresden. Sie haben zwei Kinder: Caroline und Moritz. Stefan ist Arzt und Sybille ist Programmiererin. Sie arbeitet aber nur morgens, denn Moritz ist nur morgens im Kindergarten. Im Winter gehen Sybille und Stefan vierzehn Tage zum Skilaufen in die Schweiz und die Kinder sind dann bei Stefans Mutter, Oma Schürer in Leipzig. Im Sommer gehen Stefan, Sybille und die Kinder drei oder vier Wochen nach Österreich. Sie wandern, schwimmen, surfen und segeln, und sie haben alle viel Spaß°.

Arnold Karlhuber

Arnold Karlhuber ist aus Salzburg. Er ist Automechaniker, aber im Winter arbeitet er als Skilehrer° in Kitzbühel. Arnolds Vater hat in Salzburg eine Autofirma, und Arnold arbeitet dort von April bis November. Arnolds Frau heißt Christa. Sie ist Buchhalterin° und sie arbeitet auch für Arnolds Vater. Christa ist aus München, sie ist aber jetzt Österreicherin. Arnold und Christa haben noch keine Kinder.

ski instructor

accountant

Arbeit mit dem Text

1-48 Ergänzen Sie! Fill in the missing information from the biographical sketches above. You should be able to guess the meanings of **Wohnort** and **Beruf.**

NAME	WOHNORT	BERUF	NATIONALITÄT
	Zürich		
Sybille Schürer			
		Automechaniker	
	Leipzig		
		Arzt	
			Österreicherin

Wort, Sinn und Klang

Wörter unter der Lupe

Cognates

In *Erste Kontakte* and this chapter you have seen that German and English are closely related languages. Many words are so close in sound and spelling to their English equivalents that you can easily guess their meanings. Words in different languages that are identical or similar in form and meaning are called *cognates*.

> Some words are identical or almost identical in form, but different in meaning. These are sometimes called "false friends": **arm** (*poor*), **also** (*so*), **fast** (*almost*), **bekommen** (*to receive*).

Infobox

Why German and English are similar: The Angles and Saxons

Many of the similarities between English and German can be traced back 1600 years to the time when the Angles and Saxons, Germanic tribes from what is today northern Germany, invaded Britain and settled there. Around 200 A.D. the Roman Empire encompassed not only the countries around the Mediterranean, but also present-day Austria, Switzerland, Southern Germany, France, and most of the British Isles. Beginning about the fourth century A.D., shiploads of Angle and Saxon warriors crossed the North Sea to England and attacked the increasingly vulnerable defenses of the Roman Empire. When the Romans finally retreated from Britain in the fifth century, the Angles and Saxons remained and settled the country. It was the Germanic languages of these tribes that became the foundation for present-day English.

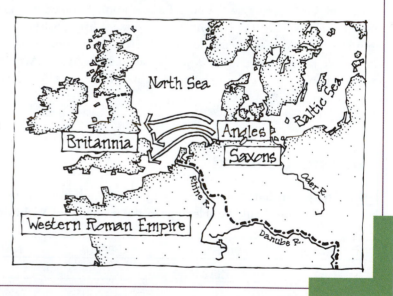

1-49 Leicht zu verstehen. Give the English cognates of the following sets of German words.

1. *Family:* die Mutter, der Vater, der Sohn, die Tochter, der Bruder, die Schwester
2. *Parts of the body:* das Haar, die Nase, die Lippe, die Schulter, der Arm, der Ellbogen, die Hand, der Finger, der Fingernagel, das Knie, der Fuß
3. *Descriptive words:* jung, alt, neu, hart, lang, laut, voll, frisch, sauer, dumm, gut, reich
4. *Animals:* der Fisch, die Ratte, die Maus, die Katze, der Hund, die Laus, der Wurm, der Fuchs, der Bulle, die Kuh
5. *Food and drink:* die Butter, das Brot, der Käse, der Apfel, das Salz, der Pfeffer, das Wasser, das Bier, der Wein, die Milch

1-50 Wie heißt das Restaurant? In the German-speaking countries, many restaurants and hotels have ornate wrought–iron signs. Look at the sampling below and match them with the names in the box.

| der Ochse | die Krone | die Sonne | das Lamm |
| der Schwan | das Kreuz | das Einhorn | die drei Könige |

Infobox (on previous page): The Norman invasion of Britain in 1066 brought further changes to the English language. French became the language of the ruling class, and evidence of this can be seen in examples like the following: It was the lower-class farmer who raised *swine, cows, and sheep,* all words of Germanic origin (in modern German **Schwein, Kuh, Schaf**). However, when the meat of these animals was served to the nobility, it was called *pork, beef,* and *mutton* (French **porc, bœuf, mouton**).

Zur Aussprache

German *ei* and *ie*

1-39 to 1-40

1-51 Hören Sie gut zu und wiederholen Sie!

| W**ei**n | W**ie**n | s**ei**n | s**ie** |
| d**ei**n | D**ie** | b**ei** | B**ie**r |

Distinguish between **ei** and **ie** by reading the following sentences aloud.

1. W**ie** v**ie**l ist dr**ei** und v**ie**r? Dr**ei** und v**ie**r ist s**ie**ben.
2. W**ie** h**ei**ßen S**ie**? Ich h**ei**ße Z**ie**gler.
3. Das ist nicht m**ei**n B**ie**r.°
4. D**ie** Schw**ei**z ist **ei**ne Demokrat**ie**.
5. D**ie**ter und Melan**ie** r**ei**sen in d**ie** Schw**ei**z.

Because of the inconsistencies of English spelling and pronunciation (e.g., N**ei**ther of my fr**ie**nds rec**ei**ved a p**ie**ce of p**ie**), English-speaking students of German often confuse the pronunciation of the German **ie** and **ei**. But unlike in English, the pronunciation of **ei** and **ie** is consistent in German. **Lerntipp:** Pick two German words you already know well to help remember the spelling and pronunciation of the sounds *ei* and *ie*, like **eins** and s**ie**ben, or even a short sentence: D**ie** Sonne sch**ei**nt.

colloquial for: *That's not my problem!*

🔊 Wortschatz 2

Nomen

der Tag, –e	day
die Woche, –n	week
der Monat, –e	month
das Jahr, –e	year
die Jahreszeit, –en	season
der Frühling	spring
der Sommer	summer
der Herbst	fall, autumn
der Winter	winter

In German the same word is used for a friend and for someone to whom one is romantically attached.

der Freund, –e	friend; boyfriend
die Freundin, –nen	friend; girlfriend
der Lehrer, –	(male) teacher
die Lehrerin, –nen	(female) teacher
der Mitbewohner, –	(male) roommate
die Mitbewohnerin, –nen	(female) roommate

Verben

arbeiten	to work
finden	to find
fliegen	to fly
glauben	to believe; to think
kosten	to cost
lernen	to learn; to study (e.g., for a test)
reisen	to travel
sitzen	to sit
spielen	to play
stehen	to stand
tanzen	to dance
tun	to do

Konjunktionen

und	and
oder	or
aber	but
denn	because

Fragewörter

wann?	when?
warum?	why?
was?	what?
wer?	who?
wie?	how?
wie viel?	how much?
wie viele?	how many?
wo?	where? (in what place?)
woher?	where … from? (from what place?)
wohin?	where? (to what place?)

Andere Wörter

besonders	particularly, especially
interessant	interesting
nichts	nothing
sehr	very
sportlich	athletic
von … bis	from … to
zusammen	together

Ausdrücke

ein bisschen	a bit
am Montag	on Monday
Ende Januar	at the end of January
im Januar	in January
im Winter	in the winter
nach Claudias Vorlesung	after Claudia's lecture
nach Florida	to Florida
Claudia kommt auch nicht.	Claudia isn't coming either.

Das Gegenteil

die Frage, –n ≠ die Antwort, –en	question ≠ answer
fragen ≠ antworten	to ask ≠ to answer
gut ≠ schlecht	good ≠ bad
hell ≠ dunkel	light ≠ dark
hier ≠ dort	here ≠ there
viel ≠ wenig	much ≠ little

Wohin gehst du?

in **die** Bibliothek	to the library
in **die** Disco	to the disco
in **die** Kneipe	to the bar/pub
in **die** Mensa	to the cafeteria
in **die** Vorlesung	to the lecture
ins Bett	to bed
ins Kino	to the movies
ins Konzert	to a concert
ins Theater	to the theater

Die Wochentage

der Montag
der Dienstag
der Mittwoch
der Donnerstag
der Freitag
der Samstag
der Sonntag

Like the months and the seasons, the days of the week are masculine.

Die Monate

der Januar	der Juli
der Februar	der August
der März	der September
der April	der Oktober
der Mai	der November
der Juni	der Dezember

Wörter im Kontext

1-52 Konjunktionen, bitte!

1. Claudia _____ Stephanie studieren in München.
2. Kommt Martin aus Berlin _____ aus Mannheim?
3. Ist es kalt? Ja, _____ nicht sehr.
4. Heute kaufe ich meine Bücher, _____ morgen beginnen die Vorlesungen.

1-53 Fragen und Antworten. Choose the appropriate response to your partner's questions.

S1:	S2:
1. Wann reisen Sie nach Italien, Frau Erb?	a. Nach Florida.
2. Wohin fliegen viele Deutsche im Winter?	b. Ja, nach Peters Vorlesung.
3. Wie lange seid ihr in Berlin?	c. Nichts.
4. Wie heißt Claudias Mitbewohnerin?	d. Von Freitag bis Sonntag.
5. Spielt ihr heute Eishockey?	e. Im Herbst.
6. Was tust du heute Abend?	f. Stephanie.

1-54 Fragen und Antworten. Choose the appropriate response to your partner's questions.

S1:	S2:
1. Wie viele Monate hat ein Jahr?	a. Hundertfünfzig Euro.
2. Wie viel kosten Peters Bücher?	b. Im Supermarkt.
3. Wie viele Tage hat eine Woche?	c. Zwölf.
4. Wo arbeitet Frau Berger?	d. Sehr gut.
5. Was macht ihr heute Abend?	e. Sieben.
6. Wie tanzt Stephanie?	f. Ich glaube, wir gehen in die Bibliothek und lernen.

Sprachnotiz lernen vs. studieren

Both verbs can mean to study, but with different connotations.

Thomas **studiert** Germanistik.	*Thomas is studying German language and literature* (as a major).
Andrea **lernt** für das Quiz.	*Andrea is studying for the quiz.*

Lernen also means *to learn,* as in English.

Andrea **lernt** Deutsch.	*Andrea is learning German* (learning the language, taking a language course).

1-55 Was passt nicht? In each group cross out the word that doesn't fit.

1. der Tag
   der Monat
   die Kneipe
   die Woche
   das Jahr

2. interessant
   sportlich
   dunkel
   lernen
   gut

3. sitzen
   nichts
   tun
   reisen
   kosten

1-56 Gegenteile.

1. Der Tag ist _____ und die Nacht ist _____.
2. Der Professor _____ und der Student _____.
3. Fünfhundert Euro sind _____ und fünf Euro sind _____.
4. Ein „A" ist _____ und ein „F" ist _____.

1-57 Ergänzen Sie!

1. Heute ist Montag und morgen ist _____.
2. Gestern war° Samstag und heute ist _____.   *was*
3. Heute ist Donnerstag und gestern war _____.
4. Heute ist Sonntag und morgen ist _____.
5. Gestern war Donnerstag und morgen ist _____.

Fischverkauf

Öffnungszeiten

Sommer   1.5. — 31.10.

Montag	:	9.00 - 18.00 Uhr
Dienstag	:	**Ruhetag**
Mittwoch	:	9.00 - 18.00 Uhr
Donnerstag	:	9.00 - 18.00 Uhr
Freitag	:	9.00 - 18.00 Uhr
Samstag	:	9.00 - 18.00 Uhr
Sonntag	:	11.00 - 18.00 Uhr

Was ist ein Ruhetag?

Freunde

Beste Freunde

Kommunikationsziele

Talking about …
- friends
- hobbies and leisure activities
- clothing and possessions

Expressing likes, dislikes, and preferences

Telling time

Describing people, places, and things

Strukturen

The verb **haben**

Verb + **gern** or **lieber**

Nominative case:
- subject
- **der**-words and **ein**-words
- adjective endings

Kultur

English loan words in German

The Black Forest and the cuckoo clock

Liechtenstein

Video-Treff: Freundschaften

Lesen: Eine Website für soziales Netzwerken

Vorschau

Uni-Sport

Just as in North America, universities in the German-speaking countries hold a variety of sports events for students throughout the year. Check out this flyer advertising a sports-related event, and glean the information you need to respond to the questions below.

2-1 Was ist das auf Deutsch?

Look for German equivalents in the flyer for the following: *tournament, drinks, running, entry/admission, information, 1:00.*

2-2 Was passt?

1. Wann ist das Fest?
   a. Im Sommer.
   b. Im Winter.
2. Wo ist das Fest?
   a. In Stockholm.
   b. In Hannover.
3. Wie viel kostet ein Ticket zum Turnier?
   a. 12 Euro.
   b. Nichts.
4. Wie groß sind die Teams für Beachvolleyball?
   a. Nicht mehr als sechs Personen.
   b. Nicht mehr als zwei Personen.
5. Wann endet das Programm?
   a. Um Mitternacht.
   b. Um Mittag.

Hochschulsport FEST

MITTWOCH // 16.06.2010

Turnier-Beginn
ab 12 Uhr // Eintritt frei

Chill & Grill
bis 24 Uhr mit Live Programm

Turnier-Anmeldung bis 13.06. // Infos: www.hochschulsport-hannover.de
Fußball Kleinfeldturnier // Team 7 Personen
Basketball Hallenturnier // Team 3 Personen
Volleyball Hallen -& Beachturnier // Team 6/4/2 Personen
Laufen 5000m // Nachmeldungen 13-15 Uhr vor Ort
Tennis // Einzel // Anmeldung 13-14 Uhr vor Ort
Side-Events & Aktionen von Sportgruppen Getränke & Kulinarisches // Promende Orchester der Königlichen Universität-Stockholm

Veranstaltungsort // Uni-Sportzentrum
Am Moritzwinkel 6
30167 Hannover tel. 0511 762 2192

Freunde

Schüler: German always distinguishes between students at a primary or secondary school (**Schüler**) and university students (**Studenten**).

Nina Ziegler sagt: Das ist mein Freund Alexander. Er ist groß und schlank, tanzt sehr gut und hat ein tolles Motorrad. Alex hat viele Hobbys: er spielt sehr gut Basketball und Eishockey, er schwimmt gern, er spielt ganz toll Gitarre, er sammelt Briefmarken und er kocht auch gern und gut. Übrigens ist Alex auch ein sehr guter Schüler.

Robert Ziegler sagt: Ich finde Alexander doof. Er telefoniert oft stundenlang mit Nina und abends ist er oft bis zehn oder elf bei uns und spielt seine blöde Gitarre. Was findet meine Schwester denn so toll an Alex? Ich finde nur sein Motorrad toll!

> The flavoring particle **denn** is frequently added to questions. It may express curiosity and interest, but it can also indicate irritation. It doesn't change the basic meaning of the question. **Denn** usually follows the subject of the question.

2-3 **Richtig oder falsch?** You will hear the two descriptions of Alexander. Indicate whether the statements about the descriptions are **richtig** or **falsch.**

	RICHTIG	FALSCH
1.	_____	_____
2.	_____	_____
3.	_____	_____

2-4 **Anders gesagt.** With a partner, read *Freunde* again and find equivalents for the following statements.

▶ Alexander ist sehr musikalisch.   =   Alexander spielt ganz toll Gitarre.

1. Alexander ist sehr sportlich.
2. Alex ist auch sehr intelligent.
3. Ich finde Alexander gar nicht toll.
4. Alex ist abends oft bis 22 oder 23 Uhr bei Zieglers.
5. Nina und Alexander telefonieren viel miteinander.

2-5 **Meine beste Freundin/Mein bester Freund.** Answer your partner's questions about your best friend.

> You will find additional vocabulary to describe personal characteristics and personality traits under **Persönliche Merkmale** in the *Anhang* on p. A19.

S1: Wie heißt deine beste Freundin/ dein bester Freund?
S2: Sie/Er heißt …

S1: Wie alt ist sie/er?
S2: Sie/Er ist …

S1: Wie ist sie/er?
S2: Sie/Er ist …

nice	groß	sehr nett°	(nicht) sehr praktisch
short	klein°	sehr intelligent	(nicht) sehr sportlich
always	schlank	immer° optimistisch	(nicht) sehr musikalisch
plump	mollig°	sehr kreativ	…

> You will find additional vocabulary for **Hobbys und Sport** and **Musikinstrumente** in the *Anhang* on pp. A15 and A16.

2-6 **Hobbys.** Now answer questions about your friend's hobbies.

S1: Was für Hobbys hat deine Freundin/dein Freund?
S2: Sie/Er … gern. (fotografiert / kocht / tanzt / schwimmt / reist / …)
   Sie/Er spielt gern …. (Tennis / Squash / Eishockey / Gitarre / Klavier° / …)

piano

Kultur / English loan words in German

Like every language, German is constantly changing, due in part to contact with other languages and cultures. **Lehnwörter** *(loan words)* entering a language usually reflect a particular area of influence from another culture. For example, words borrowed from English often relate to advertising, business, fashion, fast food, and pop culture. They include nouns like **das Marketing, das Meeting, der Blazer, der Softdrink,** and **der DJ;** adjectives like **cool**, **hip,** and **fit;** and verbs like **lunchen** and **stylen**.

German has also adopted many English words for technology. Verbs like **downloaden, chatten,** and **googeln** have become a regular part of the language, and nouns like **der Computer, die Homepage,** and **die E-Mail** are far more common than their German equivalents **die Datenverarbeitungsanlage, die Einstiegsseite,** and **die elektronische Post.**

Although these borrowed words take on German grammatical forms like gender or verb endings (*das Meeting, wir lunchen*), they usually have the same meaning as in English. However, some English words used in German have a rather unexpected meaning for speakers of English. Find the English words in the photos on this page. Which words are used in a different way from what you might expect?

2-7 **Englisch in Deutsch.** Match the German loan words with their English equivalents.

1. der Smoking
2. der Oldtimer
3. der Shootingstar
4. das Set
5. der Dressman
6. das Handy
7. das Notebook
8. der Beamer

a. suddenly successful person
b. male model
c. laptop
d. cell phone
e. place mat
f. vintage car
g. LCD projector
h. tuxedo

🔊 Wortschatz 1

///////////////////////

Nomen

die Schule, -n	school
der Schüler, -	} pupil, student in a primary
die Schülerin, -nen	or secondary school
die Briefmarke, -n	postage stamp
das Handy, -s	cell phone

Verben

haben	to have
sagen	to say
telefonieren (mit)	to talk on the phone (with)
trinken	to drink

Andere Wörter

bis	until
blöd	} stupid, dumb
doof	
immer	always
miteinander	with each other; together
nett	nice
übrigens	by the way

Ausdrücke

bei uns	at our house
bei Zieglers	at the Zieglers
Ich koche gern.	I like to cook.

Das Gegenteil

groß ≠ klein	big; tall ≠ little, small; short
intelligent ≠ dumm	intelligent ≠ stupid; dumb
mollig ≠ schlank	plump ≠ slim

Zeit

die Zeit, -en	time
die Minute, -n	minute
die Sekunde, -n	second
die Stunde, -n	hour
stundenlang	for hours
die Uhr, -en	clock; watch
zehn Uhr	ten o'clock
um zehn Uhr	at ten o'clock

die Minute, die Sekunde, die Stunde: Remember that most nouns that end in **-e** are feminine.

Getränke

das Getränk, -e	beverage, drink
das Bier	beer
die Cola	cola
der Kaffee	coffee
die Milch	milk
der Tee	tea
das Wasser	water
der Wein	wine

Sport

More sports and hobbies are listed on p. A15.

Sport machen	to do sports
Fitnesstraining machen	to work out
Basketball spielen	to play basketball
Eishockey spielen	to play hockey
Fußball spielen	to play soccer
Golf spielen	to play golf
Tennis spielen	to play tennis
joggen gehen	to go jogging
schwimmen gehen	to go swimming
snowboarden gehen	to go snowboarding
wandern gehen	to go hiking

Andere Hobbys

Hobby: Loan words like **Hobby** and **Baby** form the plural simply by adding -s.

bloggen	to blog
fotografieren	to photograph, take pictures
Gitarre spielen	to play the guitar
Klavier spielen	to play the piano
kochen	to cook
sammeln	to collect

Leicht zu verstehen

der Computer, -	downloaden
die E-Mail, -s	emailen
die Homepage, -s	kreativ
das Internet	modern
die Maus, ⸚e	musikalisch
der Softdrink, -s	praktisch

Wörter im Kontext

2-8 Was passt wo? Complete the sentences with the correct form of the appropriate verb.

kochen / haben / telefonieren / sammeln / sagen

1. Heute Nachmittag _____ wir keine Schule.
2. Alexander _____ Briefmarken.
3. Robert _____, er findet Alexanders Motorrad toll.
4. Warum _____ du immer so lang, Nina?
5. Was _____ wir heute Abend: Spagetti oder Lasagne?

Photo: This stamp commemorates the Men's Soccer World Cup held in Germany in 2006.

2-9 Was passt wo? One of the words in the list is to be used twice.

Zeit / stundenlang / Uhr / Stunde

1. Nina telefoniert oft _____ mit Alexander.
2. Für Alexander hat Nina immer _____.
3. Alexander ist abends oft bis elf _____ bei Zieglers.
4. Roberts neue Swatch ist eine sehr gute _____.
5. Eine _____ hat sechzig Minuten.

2-10 Was für Getränke passen hier?

1. In _____, in _____ und in _____ ist Koffein.
2. Babys trinken _____.
3. In _____ und _____ ist Alkohol.
4. In allen Getränken ist sehr viel _____.

2-11 Was passt wo? Some of the words in the list are to be used twice.

mollig / schlank / groß / klein

1. Elefanten sind _____ und Mäuse sind _____.
2. Fotomodelle sind sehr _____ und sehr schick.
3. Balletttänzerinnen sind nicht _____, sondern schlank.
4. Basketballspieler sind oft sehr _____.
5. Jockeys sind _____.

Photo: Bastelladen = *crafts store*

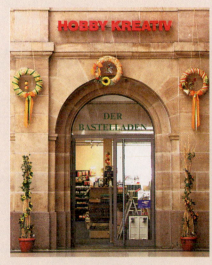

2-12 Getrennte Wörter. Reconstruct the cognates below by matching the parts appropriately.

1. mo–   a. –tisch
2. fotogra–   b. –kalisch
3. intelli–   c. –dern
4. kre–   d. –nieren
5. prak–   e. –ativ
6. telefo–   f. –fieren
7. musi–   g. –gent

Kommunikation und Formen

2-1 to 2-3

1 Expressing *to have*

The present tense of *haben*

Like English *to have*, the verb **haben** has many functions. For example, it is used to show possession or relationships, to describe the characteristics of people or things, to state amounts, and to express availability.

Peters Eltern **haben** ein schönes Haus.	*Peter's parents have a beautiful house.*
Hast du eine Freundin, Robert?	*Do you have a girlfriend, Robert?*
Ich **habe** braune Augen.	*I have brown eyes.*
Eine Minute **hat** sechzig Sekunden.	*A minute has sixty seconds.*
Wie viele Vorlesungen **habt** ihr heute?	*How many lectures do you have today?*
Heute **haben** wir viel Zeit.	*Today we have a lot of time.*

singular		plural	
ich	habe	wir	haben
du	**hast**	ihr	habt
er/es/sie	**hat**	sie	haben
	Sie haben		

Note that the **b** of the verb stem is dropped in the 2nd and 3rd person singular.

2-13 Was passt zusammen?

1.	Alexander	a. habe sehr gute Professoren.
2.	Zieglers	b. hast so schöne, braune Augen, Claudia.
3.	Du	c. habt ein schönes, großes Zimmer°.
4.	Ich	d. hat ein tolles Motorrad.
5.	Ihr	e. haben viele Freunde.

room

2-14 Fragen und Antworten. Supply the appropriate forms of **haben.**

S1:

1. _____ du heute Abend Zeit?
2. _____ Claudia blaue Augen?
3. _____ Peters Eltern ein Haus?
4. _____ ihr heute viele Vorlesungen?
5. _____ Sie ein Auto, Herr Berger?
6. Wie viele Stunden _____ ein Tag?
7. Wie viele Kinder _____ Zieglers?
8. _____ du eine Freundin, Robert?
9. Wie viel Geld _____ ihr noch?
10. Was _____ du jetzt, Politik oder Deutsch?

S2:

Nein, heute Abend _____ ich keine Zeit.
Nein, sie _____ braune Augen.
Ja, sie _____ ein sehr schönes Haus.
Nein, heute _____ wir nur zwei Vorlesungen.
Nein, aber ich _____ ein Motorrad.
Ein Tag _____ vierundzwanzig Stunden.
Sie _____ zwei Kinder.
Nein, ich _____ keine Freundin.
Wir _____ nur noch fünfzig Euro.
Zuerst _____ ich Deutsch und dann Politik.

2 Expressing likes, dislikes, and preferences

2-4 to 2-7

Verb + *gern*

In German the most common way of saying that you like to do something is to use a verb with **gern.** To say that you don't like to do something, you can use a verb with **nicht gern.**

Alexander kocht **gern.**	*Alexander **likes to** cook.*
Helga spielt **gern** Klavier.	*Helga **likes to** play the piano.*
Nina geht **gern** tanzen.	*Nina **likes to** go dancing.*
Robert lernt **nicht gern.**	*Robert **doesn't like** studying.*

2-15 Was machen diese Leute gern? The information for **S2** is in the *Anhang* on page A2.

S1: Was für Sport macht Anna gern? **S2:** Sie geht gern schwimmen.
S2: Was für Musik hört Anna gern? **S1:** Sie hört gern …
S1: Was für Spiele spielt Anna gern? **S2:** Sie spielt gern …

   … …

	SPORT	MUSIK	SPIELE
Anna		Jazz	
Peter			Karten
Maria	Tischtennis	Country and Western	
Moritz	snowboarden		Videospiele

2-16 Was machst du gern? Interview your partner about what she or he likes to do.

S1: Was für Sport machst du gern? **S2:** Ich gehe (spiele) gern …
   Was für Musik hörst du gern?   Ich höre gern …
   Was für Spiele spielst du gern? Ich spiele gern …

> You will find additional vocabulary for **Hobbys und Sport** in the *Anhang* on p. A15.

Sprachnotiz   gern haben

Gern haben is used to express fondness for someone.

STEFAN:	Liebst du Maria?	*Are you in love with Maria?*
LUKAS:	Nein, aber ich **habe** sie sehr **gern.**	*No, but I like her a lot.*

Ich gehe gern ins Museum.

Verb + *lieber*

To express a preference, German uses a verb plus **lieber**.

Was spielst du **lieber,** Karten oder Scrabble?	*What do you **prefer to** play, cards or Scrabble?*
Ich spiele **lieber** Scrabble.	*I **prefer to** play Scrabble.*

2-17 Das mache ich gern. Working with a partner, tell each other what you like or don't like to do. Follow the model. You will find additional vocabulary in the *Anhang* on pages A17 and A15 under **Essen und Trinken** and **Hobbys und Sport.**

▶ spielen: Golf / Tennis / Fußball / …

S1: Ich spiele gern Golf.　　**S2:** Ich auch.
Ich nicht,
ich spiele
lieber Tennis.

1. gehen: ins Konzert / ins Theater / ins Museum/ …
2. gehen: schwimmen / snowboarden / tanzen / …
3. spielen: Billard / Darts / Wii-Spiele
4. trinken: Kaffee / Tee / Cola / …
5. hören: Rock / Jazz / Mozart / …
6. trinken: Wein / Bier / Wasser / …

3 Telling Time

In colloquial German, telling time is similar to our system.

Wie spät ist es?

2-8 to 2-9

 eins (ein Uhr)　　　　 zwanzig vor zwei

 fünf nach eins　　　　 Viertel vor zwei

 Viertel nach eins　　　　 zehn vor zwei

halb zwei

To ask for the time, you can say either **Wie spät ist es?** or **Wie viel Uhr ist es?**

2-18 Wie spät ist es? Respond to your partner's questions.

▶

S1: Wie spät ist es?   S2: Es ist halb neun.

1.   2.   3.   4.   5.

6.   7.   8.   9.   10.

Official time: the 24-hour clock

Another way to tell time in German counts the day from 0 to 24 hours and is used for things such as train schedules, public announcements, and TV program listings. Because speakers of German see and hear this way of telling time every day, it is common to use the official forms in colloquial German as well.

Eine 24-Stunden-Uhr

13.00 Uhr		dreizehn Uhr
13.05 Uhr		dreizehn Uhr fünf
13.15 Uhr		dreizehn Uhr fünfzehn
13.30 Uhr		dreizehn Uhr dreißig
13.40 Uhr		dreizehn Uhr vierzig
13.45 Uhr		dreizehn Uhr fünfundvierzig
13.50 Uhr		dreizehn Uhr fünfzig

Note the different position of **Uhr** in writing (**13.20 *Uhr***) and speaking (**dreizehn *Uhr* zwanzig**).

2-19 Wann ist das? Use North American equivalents to answer the questions about events in this small town in the German state of Baden-Württemberg.

Samstag, 1. Februar:

Vereine / Organisationen

Jugendmusikschule: Instrumentendemonstration , 14 bis 16 Uhr, Gottlieb-Daimler-Realschule im Schulzentrum Grauhalde.
Vogel- und Aquarienverein: Hauptversammlung, 20 Uhr, Vereinsheim.
Radfahrverein „Wanderer": Mountainbiker-Treff 14 Uhr, Gmünder Straße 49.

Kultur

Manufaktur: Flamenco-Workshop, 12 bis 15.30 Uhr; Schwof mit Musik aus den 70ern, ab 22 Uhr; Bilderwand – Neue Arbeiten von Gui Ripper, Foyer, 1. Stock.

1. When does the mountain bike club meet?
2. When does a demonstration of musical instruments take place?
3. When is the workshop on flamenco?
4. What time does the bird and aquarium club meeting start?

2-20 Wie viel Uhr ist es? Respond to your partner's questions using official time.

▶  **15:10** Heute

S1: Wie viel Uhr ist es?   S2: Es ist fünfzehn Uhr zehn.

1.    2. [17:20]   3. [20:15]   4.

Infobox

The Black Forest and the cuckoo clock

Der Schwarzwald, named for its dense forests, is a wooded, mountainous region in southwestern Germany, famous for its natural beauty, picture-book villages, and handcrafted clocks, particularly the **Kuckucksuhr.**

  The clockmaking craft in the region was begun in the mid-seventeenth century by farmers who needed to supplement their meager income. Clockmaking was also a popular trade in the harsh, mountainous regions of Austria and Switzerland, but it was the clockmakers of the Black Forest who were the most successful in selling their clocks around the world. In Black Forest resorts like **Triberg** and **Titisee,** tens of thousands of cuckoo clocks are purchased annually by tourists from all over the world.

Nearly the entire Black Forest – an area about the size of the state of Connecticut – is a protected nature park.

Schwarzwälder Kuckucksuhr

Expressions of time referring to parts of the day

German has no equivalents for the terms *a.m.* and *p.m.* In colloquial German, you use the following adverbs of time to refer to the parts of a day. Note that all of these adverbs of time end in **–s.**

vormittags	*in the morning*	**abends**	*in the evening*
nachmittags	*in the afternoon*	**nachts**	*at night*

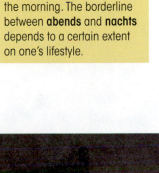

Both **morgens** and **vormittags** mean *in the morning,* but **vormittags** is not used for the very early hours in the morning. The borderline between **abends** and **nachts** depends to a certain extent on one's lifestyle.

2-21 Wie spät ist es jetzt? Take turns asking and responding in colloquial time, following the model below. Be sure to specify the part of the day.

▶ 13.45 Uhr

S1: Wie spät ist es?　　　　**S2:** Es ist Viertel vor zwei nachmittags.

1. 16.30 Uhr
2. 9.35 Uhr
3. 20.40 Uhr
4. 17.20 Uhr

5. 6.55 Uhr
6. 14.15 Uhr
7. 23.45 Uhr
8. 15.25 Uhr

Sprachnotiz

In colloquial German, the five minutes before and after the half hour are often spoken as follows:

 Es ist fünf vor halb zwei.　　 Es ist fünf nach halb zwei.

They can also be spoken as **ein Uhr fünfundzwanzig** and **ein Uhr fünfunddreißig.**

Wie spät ist es?

More on expressions of time

You just learned that adverbs like **nachmittags** and **abends** refer to parts of the day. You can also use them to express that something happens *repeatedly* or *regularly.*

Ich habe **nachmittags** Vorlesungen und **abends** gehe ich oft in die Bibliothek.
I have classes in the afternoon and in the evening I often go to the library.

You can use this same approach with days of the week or parts of days of the week, e.g., **freitags** *(on Fridays),* **sonntagabends** *(on Sunday evenings).*

Ich habe **montags** viel zu tun.
I have a lot to do on Mondays.

Ich gehe **samstagnachmittags** gern ins Kino.
I like to go to the movies on Saturday afternoons.

2-22 **Günters Stundenplan.** With a partner, complete Günter's schedule. Take turns asking your questions. The questions for **S2** are in the *Anhang* on page A2.

The questions for **S2** are in the *Anhang* on page A2.

> Note that the indefinite article **eine** will only be used when the response contains the word **-übung** *(lab)*:
> **Da hat er *eine* Matheübung.**

S1: Was hat Günter montags von acht bis zehn?

S2: Was hat Günter montags von fünfzehn bis siebzehn Uhr?

S2: Da hat er Zoologie.

S1: …

1. Was hat Günter montags von acht bis zehn?
3. Was hat Günter dienstags von zehn bis zwölf?
5. Was macht Günter mittwochs von elf bis dreizehn Uhr?
7. Was hat Günter mittwochs von dreizehn bis fünfzehn Uhr?
9. Was hat Günter donnerstags von fünfzehn bis achtzehn Uhr?
11. Was hat Günter freitags von zwölf bis vierzehn Uhr?
13. Wo ist Günter sonntags?

	Mo	Di	Mi	Do	Fr	Sa	So
8.00				Biochemie	Genetikübung	bei Helga	
9.00			Mikrobiologie		Genetikübung	bei Helga	
10.00			Mikrobiologie		Genetikübung	bei Helga	
11.00			Mikrobiologie			bei Helga	
12.00			Mikrobiologie			bei Helga	
13.00			Mikrobiologie			bei Helga	
14.00			Mikrobiologie		mit Tina	bei Helga	
15.00	Genetik				Tennis	bei Helga	
16.00	Genetik				Tennis	bei Helga	
17.00						bei Helga	
18.00						bei Helga	

2-23 **Stundenpläne.** Write your partner's name on a blank schedule and fill it in as you get answers to your questions. Follow the examples below. Then read your partner's schedule to the class. You can find a list of **Studienfächer** in the *Anhang* on page A14.

You can find a list of **Studienfächer** in the *Anhang* on page A14.

S1:

Was für Vorlesungen hast du montags?

Was hast du dienstagvormittags?

Was hast du dienstagnachmittags?

…

S2:

Von neun bis zehn habe ich Geographie.
Von dreizehn bis vierzehn Uhr habe ich Deutsch.

Dienstagvormittags habe ich keine Vorlesungen.

Von vierzehn bis sechzehn Uhr habe ich eine Physikübung.

…

2-24 **Wann ...?** Find out more about your partner's schedule. Ask the questions below and then add two of your own.

1. Wann gehst du normalerweise° in die Mensa?   *usually*
2. Gehst du abends oft in die Bibliothek?
3. Was machst du gern samstagnachmittags?
4. Um wie viel Uhr gehst du normalerweise ins Bett?

4 Answering *who* or *what*

2-12 to 2-13

The subject

A simple sentence consists of a noun or pronoun *subject* and a *predicate*. The subject is the person, place, or thing that the sentence is about. The predicate consists of a verb or a verb plus other parts of speech.

The boldfaced words in the following examples are the subjects of the verbs.

subject	predicate	
	VERB	OTHER PARTS OF SPEECH
Nina	tanzt	gern.
Nina und Alexander	gehen	oft in die Disco.
Sie	tanzen	dort oft bis zwölf Uhr nachts.

Remember that in German the subject does not always have to be the first element. If it is not first, it must immediately follow the verb.

OTHER PARTS OF SPEECH	VERB	SUBJECT	OTHER PARTS OF SPEECH
Freitagabends	gehen	**Nina und Alexander**	in die Disco.
Dort	tanzen	**sie**	oft bis zwölf Uhr.

2-25 **Alexander.** Find the subjects.

Nina sagt:
1. Alex ist abends oft bei uns.
2. Er tanzt gern und kocht auch gern und gut.
3. Abends lernen wir zusammen.

Robert sagt:
1. Ninas Freund ist viel zu oft bei uns.
2. Von morgens bis abends spielt er seine blöde Gitarre.
3. Ich finde sein Motorrad toll.

Alexander sagt:
1. Ich mache gern Sport.
2. Samstagnachmittags gehen Nina und ich joggen.
3. Dann spielen wir Videospiele.

2-12 to 2-13

The nominative case

As you progress through this text, you will learn that German grammar assigns every noun or pronoun in a sentence to one of four cases. These cases signal the function of the noun or pronoun in the sentence.

In the following examples, the forms of the definite or indefinite articles show that the nouns are in the *nominative case,* which indicates that they are the subjects.

Der Pulli kostet nur 20 Euro. *The sweater costs only 20 euros.*
Normalerweise kostet **ein** Pulli viel mehr. *Usually a sweater costs much more.*

	masculine		neuter		feminine		plural	
NOMINATIVE	der ein kein	}Pulli	das ein kein	}Hemd	die eine keine	}Jacke	die — keine	}Schuhe

Remember:
• Like *a* and *an* in English, **ein** and **eine** have no plural forms.
• **Kein** and **keine** do have a plural form.

2-26 Ich kaufe gern Kleider.

► Mantel (m)

coat **S1:** Wie viel kostet der Mantel°?
S2: Der Mantel kostet 490 Euro.

1. Rock (m)
belt 2. Bluse (f)
3. Kleid (n)
4. Schuhe (pl)

5. Sweatshirt (n)
6. Gürtel° (m)
7. Socken (pl)
8. Jacke (f)

2-14 to 2-16

The interrogative pronouns *wer* and *was*

The nominative forms of the interrogative pronouns are **wer** and **was.**

Wer ist Bill Gates? *Who is Bill Gates?*
Was ist Microsoft? *What is Microsoft?*

interrogative pronouns		
	PERSONS	THINGS OR IDEAS
NOMINATIVE	wer?	was?

2-27 Wer oder was? Complete each question with **wer** or **was.** Your partner responds appropriately from the choices given.

► _____ ist Roger Federer? Tennisspieler (m)

S1: Wer ist Roger Federer? **S2:** Roger Federer ist ein Tennisspieler.

1. _____ ist Red Bull?
2. _____ ist *Rolling Stone?*
3. _____ ist Hillary Rodham Clinton?
4. _____ ist Afrika?

5. _____ ist Mexiko?
6. _____ sind Chopin und Tschaikowski?
7. _____ sind Moskitos?
8. _____ ist J. K. Rowling?

Land (n)   Kontinent (m)
Komponisten (pl)   Magazin (n)
Getränk (n)   Politikerin (f)
Autorin (f)   Insekten (pl)

Video-Treff

Freundschaften

In this video segment Anja Szustak, André, Susann, Thomas, Karen, and Stefan Kuhlmann will introduce good friends. Be sure to complete the **Was ist das auf Englisch?** exercise before watching the video.

2-28 **Was ist das auf Englisch?**

1. Wir haben ein **gemeinsames** Hobby, und das ist Schwimmen.
2. Wir kochen nicht so **häufig** zusammen.
3. Wir **kennen uns** seit zwei Jahren.
4. Wir **sind** zusammen zur Schule **gegangen.**
5. Wir wohnen zusammen in einer **Wohngemeinschaft** in Kreuzberg.
6. Er arbeitet als **Veranstaltungstechniker.**
7. Meine Freundin ist sehr offen und **natürlich.**
8. Er ist jetzt **zirka** sechs Jahre alt.
9. Meine Freundin und ich sind beide sehr **verliebt.**

a. approximately
b. often
c. natural
d. went
e. common
f. event technician
g. have known each other
h. in love
i. shared housing

Before you watch the video, read through the exercises below. This will give you some additional information and let you know what you should be watching and listening for. Then watch the video and complete the exercises.

2-29 **Wer sagt das?** The following statements fit what Anja, André, or Susann said about their friends. Identify the person who best matches each statement.

	Anja	André	Susann
1. Meine Freundin und ich gehen gern schwimmen.	☐	☐	☐
2. Meine Freundin heißt Ines.	☐	☐	☐
3. Meine Freundin studiert in Dresden Medizin.	☐	☐	☐
4. Meine Freundin heißt Charlotte oder „Charlie".	☐	☐	☐
5. Meine Freundin und ich gehen gern ins Kino oder tanzen.	☐	☐	☐
6. Meine beste Freundin heißt Kristina.	☐	☐	☐
7. Meine Freundin und ich gehen oft zusammen joggen.	☐	☐	☐
8. Meine Freundin fotografiert sehr gern.	☐	☐	☐
9. Meine Freundin arbeitet in Berlin.	☐	☐	☐
10. Meine Freundin und ich hören beide gern Sinatra.	☐	☐	☐

2-30 Richtig oder falsch? Decide whether the following statements about Thomas, Karen, and Stefan Kuhlmann's friends are **richtig** or **falsch**. If the statement is **falsch**, provide a correct version.

	RICHTIG	FALSCH
1. Thomas: Meine Freundin ist Deutsche und kommt aus Frankfurt.	☐	☐
2. Thomas: Meine Freundin heißt Elisabeth.	☐	☐
3. Thomas: Meine Freundin ist sehr offen und natürlich.	☐	☐
4. Karen: Öcsi ist 20 Jahre alt.	☐	☐
5. Karen: Öcsi und ich sind schon vier Jahre zusammen.	☐	☐
6. Karen: Mein Freund arbeitet nicht.	☐	☐
7. Karen: Chirac ist ein großer weißer Hund.	☐	☐
8. Karen: Chirac ist etwa sechs Jahre alt.	☐	☐
9. Stefan Kuhlmann: Meine Freundin heißt Barbara.	☐	☐
10. Stefan Kuhlmann: Meine Freundin ist 22 Jahre „jung".	☐	☐

5 Describing people, places, and things

Der-words in the nominative case

2-17 to 2-18

The endings of words like **dieser** *(this)*, **jeder** *(each, every)*, and **welcher** *(which)* correspond closely to the forms of the definite article. For this reason these words, along with the definite article, are called **der–words.**

Welches deutschsprachige Land hat nur 34 000 Einwohner?
Which German-speaking country has only 34,000 inhabitants?

Ich glaube, **dieses** Land heißt Liechtenstein.
I believe **this** country is called Liechtenstein.

Diese Briefmarken kommen aus Liechtenstein.
These stamps are from Liechtenstein.

In Liechtenstein kauft fast **jeder** Tourist Briefmarken.
In Liechtenstein just about **every** tourist buys stamps.

	masculine	neuter	feminine	plural
NOMINATIVE	dies**er**	dies**es**	dies**e**	dies**e**
	(d**er**)	(da**s**)	(di**e**)	(di**e**)

2-31 Dies-, jed-, welch-?

than
1. _____ deutschsprachige Land (n) ist kleiner als° die Schweiz?
2. Woher sind _____ Briefmarken (pl)?

so...wie: *as...as*
3. Nicht _____ Land (n) hat so° schöne Briefmarken wie Liechtenstein.
4. _____ Bus (m) ist das? Ist es der Bus nach Vaduz?
5. In Vaduz kauft fast _____ Tourist (m) ein paar Briefmarken.
6. Sind _____ Touristen (pl) Amerikaner oder Kanadier?

Infobox

Liechtenstein

Nestled in the **Alpen** between Austria and Switzerland lies the principality of **Liechtenstein** (capital: **Vaduz**). With an area of only 62 square miles (15.6 miles long and 3.75 miles wide), it is the smallest of the German-speaking countries.

Liechtenstein has its own government and constitution, but since 1920 it has been using Swiss currency.

The 35,000 inhabitants of Liechtenstein enjoy a high standard of living, and taxes are so low that many foreign companies are located there. In fact, there are more companies registered in Liechtenstein than there are inhabitants.

Liechtenstein is well known to anyone who collects **Briefmarken.** Its thriving philatelic industry does millions of dollars worth of business annually.

Das Wappen von Liechtenstein

Hier residiert der Fürst von Liechtenstein.

2-19 to 2-22

Ein-words in the nominative case: *ein, kein,* and the possessive adjectives

Both **ein** and **kein** belong to a group of words called **ein–**words. Also included in this group are the possessive adjectives, which are used to indicate possession or relationships, e.g., *my* book, *my* friend. The chart below shows the personal pronouns with their corresponding possessive adjectives.

singular				plural			
PERSONAL PRONOUN		POSSESSIVE ADJECTIVE		PERSONAL PRONOUN		POSSESSIVE ADJECTIVE	
ich	*I*	**mein**	*my*	**wir**	*we*	**unser**	*our*
du	*you*	**dein**	*your*	**ihr**	*you*	**euer**	*your*
Sie	*you*	**Ihr**	*your*	**Sie**	*you*	**Ihr**	*your*
er	*he, it*	**sein**	*his, its*				
es	*it*	**sein**	*its*	**sie**	*they*	**ihr**	*their*
sie	*she, it*	**ihr**	*her, its*				

Like the formal **Sie,** the formal **Ihr** is always capitalized. The possessive adjectives take the same endings as **ein** and **kein.**

| | Wo leben **deine** besten Freundinnen jetzt, Kirsten? | *Where do **your** best friends live now, Kirsten?* |

Wo leben **deine** besten Freundinnen jetzt, Kirsten?

*Where do **your** best friends live now, Kirsten?*

Meine Freundin Maria lebt in Hamburg, und **meine** Freundin Anna und **ihr** Mann leben in Düsseldorf.

__My__ friend Maria lives in Hamburg and __my__ friend Anna and __her__ husband live in Düsseldorf.

Wie alt sind **Ihre** Kinder, Frau Ziegler?

*How old are **your** children, Ms. Ziegler?*

Unsere Tochter ist sechzehn und **unser** Sohn ist vierzehn.

__Our__ daughter is sixteen and __our__ son is fourteen.

In the following chart the possessive adjective **mein** is used to show the nominative forms of all possessive adjectives.

	masculine	**neuter**	**feminine**	**plural**
NOMINATIVE	mein Vater	mein Auto	mein**e** Freundin	mein**e** Eltern

When an ending is added to **euer**, the **e** before the **r** is dropped.

Ist **eure** Mensa gut?   *Is **your** dining hall good?*

2-32 Günter. Supply the appropriate forms of **mein**.

Ich heiße Günter, bin zwanzig Jahre alt und studiere hier in Leipzig Genetik. _____ Eltern leben auch hier in Leipzig. _____ Vater ist Polizist und _____ Mutter ist Lehrerin. _____ Bruder Stefan ist siebzehn und geht noch in die Schule. _____ Schwester Melanie ist zweiundzwanzig und studiert in Hamburg Biochemie. _____ Freundinnen heißen Helga und Tina und sie studieren auch hier in Leipzig.

2-33 Ein kleines Gespräch. Supply the appropriate forms of **ihr, Ihr,** and **unser**.

FRAU BENN: Wie alt sind _____ Kinder jetzt, Herr Haag?

HERR HAAG: _____ Tochter ist sechsundzwanzig und _____ Söhne sind einundzwanzig und siebzehn.

FRAU BENN: Und wo lebt _____ Tochter?

HERR HAAG: Laura und _____ Mann leben in Hannover.

FRAU BENN: Und _____ Söhne?

HERR HAAG: Lukas studiert in Münster und _____ Sohn Daniel ist noch hier bei uns.

2-34 Wie ist eure Uni? Imagine that you and your partner are studying at different universities. Find out about your partner's school by completing the questions and responses with the appropriate forms of **euer** and **unser**.

S1:
1. Wie alt ist _____ Uni (f)?
2. Ist _____ Campus (m) groß?
3. Wie sind _____ Vorlesungen (pl)?
4. Ist _____ Bibliothek (f) gut?
5. Sind _____ Computer (pl) up to date?
6. Wie ist _____ Mensa?
7. Sind _____ Studentenheime (pl) schön? *expensive*
8. Wie gut ist _____ Footballteam (n)?

S2:
_____ Uni ist fast 200 Jahre alt.
Nein, _____ Campus ist nicht sehr groß.
_____ Vorlesungen sind sehr interessant.
Ja, _____ Bibliothek ist sehr gut.
Ja, _____ Computer sind fast alle up to date.
_____ Mensa ist gut, aber ein bisschen zu teuer°.
Ja, _____ Studentenheime sind sehr modern und sehr schön.
_____ Footballteam ist echt spitze°.

echt spitze: *really great*

2-35 **Unsere Uni.** Gather in groups of four or five. One student plays a reporter who is interested in finding out more about your university or college. The reporter can use the questions in the previous activity as a model. Take turns responding to the reporter's questions.

2-23 to 2-26

Nominative endings of adjectives preceded by *der*-words

An adjective takes an ending when it comes directly before the noun it describes.

Diese elegant**en** Schuhe kosten nur 50 Euro.   *These elegant shoes cost only 50 euros.*

	masculine	neuter	feminine	plural
NOMINATIVE	der rot**e** Pulli	das blau**e** Hemd	die weiß**e** Jacke	die braun**en** Schuhe

In the nominative, these same endings occur after *all* **der**–words, e.g., **der** rot**e** Pulli, **dieses** blau**e** Hemd, **jede** weiß**e** Jacke, **welche** braun**en** Schuhe.

   If two or more adjectives come directly before a noun, they all have the same ending.

Wie viel kosten diese beid**en**   *How much do these two pretty blouses cost?*
   hübsch**en** Blusen?

An adjective takes an ending even if the noun to which it refers is not repeated.

Die rot**e** Bluse kostet 40 Euro und   *The red blouse costs 40 euros and*
   die gelb**e** kostet 55 Euro.   *the yellow one costs 55 euros.*

2-36 Bei Peek & Cloppenburg.

1. **S1:** Wie viel kosten diese hübsch___ Blusen?
   S2: Die rot___ Bluse kostet 40 Euro und die weiß___ Bluse kostet 35 Euro.
2. **S1:** Wie viel kosten diese schick___ Pullis?
   S2: Der weiß___ Pulli kostet 55 Euro und der rot___ kostet 60 Euro.
3. **S1:** Wie viel kosten diese toll___ Sweatshirts?
   S2: Das blau___ Sweatshirt kostet 20 Euro und das rot___ kostet 30 Euro.
4. **S1:** Wie viel kosten diese lang___ Mäntel?
   S2: Der braun___ Mantel kostet 215 Euro und der dunkelblau___ kostet 300 Euro.
5. **S1:** Wie viel kosten diese sportlich___ Jacken?
   S2: Die schwarz___ Jacke kostet 110 Euro und die weiß___ kostet 115 Euro.
6. **S1:** Wie viel kosten diese beid___ toll___ T-Shirts?
   S2: Das weiß___ T-Shirt kostet 12 Euro und das schwarz___ kostet 17 Euro.

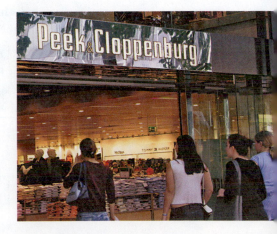

Nominative endings of adjectives preceded by *ein*-words

	masculine	neuter	feminine	plural
NOMINATIVE	**ein** rot**er** Pulli	**ein** blau**es** Hemd	eine weiß**e** Jacke	keine braun**en** Schuhe

In the chart above, you see that the **ein-**word has no ending in the masculine and neuter. In these two instances, the adjective itself shows the gender and case of the noun by taking the appropriate **der-**word ending: dies**er** Pulli, **ein** rot**er** Pulli; dies**es** Hemd, **ein** blau**es** Hemd.

CLAUDIA: Dein rot**er** Pullover ist echt toll. *Your red sweater is really fabulous.*
MARTIN: Ja, und er war nur halb so teuer *Yes, and it was only half as expensive*
         wie mein neu**es** blau**es** Hemd. *as my new blue shirt.*

2-37 Komplimente. Look at what your classmates are wearing and compliment them on a specific article of clothing.

Lisa, dein roter Rock ist sehr schick.
David, deine schwarze Jacke ist echt cool.

sehr schick   total hip   sehr interessant   echt spitze

echt toll   elegant   echt cool   schön   sehr sportlich

Sprachnotiz — The subject completion

Sometimes the predicate contains a noun that further describes what the subject is or what the subject is called. This noun is called a *subject completion*.

The boldfaced words in the following examples are subject completions. The verbs **heißt** and **ist** function like equal signs, i.e., they show that the subject and the subject completion are one and the same person or thing. Thus, like the subject, they are in the nominative case.

Ninas Freund heißt **Alexander.** (Ninas Freund = **Alexander.**)
Er ist **ein toller Tänzer.** (Er = **ein toller Tänzer.**)

74 / vierundsiebzig   **KAPITEL 2**

2-38 **Wir spielen Trivial Pursuit.** In each response, use the appropriate form of the indefinite article. The information for **S2** is in the *Anhang* on page A3.

S1: Wer ist Johnny Depp?

S2: Johnny Depp ist ein amerikanischer Filmstar.

…   …

LEUTE (WER?)		GETRÄNKE (WAS?)		GEOGRAPHIE (WAS?)	
Johnny Depp		Löwenbräu	deutsches Bier	Angola	afrikanisches Land
Margaret Atwood		Chianti		Linz	
David Cameron	englischer Politiker	Fanta		die Wolga	russischer Fluss
Maria Callas		Budweiser	amerikanisches Bier	Brandenburg	
Felix Mendelssohn	deutscher Komponist	Benedictine		der Vesuv	italienischer Vulkan

Nominative endings of unpreceded adjectives

2-23 to 2-26

	masculine	neuter	feminine	plural
NOMINATIVE	gut**er** Kaffee	gut**es** Bier	gut**e** Milch	gut**e** Oliven

Adjectives that are not preceded by a **der**–word or an **ein**–word show the gender, number, and case of the noun by taking the appropriate **der**–word ending.

Warum ist dies**er** Kaffee so teuer?
Gut**er** Kaffee ist immer teuer.

Why is this coffee so expensive?
Good coffee is always expensive.

2-39 **Herr Ziegler im Feinkostgeschäft°.**   *gourmet foods store*

▶ dieser Kaffee

S1: Warum ist dieser Kaffee so teuer?   **S2:** Guter Kaffee ist immer teuer.

1. diese Salami
2. dieses Bier
3. diese Pistazien (pl)
4. dieser Tee
5. dieser Wein
6. diese Oliven (pl)
7. dieses Olivenöl
8. diese Schokolade

Zusammenschau

Hören

Freundinnen

Listen to what Beate and Sabine will be doing between the completion of their **Abitur** and the beginning of their university studies.

NEUE VOKABELN

schon	*already*
das Geschäft	*store*
seit	*since*
die Radtour	*bicycle trip*
das Geld	*money*
suchen	*to look for*
bald	*soon*
fahren	*to travel*
durch	*through*
wieder	*again*
der Koffer, –	*suitcase*
die Wohnung	*apartment*

2-40 Erstes Verstehen. Listen to the narrative and choose the correct responses.

1. Which cities are mentioned?
   Köln   Göttingen   Schweinfurt   Schwerin
2. Which months of the year do you hear?
   Juni   Juli   August   September   Oktober
3. What types of stores do you hear?
   Feinkostgeschäft   Fotogeschäft   Schuhgeschäft   Sportgeschäft
4. Which countries are mentioned?
   Dänemark   Deutschland   Österreich   Schweden
   die Schweiz   Liechtenstein

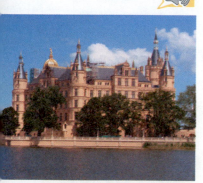

Das Schloss in Schwerin

2-41 Detailverstehen. Listen to the narrative again and answer the following questions.

1. Wo leben Beate und Sabine im Juli und wo leben sie im Oktober?
2. Was planen Beate und Sabine für September?
3. Warum suchen sie für August Arbeit?
4. Was ist Beates Hobby?
5. Wer arbeitet im Fotogeschäft und wer im Sportgeschäft?
6. Ende September sind Beate und Sabine wieder in Schwerin. Was machen sie dann?

After listening to the narrative, look at the map inside the front cover and locate the places mentioned.

Schreiben und Sprechen

2-42 **Meine beste Freundin/Mein bester Freund.** Write a description of your best friend, using the following questions to guide you. You may want to refer to the lists of **Studienfächer, Jobs und Berufe, Hobbys und Sport, Musikinstrumente,** and **Persönliche Merkmale** (*personal characteristics*) in the *Anhang* on pages A14–A16 and A19.

- Wie heißt deine beste Freundin/dein bester Freund?
- Wie alt ist sie/er?
- Wo wohnt sie/er? Im Studentenheim oder zu Hause°, oder hat sie/er ein Zimmer oder eine Wohnung?
- Was studiert sie/er oder wo arbeitet sie/er? *(Sie/Er arbeitet bei ...)*
- Was sind ihre/seine Hobbys?
- Was für Sport macht sie/er gern?
- Spielt sie/er ein Instrument?
- Wie ist sie/er?
- Was macht ihr gern zusammen?

Schreibtipp: 2-42: This writing activity divides well into three paragraphs: 1. Who is the person? (name, age, residence, work/study); 2. What does she/he like to do? (hobbies, sports, music); and 3. Why is she/he my best friend? (what she/he is like, what we do together).

at home

2-43 **Deine beste Freundin/Dein bester Freund.** Using the questions from the previous activity, find out about your partner's best friend. Fill in the information and report your findings to the class.

Name _____

Alter _____

Wohnen _____

Studienfächer/Arbeit _____

Hobbys _____

Sport _____

Musik/Instrumente _____

Wie sie/er ist _____

Gemeinsame° Interessen _____   *common*

Lesen

Zum besseren Verstehen

2-44 **Eine Website für soziales Netzwerken.** *Studentenverzeichnis* (or *StudiVZ*) is a German social networking site. Take a look at Lea Kuhnt's profile page.

1. How is this website similar to other social networking sites that you know? What strikes you as different?
2. Which words on the page are similar to English (loan words or cognates)?

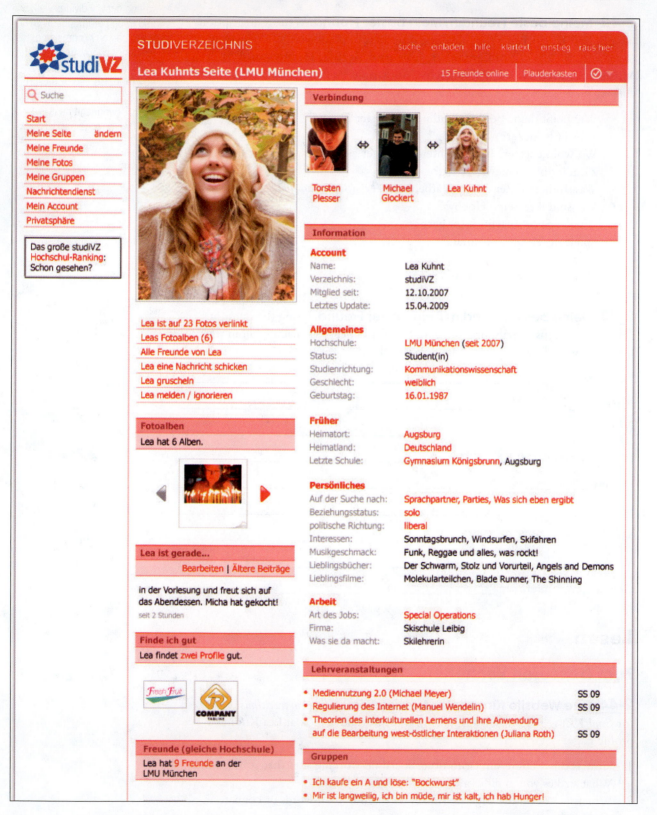

STUDIVERZEICHNIS   suche einladen hilfe klartext einstieg raus hier

studiVZ

Lea Kuhnts Seite (LMU München)   15 Freunde online | Plauderkasten

Q Suche

Start
Meine Seite   ändern
Meine Freunde
Meine Fotos
Meine Gruppen
Nachrichtendienst
Mein Account
Privatsphäre

Das große studiVZ
Hochschul-Ranking:
Schon gesehen?

Lea ist auf 23 Fotos verlinkt
Leas Fotoalben (6)
Alle Freunde von Lea
Lea eine Nachricht schicken
Lea gruscheln
Lea melden / ignorieren

Fotoalben
Lea hat 6 Alben.

Lea ist gerade...
        Bearbeiten | Ältere Beiträge

in der Vorlesung und freut sich auf
das Abendessen. Micha hat gekocht!
seit 2 Stunden

Finde ich gut
Lea findet zwei Profile gut.

Fresh Fruit   COMPANY TAGLINE

Freunde (gleiche Hochschule)
Lea hat 9 Freunde an der
LMU München

Verbindung

Torsten   Michael   Lea Kuhnt
Plesser   Glockert

Information

Account
Name: Lea Kuhnt
Verzeichnis: studiVZ
Mitglied seit: 12.10.2007
Letztes Update: 15.04.2009

Allgemeines
Hochschule: LMU München (seit 2007)
Status: Student(in)
Studienrichtung: Kommunikationswissenschaft
Geschlecht: weiblich
Geburtstag: 16.01.1987

Früher
Heimatort: Augsburg
Heimatland: Deutschland
Letzte Schule: Gymnasium Königsbrunn, Augsburg

Persönliches
Auf der Suche nach: Sprachpartner, Parties, Was sich eben ergibt
Beziehungsstatus: solo
politische Richtung: liberal
Interessen: Sonntagsbrunch, Windsurfen, Skifahren
Musikgeschmack: Funk, Reggae und alles, was rockt!
Lieblingsbücher: Der Schwarm, Stolz und Vorurteil, Angels and Demons
Lieblingsfilme: Molekularteilchen, Blade Runner, The Shinning

Arbeit
Art des Jobs: Special Operations
Firma: Skischule Leibig
Was sie da macht: Skilehrerin

Lehrveranstaltungen

• Mediennutzung 2.0 (Michael Meyer)   SS 09
• Regulierung des Internet (Manuel Wendelin)   SS 09
• Theorien des interkulturellen Lernens und ihre Anwendung
  auf die Bearbeitung west-östlicher Interaktionen (Juliana Roth)   SS 09

Gruppen

• Ich kaufe ein A und löse: "Bockwurst"
• Mir ist langweilig, ich bin müde, mir ist kalt, ich hab Hunger!

Arbeit mit dem Text

2-45 Was passt? Check all that apply.

Lea ist …
- ☐ Studentin in München.
- ☐ gar nicht sportlich.
- ☐ politisch konservativ.
- ☐ aus Augsburg.

Lea hat …
- ☐ lange, blonde Haare.
- ☐ 23 Fotoalben.
- ☐ keine Arbeit.
- ☐ amerikanische Filme gern.

Lea …
- ☐ studiert Biologie.
- ☐ hört gern klassische Musik.
- ☐ geht gern surfen.
- ☐ hat Freunde an der LMU.

2-46 Klick auf … What word would Lea need to click on in order to complete each of the following tasks?

1. Change her school and location
2. Do a search on the page
3. Add more favorite movies
4. Change her relationship status
5. Add more hobbies to her list
6. View all her friends
7. Go back to the main page
8. Visit a group she belongs to

a. Alle Freunde von Lea
b. Beziehungsstatus
c. Interessen
d. Hochschule
e. Meine Gruppen
f. Start
g. Lieblingsfilme
h. Suche

Studenten am Computer

Wort, Sinn und Klang

Wörter unter der Lupe

More on cognates

In *Kapitel 1* you saw that you often don't need a dictionary to understand cognates. If you know the "code," you will be able to add many German words to your vocabulary simply by recognizing the patterns they follow. You should have no trouble guessing the meaning of the German words in each category below. Words followed by *(v)* are the infinitive forms of verbs.

- German **f** or **ff** is English *p*
der A**ff**e	das Schi**ff**
schar**f**	hel**f**en *(v)*
die Har**f**e	o**ff**en
rei**f**	ho**ff**en *(v)*

- German **b** is English *v* or *f*
ha**b**en *(v)*	das Kal**b**
das Gra**b**	une**b**en
hal**b**	das Fie**b**er

- German **d, t,** or **tt** is English *th*
das Ba**d**	der Bru**d**er
danken *(v)*	der Va**t**er
das **D**ing	die Mu**tt**er
dick	die Fe**d**er
dünn	das Le**d**er
tausend	das We**tt**er

2-32 to 2-33

Zur Aussprache

In English the spelling of a word does not always indicate how it is pronounced (e.g., pl**ough**, thr**ough**, thor**ough**, en**ough**). English pronunciation is also a poor indicator of spelling (e.g., b**e**, s**ee**, b**e**lieve, rec**ei**ve). In German, spelling and pronunciation are much more consistent. Once you have mastered a few basic principles, you should have no trouble pronouncing and spelling new words.

The vowels *a, e, i, o,* and *u*

In a stressed syllable, each of these five vowels is either long or short. Listen carefully to the pronunciation of the following words and sentences and at the same time note the spelling. You will see that certain letter combinations indicate quite reliably whether a vowel in a stressed syllable is long or short.

Always long:
- A doubled vowel: **Haar, Tee, Boot.**
- A vowel followed by an **h**: **Jahr, geht, Sohn, Uhr.**
- An **i** followed by an **e**: **Bier, sieben.**
- A vowel followed by one consonant plus another vowel: **Nase, wenig, Kino, Monat, Minute.**
- A vowel followed by an **ß**: **groß, Straße, Fußball.**

Always short
- A vowel followed by a doubled consonant: **Wasser, Wetter, Lippe, Sommer, Suppe.**

Usually short:
- A vowel followed by two or more consonants: **Land, Mensa, trinken, Tochter, Stunde.**

2-47 **Hören Sie gut zu und wiederholen Sie!**

a (lang)

Haar
lahm
Lama
Mein Name ist Beate Mahler.
Mein Vater ist aus Saalfeld.

a (kurz)

hart
Lampe
Lamm
Tanja tanzt gern Tango.
Walter tanzt lieber Walzer.

e (lang)

Tee
gehen
leben
Peter geht im Regen segeln.

e (kurz)

Teddybär
gestern
lernen
Ein Student hat selten° Geld.

i (lang)

Liebe
Miete
Kino
Dieter liebt Lisa.

i (kurz)

Lippe
Mitte
Kinder
Fischers Fritz fischt frische Fische.

o (lang)

doof
Sohn
Ton
Warum ist Thomas so doof?

o (kurz)

Donner
Sonne
toll
Am Sonntag kommt Onkel Otto.

u (lang)

Stuhl
Schule
super
Utes Pudel frisst° nur Nudeln.

u (kurz)

Stunde
Schulter
Suppe
In Ulm und um Ulm und um Ulm herum.   *eats (feeds on)*

Peter geht im Regen segeln.

Nomen

die Freundschaft, –en	friendship
die Arbeit	work
das Geld	money
die Radtour, –en	bicycle trip
das Wochenende, –n	weekend
das Haus, ¨er	house
das Land, ¨er	country
die Leute (pl)	people
die Stadt, ¨e	city; town
die Straße, –n	street
die Wohnung, –en	apartment
das Zimmer, –	room
der Nachbar, –n }	neighbor
die Nachbarin, –nen	

Universitätsleben

das Fach, ¨er }	field of study; subject
das Studienfach, ¨er	
das Studentenheim, –e	student residence, dormitory
der Stundenplan, ¨e	schedule, timetable
die Übung, –en	lab; discussion section
an der Uni	at the university
zur Uni	to the university

Kleidungsstücke

das Kleidungsstück, –e	article of clothing
der Anzug, ¨e	(men's) suit
die Bluse, –n	blouse
der Gürtel, –	belt
das Hemd, –en	shirt
die Hose, –n	pants
die Jacke, –n	jacket
die Jeans (pl)	jeans
das Kleid, –er	dress
die Kleider (pl)	clothes
der Mantel, ¨	coat
der Pulli, –s	light sweater
der Pullover, –	sweater
der Rock, ¨e	skirt
der Schuh, –e	shoe

die Shorts (pl)	shorts
die Socke, –n	sock
der Stiefel, –	boot
das Sweatshirt, –s	sweatshirt
das T-Shirt, –s	T-shirt

Verben

bedeuten	to mean
besuchen	to visit
hören	to hear
leben	to live (in a country or city)
wohnen	to live (in a building or on a street)

Andere Wörter

bald	soon
beide	both; two
gemeinsam	common
hübsch	pretty
schick	chic
schon	already
wieder	again

Ausdrücke

Um wie viel Uhr …?	(At) what time …?
Wie spät ist es? }	What time is it?
Wie viel Uhr ist es?	
zu Ende sein	to be over
echt spitze	really great
so … wie	as … as
Heute ist es nicht so kalt wie gestern.	Today it's not as cold as yesterday.

Was bedeutet „bunt"?

Das Gegenteil

der Mann, ⸚er ≠ die Frau, -en	husband; man ≠ wife; woman
suchen ≠ finden	to look for ≠ to find
dick ≠ dünn	thick; fat ≠ thin; skinny
lang ≠ kurz	long ≠ short
teuer ≠ billig	expensive ≠ cheap
immer ≠ nie	always ≠ never

Leicht zu verstehen

der Euro	die Olive, -n
der Film, -e	das Olivenöl
der Job, -s	die Salami
das Konzert, -e	die Schokolade
das Magazin, -e	cool
das Museum, Museen	elegant
die Oper, -n	hip

Wörter im Kontext

2-48 Was passt nicht?

1. das Hemd
   die Hose
   die Bluse
   der Pullover

2. die Jeans
   der Rock
   die Hose
   die Bluse

3. die Jacke
   der Gürtel
   der Mantel
   das Kleid

4. die Schuhe
   der Pullover
   das Sweatshirt
   das Hemd

2-49 *Leben* oder *wohnen?*

1. Stephanie und Claudia _____ beide im Studentenheim.
2. Stephanies Eltern _____ in Chicago.
3. Maria ist aus Salzburg, aber sie _____ jetzt in Wien und _____ dort bei ihrer Großmutter.

> **Leben** and **wohnen: Leben** is usually used in connection with the country or city of residence. **Wohnen** is used in connection with a building, street, or family (e.g., **Michael lebt in Berlin und wohnt in der Crellestraße**).

2-50 Was ist die richtige Reihenfolge? What's the proper sequence?
Number the following items from largest to smallest (1 to 5).

_____ das Haus   _____ das Land
_____ die Stadt   _____ die Straße
_____ die Wohnung

2-51 Was passt wo?

dick ≠ dünn / immer ≠ nie / lang ≠ kurz / billig ≠ teuer

1. Im Winter sind die Tage _____ und die Nächte _____.
2. Silber ist nicht _____, aber es ist nicht so _____ wie Gold.
3. Sweatshirts sind _____ und T-Shirts sind _____.
4. Warum hörst du _____ nur Rock und _____ Mozart oder Beethoven?

Familie

Eine österreichische Familie im Sommer

Kommunikationsziele

Talking about …
- family
- shopping and other activities
- useful everyday objects
- occupations

Expressing preferences and favorites

Describing people, places, and things

Strukturen

Accusative case:
- direct object
- **der**-words and **ein**-words
- adjective endings
- time phrases

Word order: More on the position of **nicht**

Verbs with stem changes in the present tense

Kultur

Austria

Family policies in Germany and Austria

Video-Treff: Meine Familie

Lesen: Mozart, das musikalische
  Wunderkind Österreichs

 Vorschau

Ein Familienauto?

3-1 **Was für ein Auto! Der Mercedes-Benz SLS AMG.** German engineering is valued worldwide. Look at the car ad and select the appropriate completions to describe this amazing automobile.

1. Der Mercedes–Benz SLS AMG ist ein Auto …
2. Der SLS AMG ist aber kein Auto …
3. Der SLS AMG ist …
4. Das Auto hat zwei …
5. Das Auto fliegt …
6. Man findet im Internet …

a. für Familien.
b. mit Cockpit.
c. Informationen über das Auto.
d. ein Flugzeug für die Straße.
e. sportliche Flügel.
f. auf der Straße.

Verwandte

Oma Ziegler sagt: Das ist meine Tochter Bettina. Sie ist nicht verheiratet und hat keine Kinder, aber sie ist eine sehr gute Physiotherapeutin. Bettina kauft gern teure Kleider, sie hat einen viel zu teuren Wagen und sie fährt auch oft zu schnell. Und warum reist Bettina denn immer so viel?

Nina sagt: Tante Bettina ist meine Lieblingstante. Sie hat ein echt tolles Leben: viel Geld, schicke Kleider, große Reisen (auch nach Nordamerika, denn sie spricht sehr gut Englisch) und ein rotes Sportcoupé.

 3-2 **Richtig oder falsch?** You will hear the two descriptions of Bettina Ziegler. Indicate whether the statements following the descriptions are **richtig** or **falsch**.

	RICHTIG	FALSCH		RICHTIG	FALSCH
1.	_____	_____	3.	_____	_____
2.	_____	_____	4.	_____	_____

3-3 **Anders gesagt.** With a partner, read *Verwandte* again, and find equivalents for the following statements.

▶ Oma Ziegler ist Bettinas Mutter.   =   Oma Ziegler sagt: Das ist meine Tochter Bettina.

1. Bettina hat keinen Mann.
2. Bettinas Kleider kosten viel Geld.
3. Bettina macht zu viele Reisen.
4. Bettina hat einen sehr sportlichen Wagen.

3-4 **Eine Familie.** The following well-known children's rhyme describes one family. Read the poem. Then study the family tree and answer the questions.

Illustration of family:
(from left to right) Benjamin, Sebastian, Susanna, Katharin, Daniel, Michael, Regine, Rosine, Johanna, Ottilie, Christian.

Der Vater, der heißt Daniel,
der kleine Sohn heißt Michael,
die Mutter heißt Regine,
die Tochter heißt Rosine,
male cousin der Bruder, der heißt Christian,
know der Onkel heißt Sebastian,

die Schwester heißt Johanna,
die Tante heißt Susanna,
der Vetter°, der heißt Benjamin,
die Kusine, die heißt Katharin,
die Oma heißt Ottilie –
jetzt kennst° du die Familie.

Ein Stammbaum

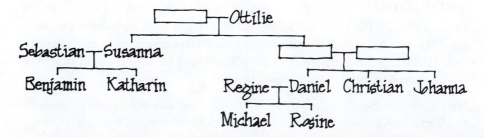

1. Wie heißen Johannas Brüder?
2. Wie heißen Susannas Kinder?
3. Wie heißt Michaels Schwester?
siblings 4. Wie heißen Daniels Geschwister°?
5. Wie heißen Katharins Vettern?

6. Wie heißt Ottilies Tochter?
7. Wie heißt Benjamins Kusine?
8. Wie heißt Rosines Tante?
9. Wie heißt Johannas Großmutter?
10. Wie heißen Katharins Eltern?

3-5 Lieblingsverwandte. Answer your partner's questions about your favorite relative. You will find additional vocabulary to describe personal characteristics and personality traits under **Persönliche Merkmale** in the *Anhang* on page A19.

S1: Wer ist …
  deine Lieblingsverwandte (f)?

  dein Lieblingsverwandter (m)?

S1: Wie alt ist sie/er?
S1: Warum ist sie/er deine
  Lieblingsverwandte/dein
  Lieblingsverwandter?

S2: Das ist …
  meine Oma/Tante/Kusine
  (name of relative).
  mein Opa/Onkel/Vetter
  (name of relative).

S2: Sie/Er ist …
S2: Sie/Er ist …

ist immer freundlich
ist immer optimistisch
ist so intelligent
ist so sportlich

hat viel Fantasie
hat viel Humor
versteht° meine Probleme
lacht° viel

kocht gut
bäckt° gut
…

bakes
understands

laughs

3-6 Lieblingsdinge. What are your partner's favorite things or activities? Write the information in the spaces provided and report your findings to the class.

S1: Was ist dein Lieblings_____?   **S2:** Mein Lieblings_____ ist …

Lieblingsmusik (f) _____
Lieblingssport (m) _____
Lieblingssong (m) _____
Lieblingsfilm (m) _____
Lieblingsband (f) _____

Lieblingsfach (n) _____
Lieblingsbuch (n) _____
Lieblingsgetränk (n) _____
Lieblingsauto (n) _____
…

Kultur / Österreich

A Rich and Diverse History

Until World War I, **Österreich** was the center of the vast multinational Austro-Hungarian Empire, which included not only Austrians and Hungarians, but also many Slavic peoples. After the war, the German-speaking part of the empire became the Republic of Austria, only to be annexed by Nazi Germany in 1938. After World War II, Austria was occupied by the Allies, and in 1955 it again became an independent, democratic state.

The map from 1914 shows how this once vast empire extended much farther to the east and encompassed multiple cultures and language groups. The country's current population is around 8.4 million, about 11% of whom are foreigners, primarily from former Yugoslavia. Austria's capital, **Wien**, was always a crossroads for diverse cultures, and remains so today.

Austria's Role in the World Today

In 1995 Austria became a member of the **EU (Europäische Union)** and in 2002 it adopted the **Euro** as its currency. Today, Vienna easily rivals Geneva as a center for international conferences and headquarters for international organizations. One of these, the International Atomic Energy Agency (IAEA), promotes the peaceful, non-military use of nuclear energy and was awarded the Nobel Peace Prize for its work in 2005. Austria now plays an active role in the peacekeeping efforts of the United Nations. Because the country has declared itself a neutral state, it is not a member of NATO.

Das UNO-Gebäude in Wien

Österreich-Ungarn, 1914

Natural Beauty in Winter and Summer

Because of the country's beautiful alpine landscapes, Austria attracts over 21 million vacationers annually. With 3500 lifts for ski and snowboard enthusiasts, Austria is also a leader in alpine ski technology. The city of Kitzbühel hosts frequent World Cup ski events, and Innsbruck, a city in the state of **Tirol,** has hosted two Winter Olympics. In the summer, thousands of kilometers of trails attract hikers and mountain climbers.

Skigebiet, Zell am See

Eine Sommerwanderung

Die Hundertwasserkirche in Bärnbach (Steiermark).

Music, Art, and Architecture

Austria has a rich cultural tradition and has been home to many famous composers. Haydn, Mozart, Schubert, and Johann Strauß were born in Austria. Beethoven, though born in Germany, lived and worked in Vienna until his death. Today, Vienna's glittering opera houses and theaters are synonymous with excellence, and Salzburg's **Festspiele** (an annual summer festival featuring opera, drama, and concerts) are known worldwide.

Early twentieth-century Austrian artists are also world-renowned. The painter Gustav Klimt contributed to the **Jugendstil** (art nouveau) movement, which in turn influenced the Austrian artist and architect Friedensreich Hundertwasser. In addition to creating richly colorful paintings and prints, Hundertwasser, an avid environmentalist, designed buildings that defied more traditional approaches to architecture.

Film and Literature

With actors such as Klaus Maria Brandauer, Christoph Waltz, and Arnold Schwarzenegger, and directors like Billy Wilder (*Some Like It Hot*, starring Marilyn Monroe), Austrians and Austrian emigrants have made their mark on Hollywood. In Austria, Michael Haneke directed the award-winning film **Die Klavierspielerin** (English title: *The Piano Teacher*), based on a novel by Austrian writer Elfriede Jelinek, who won the Nobel Prize for Literature in 2004. Jelinek's highly controversial work is sharply critical of many aspects of contemporary society. Stefan Ruzowitzky's **Die Fälscher** (*The Counterfeiters*), an Austrian-German co-production, won the 2007 Oscar for Best Foreign Language Film, and Haneke's **Das weiße Band** (*The White Ribbon*) received two nominations for the 2009 Academy Awards. In 2010, Austria's Christoph Waltz won an Oscar for his supporting role in Inglourious Basterds.

Schauspieler Christoph Waltz (*Inglourious Basterds*)

3-7 Snow & Spaß. As you've seen, Austria has plenty of natural beauty and outdoor entertainment, summer and winter. Read the following ad for a popular winter ski location, and mark all correct responses according to the text.

1. Bei Snow & Spaß kann man

   ☐ nachts Ski laufen   ☐ Skilaufen lernen   ☐ Skihütten finden

2. Erwachsene heißt auf Englisch

   ☐ children   ☐ youth   ☐ grown-ups

3. Snow & Spaß ist eine Attraktion für

   ☐ junge Skiläufer   ☐ Familien   ☐ Senioren

4. Die Schneemännchen-Tageskarte für 4 Euro ist für:

   ☐ Teenager   ☐ Schulkinder   ☐ sehr junge Kinder

Snow & Spaß in Österreich

Optimales Skivergnügen für jung und alt!

Mit 10 Liften (1 Vierersessellift, 8 Schlepplifte, 1 Übungslift) ist **Snow & Spaß** ein attraktives Skigebiet für die ganze Familie.

✶ **Skischule** ✶ **Skikindergarten**
✶ **Skiverleih** ✶ **Skihütten**

TAGESKARTEN

	1/2 Tag	Tag
Kinder*	6,00	11,50
Erwachsene	11,00	21,50
Senioren	10,00	19,50

*auch Schneemännchen-Tageskarte (für Kinder unter 6 Jahren) 4,00

Betriebszeiten:
Mo. bis So. von 09.00 bis 18.00 Uhr

Nomen

das Ding, -e	thing
die Fantasie	imagination
das Leben	life
der Liebling, -e	darling; favorite
die Reise, -n	trip

Die Familie

die Familie, -n	family
die Eltern (pl)	parents
die Mutter, ¨	mother
die Stiefmutter, ¨	stepmother
der Vater, ¨	father
der Stiefvater, ¨	stepfather
das Kind, -er	child
das Einzelkind, -er	only child
die Tochter, ¨	daughter
der Sohn, ¨e	son
die Schwester, -n	sister
der Bruder, ¨	brother
die Geschwister (pl)	sisters and brothers, siblings
der/die Verwandte, -n	relative
die Großeltern (pl)	grandparents
die Großmutter, ¨	grandmother
die Oma, -s	grandma
der Großvater, ¨	grandfather
der Opa, -s	grandpa
der Enkel, -	grandson; grandchild
die Enkelin, -nen	granddaughter
die Tante, -n	aunt
der Onkel, -	uncle
die Kusine, -n	(female) cousin
der Vetter, -n	(male) cousin
die Nichte, -n	niece
der Neffe, -n	nephew
das Haustier, -e	pet
der Hund, -e	dog
die Katze, -n	cat

Fahrzeuge

das Fahrzeug, -e	vehicle
das Auto, -s	car
der Wagen, -	
der Bus, -se	bus
das Fahrrad, ¨er	bicycle
das Rad, ¨er	bike; wheel
das Motorrad, ¨er	motorcycle
der Zug, ¨e	train
das Flugzeug, -e	airplane
der Flügel, -	wing

Verben

kennen	to know; to be acquainted with
lachen	to laugh
verstehen	to understand

Ausdrücke

viel zu schnell	much too fast
Was ist dein Lieblingsbuch?	What's your favorite book?

Das Gegenteil

freundlich ≠ unfreundlich	friendly ≠ unfriendly
interessant ≠ langweilig	interesting ≠ boring
schnell ≠ langsam	fast ≠ slow(ly)
verheiratet ≠ ledig	married ≠ single
verheiratet ≠ geschieden	married ≠ divorced
oft ≠ selten	often ≠ seldom

Leicht zu verstehen

der Humor	das Problem, -e
die Fantasie	pessimistisch
der Partner, -	optimistisch
die Partnerin, -nen	

Wörter im Kontext

3-8 Die Familie. What are the male or female counterparts?

1. die Kusine
2. die Schwester
3. die Großmutter
4. der Onkel
5. der Opa
6. der Vater
7. die Tochter
8. die Enkelin
9. der Neffe

3-9 Was passt zusammen? See how many new compound words you can understand by looking at the words below and matching appropriately. What does the word **Zeug** seem to mean after you've seen it in several combinations?

1. Stiefvater
2. Stiefbruder
3. Haustier
4. Hausschuhe
5. Flugzeug
6. Schreibzeug
7. Bettzeug
8. Spielzeug

a. stepbrother
b. airplane
c. slippers
d. writing implement *(pen, pencil, etc.)*
e. stepfather
f. sheets, bedclothes
g. toy, plaything
h. pet

3-10 Was passt wo?

Zug / Fahrräder / Flugzeug / Motorräder / Wagen

1. Der Mercedes-Benz SLS AMG ist ein sehr guter und sehr teurer _____.
2. _____ und _____ haben nur zwei Räder.
3. Ein Bus ist nicht so lang wie ein _____.
4. Mit dem _____ fliegt man schnell nach Deutschland.

3-11 Was passt wo?

interessant / langweilig / schnell / langsam / optimistisch / pessimistisch

1. Daniel ist immer sehr _____ und hat oft Depressionen.
2. Laura lacht gern und ist immer _____.
3. _____, bitte! Ich verstehe noch nicht so gut Deutsch.
4. Ist das Buch _____?
   Nein, ich finde es sehr _____.
5. Fahrräder fahren nicht so _____ wie Motorräder.

1 Answering *whom* or *what*

3-1 to 3-14

The direct object

You already know that a simple sentence consists of a *subject* and a *predicate* and that the predicate is whatever is said about the subject. The predicate consists of a verb and often other parts of speech as well.

One of the "other parts of speech" is often a noun or pronoun that is the target of what is expressed by the verb. This noun or pronoun is called the *direct object*. The boldfaced words in the following examples are the direct objects.

subject	predicate	
	VERB	DIRECT OBJECTS AND OTHER PARTS OF SPEECH
Aunt Bettina	visits	**exotic countries.**
She	meets	**interesting people** there.
She	wears	**expensive clothes.**
Nina	finds	**her aunt's life** exciting.

3-12 Onkel Alfred. Robert Ziegler and his father are talking about another family relative, the rich but boring Uncle Alfred. Find the subjects and direct objects.

	SUBJECT		DIRECT OBJECT
earns	Mein Bruder Alfred	verdient°	viel Geld.
reads	Er	liest°	langweilige Bücher.

Herr Ziegler sagt:
1. Kennen Sie meinen Bruder Alfred?
2. Seinen großen Mercedes finde ich toll.
3. Er trinkt teure Weine.
4. Er kauft auch teure Anzüge.

Robert sagt:
5. Onkel Alfred hat keine Familie und keine Freunde.
6. Er liest nur langweilige Bücher!
7. Er macht keinen Sport und macht auch keine Reisen.
8. Ich finde meinen Onkel doof und sein Leben stinklangweilig.

> Note how the second sentence in this exercise starts with the direct object, which gives the direct object more emphasis.

3-1 to 3-11

The accusative case

The masculine forms of both the definite article (**der**) and the indefinite article (**ein**) change depending on whether they are part of the subject or the direct object.

SUBJECT FORMS	DIRECT OBJECT FORMS
Der Pullover ist schön.	Ich kaufe **den** Pullover.
Ein Pullover ist teuer.	Ich brauche° **einen** Pullover.

need

The neuter and feminine forms of the definite article **(das, die)** and of the indefinite article **(ein, eine)** remain unchanged, regardless of whether they are part of the subject or the direct object.

Das Sweatshirt ist schön.   Ich kaufe **das** Sweatshirt.
Ein Sweatshirt ist teuer.   Ich brauche **ein** Sweatshirt.

Die Jacke ist schön.   Ich kaufe **die** Jacke.
Eine Jacke ist teuer.   Ich brauche **eine** Jacke.

The plural form of the definite article **(die)** also remains unchanged.

Die Schuhe sind schön.   Ich kaufe **die** Schuhe.

You already know that subjects and subject completions are in the *nominative case*. Direct objects are in the *accusative case*.

nominative case	=	subject and subject completion
accusative case	=	direct object

	masculine	neuter	feminine	plural
NOMINATIVE	der ⎫ ein ⎬ Rock kein ⎭	das ⎫ ein ⎬ Kleid kein ⎭	die ⎫ eine ⎬ Jacke keine ⎭	die ⎫ — ⎬ Schuhe keine ⎭
ACCUSATIVE	d**en** ⎫ ein**en** ⎬ Rock kein**en** ⎭	das ⎫ ein ⎬ Kleid kein ⎭	die ⎫ eine ⎬ Jacke keine ⎭	die ⎫ — ⎬ Schuhe keine ⎭

Note that the only accusative forms that differ from the nominative are the masculine (**den, einen,** and **keinen**). All other accusative forms stay the same.

3-13 Brauchst du das?

▶

S1: Brauchst du einen Pullover?   **S2:** Ja, ich brauche einen Pullover.
Nein, ich brauche keinen Pullover.

1.   2.   3.   4.   5.   6.

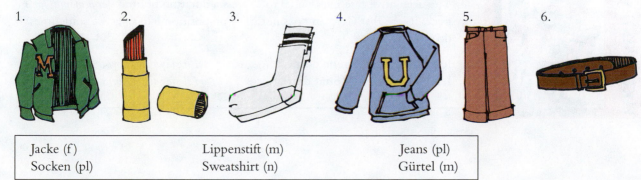

Jacke (f)	Lippenstift (m)	Jeans (pl)
Socken (pl)	Sweatshirt (n)	Gürtel (m)

3-14 **Was für Klamotten brauchst du und wo kaufst du sie?** Respond to your classmates' questions according to the model. Practice with several different clothing items from the previous exercise or from the list in the *Anhang* on p. 16.

p. 16

Klamotten: This is an informal expression originally used to describe shabby clothes. It is commonly used among students instead of **Kleider.**

S1: Was für Klamotten brauchst du?　　S2: Ich brauche eine Jacke.
S1: Und wo kaufst du die Jacke?　　　S2: Ich kaufe die Jacke bei Gap.
S2: Was für Klamotten brauchst du?　　S3: Ich brauche …

3-12

The interrogative pronoun *wen*

Many speakers of American English don't make a distinction between *who* and *whom* and use *who* as the only interrogative pronoun (question word), for people. But in German the interrogative pronoun for a person changes depending on its case. If it is *nominative* (the subject), it is **wer;** if it is *accusative* (the object), it is **wen.**

Nominative

Wer arbeitet als Physiotherapeutin?　　*Who works as a physical therapist?*
Wer ist Ninas Lieblingstante?　　　　*Who is Nina's favorite aunt?*

Accusative

Wen besucht Nina in Salzburg?　　*Whom does Nina visit in Salzburg?*
Wen findet Robert langweilig?　　*Whom does Robert find boring?*

Ein Brunnen in Salzburg

interrogative pronouns for people	
NOMINATIVE	wer?
ACCUSATIVE	wen?

Sprachnotiz　Expressing time with the accusative case

To express definite points of time, German often uses time phrases in the accusative case.

Ich fliege **diesen Freitag** nach Kanada.　　*I'm flying to Canada this Friday.*

The accusative case is also used to express a duration of time (*for a month, for a week*). Note that German does not use a preposition like *for* as we sometimes do in English.

Ich bleibe **eine Woche** dort.　　*I'll stay there (for) a week.*
Ich bleibe **einen Monat** dort.　　*I'll stay there (for) a month.*

3-15 **Was machst du?** Complete each question with **wer** or **wen**.

S2 selects the correct response from the options in the second column.

S1:   **S2:**

1. _____ besuchst du am Wochenende?   Nein, sie heißt Maria Braun.
   _____ ist das? Birgit?   Eine gute Freundin.

2. _____ ist dein Deutschlehrer?   Den alten Professor Seidlmeyer.
   Und _____ hast du für Physik?   Er heißt Rothermundt.

3. _____ ist dein Lieblingsautor?   Ich lese Crichton auch gern.
   Und _____ liest du gern?   Das ist Michael Crichton.

Der-words in the accusative case

3-13

In the accusative case, as in the nominative, the endings of words like **dieser** *(this)*, **jeder** *(each, every)*, and **welcher** *(which)* correspond closely to the forms of the definite article (**der**).

Ich verstehe **diesen** Text nicht.   *I don't understand **this** text.*
Ich finde **jeden** Satz schwer!   *I find **every** sentence hard!*

	masculine	neuter	feminine	plural
NOMINATIVE	dieser	dieses	diese	diese
ACCUSATIVE	diesen	dieses	diese	diese

Lerntipp: The other **der**-words you have learned (**jeder, welcher**) take the same endings as **dieser** in this chart. The only accusative form that differs from the nominative is **diesen** (**jeden, welchen**).

3-16 **Das Familienalbum.** Nina and a friend are looking at the Ziegler family photo album. Supply the appropriate nominative or accusative endings.

SABINE: Wer ist denn dies____ elegante Frau?
NINA: Das ist meine Tante Bettina.
SABINE: Fährt sie dies____ tolle, rote Sportcoupé (n)?
NINA: Ja. – Hier ist sie in Australien. Sie macht jeden Sommer so eine große
          Reise. – Dies____ Foto (n) zeigt° meine ganze Familie. Kennst du   *shows*
          dies____ Mann da?
SABINE: Ist dies____ Mann dein Vater?
NINA: Nein, das ist mein langweiliger Onkel Alfred. Dies____ große Mann hier
          ist mein Vater.

3-17 **Meine Familie.** Bring a family photo to class. Discuss your photo with a partner, and take turns asking who individual people are. Here are some phrases that will help. You can also use the previous activity as a guide.

S1:   **S2:**

Wer ist **dieser** große Mann da? Dein Onkel?   **Nein, das ist mein Vater.**
Wie heißt **dieses** kleine Kind? Ist das dein Neffe? **Nein, das ist mein …**
Wie heißt **diese** elegante Frau? Ist das deine Mutter? **Das ist meine …**
Wer sind **diese** zwei Kinder?   **Das sind meine zwei …**

Ein-words in the accusative case

3-14

You already know that the **ein**–words are **ein, kein,** and the possessive adjectives, and that all **ein**–words take the same endings. The chart below reviews the possessive adjectives.

possessive adjectives			
mein	*my*	**unser**	*our*
dein	*your*	**euer**	*your*
sein	*his, its*	**ihr**	*their*
ihr	*her, its*		
		Ihr	*your*

Remember that just like the formal **Sie,** the formal **Ihr** is always capitalized.

Warum verkaufen Sie **Ihren** Wagen, Herr Ziegler?

*Why are you selling **your** car, Mr. Ziegler?*

Und warum verkaufen Sie **Ihre** Kamera?

And why are you selling your camera?

In the chart below, **mein** shows the nominative and accusative endings of *all* possessive adjectives.

Lerntipp: The only accusative form that differs from the nominative is masculine accusative (**meinen, deinen, seinen, ihren, unseren,** etc.).

	masculine	neuter	feminine	plural
NOMINATIVE	mein Freund	mein Auto	meine Freundin	meine Eltern
ACCUSATIVE	mein**en** Freund	mein Auto	meine Freundin	meine Eltern

Remember that when an ending is added to **euer** *(your),* the **e** before the **r** is dropped: **eure, euren.**

Warum verkauft ihr **euren** Wagen? *Why are you selling **your** car?*

3-18 Warum denn? Why are these people selling the things mentioned? **S1** completes the questions with the proper forms of **dein, euer,** or **Ihr. S2** selects the appropriate response from the options in the second column.

S1:

1. Warum verkaufen Sie _____ Kamera?
2. Warum verkauft ihr _____ Fahrräder (pl)?
3. Warum verkaufst du _____ Keyboard (n)?
4. Warum verkaufen Sie _____ Wagen (m)?
5. Warum verkauft ihr _____ Haus (n)?

S2:

Ich spiele viel lieber Gitarre.
Es ist viel zu klein für uns.
Ich nehme jetzt immer den Bus.
Wir haben jetzt einen Wagen.
Ich mache jetzt nur noch Videos.

3-19 **Besuche bei Freunden und Verwandten.** Ask whom your partner is planning to visit at the times below. **S2** can use family vocabulary from *Wortschatz 1* as a guide.

S1: Wen besuchst du im Dezember?   **S2:** Ich besuche meine Oma (f.)/meinen Opa (m.) …

S2: Und du? Wen besuchst du an Thanksgiving?

im Dezember / an Thanksgiving / jeden Sommer / nächstes Jahr

3-20 Besuche am Wochenende.

S1 asks the question using the appropriate form of **machen.**

S2 answers by completing the phrase directly opposite with the correct form of the missing possessive adjective (**sein, ihr,** or **unser**).

▶   Was … Frau Ziegler?   Sie besucht … Schwester.

  S1: Was macht Frau Ziegler?   **S2:** Sie besucht ihre Schwester.

1. Was … Nina?   Sie besucht … Lieblingstante.
2. Was … Robert?   Er besucht … langweiligen Onkel Alfred.
3. Was … Oma Ziegler?   Sie besucht … Sohn Klaus.
4. Was … Alexander?   Er besucht … Freundin Nina.
5. Was … Zieglers am Sonntag?   Sie besuchen … Freunde in München.

6. Was … Bergers?   Sie besuchen … Tochter Claudia in München.
7. Was … ihr am Samstag?   Wir besuchen … Großmutter.
8. Was … ihr am Sonntag?   Wir besuchen … Onkel Karl.

3-21 Was hast du alles? Ask each other questions about some of the items below, as in the examples.

S1: Hast du einen Wagen?   **S2:** Ja, ich habe einen Wagen.
S2: Hast du ein Motorrad?   **S1:** Nein, ich habe kein Motorrad.

ein Fahrrad	ein Motorrad	einen Hund	eine Katze
ein Wii-Set	einen iPod	einen Scanner	eine Digitalkamera

Sprachnotiz | Omission of the indefinite article

When stating someone's membership in a specific group (e.g., nationality, place of residence, occupation, or religious affiliation), German does not use the indefinite article.

Maria ist **Österreicherin.** *Maria is **an** Austrian.*
Wolfgang ist **Deutscher.** *Wolfgang is **a** German.*
Ich bin **Berliner.** *I am **a** Berliner.*
Kurt ist **Koch.** *Kurt is **a** cook.*

Video-Treff

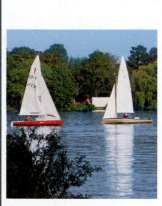

Mein Vater hat ein Segelboot.

Meine Familie

Maiga, Stefan Meister, Anja Peter, Thomas, André, and Karen are talking about their families. Be sure to complete the **Was ist das auf Englisch?** exercise before watching the video.

3-22 Was ist das auf Englisch?

1. Meine Eltern leben seit drei Jahren **getrennt.**   a. sailboat
2. Mein Bruder geht in **die 11. Klasse.**   b. in a great area
3. Mein Vater hat ein **Segelboot.**   c. different
4. Ich habe eine **supersüße** Nichte.   d. makes … herself
5. Meine Eltern haben ein schönes Haus **in einer**   e. eleventh grade
   tollen Gegend.
6. Sie wohnen jetzt **außerhalb von** Berlin.   f. separated
7. Meine Schwester **macht** ihre Klamotten **selber.**   g. older
8. Ich habe zwei Halbgeschwister; wir haben alle   h. outside of
   drei **unterschiedliche** Mütter.
9. Ich habe eine **ältere** Schwester.   i. very sweet

3-23 Was ist die richtige Antwort? Choose the appropriate answer to the following questions about the families of Maiga, Stefan, and Anja.

MAIGA

1. Maigas Mutter heißt   Bettina.   ☐   Regina.   ☐
2. Maigas Eltern wohnen in   Göttingen.   ☐   Berlin.   ☐
3. Maigas Bruder Philipp ist   Schüler.   ☐   Student.   ☐
4. Ihr Bruder Philipp spielt gern   Fußball. ☐   Gitarre.   ☐

STEFAN

5. Stefans Vater heißt   Hansjürgen. ☐   Karlheinz. ☐

6. Sein Vater ist … von Beruf.   Lehrer ☐   Kaufmann ☐

7. Als Hobby geht Stefans Vater gern   segeln. ☐   angeln. ☐

8. Stefan hat   eine Schwester. ☐   einen Bruder. ☐

ANJA

9. Anja hat   keine Geschwister. ☐   einen Bruder. ☐

10. Ihre Eltern haben   eine schöne Wohnung. ☐   ein schönes Haus. ☐

3-24 Wer sagt das? Select the name of the person who matches the statement best.

	Thomas	André	Karen
1. Mein Vater heißt Wolfgang.	☐	☐	☐
2. Meine Mutter und mein Vater sind 51 Jahre alt.	☐	☐	☐
3. Mein Vater ist Manager von Beruf.	☐	☐	☐
4. Meine Schwester kauft sehr gern Schuhe.	☐	☐	☐
5. Mein Bruder studiert Theologie und Germanistik.	☐	☐	☐
6. Meine Eltern wohnen nicht weit von Berlin.	☐	☐	☐
7. Ich habe zwei Halbgeschwister.	☐	☐	☐
8. Meine Eltern sind geschieden.	☐	☐	☐
9. Meine Mutter ist Lehrerin.	☐	☐	☐

2 Describing people, places, and things

Accusative endings of adjectives preceded by *der*-words

3-15 to 3-19

	masculine	neuter	feminine	plural
NOMINATIVE	der neue Drucker	das teure Notebook	die neue Maus	die tollen CDs
ACCUSATIVE	den neuen Drucker	das teure Notebook	die neue Maus	die tollen CDs

- Note that the adjective endings are identical in both cases, except for the masculine accusative singular.
- In the masculine accusative singular, the ending will be **–en.**
- Adjectives that end in **–er** or **–el** drop the **e** when they take an ending **(teuer: den teuren Drucker; dunkel: das dunkle Notebook)**

CHRISTA: Welch**en** Drucker kaufst du, **den** teur**en** oder **den** billig**en**?   *Which printer are you going to buy, the expensive one or the cheap one?*

ANNA: Ich glaube, ich kaufe **den** billig**en.**   *I think I'm going to buy the cheap one.*

3-25 Bei Saturn You and your partner are shopping at Saturn, an electronics superstore. Complete the dialogues by supplying the missing adjective endings according to the example. Note that both speakers are practicing accusative endings.

> Welchen Computer / hell, dunkel

S1: Welchen Computer kaufst du, den hellen oder den dunklen? **S2:** Ich glaube, ich kaufe den dunklen.

1. Welches Handy / blau, schwarz
2. Welche CDs / deutsch, amerikanisch
3. Welchen iPod / weiß, schwarz
4. Welchen CD-Spieler / japanisch, deutsch
5. Welchen Scanner / preisgünstig, teuer
6. Welches Notebook / japanisch, deutsch

Accusative endings of adjectives preceded by *ein*-words

3-15 to 3-19

	masculine	**neuter**	**feminine**	**plural**
NOMINATIVE	ein neuer Drucker	ein teures Notebook	eine neue Maus	meine tollen CDs
ACCUSATIVE	einen neuen Drucker	ein teures Notebook	eine neue Maus	meine tollen CDs

- Just as you saw with the adjective endings following **der-**words, the adjective endings following **ein-**words are identical in both cases, except for the masculine accusative singular.
- The masculine accusative singular always ends in **-n.**
- Remember that wherever the **ein-**word has no ending (nominative masculine and neuter, and accusative neuter), the ending that shows gender goes on the adjective instead: Das ist ein neu**er** Drucker. Ich kaufe ein teur**es** Notebook.

VERKÄUFER:	Möchten Sie ein**en** preisgünstig**en** Drucker?	*Would you like an inexpensive printer?*
SIE:	Ja, ich möchte ein**en** preisgünstig**en** japanisch**en.**	*Yes, I'd like an inexpensive Japanese one.*

Large-scale warehouses for electronics are as popular in Germany as they are in North America. Saturn is the go-to place for everything electronic in almost every German city.

3-26 Im Elektronikgeschäft. Now you're ready to talk to the salesperson at Saturn about what products to buy. **S1** is the salesperson and **S2** expresses a preference.

▶ das Handy, grau, schwarz

  S1: Möchten Sie ein graues oder   **S2:** Ich möchte ein graues.
      ein schwarzes Handy?

1. der DVD-Spieler: japanisch, deutsch
2. das Notebook: weiß, schwarz
3. der Scanner: preisgünstig, klein
4. die Computerspiele (pl): deutsch, amerikanisch
5. das Handy: koreanisch, deutsch

3-27 Im Kleidergeschäft. You are in a clothing store and your friend keeps showing you things in colors you don't want.

▶ das T-Shirt, blau   blau, rot

  S1: Hier ist ein schönes blaues   **S2:** Aber ich möchte kein blaues T-Shirt,
      T-Shirt.   ich möchte ein rotes.

1. die Jacke, braun   braun, grau
2. der Mantel, schwarz   schwarz, dunkelblau
3. das Polohemd, blau   blau, weiß
4. der Pullover, schwarz   schwarz, grau
5. das Sweatshirt, grün   grün, weinrot
6. die Hose, braun   braun, schwarz

> **Lerntipp:** When several adjectives appear in a series, they all take the same ending: **ein schön*es*, blau*es* T-Shirt.**

3-28 Was trägt Lisa? Using adjectives from each of the two groups below, write descriptions of what two of your classmates are wearing today. Then read your descriptions to a group of your classmates. Express shades of color by adding **dunkel–** or **hell–.** You will find a list of **Kleidungsstücke** in the *Anhang* on page A16.

S: Lisa trägt einen wunderschönen dunkelroten Pulli und einen langen schwarzen Rock. David trägt …

cool	praktisch	blau	rosarot
elegant	schick	braun	rot
interessant	schön	gelb	schwarz
kurz	toll	grau	violett
lang	sportlich	grün	weiß

3-15 to 3-19

Accusative endings of unpreceded adjectives

	masculine	neuter	feminine	plural
NOMINATIVE	guter Kaffee	gutes Bier	gute Salami	gute Oliven
ACCUSATIVE	gut**en** Kaffee	gutes Bier	gute Salami	gute Oliven

- In the masculine accusative singular, the ending of an unpreceded adjective is **–en.**
- The other accusative endings are identical to those in the nominative.

server	KELLNER°:	Möchten Sie lieber schottisch**en** oder kanadisch**en** Lachs?	*Would you rather have Scottish or Canadian salmon?*
guest	GAST°:	Heute esse ich mal kanadisch**en** Lachs.	*Today I'm going to eat Canadian salmon for a change.*

3-29 Im Hotel. Use **essen** or **trinken** in the responses to the server's questions.

▶ Wein (m), italienisch, spanisch

KELLNERIN:	Möchten Sie lieber italienischen oder spanischen Wein?		GAST:	Heute trinke ich mal spanischen Wein.

1. Oliven (pl), griechisch, türkisch
2. Salami (f), italienisch, ungarisch
3. Bier (n), deutsch, belgisch
4. Käse (m), holländisch, französisch
5. Mineralwasser (n), deutsch, italienisch
6. Tee (m), chinesisch, indisch
7. Kaffee (m), arabisch, kolumbianisch

3 Word Order

3-20

More on the position of *nicht*

Nicht usually follows the direct object.

Mein Freund kennt den Film *Good Bye, Lenin!* **nicht.**
Warum verstehen meine Eltern meine Probleme **nicht?**
Ich glaube, ich kaufe den Scanner **nicht.**

Remember that nouns preceded by the indefinite article **ein** or nouns without an article are negated with **kein.**

Ein Yugo ist **kein** BMW!
Ich habe **keine** Zeit!

3-30 Immer negativ!

S1: Kennst du diese Familie?   **S2:** Nein, ich kenne diese Familie nicht.

1. Kaufen Zieglers ein Haus?   Nein, sie …
2. Hat Roberts Kusine Geschwister?   Nein, sie …
3. Kaufen Zieglers einen Hund?   Nein, sie …
4. Kennst du Roberts Tante?   Nein, ich…
5. Haben Roberts Verwandte ein großes Haus?   Nein, sie …
6. Kennst du Ninas Vetter?   Nein, ich …
7. Verstehen Ninas Eltern ihre Probleme?   Nein, sie …

3-31 Ein kleines Interview.

Ask each other the following questions and answer truthfully, using **nicht** or a form of **kein** if the answer is no. Formulate a few questions of your own at the end.

1. Hast du ein gutes Notebook?
2. Hast du einen Mercedes-Benz SLS-AMG mit Cockpit und Flügeln?
3. Hast du ein Motorrad?
4. Hast du viele Geschwister?
5. Leben deine Eltern hier?
6. Trinkst du gern Kaffee?
7. Hast du einen Wagen?
8. Gehst du gern ins Kino?
9. Kennst du einen guten deutschen Film?
10. Trinkst du gern deutsches Bier?
11. Kennst du ein gutes deutsches Restaurant hier?
12. …

4 Expressing actions in the present and future

Verbs with stem-vowel changes in the present tense

3-21 to 3-25

Some German verbs have a stem-vowel change in the **du-**form and in the **er/es/sie-**form of the present tense. Note that the stem vowel changes *only* in the **du-**form and in the **er/es/sie-**form.

e → i		e → ie		a → ä		au → äu	
sprechen		lesen		fahren		laufen	
ich	spreche	ich	lese	ich	fahre	ich	laufe
du	sprichst	du	liest	du	fährst	du	läufst
er/es/sie	spricht	er/es/sie	liest	er/es/sie	fährt	er/es/sie	läuft
wir	sprechen	wir	lesen	wir	fahren	wir	laufen
ihr	sprecht	ihr	lest	ihr	fahrt	ihr	lauft
sie/Sie	sprechen	sie/Sie	lesen	sie/Sie	fahren	sie/Sie	laufen

In dictionary lists of irregular verbs, verbs that have vowel changes in the present tense are usually listed as follows:

sprechen (spricht)	*to speak*
fahren (fährt)	*to drive*

Verbs with stem-vowel change from *e → i* or *ie*

e → i				
essen	*to eat*	ich esse	du **isst**	er **isst**
geben	*to give*	ich gebe	du **gibst**	er **gibt**
nehmen	*to take*	ich nehme	du **nimmst**	er **nimmt**
sprechen	*to speak*	ich spreche	du **sprichst**	er **spricht**
verprechen	*to promise*	ich verspreche	du **versprichst**	er **verspricht**
werden	*to become; to get; to be*	ich werde	du **wirst**	er **wird**
e → ie				
lesen	*to read*	ich lese	du **liest**	er **liest**
sehen	*to see*	ich sehe	du **siehst**	er **sieht**

3-32 Was passt? Complete each sentence with the correct form of the verb given. Then substitute the new subject in parentheses and change the verb accordingly.

1. **essen:** Nina _____ zu viel Schokolade. (ich)
2. **geben:** Claudia und Stephanie _____ morgen Abend eine Party. (Robert)
3. **nehmen:** Ich _____ immer den Bus zur Uni. (du)
4. **nehmen:** Wir _____ oft ein Taxi. (ihr)
5. **sprechen:** Stephanie _____ sehr gut Deutsch. (wir)
6. **sprechen:** Tante Bettina _____ sehr gut English. (ihr)
7. **werden:** Peter _____ morgen einundzwanzig. (ich)
8. **werden:** Wann _____ du einundzwanzig? (ihr)
9. **lesen:** Mein Vater _____ jeden Morgen die Zeitung°. (ich) *newspaper*
10. **sehen:** Wir _____ heute Abend einen deutschen Film. (Nina)

Two common expressions using **es gibt: Was gibt's?** *(What's up?)* and **Was gibt's Neues?** *(What's new?)*

Es gibt sie noch, die guten Dinge.

Sprachnotiz **The expression** *es gibt*

German conveys *there is* or *there are* using the expression **es gibt** (from the verb **geben**). Note that **es gibt** always has an accusative object.

Es gibt viele McDonald's in Hamburg.
There are many McDonald's in Hamburg.

Heute **gibt es** keinen Nachtisch.
Today there's no dessert.

3-33 Was für eine Touristenattraktion gibt es in …? Match the locations with the appropriate attractions.

1. In San Francisco gibt es
2. In Arizona gibt es
3. In Japan gibt es
4. In Wyoming gibt es
5. In Ägypten gibt es
6. In Paris gibt es
7. In Indien gibt es

a. den Fudschijama
b. die Pyramiden
c. den Eiffelturm
d. die Golden-Gate-Brücke
e. das Taj Mahal
f. den Yellowstone Nationalpark
g. den Grand Canyon

3-34 Bei uns gibt es ... Working in small groups, make a list of at least five attractions in your university/college town. Consider what adjectives you could use to describe each attraction, using the suggestions below or adding some of your own. Then present your list to the class.

Hier in …	**gibt es**	ein**en** fantastisch**en** Zoo (m).
		ein erstklassig**es** Theater (n).
		eine toll**e** Disco (f).

Suggestions:
Kino (n), Restaurant (n), Bibliothek (f), Museum (n), Galerie (f), Sinfonieorchester (n)

Verbs with stem-vowel change from *a → ä* or *au → äu*

a → ä				
backen	*to bake*	ich backe	du **bäckst**	er **bäckt**
fahren	*to drive*	ich fahre	du **fährst**	er **fährt**
halten	*to hold; to stop; to keep*	ich halte	du **hältst**	er **hält**
lassen	*to let; to leave*	ich lasse	du **lässt**	er **lässt**
schlafen	*to sleep*	ich schlafe	du **schläfst**	er **schläft**
tragen	*to wear*	ich trage	du **trägst**	er **trägt**
waschen	*to wash*	ich wasche	du **wäschst**	er **wäscht**
au → äu				
laufen	*to run*	ich laufe	du **läufst**	er **läuft**

3-35 Was passt? Complete each sentence with the correct form of the verb given. Then substitute the new subject in parentheses and change the verb accordingly.

1. **backen:** Oma Ziegler _____ einen guten Kuchen. (ich)
2. **fahren:** Was für einen Wagen _____ du? (Sie)
3. **halten:** Entschuldigung, wo _____ hier der Bus? (die Busse, *pl.*)
4. **lassen:** Meine Schwester _____ den Hund ins Haus. (meine Eltern)
5. **schlafen:** Ich _____ jeden Sonntagmorgen bis halb zwölf. (dein Freund)
6. **schlafen:** _____ du auch am Wochenende so lang? (ihr)
7. **tragen:** Tante Bettina _____ elegante Kleider. (du)
8. **tragen:** Viele Studenten _____ oft Uni-Sweatshirts. (Robert)
9. **waschen:** Robert _____ jede Woche sein Auto. (ich)
10. **waschen:** _____ du jeden Tag die Haare? (sie *pl.*)
11. **laufen:** Alexander _____ die hundert Meter sehr schnell. (ich)

3-36 **Ein Samstagnachmittag bei Zieglers.** Complete the sentences with the appropriate verbs from the list.

backen / fahren / waschen / essen / werden / schlafen / lesen / halten

1. Nina _____ einen Apfel und _____ ein Buch.
2. Oma Ziegler _____ einen Kuchen, denn Nina _____ morgen siebzehn.
3. Frau Ziegler ist im Bett und _____.
4. Dann geht Frau Ziegler joggen, denn Joggen _____ fit.
5. Herr Ziegler und Robert _____ den Wagen.
6. Dann _____ Herr Ziegler in die Stadt.

3-37 **Herr Ziegler kritisiert heute alles!** Complete his questions by using the correct form from the list below.

essen / sprechen / halten / geben / tragen / nehmen

1. Warum _____ du denn keinen Brokkoli, Robert?
2. Warum _____ es denn heute keinen Nachtisch?
3. Warum _____ du denn so laut?
4. Warum _____ du denn immer dieses blöde T-Shirt, Nina?
5. Warum versprechen Politiker so viel und _____ es fast nie?
6. Warum _____ du nicht den Bus?

3-38 **Was machen diese Leute?**

S1: Was macht Tanja?   **S2:** Sie läuft Ski.

▶ … Ski.

1. Was macht Helga?   2. Was macht Günter?

… ein Bad.   … alles doppelt.

3. Was macht Ralf?   4. Was macht Herr Lukasik?

… sein Motorrad.   … seinen Wagen.

5. Was macht Frau Schneider?

… ein Buch.

6. Was macht Tina?

… einen Apfel.

7. Was macht Charlyce?

… mit Bernd.

8. Was macht Monika?

…

 3-39 Was machen diese Leute gern? The information for **S2** is in the *Anhang* on page A3.

S2: Was isst Maria gern?
S1: Was isst Thomas gern?
S2: Was essen Tina und Lisa gern?

S1: Sie isst gern Spaghetti.
S2: Er isst gern Nudeln.
S1: Sie essen gern Pizza.

	MARIA	THOMAS	TINA UND LISA
ESSEN	Spaghetti		Hotdogs
LESEN		Zeitungen	
SEHEN		Dokumentarfilme	Sportreportagen
SPRECHEN	Spanisch		Deutsch
FAHREN		Auto	
TRAGEN	Jeans		

3-40 Ein Interview. Interview your partner and report your findings to the class.

Was isst du gern?

Was liest du gern?

Welche Fernsehprogramme° siehst du gern?

Wie viele Sprachen° sprichst du? Welche?

Was für einen Wagen fährst du?

Was für Kleider trägst du gern?

Wie lange schläfst du denn am Wochenende?

TV programs

languages

Infobox

Familienpolitik in Deutschland und Österreich

What do you know about policies in your home country that are meant to support families and allow parents to continue working while raising a family?

Recent statistics show that most young people want to have children, yet Germany and Austria have the lowest birth rates in the European Union. In both countries, government policies are in place to encourage couples to start a family and have more than one child. This assistance includes job protection, benefits that replace lost income when a parent stays home to care for a child, and a monthly allowance for each child in the household. Such benefits are typical in the social democracies of Europe.

In Germany and Austria, both parents have the right to a long period of **Elternzeit** (parental leave), during which the parent's job is protected. In Germany, **Elterngeld** is provided to replace 67% of the caregiver's net income for a period of up to a year. In Austria, maternity leave for women starts eight weeks before the birth and lasts for eight weeks afterwards, and insurance funds pay the mother's net salary until the child is born. As in Germany, Austrian parents staying home to care for children are also compensated with a monthly allowance, called **Kinderbetreuungsgeld.**

Germans and Austrians also receive a monthly allowance to offset the costs of raising a family. This benefit is offered in addition to the salary replacement for caregivers.

Austrian children who are completing their education or job training qualify for **Familienbeihilfe** until the age of 24; German children receive **Kindergeld** until age 25.

Monatliche Unterstützung für Kinder		
	Deutschland (Kindergeld)	Österreich (Familienbeihilfe)
1–2 Kinder	184 Euro pro Kind	105–164 Euro pro Kind
3 Kinder	+ 190 Euro	+ 153–212 Euro
4+ Kinder	+ 215 Euro	+ 203–310 Euro

Zusammenschau

Hören

Wie erkennen wir einander?

Before Stephanie arrived in **München** in mid-October, she spent two weeks visiting relatives in **Köln**. In the conversation you are about to hear, Stephanie is calling from Chicago to make arrangements to have her cousins Michael and Martina, whom she has never met, pick her up at the international airport in **Düsseldorf**.

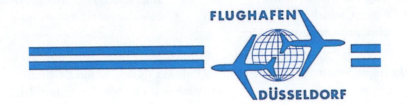

NEUE VOKABELN

mich	*me*	**die Flugnummer**	*flight number*
zum Flughafen	*to the airport*	**ganz kurz**	*very short*
übermorgen	*the day after tomorrow*	**erkennen**	*to recognize*

3-41 Erstes Verstehen. In which sequence do you hear the following statements and questions?

_____ Nein, meine Haare sind jetzt kurz und blond.
_____ Na, dann tschüss bis übermorgen, Stephanie, und gute Reise.
_____ Dann bist du übermorgen in Deutschland.
_____ Martina! Was trägst du übermorgen?
_____ Hier spricht deine Kusine Stephanie aus Chicago.
_____ Ja, wie erkennen wir einander dann?

3-42 Detailverstehen. Listen to the telephone conversation again and write short responses to the following questions.

1. Was ist Michaels Familienname?
2. Wann fahren Stephanie und ihr Vater zum Flughafen?
3. Wie kommen Michael und Martina zum Flughafen in Düsseldorf?
4. Wer ist blond und wer ist brünett?
5. Wer hat ganz kurze Haare und wer hat lange Haare?
6. Wer kommt übermorgen in Blau, wer in Weiß und wer in Schwarz?

Schreiben und Sprechen

3-43 **Wer ist das?** Working in small groups, take turns describing the style and color of a classmate's hair and clothing. The rest of your group will guess who is being described. Use the descriptive adjectives below and be sure to attach the correct endings in the accusative.

KLEIDER

sunglasses

S1: Sie trägt ein**en** lang**en** blau**en** Pullover (m), ein toll**es** dunkelrot**es** T-Shirt (n) und ein**e** schwarz**e** Sonnenbrille° (f).

straight / curly / wavy

- lang, kurz, groß, klein
- elegant, schick, schön, toll, hübsch
- blau, grün, rosarot, schwarz, hellblau, dunkelrot …

HAARE

S2: Sie hat lang**e**, blond**e**, schön**e** Haare.

- lang, kurz, glatt°, lockig°, wellig°
- blond, brünett, rot, schwarz …

Sie/Er trägt   einen   _____en, _____en Pullover (Rock, Mantel, Gürtel)

ein   _____es, _____es Polohemd (T-Shirt, Sweatshirt, Kleid)

eine   _____e, _____e Hose (Jogginghose, Jacke, Bluse)

_____e, _____e Jeans (Shorts, Socken, Schuhe, Stiefel, Sandalen)

3-44 **Meine Familie.** Write a description of a few people in your family using the following questions as a guide. You will find vocabulary for **Jobs und Berufe** and **Hobbys und Sport** in the *Anhang* on pages A14 and A15.

Wie heißen sie?
Wo wohnen sie?
Was sind sie von Beruf?

Was für einen Wagen fahren sie?
Haben sie einen Hund oder eine Katze?
Wie alt sind sie?

Was für Hobbys haben sie?
Spielen sie ein Instrument?
Sind sie sportlich?

Familienwanderung in Amerika

Taufe in Deutschland

Lesen

Zum besseren Verstehen

3-45 **Wolfgang Amadeus Mozart.** What do you associate with Mozart? Mark all that apply.

a famous composer

☐ klassische Musik
☐ eine musikalische Familie

☐ ein berühmter Komponist°
☐ ein Wunderkind

☐ Mozartkugeln
☐ Klaviermusik

3-46 Was ist das auf Englisch?

1. Der Konzertmeister in einem Orchester spielt **ausgezeichnet** Violine.
2. Ein guter **Geschäftsmann** verdient sehr gut.
3. Maria Theresia war die **Kaiserin** von Österreich.
4. In der katholischen Kirche in Salzburg gibt es einen **Erzbischof.**
5. Mozart macht eine musikalische **Tournee,** als er noch sehr jung ist.
6. Eine populäre Mozart-Oper heißt *Die* **Hochzeit** *des Figaro.*
7. Der 35-jährige Mozart wird in Wien sehr **krank**.
8. Im Dezember 1791 ist der junge Mozart schon **tot**.
9. Über 200 Jahre nach seinem **Tod** hört und spielt man immer noch die Musik dieses Wunderkinds.

a. sick
b. tour
c. dead
d. excellent(ly)
e. businessman
f. death
g. marriage
h. empress
i. archbishop

Mozart verkauft Mozartkugeln.

Mozart, das musikalische Wunderkind Österreichs

Ein Wunderkind

Am 27. Januar 1756 kommt Wolfgang Amadeus Mozart in diesem Haus in der Getreidegasse in Salzburg, auf die Welt. Sein Vater, Leopold Mozart, ist Violinist im Orchester des Erzbischofs und auch Musiklehrer und Komponist. Das kleine Wunderkind Wolfgang schreibt schon mit vier Jahren seine ersten Kompositionen. Mozarts Schwester Nannerl ist eine ausgezeichnete Pianistin.

Erstes Konzert in Wien

Im Jahre 1762 reist die ganze Familie nach Wien. Dort spielen die beiden Wunderkinder – Nannerl ist jetzt elf und Wolfgang sechs – für die Kaiserin Maria Theresia. Die Kinder bekommen schöne Kleider und verdienen viel Geld.

Musikalische Sensation in Europa

Mozarts Vater Leopold ist nicht nur ein guter Musiker, sondern auch ein guter Geschäftsmann. Er organisiert für seine Kinder eine große Tournee. Von 1763 bis 1767 – fast vier Jahre lang – reisen die Mozarts Tausende von Kilometern durch Deutschland, Belgien, Frankreich, England und Holland und geben Hunderte von Konzerten. Im Jahre 1769 reist der jetzt 13-jährige Wolfgang mit seinem Vater nach Italien. Fünfzehn Monate lang ist der junge Pianist und Komponist auch dort die große Sensation.

Arbeit im Orchester und als Komponist

1772 ist Wolfgang wieder in Salzburg und wird sechzehn Jahre alt. Aber jetzt ist er kein Wunderkind und keine Sensation mehr, sondern nur ein ganz normaler Musiker im Orchester des Erzbischofs.

Familie Mozart: Schwester Nannerl, Wolfgang, und Leopold

This famous painting by Johann Nepomuk della Croce shows Wolfgang and his sister Nannerl at the harpsichord and father Leopold with his violin. The mother, who died before the portrait was painted, is included by means of the painting on the wall. Leopold and his wife Anna had seven children, but only two survived.

Hochzeit mit Konstanze Weber

1781 geht Mozart mit 25 Jahren wieder nach Wien und verdient dort als Pianist und Komponist wieder ganz gut. 1782 heiratet er die Wienerin Konstanze Weber. Er lebt mit seiner Frau wie ein König und braucht immer mehr Geld. Mozart arbeitet Tag und Nacht und verdient jedes Jahr mehr. Im Jahr 1791, seinem letzten Lebensjahr, schreibt Mozart zwei Opern, ein Klavierkonzert, ein Klarinettenkonzert, ein Quintett und eine Kantate und arbeitet an einem Requiem. Aber im November 1791 wird er sehr krank und kann nicht mehr arbeiten. Am fünften Dezember ist Mozart tot. Er ist erst fünfunddreißig Jahre alt.

Arbeit mit dem Text

3-47 Biografische Information. Complete the table with the choices below.

JAHR	MOZART IST	BIOGRAFISCHE INFORMATIONEN
1762	6 J.	
1763–7	7–11 J.	
1769	13 J.	
1772	16 J.	
1781	25 J.	
1782	26 J.	
1791	35 J.	

Reise nach Italien – Mozart ist die große Sensation!
Orchesterposten beim Erzbischof in Salzburg   Lange Tournee durch Europa
Konzert vor der Kaiserin Maria Theresia   Hochzeit mit Konstanze Weber
Arbeit als Pianist und Komponist in Wien   Mozarts Tod

3-48 Was ist die richtige Antwort? Your instructor will read eight questions about Mozart and his life. Select the correct responses.

1. ___ Erzbischof
   ___ Musiker.
2. ___ Klavier.
   ___ Violine.
3. ___ Für die Kaiserin.
   ___ Für den Erzbischof.
4. ___ Sie sind in Italien.
   ___ Sie reisen durch halb Europa.

5. ___ Er spielt nicht mehr so gut.
   ___ Er ist keine Sensation mehr.
6. ___ In Salzburg.
   ___ In Wien.
7. ___ Er lebt wie ein König.
   ___ Er verdient nicht viel.
8. ___ 53.
   ___ 35.

Wort, Sinn und Klang

Wörter unter der Lupe

More cognates

In *Kapitel 2* you saw that it is often quite simple to decode the English meanings of certain cognates. Below is another list with the "code" that will help you figure out the English meanings. In some cases it helps to say the German words out loud. Words followed by *(v)* are verbs in their infinitive form.

- German **s, ss,** or **ß** is English *t* or *tt*

  das Wa**ss**er   ra**ss**eln *(v)*   verge**ss**en *(v)*   der Fu**ß**   der Ke**ss**el
  ha**ss**en *(v)*   be**ss**er   bei**ß**en *(v)*   die Nu**ss**   wa**s**

- German **z** or **tz** is English *t* or *tt*

  se**tz**en *(v)*   die Ka**tz**e   grun**z**en *(v)*   **z**ehn
  si**tz**en *(v)*   die Min**z**e   die War**z**e   **z**wölf
  der Si**tz**   das Sal**z**   **z**u   die **Z**unge
  glit**z**ern *(v)*   das Ne**tz**

- German **pf** is English *p* or *pp*

  der A**pf**el   der **Pf**ennig   das **Pf**und   der **Pf**ad (**d** → *th!*)
  der Kram**pf**   die **Pf**lanze (**z** → *t!*)   der **Pf**effer (**f** → *p!*)   die **Pf**eife (**f** → *p!*)
  die **Pf**anne   der **Pf**osten

Words as chameleons: *wie*

In different contexts, the word **wie** can take on a number of different meanings.

- **Wie** can mean *how:*

  Wie alt sind Sie?   ***How** old are you?*
  Wie geht's?   ***How** are you?*

- **Wie** can mean *what:*

  Wie ist Ihr Name und   ***What** is your name and*
     Ihre Adresse?   *your address?*
  Wie heißt du?   ***What** is your name?*

- **Wie** can mean *what . . . like:*

  Wie ist Ihre neue Wohnung?   ***What** is your new apartment **like?**

- **Wie** can mean *like:*

  Eine Wohnung **wie** meine   *An apartment **like** mine costs a*
     kostet viel Geld.   *lot of money.*

- **Wie** means *as* in the expression **so ... wie:**

  Meine Wohnung kostet nicht   *My apartment doesn't cost as much*
     so viel **wie** deine.   *as yours.*

3-49 Was bedeutet *wie*? Match the number given after each occurrence of **wie** with the appropriate English equivalent.

1. LAURA: **Wie** (1) heißt Lenas neuer Freund und **wie** (2) alt ist er?

    MARIA: Er heißt Florian und er ist 22 Jahre alt.

    LAURA: Und **wie** (3) ist er? Ist er so doof **wie** (4) ihr letzter Freund?

    how _____ what _____ what … like _____ as _____

2. JULIA: **Wie** (1) ist das Wetter? Ist es immer noch so schön **wie** (2) heute Morgen?

    crazy   LUKAS: Nein, jetzt regnet es **wie** (3) verrückt°.

    what … like _____ like _____ as _____

3. PETER: **Wie** (1) geht's, Claudia? **Wie** (2) ist deine neue Mitbewohnerin? Ist sie so nett **wie** (3) die letzte?

    CLAUDIA: Klar. Stephanie und ich sind schon fast **wie** (4) gute, alte Freundinnen.

    how _____ what … like _____ like _____ as _____

Zur Aussprache

3-32 to 3-34

The diphthongs

A diphthong is a combination of two vowel sounds. There are three diphthongs in German.

3-50 Hören Sie gut zu und wiederholen Sie!

The diphthong **ei** (also spelled **ey, ai, ay**) is pronounced like the *i* in *mine*.

eins	zw**ei**	dr**ei**
Herr M**ey**er	Herr S**ai**ler	Herr B**ay**er

H**ei**ke B**ay**er und H**ei**nz Fr**ey** h**ei**raten am zw**ei**ten M**ai**.

The diphthong **au** is pronounced like the *ou* in *house*.

br**au**chen	l**au**fen	k**au**fen
bl**au**	br**au**n	gr**au**

P**au**l, du bist zu l**au**t. Ich gl**au**be, du bist bl**au**.
Br**au**tkleid bleibt Br**au**tkleid und Bl**au**kr**au**t bleibt Bl**au**kr**au**t.

The diphthong **eu** (also spelled **äu**) is pronounced like the *oy* in *boy*.

h**eu**te	t**eu**er	n**eu**
H**äu**ser	M**äu**se	Verk**äu**fer

Wer ist Frau B**äu**erles n**eu**er Fr**eu**nd?
Ein Verk**äu**fer aus Bayr**eu**th.

WIR SUCHEN EINE

freundliche Verkäuferin

bitte im Laden melden

🔊 Wortschatz 2

Nomen

der Familienname, -n	last name
der Vorname, -n	first name
der Flug, ⸚e	flight
der Flughafen, ⸚	airport
die Flugnummer, -n	flight number
das Geschäft, -e	store; business
der Geschäftsmann, -leute	businessman
die Geschäftsfrau, -en	businesswoman
das Kleidergeschäft, -e	clothing store
die Klamotten (pl)	clothes
das Kaufhaus, ⸚er	department store
der Verkäufer, – } die Verkäuferin, -nen }	sales clerk
die Hochzeit, -en	wedding
der Tod	death
die Kaffeemaschine, -n	coffee maker
die Sonnenbrille	sunglasses
die Sprache, -n	language
die Zeitung, -en	newspaper

Verben

bekommen	to get; to receive
bezahlen	to pay
brauchen	to need
erkennen	to recognize
heiraten	to marry
verdienen	to earn
backen (bäckt)	to bake
fahren (fährt)	to drive
halten (hält)	to hold; to stop; to keep
lassen (lässt)	to let; to leave
laufen (läuft)	to run
schlafen (schläft)	to sleep
tragen (trägt)	to wear
waschen (wäscht)	to wash
essen (isst)	to eat
geben (gibt)	to give
lesen (liest)	to read

nehmen (nimmt)	to take
sehen (sieht)	to see
sprechen (spricht)	to speak
versprechen (verspricht)	to promise
werden (wird)	to become; to get; to be

Andere Wörter

ausgezeichnet	excellent
laut	loud
offen	open
preisgünstig	inexpensive
tot	dead
wunderbar	wonderful
wunderschön	very beautiful
blond	blonde
brünett	brunette
glatt	straight (of hair)
lockig	curly
gestern	yesterday
mehr	more
immer mehr	more and more

Bekommen is a "false friend;" the word for *to become* is **werden**.

BIPA FOTO SHOP

Digitalbilder werden zu Fotos!

Ausdrücke

es gibt (+ *acc*)	there is, there are
ganz kurz	very short
die ganze Famlie	the whole family
nächstes Jahr	next year
Er arbeitet nicht mehr.	He's not working any more.
Sie wird zwanzig.	She's turning twenty.
Was sind Sie von Beruf?	What is your occupation?
nicht X, sondern Y	not X, but rather Y

Das Gegenteil

die Hausfrau, -en ≠ der Hausmann, ¨-er	housewife ≠ househusband
kaufen ≠ verkaufen	to buy ≠ to sell
erst ≠ letzt	first ≠ last
krank ≠ gesund	sick ≠ healthy
neu ≠ alt	new ≠ old
alles ≠ nichts	all ≠ nothing
jemand ≠ niemand	somebody ≠ nobody
vorgestern ≠ übermorgen	the day before yesterday ≠ the day after tomorrow

Leicht zu verstehen

die CD, -s	das Orchester, -
der CD-Spieler, -	die Person, -en
das Interview, -s	der Preis, -e
die Kamera, -s	die Sandale, -n
die Klasse, -n	die Sensation, -en
der Komponist, -en	die Tournee, -n
das Mineralwasser	kritisieren
das Mountainbike, -s	

Person: Although this noun can refer to males or females, it is always feminine.

Wörter im Kontext

3-51 Jennifers Familie. Jennifer's parents are American but have German ties. Soon they will visit their daughter who is studying abroad. Complete with words from the list.

nimmt / wird / von Beruf / nächste / niemand / Flughafen / gibt es / bekommt / offen / übermorgen

1. Jennifers Vater und ihr Bruder Kurt sind beide Koch _____.
2. Im Restaurant von Jennifers Eltern _____ oft deutsche Spezialitäten.
3. Montags ist das Restaurant nicht _____, denn montags isst fast _____ im Restaurant.
4. _____ fliegt Jennifers Mutter nach Deutschland, denn Jennifer _____ _____ Woche einundzwanzig.
5. Ihr Flugzeug landet auf dem Hamburger _____, und von dort _____ sie dann den Zug nach Kiel.
6. Jennifer _____ von ihren Eltern dreihundert Euro zum Geburtstag.

3-52 Was passt zusammen? For each sentence in the first column, find the most appropriate statement in the second column and complete it with the correct form of a suitable verb from the following list.

essen / tragen / schlafen / waschen / sehen / fahren

1. Er ist Polizist.
2. Sie ist Studentin.
3. Er ist ein Gourmet.
4. Das ist ein Bär.
5. Das ist eine Katze.
6. Er ist Hausmann.

a. Er kocht und bäckt und _____.
b. Er _____ fast den ganzen Winter.
c. Er _____ eine Uniform.
d. Sie _____ jeden Morgen zur Uni.
e. Er _____ gern Kaviar.
f. Sie _____ auch bei Nacht sehr gut.

KLAMOTTE

Die Boutique
für
small & big

Größe 36 -52

3-53 Anders gesagt. Decide which two sentences in each group have approximately the same meaning.

1. a. Anna ist Verkäuferin.
   b. Anna kauft Klamotten.
   c. Anna verkauft Klamotten.

2. a. Wie viel Geld verdienst du?
   b. Wie viel Geld bekommst du?
   c. Wie viel Geld brauchst du?

3. a. Tom und Maria heiraten morgen.
   b. Maria wird morgen Toms Frau.
   c. Maria und Tom sind nicht mehr verheiratet.

4. a. Tom spricht viele Sprachen.
   b. Toms Muttersprache ist Englisch.
   c. Toms Englisch ist ausgezeichnet.

5. a. Mein Familienname ist Müller.
   b. Ich heiße Stefan Müller.
   c. Ich heiße Müller.

Alltagsleben

Obst- und Gemüsemarkt in Biel, Schweiz

Kommunikationsziele

Talking about ...
- daily routines
- food and meals
- abilities, necessities, and obligations

Expressing permission, wishes, and likes

Telling someone what to do

Making requests and giving advice

Giving reasons and conditions

Strukturen

Modal verbs

Separable-prefix verbs

The imperative

Word order: Position of the verb in independent and dependent clauses

Kultur

Meal traditions in the German-speaking countries

Switzerland

Railways in the German-speaking countries

Video-Treff: Ein typischer Tag

Lesen: Schweizer Innovation: Die Firma Victorinox

Vorschau

Wie frühstückt man?

4-1 **Frühstücksgewohnheiten.** Read some results from a recent survey about breakfast habits in Germany done by Ferrero, the company that makes the hazelnut–chocolate spread Nutella®. Would you give similar reasons for why you eat breakfast?

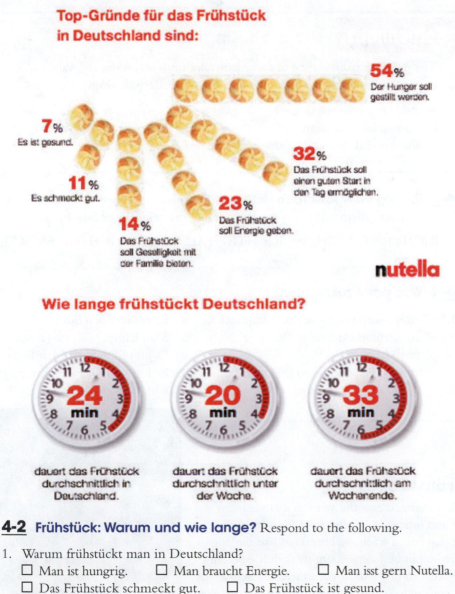

Top-Gründe für das Frühstück in Deutschland sind:

54% Der Hunger soll gestillt werden.

7% Es ist gesund.

11% Es schmeckt gut.

14% Das Frühstück soll Geselligkeit mit der Familie bieten.

23% Das Frühstück soll Energie geben.

32% Das Frühstück soll einen guten Start in den Tag ermöglichen.

nutella

Wie lange frühstückt Deutschland?

24 min — dauert das Frühstück durchschnittlich in Deutschland.

20 min — dauert das Frühstück durchschnittlich unter der Woche.

33 min — dauert das Frühstück durchschnittlich am Wochenende.

4-2 **Frühstück: Warum und wie lange?** Respond to the following.

1. Warum frühstückt man in Deutschland?
   ☐ Man ist hungrig.   ☐ Man braucht Energie.   ☐ Man isst gern Nutella.
   ☐ Das Frühstück schmeckt gut.   ☐ Das Frühstück ist gesund.
2. Montags bis freitags dauert das Frühstück
   ☐ 20 Minuten.   ☐ 24 Minuten.   ☐ 33 Minuten.
3. Man frühstückt am Wochenende … länger als an Wochentagen.
   ☐ 33 Minuten   ☐ 20 Minuten   ☐ 13 Minuten

So bin ich eben

MARTIN: *(steht auf und gähnt)* Was?! Du bist schon auf? Wie spät ist es denn?

PETER: Fast acht Uhr. Ich muss mein Referat für Professor Weber fertig schreiben. Das Seminar fängt schon um elf an.

MARTIN: *(lacht)* Ja ja, du und deine Referate: viel Stress, viel Kaffee, kein Frühstück. Iss doch eine Scheibe Brot. Und hier sind auch Butter, Wurst und Käse dazu.

PETER: Ich kann jetzt nicht aufhören, ich muss das Ding fertig schreiben.

MARTIN: Du bist echt doof, Peter. Warum fängst du immer so spät an?

PETER: Ich brauche den Stress, Martin. So bin ich eben.

Sprachnotiz   The pronoun *man*

The pronoun **man** is used to make generalizations and is the equivalent of *one, you, they,* or *people*. The word **man** (not capitalized) is always singular.

Wie sagt **man** das auf Deutsch?	*How does **one** (do **you**) say that in German?*
In Deutschland isst **man** oft Wurst und Käse zum Frühstück.	*In Germany **they (people)** often eat cold cuts and cheese for breakfast.*

4-3 Richtig oder falsch. You will hear the conversation between Martin and Peter. Indicate whether the statements that follow are **richtig** or **falsch.**

RICHTIG	FALSCH		RICHTIG	FALSCH		RICHTIG	FALSCH
1. _____	_____	2. _____	_____		3. _____	_____	

4-4 Was passt zusammen?

1. Warum essen viele Deutsche Frühstück?
2. Warum frühstückt man an Wochentagen nicht so lang?
3. Warum ist Peter schon so früh auf?
4. Warum fängt Peter immer so spät an?

a. Er braucht den Stress.
b. Man hat nicht so viel Zeit.
c. Es gibt Energie für den Tag.
d. Er muss sein Referat fertig schreiben.

Infobox

Was gibt's zum Frühstück?

The German **Frühstück** has changed over the years to include many new products from abroad and to respond to the need for some people to have a faster start to the day. Still, a traditional breakfast like the one pictured here is a treat many continue to enjoy. On weekends especially, it is common to visit the bakery to buy two or even three different kinds of fresh breakfast rolls. Travelers who stay in vacation apartments can even sign up for **Brötchenservice** to have rolls delivered to their door each morning.

Since World War II, American breakfast cereals have become widely available in the German-speaking countries. German doesn't have a generic word for *cereal*, but uses the individual product names in English (e.g., Rice Krispies®) instead. Recently, **Bagels** and **Muffins** (both pronounced as in English) have appeared on the scene in Germany, although **Muffins** are more of an afternoon treat than a breakfast food.

The great North American weekend favorite, pancakes, are not eaten at breakfast at all in the German-speaking countries, but are served for lunch or dinner. **Pfannkuchen** are thinner, larger, and more closely resemble the French crepe. They are often eaten with a fruit compote. Fried potatoes **(Bratkartoffeln)**, are also not eaten at breakfast, but are popular as part of a main meal. They are prepared with onions and sometimes with small bits of bacon.

4-5 Was isst und trinkst du zum Frühstück? Working with a partner, interview each other about your breakfast habits. Take notes so you can report your findings to the class.

S1:	S2:
Was isst du an Wochentagen zum Frühstück?	An Wochentagen esse ich …
Was trinkst du an Wochentagen?	An Wochentagen trinke ich …
Und am Wochenende? Was isst du dann?	Am Wochenende esse ich meistens° … *usually*
Und was trinkst du am Wochenende zum Frühstück?	Am Wochenende trinke ich gern …

4-6 Unsere Frühstücksgewohnheiten. Report to the class on the breakfast habits of your partner. Here are some phrases to get you started.

S: An Wochentagen isst [*Name*] … Und er/sie trinkt …
  Aber am Wochenende isst sie/er … Und er/sie trinkt …

Kultur / Die Schweiz

Schweizer Alpen: Lidernenhütte

Diverse cultures and languages, rugged terrain

Die Schweiz is a country of four distinct cultures and four official languages: **Deutsch, Französisch, Italienisch,** and **Rätoromanisch**. Of a population of about 7.4 million, 64% speak German, 20% speak French, 6.5% speak Italian, and about 0.5% speak Rhaeto-Romanic. About 70 percent of the country has a rugged Alpine landscape. The topography led to the development of many isolated regions, each of which developed autonomously, giving rise to the 26 **Kantone** that later came together to form the **Schweizerische Eidgenossenschaft** (Swiss Confederation) we know today.

Ingenuity in industry, Swiss style

Though Switzerland has only limited natural resources, it enjoys one of the highest standards of living in the world. Persistence and ingenuity have allowed the Swiss to develop many prosperous industries in this tiny country. Today, Swiss cheeses, milk chocolate, and baby foods are known internationally through brand names like Lindt and Nestlé. The Swiss are leaders in chemicals, high-fashion textiles, banking, and insurance. Switzerland also holds a niche in small- and large-scale precision products, producing everything from the smallest watches to enormous diesel engines.

Victorinox SwissFlash

Fast Facts

- The country code for Switzerland (Confoederatio Helvetica) is CH.
- The symbol of the International Red Cross is the reverse image of the Swiss flag.
- Switzerland is not a member of the EU, yet many important trading partners are EU countries.
- The (male) electorate did not grant women the right to vote in Switzerland until 1971.
- Switzerland is the world's second largest producer of watches.

Confoederatio Helvetica: Swiss history in brief

The **Confoederatio Helvetica** (CH) originated in 1291 when the cantons **Schwyz**, **Uri**, and **Unterwalden** united against their oppressors, the Habsburgs (the dynasty that later ruled the Austrian empire). In 1815, Switzerland declared itself permanently neutral, which has allowed the country to play a unique role in international politics. Geneva has long been the headquarters for many international organizations and a neutral site for dialogue between nations with opposing ideologies. Although military service is compulsory, the military's sole mission is to defend the country and assist in peace-keeping and humanitarian activities.

Swiss roots of the Red Cross: Nobel Prize winner Henry Dunant

Das Internationale Rote Kreuz was founded in 1863, based on the ideas of Swiss citizen Henry Dunant. Having witnessed the aftermath of the bloody Battle of Solferino in Italy in 1859, he wrote about the horrors of war in a book that was translated into many languages. The questions he raised led to the founding of the Red Cross and soon after to the adoption of the first Geneva Convention for the protection of wounded or imprisoned soldiers in wartime. Both the Red Cross and the Geneva Convention continue to play a crucial role in countries all over the world.

Ausblick bei einer Tageswanderung

Kühe in der Alpenlandschaft

Alpine landscapes

The natural beauty and recreational opportunities of this mountainous country are the basis for Switzerland's flourishing tourist trade. The **Schweizer Alpen** provided the setting for Johanna Spyri's classic children's novel *Heidi*, and Swiss landscapes figure prominently in many other poems, novels, and literary works from Switzerland.

4-7 **Kleine Prosa: Schneien** Swiss modernist writer Robert Walser (1878–1956) captures the essence of the Swiss winter landscape in this excerpt from "Snowing."

Excerpt from Schneien

ROBERT WALSER

Es schneit, schneit, was vom Himmel herunter[1] mag[2], und es mag Erklecklichles[3] herunter. Das hört nicht auf, hat nicht Anfang und nicht Ende. Einen Himmel gibt es nicht mehr, alles ist ein graues weißes Schneien. Eine Luft[4] gibt es auch nicht mehr, sie ist voll von Schnee. Eine Erde[5] gibt es auch nicht mehr, sie ist mit Schnee und wieder mit Schnee zugedeckt[6].

[1]*down*   [2]*= möchte*   [3]*a lot*   [4]*air*   [5]*earth*   [6]*covered up*

---

1. What kind of "snowing" do you think Walser is describing? Support your answer with words or short phrases from the text.
2. What descriptive words would you use to express the feeling that this text evokes?

Nomen

das Frühstück	breakfast
zum Frühstück	for breakfast
das Brot	bread
belegte Brote (pl)	(open-faced) sandwiches
das Brötchen, -	roll
das Ei, -er	egg
das Rührei (sing)	scrambled eggs
das Spiegelei, -er	fried egg (sunny side up)
der Honig	honey
der Joghurt	yogurt
der Käse	cheese
die Marmelade	jam
das Müsli	muesli
der Müsliriegel, -	granola bar
der Orangensaft	orange juice
der Zucker	sugar
der Becher, -	cup; container
ein Becher Joghurt	a container of yogurt
das Glas, ̈er	glass
ein Glas Orangensaft	a glass of orange juice
die Scheibe, -n	slice
eine Scheibe Brot	a slice of bread
die Schüssel, -n	bowl
eine Schüssel Müsli	a bowl of muesli
die Tasse, -n	cup
eine Tasse Kaffee	a cup of coffee
das Mittagessen	noon meal; lunch
zum Mittagessen	for lunch
das Abendessen	evening meal
zum Abendessen	for supper; for dinner
das Abendbrot	evening meal of bread and cold cuts
das Fleisch (sing)	meat
das Gemüse (sing)	vegetables
die Kartoffel, -n	potato
die Bratkartoffeln (pl)	fried potatoes
die Pommes frites	French fries
die Pommes	
die Wurst, ̈e	sausage; cold cuts

der Nachtisch	dessert
zum Nachtisch	for dessert
das Eis	ice cream; ice
das Obst (sing)	fruit
der Nachmittagskaffee	afternoon coffee
zum Nachmittagskaffee	for afternoon coffee
der Kuchen, -	cake
die Torte, -n	layer cake
das Stück, -e	piece
ein Stück Torte	a piece of layer cake

Verben

an·fangen (fängt an)	to begin; to start
auf·hören	to end, to stop
auf·stehen	to get up
dauern	to last
frühstücken	to have breakfast
schmecken	to taste; to taste good

> **an·fangen**, etc.: The raised dot indicates that these are separable-prefix verbs. You will learn more about them later in this chapter.

Andere Wörter

fertig	finished; ready
genau	exact(ly); carefully
meistens	most of the time, usually
normalerweise	normally, usually

Ausdrücke

Bist du heute Abend zu Hause?	Will you be (at) home tonight?
Gehst du nach Hause?	Are you going home?
So bin ich eben.	That's just the way I am.
Wann isst du zu Mittag (zu Abend)?	When do you have lunch (supper)?
Wie sagt man das auf Deutsch?	How does one (do you) say that in German?

Das Gegenteil

früh ≠ spät	early ≠ late
manchmal ≠ oft	sometimes ≠ often

Leicht zu verstehen

der Bagel, –s	der Fisch, –e	die Orange, –n	das Sauerkraut
die Banane, –n	die Grapefruit, –s	der Pudding	der Toast
der Brokkoli	der Muffin, –s	der Reis	
die Butter	die Nudel, –n	der Salat, –e	

Wörter im Kontext

4-8 Was passt nicht?

1. das Fleisch	2. die Nudel	3. der Becher	4. der Pudding
der Orangensaft	der Nachtisch	das Glas	das Eis
der Käse	die Kartoffel	die Scheibe	das Obst
die Wurst	der Reis	die Tasse	der Brokkoli

4-9 *Nach Hause* oder *zu Hause?*

Zieglers fahren nach Hause

Zieglers sind zu Hause

1. Isst du heute im Restaurant oder _____?
2. Wann kommt Stephanie _____?
3. Ich gehe jetzt _____.
4. Ich muss um sieben _____ sein.
5. Wohnt Stefan noch _____?

4-10 Was passt wo?

zum Mittagessen / zum Frühstück / zum Nachtisch / manchmal

1. _____ esse ich Brötchen oder eine Schüssel Müsli.
   _____ esse ich Fleisch und Gemüse.
   _____ esse ich Obst oder italienisches Eis.
   Am Wochenende esse ich _____ Frühstück.

Joghurt / Pommes frites / Käse / Chips / Butter

2. _____, _____ und _____ macht man aus Milch.
   _____ und _____ macht man aus Kartoffeln.

eine Scheibe / eine Tasse / einen Becher / ein Glas / ein Stück

3. Zum Frühstück trinke ich normalerweise _____ kalten Orangensaft und _____
   schwarzen Kaffee und esse _____ Toast dazu. Zum Nachmittagskaffee esse
   ich _____ Torte und abends esse ich zum Nachtisch oft _____ Fruchtjoghurt.

1 Modifying the meaning of verbs: modal verbs

4-1 to 4-4

Meaning and position of modal verbs

Verbs like the English *can, must,* and *want to* are called modal verbs. They modify the meaning of other verbs (*I **can** go now; I **must** go now, I **want** to go now*).

In German there are six modal verbs. When you use a modal verb, the main verb is placed at the end of the sentence. It completes the thought.

Wir müssen leider

draußen bleiben.

Ich **kann** gleich **anfangen**.   *I can begin right away.*
Ich **muss** gleich **anfangen**.   *I must begin right away.*
Ich **will** gleich **anfangen**.   *I want to begin right away.*

The modal verb **können** is also used to express that a person can speak a foreign language. When it is used in this special way, there is no main verb at all, because the meaning is understood from context.

Ich **kann** Deutsch und Spanisch.   *I **can speak** German and Spanish.*

The modals *können, müssen,* and *wollen*

Below are the present tense forms of **können** *(to be able to, to know how to, can),* **müssen** *(to have to, must),* and **wollen** *(to want to).*

können		müssen		wollen	
ich	kann	ich	muss	ich	will
du	kannst	du	musst	du	willst
er/es/sie	kann	er/es/sie	muss	er/es/sie	will
wir	können	wir	müssen	wir	wollen
ihr	könnt	ihr	müsst	ihr	wollt
sie/Sie	können	sie/Sie	müssen	sie/Sie	wollen

Note:
- These modals have a stem-vowel change in the **ich-, du-,** and **er/es/sie-**forms. None of the singular forms of modals has an umlaut.
- Modals have no endings in the **ich-**form and the **er/es/sie-**form, and these two forms are identical.

4-11 Wer kann was besonders gut?

1. Herr und Frau Ziegler _____ ziemlich gut Spanisch.
2. Nina _____ sehr gut Klavier spielen.
3. Alexander _____ ausgezeichnet kochen.

LEHRER/IN: Und Sie? Was können Sie besonders gut?
STUDENT/IN: Ich _____ ziemlich gut (sehr gut, ausgezeichnet) …

4-12 Was müssen Zieglers alles tun?

1. Herr und Frau Ziegler _____ beide arbeiten und Geld verdienen.
2. Nina und Robert _____ jeden Morgen in die Schule gehen und jeden
   Abend _____ sie ihre Hausaufgaben° machen.   *homework*
3. Herr Ziegler _____ jeden Morgen das Frühstück machen und jeden Samstag
   das Haus putzen°.   *clean*
4. Frau Ziegler _____ jeden Abend kochen und jeden Samstag waschen.

LEHRER/IN: Und Sie? Was müssen Sie alles tun?
STUDENT/IN: Ich _____ …

4-13 Was wollen Nina, Robert und Alexander werden?

1. Nina _____ Journalistin werden.
2. Robert _____ Fußballprofi° werden.   **Profi:** *pro*
3. Alexander _____ Ingenieur werden.

LEHRER/IN: Und Sie? Was wollen Sie werden?
STUDENT/IN: Ich _____ …
LEHRER/IN: Und warum wollen Sie … werden?
STUDENT/IN: Ich finde diesen Beruf sehr interessant.
  Ich arbeite gern mit Kindern / mit alten Leuten / mit Tieren / …
  Ich kann sehr gut schreiben / fotografieren / …
  Ich will viel Geld verdienen.

4-14 Mal ganz ehrlich. *(Let's be honest.)* Ask your partner what she/he is not so good at. Report your findings to the class.

S1: Was kannst du nicht so gut?   **S2:** Ich kann nicht so gut …
                                        Ich kann gar nicht gut …

The modals *dürfen, sollen,* and *mögen*

Below are the present tense forms of **dürfen** *(to be allowed to, to be permitted to, may)*, **sollen** *(to be supposed to, should)*, and **mögen** *(to like)*.

dürfen		sollen		mögen	
ich	darf	ich	soll	ich	mag
du	darfst	du	sollst	du	magst
er/es/sie	darf	er/es/sie	soll	er/es/sie	mag
wir	dürfen	wir	sollen	wir	mögen
ihr	dürft	ihr	sollt	ihr	mögt
sie/Sie	dürfen	sie/Sie	sollen	sie/Sie	mögen

Ich darf hier nicht hinein !

Signs like these are common in Germany, because people sometimes bring their dogs on short shopping trips in town.

Remember, if you want to say you like to do something, use **gern** rather than a modal: *Ich spiele gern Tennis. Ich trinke gern Kaffee.*

Note:
- **Sollen** is the only modal that does not have a stem-vowel change in the **ich-, du-,** and **er/es/sie-**forms.
- Like the other modals you have learned, the **ich-** and **er/es/sie-**forms are identical and have no endings.
- **Mögen** is usually used without an infinitive.

Ich **mag** Stephanie.   *I **like** Stephanie.*
Warum **mögt** ihr kein Gemüse?   *Why **don't** you **like** vegetables?*

4-15 Was dürfen Zieglers alles nicht tun?

1. Herr und Frau Ziegler _____ keinen Kaffee trinken.
2. Ihre Tochter Nina ist erst sechzehn und _____ noch nicht Auto fahren.
3. Ihr Sohn Robert ist vierzehn und _____ nicht nach Mitternacht nach Hause kommen.

LEHRER/IN: Und Sie? Was dürfen Sie alles nicht tun?
STUDENT/IN: Ich _____ nicht …

4-16 Was sollen Zieglers nächsten Samstag alles tun?

1. Frau Ziegler und Nina _____ nächsten Samstag Oma Ziegler besuchen.
2. Robert _____ nächsten Samstag Vaters Wagen waschen.
3. Herr Ziegler _____ nächsten Samstag die Waschmaschine reparieren.

LEHRER/IN: Und Sie? Was sollen Sie nächsten Samstag alles tun?
STUDENT/IN: Ich _____ nächsten Samstag …

4-17 Was mögen Zieglers alles nicht?

1. Herr Ziegler _____ keine Kartoffeln und keine Nudeln.
2. Die beiden Teenager _____ kein Gemüse und keinen Salat.
3. Frau Ziegler _____ kein Fleisch.

LEHRER/IN: Und Sie? Was mögen Sie alles nicht?
STUDENT/IN: Ich _____ kein__ …

4-18 Was magst du und was magst du nicht? You and your partner ask each other what you especially like to eat and what you don't like at all. You will find additional food items under **Essen und Trinken** in the *Anhang* on p. A17.

> When you want to express that you really don't like something at all, use **gar nicht**, not **kein: Reis mag ich gar nicht.**

S1: Was magst du besonders gern?
    Was magst du gar nicht?

S2: … mag ich besonders gern.
    … mag ich gar nicht.

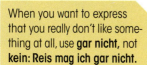

Möchte versus *mögen*

Although the modal **möchte** is derived from **mögen,** it is not used to express what one likes or dislikes, but what one *would like* to have or to do. **Ich möchte** is therefore a more polite way of saying **ich will. Möchte** is used when making requests and ordering food.

Ich **mag** Käsekuchen.   *I like cheesecake.*
Ich **möchte** ein Stück Käsekuchen.   *I would like a piece of cheesecake.*

It would be impolite to say:

Ich **will** ein Stück Käsekuchen.   *I want a piece of cheesecake.*

singular		plural	
ich	möchte	wir	möchten
du	möchtest	ihr	möchtet
er/es/sie	möchte	sie	möchten
	Sie	möchten	

4-19 Wer möchte was?

1. Frau Ziegler _____ eine Weltreise° machen.
2. Herr Ziegler _____ einen Porsche.
3. Robert _____ ein neues Mountainbike.
4. Nina _____ ein Jahr in Amerika studieren.

trip around the world

LEHRER/IN: Und Sie? Was möchten Sie?
STUDENT/IN: Ich _____ ...

Omission of the infinitive after modal verbs

4-7 to 4-10

If the meaning of a sentence containing a modal is clear without an infinitive, the infinitive is often omitted.

Ich muss jetzt nach Hause.   *I have to **go** home now.*

4-20 Welcher Infinitiv passt?

trinken / gehen / essen / fliegen / sprechen

1. Wir müssen jetzt in die Vorlesung.
2. Können deine Eltern Deutsch?
3. Möchten Sie ein Stück Kuchen?
4. Darf deine kleine Schwester immer noch nicht in die Disco?
5. Möchtest du auch nach Australien?
6. Wollt ihr lieber Bier oder Wein?
7. Im Winter mag ich kein Eis.
8. Warum willst du denn nicht ins Kino?

Position of *nicht* in sentences with modal verbs

4-11

You know how to negate a particular word or expression with **nicht**: Put **nicht** directly before it. The same rule applies in sentences with modal verbs.

Ich muss **nicht jede Woche** so viel lesen. *I don't have to read so much every week.*
Ich muss **nicht beide Artikel** lesen. *I don't have to read both articles.*

However, when you want to negate the main verb, **nicht** comes directly before the infinitive.

Professor Raabe kann morgen **nicht** kommen. *Professor Raabe can't come tomorrow.*
Toll! Dann muss ich seinen Artikel *Great! Then I don't have to read*
   nicht lesen. *his article.*

4-21 Immer negativ.

S1: Kannst du kochen?   S2: Nein, ich kann nicht kochen.

1. Kann Martin gut kochen?   Nein, er kann ...
2. Dürfen wir den Apfelkuchen essen?   Nein, ihr dürft ...
3. Muss ich dieses Buch lesen?   Nein, du musst ...
4. Kannst du Peter nach Hause fahren?   Nein, ich kann ...
5. Will Claudia den ganzen Abend zu Hause bleiben?   Nein, sie will ...
6. Möchtest du mein Referat lesen?   Nein, ich möchte ...

4-22 So bin ich eben. Write about yourself, using the modal verbs in the questions to guide you.

Was kannst du besonders gut?
Was kannst du gar nicht gut?
Wen magst du besonders gern? Warum?
Was magst du besonders gern?
Was magst du gar nicht?
Was möchtest du gern tun und darfst es nicht?
Was sollst du tun und tust es nicht?

2 Modifying the meaning of verbs: prefixes

4-12 to 4-13

Meaning of separable-prefix verbs

In English the meaning of certain verbs is modified or changed when you add a preposition or an adverb after the verb. In German the same effect is achieved by adding a prefix to the verb. In pronunciation, the stress always falls on the separable prefix.

*to go **out***	**aus**gehen	*to try **out***	**aus**probieren
*to go **away***	**weg**gehen	*to clean **up***	**auf**räumen
*to come **back***	**zurück**kommen	*to stand **up**;*	**auf**stehen
*to come **home***	**heim**kommen	*to get **up***	
*to try **on***	**an**probieren		

Separable-prefix verbs are not always similar to their English equivalents.

abfahren	*to depart, to leave*	**ein**laden	*to invite*
ankommen	*to arrive*	**ein**schlafen	*to fall asleep*
anfangen	*to begin, to start*	**fern**sehen	*to watch TV*
aufhören	*to end, to stop*	**herum**hängen	*to hang out*
anhören	*to listen to*	**vor**haben	*to plan, to have planned*
anrufen	*to call (on the phone)*		

The verb **herumhängen** (*to hang out*) is a casual expression and usually gets shortened to **rumhängen**.

Sprachnotiz **More about separable prefixes**

By combining prefixes with verbs, German creates a host of new verbs. In each set below, look at the first example and its English equivalent. Then figure out the meaning of the other verbs.

mitkommen *(to come **along**):* mitbringen, mitnehmen, mitlesen, mitsingen
weggehen *(to go **away**):* wegfahren, wegsehen, weglaufen, wegnehmen
weiterlesen *(to continue reading):* weiterarbeiten, weiteressen, weiterfahren
zurückrufen *(to call **back**):* zurückbringen, zurückfahren, zurückgeben

---

Position of the separable prefix

In the infinitive form, the prefix is attached to the front of the verb (**aus**gehen, **heim**kommen, etc.). In the present tense, the prefix is separated from the verb and placed at the end of the sentence.

Ich **gehe** jetzt **aus**.　　　　　　*I'm going out* now.
Ich **komme** sehr spät **heim**.　　　*I'm coming home* very late.

4-23 **Was machst du heute Nachmittag?** Use one of the verbs in the boxes below to respond to your partner's questions.

▶ du heute Nachmittag　　　　　　　　meine neue CD anhören

S1: Was machst du heute Nachmittag?　　**S2:** Da höre ich meine neue CD an.

Since each answer starts with the word *da* instead of the subject, the verb will be next, followed by the subject.

1. du am
   Samstagmorgen

2. du am
   Samstagabend

3. du morgen
   Abend

4. ihr am
   Sonntagabend

fernsehen	mit Claudia ausgehen
erst um elf aufstehen	mein Zimmer aufräumen

5. du heute
   Abend

6. ihr bei
   Karstadt

7. du am
   Bodensee

8. ihr am
   Freitagabend

The **Bodensee** (*Lake Constance*) borders Switzerland, Austria and Germany, and is a popular tourist destination.

rumhängen	mein Surfbrett ausprobieren
meine Eltern anrufen	ein paar Kleider anprobieren

4-12 to 4-13

Position of separable-prefix verbs with modals

When used with a modal, the separable-prefix verb appears as an infinitive at the end of the sentence, just like other verbs.

Du **musst** jetzt **aufstehen.**   *You have to get up now.*
Du **musst** jetzt **essen.**   *You have to eat now.*

4-24 Kleine Gespräche.

▶ aufstehen
  Warum _____ du denn so
  früh _____?

  anrufen
  Ich will meine Kusine in
  Deutschland _____.

S1: Warum stehst du denn
    so früh auf?

S2: Ich will meine Kusine in
    Deutschland anrufen.

1. ausgehen
   _____ du heute Abend mit
   uns _____?

   aufräumen
   Nein, ich muss endlich mal° mein
   Zimmer _____.

2. anhören
   Möchtest du meine neue
   CD _____?

   ausprobieren
   Nein, ich möchte lieber deinen neuen
   Computer _____.

3. vorhaben
   Was _____ du heute _____?

   anprobieren
   Ich will bei Karstadt Kleider _____.

4. anrufen
   Kann ich Claudia abends um
   zehn noch _____?

   fernsehen
   Klar! Sie _____ jeden Abend bis nach
   Mitternacht _____.

5. heimgehen
   Können wir jetzt endlich _____?

   aufhören
   Nein, erst muss der Regen _____.

endlich mal: finally

Sprachnotiz   **Position of *nicht* with separable-prefix verbs**

When you want to negate a separable-prefix verb, **nicht** is the second-to-last element.

Ich gehe heute **nicht** aus.   *I'm **not** going out today.*
Ich will heute **nicht** ausgehen.   *I **don't** want to go out today.*

4-25 Ich will mein Leben ändern. Tell your classmates about three things you want to change in your life.

Ich will nicht mehr so viel (so oft, so spät, so lange) …		Ich will mehr …
fernsehen	in die Kneipe gehen	Milch trinken
schlafen	Bier trinken	Gemüse und
aufstehen	Junkfood essen	Obst essen
ausgehen	Kaffee trinken	lernen
rauchen°	ins Bett gehen	Sport machen
…	…	…

to smoke

4-26 **Was machst du den ganzen Tag?** Ask your partner about a typical day. Practice using **meistens** to say *most of the time*.

S1:

Wann stehst du morgens auf?

Wann fangen deine
   Vorlesungen an?

Wann kommst du heim?

Gehst du abends oft aus?

S2:

Ich _____ meistens um … _____.

Meine Vorlesungen _____ meistens
   um … _____.

Ich _____ meistens um … _____.

Ja, ich _____ abends oft _____. /

Nein, ich _____ abends nur sehr
   selten° _____.   *seldom*

4-27 **Verkehrszeichen.** Ask each other what these German traffic signs mean. The information for **S2** is in the *Anhang* on page A4.

S1: Was bedeutet Verkehrszeichen
   Nummer 1?

S2: Hier kommt gleich eine
   scharfe Rechtskurve.

1	2 Hier fängt die Autobahn an.	3
4	5 Hier geht es zur Autobahn nach Berlin.	6 Hier darf man nur nach rechts fahren.
7	8 Hier darf man nicht halten.	9
10 Autos und Motorräder dürfen hier nicht hineinfahren.	11 Hier darf man nur drei Minuten halten.	12

> The red border around a round German traffic sign indicates that something is restricted or prohibited.

Verb-noun and verb-verb combinations

Some verbs are so closely associated with a noun or another verb that they function like separable-prefix verbs.

With nouns this happens most frequently with the verbs **spielen, laufen,** and **fahren.**

Im Sommer **fährt** David fast jeden Tag **Rad.**	*In the summer David goes cycling almost every day.*
Im Winter **läuft** er fast jedes Wochenende **Ski.**	*In the winter he skis almost every weekend.*

With verbs this happens most frequently with the verb **gehen.**

Er **geht** jeden Abend **joggen.**	*He goes jogging every evening.*

If a modal is used, both parts of these verb-noun or verb-verb combinations appear at the end of the sentence. They work together as one element, like separable-prefix verbs, but they are written as separate words.

Ich **will** im Sommer **Rad fahren.**	*I want to go biking in the summer.*
Ich **kann** in der Schweiz **Ski laufen.**	*I can ski in Switzerland.*
Ich möchte die Schweiz **kennen lernen.**	*I'd like to get to know Switzerland.*

Again, when **nicht** is used to negate the verb, it is the second-to-last element. If there is a modal, as in the second sentence below, the **nicht** precedes the entire combination.

Claudia geht heute **nicht spazieren.**	*Claudia isn't going for a walk today.*
Sie will auch **nicht Tennis spielen.**	*She also doesn't want to play tennis.*

4-28 Was Tanja, Dieter und Laura können oder nicht können. Look at the first column of the table to determine what Tanja does well or doesn't do. Then do the same for Dieter and Laura.

	TANJA	DIETER	LAURA
Motorrad fahren	sehr gut	nicht	sehr gut
Gitarre spielen	nicht	sehr gut	sehr gut
Ski laufen	sehr gut	sehr gut	nicht

1. Tanja fährt … und sie läuft auch …, aber sie kann …
2. Dieter spielt … und er läuft auch …, aber er kann …
3. Laura fährt … und sie spielt auch …, aber sie kann …

136 / hundertsechsunddreißig

KAPITEL 4

Infobox

Die Bahn

In the German-speaking countries, train transportation is a vital part of life. The railway systems are renowned for their fast and efficient passenger service, and companies in industrial regions of Germany and nearly all of mountainous Switzerland depend on trains to transport raw materials and finished products.

Der ICE: dritte Generation

The fastest passenger trains of the **Deutsche Bahn** are the **ICE (InterCityExpress)** and **ICE International.** These trains connect major German cities to each other and to other cities in Europe at speeds up to 300 km/h (about 186 mph) and have restaurant cars and comfortable workspaces, often with wireless internet (**W-LAN**). Even the regular **RE (RegionalExpress)** trains that connect larger cities are capable of speeds up to 160 km/h (100 mph). These factors and the dense network of rail lines in Europe make trains a viable and convenient alternative to traveling by car.

Although Germany is about the size of the state of Montana, it has approximately 5,400 **Bahnhöfe** *(train stations)*. Both Austria and Switzerland have built an extensive mountain rail system in addition to the city-to-city routes of the **Österreichische Bundesbahn (ÖBB)** and the **Schweizerische Bundesbahn (SBB)**. Apart from connecting millions of skiers to alpine slopes, train companies offer scenic trips such as the Swiss **Glacier Express,** a day-long ride that traverses 291 bridges, 91 tunnels, and navigates the 2033-meter-high (6670 feet) Oberalp Pass.

When traveling by train, be sure to buy a ticket before you board, since traveling without one (**Schwarzfahren**) can incur a hefty fine.

Der Glacier Express

In Germany, **Ländertickets** for regional trains in each state allow groups of up to five people to travel on local and regional trains all day for only around 35 euros. The same group of five can use the **Schönes-Wochenende-Ticket** to travel across the country for just under 40 euros, if the group uses regional rather than Intercity or ICE trains.

For North American students, a popular way to explore Europe is with the Eurail Pass, which provides unlimited travel for a period of time on a total of 280,000 kilometers (174,000 miles) of track through 22 European countries. And most countries have country-specific Flexipasses that let travelers pay for a specific number of travel days within a stay abroad.

4-29 Verben im Kontext. Many verbs for traveling have separable prefixes. Read the following description of a train trip and match the verbs for train travel with their English equivalents from the list below.

Zuerst **steigen** wir in Dortmund in den ICE 209 **ein**.

Wir **fahren** um 13:37 **ab**.

Der Zug **hält** um 15:51 in Frankfurt am Flughafen kurz **an**.

Aber wir **steigen** nicht **um**. Der Zug **fährt** in 3 Minuten **weiter.**

Er hält nur kurz in Großstädten. So **kommen** wir schon um 18:47 in Basel **an**.

to arrive	to depart	to stop
to continue	to change trains	to board the train

DB BAHN

Kontakt | Hilfe | Sitemap a a+ a++   Frage oder Suchbegriff eingeben... [Suchen]

Startseite | Angebotsberatung | **Fahrplan & Buchung** | Services | BahnCard | Urlaub   Meine Bahn

Fahrtinformationen
ICE 209

Halt	Ankunft	Abfahrt	Gleis	Aktuelles
aktuelle Zeit: 23:47				
Dortmund Hbf		13:37		
Hagen Hbf	13:55	13:57	9/10	
Wuppertal Hbf	14:12	14:14		
Solingen Hbf	14:25	14:27		
Köln Hbf	14:45	14:55		
Siegburg/Bonn	15:09	15:11		
Frankfurt(M) Flughafen Fernbf	15:51	15:54	Fern 5	
Mannheim Hbf	16:24	16:36		
Karlsruhe Hbf	16:58	17:00		
Offenburg	17:27	17:29		
Freiburg(Breisgau) Hbf	17:59	18:01		
Basel Bad Bf	18:36	18:41		
Basel SBB	18:47			

Verkehrstage: Mo - Fr, nicht 22., 25. Apr, 13. Jun, 3. Okt (Dortmund Hbf --> Karlsruhe Hbf)
Mo - Fr, nicht 22., 25. Apr, 13. Jun, 1. Aug bis 2. Sep 2011, 3. Okt (Karlsruhe Hbf --> Basel SBB)

Bemerkungen: **Bordbistro**
WLAN verfügbar zwischen Dortmund-Köln-Frankfurt-Stuttgart-München (Dortmund Hbf --> Mannheim Hbf)

→ Schließen

Alle Angaben ohne Gewähr.

🖶 Seite drucken   ⇧ Zum Seitenanfang

© Deutsche Bahn AG | AGB | Impressum | Datenschutzgrundsätze | www.deutschebahn.com

4-30 Eine Reise in die Schweiz! Take a look at the train schedule for the ICE train from Dortmund to Basel, Switzerland. Imagine you are starting in **Köln** (Cologne) and using a rail pass, so you can get on and off the train as you like. Choose a German city you could visit on your way to Switzerland and plan a trip with your partner. When and where will you board the train, and where will you get off? Use some of the verbs below.

in den Zug einsteigen / aussteigen / weiterfahren / anhalten / ankommen

Video-Treff

Ein typischer Tag

Christina Brieger, Ursula, André, Maiga, and Stefan Kuhlmann talk about their daily routines. Be sure to complete the **Was ist das auf Englisch?** exercise before watching the video.

Ich gehe joggen.

4-31 Was ist das auf Englisch?

1. Ich **bringe** dann die Wohnung **in Ordnung.**
2. Ich habe eine Vorlesung in **Sinologie** und lerne chinesische Aussprache.
3. Ich esse **entweder** ein Brot von zu Hause **oder** ich gehe in die Mensa.
4. Wenn ich **großen Hunger habe,** dann gehe ich in die Mensa.
5. Ich gehe um eins oder zwei ins Bett. Ich bin **ein Nachtmensch.**
6. Ein typischer Tag fängt **ohne** Frühstück an, weil ich nicht gern frühstücke.
7. Danach fahre ich mit dem Fahrrad in die Uni, meistens **etwas knapp.**

a. either . . . or
b. without
c. a night person
d. Chinese Studies
e. just barely in time
f. am really hungry
g. tidy up

4-32 Was passt? Choose the appropriate information to complete these sentences about Christina Brieger, Ursula, and André.

1. Christina steht morgens gegen _____ auf.
   ☐ sechs Uhr   ☐ sieben Uhr

2. Manchmal essen Christina und Nicolai _____ zum Frühstück.
   ☐ Schokomüsli mit Joghurt   ☐ Toast mit Marmelade

3. _____ bringt Nicolai zum Kindergarten.
   ☐ Christoph   ☐ Christina

4. Christina arbeitet _____.
   ☐ im Büro   ☐ zu Hause

5. Ursula steht meistens um _____ auf.
   ☐ 7.30   ☐ 8.30

6. Dann geht sie _____ im Park joggen.
   ☐ 30 Minuten   ☐ 15 Minuten

7. Ursula arbeitet ____.
   ☐ zu Hause   ☐ im Büro

8. André steht im Semester immer _____ auf.
   ☐ früh   ☐ spät

9. Wenn André frühstückt, _____.
   ☐ sieht er oft fern ☐ liest er oft Zeitung

10. Wenn er nachmittags frei hat, _____.
    ☐ lernt er zu Hause ☐ geht er in die Bibliothek

4-33 Richtig oder falsch? Decide whether the following statements about Maiga and Stefan Kuhlmann are **richtig** or **falsch**. If the statement is **falsch**, provide a correct version.

	RICHTIG	FALSCH
1. Wenn Maiga eine Vorlesung hat, steht sie so gegen halb 9 oder 9 Uhr auf.	☐	☐
2. Zum Frühstück isst sie nichts, weil sie keinen Hunger hat.	☐	☐
3. Maiga nimmt den Bus zur Uni.	☐	☐
4. Maiga bringt ihr Mittagessen oft zur Uni mit.	☐	☐
5. Maiga ist bis 16 Uhr an der Uni.	☐	☐
6. Stefan isst immer ein großes Frühstück.	☐	☐
7. Stefan trinkt morgens eine Tasse Tee.	☐	☐
8. Stefan hört morgens Musik.	☐	☐
9. Abends sieht Stefan oft fern, oder er geht ins Kino.	☐	☐
10. Stefan geht meistens früh ins Bett.	☐	☐

3 Expressing commands and requests, and giving advice

Imperatives

You can use the imperative form of a verb to express a command, make a request, or give advice. Since English has only one form of address *(you),* it has only one imperative form. German has three forms of address **(Sie, ihr,** and **du),** and so it has three imperative forms. In written German, imperative sentences often end with an exclamation mark.

> **Kommen Sie!**
> **Kommt!**   } *Come!*
> **Komm!**

 ### The *Sie*-imperative

4-17 to 4-24

The **Sie**-imperative is the infinitive of the verb followed directly by **Sie.**

Wiederholen Sie bitte, was ich sage!   *Please repeat what I say.*

The prefix of a separable verb appears at the end of the imperative sentence.

Hören Sie bitte gut **zu!**   *Please listen carefully.*

Again, verb-noun and verb-verb combinations function like separable-prefix verbs.

Spielen Sie doch mit uns **Volleyball!**   *Play volleyball with us.*
Gehen Sie nicht allein **schwimmen!**   *Don't go swimming alone.*

The verb **sein** is slightly irregular in the **Sie**-imperative.

Seien Sie doch nicht so nervös!   *Don't be so nervous.*

4-34 **Frau Ziegler geht zum Arzt.** Match Frau Ziegler's problem at the left with the appropriate suggestion from her doctor at the right.

1. Ich bin immer so müde.
2. Ich kann nicht gut schlafen.
3. Ich werde mollig.
4. Ich bin abends so nervös!
5. Vormittags habe ich keine Energie.

a. Dann trinken Sie nicht so viel Kaffee!
b. Dann gehen Sie früh ins Bett!
c. Dann trinken Sie abends ein Glas Wein!
d. Dann gehen Sie mal in das Fitnessstudio!
e. Dann essen Sie mal ein gesundes Frühstück!

4-35 **In Professor Kuhls Deutschkurs.**

1. _____ bitte ein bisschen lauter! (sprechen)
2. _____ bitte das Wort, Kevin! (wiederholen)
3. _____ das Wort bitte _____! (auf•schreiben)
4. _____ bitte _____, Andrea! (weiter•lesen)
5. _____ doch nicht so nervös! (sein)
6. _____ jetzt bitte gut _____! (zu•hören)
7. _____ diese Übung bitte schriftlich°! (machen)   *in writing*

The *ihr*-imperative

4-17 to 4-24

The **ihr**-imperative is the **ihr**-form of the verb without the pronoun.

Kommt, Kinder! Wir gehen schwimmen.   *Come on, children! We're going swimming.*
Nehmt eure Badeanzüge **mit!**   *Take your bathing suits along.*
Seid doch bitte nicht so laut!   *Please don't be so noisy.*

4-36 Ein Picknick. You and your friends are going on a picnic. Your mother gives last-minute instructions.

1. _____ viele Getränke _____! (mit·nehmen)
2. _____ das Frisbee _____! (mit·nehmen)
3. _____ auch eure Badeanzüge _____! (ein·packen)
4. _____ genug° Sonnencreme _____! (mit·nehmen)   *enough*
5. _____ auch ein paar schöne Fotos! (machen)
6. _____ genug Brote _____! (ein·packen)
7. _____ bitte nicht zu schnell! (fahren)
8. _____ bitte nicht zu viel! (trinken)
9. _____ bitte vor neun wieder zurück! (sein)
10. _____ doch endlich _____! (ab·fahren)

> Until recently, **Halloween** was known to Germans only through American movies. Today it is not uncommon to see children wearing costumes and knocking on doors calling **Streich oder Süßigkeiten!**

The *du*-imperative

4-17 to 4-24

The **du**-imperative is simply the stem of the verb.

Lass mich in Ruhe!   *Stop bothering me!*
Komm nicht wieder so spät **heim!**   *Don't come home so late again!*
Sei doch nicht immer so unordentlich, Peter!   *Don't always be so sloppy, Peter!*

Verbs that have a stem-vowel change from **e** to **i** or **ie** in the 2nd and 3rd person singular of the present tense (e.g., **ich lese, du liest, er liest**) use the changed stem in the **du**-imperative.

Nimm doch nicht so viel Fleisch, Robert!   *Don't take so much meat, Robert!*
Iss nicht wieder den ganzen Kuchen!   *Don't eat all the cake again!*

Verbs with stems ending in **–d** or **–t** add an **–e** in the **du**-imperative.

Rede doch nicht so viel!   *Don't talk so much.*
Antworte bitte so bald wie möglich!   *Please answer as soon as possible.*

4-37 Mach bitte, was ich sage! You and your partner are siblings. One tries to lord it over the other, but it isn't working.

► _____ doch endlich _____! (auf·stehen)   _____ still und _____ mich schlafen! (sein, lassen)

S1: Steh doch endlich auf!   S2: Sei still und lass mich schlafen!

1. _____ doch endlich mal deine Cornflakes! (essen)   _____ still und _____ deinen Kaffee! (sein, trinken)
2. _____ doch nicht immer _____! (rumhängen)   _____ mich in Ruhe und _____ deine Vokabeln! (lassen, lernen)

3. _____ bitte gleich dein Zimmer _____! (auf·räumen)

_____ still und _____ dein Referat fertig! (sein, schreiben)

4. _____ deinen Freund doch nicht schon wieder _____! (an·rufen)

_____ mich in Ruhe und _____ dein Müsli! (lassen, essen)

5. _____ nur ein Stück Kuchen! (nehmen)

_____ still und _____ dein Buch! (sein, lesen)

6. _____ bitte gleich meinen Wagen! (waschen)

_____ deinen Wagen doch selbst°! (waschen)   *yourself*

4-38 Du nervst mich! Using the suggestions below, tell your roommate or a family member to stop doing things that get on your nerves.

▶ doch nicht so schnell fahren

S1: Fahr doch nicht so schnell!

doch nicht so langsam fahren
doch nicht so laut schnarchen°   *snore*
doch nicht immer nur Junkfood essen
doch nicht immer so lange telefonieren
doch nicht so schnell essen
doch nicht immer so viel reden

doch nicht so schnell / langsam sprechen
doch nicht immer nur deine doofen Comics lesen
doch nicht immer nur vor dem Fernseher° sitzen   *in front of the TV*

4-39 Guter Rat. One of you (**S1**) plays the person or persons asking for advice. The other (**S2**) responds with advice, using the **Sie-, ihr-,** or **du-**imperative, depending on who is asking for advice.

▶ einen Audi

FRAU FISCHER: Was soll ich kaufen, einen VW oder einen Audi?

S2: Kaufen Sie lieber einen Audi.

1. EVA UND TANJA: Wo sollen wir studieren, in Freiburg oder in Berlin?   in Freiburg

2. FRAU BRAUN: Wann soll ich fliegen, am Donnerstag oder am Freitag?   am Donnerstag

3. BERND: Was soll ich lesen, ein Buch oder die Zeitung?   ein Buch

4. TIM UND SILKE: Wann sollen wir kommen, um zwei oder um drei?   schon um zwei

5. RALF: Was soll ich trinken, Bier oder Wein?   ein Glas Wein

6. KURT UND JAN: Wann sollen wir morgen aufstehen, um sieben oder um acht?   schon um sieben

7. TOURIST: Wo soll ich essen, im Wienerwald° oder bei McDonald's?   im Wienerwald

a restaurant chain specializing in chicken

4 Word Order

4-25 to 4-28

Position of the verb in independent and dependent clauses

You already know four of the following conjunctions. The final one (**nicht … sondern**) is new.

und	*and*	**aber**	*but*
denn	*because, for*	**nicht … sondern**	*not … but rather …*
oder	*or*		

These conjunctions are called coordinating conjunctions. They connect independent clauses, i.e., clauses that can stand alone as complete sentences. Coordinating conjunctions do not affect the position of the verb.

independent clause	conjunction	independent clause
Bernd hat endlich ein Zimmer	**und**	es kostet nur 150 Euro im Monat.
Es ist nur ein kleines Zimmer,	**aber**	es ist groß genug für Bernd.
Bernd geht **nicht** zu Fuß zur Uni,	**sondern**	er nimmt den Bus.

- The conjunctions **aber** and **sondern** are always preceded by a comma.
- The clause preceding **sondern** states what is *not* happening. The clause following **sondern** states what is happening *instead*.

4-40 Bernd hat ein Problem. Make Bernd's story read more smoothly. Using the appropriate coordinating conjunctions, connect the sentences in the left column with those directly opposite in the right column.

1. Ich habe endlich ein Zimmer! — Es kostet nur 150 Euro im Monat!
far 2. Das Zimmer ist sehr schön. — Von hier zur Uni ist es sehr weit°.
thus 3. Ich brauche also° einen Wagen. — Ich muss jeden Tag zur Uni.
4. Soll ich jetzt einen Wagen kaufen? — Soll ich ein anderes Zimmer suchen?

The following conjunctions are called subordinating conjunctions:

bevor	*before*	**weil**	*because*
obwohl	*although; even though*	**wenn**	*if; when*

Subordinating conjunctions introduce dependent clauses, i.e., clauses that make sense only in connection with an independent clause. Subordinating conjunctions affect the position of the verb: the verb stands at the end of the clause. A dependent clause is *always* separated from the independent clause by a comma.

independent clause	dependent clause
Bernd möchte das Zimmer,	**weil** es schön und preisgünstig ist.
Er möchte das Zimmer,	**obwohl** es von dort zur Uni sehr weit ist.

4-41 **Wie löst Bernd sein Problem?** Describe how Bernd solves his problem. Using the subordinating conjunctions provided, connect the sentences in the left column with those directly opposite in the right column.

1. Bernd möchte einen Wagen.   weil   Seine Wohnung ist weit von der Uni.
2. Er ruft seine Eltern an.   weil   Er braucht Geld für einen Wagen.
3. Bernd geht zu Auto-Müller.   wenn   Er hat das Geld.
4. Er kauft einen alten VW Polo.   bevor   Er nimmt das Zimmer.

In clauses introduced by a subordinating conjunction, modal verbs appear at the end of the clause and separable-prefix verbs are no longer separated.

independent clause	dependent clause
Peter steht früh auf,	**weil** er sein Referat fertig schreiben **muss.**
Claudia steht früh auf,	**weil** ihre erste Vorlesung um halb neun **anfängt.**

4-42 **Warum steht Peter heute so früh auf?** Describe Peter's morning. Using the conjunctions provided, connect the sentences in the left column with those directly opposite in the right column.

1. Peter steht heute schon um fünf auf.   weil   Er muss sein Referat fertig schreiben.
2. Es sind nur noch wenige Stunden.   bevor   Das Seminar bei Professor Weber fängt an.
3. Peter hat mehr Zeit für das Referat   wenn   Er frühstückt nicht.
4. Peter will das Referat noch genau durchlesen.   bevor   Er muss wegfahren.
5. Peter nimmt ein Taxi.   obwohl   Das kostet viel Geld.

Sprachnotiz **Word order when the dependent clause comes first**

If the dependent clause comes at the beginning of the sentence, the entire clause serves as the first element. It is followed by a comma and then the conjugated verb of the independent clause. The conjugated verbs of both clauses thus appear side by side, separated by a comma.

Bevor ich **aufstehe, sehe** ich eine halbe Stunde fern.
Wenn du fit bleiben **willst, musst** du Sport machen.

4-43 Fragen, Fragen, Fragen. You and your partner are sharing information about Kathrin, Florian, and Frau Özal. Begin the responses to your partner's requests for information with the conjunctions provided. The questions and responses for **S2** are in the *Anhang* on page A5.

S1: Warum geht Florian nicht ins Kino?   **S2:** Weil er ein Referat schreiben muss.
S2: Warum geht Kathrin nicht ins Kino?   **S1:** Weil sie …

		KATHRIN	FLORIAN	FRAU ÖZAL
Warum geht … nicht ins Kino?	weil	Sie muss E-Mails schreiben.		Sie kann keine Babysitterin finden.
Geht … heute schwimmen?	wenn		Es wird sehr heiß.	
Wann geht … nach Hause?	wenn	Der Regen hört auf.	Seine Vorlesungen sind zu Ende.	
Wann sieht … gern fern?	bevor	Sie steht auf.		
Warum arbeitet …?	weil	Sie will weiterstudieren.	Er will einen Wagen kaufen.	

4-44 Lebst du gesund oder ungesund? Choose the responses from the right-hand column that reflect your lifestyle.

S1: Trinkst du Kaffee?   **S2:** Nein, ich trinke keinen Kaffee. / Ja, ich trinke Kaffee.
S1: Warum nicht? / Warum?   **S2:** Weil …

1. Trinkst du Kaffee?   Ich will fit bleiben°   *stay*
2. Trinkst du Alkohol?   Ich bin viel zu nervös.
3. Rauchst du?   Ich will nicht krank werden.
4. Trinkst du viel Milch?   Ich kann dann besser denken.
5. Frühstückst du jeden Morgen?   Ich habe keine Zeit.
6. Isst du viel Fleisch?   Ich muss meinen Kaffee haben.
7. Machst du Sport?   Ich brauche meine Zigaretten.
8. Nimmst du Vitamine?   Ich bin Vegetarier(in).
                                          …

Infobox

Was isst man zu Mittag und danach?

Mittagessen in the German-speaking countries is usually the main meal of the day. A more formal meal at home or in a restaurant might have three courses: a **Vorspeise**, a **Hauptgericht**, and a **Nachtisch**. Salads often serve as the vegetable and usually accompany the main course.

The evening meal (**Abendessen**) is also sometimes called **Abendbrot,** which is usually a cold meal of open-faced sandwiches **(belegte Brote)**. Given the hundreds of types of ham, salami, sausage, and cheeses available in Europe, this meal has a lot of variety.

On the weekends, most typically on Sunday afternoons, family and friends meet for **Kaffee und Kuchen**, often after taking a walk outdoors. Many pastry shops are open for a few hours on Sunday to sell fresh pastries and cakes. Cafés in beautiful natural settings are also popular destinations for those who are out on a walk.

Zusammenschau

Hören

Ein typischer Tag in Lisas Leben

Listen as Lisa describes a typical day in her life.

NEUE VOKABELN

Punkt halb sieben	*six-thirty on the dot*	**auf·passen**	*to pay attention*
die Dusche	*shower*	**mit·schreiben**	*to take notes*
dazu	*with it*	**sobald**	*as soon as*
eineinhalb	*one and a half*	**damit**	*so that*

4-45 Erstes Verstehen. Check off which words or expressions you hear in the three categories.

ESSEN UND TRINKEN	AKTIVITÄTEN	TAGESZEITEN
_____ Müsli	_____ ausgehen	_____ Viertel vor acht
_____ Joghurt	_____ aufstehen	_____ halb acht
_____ Milch	_____ mitgehen	_____ Viertel nach acht
_____ Kaffee	_____ mitschreiben	_____ halb elf
_____ Apfel	_____ lesen	_____ Viertel vor zwölf
_____ Käse	_____ kochen	_____ halb fünf

4-46 Detailverstehen. Listen to the narrative again and write short responses to the following questions.

1. Warum geht Lisa jeden Morgen um halb sieben joggen? *Weil …*
2. Was isst und trinkt Lisa zum Frühstück?
3. Wann fängt Lisas erste Vorlesung an?
4. Wann geht Lisa in die Cafeteria? *Wenn …*
5. Was macht Lisa, bevor sie zu Mittag isst?
6. Warum kommt Lisa erst um fünf nach Hause? *Weil …*
7. Warum kocht Lisa ein gutes Abendessen, bevor sie ihre Hausaufgaben macht? *Weil …*

Schreiben und Sprechen

4-47 Ein Interview. Wie ist dein Tag? Interview your partner to find out about his/her typical day.

Wann stehst du auf? Warum so früh/so spät?

Was isst und trinkst du zum Frühstück?

Wann musst du zur Uni?

Was sind deine Lieblingsvorlesungen? Warum?

Machst du Sport? Warum?/Warum nicht? Wann machst du das?

Hast du einen Job? Wann und wo arbeitest du?

Wann und wo lernst du?

Gehst du abends oft aus? Wohin gehst du?

Isst du mittags oder abends warm?

Was isst du gern zum Mittagessen?

Isst du gern belegte Brote?

Was isst du gern am Wochenende?

Kochst du zu Hause oder gehst du ins Restaurant?

Was ist dein Lieblingsnachtisch?

4-48 Das ist mein Tag. Write about a typical day in your own life, using the questions from **4–47** to guide you. Try to vary your sentence structure by sometimes starting with a **weil–** clause. Note that when the sentence starts this way, the verb is always the second element (directly after the dependent clause, set off by a comma).

Wenn ich Vorlesungen habe, stehe ich meistens um _____ auf.
Wenn ich Hunger habe, esse ich manchmal _____.

Lesen

4-49 The Swiss Army Knife.

1. Do you own a **Taschenmesser** such as an original Swiss Army Knife?
2. Do you know the name of the company that manufactures this and other Swiss products?
3. How many products pictured on this page have you seen before?

4-50 Was ist das auf Englisch?

1. Ein **Messerschmied** macht Messer aus Metal.
2. Ein Messerschmied arbeitet in einer **Werkstatt.**
3. Wenn viele Messerschmiede zusammen arbeiten wollen, **gründen** sie einen **Messerschmiedverband.**
4. Karl Elsener möchte um 1890 Messer für **Soldaten** produzieren.
5. Später **entwickelt** Karl Elsener das Schweizer „Offiziersmesser".
6. Moderne Taschenmesser macht man aus **rostfreiem Stahl.**
7. 1945 ist der **Zweite Weltkrieg** zu Ende und die Taschenmesser werden populär.
8. Die Firma Victorinox ist heute noch sehr **erfolgreich.**
9. Victorinox Produkte sind heute in vielen Ländern **bekannt.**

a. stainless steel
b. develops
c. soldiers
d. successful
e. found . . . knifesmiths' association
f. Second World War
g. knifesmith
h. well-known
i. workshop

Modernes Offiziersmesser

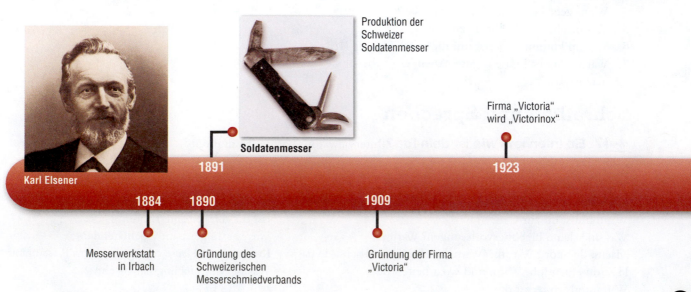

Produktion der Schweizer Soldatenmesser

Firma „Victoria" wird „Victorinox"

Soldatenmesser

Karl Elsener

1891

1923

1884

1890

1909

Messerwerkstatt in Irbach

Gründung des Schweizerischen Messerschmiedverbands

Gründung der Firma „Victoria"

Schweizer Innovation: Die Firma Victorinox

Karl Elsener, Schweizer Messerschmied

Im Jahre 1884 eröffnet Karl Elsener in Irbach im Kanton Schwyz eine kleine Messerwerkstatt. Es gibt in der Schweiz noch keine industrielle Massenproduktion, und die Schweizer Armee kauft für ihre Soldaten Taschenmesser in Deutschland. Aber Elsener will die „Soldatenmesser" in der Schweiz produzieren. Deshalb[1] gründet er mit fünfundzwanzig Kollegen den Schweizerischen Messerschmiedverband. Schon 1891 beginnt die Produktion des Schweizer Soldatenmessers.

Das Schweizer Offiziersmesser und die Firma *Victorinox*

Mit der Zeit produziert Elsener noch schönere[2] Messer, auch elegante „Offiziersmesser", die die Offiziere selber bezahlen müssen. Diese Messer sind so schön, dass auch andere die Messer kaufen wollen. Bald aber kommen billige Imitationen aus Deutschland. 1909 darf Elsener sein Offiziersmesser mit dem Schweizer Kreuz schützen[3]. In diesem Jahr stirbt[4] auch seine Mutter Victoria, und er nennt seine Firma „Victoria". 1923 sind die Messer dann aus dem rostfreien Stahl *Inox* und Elseners Firma heißt „Victorinox".

Export in alle Länder: Schweizer Innovation

Elseners Messer werden nach dem zweiten Weltkrieg bei den vielen amerikanischen Soldaten in Deutschland bekannt. So beginnt der Export in viele andere Länder.
Heute produziert Victorinox täglich 34 000 Taschenmesser und exportiert Messer und weitere Victorinox-Produkte in über hundert Länder. Heute leitet Carl Elsener IV. die Firma seiner Familie. Man findet auch in amerikanischen Kleinstädten die innovativen Schweizer Produkte von Victorinox: Rucksäcke, Wasserflaschen und das superdünne „Swiss Bit Schweizer Offiziersmesser mit Memory Stick".

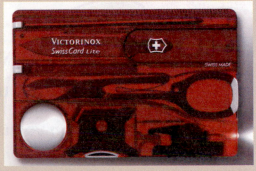

SwissCard Lite

[1]*because of this*   [2]**noch schönere:** *even more beautiful*   [3]*protect (against imitation)*   [4]*dies*

großer Export ins
Ausland beginnt,
zuerst nach Amerika
und in *PX Stores* weltweit

Carl Elsener IV. Geschäftsführer von Victorinox

1945

2000

2009

Produktion von dem
Victorinox-USB
Stick beginnt

Victorinox feiert
125. Jubiläum

Arbeit mit dem Text

4-51 Wer oder was ist das? Match the following items from the story of the Swiss Army Knife appropriately.

1. Victoria Elsener
2. Soldatenmesser
3. Inox
4. Carl Elsener IV.
5. Schweizer Kreuz

a. Taschenmesser für Schweizer Soldaten
b. Schweizer Nationalsymbol
c. Karl Elseners Mutter
d. rostfreier Stahl
e. jetziger Direktor von Victorinox

4-52 Das Schweizer Offiziersmesser. Respond briefly with information from the text.

1. Warum heißt die Firma heute „Victorinox"?
2. Warum ist die Firma heute noch so erfolgreich?
3. Was für Produkte exportiert Victorinox weltweit?
4. Haben Sie ein Victorinox-Taschenmesser oder ein anderes Produkt von Victorinox?

Wort, Sinn und Klang

Wörter unter der Lupe

Denn versus *dann*

The words **denn** and **dann** occur very frequently in German. Because these words are so similar in sound and appearance and because **denn** has two very different meanings, they deserve a closer look.

- The flavoring particle **denn** occurs only in questions. It expresses curiosity and interest, and sometimes irritation.

  Wann stehst du **denn** endlich auf?   *When are you finally going to get up?*

- The coordinating conjunction **denn** introduces a clause that states the reason for something. Its English equivalents are *because* and *for*.

  Ich esse jeden Tag Frühstück, **denn** ich habe morgens immer Hunger!

- The adverb **dann** is an equivalent of English *then*. It expresses that a certain thing or action follows another thing or action.

  Zuerst koche ich Kaffee und **dann** esse ich ein Brötchen mit Butter und Käse.

4-53 *Denn* or *dann*?

1. HEIKE: Was schreibst du _____ da?
   SYLVIA: Einen Brief an meine Eltern.
   HEIKE: Und _____? Was machst du _____?
   SYLVIA: _____ rufe ich Holger an, _____ wir wollen heute Abend zusammen ins Kino gehen.
2. SONJA: Wann rufst du _____ endlich deine Eltern an?
   definitely   LAURA: Erst heute Abend, _____ _____ sind sie bestimmt° zu Hause.

Zur Aussprache

The vowels *ä, ö,* and *ü*

The vowels **a, o,** and **u** can be umlauted: **ä, ö,** and **ü.** These umlauted vowels can be long or short. Listen carefully and you will hear the difference between **a, o, u** and their umlauted equivalents.

4-54 **Hören Sie gut zu und wiederholen Sie!**

a (lang)	ä (lang)	a (kurz)	ä (kurz)
Glas	Gläser	alt	älter
Rad	Räder	kalt	kälter
Vater	Väter	lang	länger

o (lang)	ö (lang)	o (kurz)	ö (kurz)
Brot	Brötchen	oft	öfter
Sohn	Söhne	Tochter	Töchter
groß	größer	Wort	Wörter

If you have trouble producing the sound **ö,** pucker your lips as if to whistle, hold them in this position, and say *eh.*

u (lang)	ü (lang)	u (kurz)	ü (kurz)
Buch	Bücher	Mutter	Mütter
Bruder	Brüder	jung	jünger
Fuß	Füße	dumm	dümmer

If you have trouble producing the sound **ü,** pucker your lips as if to whistle, hold them in this position, and say *ee.*

> **Brötchen:** The **ö** and the suffix **-chen** signal that this is the diminutive form of **Brot** (compare English **pig** and **piglet**). The diminutive forms of nouns with **a, o, u** and **au** add an umlaut. What are the diminutive forms of **Haus, Bett, Hund,** and **Sohn?** You will encounter more diminutive forms in the story below.

4-55 **Das Rübenziehen.** In the following story about pulling out a turnip, long and short vowels, including umlauts, stand in sharp contrast to one another. Listen carefully and try to imitate the speaker.

Väterchen hat Rüben gesät°. Er will eine dicke Rübe herausziehen; er packt° sie beim Schopf°, er zieht und zieht und kann sie nicht herausziehen. Väterchen ruft Mütterchen: Mütterchen zieht Väterchen, Väterchen zieht die Rübe, sie ziehen und ziehen und können sie nicht herausziehen.

    Kommt das Söhnchen: Söhnchen zieht Mütterchen, Mütterchen zieht Väterchen, Väterchen zieht die Rübe, sie ziehen und ziehen und können sie nicht herausziehen.

    Kommt das Hündchen: Hündchen zieht Söhnchen, Söhnchen zieht Mütterchen, Mütterchen zieht Väterchen, Väterchen zieht die Rübe, sie ziehen und ziehen und können sie nicht herausziehen.

    Kommt das Hühnchen: Hühnchen zieht Hündchen, Hündchen zieht Söhnchen, Söhnchen zieht Mütterchen, Mütterchen zieht Väterchen, Väterchen zieht die Rübe, sie ziehen und ziehen und können sie nicht herausziehen.

    Kommt das Hähnchen: Hähnchen zieht Hühnchen, Hühnchen zieht Hündchen, Hündchen zieht Söhnchen, Söhnchen zieht Mütterchen, Mütterchen zieht Väterchen, Väterchen zieht die Rübe: sie ziehen und ziehen – schwupps°, ist die Rübe heraus, und das Märchen° ist aus.

hat … gesät: *has sown / grabs by the top*

whoosh
fairy tale

🔊 Wortschatz 2

Nomen

die Autobahn, -en	freeway
der Bahnhof, ⸚e	train station
der Fahrplan, ⸚e	train or bus schedule
die Hausaufgabe, -n	homework (assignment)
das Referat, -e	(oral) report; paper
das Seminar, -e	seminar course
der Fernseher, -	television set
vor dem Fernseher	in front of the TV
der Schnee	snow
das Messer, -	knife
die Tasche, -n	pocket; bag
das Taschenmesser, -	pocket knife

Verben

bleiben	to stay, to remain
rauchen	to smoke
reden	to talk, to speak
schneien	to snow
vergessen (vergisst)	to forget
ab·fahren (fährt ab)	to leave, to depart
an·halten (hält an)	to stop
an·hören	to listen to
an·kommen	to arrive
an·probieren	to try on
an·rufen	to call *(on the phone)*
auf·passen	to pay attention
auf·räumen	to clean up
auf·wachen	to wake up
aus·gehen	to go out
aus·probieren	to try out
aus·steigen	to get off *(train, bus, etc.)*
durch·lesen (liest durch)	to read through
ein·laden (lädt ein)	to invite
ein·schlafen (schläft ein)	to fall asleep
ein·steigen	to board, get on *(train, bus, etc.)*
fern·sehen (sieht fern)	to watch TV
heim·kommen	to come home
mit·kommen	to come along
um·steigen	to change (trains)

vor·haben	to plan, to have planned
weg·fahren (fährt weg)	to drive away
weiter·fahren (fährt weiter)	to continue driving; to continue traveling
weiter·lesen (liest weiter)	to continue reading
zurück·kommen	to come back
kennen lernen	to get to know
Rad fahren (fährt Rad)	to ride a bike, to go cycling
spazieren gehen	to go for a walk

Konjunktionen

bevor	before
obwohl	although, even though
weil	because
wenn	if; when

Andere Wörter

bekannt	well-known
deshalb	therefore; that's why
endlich	finally, at last
erfolgreich	successful(ly)
genug	enough
gleich	right away
schriftlich	in writing; written
selbst	myself, yourself, herself, etc.
sondern	*(but)*... instead, but rather

Ausdrücke

nach Mitternacht	after midnight
zu Fuß gehen	to walk
Lass mich in Ruhe!	Stop bothering me!

Das Gegenteil

der Anfang, ⸚e ≠ das Ende, -n	beginning ≠ end
gesund ≠ ungesund	healthy ≠ unhealthy
möglich ≠ unmöglich	possible ≠ impossible
oft ≠ selten	often ≠ seldom, rarely
ordentlich ≠ unordentlich	neat, tidy ≠ messy, sloppy
rechts ≠ links	right, to the right ≠ left, to the left
zuerst ≠ zuletzt	first ≠ last

> **Autobahn, Bahnhof:** The literal meaning of **Bahn** is *path* or *track*. By itself, **die Bahn** is now used to refer to the whole German railway system.

> A **Referat** is usually presented orally in a **Seminar** and then handed in in written form for final grading.

Leicht zu verstehen

der Alkohol	die Innovation, –en	joggen	nervös
die Firma, Firmen	der Stress	innovativ	typisch
das Foto, –s	die Zigarette, –n		

Wörter im Kontext

4-56 Welches Präfix passt hier?

weg / auf / ein / vor / heim

1. Wachst du immer so früh _____?
2. Wann fährst du morgens _____ und wann kommst du abends _____?
3. Was hast du heute Nachmittag _____?
4. Schläfst du in Professor Altmanns Vorlesung auch immer _____?

fern / an / mit / weiter / aus / ab

5. Heute Abend gehen wir alle _____. Kommst du _____?
6. Siehst du immer so viel _____?
7. Warum hörst du denn auf, Matthias? Lies doch _____.
8. Wann fährt euer Zug in Frankfurt _____ und wann kommt er in Hannover _____?

4-57 Was macht hier Sinn? Imagine you are taking a trip from Berne, Switzerland, to Berlin. Put the sentences in the most sensible order. The first one is completed for you.

1. Ich komme sechs Stunden später in Berlin an. _____
2. Ich steige in der Schweiz in den Zug ein. __1__
3. Der Zug fährt von Bern ab. _____
4. Ich fahre bis Mannheim, denn ich muss in Mannheim umsteigen. _____
5. Bald kommt in Mannheim der nächste Zug. _____
6. Dieser Zug fährt ab. _____

4-58 Was passt wo?

bekannt / in Ruhe / endlich / genug / zu Fuß / innovativ

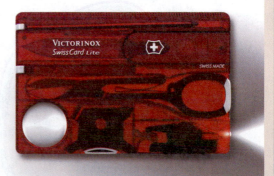

1. Die Firma Victorinox ist für ihre Innovation _____.
2. Die Schweizer Taschenmesser sind besonders _____.
3. Hast du noch _____ Geld?
4. Warum kannst du mich denn nicht endlich _____ lassen?
5. Nehmt ihr den Bus oder geht ihr _____?
6. Ich nehme den Bus, wenn er _____ kommt!

4-59 Gegenteile.

selten / ungesund / möglich / rechts / oft / links / gesund / unmöglich

1. Sport machen ist _____. Rauchen ist _____.
2. In Finnland schneit es _____. In Sizilien schneit es nur sehr _____.
3. In England fährt man _____. In Nordamerika fährt man _____.
4. Ich fahre so schnell wie _____, aber ich kann _____ in zehn Minuten zu Hause sein.

Freizeit – Ferienzeit

Kajaker auf der
Müritz-Elde-Wasserstraße

Kommunikationsziele

Making plans …
- for a vacation
- for a day off

Expressing personal opinions and tastes

Comparing qualities and characteristics

Talking about …
- whom and what you know
- events in the past

Strukturen

More on the accusative:
- personal pronouns
- prepositions

The comparative and superlative

Word order: Position of the verb in object
clauses

Wissen

Simple past tense of **haben, sein,** and the
modal verbs

Kultur

Affordable travel

Soccer

Paid vacation in Europe and North America

Munich

South Tyrol

Video-Treff: Ferienzeit

Lesen: Ludwig II. von Bayern

Vorschau

Am Grundlsee

The hotel you see below is situated on a hill at the head of the Grundlsee, an alpine lake in the Ausseerland region in the Austrian state of Styria (**Steiermark**). The region offers visitors spectacular natural beauty and a wide range of sport and leisure activities throughout the year. Take a look at this ad for a special package deal when the daffodils (**Narzissen**) are in bloom and respond to the questions below.

Narzissenblüte im Ausseerland

Datum: 28.04.2011 - 19.05.2011

Preis: € 198,00 pro Person/Aufenthalt im Doppelzimmer

Leistungen Narzissenblüte:

- 4 oder 5 Tage im Doppelzimmer
  (Donnerstag-Sonntag oder Sonntag-Donnerstag)
- tägliches Frühstücksbuffet im Restaurant Seeblick
- Verwöhnarrangement in Ihrem Zimmer bei der Anreise
  (1 Flasche Sekt, Obstkorb)
- Gemütliche Wanderung durch blühende Wiesen zu den schönsten Plätzen des Ausseerlandes
- Freie Nutzung des Panorama Wellness Bereichs

€ 198,00 pro Person im Doppelzimmer (exklusive Ortstaxe)
Einzelzimmerzuschlag: € 45,00

⇨ unverbindl. Anfrage

5-1 Was ist das auf Englisch? Find the following words in the ad and choose the meaning that best fits the context.

1. Verwöhnarrangement
2. Sekt
3. Wellness Bereich
4. Zuschlag
5. Nutzung

a. surcharge
b. spa
c. sparkling wine
d. use
e. "Let us spoil you" package

5-2 Was ist richtig?

1. Die Narzissen blühen am Grundlsee normalerweise im Monat _____.
   a. Juni
   b. Mai
2. In einem Doppelzimmer ist Platz für _____.
   a. eine Person
   b. zwei Personen
3. Das Paket „Narzissenblüte" kostet für 2 Personen _____ für 5 Tage.
   a. 198 Euro
   b. 396 Euro
4. Wenn man allein reist, kostet das Paket „Narzissenblüte" _____ für 5 Tage.
   a. 198 Euro
   b. 243 Euro
5. Welche Leistung ist im Paket „Narzissenblüte" *nicht* inklusive?
   a. Frühstück im Restaurant Seeblick
   b. eine gemütliche Bootsfahrt
   c. eine Wanderung durch die Wiesen
   d. eine Flasche Sekt

Ferienpläne

Frau Ziegler will nicht, was ihre Kinder wollen, aber Herr Ziegler findet eine gute Lösung.

Der Grundlsee in Österreich

NINA: Mitte Juli beginnen die Sommerferien, Vati. Fahren wir wieder zum Grundlsee? Der Campingplatz dort war echt spitze.

VATER: Aber du weißt doch, dass Mutti nicht dafür ist. Sie wollte schon letztes Jahr nicht mehr campen gehen.

ROBERT: Aber wir hatten doch so viel Spaß dort.

MUTTER: Spaß? Fast jeden Tag Regen und alles nass im Zelt. Und diese primitive Kocherei! Weißt du, Robert, das ist kein Urlaub für mich.

NINA: Aber wir hatten so gute Freunde, Robert und ich. Sie sind dieses Jahr bestimmt wieder dort.

MUTTER: Ich weiß, ich weiß, aber ich brauche auch mal Urlaub und möchte am liebsten in ein Hotel. Und bitte nicht in das billigste, Klaus.

VATER: Auch am Grundlsee?

MUTTER: Wenn es schön ist, habe ich nichts dagegen.

VATER: Ich kenne da nämlich ein kleines, aber sehr komfortables Hotel, nicht weiter als einen halben Kilometer vom Campingplatz. Dann haben die Kinder ihre Freunde, ich kann zum See und angeln gehen …

MUTTER: Und ich kann endlich auch mal ein bisschen ausspannen.

> The flavoring particles **doch** and **mal** are often used in colloquial German, but have no direct equivalent in English. **Doch** is often used as an intensifier, and **mal** makes a statement or question sound more casual.

5-3 **Richtig oder falsch?** You will hear the conversation on page 156. Indicate whether the statements that follow are **richtig** or **falsch.**

	RICHTIG	FALSCH
1.	_____	_____
2.	_____	_____
3.	_____	_____
4.	_____	_____

5-4 **Was ist die richtige Antwort?** Indicate whether the responses below answer question 1 or question 2 by entering the appropriate number in the spaces provided.

1. Warum wollen Nina und Robert diesen Sommer wieder zum Grundlsee?
2. Warum will Frau Ziegler nicht mehr campen gehen?

_____ Weil sie die primitive Kocherei nicht mag.

_____ Weil der Campingplatz dort echt spitze war.

_____ Weil sie dort so gute Freunde hatten.

_____ Weil im Zelt alles nass wird, wenn es zu viel regnet.

_____ Weil das für sie kein Urlaub ist.

_____ Weil sie dort so viel Spaß hatten.

5-5 **Eine Umfrage.** Walk around the classroom and survey three or four classmates about their vacation preferences. Fill in the questionnaire as you do so. Then report to the class.

S1: Wann machst du am liebsten Ferien?
Wo machst du am liebsten Ferien?
Warum machst du dort am liebsten Ferien?

S2: Ich mache am liebsten … Ferien.
Ich mache am liebsten … Ferien.
Weil …

PERSON	WANN?	WO?	WARUM?
Lisa	*im Winter*	*in Whistler, B.C.*	*Weil sie gern Ski läuft.*
_____	_____	_____	_____
_____	_____	_____	_____
_____	_____	_____	_____
_____	_____	_____	_____

Kultur / Affordable travel

Die Jugendherberge in Windischleuba, Thüringen

Many young people enjoy hiking and biking in the German-speaking countries; hiking trails and bike paths can be found everywhere. A network of over 700 **Jugendherbergen** *(youth hostels)* in Germany, Austria, and Switzerland provides reasonably priced, clean overnight accommodations and meals. Accommodations are often dorm-like but much cheaper than a room in a hotel, and some **Jugendherbergen** are housed in interesting old buildings such as medieval castles. In addition to a range of outdoor activities, many hostels offer cultural and educational events for individual travelers or groups. They are a good place to get to know other young people from all over the world.

Campingplatz an der Nordsee

There are also thousands of **Campingplätze** *(campgrounds)* in the German-speaking countries. As in North America, they are usually situated in areas that offer lots of recreational activities. **Campen** is a favorite way of vacationing for families with children. In Germany, the number of campground users has been steadily increasing.

5-6 Campen im Erzgebirge. Lisa und Ralf haben bald vierzehn Tage Urlaub, wollen campen gehen und studieren deshalb eine Broschüre von Campingplätzen im Erzgebirge. Sie gehen beide gern baden[1] und sie möchten auch ein paar kleine Radtouren machen. Ralf möchte gern einen Campinglatz mit Fitnesscenter und Sauna. Lisas Lieblingssport ist Segeln, und weil Lisa und Ralf passionierte Angler sind, suchen sie einen Campingplatz, wo sie auch angeln gehen können. Finden Sie den idealen Campingplatz für Lisa und Ralf!

- Suchen Sie zuerst die vier Campingplätze, wo die beiden angeln gehen können, und schreiben Sie die Namen von diesen Campingplätzen in die ersten vier Lücken[2].
- Markieren Sie dann, welche von diesen vier Campingplätzen auch Bademöglichkeit, Fahrradverleih[3], Fitnesscenter, Sauna und Segeln haben.

[1]swimming [2]spaces [3]bike rental

Angeln	1. _____	2. _____	3. _____	4. _____
Bademöglichkeit	_____	_____	_____	_____
Fahrradverleih	_____	_____	_____	_____
Fitnesscenter	_____	_____	_____	_____
Sauna	_____	_____	_____	_____
Segeln	_____	_____	_____	_____

	Bademöglichkeit	Tankstelle	Einkaufsmöglichkeit	Sportgeräteausleih/Fahrradverleih	Bootsverleih	Haustiere möglich	Gaststätte	Surfen/Segeln	Wasch-, Trockenautomat	Fitnesscenter	Sauna	Duschen, Waschraum, WC	Kinderspielplatz	Angeln	Einrichtungen für Behinderte
Altenberg	●	●	●				●	●			●	●		●	
Freiberg	●	●					●				●	●			●
Königswalde		●	●	●							●	●			
Lindenau	●	●			●		●				●	●			
Malter	●	●	●		●	●	●	●	●		●	●	●	●	
Oberrabenstein	●	●	●	●	●	●		●			●	●	●	●	
Paulsdorf	●	●	●						●		●	●		●	
Reichenbach	●	●	●	●			●		●		●	●		●	
Stollberg	●	●		●			●		●		●	●		●	

Legende:
- Bademöglichkeit
- Tankstelle
- Einkaufsmöglichkeit
- Sportgeräteausleih/Fahrradverleih
- Bootsverleih
- Haustiere möglich
- Gaststätte
- Surfen/Segeln
- Wasch-, Trockenautomat
- Fitnesscenter
- Sauna
- Duschen, Waschraum, WC
- Kinderspielplatz
- Angeln
- Einrichtungen für Behinderte

Nomen

die Freizeit	free time,
die Ferien (pl)	vacation (*generally of students*)
der Urlaub	vacation (*generally of people in the workforce*)
der Aufenthalt, -e	stay
die Bademöglichkeit, -en	(place to go) swimming; swimming facility
der Campingplatz, ⸚e	campground; campsite
der Fahrradverleih, -e	bike rental
die Jugendherberge, -n	youth hostel
der Platz, ⸚e	place; space, room
das Zelt, -e	tent
der Baum, ⸚e	tree
der Berg, -e	mountain
das Dorf, ⸚er	village
das Feld, -er	field
der Fluss, ⸚e	river
das Gebirge, -	mountain range

die Insel, -n	island
die Landschaft, -en	landscape
der Regen	rain
das Schloss, ⸚er	castle
der See, -n	lake
der Strand, ⸚e	beach
das Tal, ⸚er	valley
der Wald, ⸚er	woods; forest
die Wolke, -n	cloud
die Flasche, -n	bottle
der Sekt	sparkling wine

Verben

angeln	to fish
aus·spannen	to relax
baden	to swim; to bathe
blühen	to blossom; to flourish
fließen	to flow
wissen (weiß)	to know

> **Bademöglichkeit: Möglichkeit** actually means *possibility* or *opportunity*. What is the literal meaning of **Einkaufsmöglichkeit, Kochmöglichkeit, Parkmöglichkeit,** and **Schlafmöglichkeit?** What do you think their English equivalents might be?

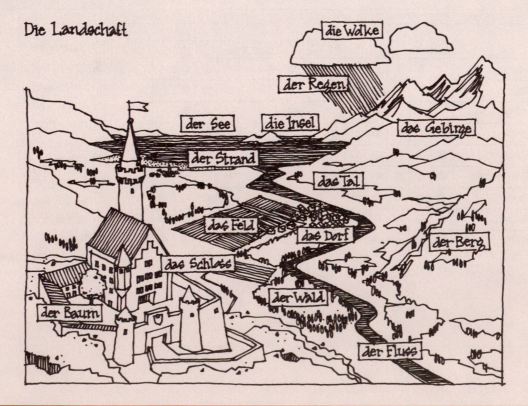

Die Landschaft

Andere Wörter

bestimmt	definite(ly); for sure
frei	free *(of time)*
gemütlich	cozy; comfortable

Ausdrücke

Anfang Juli	(at) the beginning of July
Ende Juli	(at) the end of July
Mitte Juli	(in) mid-July
eine Reise machen	to go on a trip, to take a trip
Ferien (Urlaub) machen	to go on vacation
Wo machst du am liebsten Ferien?	Where's your favorite vacation spot?
Spaß haben	to have fun
vierzehn Tage	two weeks

Das Gegenteil

das Problem, -e ≠ die Lösung, -en	problem ≠ solution
alt ≠ jung	old ≠ young
nass ≠ trocken	wet ≠ dry
weit ≠ nah	far ≠ near

Leicht zu verstehen

der Angler, -	der Plan, ¨e
die Anglerin, -nen	die Sauna, -s
die Broschüre, -n	campen
das Campen	ideal
das Fitnesscenter, -	komfortabel
der Garten, ¨	passioniert
das Hotel, -s	primitiv

Wörter im Kontext

5-7 **Was passt zusammen?** Match appropriately in each set.

1. Schlösser
2. Lösungen
3. Fische
4. Sekt
5. Hotelzimmer

a. angelt man.
b. reserviert man.
c. fotografiert man.
d. sucht man.
e. trinkt man.

6. Wenn man Urlaub macht,
7. Wenn man im Regen steht,
8. Wenn die Sonne scheint,
9. Wenn es Frühling ist,

f. blühen die Narzissen.
g. will man ausspannen.
h. wird man nass.
i. bleibt man trocken.

5-8 **Was passt zusammen?**

1. Herr und Frau Ziegler machen immer dann Urlaub,
2. Weil es im Zelt so primitiv war,
3. Nina und Robert möchten wieder zum Grundlsee,
4. Herr Ziegler braucht einen See,
5. Wenn man eine Radtour machen will und kein Rad hat,

a. möchte Frau Ziegler diesen Sommer mal in ein komfortables Hotel.
b. weil sie dort so viel Spaß hatten.
c. weil er ein passionierter Angler ist.
d. geht man zum Fahrradverleih.
e. wenn ihre Kinder Schulferien haben.

5-9 **Was passt wo?** Complete the description, using the illustration „Die Landschaft."

Wolken / Tal / Strand / Berg / fließt / Dorf / Insel / Schloss / Felder / Gebirge / baden

Links in der Illustration „Die Landschaft" ist ein altes _____, in der Mitte sind ein kleiner Wald und ein Fluss und rechts ist ein _____. Der Fluss _____ durch ein schönes _____ in einen großen See. Direkt am Fluss ist ein kleines _____ und links von dort sind ein paar _____. Im See ist eine kleine _____. Oft _____ auch viele Leute an dem sandigen _____. Am Himmel sind zwei _____, und im _____ regnet es schon.

Kommunikation und Formen

1 Talking about persons or things without naming them

5-1 to 5-6

Personal pronouns in the accusative case

In English the object forms of the personal pronouns are often different from the subject forms, e.g., *I love **him** and he loves **me** too.*

The same is true in German, where the accusative (object) forms of the personal pronouns are often different from the nominative (subject) forms.

Ich liebe **ihn** und er liebt **mich** auch.   *I love **him** and he loves **me** too.*

Remember that *things* also have gender in German and that this is reflected in the pronoun forms.

Warum liest du **den Roman**   *Why don't you finish reading **the novel?***
  nicht fertig?
Ich finde **ihn** langweilig.   *I find **it** boring.*

personal pronouns							
SINGULAR				**PLURAL**			
NOMINATIVE		ACCUSATIVE		NOMINATIVE		ACCUSATIVE	
ich	*I*	**mich**	*me*	**wir**	*we*	**uns**	*us*
du	*you*	**dich**	*you*	**ihr**	*you*	**euch**	*you*
er	*he, it*	**ihn**	*him, it*				
es	*it*	**es**	*it*	**sie**	*they*	**sie**	*them*
sie	*she, it*	**sie**	*her, it*				
Sie	*you*	**Sie**	*you*	**Sie**	*you*	**Sie**	*you*

5-10 **Reisepläne.** You and your partner are making plans for a trip. Respond to your partner's questions using the appropriate pronouns.

S1: Kennst du den Grundlsee?   **S2:** Ja, ich kenne ihn.

1. Kennst du den Campingplatz? (die Jugendherberge, den Strand, das Schloss)
2. Nehmen wir das Zelt mit? (die Wanderschuhe, die Fahrräder, den Kajak)
3. Hast du die Kreditkarten? (den Fahrplan, die Kamera, das Handy)
4. Nehmen wir Sylvia mit? (Thomas, Maria und ihren Freund Daniel)

5-11 *Lieben* **und** *mögen.* Supply the appropriate personal pronouns.

1. Philipp loves Vanessa but, although she is fond of him, Vanessa doesn't love Philipp.

    PHILIPP: Ich liebe dich, Vanessa, liebst du _____ auch?
    VANESSA: Ich mag _____, Philipp, aber ich liebe _____ nicht.

2. Sarah quizzes Philipp about his feelings for Vanessa.

SARAH: Liebst du Vanessa?

PHILIPP: Ja, ich liebe _____, ich liebe _____ sehr.

SARAH: Und Vanessa? Liebt sie _____ auch?

PHILIPP: Sie sagt, sie mag _____, aber sie liebt _____ nicht.

3. Sarah quizzes Vanessa about her feelings for Philipp.

SARAH: Liebst du Philipp?

VANESSA: Ich mag _____, aber ich liebe _____ nicht.

SARAH: Und Philipp? Liebt er _____?

VANESSA: Er sagt, er liebt _____ sehr.

5-12 **Wie findest du Davids Pullover?** Look at your fellow students. How do you like their clothes, hairdos, beards, glasses, jewelry?

S1: Wie findest du Davids Pullover?   **S2:** Ich finde ihn echt spitze.

S2: Wie findest du …?   **S3:** Ich finde …

…

der Pulli	sehr schön	
der Pullover	sehr elegant	
das Sweatshirt	echt spitze	
das T-Shirt	sehr schick	
das Hemd	echt toll	
die Jeans	sehr hübsch	
die Hose	echt cool	
der Rock	sehr geschmackvoll°	*tasteful*
die Schuhe	gar nicht schlecht	

die Frisur

der Ohrring, -e

das Armband, ̈er

die Tätowierung, -en

der Ring, -e

die Halskette, -n

die Brille

der Nasenstecker, -

der Haarschnitt

der Bart

der Schnurrbart

die Baseballkappe, -n

2 Expressing direction, destination, time, manner, and place

5-7 to 5-11

Accusative prepositions

A preposition is a word that combines with a noun or pronoun to form a phrase.

For whom are you printing out this train schedule, *for David* or *for me?*

The noun or pronoun in the prepositional phrase is called the object of the preposition. After the following German prepositions, the noun or pronoun object appears in the accusative case.

durch	through	Nächsten Sommer möchte ich mit dir **durch die Schweiz** reisen.
für	for	**Für wen** druckst du diese Broschüre aus, **für mich?**
gegen	against	Ja, hast du etwas **gegen meine Idee?**
	around (with time)	Nein, ich möchte die Reise mit dir planen. Hast du morgen **gegen neun** Zeit?
ohne	without	Ja, aber mach bitte keine Pläne **ohne mich!**
um	around	Das nächste Reisebüro ist gleich **um die Ecke°**.
	at (with time)	Das Reisebüro öffnet morgen **um acht.**

corner

Briefkasten links um die Ecke

Sprachnotiz | **Accusative prepositions in contractions**

In colloquial German the prepositions **durch, für,** and **um** are often contracted with the article **das: durchs, fürs, ums.**

Wir laufen **durchs** Hotel.
In deutschen Hotels muss man **fürs** Frühstück nicht extra bezahlen.
Ums Parkhotel stehen viele alte Bäume.

We're walking through the hotel.
In German hotels you don't have to pay extra for breakfast.
There are many old trees around the Park Hotel.

5-13 Ich reise nie ohne ... What would you never travel without? Check off some items in the list below and add some of your own. Tell your classmates one item that is important to you and then call on another student. Follow the example.

S1: Ich reise nie ohne ein gutes Buch. Und du, David?　　**S2:** Ich reise nie ohne …

☐ eine Packung Aspirin
☐ meinen Regenmantel
☐ meine ATM Karte
☐ meine Kreditkarte
☐ eine warme Jacke
☐ meinen iPod
☐ _____

☐ meinen Pass
☐ meine Zahnbürste°　　　　　　toothbrush
☐ meinen Regenschirm°　　　　　umbrella
☐ eine Flasche Wasser
☐ meinen Studentenausweis°　　　student I.D.
☐ mein Handy
☐ _____

5-14 Kleine Gespräche.

▶ Für wen sind diese Fotos?　　　　　dein__ Schwester
　 Für mein__ Bruder?

S1: Für wen sind diese Fotos?　　　**S2:** Nein, für deine Schwester.
　　 Für meinen Bruder?

1. Für wen kaufen Sie das Flugticket?　　sein__ Frau
　 Für Ihr__ Chef°?　　　　　　　　　　　　　　　　boss
2. Gegen wen spielt das deutsche　　　d__ Dänen (pl)
　 Team nächsten Samstag? Gegen d__
　 Engländer (pl)?
3. Für wen ist diese Broschüre? Für　　dein__ Freund
　 mein__ Mitbewohnerin?

5-15 Durch, für, gegen, ohne, um? Supply the appropriate prepositions.

1. Sind deine Eltern _____ oder _____ diese Reise?
2. Hier ist ein Brief _____ dich.
3. Heute müsst ihr mal _____ mich angeln gehen.
4. Wohnt Bernd immer noch _____ die nächste Ecke?
5. Trinkst du deinen Kaffee immer _____ Milch und Zucker?
6. _____ dich mache ich diese Radtour nicht.
7. Spielt Mainz 05 morgen _____ Hansa Rostock?
8. Fährt der Zug nach München _____ 17.35 Uhr oder _____ 18.35 Uhr?
9. _____ sieben ist nicht Punkt° sieben. Es ist ein bisschen vor oder nach sieben.　　on the dot
10. Im Sommer wollen wir eine Reise _____ Österreich machen.

The Northern German city of **Rostock** was once a member of the **Hansa**, a league of merchant cities that dominated trade in the North and Baltic Seas between 1356 and circa 1670. The word **Hansa** and the typically round-bodied trading vessel in the club's logo commemorate the city's trading past. The number often seen in the names of German soccer clubs like **Mainz 05** refers to the year of their founding and shows that soccer became popular in Germany around the year 1900. **Mainz 05** is also known as **Die Nullfünfer.**

Infobox

Fußball: King of sports in Germany

Fußball is so much a part of German sports culture that it's hard to imagine it hasn't always been that way. Before World War II, Germany had only a lackluster national team, especially compared to its successful competitors in Austria, Hungary, and England. It was not until 1954, when the West German national team won its first World Cup in Bern, Switzerland, that **Fußball** really came into its own. This unexpected win over the strongly favored Hungarians has become legendary and is seen by many as a first moment of post–World War II national pride. For the German Democratic Republic, a similarly triumphant soccer moment occurred when the East German national team defeated the West Germans in the 1974 World Cup.

Frauenfußballweltmeisterschaft 2003: Deutschland vs. USA

Today **Fußball** is a multimillion-euro business. Top **Fußballspieler** enjoy celebrity status and earn large salaries. Many players from other countries play in the professional leagues in Germany. On soccer season weekends, about 300,000 fans flock to the stadiums to cheer on their favorite teams in the **Bundesliga.** With 6 to 7 million viewers, televised games pull in huge advertising revenues. Once considered a working-class sport, **Fußball** has become a national passion.

While not as lucrative as men's soccer, professional women's soccer holds its own: the German national team has won two World tournaments as well as bronze medals at the Olympic games in 2000, 2004, and 2008.

> A **Bundesliga** team can hire five **Nichteuropäer.** There is no limit to the number of players from other EU countries, as long as there are 12 German members on the team.

Fußball is more than just a spectator sport in Germany. The game is played by young and old, male and female, mostly as a leisure-time activity. Just about every town has an amateur soccer team and each team belongs to the **Deutscher Fußball-bund.** With 6.7 million members, this umbrella organization is the largest sporting association in the country.

Sprachnotiz   *Dafür* and *dagegen*

The German equivalents of the prepositional phrases *for it* and *against it* are **dafür** and **dagegen.**

Ist Frau Ziegler für den Campingurlaub am Grundlsee?

Nein, sie ist nicht **dafür.**

Is Ms. Ziegler for the camping vacation at the Grundlsee?

*No, she isn't **for it**.*

Hat sie etwas gegen einen Aufenthalt im Hotel?

Nein, sie hat nichts **dagegen.**

Does she have anything against a stay in a hotel?

*No, she has nothing **against it**.*

Sie denken an später – aber was tun Sie dafür?

Finanzielle Vorsorge,
systematischer
Vermögensaufbau,
zusätzliches Einkommen
im Alter –
unsere Spezialisten
beraten Sie.

Beratungstage „Finanzielle Vorsorge".
Vom 7.10 bis 11.10

Deutsche Bank

3 Making comparisons

5-12 to 5-14

The comparative of adjectives and adverbs

You can compare characteristics and qualities by using the comparative forms of adjectives and adverbs. In contrast to English, German has only one way of forming the comparative: by adding **-er** to the adjective or adverb, e.g., **klein*er*, schnell*er*, schön*er*, primitiv*er*.** Note that the German equivalent of *than* is **als.**

Vom Hotel ist es ein bisschen **weiter** zum See **als** vom Campingplatz.	*From the hotel it's a bit **farther** to the lake **than** from the campground.*
Robert und Nina finden den Campingplatz **interessanter als** ein Hotel.	*Robert and Nina find the campground **more interesting than** a hotel.*

Most German one-syllable adjectives or adverbs with the vowels **a, o,** or **u** are umlauted in the comparative.

a → ä	o → ö	u → ü
nah – näher	oft – öfter	jung – jünger
warm – wärmer	groß – größer	kurz – kürzer

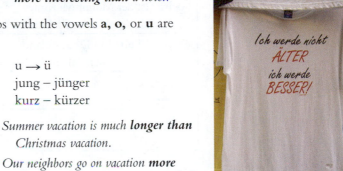

Die Sommerferien sind viel **länger als** die Weihnachtsferien.	*Summer vacation is much **longer than** Christmas vacation.*
Unsere Nachbarn machen **öfter** Urlaub **als** wir.	*Our neighbors go on vacation **more often than** we do.*

5-16 Wie alt und wie groß bist du? Walk around the classroom and find out the age and height of your classmates. Use the scale to convert feet and inches to metric measure.

S1: Wie alt bist du? **S2:** Ich bin …

S1: Dann bist du | so alt wie ich.
älter als ich.
jünger als ich.

S1: Und wie groß bist du? **S2:** Ich bin …

S1: Dann bist du | so groß wie ich.
größer als ich.
kleiner als ich.

> Remember how heights are read: **1,68 = eins achtundsechzig (ein Meter und achtundsechzig Zentimeter).** Note that a comma is used where English would use a decimal point.

Adjectives that end in **-er** or **-el** drop the **e** in the comparative.

teuer – **teurer**   dunkel – **dunkler**

Ein gutes Hotel ist **komfortabler als** eine Jugendherberge.	*A good hotel is **more comfortable than** a youth hostel.*

As in English, a few adjectives and adverbs have irregular comparative forms.

gut – **besser**	hoch° – **höher**	*high*
viel – **mehr**	gern – **lieber**	

Ich übernachte **lieber** in Jugendherbergen **als** in Hotels.	*I would **rather** stay in youth hostels **than** in hotels.*
In Österreich sind die Berge **höher als** in Deutschland.	*In Austria the mountains are **higher than** in Germany.*

5-17 Weißt du das? You and your partner are sharing general knowledge. Use the comparative forms for the adjectives given. **S2**'s questions are in the *Anhang* on page A5.

S1: Ist der Rhein länger als die Donau?

S2: Nein, der Rhein ist kürzer als die Donau.

FRAGEN	ANTWORTEN
lang: Ist der Rhein _____ als die Donau?	
	warm: Nein, in Island ist es _____ als in Grönland.
hoch: Ist der Mount McKinley _____ als der Mount Fudschi?	
wenig: Leben in Deutschland _____ Menschen° als in Kalifornien?	
	klein: Nein, Deutschland ist _____ als Kalifornien.
	teuer: Ja, der Audi A4 ist _____ als der Volkswagen Golf.

people

5-18 Wie heißt die Stadt? Think of a large American or Canadian city. Take turns asking the following questions to find out which city each of you has in mind. Use the comparative forms of the adjectives and adverbs.

1. Ist die Stadt in Amerika oder in Kanada?
2. Ist die Stadt im Norden, im Süden, im Osten oder im Westen von Amerika/Kanada?
3. Ist die Stadt _____ oder _____ als *(name of your college or university town)?* (groß, klein)
4. Ist der Sommer dort _____ oder _____ als der Sommer hier? (heiß, kühl)
5. Ist der Winter dort _____ oder _____ als der Winter hier? (kalt, warm)
6. Regnet es dort _____ oder _____ als hier? (viel, wenig)
7. Schneit es dort _____ oder _____ als hier? (viel, wenig)
8. Heißt die Stadt _____?

An adjective in the comparative before a noun

When you put an adjective in the comparative before a noun, you add an adjective ending to the comparative form. Remember to add the adjective ending even if you don't repeat the noun to which it refers.

Wer hat das größer**e** Zimmer, Laura oder Maria?
Laura hat ein klein**es** Zimmer und möchte ein größer**es.**

5-19 Entscheidungen. The arrows show **S2** which decision to make.

▶ Welches Fahrrad kaufst du,
das teurer___ oder das billiger___?

S1: Welches Fahrrad kaufst du,
das teurere oder das billigere?

S2: Ich kaufe das teurere Fahrrad.

1. Welchen Apfel möchtest du, den
kleiner__ oder den größer__?

2. Welche Wurst möchtest du,
die dicker__ oder die dünner__?

3. Welches Stück Torte möchtest du,
das kleiner__ oder das größer__?

4. Welchen Wagen kaufst du,
den älter__ oder den neuer__?

5. Welchen Mantel nimmst du,
den heller__ oder den dunkler__?

6. Welche Jacke nimmst du,
die länger__ oder die kürzer__?

7. Welche Wanderschuhe kaufst du,
die leichter__° oder die schwerer__°?

lighter / heavier

8. Welchen ICE nimmst du,
den früher__ oder den später__?

5-15 to 5-16

The superlative

You can indicate the greatest level of a quality or a characteristic in relation to others by using the superlative forms of adjectives and adverbs. Unless the superlative precedes a noun (see below), you form it by using the pattern **am _____sten** (e.g., **am** schnell**sten**).

Maria spricht schnell, Anna spricht schneller als Maria, aber Tina spricht **am schnellsten.**

Maria talks fast, Anna talks faster than Maria, but Tina talks ***the fastest.***

If the adjective or adverb ends in **-d, -t,** an **s**-sound, or a vowel, you add an **e** before the **st** (e.g., **am leichtesten, am heißesten, am neuesten**). In contrast to English, German uses the pattern **am _____(e)sten** with all adverbs and adjectives, regardless of their length (e.g., **am interessantesten**).

Evas Referat war interessant, Davids Referat war noch interessanter, aber Lauras Referat war **am interessantesten.**

Eva's report was interesting, David's report was even more interesting, but Laura's report was ***the most interesting***.

Most one-syllable adjectives or adverbs with the stem vowels **a, o,** or **u** are umlauted in the superlative, just as they are in the comparative (e.g., **am kältesten, am wärmsten, am jüngsten**).

Im Juli und im August ist es hier **am wärmsten.**

In July and in August it's ***warmest*** *here.*

A few adjectives and adverbs have irregular superlative forms.

gut	besser	**am besten**
viel	mehr	**am meisten**
groß	größer	**am größten**
gern	lieber	**am liebsten**
hoch	höher	**am höchsten**
nah	näher	**am nächsten**

5-20 Ein paar persönliche Fragen. Using the superlative forms of the words provided, ask each other the following questions.

1. Welche Sprache sprichst du am _____? (gut)
2. Welches Fach findest du am _____? (interessant)
3. Für welches Fach musst du am _____ lernen? (viel)
4. Was für einen Wagen möchtest du am _____? (gern)
5. Was isst und trinkst du am _____? (gern)
6. Was für Musik findest du am _____? (schön)

5-17 to 5-18

An adjective in the superlative before a noun

If an adjective in the superlative precedes a noun, you don't use the pattern **am _____(e)sten.** Instead, you add **-(e)st** plus an adjective ending. Remember that you add the adjective ending even if you don't repeat the noun to which it refers.

David hat jetzt das neu**este** Notebook, aber es ist natürlich auch das teuer**ste.**

David now has the newest notebook, but of course it's also the most expensive one.

5-21 Superlative. Supply the appropriate superlatives with the proper endings.
S2 chooses the appropriate adjective from the box.

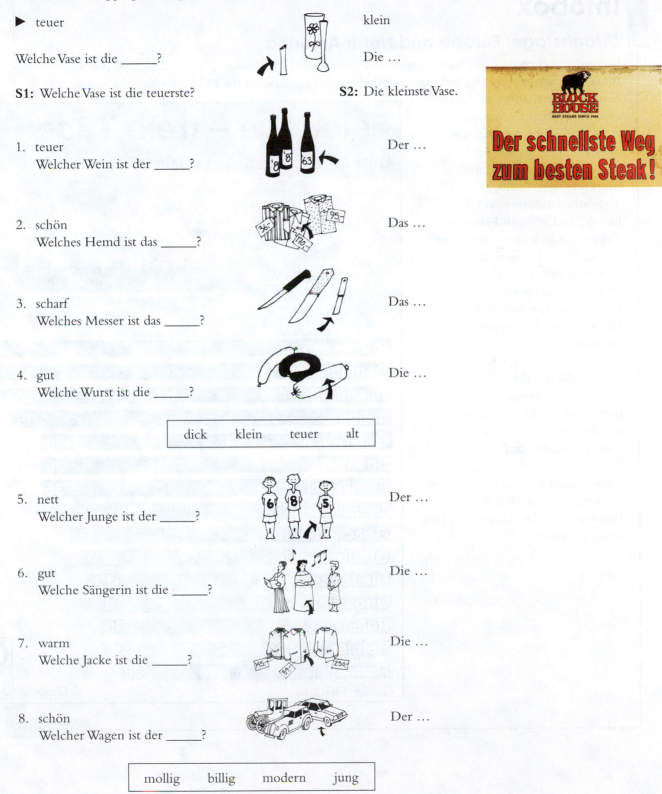

► teuer

Welche Vase ist die _____?

klein

Die …

S1: Welche Vase ist die teuerste?   **S2:** Die kleinste Vase.

1. teuer
   Welcher Wein ist der _____?   Der …

2. schön
   Welches Hemd ist das _____?   Das …

3. scharf
   Welches Messer ist das _____?   Das …

4. gut
   Welche Wurst ist die _____?   Die …

| dick | klein | teuer | alt |

5. nett
   Welcher Junge ist der _____?   Der …

6. gut
   Welche Sängerin ist die _____?   Die …

7. warm
   Welche Jacke ist die _____?   Die …

8. schön
   Welcher Wagen ist der _____?   Der …

| mollig | billig | modern | jung |

Infobox

Urlaubstage: Europe and North America

European workers generally have a greater number of paid **Urlaubstage** per year than their North American counterparts. **Die Schweiz** and the member countries of the **EU** have a legally mandated minimum number of paid vacation days. However, most European employers offer more than this minimum number as a result of various kinds of collective bargaining agreements.

Workers are also paid for national and religious **Feiertage** *(holidays),* which vary from country to country and often from state to state as well. With 42 days off per year, **Schweden** was **Freizeitweltmeister** in 2008, with **Deutschland** and **Österreich** not far behind.

In North America, **Kanada** also has a legally mandated minimum number of paid vacation days. In contrast, the U.S. Fair Labor Standards Act makes no such provision. Aside from federal holidays, the number of paid **Urlaubstage** enjoyed by American workers is typically based on the length of time they have worked for an employer.

Feiertage – freie Tage

Urlaubs- und Feiertage im Jahr 2008

Land	Tage
Schweden	42
Deutschland	40,5
Dänemark	40
Italien	39
Österreich	36
Spanien	36
Frankreich	36
Tschechien	35
Griechenland	33
Großbritannien	32,7
Niederlande	31,6
Ungarn	30
Polen	30
Belgien	30
Rumänien	28

Quelle: EIRO, iw

© Globus
3142

Video-Treff

Ferienzeit

Christoph and Christina Brieger, Stefan Meister, André, and Stefan Kuhlmann talk about their vacation preferences. Be sure to complete the **Was ist das auf Englisch?** exercise before watching the video.

5-22 Was ist das auf Englisch?

1. Wir machen **zweimal** im Jahr Urlaub
2. Wir fahren **ans Meer** und sind viel am Strand.
3. Englisch ist die Fremdsprache, die ich am besten **beherrsche.**
4. Man kann im **Mittelmeer** schwimmen.
5. Das war unser **Mietwagen:** der Ford Ka.
6. Ich **habe mich** in die Frau und in das Land **verliebt.**
7. Australien ist das schönste Land **der Welt.**

a. Mediterranean Sea
b. know
c. in the world
d. rental car
e. fell in love
f. to the ocean
g. twice

5-23 Richtig oder falsch?
Decide whether the following statements about the Briegers and Stefan Meister are **richtig** or **falsch**. If the statement is **falsch**, provide a correct version.

	RICHTIG	FALSCH
1. Christoph und Christina machen im Sommer und im Winter Urlaub.	☐	☐
2. Im Sommer fahren sie am liebsten nach Holland.	☐	☐
3. Im Winter fahren sie gern in den schweizerischen Bergen Ski.	☐	☐
4. Im Urlaub geht Christina gern tauchen.	☐	☐
5. Stefan Meister fährt am liebsten nach Amerika, Neuseeland und Australien, weil es für ihn dort sehr billig ist.	☐	☐
6. Stefan sagt, er kann gut Spanisch.	☐	☐
7. Stefan macht Urlaub, wenn es warm ist und wenn man nur ein T-Shirt tragen kann.	☐	☐
8. Stefan zeigt Fotos vom Wassersport in Australien.	☐	☐

5-24 Wer ist das? The following statements fit what André or Stefan Kuhlmann said about vacation preferences. Identify the person who best matches each statement.

André   Stefan Kuhlmann

1. Er macht gern Ferien, wenn es sehr warm ist.   ☐   ☐
2. Er glaubt, „Oz" ist das schönste Land der Welt.   ☐   ☐
3. Er findet die spanische Kultur sehr schön.   ☐   ☐
4. Er macht nicht sehr oft Urlaub.   ☐   ☐
5. Er war mit seiner Freundin letztes Jahr in Andalucia.   ☐   ☐
6. Er sagt, man kann in der Sierra Nevada im Sommer Ski laufen.   ☐   ☐
7. In Australien hatte er eine Freundin.   ☐   ☐

4 Word order

Object clauses introduced by *dass*

5-19

Sometimes the object of a verb is not a noun or a pronoun, but a clause. When you introduce this object clause with the conjunction **dass** *(that)*, it becomes a dependent clause. You must therefore put the conjugated verb at the end of the clause.

verb	object clause introduced by *dass*
Ich hoffe°,	**dass** ihr immer schönes Wetter **habt.**
Ich hoffe,	**dass** ihr dort viel wandern **könnt.**
Ich hoffe,	**dass** ihr total fit **zurückkommt.**

hope

> Remember that **doch** and **mal** are often used when giving advice.

5-25 Meine überkritische Freundin. Using clauses with **dass,** talk about your friend's criticisms. Your partner responds with advice.

▶ Ich arbeite zu lange.   gehen / doch mal ein bisschen früher nach Hause

S1: Meine Freundin denkt, dass ich zu lange arbeite.

S2: Dann geh doch mal ein bisschen früher nach Hause.

1. Ich bin zu dünn.   essen / doch ein bisschen mehr
2. Ich kann nicht gut tanzen.   nehmen / doch mal einen Tanzkurs
3. Ich schlafe nicht genug.   gehen / doch früher ins Bett
4. Ich kann nicht gut kochen.   nehmen / doch mal einen Kochkurs
5. Ich sitze zu viel am Computer. lesen / doch mal einen guten Roman
6. Ich bin zu nervös.   trinken / doch weniger Kaffee

5-26 Ratschläge geben. Tell your classmates about something you do that annoys members of your family or your friends. Your classmates should have some advice for you.

S1: Meine Eltern denken, dass ich zu viel fernsehe.

S2: Dann lies doch mal ein gutes Buch.
S3: Dann mach doch ein bisschen mehr Sport.

S4: Mein Mitbewohner denkt, dass ...

S5: ...

Information questions as object clauses

5-20 to 5-22

You can introduce information questions with phrases like **Weißt du, ...** or **Entschuldigung, wissen Sie, ...** The information questions then become object clauses. These object clauses are dependent clauses, and you must therefore put the conjugated verb at the end of the clause.

information question	introductory phrase + object clause	
Wie viel Uhr **ist** es?	Weißt du,	wie viel Uhr es **ist**?
Wann **fängt** das Konzert **an**?	Weißt du,	wann das Konzert **anfängt**?
Wo **kann** man Karten bekommen?	Weißt du,	wo man Karten bekommen **kann**?

5-27 Höfliche Fragen. You are a stranger in town. Politely ask a passerby for directions and information.

▶ Wie komme ich zum Fußballstadion?   nehmen / am besten ein Taxi

S1: Entschuldigung, wissen Sie, wie ich zum Fußballstadion komme?

S2: Nehmen Sie am besten ein Taxi.

1. Wo kann man hier billig übernachten?   gehen / am besten in die Jugendherberge
2. Wie komme ich zur Jugendherberge?   nehmen / am besten die S-Bahn
3. Wo kann man hier gut und billig essen?   gehen / am besten ins Ristorante Napoli
4. Wann fängt das Fußballspiel an?   fragen / am besten den Kellner
5. Wie komme ich zum Bahnhof?   nehmen / am besten die Buslinie 10

Yes/no questions as object clauses

5-20 to 5-22

You can also introduce a yes/no question with phrases like **Weißt du, ...** or **Könnten Sie mir bitte sagen, ...** When a yes/no question is the object of an introductory phrase, it begins with the conjunction **ob** *(whether)*, and you must put the conjugated verb at the end of the clause.

yes/no question	introductory phrase + object clause
Ist Claudia zu Hause?	Weißt du, **ob** Claudia zu Hause **ist**?
Hat sie heute Abend etwas **vor**?	Weißt du, **ob** sie heute Abend etwas **vorhat**?
Möchte sie mit uns ausgehen?	Weißt du, **ob** sie mit uns ausgehen **möchte**?

Infobox

München

München, the capital of **Bayern** *(Bavaria),* is one of Germany's major cultural centers. It boasts over 60 theaters and six orchestras. The most famous of its many art museums are the **Alte Pinakothek,** the **Neue Pinakothek,** and the **Pinakothek der Moderne. München** is also the home of the largest technical museum in the world, the **Deutsches Museum.** The **Deutsches Museum** is so large that viewing all the exhibits requires a ten-mile walk.

München: Deutsches Museum

With close to 60,000 students, the **Ludwig-Maximilians-Universität** in **München** is the largest university in the Federal Republic. Adjoining the university is the **Englischer Garten,** a 925-acre park in the heart of the city. The park is a favorite playground for students, who spend their free time strolling, cycling, sunbathing, or swimming in the chilly waters of the **Eisbach.**

The **Eisbach** stays cold for a long time because it springs from the glaciers in the Alps south of Munich.

Oktoberfest: 2010 marked the 200th anniversary of the Oktoberfest. 6.4 million visitors drank 7 million **Maß Bier (die Maß = 1 Liter),** and consumed ca. 530,000 grilled chickens and ca. 300,000 sausages. The 14 beer tents provide seating capacity for 100,000 people.

München, the home of **BMW (Bayerische Motorenwerke), MAN (Maschinenfabrik Augsburg–Nürnberg), Siemens,** and the German headquarters of Microsoft, is also an important industrial and high tech center.

The end of September marks the beginning of **München**'s 16-day **Oktoberfest,** the world's largest **Volksfest,** which each year employs about 12,000 people and attracts about six million visitors from all over the world.

5-28 Höfliche Fragen.

The **Englischer Garten** was designed by an Englishman, Sir Benjamin Rumford, and officially opened in 1789.

▶ Fährt dieser Bus zum Bahnhof?

Nein, er fährt zum …

S1: Wissen Sie, ob dieser Bus zum Bahnhof fährt?

S2: Nein, er fährt zum Englischen Garten.

1. Fährt dieser Bus zum Flughafen?

Nein, er fährt zum …

2. Ist das die Alte Pinakothek?

Nein, das ist …

The **Alte Pinakothek** houses 14th–18th century art; the **Neue Pinakothek**, 18th–20th century art; and the **Pinakothek der Moderne**, 20th–21st-century art.

3. Beginnt das Konzert um 20 Uhr?

Nein, ich glaube, es beginnt …

4. Ist das das Deutsche Museum?

Nein, das ist …

Die Alte Pinakothek

5. Fährt dieser Zug nach Hamburg?

Nein, das ist der Intercity …

5 Talking about what and whom you know

The verb *wissen*

5-23

The present tense of **wissen** *(to know)* is irregular in the singular.

singular		plural	
ich	**weiß**	wir	wissen
du	**weißt**	ihr	wisst
er/es/sie	**weiß**	sie	wissen
		Sie wissen	

As you have already seen, the object of the verb **wissen** can be a dependent clause. It can also be a pronoun like **das, es, alles,** or **nichts.**

Weißt du, **ob wir morgen eine Klausur schreiben?**

Nein, **das** weiß ich nicht.

*Do you know **whether we have a test tomorrow?***

*No, I don't know **(that).***

5-29 Wer weiß das? Supply the appropriate forms of **wissen.**

1. KURT: _____ deine Eltern, dass du so schlechte Zensuren° hast?

   GÜNTER: Meine Mutter _____ es, aber mein Vater _____ es noch nicht.

   grades

2. TOURISTIN: Entschuldigung, _____ Sie, wohin dieser Bus fährt?

   TOURIST: Nein, das _____ ich leider° auch nicht.

   unfortunately

3. BERND: _____ ihr, wo Peter ist?

   MARTIN: Nein, das _____ wir auch nicht.

   CLAUDIA: Frag doch Stephanie! Sie _____ es bestimmt.

4. FRAU KOHL: Warum _____ du denn nicht, wie man Sauerkraut kocht?

   HERR KOHL: Ich kann doch nicht alles _____.

Kennen Sie wirklich Ihren Hauttyp? Haartyp? Sonnentyp?

bei uns wissenschaftliche Analyse von

Haut & Haar

mit Phototyp-bestimmung/Melaninmessung

Sprachnotiz *Wissen* versus *kennen*

Whereas **wissen** means *to know something as a fact,* **kennen** means *to know* in the sense of *to be acquainted with someone* or *to be familiar with something.* **Kennen** is always followed by a direct object. It cannot be followed by an object clause.

Kennst du Günters neue Freundin?	*Do you **know** Günter's new girlfriend?*
Ja, ich **kenne** sie sehr gut.	*Yes, I **know** her very well.*
Weißt du, wie alt sie ist?	*Do you **know** how old she is?*
Nein, das **weiß** ich nicht.	*No, that I don't **know**.*

6 Talking about events in the past

5-24 to 5-28

The simple past of *sein, haben,* and the modal verbs

When writing or speaking about events that occurred in the past, speakers of German generally use the simple past tense with common verbs such as **sein,** **haben,** and the modal verbs (**dürfen, können, mögen, müssen, sollen, wollen**).

Warum **warst** du gestern Abend nicht auf Lisas Party?	*Why **weren't** you at Lisa's party last night?*
Ich **hatte** keine Zeit. Ich **musste** für eine Klausur lernen.	*I **didn't have** time. I **had to** study for a test.*

The simple past of *sein*

The simple past stem of **sein** is **war.** Note that there are no personal endings in the 1st and 3rd person singular.

singular		plural	
ich	war	wir	waren
du	warst	ihr	wart
er/es/sie	war	sie	waren
	Sie waren		

5-30 **Kleine Gespräche.** Use the simple past of **sein** in the following mini-conversations. **S2** answers with the appropriate phrase from the box below.

▶ Wo _____ ihr gestern Abend?

_____ der Film gut?

im Kino

Nein, … viel zu sentimental.

S1: Wo wart ihr gestern Abend? War der Film gut?	**S2:** Wir waren im Kino. Nein, er war viel zu sentimental.

1. Wo _____ ihr letztes Wochenende?

   _____ das Wasser warm?   Nein, ... noch ziemlich° kalt.   *quite*

2. Wo _____ Sie letzten Sommer?

   _____ es heiß?   Ja, ... sehr heiß.

3. Wo _____ du am Sonntagnachmittag?

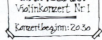

   _____ es interessant?   Ja, ... sehr interessant.

4. Wo _____ ihr am Samstagnachmittag?

   _____ das Bier gut?   Ja, ... sehr gut.

5. Wo _____ du am Sonntagabend?

   ```
   W.A. MOZART
   Violinkonzert Nr. 1
   Konzertbeginn: 20.30
   ```

   _____ der Solist gut?   Ja, ... ganz fabelhaft.

6. Wo _____ Sie letzten Sommer?

   _____ das Wetter schön?   Ja, ... fast immer warm und schön.

im Biergarten	im Konzert	am Starnberger See
in Österreich	in Italien	im Deutschen Museum

The simple past of *haben*

The simple past stem of **haben** is **hatt–**.

singular		plural	
ich	hatte	wir	hatten
du	hattest	ihr	hattet
er/es/sie	hatte	sie	hatten
	Sie hatten		

5-31 Warum? In the questions use the simple past of **sein,** and in the responses the simple past of **haben.**

▶ ihr nicht auf Lisas Party   wir / zu viel zu tun

S1: Warum wart ihr nicht auf Lisas Party?   **S2:** Wir hatten zu viel zu tun.

1. du gestern Nachmittag nicht zu Hause   ich / Vorlesungen
2. ihr am Samstag nicht beim Fußballspiel   wir / zu viele Hausaufgaben
3. Martin nicht beim Mittagessen   er / keinen Hunger
4. ihr gestern Nachmittag nicht im Biergarten   wir / keine Zeit
5. Stephanie nicht mit euch am Starnberger See   sie / eine Klausur
6. Meyers letzten Sommer nicht in Italien   sie / kein Geld

The simple past of modal verbs

You form the simple past of modal verbs by adding the past tense marker **–t–** to the verb stem and then adding the personal endings. When a modal has an umlaut in the infinitive form, you drop the umlaut in the simple past. Note that the **g** of **mögen** becomes **ch.**

dürfen	können	mögen	müssen	sollen	wollen
ich durfte	ich konnte	ich mochte	ich musste	ich sollte	ich wollte

In the simple past, all modals follow the pattern shown in the table below.

Lerntipp: The personal endings for modal verbs in the simple past tense are the same as those for the simple past tense of **haben.**

singular		plural	
ich	konnte	wir	konnten
du	konntest	ihr	konntet
er/es/sie	konnte	sie	konnten
	Sie konnten		

Weißwürste are a Bavarian specialty made from veal and spices. The **Donisl** is a famous restaurant on the **Marienplatz**, the city's central square that also features the famous **Glockenspiel** in the tower of the New City Hall.

5-32 Freizeit – Ferienzeit. Complete, using modal verbs in the simple past.

1. Martin _____ (wollen) gestern mit Claudia in die Alte Pinakothek gehen.
2. Aber diesmal _____ (müssen) er mit Claudia zuerst zum Donisl und dann ins Deutsche Museum.
3. Die Weißwürste beim Donisl waren so gut, dass auch Martin sie _____ (mögen).

4. Im Deutschen Museum _____ (können) sie nur zwei Stunden bleiben, weil Martin für seine Eltern ein paar Broschüren aus dem Reisebüro mitbringen _____ (sollen).

5. Seine Eltern _____ (wollen) bald einen Aufenthalt in der Schweiz buchen.

5-33 Weißt du das noch? Ask each other about childhood memories and note down your partner's responses. Then report your findings to the class. You will find vocabulary to describe **Jobs und Berufe** and **Essen und Trinken** in the *Anhang* on pages A14 and A17.

S1:

1. Was wolltest du als Kind werden?
2. Was durftest du als Kind nicht?
3. Was konntest du als Kind besser als andere Kinder?
4. Was mochtest du als Kind nicht essen?
5. Musstest du das dann trotzdem° essen?

S2:

Ich wollte … werden.
Ich durfte nicht …
Ich konnte besser …

Ich mochte kein__ …
Ja, das musste ich. / Nein, das musste ich nicht.

anyway

Infobox

Südtirol

The northern Italian province of **Südtirol** (**Alto Adige** in Italian), with its spectacular mountains and its valleys of orchards and vineyards, is a mecca for tourists. However, this area has had a turbulent history. At the beginning of the twentieth century it was part of the Austrian province of **Tirol.** In 1919 **Südtirol** was ceded to Italy, and the Italian government prohibited the use of German in public life and worked to attract Italian-speaking settlers to the region. In 1939, Hitler and Mussolini signed an agreement to resettle the population of **Südtirol** in German territory. Because of World War II, the resettlement never came about.

Schloss Tirol.

Ladin: A Rhaeto-Romance (**rätoromanisch**) dialect spoken in several valleys of the Dolomites in northeast Italy. It is similar to the Rhaeto-Romance dialect spoken in Switzerland. You can find **Südtirol** on the map of **Österreich** inside the front cover.

After 1945, **Südtirol** became an autonomous Italian province with three official languages. Of a population of 463,000, 69 percent speak German, 26 percent speak Italian, and 4 percent speak Ladin.

In **Südtirol** all laws are published in German and Italian, and civil servants must be competent in both languages. The autonomy of **Südtirol** has been hailed as an outstanding example of the protection of ethnic minorities.

Südtirol is situated in the **Alpen,** and tourism employs over half of the work force. Of the 5 million tourists who visit annually, most come from Germany. The top quality fruit and wine from **Südtirol** are found in markets throughout Europe.

Zusammenschau

Hören

Morgen haben wir keine Vorlesungen

Claudia tells Stephanie about her plans for spending a free day with Martin in Munich.

NEUE VOKABELN

ab·holen	*to pick up*	**an·schauen**	*to look at*
schleppen	*to drag*	**arm**	*poor*
denkste	**= denkst du**	**aus·geben**	*to spend (money)*
lecker	*delicious*	**Mövenpick**	*a Swiss restaurant chain*

 5-34 **Erstes Verstehen.** Listen to the conversation and indicate whether the statements that follow each conversation are **richtig** or **falsch.**

	RICHTIG	FALSCH
1.	_____	_____
2.	_____	_____
3.	_____	_____
4.	_____	_____

 5-35 **Detailverstehen.** Listen to the conversation again and write responses to the following questions.

1. Warum will Claudia nicht in die Alte Pinakothek? *Weil ...*
2. Warum will Claudia Weißwürste beim Donisl zu Mittag essen? *Weil ...*
3. Warum will Claudia ins Deutsche Museum? *Weil ...*
4. Warum will sie nicht im Eisbach baden gehen? *Weil ...*
5. Wo will Claudia mit Martin zu Abend essen? *Sie ...*

Schreiben und Sprechen

5-36 **Mein Kalender.** Draw up your calendar for this week, listing the days and times of some activities you plan to do. You may find some ideas in the box on the next page.

Montag	9–10	Cafeteria: mit Lisa deutsche Vokabeln lernen
	10–11	Deutsch (Wortschatzquiz!)
	19–?	Kino + Kneipe
Dienstag	...	

• bis _____ Uhr schlafen	• fernsehen (Meine Lieblingsprogramme sind …)
• E-Mails schreiben	• mit Freunden rumhängen
• Freunde besuchen	• Tennis (Computerspiele, Wii-Spiele, …) spielen
• meine Wäsche waschen	• ins Kino (ins Konzert, ins Fitnesscenter, …) gehen
• Muffins backen	• ein gutes Buch lesen
• einkaufen gehen	• ein paar Songs runterladen
• meinen nächsten Urlaub planen	• neue Fotos auf meine Facebook-Seite stellen
• mein Zimmer aufräumen	• durch den Park (Campus, Wald, …) joggen

5-37 Gehst du mit? Using your calendar entries from **5–36,** find a good time for meeting a friend to do something together. Then call up your friend and ask whether she or he is free to join you. You may want to use phrases like the ones below.

S1: *(wählt°)*   **S2:** _____ hier.   *dials*

S1: Ich bin's, _____. Du, _____, ich möchte mal wieder ins Kino und dann in die Kneipe.

S2: Ich auch. Wann hast du Zeit?

S1: Für heute Abend habe ich nichts im Kalender. Geht das?

S2: Heute kann ich leider nicht. Ich muss …

S1: Und wie ist's mit Mittwoch um _____ Uhr?

S2: Am Mittwoch habe ich … Aber Freitag ist gut.

S1: Super! Da habe ich auch nichts vor.

S2: …

Lesen

Zum besseren Verstehen

5-38 Touristenattraktionen.

1. Have you ever visited a castle? Tell your classmates what you found interesting.
2. Can you give examples of extravagant buildings or monuments that have become major tourist attractions?

5-39 Was ist das auf Englisch?

1. Kinder hören gern **Märchen.**
2. *Rapunzel* ist ein **berühmtes** deutsches Märchen.
3. **Könige** leben in Schlössern.
4. Könige **bauen** gern Schlösser.
5. Weißt du **etwas** von König Ludwigs Schlössern?
6. Neuschwanstein ist ein **märchenhaftes** Schloss.
7. München ist die **Hauptstadt** von Bayern.
8. In München gibt es viele **Kunstgalerien.**

a. famous
b. fairy-tale
c. something
d. capital
e. fairy tales
f. art galleries
g. kings
h. build

> **Hauptstadt: Haupt-** prefixed to a noun indicates *main* or *major*. What are the English equivalents of **Hauptfach, Hauptstraße, Hauptbahnhof, Hauptreisezeit?**

Ludwig II. von Bayern und seine Märchenschlösser

Ein 18-Jähriger wird König

Die größte Touristenattraktion in Bayern sind die märchenhaften Schlösser von König Ludwig (1845–1886). Jedes Jahr kommen Tausende von Touristen aus aller Welt, marschieren in Gruppen durch eine fantastische Märchenwelt und hören von Ludwigs extravagantem Lebensstil und von seinem mysteriösen Tod.

In seiner Jugend ist Ludwig am liebsten auf Schloss Hohenschwangau in den bayerischen Bergen, wo er durch die wundervolle Bergwelt wandert. Er liebt Kunst, Musik und Literatur, aber von Finanzen und Politik versteht er fast nichts. Im Jahr 1864 wird der 18-jährige Ludwig König. Er hat große Pläne für seine Hauptstadt: München soll ein Zentrum für Kunst und Musik werden.

König Ludwig und Richard Wagner

Weil er die romantischen Opern von Richard Wagner so liebt, holt Ludwig den berühmten Komponisten nach München und finanziert Wagners verschwenderischen Lebensstil. Ludwig hilft Wagner auch bei der Finanzierung eines sehr teuren, neuen Opernhauses in Bayreuth. Für Ludwigs konservative Minister ist Wagner nicht die richtige Gesellschaft[1] für den jungen König. Der Komponist muss gehen, und Ludwig ist so verbittert, dass er nicht mehr oft in München ist und lieber in seinen geliebten bayerischen Bergen residiert.

Märchenschlösser

Wenn er aus München keine Märchenstadt machen darf, so will er jetzt hier in den Bergen eine Märchenwelt bauen: die drei berühmten Schlösser Neuschwanstein, Linderhof und Herrenchiemsee. Linderhof, das kleinste der drei Schlösser, wird 1878 fertig, und Ludwig wohnt dort ein paar Jahre, aber die anderen beiden Schlösser werden nie fertig. Herrenchiemsee liegt im Alpenvorland, auf einer Insel im Chiemsee. Das Modell für Herrenchiemsee war das weltberühmte Schloss Versailles in Paris.

Neuschwanstein

Das mysteriöse Ende

Ludwigs Schlösser kosten natürlich sehr viel Geld. Im Jahr 1886 hat der König so viel Schulden[2], dass die Minister in München etwas dagegen tun müssen. Vier Ärzte[3] müssen den König für verrückt erklären[4], und am 12. Juni 1886 bringt man ihn ins Schloss Berg am Starnberger See. Dort gehen Ludwig und ein Arzt am nächsten Abend spazieren, und wenige Stunden später findet man sie beide tot im See.

[1]*company*   [2]*debt*   [3]*physicians*   [4]*declare insane*

Arbeit mit dem Text

5-40 Anders gesagt. Find equivalents for these statements in the reading.

1. Schlösser sind sehr teuer.
2. Ludwig ist kein guter Finanzier und kein guter Politiker.
3. Richard Wagner darf nicht in München bleiben.
4. Vier Ärzte müssen sagen, dass Ludwig nicht normal ist.
5. Ludwig schaut gern schöne Bilder° an, hört gern Musik und liest gern. *paintings*
6. In Bayern schauen die meisten Touristen die Schlösser von König Ludwig an.
7. Ludwig bezahlt für Wagners extravagantes Leben.
8. Ludwig will, dass München eine berühmte Kunst- und Musikstadt wird.

5-41 Was ist die richtige Antwort? You will hear six questions about *Ludwig II. von Bayern*. Mark the correct answers.

1. _____ Mysteriös.
   _____ Extravagant.
2. _____ Auf Schloss Hohenschwangau.
   _____ In München.
3. _____ Von Finanzen und von Politik.
   _____ Von Kunst und von Literatur.
4. _____ Romantisch.
   _____ Konservativ.
5. _____ In den bayerischen Bergen.
   _____ In München.
6. _____ Seine Minister.
   _____ Vier Ärzte.

Wort, Sinn und Klang

Wörter unter der Lupe

Predicting gender

The gender of many German nouns is indicated by their suffixes. Here are some examples.

- Nouns with the suffixes **–or** and **–ent** are masculine.

  der Profess**or**   **der** Stud**ent**

- Nouns with the suffix **–er** that are derived from verbs are always masculine. These nouns can refer to people as well as things.

  arbeiten   **der** Arbeit**er**   fernsehen   **der** Fernseh**er**

- Nouns with the suffix **–in** added to a masculine noun are feminine.

  die Profess**orin**   **die** Arbeit**erin**

- Nouns with the suffix **–ur** are almost always feminine.

  die Temperat**ur**   **die** Zens**ur**   **die** Klaus**ur**

- Nouns with the suffix **–ment** are almost always neuter.

  das Instru**ment**   **das** Experi**ment**   **das** Argu**ment**

- Nouns with the suffix **–(i)um** are almost always neuter.

  das For**um**   **das** Gymnas**ium**

- Nouns with the diminutive suffixes **–chen** and **–lein** are always neuter. These two suffixes (compare English -*kin* in mani*kin* and lamb*kin*, or -*let* in star*let*, book*let*, and pig*let*) can be affixed to virtually every German noun to express smallness. This also explains why both **Mädchen** *(girl)* and **Fräulein** *(Miss; young lady)* are neuter. The vowels **a, o, u,** and the diphthong **au** are umlauted when a diminutive suffix is added to the noun. Remember that with the diphthong **au** it is the **a** that is umlauted.

  die Stadt   **das** Städt**chen**   **der** Bruder   **das** Brüder**lein**

  die Tochter   **das** Töchter**lein**   **das** Haus   **das** Häus**chen**

5-42 *Der, das oder die?* Say the following nouns with their definite articles. If a noun has a corresponding feminine form, give that form and the corresponding article as well.

1. Präsident	7. Frisur	13. Kätzchen	19. Projektor
2. Element	8. Assistent	14. Besucher	20. Patient
3. Mäuschen	9. Fahrer	15. Dokument	21. Ornament
4. Motor	10. Kompliment	16. Agent	22. Medium
5. Verkäufer	11. Fischlein	17. Autor	23. Lautsprecher
6. Aquarium	12. Mentor	18. Individuum	24. Diktatur

Suffix -er: English also derives many so-called agent nouns from verbs. As in German, they do not always refer to people: *to work/worker; to serve/server; to wash/washer; to dry/dryer.*

Suffix -ur: *das Abitur* is an exception.

Fräulein: Before the feminist movement exerted its influence on gender-related vocabulary, this word referred to unmarried women of any age. Now the term has become archaic.

5-40 to 5-41

Zur Aussprache

German *ch*

German **ch** is one of the few consonant sounds that has no equivalent in English.

- **ch** after **a, o, u,** and **au**

  When **ch** follows the vowels **a**, **o**, **u**, or **au**, it resembles the sound of a gentle gargling.

  > Frau Ba**ch** kommt Punkt a**ch**t.
  > Am Wo**ch**enende ko**ch**t immer meine To**ch**ter.
  > Warum su**ch**st du denn das Ko**ch**bu**ch**?
  > Ich will versu**ch**en°, einen Ku**ch**en zu backen.   *try*
  > Hat Herr Rau**ch** au**ch** so einen Bierbau**ch**° wie Herr Strau**ch**?   *beer belly*

- **ch** after all other vowels and after consonants

  The sound of **ch** after all other vowels (including the umlauted vowels) and after consonants is similar to the sound of a loudly whispered *h* in *huge* or *Hugh*.

  > Mi**ch**aels Kätz**ch**en mö**ch**te ein Teller**ch**en° Mil**ch**.   *little dish*

  The ending **–ig** is pronounced as if it were spelled **–ich**, unless it is followed by a vowel.

  > Es ist sonn**ig**, aber sehr wind**ig**.

- The two types of **ch** sounds are often found in the singular and plural forms of the same noun.

die Na**ch**t	die Nä**ch**te	das Bu**ch**	die Bü**ch**er
die To**ch**ter	die Tö**ch**ter	der Bierbau**ch**	die Bierbäu**ch**e

- The combination **–chs** is pronounced like English *x*.

das Wa**chs**	se**chs**	der **Ochs**e	der Fu**chs**

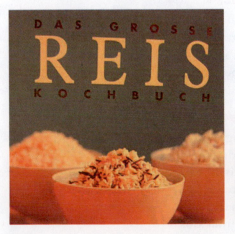

Nomen

die Hauptstadt, ⸚e	capital city
der Pass, ⸚e	passport
das Reisebüro, –s	travel agency
der Studentenausweis, –e	student ID
die Welt, –en	world
das Bild, –er	picture; painting
die Kunst, ⸚e	art
das Märchen, –	fairy tale
der Roman, –e	novel
der Arzt, ⸚e ⎫ die Ärztin, –nen ⎭	physician; doctor
der Chef, –s ⎫ die Chefin, –nen ⎭	boss
die Jugend (sing)	youth
der Mensch, –en	human being; person; (pl) people
der Bart, ⸚e	beard
der Schnurrbart, ⸚e	mustache
die Frisur, –en	hair style; hairdo
der Haarschnitt, –e	haircut
die Brille, –n	(eye)glasses
die Kontaktlinse, –n	contact lens

> **Brille** is used in the plural only when it refers to more than one pair.

das Armband, ⸚er	bracelet
die Halskette, –n	necklace
der Nasenstecker, –	nose stud
der Ohrring, –e	earring
die Klausur, –en	test
das Quiz, –	quiz
die Zensur, –en	grade

> **Quiz** has no ending in the plural

die Ecke, –n	corner

Verben

ab·holen	to pick up
an·schauen	to look at
aus·geben	to spend (*money*)
buchen	to book
ein·kaufen	to shop
hoffen	to hope
lieben	to love
schleppen	to drag
übernachten	to spend the night; to stay overnight

> **Schleppen** has come into English via Yiddish.

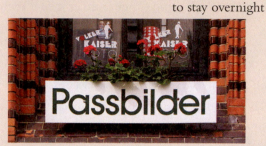

Andere Wörter

berühmt	famous
hoch	high
kühl	cool (*of weather*)
lecker	delicious
leider	unfortunately
märchenhaft	fairy-tale, fantastic
natürlich	of course
trotzdem	anyway; nevertheless
verrückt	crazy; insane
ziemlich	quite; rather

Ausdrücke

als Kind	as a child
Punkt halb zwei	at one-thirty on the dot
Ich bin's.	It's me.
Ich habe Durst.	I'm thirsty.
Ich habe Hunger.	I'm hungry.

Das Gegenteil

der Junge, –n ≠ das Mädchen, –	boy ≠ girl
altmodisch ≠ modern	old-fashioned ≠ modern
arm ≠ reich	poor ≠ rich
geschmackvoll ≠ geschmacklos	tasteful ≠ tasteless
dafür ≠ dagegen	for it ≠ against it
etwas ≠ nichts	something ≠ nothing
mit ≠ ohne	with ≠ without

Leicht zu verstehen

das Argument, -e   das Kompliment, -e   das Museum, Museen   fantastisch
die ATM-Karte, -n   die Kreditkarte, -n   der Tourist, -en   konservativ
die Baseballkappe, -n   der Kurs, -e   die Touristin, -nen   romantisch
das Experiment, -e   die Literatur, -en   finanzieren   sentimental
der Kalender, -   die Maschine, -n   arrogant

Wörter im Kontext

> **Museum, Museen:** Remember that nouns that end in **-um** are almost always neuter, and many form the plural this way. What are the singular forms for **Alben, Zentren, Daten**?

5-43 Was passt zusammen?

1. Wenn man schöne Bilder anschauen möchte,	a. geht man zum Reisebüro.
2. Wenn man sehr teure Ohrringe kaufen will,	b. geht man in die Jugendherberge.
3. Wenn man eine ATM-Karte braucht,	c. geht man zum Optiker.
4. Wenn man krank ist,	d. geht man zum Juwelier.
5. Wenn man eine Reise buchen will,	e. geht man ins Museum.
6. Wenn man einen guten Roman lesen will,	f. geht man zum Arzt.
7. Wenn man billig übernachten will,	g. geht man zur Bank.
8. Wenn man eine Brille oder Kontaktlinsen braucht,	h. geht man in die Bibliothek.

> The German equivalent of *to take a test* or *to have a test* is **eine Klausur schreiben.**

5-44 Was passt zusammen?

1. Wenn ich kein Geld habe,	a. muss ich leider einen neuen Job finden.
2. Wenn ich meinen Chef nicht mag,	b. kann ich nicht einkaufen gehen.
3. Wenn ich gute Zensuren will,	c. brauche ich einen Studentenausweis.
4. Wenn ich in München historische Maschinen anschauen will,	d. muss ich mit meinem Professor sprechen.
5. Wenn ich eine Klausur nicht schreiben will,	e. muss ich viel lernen.
6. Wenn ich für eine Konzertkarte weniger bezahlen will,	f. gehe ich ins Deutsche Museum.

5-45 Was passt zusammen? Match appropriately in each set.

1. die ATM-Karte	a. die Galerie	4. der Pass	d. die Weltreise
2. der Kalender	b. das Geld	5. der Kurs	e. der Roman
3. die Kunst	c. das Jahr	6. die Literatur	f. die Klausur

> **geschmacklos:** Many words form their opposites in meaning by adding the suffix **-voll** or **-los.** What are the English equivalents of the following sets of opposites: **liebevoll ≠ lieblos; humorvoll ≠ humorlos; taktvoll ≠ taktlos; respektvoll ≠ respektlos?**

5-46 Kleine Gespräche.

leider / verrückt / Durst / trotzdem / reich / etwas / einkaufen

1. STEFAN: Ich habe _____. Hast du _____ zu trinken für mich?
   HORST: Nein, _____ nicht.
2. ANNA: Ist es richtig, dass Ludwig II. _____ war?
   JULIA: Ja, aber seine Schlösser sind _____ schön.
3. MARIA: Laura geht ziemlich oft _____.
   LUKAS: Ja, ihre Eltern sind sehr _____.

Ein Blick zurück

1924: Einwandererkinder auf Ellis Island

Kommunikationsziele

Describing past events …
- in conversational situations
- in personal narratives

Talking about …
- one's ancestors
- education and job qualifications

Describing someone's appearance

Strukturen

The perfect tense

Ordinal numbers

Hin and **her**

Kultur

German roots in North America

The German language in North America

Video-Treff: **Mein erster Job**

Lesen: **Aus Christian Köchlings Tagebuch**

Vorschau

Ein deutscher Auswanderer

Hans Keilhau ist im Sommer 1930 nach Amerika ausgewandert und hat kurz vorher diesen Pass bekommen. Schauen Sie den Pass genau an.

1. Wann hat Herr Keilhau diesen Pass bekommen?
2. Was war Hans Keilhau von Beruf?
3. Wo ist er geboren?
4. Wann ist er geboren?
5. Wo in Deutschland hat Herr Keilhau im Juni 1930 gewohnt?
6. Ist er groß, klein oder mittelgroß?
7. Welche Form hat sein Gesicht? *Es ist …*
8. Welche Farbe haben seine Augen? *Sie sind …*
9. Welche Farbe hat sein Haar? *Es ist …*
10. Wie heißt der Ringfinger in Hans Keilhaus Pass?
11. Wie weiß man, dass Hans Keilhau nicht verheiratet ist?

Ein deutscher Einwanderer sucht Arbeit

Hans Keilhaus Freund Paul Richter kommt auch aus Deutschland. Er arbeitet bei *Hutton Machine and Tool* und er erzählt Hans, dass seine Firma einen Schlosser sucht. Hans kann mit dem Personalchef, der aus Österreich kommt, Deutsch sprechen.

PERSONALCHEF:	Guten Tag, Herr Keilhau. Sie sind Schlosser?
HANS:	Ja, ich habe Schlosser gelernt.
PERSONALCHEF:	Wo haben Sie gelernt?
HANS:	In Werdau in Sachsen.
PERSONALCHEF:	Und wo haben Sie zuletzt gearbeitet?
HANS:	Bei Escher in Leipzig.
PERSONALCHEF:	Das ist eine gute Firma. Warum sind Sie dort nicht geblieben?
HANS:	Escher hatte immer weniger Aufträge und letztes Jahr bin ich arbeitslos geworden. Ich habe in ganz Deutschland Arbeit gesucht und nichts gefunden. Deshalb bin ich dann ausgewandert.
PERSONALCHEF:	Haben Sie hier Arbeit gefunden?
HANS:	Ja, aber nicht als Schlosser. Ich arbeite jetzt bei *Garden State Nurseries* als Gärtner.
PERSONALCHEF:	Warum sind Sie Schlosser geworden?
HANS:	Mein Großvater war Schlosser, mein Vater war Schlosser und deshalb habe auch ich Schlosser gelernt.
PERSONALCHEF:	Ah, Familientradition. Sagen Sie, wer hat Sie zu *Hutton Machine and Tool* geschickt?
HANS:	Paul Richter. Er ist mein Freund.
PERSONALCHEF:	Paul Richter ist Ihr Freund? Er ist ein sehr guter Arbeiter. Wenn Paul Richter Sie geschickt hat, sind Sie bestimmt auch gut. Sie können morgen anfangen.

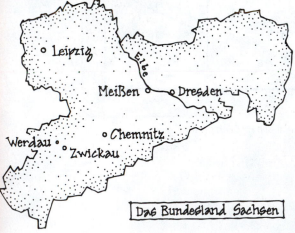

Hans Keilhau ist Schlosser von Beruf.

Das Bundesland Sachsen

6-1 Richtig oder falsch? You will hear the conversation between the personnel manager and Hans Keilhau. Indicate whether the statements that follow are **richtig** or **falsch**.

	RICHTIG	FALSCH		RICHTIG	FALSCH
1.	_____	_____	4.	_____	_____
2.	_____	_____	5.	_____	_____
3.	_____	_____			

6-2 Stephanies Stammbaum.

1. Wo ist Stephanies Mutter geboren?
2. Wie heißt Stephanies Großvater mütterlicherseits?
3. Wo ist er geboren?
4. Wie heißt Stephanies Großmutter mütterlicherseits?
5. Woher kommen Sophia Castellos Eltern?
6. Wie heißt Stephanies Großmutter väterlicherseits?
7. Woher sind Christa Bauers Eltern?

6-3 Ich zeichne° meinen Stammbaum. Draw your family tree. Write your ancestors' names and where they come from.

draw

6-4 Familiengeschichte°: Woher sind deine Vorfahren°?
Answer your partner's questions about your family tree.

family history / ancestors

1. Wo sind deine Eltern geboren?
2. Woher kommen deine Großeltern mütterlicherseits?
3. Woher kommen deine Großeltern väterlicherseits?
4. Woher sind deine beiden Urgroßväter° mütterlicherseits?
5. Woher …

great-grandfathers

6-5 Was steht in Lauras Pass? You want to know what Laura and Philipp look like and your partner wants information about Thomas and Bettina. The information for **S2** is in the *Anhang* on page A6.

S1: Ist Laura groß oder klein?
Was für eine Form hat ihr Gesicht?
Was für Augen hat sie?
Was für Haar hat sie?

S2: Sie ist …
Sie hat ein _____es Gesicht.
Sie hat _____e Augen.
Sie hat _____es, _____es Haar.

	LAURA	THOMAS	BETTINA	PHILIPP
Größe		ziemlich groß	ziemlich klein	
Gesichtsform		schmal°	rund	
Augen		dunkelbraun	blau	
Haar		hellbraun, kurz	blond, lockig	

thin

Kultur / German roots in North America

Today's North American population has strong roots in the German-speaking world. Hundreds of towns in North America are named after the German, Swiss, or Austrian birthplaces of their founders. The United States has 26 Berlins, and place names like Baden, Bern(e), Bismarck, Frankfort, Germantown, Hamburg, Hanover, Heidelberg, Saltsburg, or Zurich can be found across the continent.

First settlers

The first German settlers, 13 Pietist families from Northern Germany, came to America in 1683 seeking freedom from religious persecution. They came at the invitation of William Penn, the Quaker who had founded Pennsylvania. These first settlers built a community that they named Germantown. Other such immigrants followed, among them the Mennonites, who also settled in Pennsylvania and later branched out into other states and Canada.

The 19th century

Political turmoil, persecution, and economic hardship drove many from the German-speaking regions to seek a better life in North America in the 19th century. German immigrant and civil engineer **John Roebling** left Prussia in 1831 and later designed the world-famous Brooklyn Bridge. After the failed liberal revolution in Germany, **Carl Schurz** emigrated to the United States in 1852 with his wife, **Margarethe Meyer-Schurz**. He went on to become a general of the Northern States in the Civil War, a senator from Wisconsin, and Secretary of the Interior from 1877–91, while she founded the first kindergarten in the US. The **Carl Schurz Society**, which fosters German-American relations, was founded in 1930.

The 20th century

The twentieth century saw far fewer immigrants from the German-speaking countries. In the 1920s and 1930s quotas were established. Many of the people who immigrated in the 1930s were fleeing Hitler's totalitarian and anti-Semitic regime, and their emigration was an immeasurable loss to Germany and Austria. From 1933 to 1938 approximately 130,000 German Jews came to North America, among them physicist **Albert Einstein,** psychologists **Erich Fromm** and **Ruth Westheimer,** composers **Arnold Schoenberg, Kurt Weill,** and **Erich Wolfgang Korngold,** actor **Peter Lorre,** and film director **Billy Wilder. Korngold** became famous for his film scores in Hollywood, while Lorre appeared in such Hollywood classics as *The Maltese Falcon* and *Casablanca*. Others who came to North America include architects **Walter Gropius** and **Ludwig Mies van der Rohe,** writers **Thomas Mann** and **Bertolt Brecht**, as well as stage and film stars **Lotte Lenya** and **Marlene Dietrich,** who actively supported the American war effort against Nazi Germany by helping to raise war bonds and touring for the troops.

After 1945

After World War II, over 800,000 refugees from former German territories in eastern Europe and other disillusioned Germans crossed the Atlantic. Among this group of so-called "Displaced Persons" were also many fugitives from the Soviet zone of Germany. In more recent times, several notable immigrants from the German-speaking countries, such as writer **Ursula Hegi**, actor turned politician **Arnold Schwarzenegger**, or model and TV personality **Heidi Klum**, have made their mark on American culture and politics.

6-6 Was haben diese berühmten Einwanderer und Einwanderinnen gemacht?

1. Der Ingenieur John Roebling (geb. Johann August Röbling)
2. Die Sängerin Marlene Dietrich (geb. Maria Magdalena Dietrich)
3. Die Psychologin Ruth Westheimer (geb. Karola Ruth Siegel)
4. Die Autorin Ursula Hegi
5. Das Fotomodell Heidi Klum
6. Der Unternehmer Levi Strauss (geb. Löb Strauß)
7. Der Schauspieler Arnold Schwarzenegger
8. Die Pädagogin Margarethe Meyer-Schurz
9. Der Komponist Erich Wolfgang Korngold

a. hat den Bestseller *Stones from the River* (1994) geschrieben.
b. ist 2003 Gouverneur von Kalifornien geworden.
c. hat in Wisconsin den ersten Kindergarten in den USA gegründet.
d. hat im Zweiten Weltkrieg Konzerte für amerikanische Truppen gegeben.
e. hat die Brooklyn Bridge entworfen.
f. hat den Oscar für die Musik zu dem Film *The Adventures of Robin Hood* (1938) gewonnen.
g. hat am Ende der Fernseh-Show *Project Runway* „Auf Wiedersehen" gesagt (und davon kommt: „You've been auffed").
h. ist mit der Radio-Show *Sexually Speaking* populär geworden.
i. hat in San Francisco die ersten Denim Jeans produziert.

Nomen

der Geburtsort, -e	place of birth
der Wohnort, -e	place of residence
die Geschichte, -n	history; story
das Land, ̈er	country; state
der Stammbaum, ̈e	family tree
die Urgroßeltern (pl)	great-grandparents
die Urgroßmutter, ̈	great-grandmother
der Urgroßvater, ̈	great-grandfather
die Vorfahren (pl)	ancestors
die Größe, -n	height; size
der Personalchef, -s	personnel manager

Das Gesicht

das Gesicht, -er	face
das Haar, -e	hair
die Stirn	forehead
das Auge, -n	eye
das Ohr, -en	ear
die Nase, -n	nose
der Mund, ̈er	mouth
der Zahn, ̈e	tooth
das Kinn	chin

> **Land:** Within Germany and Austria the states are called **Länder** or **Bundesländer**. In Switzerland they are called **Kantone**.

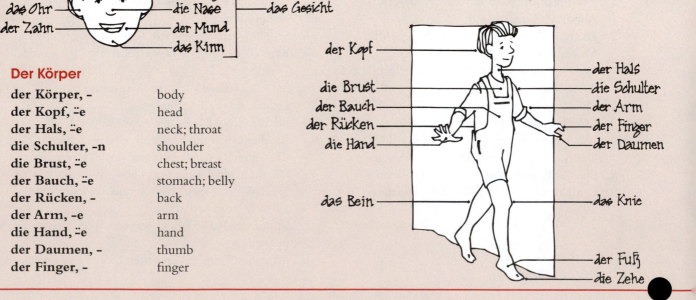

Der Körper

der Körper, -	body
der Kopf, ̈e	head
der Hals, ̈e	neck; throat
die Schulter, -n	shoulder
die Brust, ̈e	chest; breast
der Bauch, ̈e	stomach; belly
der Rücken, -	back
der Arm, -e	arm
die Hand, ̈e	hand
der Daumen, -	thumb
der Finger, -	finger

das Knie, -	knee
das Bein, -e	leg
der Fuß, ̈e	foot
die Zehe, -n	toe

Verben

erzählen	to tell
schicken	to send
zeichnen	to draw (a picture)

Andere Wörter

arbeitslos	unemployed

Ausdrücke

Wann bist du geboren?	When were you born?
Am ersten Juni 1994.	On the first of June 1994.

Das Gegenteil

der Auswanderer, - ≠ der Einwanderer, -	emigrant ≠ immigrant
aus·wandern ≠ ein·wandern	to emigrate ≠ to immigrate
väterlicherseits ≠ mütterlicherseits	paternal ≠ maternal
vorher ≠ nachher	before ≠ after

Leicht zu verstehen

der Emigrant, -en	die Immigrantin, -nen
die Emigrantin, -nen	die Form, -en
der Immigrant, -en	die Region, -en

Wörter im Kontext

6-7 Sylvias Vorfahren.

ausgewandert / Stammbaum / Vorfahren / Familiengeschichte / väterlicherseits

Sylvia schreibt ihre _____ und als Illustration zeichnet sie einen schönen, großen _____. Ihre _____ mütterlicherseits kommen aus Italien. Ihre Vorfahren _____ sind im neunzehnten Jahrhundert aus Österreich nach Amerika _____.

6-8 Was passt wo?

Urgroßeltern / Emigrantin / Geburtsort / Wohnort / Emigrant

1. Wenn ich in ein anderes Land auswandere, bin ich ein _____ oder eine _____.
2. Die Großeltern von meinen Eltern sind meine _____.
3. Wenn ich in Boston geboren bin, dann ist Boston mein _____.
4. Wenn ich in Hamburg lebe und wohne, dann ist diese Stadt mein _____.

6-9 Was passt zusammen? Match appropriately in each set.

1. der Kopf	a. sehen	7. der Fuß	g. die Brille
2. das Auge	b. denken	8. der Finger	h. die Zahnbürste
3. das Ohr	c. schreiben	9. der Hals	i. die Frisur
4. die Hand	d. hören	10. die Augen	j. der Schuh
5. das Bein	e. sprechen	11. das Haar	k. die Halskette
6. der Mund	f. gehen	12. die Zähne	l. der Ring

6-10 Was steht in Hans Keilhaus Pass?

wohnt / Beruf / Haar / Augen / geboren / Gesicht

In Hans Keilhaus Pass steht, …

1. was er von _____ ist.
2. wo und wann er _____ ist und wo er _____.
3. wie groß er ist und was für eine Form sein _____ hat.
4. was für eine Farbe seine _____ und sein _____ haben.

Kommunikation und Formen

1 Talking about events in the past

The perfect tense

6-1 to 6-2

To talk about past events in conversational situations, you use the perfect tense in German. In English we generally use the simple past for this purpose.

> The perfect tense is sometimes referred to as the present perfect tense or the conversational past.

Was **hast** du gestern **gemacht?**   *What **did** you **do** yesterday?*
Ich **habe** mit Peter Tennis **gespielt.**   *I **played** tennis with Peter.*

The perfect tense consists of an auxiliary verb (usually **haben**) that takes personal endings and a past participle that remains unchanged.

	singular		plural
ich	habe gespielt	wir	haben gespielt
du	hast gespielt	ihr	habt gespielt
er/es/sie	hat gespielt	sie	haben gespielt
		Sie haben gespielt	

> The auxiliary verb is sometimes called the helping verb. Why do you think this is so?

Depending on the context, the German perfect tense can correspond to any of the following English verb forms.

ich habe gespielt	*I played*
	I have played
	I have been playing
	I was playing
	I did play

Position of auxiliary verb and past participle

The auxiliary verb takes the regular position of the verb and the past participle stands at the end of the sentence.

Hast du deinen Flug schon **gebucht?**   *Have you booked your flight yet?*
Ja, ich **habe** ihn gestern Nachmittag   *Yes, I **booked** it yesterday*
  gebucht.   *afternoon.*
Und was **hast** du gestern Nachmittag   *And what else **did** you **do** yesterday*
  noch **gemacht?**   *afternoon?*
Ich **habe** einen neuen Koffer **gekauft.**   *I **bought** a new suitcase.*

The past participle of regular verbs

Most German verbs form the past participle by adding the prefix **ge-** and the ending **-t** or **-et** to the verb stem. The ending **-et** is used if the verb stem ends in **-d, -t,** or certain consonant combinations.

	prefix	verb stem	ending
lernen	ge	lern	t
arbeiten	ge	arbeit	et
baden	ge	bad	et
zeichnen	ge	zeichn	et

Past participles of verbs ending in **-ieren** do not have the prefix **ge-**.

	prefix	verb stem	ending
reparieren		reparier	t

6-11 **Was haben Yusuf, Maria und Jennifer gestern gemacht?**
The information for **S2** is in the *Anhang* on page A6.

S1: Was hat Yusuf gestern Vormittag gemacht?

S2: Gestern Vormittag hat er seinen Wagen repariert.

	MARIA	YUSUF	JENNIFER
gestern Vormittag	stundenlang mit Julia telefoniert		ihren Flug nach Deutschland gebucht
gestern Nachmittag			einen neuen Koffer gekauft
gestern Abend	im Internet gesurft	bei McDonald's gearbeitet	

6-12 **Was hast du gestern gemacht?** Use a few of the following expressions to tell each other some of the things you did yesterday.

Gestern habe ich …

- Karten (Fußball, …) gespielt
- für eine Klausur (ein Quiz) in _____ gelernt
- ein paar Stunden gearbeitet
- mein Fahrrad repariert
- das neue Lied° (Album) von _____ gehört

- mit _____ telefoniert
- im Internet gesurft
- Hausaufgaben gemacht
- Klamotten gekauft
- stundenlang gebloggt
- für ein Referat recherchiert

song

Position of auxiliary verb and past participle in a dependent clause

In a dependent clause, the auxiliary verb stands at the end of the clause, and the past participle precedes it.

Heute bin ich müde, **weil** ich gestern so viel **gearbeitet habe.**

*I'm tired today, **because** I **worked** so much yesterday.*

Position of *nicht* in sentences in the perfect tense

The rules you learned about the position of **nicht** on pages 34 and 104 still apply.

In the present perfect tense, **nicht** is placed directly before the past participle, unless a particular word or expression is negated.

Warum **hast** du deine Hausaufgaben   *Why **didn't** you **do** your homework?*
    nicht gemacht?

6-13 Warum hast du das nicht gemacht?

▶

    deinen Koffer packen   mit Monika telefonieren

S1: Warum hast du deinen Koffer nicht   **S2:** Weil ich mit Monika telefoniert
gepackt?   habe.

1.

2.

3.

| Radio hören | frühstücken | deine Vokabeln lernen |
| den Hund füttern | Karten spielen | Tennis spielen |

4.

5.

6.

lawn

| Klavier üben | den Rasen° mähen | die Fenster putzen |
| Gitarre spielen | Fußball spielen | dein Fahrrad reparieren |

The past participle of irregular verbs

Irregular verbs are a small but frequently used group of verbs. The past participles of these verbs end in **–en.** The verb stem often undergoes a vowel change and sometimes consonant changes as well.

	prefix	verb stem	ending
finden	ge	fund	en
nehmen	ge	nomm	en
schlafen	ge	schlaf	en

The list below shows the past participles of some common irregular verbs. Be sure to learn them.

backen	**gebacken**	finden	**gefunden**	singen	**gesungen**	
essen	**gegessen**	gießen°	**gegossen**	sitzen	**gesessen**	*to water*
lesen	**gelesen**	liegen°	**gelegen**	sprechen	**gesprochen**	*to lie*
schlafen	**geschlafen**	nehmen	**genommen**	stehen	**gestanden**	
sehen	**gesehen**	schneiden°	**geschnitten**	streichen°	**gestrichen**	*to cut / to paint*
waschen	**gewaschen**	schreiben	**geschrieben**	trinken	**getrunken**	

6-14 **Was haben Julia, Moritz und Lisa gestern gemacht?** The information for **S2** is in the *Anhang* on page A6.

S1: Was hat Julia gestern Vormittag gemacht?

S2: Gestern Vormittag hat sie eine Torte gebacken.

	JULIA	MORITZ	LISA
gestern Vormittag			Bernds Haare geschnitten
gestern Nachmittag	mit Sophia Kaffee getrunken	ein Referat für Deutsch geschrieben	
gestern Abend			ein heißes Bad genommen

6-15 Morgen, morgen, nur nicht heute ...

▶

die Zimmerpflanzen gießen

S1: Hast du die Zimmerpflanzen gegossen?

Was hast du denn gemacht?

mit Eva vor dem Fernseher sitzen

S2: Nein, noch nicht.

Ich habe mit Eva vor dem Fernseher gesessen.

1.

2.

3.

| dein Referat schreiben | die Zeitung lesen | ein Stück Torte essen |
| mit Professor Berg sprechen | deinen Wagen waschen | mit Eva Kaffee trinken |

4.

5.

6.

| den Zaun streichen | ein Bad nehmen | die Hecke schneiden |
| ein Buch lesen | einen Kuchen backen | ein bisschen schlafen |

6-16 Was Eva gestern alles gemacht hat. Listen as your instructor narrates what Eva did yesterday. Then take turns telling the story with a partner. Begin the sentences as indicated and use the verbs provided.

1. Um halb sieben hat Eva noch im Bett gelegen und geschlafen.
2. Um … (nehmen)
3. Um … (trinken, lesen)
4. Dann … (gießen)
5. Später … (schreiben)
6. Um … (sprechen)

7. Um … (essen)
8. Am Nachmittag …
   (Wäsche [f] waschen)
9. Danach …
   (Pizza [f] backen)
10. Später … (sitzen)
11. Und am Abend … (singen)

6-17 Ein paar persönliche Fragen. Respond to your partner's questions, using the perfect tense. Add one or two questions of your own.

Bis wann hast du heute Morgen geschlafen?

Was hast du zum Frühstück (zum Mittagessen) gegessen und getrunken?

Welche interessanten Bücher hast du in letzter Zeit° gelesen?

Was hast du in letzter Zeit im Fernsehen gesehen?

Wie viele Klausuren hast du letzte Woche geschrieben? …

in letzter Zeit: *recently*

The verb *sein* as auxiliary in the perfect tense

In English you always use the verb *to have* as the auxiliary in the perfect tense. In German you usually use **haben,** but for verbs that express a change of location or a change of condition, you use **sein.** These verbs can be regular or irregular.

singular		plural	
ich	bin gekommen	wir	sind gekommen
du	bist gekommen	ihr	seid gekommen
er/es/sie	ist gekommen	sie	sind gekommen
	Sie sind gekommen		

Change of location:

Ist Eva ins Kino **gegangen?**   *Has Eva **gone** to the movies?*

Some common verbs that express a change of location:

fahren	**ist gefahren**	kommen	**ist gekommen**
fliegen	**ist geflogen**	reisen	**ist gereist**
gehen	**ist gegangen**	wandern	**ist gewandert**

Change of condition:

Opa Ziegler **ist** plötzlich sehr krank   *Grandpa Ziegler suddenly **became** very*
  geworden und **gestorben.**   *ill and **died.***
Wann **ist** das **passiert?**   *When **did** that **happen**?*

Some common verbs that express a change of condition:

werden	**ist geworden**	*to become*
sterben	**ist gestorben**	*to die*
passieren	**ist passiert**	*to happen*

Two very common verbs use **sein** as an auxiliary although they express neither a change of location nor a change of condition:

bleiben	**ist geblieben**	*to stay; to remain*
sein	**ist gewesen**	*to be*

Warum **ist** Sylvia zu Hause **geblieben?**   *Why **did** Sylvia **stay** home?*
Wo **bist** du **gewesen,** Sylvia?   *Where **have** you **been,** Sylvia?*

The list below shows the past participles of some common irregular verbs that use **sein** as an auxiliary. Be sure to learn them.

bleiben	**ist geblieben**	kommen	**ist gekommen**
fahren	**ist gefahren**	sein	**ist gewesen**
fliegen	**ist geflogen**	sterben	**ist gestorben**
gehen	**ist gegangen**	werden	**ist geworden**

6-18 Opa Ziegler ist gestorben. Brigitte Ziegler calls her friend Beverly and tells her why she and Klaus can't come for dinner tonight. Supply the appropriate perfect forms.

ist … geworden / ist … passiert / ist … gefahren / ist … gestorben / ist … gekommen

1. BRIGITTE: Du Beverly, wir können leider nicht zum Abendessen kommen.
                Klaus musste ganz schnell zu seinen Eltern nach Hamburg.
   BEVERLY: Was _____ denn _____?
2. BRIGITTE: Opa Ziegler _____ plötzlich° sehr krank _____.   *suddenly*
   BEVERLY: Ist er im Krankenhaus?
3. BRIGITTE: Ja, und dort _____ er heute Morgen um zehn _____.
   BEVERLY: Hoffentlich° _____ Klaus nicht zu spät _____.   *I hope*
4. BRIGITTE: Nein. Er _____ vom Bahnhof direkt ins Krankenhaus _____ und
                konnte noch ein paar Worte mit Opa sprechen.

Sprachnotiz   The perfect tense of *sein* and *haben*

In Austria, Southern Germany, and Switzerland, the perfect tense of **sein** and **haben** is used quite frequently in conversational situations.

Wo **bist** du gestern **gewesen?**	Where **were** you yesterday?
Wie viele Vorlesungen **hast** du gestern **gehabt?**	How many courses **did** you **have** yesterday?

But remember that most speakers of German use the simple past of these verbs.

Ich **war** den ganzen Tag zu Hause.	I **was** home all day.
Ich **hatte** nur eine Vorlesung.	I **had** only one lecture.

6-19 Eine Urlaubsreise nach Spanien. Beverly asks Brigitte Ziegler about the vacation Brigitte and Klaus had last summer. Supply the appropriate forms of **haben** or **sein.**

1. BEVERLY: _____ Klaus und die Kinder dich letzten Sommer wieder zum
                Grundlsee geschleppt?
   BRIGITTE: Nein, letzten Sommer _____ wir mal ohne Kinder an die Costa
                Brava gereist.
2. BEVERLY: _____ ihr gefahren oder geflogen?
   BRIGITTE: Wir _____ von Frankfurt direkt nach Barcelona geflogen.
3. BEVERLY: Wie lang _____ ihr in Barcelona geblieben?
   BRIGITTE: Nur einen Tag. Aber wir _____ trotzdem viel gesehen.
4. BEVERLY: Wie _____ ihr zur Costa Brava gekommen?
   BRIGITTE: Wir _____ einen Wagen gemietet°.   *rented*
5. BEVERLY: Was _____ ihr denn den ganzen Tag gemacht?
   BRIGITTE: Wir _____ jeden Tag zweimal° schwimmen gegangen, _____ viel   *twice*
                Tennis gespielt und sehr gut gegessen.

6-20 Auch das kann im Urlaub passieren. S1 has all kinds of aches and pains. S2 offers an explanation for each one of them by choosing the appropriate response with the verbs given.

pain ▶ Schmerzen° im rechten Arm

Du hast bestimmt zu viel Tennis _____.

spielen

S1: Warum habe ich denn solche Schmerzen im rechten Arm?

S2: Du hast bestimmt zu viel Tennis gespielt.

Ein starker Rücken kennt keine Schmerzen

KIESER TRAINING

1. Zahnschmerzen
2. Kopfschmerzen

3. Schmerzen im Knie
4. Hals- und Ohrenschmerzen
5. Bauchschmerzen

sweets 6. Rückenschmerzen

Du hast bestimmt zu viel Bier _____.
Du hast bestimmt zu viel Beachvolleyball _____.
Du bist bestimmt zu lang im Wasser _____.
Du hast bestimmt zu viel Eis _____.
Du hast bestimmt zu viele schwere Koffer _____.
Du hast bestimmt zu viele Süßigkeiten° _____.

| trinken | bleiben | essen (2x) | spielen | schleppen |

6-21 Meine letzte Reise. Respond to your partner's questions using the perfect tense.

Wann hast du deine letzte Reise gemacht?
Wohin bist du gereist? Bist du geflogen oder gefahren?
Wie lang bist du geblieben und was hast du dort gemacht?
Bist du mit Schmerzen nach Hause gekommen? Wenn ja, was für Schmerzen und warum?

Infobox

The German language in North America

Like many immigrant groups, German-speaking **Einwanderer** continued to use their native language long after they arrived in **Nordamerika.** Even today, with about 1.1 million speakers, German ranks sixth among foreign languages spoken at home in the United States, following Spanish, Chinese, French (including Cajun French), Tagalog, and Vietnamese. In Canada, about 622,000 people speak German at home on a regular basis. German-language newspapers were published in the United States as far back as the eighteenth century. In fact, North America's first German-language newspaper, the *Philadelphische Zeitung,* was published by Benjamin Franklin in 1732.

(No. II.)

Philadelphifche ZEITUNG.

SONNABEND, den 24 Jun. 1732.

6-22 „Claudias Mittwoch" oder „Das Studentenleben ist schwer°!" *hard*

Listen as your instructor tells what Claudia did on Wednesday. Then, taking turns
with a partner, retell the story. Begin the sentences as indicated and use the verbs
provided.

1. Am Mittwoch hat Claudia bis neun geschlafen.

2. Dann … (nehmen)

3. Ein bisschen später …
   (frühstücken)

4. Dann … (telefonieren)

5. Dann … (fahren)

6. Von … bis … (haben)

7. Um … (essen)

8. Dann … (spielen)

9. Um … (gehen, lernen)

10. Um … (gehen)

11. Danach … (gehen)

12. Später … (gehen, tanzen)

13. Dann … (fahren)

14. Zu Hause … (gehen, lesen)

15. Um … (schlafen)

Mein erster Job

Susann, Thomas, Stefan Meister, and Stefan Kuhlmann talk about their first jobs. Be sure to complete the **Was ist das auf Englisch?** exercise before watching the video.

6-23 Was ist das auf Englisch?

1. Ich habe in einem Restaurant **gekellnert.**
2. **Während** der Schulzeit habe ich oft dort gearbeitet.
3. Ich habe 10 Mark **pro Stunde** verdient.
4. Das war **damals** noch die D-Mark-Zeit.
5. Ich habe den Job durch eine **Empfehlung** von Freunden bekommen.
6. Die Nachbarn wollten, dass es im Garten kein **Unkraut** gibt.
7. Als Kellner kann man viel **Trinkgeld** verdienen.
8. Ich musste im Supermarkt die **Regale** mit Hundefutter auffüllen.
9. Das war eine Menge Geld für einen **Zwölfjährigen.**

a. recommendation
b. waited tables
c. 12-year-old
d. shelves
e. weeds
f. back then
g. during
h. tips
i. per hour

6-24 Wer sagt das? The following statements fit what Susann or Thomas said about their first job. Identify the person who best matches each statement.

Susann   Thomas

1. Mein erster Job war im Supermarkt.   ☐   ☐
2. Ich habe in einem Restaurant für Touristen gekellnert.   ☐   ☐
3. Ich habe den Job durch Freunde bekommen.   ☐   ☐
4. Ich habe 10 Mark pro Stunde und dazu auch Trinkgeld verdient. ☐   ☐
5. Ich habe zwei- bis dreimal in der Woche dort gearbeitet.   ☐   ☐
6. Ich habe die Regale mit Hunde- und Katzenfutter aufgefüllt.   ☐   ☐
7. Ich habe viel Geld für CDs ausgegeben.   ☐   ☐

6-25 **Was passt?** Complete the sentences with the appropriate information according to what you heard from Stefan Meister and Stefan Kuhlmann.

1. Stefan Meisters erster Job war _____.
   ☐ im Garten
   ☐ im Supermarkt
2. Er war damals _____ Jahre alt.
   ☐ 16
   ☐ 12
3. Er hat _____ gearbeitet.
   ☐ fünf Stunden pro Tag
   ☐ fünf Stunden pro Woche
4. Er hat _____ im Monat verdient.
   ☐ 200 Mark
   ☐ 20 Mark
5. Stefan Kuhlmanns erster Job war _____.
   ☐ im Supermarkt
   ☐ im Restaurant
6. Er war damals _____ Jahre alt.
   ☐ 17
   ☐ 16
7. Stefan Kuhlmann hat in der _____ gearbeitet.
   ☐ Kneipe
   ☐ Getränkeabteilung
8. Stefan gibt sehr viele Beispiele° von _____.   *examples*
   ☐ nichtalkoholischen Getränken
   ☐ alkoholischen Getränken
9. Er musste _____ acht Stunden arbeiten.
   ☐ jeden Tag
   ☐ jede Woche

2 More on the past

The past participle of verbs with separable prefixes

6-11 to 6-12 To form the past participle of separable-prefix verbs, you simply attach the prefix to the past participle of the base verb. Separable-prefix verbs can be regular or irregular.

regular verbs		irregular verbs	
INFINITIVE	PERFECT TENSE	INFINITIVE	PERFECT TENSE
anhören	hat **an**gehört	**fern**sehen	hat **fern**gesehen
abreisen	ist **ab**gereist	**mit**singen	hat **mit**gesungen
anprobieren	hat **an**probiert	**auf**stehen	ist **auf**gestanden

Remember:

- Verbs that express a change of location or condition use **sein** as an auxiliary.
- Past participles of regular verbs ending in **-ieren** do not add **ge-** to the verb stem.

6-26 Was hast du letzte Woche gemacht?

▶

du am Samstag	zu Hause rumgehangen
S1: Was hast du am Samstag gemacht?	**S2:** Ich habe zu Hause rumgehangen.

1. du am Sonntagvormittag

2. ihr am Sonntagnachmittag

3. ihr am Sonntagabend

4. du am Montag früh

bis nachts um eins ferngesehen erst um elf aufgestanden	Bilder von Rembrandt angeschaut mein Zimmer aufgeräumt

5. ihr am Dienstagabend

6. ihr am Mittwochnachmittag

7. du am Donnerstagabend

8. ihr am Freitagabend

alle zusammen ausgegangen bei Karstadt Kleider anprobiert	im Studentenchor mitgesungen ein paar Songs runtergeladen

The past participle of verbs with inseparable prefixes

6-13 to 6-14

Many regular and irregular verbs have inseparable prefixes. The three most common inseparable prefixes are **be–, er–,** and **ver–.** The past participles of verbs with inseparable prefixes do not add **ge–.** Whereas separable prefixes are *stressed* in pronunciation, inseparable prefixes are *unstressed.*

regular verbs		irregular verbs	
INFINITIVE	PERFECT TENSE	INFINITIVE	PERFECT TENSE
besuchen	hat **besucht**	bekommen	hat **bekommen**
erzählen	hat **erzählt**	ertrinken	ist **ertrunken**
verkaufen	hat **verkauft**	verstehen	hat **verstanden**

6-27 Kleine Gespräche. Complete the mini-dialogues with the perfect tense of the verbs given in parentheses.

1. STEFAN: _____ Professor Kluge die Relativitätstheorie gut _____? (erklären°)   *to explain*

   MATTHIAS: Ja, aber ich _____ trotzdem nicht alles _____. (verstehen)

2. MICHAEL: _____ du letzten Sommer gut _____? (verdienen)

   VERONIKA: Ja, meine Chefin _____ mich sehr gut _____. (bezahlen)

3. FRAU FELL: Stimmt es°, dass Bergers ihr Haus _____ _____? (verkaufen)   *is it true*

   FRAU HOLZ: Ja, das stimmt. Sie _____ fast eine halbe Million Euro dafür _____. (bekommen)

4. KATHRIN: Was _____ euer Reiseleiter° von König Ludwig _____? (erzählen)   *tour guide*

   SYLVIA: Dass er im Starnberger See _____ _____. (ertrinken°)   *to drown*

5. HORST: _____ du in Berlin auch deine Kusine Sophia _____? (besuchen)

   INGRID: Ich _____ es _____. Aber sie war nie zu Hause. (versuchen°)   *to try*

The past participle of mixed verbs

6-15 to 6-21

There is a small group of verbs that have characteristics of regular *and* irregular verbs. The past participle of these mixed verbs has a stem change like an irregular verb and ends in **–t** like a regular verb. Be sure to learn these common verbs.

infinitive	perfect tense	
bringen	hat **gebracht**	*to bring*
denken	hat **gedacht**	*to think*
kennen	hat **gekannt**	*to know (be acquainted with)*
nennen	hat **genannt**	*to name, to call*
rennen	ist **gerannt**	*to run*
wissen	hat **gewusst**	*to know (a fact)*

6-28 **Der falsche Monat.** Complete with the appropriate past participles.

gedacht / gekannt / gebracht / genannt / gewusst / gerannt

Tina und ich haben einander schon im Gymnasium gut _____ und ich habe

her / flowers / birthday ihr° oft Blumen° zum Geburtstag° _____.

Heute Morgen habe ich beim Frühstück meinen Kalender angeschaut und gesehen, dass heute der erste Juni ist. „Der erste Juni?!" habe ich _____, „das ist

immediately doch Tinas Geburtstag!" Ich bin sofort° zum nächsten Blumengeschäft _____, und weil Tina dieses Jahr einundzwanzig wird, habe ich einundzwanzig rosarote

carnations / astonished Nelken° gekauft. Tina hat die einundzwanzig Nelken zuerst nur verwundert°

guy angeschaut. Dann hat sie gelacht, mich einen lieben Kerl° _____ und gesagt: „Den Tag hast du richtig _____, aber der Monat ist falsch. Mein Geburtstag ist nicht am ersten Juni, sondern am ersten Juli."

6-29 **Kleine Gespräche.** Complete the mini-dialogues with the perfect tense of the verbs given in parentheses.

1.   HOLGER: Warum _____ Paul denn plötzlich _____? (wegrennen)
         KARL: Weil du ihn einen Esel _____ _____. (nennen)
2.   KATHRIN: Warum _____ du Tina Blumen _____? (bringen)
     GERHARD: Ich _____ _____, sie hat heute Geburtstag. (denken)
3.   HERR KRUG: _____ Sie Frau Merck gut _____? (kennen)
     FRAU FELL: Ja, aber dass sie so plötzlich gestorben ist, _____ ich nicht _____. (wissen)

3 Ranking people and things

📖 **Ordinal numbers**

6-22 to 6-25

Ordinal numbers indicate the position of people and things in a sequence (e.g., the first, the second).

Der **erste** Zug fährt um sieben.	*The **first** train leaves at seven.*
Dann nehme ich lieber den **zweiten.**	*Then I'd rather take the **second** one.*

For the numbers 1 through 19, you form the ordinal numbers by adding **–t–** and an adjective ending to the cardinal number. The few irregular forms are indicated below in boldface.

der **erst**e	der **siebt**e	der dreizehnte
der zweite	der **acht**e	der vierzehnte
der **dritt**e	der neunte	der fünfzehnte
der vierte	der zehnte	der sechzehnte
der fünfte	der elfte	der siebzehnte
der sechste	der zwölfte	der achtzehnte
		der neunzehnte

From the number 20 on, you form the ordinal numbers by adding **–st–** and an adjective ending to the cardinal number.

der zwanzigste	der dreißigste
der einundzwanzigste	etc.
der zweiundzwanzigste	

Dates

To ask for and give the date, you use the following expressions.

Der Wievielte ist heute?   *What's the date today?*
Heute ist der Fünfzehnte.   *Today is the fifteenth.*

Den Wievielten haben wir heute?   *What's the date today?*
Heute haben wir den Fünfzehnten.   *Today is the fifteenth.*

Note that **Wievielt–** and ordinal numbers are capitalized unless they are followed by a noun.

When written as a numeral, an ordinal number is indicated by a period. Note that the day always precedes the month.

WRITTEN: Heute ist der 23. Mai.
SPOKEN: Heute ist der dreiundzwanzigste Mai.

The month is also frequently written as an ordinal number.

WRITTEN: Lisa ist am 23. 5.1994 geboren.
SPOKEN: Lisa ist am dreiundzwanzigsten Fünften
                  neunzehnhundertvierundneunzig geboren.

6-30 Daten. You and your partner take turns asking each other and responding to the following questions.

> **Der Wievielte ist heute?** and **Den Wievielten haben wir heute?** and their respective responses are synonymous.

S1:
1. Den Wievielten haben wir heute?
2. Der Wievielte ist morgen?
3. Der Wievielte ist Sonntag?
4. Den Wievielten hatten wir letzten Sonntag?
5. Wann ist Valentinstag?
6. Wann ist Halloween?
7. Wann ist Neujahr?
8. Wann gibt es ein Feuerwerk in den USA?

S2:
Heute haben wir den _____.
Morgen ist der _____.
Sonntag ist der _____.
Letzten Sonntag hatten wir den _____.
Valentinstag ist am _____ _____.
Halloween ist am _____ _____.
Neujahr ist am _____ _____.
Es gibt ein Feuerwerk am _____ _____.

6-31 Wann hast du Geburtstag? Draw a grid showing the months of the year. Walk around the classroom, tell your classmates when your birthday is, ask for theirs, and record them on the grid.

S1: Ich habe am zehnten Juli Geburtstag. Wann ist dein Geburtstag?
S2: Mein Geburtstag ist am einundzwanzigsten Mai.
     …

4 Indicating direction away from and toward

6-26 to 6-27

Hin and her as directional suffixes and prefixes

You already know that **hin** and **her** are used as suffixes with the question word **wo.**

Wo bist du?	*Where are you?*
Wo**hin** gehst du?	*Where are you going (to)?*
Wo**her** kommst du?	*Where are you coming from?*

Hin indicates motion or direction *away from* the speaker.
Her indicates motion or direction *toward* the speaker.

The question words **wohin** and **woher** are often split. The question then begins with **wo** and ends with **hin** or **her.**

Wo gehst du **hin?** **Wo** kommst du **her?**

Hin and **her** are also used as separable prefixes or as parts of separable prefixes.

RALF:	Arbeitest du immer noch in Bernau?	*Do you still work in Bernau?*
LISA:	Ja, ich **fahre** immer noch jeden Tag **hin** und **her.**	*Yes, I still **drive there** and **back** every day.*
KURT:	Sollen wir **hineingehen?**	*Should we **go in?***
EVA:	Nein, wir warten lieber, bis Frau Borg **herauskommt.**	*No, we'd better wait until Ms. Borg **comes out**.*

6-32 Was sagen diese Leute? Look at the drawings and complete the sentences for each speech bubble with the appropriate prefix.

▶ hinunter / herunter
Passen Sie auf, dass Sie nicht _____fallen!
Passen Sie auf, dass Sie nicht herunterfallen!

1. hinunter / herunter
Passen Sie auf, dass Sie nicht
_____fallen!

2. hinauf / herauf
Keine Angst! Wir ziehen Sie
gleich _____.

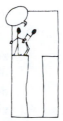

3. hinüber / herüber
Warum springen Sie denn
nicht _____?

4. hinüber / herüber
Warum springen Sie denn
nicht _____?

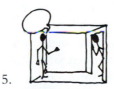

5. hinein / herein
Kommen Sie doch _____,
bitte!

6. hinaus / heraus
Gehen Sie sofort _____!

7. hinein / herein
Sollen wir _____gehen?

8. hinaus / heraus
Kommen Sie sofort _____!

Sprachnotiz *Away from* and *toward* in colloquial German

In colloquial German, prefixes like **hinaus-, herein-, hinauf-,** and **herunter-** are (somewhat illogically) abbreviated to **raus-, rein-, rauf-, runter-.**

Gehen wir **hinein** oder warten wir, bis Dieter **herauskommt**?
Gehen wir **rein** oder warten wir, bis Dieter **rauskommt**?

Zusammenschau

This interview begins with Martin knocking on Ms. Borg's door. In the German-speaking countries, office doors are generally closed.

Hören

Martin sucht einen Ferienjob

Es ist Mitte Juli. Martin hat heute Vormittag seine letzte Klausur geschrieben und sucht jetzt einen Ferienjob. Er geht deshalb zum Studentenwerk und spricht dort mit Frau Borg.

NEUE VOKABELN

zum Beispiel	*for example*
die Arbeitserfahrung	*work experience*
der Maler	*painter*
vielleicht	*perhaps*

6-33 Erstes Verstehen. Who says the following? Mark M for Martin and B for Frau Borg.

_____ Interessiert Sie das?

_____ Ich habe heute Vormittag noch meine letzte Klausur geschrieben.

_____ Ich fahre dann gleich hin.

_____ Vielleicht können Sie mich dann jeden Tag kurz anrufen, ja?

_____ Was für Arbeitserfahrung haben Sie?

_____ Auch keine Tagesjobs?

Studentenwerk Leipzig
Anstalt des öffentlichen Rechts

Amt für Ausbildungsförderung
Studentisches Wohnen
Jobvermittlung
Verwaltung

6-34 Detailverstehen. Listen to the conversation again and answer the following questions.

1. Warum ist Martin nicht früher zum Studentenwerk gegangen?
2. Was für eine Arbeit hat Frau Borg für Donnerstag und Freitag? Was muss Martin alles tun?
3. Wie viel kann er verdienen?
4. Was ist Frau Fischers Adresse? Wann will Martin hinfahren?
5. Warum findet Frau Borg es so gut, dass Martin schon als Maler gearbeitet hat?
6. Was soll Martin von jetzt ab jeden Tag tun? *Er soll …*

Sprachnotiz **The expression *Bitte schön!***

You can use **Bitte schön!** or just **Bitte!** as a response to **Danke, Danke schön,** or **Vielen Dank** to mean *You're welcome!* or *Don't mention it!*

Vielen Dank für Ihre Hilfe!	*Thanks a lot for your help!*
Bitte schön!	*You're welcome!*

Sprechen

6-35 Was für Arbeitserfahrung haben Sie?

You work at the **Studentenwerk** as a job counselor and are interviewing a student looking for a summer job. Find out about her or his work experience. You will find a list of **Jobs und Berufe** in the *Anhang* on page A14. The following questions will help you get started.

Was für Arbeitserfahrung haben Sie? *Ich habe als _____ gearbeitet. Und auch als _____ …*
Was mussten Sie alles tun?
Was haben Sie am liebsten gemacht? Warum?
Was haben Sie nicht so gern gemacht? Warum?
Wo haben Sie am meisten gelernt?
Was sind Ihre Stärken° und Schwächen°?
…

Als Kellner kann man gut verdienen.

strengths / weaknesses

Lesen

Zum besseren Verstehen

6-36 Auswanderer.

1. Do you know any immigrants who have come to this country recently? What sorts of hardships are they encountering?
2. Many immigrants to North America began their lives here doing hard physical labor. What is the occupation of the men in the photo on the following page? Describe how you imagine life was like for them.
3. If you were to emigrate, where would you want to go? Why? What sorts of hardships can you imagine encountering?

6-37 Wo war Christian Köchling am …? Scan the reading text, find out where each diary entry was written, and number the locations accordingly.

S1: Wo war Christian Köchling am achtundzwanzigsten Sechsten neunzehnhundertdreißig?

S2: Da war er …

1. 28. 6. 1930   _____ in Watford.
2. 4. 7. 1930   _____ an Bord der Karlsruhe.
3. 16. 7. 1930   _____ in Bremen.
4. 7. 8. 1930   _____ in Kenora.
5. 15. 12. 1930   _____ im Zug von Montreal nach Toronto.

6-38 Was ist das auf Englisch?

1. Wir lesen nicht das ganze Tagebuch von Christian Köchling, sondern nur ein paar **Auszüge.**
2. Christian ist **über** Hannover nach Bremen gefahren.
3. Die **Bahnfahrt** war sehr schön.
4. In Bremen waren Auswanderer aus ganz Europa, aber die **Mehrzahl** waren Deutsche.
5. Ein **Holzfäller** arbeitet im Wald und fällt dort Bäume.
6. Wenn Christian jeden Tag einen Dollar **spart,** hat er bis zum Frühling hundert Dollar.
7. Er kann dann in Toronto ein kleines Zimmer **mieten.**

a. via
b. lumberjack
c. train trip
d. rent
e. saves
f. excerpts
g. majority

Christian Köchling (ganz rechts) als Holzfäller

Aus Christian Köchlings Tagebuch

Christian Köchling, ein junger deutscher Goldschmied, ist im Sommer 1930 nach Kanada ausgewandert. Die folgenden Auszüge aus Christians Tagebuch zeigen[1], was für ein schweres Leben viele Auswanderer hatten.

Bremen, den 28. 6. 1930

Nach einer langen, schönen Bahnfahrt durch den Harz[2] und über Hannover bin ich endlich in Bremen angekommen. Ganz Europa ist hier vertreten[3], doch die Mehrzahl sind Deutsche.

An Bord der Karlsruhe[4], den 4. 7. 1930

Am 1. 7. sind wir in Bremerhaven aufs Schiff gegangen. Zuerst hatten wir wunderbares Wetter, aber im Englischen Kanal ist es stürmisch geworden. Wir waren alle seekrank.

Im Zug von Montreal nach Toronto, den 16. 7. 1930

Am 11. 7. sind wir in Halifax angekommen und nach 29-stündiger Bahnfahrt waren wir in Montreal. Wir haben da aber nur gehört: „Was wollt ihr denn hier? Wir haben doch selbst keine Arbeit!" Deshalb sind wir heute weitergefahren. Ich habe nur noch 25 Dollar, denn Montreal war sehr teuer: $1,– für eine Übernachtung mit Frühstück!

[1]*show* [2]*the Harz mountains* [3]*represented* [4]*name of the ship*

Watford, den 7. 8. 1930, bei Farmer Robertson

Ich war fast zwei Wochen in Toronto, habe aber keine Arbeit gefunden. Ich habe gehört, dass Farmer im Sommer Hilfe brauchen. Deshalb bin ich hierher gefahren und habe sofort Arbeit gefunden. Aber was für eine Arbeit für einen Goldschmied! Mist laden[5] von morgens bis abends, und nur fürs Essen und ein schlechtes Bett!

Kenora, den 15. 12. 1930

Ich bin jetzt Holzfäller hier im Norden von Kanada. Es ist sehr kalt und die Arbeit ist schwer, aber ich verdiene endlich ein bisschen Geld. Und wenn die anderen abends Karten spielen, wasche ich ihre Socken (10 Cent für ein Paar Socken). Bis zum Frühling möchte ich so viel sparen, dass ich in Toronto eine kleine Werkstatt[6] mieten und endlich wieder als Goldschmied arbeiten kann.

[5]loading manure   [6]workshop

Arbeit mit dem Text

6-39 Anders gesagt. Find the equivalents for the following statements in *Aus Christian Köchlings Tagebuch.*

1. Hier sind Menschen aus ganz Europa, aber die meisten kommen aus Deutschland.
2. Am Anfang war das Wetter sehr schön …
3. Am 11.7. ist unser Schiff in Halifax gelandet …
4. … und haben dann bis Montreal noch 29 Stunden im Zug gesessen.
5. Wir sind doch auch alle arbeitslos!
6. … dass es auf Farmen im Juli und im August Arbeit gibt.
7. … und ich bekomme kein Geld dafür, aber darf hier essen und schlafen.

Schreiben

6-40 Aus meinem Tagebuch. Following the model of Christian Köchling's diary, write diary entries about what you did last week. The expressions below will give you some ideas. Writing diaries is considered a conversational situation, so remember to use the perfect tense. (But use the simple past for **haben, sein,** and the modal verbs.) Be sure to include places and dates and avoid beginning each sentence with **Dann …** by using expressions like **Am Nachmittag …, Später …, Um _____ Uhr …, Am Abend …**

- erst/schon um _____ Uhr aufstehen
- zum Frühstück … essen und … trinken
- mein Zimmer aufräumen
- in den Waschsalon° gehen und meine Wäsche waschen
- für die ganze nächste Woche einkaufen
- mein Fahrrad (mein Auto) putzen (reparieren)
- meine Eltern (meine Freundin, meinen Freund) besuchen (anrufen)
- im Fernsehen ein Eishockeyspiel (Basketballspiel) anschauen
- ins Fitnesscenter gehen
- mit _____ ins Kino (ins Konzert, in die Disco, auf eine Party) gehen …

Schreibtipp: Using the perfect tense to relate events that occurred in the past lends familiarity to a personal narrative.

laundromat

Wort, Sinn und Klang

Wörter unter der Lupe

Predicting gender

All nouns with the suffix **–ung** are feminine. Like most English nouns with the suffix *-ing,* most of these nouns are derived from verbs. Note that the plural forms always end in **–en.**

| warnen | to warn | **die** Warn**ung, –en** | *warning* |
| landen | to land | **die** Land**ung, –en** | *landing* |

However, many English equivalents of German nouns with the suffix **–ung** do not have the suffix *-ing.*

üben	to practice	**die** Üb**ung, –en**	*exercise*
wohnen	to live	**die** Wohn**ung, –en**	*apartment*
erzählen	to tell	**die** Erzähl**ung, –en**	*story*
ausstellen	to exhibit	**die** Ausstell**ung, –en**	*exhibition*

6-41 Was ist das? Form nouns from the following verbs and give their English equivalents.

1. erklären   *to explain*   6. übersetzen   *to translate*
2. bestellen   *to order*   7. bedeuten   *to mean*
3. beschreiben   *to describe*   8. verbessern   *to correct*
4. lösen   *to solve*   9. einladen   *to invite*
5. bezahlen   *to pay*   10. übernachten   *to stay overnight*

Giving language color

Like other languages, German uses the names of parts of the body in many colorful expressions. Below is a sampling.

Er ist nicht auf den Kopf gefallen.   *He's no fool.*
Ich habe die ganze Nacht kein Auge   *I didn't sleep a wink all night.*
  zugetan.
Er hat wieder mal die Nase zu tief   *He drank too much again.*
  ins Glas gesteckt.
Nimm doch den Mund nicht   *Don't always talk so big!*
  immer so voll!
Hals- und Beinbruch!   *Good luck!*
Das hat Hand und Fuß.   *That makes sense.*

Hals- und Beinbruch: This expression stems from Hebrew and entered the German language through Yiddish. After a successful business transaction, Yiddish-speaking Jews wished each other **hazloche und broche** *(success and blessings)*. Speakers of German understood this as **Hals- und Beinbruch.** The English equivalent *Break a leg!* is often used in theatrical circles to wish an actor luck. It entered the English language in the 1920s and some sources surmise that it also has its roots in Yiddish, since many German Jews worked in the theater at this time.

6-42 Was passt zusammen?

1. Warum magst du Günter nicht?
2. Warum lässt du mich denn nicht fahren?
3. Warum bist du denn so müde?
4. Warum bekommt Maria für ihre Referate immer so gute Zensuren?
5. Ich muss jetzt gehen. Wir schreiben gleich eine Klausur.
6. Ist es wahr°, dass Paul die Lösung für dieses Problem gefunden hat?

a. Na, dann Hals- und Beinbruch!
b. Weil alles, was sie schreibt, Hand und Fuß hat.
c. Klar. Er ist doch nicht auf den Kopf gefallen.
d. Weil du wieder mal die Nase zu tief ins Glas gesteckt hast.
e. Weil er den Mund immer so voll nimmt.
f. Weil ich die ganze Nacht kein Auge zugetan habe.

true

Zur Aussprache

 6-35 to 6-36

German *l*

In English the sound represented by the letter *l* varies according to the vowels and consonants surrounding it. (Compare the *l* sound in *leaf* and *feel*.) In German the sound represented by the letter **l** never varies and is very close to the *l* in English *leaf*. Try to maintain the sound quality of the *l* in *leaf* throughout the exercise below.

6-43 Hören Sie gut zu und wiederholen Sie!

Lilo lernt Latein°.
Latein ist manchmal langweilig.
Lilo lernt Philipp kennen.
Philipp hilft° Lilo Latein lernen.
Philipp bleibt lange bei Lilo.
Lilo lernt viel.
Lilo lernt Philipp lieben.

Latin

helps

Nomen

die Arbeitserfahrung –en	work experience
die Bezahlung	pay; wages
der Ferienjob, –s	summer job
das Gymnasium, –ien	(academic) high school
der Maler, -	painter; artist
die Malerin, –nen	
das Studentenwerk	student center

Krankenhaus!
Bitte
langsam fahren

das Krankenhaus, ⏜er	hospital
der Schmerz, –en	ache; pain
die Blume, –n	flower
der Geburtstag, –e	birthday
die Hecke, –n	hedge
der Rasen, -	lawn
der Zaun, ⏜e	fence
die Zimmerpflanze, –n	house plant
das Lied, –er	song
der Koffer, -	suitcase
das Tagebuch, ⏜er	diary
der Waschsalon, –s	laundromat

Verben

bringen, gebracht	to bring
erklären	to explain
füttern	to feed
gießen, gegossen	to water
liegen, gelegen	to lie; to be situated
mähen	to mow
malen	to paint (a picture)
mieten	to rent

Past participles are listed in vocabularies only for irregular and mixed verbs. The auxiliary verb is provided only when it is **sein.**

passieren, ist passiert	to happen
putzen	to clean
recherchieren	to do research
rennen, ist gerannt	to run
rumhängen, rumgehangen	to hang out
schneiden, geschnitten	to cut
sparen	to save
stehen, gestanden	to stand; to say
sterben (stirbt) ist gestorben	to die
streichen, gestrichen	to paint (e.g., a fence, a house)
üben	to practice
übersetzen	to translate
verbessern	to correct
warten	to wait

Recherchieren derives from French, so **ch** is pronounced **sch.**

Stehen means *to say* in expressions like **Im Pass steht …**, etc.

Andere Wörter

hoffentlich	hopefully, I hope (so)
müde	tired
plötzlich	suddenly
sofort	immediately
vielleicht	perhaps
wahr	true
zweimal	twice

Ausdrücke

Danke schön!	Thank you!
Das (Es) stimmt.	That's true (right).
Vielen Dank!	Many thanks!
Bitte schön!	You're welcome!
Hals- und Beinbruch!	Break a leg! Good luck!
in letzter Zeit	recently
die Wäsche waschen	to do the laundry
Den Wievielten haben wir heute?	What's the date today?
Der Wievielte ist heute?	
zum Beispiel (z. B.)	for example (e.g.)

Das Gegenteil

starten, ist gestartet ≠ landen, ist gelandet	to take off ≠ to land
starten ≠ stoppen	to start (something) ≠ to stop (something)

schwer ≠ leicht	difficult; heavy ≠ easy; light	**Leicht zu verstehen**
		das Album, Alben
stark ≠ schwach	strong ≠ weak	an Bord
die Stärke, –n ≠ die Schwäche, –n	strength ≠ weakness	
packen ≠ aus·packen	to pack ≠ to unpack	

warnen
die Warnung, –en

Wörter im Kontext

6-44 Was passt zusammen?

1. Hast du die Zimmerpflanzen
2. Hast du den Zaun
3. Hast du die Hecke
4. Hast du die Wohnung
5. Hast du den Rasen
6. Hast du den Hund
7. Hast du die Vokabeln

a. geübt?
b. gemietet?
c. gemäht?
d. geschnitten?
e. gegossen?
f. gestrichen?
g. gefüttert?

Zaun: You have learned that a German **z** is often a *t* in the related English word: **zehn** – *ten,* **zwölf** – *twelve,* **Zunge** – *tongue.* Applying this principle to **Zaun** gives you *town.* How do you think these two words are related in meaning?

People in the German-speaking countries treasure their privacy, and most yards are enclosed by fences or hedges.

6-45 Warum David so spät nach Hause gekommen ist.

gelegen / erklärt / gewartet / gerannt / hereingerannt / warten / passiert / starten

Gestern Nacht habe ich stundenlang auf David _____. Als ich dann schon im Bett _____ habe, ist er plötzlich zur Tür _____. „Was ist denn _____, David?" habe ich gefragt, und er hat _____, dass er seinen Wagen nicht _____ konnte, dass er viel zu lange auf den ADAC° _____ musste und dass er dann den ganzen langen Weg nach Hause _____ ist.

ADAC: North American equivalents are the *AAA* (U.S.) and the *CAA* (Canada).

Allgemeiner Deutscher Automobil–Club

6-46 Was ist hier identisch? Read the following sets of sentences aloud and decide which two in each set convey approximately the same meaning.

1. Was bedeutet dieses Wort?
   Ich verstehe dieses Wort nicht.
   Hast du dieses Wort verbessert?

2. Opa Ziegler ist im Krankenhaus.
   Opa Ziegler lebt nicht mehr.
   Opa Ziegler ist gestorben.

3. Das stimmt nicht.
   Das kann warten.
   Das ist nicht wahr.

4. Wie ist die Bezahlung?
   Wie viel musst du bezahlen?
   Wie viel verdienst du?

Martin-Luther-Gymnasium: This school was designed by an architect you read about in *Kapitel 3.* Do you remember his name?

6-47 Der ideale Ferienjob.

schwer / sparen / Hoffentlich / Tagebuch / sofort / Bezahlung

Aus Annas _____:

Mein idealer Ferienjob muss _____ am ersten Ferientag beginnen und ich möchte bis zum letzten Ferientag arbeiten. Die _____ muss gut sein, am besten acht oder neun Euro die Stunde, damit ich viel Geld _____ kann und mein nächstes Studienjahr fast ganz selbst bezahlen kann. Die Arbeit soll interessant und nicht zu _____ sein. _____ kann ich bald so einen Job finden.

Das Martin-Luther-Gymnasium in Wittenberg

Feste und Feiertage

Fasnacht in Basel, Schweiz

Kommunikationsziele

Talking about …
- birthdays and holidays
- buying and giving gifts
- personal tastes and opinions

Expressing congratulations, best wishes, and thanks

Strukturen

The dative case:
- indirect object
- personal pronouns
- dative verbs
- dative prepositions
- **da**-compounds
- adjective endings

Word order: Sequence of objects

Kultur

KaDeWe in Berlin

Holidays and celebrations in the German-speaking countries

Parties and presents

Video-Treff: **Mein bestes Geschenk**

Lesen: **Glückwunschanzeigen**

Vorschau

Eine Geburtstagskarte

Beginning in this chapter, all directions for exercises except those in the *Wort, Sinn und Klang* sections are in German.

7-1 **Ein Gutschein zum Geburtstag.** Schauen Sie die Geburtstagskarte an und beantworten Sie die Fragen.

1. Wer hat diese Geburtstagskarte geschrieben?
2. Wer hat Geburtstag?
3. Wann hat Peter diese Karte geschrieben?
4. Wann hilft Peter seiner Mutter?
5. Was tut er alles für sie?

zum GEBURTSTAG eine ÜBERRASCHUNG

GUTSCHEIN
für meine Mutter:

Ich übernehme am __3.4.__

und am __3.5.__ oder am __8.6.__

⊗ Kochen
O Frühstück
O Tisch decken
⊗ Abwasch
O Schuhe putzen
O Großeinkauf
⊗ Betten machen
O Mülleimer leeren
⊗ Fenster putzen
O _____

Datum __2.4.__

Unterschrift __Peter__

Das Geburtstagsgeschenk

NICOLE: Du, Maria, was soll ich denn meinem kleinen Bruder zum Geburtstag schenken?

MARIA: Schenk ihm doch eine Baseballkappe. Oder eine Armbanduhr – eine coole Swatch! Oder eine DVD. Was schaut er denn gern an? Oder kauf ihm ein Computerspiel. Ja! Einem Dreizehnjährigen schenkt man heutzutage sowieso Computerspiele!

NICOLE: Das hat David alles schon und außerdem ist mir ein gutes Computerspiel viel zu teuer.

MARIA: Dann fahren wir doch zum KaDeWe! Wenn wir sehen, was es alles gibt, fällt uns bestimmt etwas ein.

NICOLE: Gute Idee, Maria!

Infobox

KaDeWe

KaDeWe stands for **Kaufhaus des Westens.** Situated in former West Berlin, this huge department store is the second largest in continental Europe, employing about 2,000 people and drawing about 40,000 visitors a day. Each of its eight floors focuses on a different kind of merchandise, such as **Luxus & Beauty** on the first floor and **Herren-Fashion** on the second. Its legendary gourmet food department, the so-called **Schlemmer-Etage** on the 7th floor, features food delicacies from around the world (**schlemmen** = *to feast* or *indulge*).

When it was repaired and reopened after World War II, **KaDeWe** represented West Germany's remarkable economic recovery, known as the **Wirtschaftswunder** *(economic miracle).* While Germany was divided, the store's wide variety of luxury consumer items also provided a conspicuous display of the affluence of West Berlin compared to the poorer East.

Beim KaDeWe

Beim KaDeWe hat gerade der Winterschlussverkauf begonnen und alle Preise sind stark reduziert. Die beiden Freundinnen gehen deshalb noch schnell in die Damenabteilung, bevor sie ein Geschenk für David suchen. Maria kauft dort eine schicke, warme Winterjacke und Nicole gibt fast ihr ganzes Geld für einen eleganten, schwarzen Pulli aus. Dann schaut sie ein bisschen beschämt auf die paar Euro in ihrer Geldtasche und sagt: „Wie soll ich denn damit meinem Bruder ein Geburtstagsgeschenk kaufen?" Aber Maria hat eine gute Idee: „Kauf ihm doch eine lustige Geburtstagskarte, und zusammen mit dieser Karte schickst du ihm einen Schuldschein mit den Worten: ‚Lieber David, ich schulde dir ein Geburtstagsgeschenk. Du bekommst es, sobald ich wieder Geld habe.'"

statements

7-2 Richtig oder falsch? Sie hören die beiden Texte und nach jedem Text ein paar Aussagen°. Sind diese Aussagen **richtig** oder **falsch?**

DAS GEBURTSTAGSGESCHENK			BEIM KADEWE	
RICHTIG	FALSCH		RICHTIG	FALSCH
1. _____	_____	1.	_____	_____
2. _____	_____	2.	_____	_____
3. _____	_____	3.	_____	_____
4. _____	_____	4.	_____	_____

7-3 Was kann man dir zum Geburtstag schenken?

S1: Ich trinke viel Kaffee.   **S2:** Dann kann man dir eine Kaffeemaschine schenken.

1. Ich fahre immer mit dem Rad zur Uni.
2. Mein Zimmer muss wie ein Garten aussehen°.   *look, appear*
3. Ich möchte nächsten Sommer durch den Schwarzwald wandern.
4. Ich komme morgens oft zu spät zur Vorlesung.
5. Ich kann nicht kochen.
6. Die UV-Strahlen machen meine Augen kaputt.
7. Ich möchte mein Deutsch verbessern.
8. Ich möchte fit werden.
9. Ich höre gern Musik.

der Heimtrainer die Zimmerpflanze die Kaffeemaschine das Wörterbuch DUDEN der Rucksack der Fahrradhelm das Kochbuch der iPod die Geschenkkarte der Wecker die Sonnenbrille

7-4 Geburtstagsgeschenke. Sagen Sie, was Sie Ihren Mitstudenten° zum   *fellow students*
Geburtstag schenken wollen und warum.

S: Ich schenke David eine Lederjacke, weil er gern schicke Kleidung trägt.
S: Ich schenke Julia eine iTunes Geschenkkarte°, weil sie immer Musik hört.   *gift card*

Alles Gute zum
Geburtstag

Kultur / Feste und Feiertage

The German-speaking countries enjoy a wider array of public holidays than the United States or Canada. Many of these holidays have their roots in Christian traditions, although an increasingly secular society celebrates them without giving much thought to their religious origin.

The Christmas Season

As in North America, **Weihnachten** is still the biggest and most important holiday, and preparation begins four weeks in advance. Beginning on December 1, many children count down the 24

Weihnachtsmarkt in Bremen

days to Christmas Eve **(der Heilige Abend)** with the help of an **Adventskalender.** Each day they open a door or window on the calendar and find motifs related to **Weihnachten** or a small gift. On the eve of **Nikolaustag** (December 6), children put their shoes outside their bedroom door for **Sankt Nikolaus** (the patron saint of children) to fill with candy, chocolate, fruit, and nuts. As in other countries, **Weihnachten** is associated with a Christmas tree **(der Weihnachtsbaum)** and gift-giving **(die Bescherung)**. In the German-speaking countries the **Weihnachtsbaum** is frequently not put up until December 24, **am Heiligen Abend,** which is also when the **Bescherung** takes place. On December 25 **(der erste Weihnachtsfeiertag),** families gather for a traditional dinner that often centers around a Christmas goose **(die Weihnachtsgans).**

The root of the word **Bescherung** is related to English *share.*

On December 26 **(der zweite Weihnachtsfeiertag),** it is customary to visit relatives and friends.

In the New Year

New Year's Eve **(Silvester)** is an evening of parties and revelry culminating at midnight with spectacular displays of fireworks even in smaller towns.

In the time between New Year's and Lent, people in the German-speaking countries celebrate **Karneval** (as it is called in the **Rheinland**) or **Fastnacht / Fasching** (as it is called in Southern Germany, Austria, and Switzerland). **Karneval** celebrations include huge parades with marching bands, elaborate costumes, and huge floats. These floats often depict in satirical fashion scenes critical of politicians and unpopular government policies.

Easter Holidays

Spring brings Easter **(Ostern)**. Businesses are closed on Good Friday **(Karfreitag)** and on **Ostermontag.** On **Ostersonntag** children receive colored eggs and chocolate goodies from the **Osterhase**. The week before and after **Ostern** are school holidays. Pentecost or Whitsun **(Pfingsten)** is celebrated on the seventh Sunday and Monday after **Ostern** and brings with it another week of vacation from school.

Schöne Osterhasen

Secular Holidays

Secular holidays in the German-speaking countries include the **Tag der Arbeit** or **Maifeiertag** on May 1 as well as national holidays for each country. On October 3, Germany celebrates the **Tag der deutschen Einheit** to commemorate the reunification in 1990 of the **Bundesrepublik Deutschland (BRD)** and the former **Deutsche Demokratische Republik (DDR).** Austria has set aside October 26 **(Tag der Fahne)** to celebrate the day in 1955 when it became a neutral state. On August 1, Switzerland celebrates the beginning of the Swiss confederation **(Confœderatio Helvetica),** which took place in 1291.

Regional and Local Festivals

Aside from celebrating the bigger holidays in their own traditional ways, individual regions also hold festivals to honor or celebrate their own local history and culture. Some have become world famous, like Munich's annual **Oktoberfest** in southern Germany, and **Kieler Woche,** the world's largest sailing festival, in northern Germany. As in North America, locally grown products are celebrated in yearly seasonal festivals, such as **Weinfeste**.

7-5 Was sind Ihre Feste und Feiertage?

1. Feiern Sie Weihnachten? Wenn ja, wann ist die Bescherung? Wenn nein, wie heißt Ihr wichtigster° Feiertag und wie feiern Sie ihn?   *most important*
2. Wann ist der Tag der Arbeit in Ihrem Land?
3. Wie heißt Ihr Nationalfeiertag? Wann ist er und wie feiern Sie ihn?
4. Was für regionale Feste gibt es dort, wo Sie wohnen? Was und wie feiert man da?

7-6 Feste an der Mosel. Beantworten Sie die Fragen über die Mosel Weinfeste und Veranstaltungen.

1. Welche Spezialität hat diese Region?
2. Wann sind die meisten Feste hier? Warum, glauben Sie, ist das so?
3. Welches Fest hat nichts mit der regionalen Spezialität zu tun?
4. Zu welchem Fest möchten Sie gern gehen?

Locate the **Mosel** river on the map inside the front cover of this book. What other countries does this river flow through?

Mosel Weinfeste & Veranstaltungen

10.06. - 12.06.	Senheim-Senhals	Pfingstweinfest in Senheim
19.08. - 21.08.	Bernkastel-Kues	Wein- und Straßenfest in der Weingartenstraße
05.08. - 07.08.	Ürzig	HARLEY & WEIN Internationales Harley-Davidson-Treffen am Moselufer mit großer Riesling-Weinprobe
02.09. - 04.09.	Reil	Straßenweinfest in der Dorfstraße
23.09. - 25.09.	Burg	Schlurpstour – Weinschlürfertage
30.09. - 02.10.	Ediger-Eller	Wein und mehr in den Kellern von Eller
30.09. - 12.11.	Klotten	Weinerntefest
29.10.	Kröv	Herbstweinfest zum Saisonabschluss
31.10.	Zell	Halloween Rockparty: Die Nacht des Grauens

Nomen

der Feiertag, -e	holiday
das Fest, -e	celebration; festival
Ostern	Easter
Silvester	New Year's Eve
Weihnachten	Christmas
der Weihnachtsbaum, ̈-e	Christmas tree
das Geschenk, -e	present
die Geschenkkarte, -n	gift card
die Überraschung, -en	surprise
die Abteilung, -en	department
die Damenabteilung	women's department
die Herrenabteilung	men's department
der Schlussverkauf, ̈-e	clearance sale
die Aussage, -n	statement
die Idee, -n	idea
die Armbanduhr, -en	wristwatch
der Fahrradhelm, -e	bicycle helmet
die Geldtasche, -n	wallet
der Gutschein, -e	voucher
der Heimtrainer, -	exercise bike
der Schuldschein, -e	IOU
der Wecker, -	alarm clock

Verben

aussehen (sieht aus), ausgesehen (wie)	to look (like), appear
feiern	to celebrate
kaputt machen	to ruin; to break
schauen (auf)	to look (at)
schenken	to give (a gift)
schulden	to owe

Andere Wörter

außerdem	besides; in addition
gerade	just, just now
heutzutage	nowadays
lustig	funny, humorous; happy
wichtig	important

Ausdrücke

den Abwasch machen	to do the dishes
den Mülleimer leeren	to empty the garbage can
den Tisch decken	to set the table
stark reduziert	sharply reduced
zum Geburtstag	for one's birthday
Herzliche Glückwünsche zum Geburtstag!	Happy Birthday!
zu Weihnachten	for Christmas
Frohe Weihnachten!	Merry Christmas!
Ein gutes neues Jahr! (Einen) guten Rutsch!	} Happy New Year!

> **Einen guten Rutsch:** Although most speakers of German understand **Rutsch** as coming from **rutschen** (to slide), it probably stems from the Hebrew word **rosh** (head, beginning) as in Rosh Hashanah, the Jewish New Year. It is thought that the word came into German via Yiddish.

Das Gegenteil

leer ≠ voll	empty ≠ full

Leicht zu verstehen

kaputt	der Text, -e
das Computerspiel -e	das Wort, ̈-er
das Kochbuch, ̈-er	das Wörterbuch, ̈-er

Brauchst du ein Kochbuch …

… oder ein Wörterbuch?

Wörter im Kontext

7-7 Was ist die richtige Reihenfolge°?

sequence

_____ das Essen kochen   _____ den Abwasch machen   _____ einkaufen

_____ essen   _____ den Tisch decken   _____ Freunde einladen

7-8 Was passt zusammen?

1. Wenn es dunkel ist,   a. braucht man keinen Wecker.
2. Wenn man von selbst aufwacht,   b. braucht man keinen Fahrradhelm.
3. Wenn man fit ist,   c. braucht man kein Kochbuch.
4. Wenn man immer nur Auto fährt,   d. braucht man keine Sonnenbrille.
5. Wenn man immer in der Mensa isst,   e. braucht man keinen MP3-Spieler.
6. Wenn man nicht gern Musik hört,   f. braucht man keinen Heimtrainer.

7-9 Was ich tue, wenn …

1. Wenn meine Geldtasche leer ist,   a. muss ich ihn leeren.
2. Wenn ich nicht weiß, wie spät es ist, b. schenke ich ihr immer ein gutes
3. Wenn der Mülleimer voll ist,   Buch.
4. Wenn ich Geburtstag habe,   c. feiere ich mit meiner Familie.
5. Wenn meine Freundin Geburtstag   d. bezahle ich mit meiner Kreditkarte.
   hat,   e. schaue ich auf meine Armbanduhr.
6. Wenn ich eine Bluse kaufen   f. gehe ich in die Damenabteilung.
   möchte,

7-10 Was brauche ich da? Beginnen Sie alle Antworten mit *Da brauche ich …*

1. Ich möchte fit werden.   a. ein Wörterbuch
2. Ich muss das Frühstück machen.   b. ein Geschenk
3. Ich will ein Comicbuch schreiben.   c. eine lustige Idee
4. Ich weiß nicht, wie man Wiener   d. eine Kaffeemaschine
   Schnitzel macht.   e. einen Heimtrainer
5. Meine beste Freundin hat   f. ein Kochbuch
   Geburtstag.
6. Ich weiß nicht, wie man auf
   Deutsch *Happy Birthday!* sagt.

7-11 Bettina Zieglers Geburtstag.

gerade / Überraschung / lustig / feiert / außerdem / Fest / geschenkt

Bettina Ziegler _____ heute ihren dreißigsten Geburtstag und hat zu
diesem _____ die ganze Familie und alle ihre Freunde eingeladen.
Sie haben _____ ein paar Flaschen Champagner getrunken und sind
deshalb alle sehr _____. Als _____ haben Bettinas Freunde ihr eine Reise
nach Kalifornien _____ und von ihrer Familie hat sie _____ dreihundert
Euro bekommen.

Kommunikation und Formen

1 Indicating the person *to whom* or *for whom* something is done

7-1 to 7-5

The dative case: the indirect object

In *Kapitel 3* you learned that many verbs take direct objects and that the direct object is signaled by the accusative case.

Klaus möchte **einen iPod.**	*Klaus would like **an iPod.***

Some verbs take not only a direct object, but an *indirect object* as well. The indirect object indicates *to whom* or *for whom* something is done and is therefore almost always a *person*. In German the indirect object is signaled by the *dative case*.

Brigitte kauft **ihrem Mann** einen iPod.	*Brigitte buys **her husband** an iPod.*
Sie schenkt **ihrem Mann** den iPod zum Geburtstag.	*She gives **her husband** the iPod for his birthday.*

It is important to remember that German signals the indirect object with the dative case, never with the preposition **zu** *(to)*.

	masculine		neuter		feminine		plural	
NOMINATIVE	der mein	Vater	das mein	Kind	die meine	Mutter	die meine	Kinder
ACCUSATIVE	den meinen	Vater	das mein	Kind	die meine	Mutter	die meine	Kinder
DATIVE	**dem** **meinem**	Vater	**dem** **meinem**	Kind	**der** **meiner**	Mutter	**den** **meinen**	Kinder**n**

- The other possessive adjectives (**dein, sein, ihr, unser, euer, ihr, Ihr**) and **ein** and **kein** take the same endings as **mein.**
- In the dative plural, all nouns take the ending **–n** unless the plural form already ends in **–n** (**die Freundinnen, den Freundinnen**) or if it ends in **–s** (**die Chefs, den Chefs**).

7-12 Ein bisschen Grammatik. Finden Sie die indirekten Objekte!

▶ Brigitte Ziegler schenkt <u>ihrem Mann</u> einen iPod.

1. Stephanie feiert dieses Jahr Weihnachten nicht zu Hause in Chicago, sondern in München, und sie schickt deshalb ihrer Familie ein großes Paket. Sie schickt ihrem Großvater ein gutes Buch, ihrem Vater ein schönes Bierglas und ihrer Mutter einen Kalender mit Bildern von München.

2. Und was schenkt Stephanie ihren Freunden in München? Sie schenkt ihrem Freund Peter ein Sweatshirt, ihrer Mitbewohnerin Claudia ein Paar Ohrringe und Claudias Freund Martin ein tolles Buch.

 7-13 **Geschenke.** Die Information für **S2** ist im *Anhang* auf Seite A7.

S2: Was schenkt Florian seinen Eltern?

S1: Florian schenkt seinen Eltern Weingläser.

	DAVID	FLORIAN
seinen Eltern		Weingläser
seiner Schwester		eine coole Sonnenbrille
seinem Bruder	ein warmes Sweatshirt	
seiner Freundin	einen schwarzen Fahrradhelm	

 7-14 **Was schenkst du …?**

S1: Was schenkst du deinen Eltern zu Weihnachten?

S2: Ich schenke meinen Eltern ____ zu Weihnachten.

Was schenkst du	deiner Schwester	zum Geburtstag
	deinem Freund	zu Chanukka
	deiner Freundin	zum Valentinstag
	unserem Deutschlehrer	zu Halloween
	unserer Deutschlehrerin	…
	…	

The interrogative pronoun in the dative case

7-6 to 7-7

The dative form of the interrogative pronoun wer has the same ending as the dative form of the masculine definite article.

	interrogative pronoun	masculine definite article
NOMINATIVE	wer	der
ACCUSATIVE	wen	den
DATIVE	**wem**	**dem**

Wer ist der Mann dort?
Der Briefträger.

Who is that man there?
The letter carrier.

Wen hat Ihr Hund gebissen?
Den Briefträger.

Whom did your dog bite?
The letter carrier.

Wem schenken Sie den Wein?
Dem Briefträger.

***To whom** are you giving the wine?*
***To the** letter carrier.*

things

7-15 **Wem schenkst du das alles?** **S2** hat schon alle Weihnachtsgeschenke gekauft. **S1** fragt, wem **S2** diese Sachen° schenkt.

▶ es mein___ Mutter

S1: Wem schenkst du das Parfüm? **S2:** Ich schenke es meiner Mutter.

1. 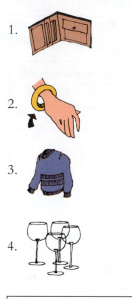 sie mein___ Vater

2. es mein___ Schwester

3. ihn mein___ Bruder

4. sie mein___ Großeltern

| das Armband | die Geldtasche | die Weingläser | der Pullover |

Personal pronouns in the dative case

7-8 to 7-9

In English, personal pronouns have only one object form. This one form can function as a direct object and as an indirect object. In German, personal pronouns have two object forms. You are familiar with the accusative form, which is used for the direct object. The dative form is used for the indirect object.

Kannst du **mir** eine Tasse Kaffee machen? | *Can you make **me** a cup of coffee?*

nominative	accusative	dative
ich	mich	mir
du	dich	dir
er	ihn	ihm
es	es	ihm
sie	sie	ihr
wir	uns	uns
ihr	euch	euch
sie	sie	ihnen
Sie	Sie	Ihnen

7-16 **Geschenke.** Die Information für **S2** ist im *Anhang* auf Seite A7.

S2: Weißt du, was Sophia Onkel Thomas und Tante Barbara schenkt?

S1: Ich glaube, sie schenkt ihnen eine Safari in Südafrika.

	DANIEL	SOPHIA
Onkel Thomas und Tante Barbara		ihnen eine Safari in Südafrika
Silvia	ihr ein Paar Socken	
Frank		ihm ein Rolex Armbanduhr mit Diamanten

7-17 **Was soll ich diesen Leuten schenken?**

▶ mein__ Großmutter

S1: Was soll ich meiner Großmutter schenken?

S2: Schenk ihr doch ein Paar warme Hausschuhe.

1. mein__ Vater

2. mein__ besten Freundin

3. mein__ Mutter

4. unser__ neuen Nachbarn (pl)

einen Kugelschreiber	ein paar Flaschen Wein
ein Paar Handschuhe	einen Hockeyschläger

Ein Paar means *a pair,* i.e., *two* of something, like shoes or gloves. **Ein paar** means *a couple (of)* in the sense of *a few.*

7-18 **Vorschläge.** Sagen Sie einander, was Ihre Freunde und Verwandten gern tun, und machen Sie einander dann Vorschläge° für passende° Geschenke.

suggestions / appropriate

S1: Meine Freundin spielt gern Tennis.

S2: Dann schenk ihr doch einen Tennisschläger.

Mein Freund (Mein Bruder, Meine Schwester, Meine Eltern, Meine Kusine, Mein Mitbewohner …)

- hört gern Rapmusik (Country, Jazz, …)
- geht gern einkaufen
- spielt gern Computerspiele (Wii, …)
- liest gern Comics
- trinkt gern Bier (Kaffee, Likör, …)

- trägt gern Schmuck°
- reist gern
- liebt Süßigkeiten°
- spielt gern Golf (Baseball, Frisbee, …)
- hat keine Hobbys oder Interessen

jewelry

candy

Infobox

Parties and presents

In the German-speaking countries, the person celebrating a birthday is expected to organize and host the party (**die Fete** or **die Party**). The invited guests of course bring presents. It's considered unlucky to celebrate a birthday—or even wish someone a happy birthday—before the actual date. A popular approach is ***hinein*feiern** (or ***rein*feiern**): You invite your guests to a party that begins late on the evening *before* your birthday; the partying starts before midnight, but friends are careful not to give birthday presents or wishes until the clock strikes 12.

If you are invited for a meal (**zum Essen**) or **zu Kaffee und Kuchen** in a German-speaking country, it is customary to bring a small gift (**ein Mitbringsel**) for your hostess or host. The most common gifts are chocolates, a bottle of wine, or flowers. A small bouquet should contain an odd number of flowers because this is considered more pleasing to the eye.

Word order: sequence of objects

7-10 to 7-11

The dative object (the indirect object) precedes the accusative object (the direct object) *unless the accusative object is a pronoun.*

	DATIVE	ACCUSATIVE	
Maria schenkt	**ihrem Vater**	**ein Buch**	zum Vatertag.
Sie schenkt	**ihm**	**ein Kochbuch.**	
	ACCUSATIVE	DATIVE	
Sie kann	**es**	**ihrem Vater**	nicht persönlich geben.
Sie muss	**es**	**ihm**	schicken.

Note: Pronoun objects always come before noun objects, regardless of case.

Lerntipp: Remember: The dative object comes first unless the accusative object is a pronoun.

supply
order

7-19 Kleine Gespräche. Ergänzen° Sie die Akkusativobjekte und Dativobjekte in der richtigen Reihenfolge°.

1. KIND: Kaufst du _____ _____, Vati?   mir, das Fahrrad
   VATER: Ja, ich kaufe _____ _____.   dir, es
2. MUTTER: Kaufen wir _____ _____?   unserem Sohn, die Kamera
   VATER: Ja, ich glaube, wir kaufen   ihm, sie

   _____ _____.

shown
probably

3. TOM: Hast du _____ _____ gezeigt°?   deinem Vater, deine Zensuren
   ROBERT: Nein, ich zeige _____ wohl°   meiner Mutter, sie

   nur _____.

lend

4. BERND: Kannst du _____ _____ leihen°, Eva?   mir, dein Chemiebuch
   EVA: Wenn du _____ _____ morgen   mir, es

   früh zurückgibst.

5. ERGÜN: Hast du _____ _____ geschenkt?   deinen Eltern, den Toaster
   ANNE: Nein, ich habe _____ _____   meinen Großeltern, ihn

   geschenkt.

Dative verbs

7-12 to 7-13

There are a few German verbs that take only a dative object.

antworten	Warum antwortest du **mir** nicht?	*Why don't you answer* **me?**
danken	Ich danke **dir** für deine Hilfe.	*I thank* **you** *for your help.*
gehören	Gehört dieser Wagen **dir**?	*Does this car belong* **to you?**
gratulieren	Ich gratuliere **Ihnen** zu Ihrem Erfolg!	*I congratulate* **you** *on your success!*
helfen	Kannst du **mir** bitte helfen?	*Can you help* **me** *please?*

> Note that **gratulieren** is also used to wish someone a happy birthday: **Ich möchte dir zum Geburtstag gratulieren.**

7-20 **Kleine Gespräche.** Ergänzen Sie passende Dativverben.

1. ALEXANDER: Wem _____ denn dieser tolle Wagen?
   SEBASTIAN: Meiner Freundin.
2. MARIA: Warum schreibst du denn deinem Bruder nie?
   NICOLE: Weil er mir auch nie _____.
3. STEFAN: Warum kommst du nicht zu unserer Party?
   ROBERT: Weil ich meinem Vater _____ muss.
4. HELGA: Warum rufst du Claudia an?
   SABINE: Sie hat heute Geburtstag und ich möchte ihr _____.
5. FRAU BERG: Aber Frau Kuhn! Warum bringen Sie mir denn Blumen?
   FRAU KUHN: Weil ich Ihnen für Ihre Hilfe _____ möchte.

7-21 **Kleine Gespräche.** Ergänzen Sie **mir, mich, dir** oder **dich.**

1. LUKAS: Warum antwortest du _____ nicht?
   HORST: Du hast _____ doch gar nichts gefragt.
2. BEATE: Heute früh hat Markus _____ besucht. Er hat _____ zum Geburtstag gratuliert und hat _____ diese wunderschönen roten Rosen gebracht. Glaubst du, dass er _____ liebt?
   SOPHIA: Wenn er _____ rote Rosen bringt, liebt er _____ bestimmt.
3. PAUL: Gehört _____ dieses tolle Fahrrad?
   SARA: Ja, meine Eltern haben es _____ gekauft.
4. STEFAN: Ich danke _____, dass du _____ bei meinem Referat so viel geholfen hast.
   MARIA: Wenn du _____ jetzt zum Essen einlädst, helfe ich _____ gern wieder.

The dative case with adjectives

7-14 to 7-16

The dative case is often used with adjectives to express a personal opinion, taste, or conviction.

| Das ist **mir** sehr wichtig. | *That's very important* **to me.** |
| Rockmusik ist **meiner Oma** zu laut. | *Rock music is too loud* **for my grandma.** |

7-22 **Warum?** Ergänzen Sie passende Personalpronomen im Dativ.

▶ Sie ist _____ zu laut.

S1: Warum mögen deine Großeltern
   keine Rockmusik?

S2: Sie ist ihnen zu laut.

1. Warum kaufen Müllers das Haus nicht?   Es ist _____ zu klein.
2. Warum liest du den Roman nicht fertig?   Er ist _____ zu langweilig.
3. Warum trinkt Ingrid ihren Wein nicht?   Er ist _____ zu sauer.
4. Warum geht Robert nicht schwimmen?   Es ist _____ zu kalt.
5. Warum mag Maria diesen Film nicht?   Er ist _____ zu sentimental.
6. Warum nehmt ihr die Wohnung nicht?   Sie ist _____ zu dunkel.
7. Warum kauft Peter den Wagen nicht?   Er ist _____ zu teuer.

different **7-23** **Die Geschmäcker sind verschieden°.** Schauen Sie Ihre
Mitstudenten an und sagen Sie, was für ein Kleidungsstück Sie ihnen zum
Geburtstag schenken wollen, und warum.

S1: Ich schenke Anna ein Sweatshirt. Ihr Sweatshirt
   ist mir ein bisschen zu verrückt.

S2: Ich schenke Justin …

> You can also begin the sentence with the indirect object for emphasis: **Justin schenke ich …**

ein bisschen zu verrückt   nicht hip genug
viel zu konservativ   ein bisschen zu altmodisch
nicht sportlich genug   viel zu trendy

The dative case in idiomatic expressions

7-14 to 7-16

The dative case also appears in the following common expressions:

Wie geht es **Ihnen**?   *How are you?*
(Es) tut **mir** leid.   *I'm sorry.*
Das ist **mir** egal.   *I don't care.*
Wie gefällt **dir** mein Mantel? *How do you like my coat?*
Diese Jacke steht **dir.**   *This jacket looks good on you.*

7-24 Was passt zusammen?

1. Mir geht es heute gar nicht gut.
2. Die Jacke steht dir. Warum nimmst
   du sie denn nicht?
3. Wie gefällt dir meine neue Jacke?
4. Weiß Jonas, dass du einen neuen
   Freund hast?
5. Ist Lisa immer noch so krank?

a. Nein, es geht ihr schon wieder viel
   besser.
b. Ja, aber ich glaube, es ist ihm egal.
c. Weil sie mir zu teuer ist.
d. Sie steht dir sehr gut.
e. Das tut mir aber leid.

7-25 Was gefällt Ihnen an Ihren Mitstudenten?

S1: An° Lana gefällt mir, dass sie so freundlich ist.   *about*
S2: An Thomas gefällt mir, dass er …

freundlich		witzig°	natürlich°	optimistisch
	lustig	praktisch	höflich°	sportlich
ordentlich		spontan	pünktlich	…

witty
natural
polite

Video-Treff

Mein bestes Geschenk

Stefan Kuhlmann, Stefan Meister, Ursula und André
erzählen von ihrem besten Geschenk. Machen Sie
die erste Aufgabe, **Was ist das auf Englisch?,**
bevor Sie das Video anschauen.

7-26 Was ist das auf Englisch?

1. Das ist das Cover der Comic-**Ausgabe** von *Der kleine Hobbit*.
2. Das beste Geschenk ist ein **selbstgemachtes** T-Shirt.
3. Ich habe dieses Geschenk von meiner **damaligen** Freundin bekommen.
4. Termiten haben diesen Baum **ausgehöhlt.**
5. Ich habe dann selber **daran** gearbeitet.
6. Ich habe Inlineskates. Meine Freundin hat auch **welche.**
7. Sie sagte, dass ihre Familie diese Instrumente selber **herstellt.**
8. Madame Sec hat von **sich** erzählt.

a. herself
b. some
c. on it
d. at that time
e. hollowed out
f. produces
g. edition
h. homemade

7-27 Richtig oder falsch? Lesen Sie die Aussagen über Stefan Kuhlmann
und Stefan Meister und ihre besten Geschenke. Sind diese Aussagen richtig oder
falsch? Wenn eine Aussage falsch ist, korrigieren Sie sie!

	RICHTIG	FALSCH
1. Stefan Kuhlmann hat das T-Shirt von einer alten Freundin bekommen.	☐	☐
2. Das Bild auf dem T-Shirt ist von der Comic-Ausgabe von „Der kleine Hobbit".	☐	☐
3. Stefan findet es nicht gut, dass das T-Shirt selbstgemacht ist.	☐	☐
4. Auf dem T-Shirt steht auch „Für Stefan".	☐	☐
5. Stefan Meister hat das Didgeridoo von einer australischen Freundin bekommen.	☐	☐
6. Das Instrument kommt aus einem teuren Souvenirgeschäft.	☐	☐
7. Das war ein besonderes Geschenk für ihn, weil es typisch australisch ist.	☐	☐

7-28 Was passt? Ergänzen Sie die Aussagen über Ursula and André.

1. Die Inlineskates hat Ursula _____ bekommen.

   ☐ zu Weihnachten   ☐ zum Geburtstag

2. Sie hat die Inlineskates _____ bekommen.

   ☐ vor zwei Wochen   ☐ vor zwei Tagen

3. Das war ein Geschenk von _____.

   ☐ ihrer Mutter   ☐ ihrer besten Freundin

4. Ursulas _____ hat auch Inlineskates und jetzt können sie zusammen fahren.

   ☐ Freundin Anke   ☐ Mutter Anke

5. André hat _____ zwei Geschenke bekommen: eine traditionelle afrikanische Trommel und ein Etui.

   ☐ vor fünf Jahren   ☐ vor vier Jahren

6. Das Etui ist für _____.

   ☐ Kleinigkeiten   ☐ die Djembé

7. André hat Madame Sec _____ kennen gelernt.

   ☐ im Senegal   ☐ in seiner französischen Klasse

8. André findet die Djembé ein gutes Geschenk, _____.

   ☐ obwohl er selbst nicht spielen kann   ☐ weil er selbst gut spielen kann

---

Sprachnotiz   Word order: time/manner/place

You have already learned that expressions of time precede expressions of place.

Claudia und Stephanie fahren **morgen nach Hamburg.**

When an expression of manner is added (i.e., when you want to say *how* something is done) the order is *time / **manner** / place.*

Claudia und Stephanie fahren **morgen *mit dem Zug* nach Hamburg.**

Der Hamburger Hauptbahnhof

2 Expressing origin, destination, time, manner, and place

The dative prepositions

7-17 to 7-20
In *Kapitel 5* you learned the prepositions that are followed by an object in the accusative case: **durch, für, gegen, ohne, um**. The prepositions that are always followed by an object in the *dative case* are **aus, außer, bei, mit, nach, seit, von, zu**.

aus	*out of*	Nimm den Weißwein **aus dem Kühlschrank°**!	*refrigerator*
	from	Der Wein ist **aus dem Rheintal.**	
außer	*except for*	**Außer meinem Bruder** sind alle hier.	
bei	*for*	Mein Bruder arbeitet **bei der Bahn** und konnte nicht kommen.	
	at, at the home of	Diesmal feiern wir Muttis Geburtstag **bei meiner Schwester** in Potsdam.	
	near	Potsdam ist **bei Berlin.**	
mit	*with*	Der Kuchen **mit den 50 Kerzen°** ist von Tante Anna.	*candles*
	by	Ich bin **mit dem Zug** nach Potsdam gekommen.	
nach	*after*	**Nach dem Geburtstagsessen** haben wir einen Spaziergang gemacht.	
	to	Ich fahre morgen **nach Bonn** zurück.	
seit	*since*	Ich lebe **seit dem letzten Sommer** in Bonn.	
	for	Meine Schwester lebt **seit zehn Jahren** in Potsdam.	
von	*from*	**Von meiner Schwester** hat Mutti ein schönes Bild bekommen.	
	of	Eine Freundin **von Mutti** hat ihr ein goldenes Armband geschickt.	
	about	Mutti hat uns oft **von dieser Freundin** erzählt.	
zu	*to*	Wir kommen alle sehr gern **zu meiner Schwester.**	
	for	**Zu ihrem 50. Geburtstag** hat Mutti von uns allen eine Reise nach Hawaii bekommen.	
	with	**Zu dem leckeren Geburtstagskuchen** haben wir Muttis Lieblingstee getrunken.	

stellen Fragen:
ask questions

7-29 **Was weißt du von diesen Leuten?** S1 stellt Fragen° über Sabine und Osman, und S2 möchte Information über Wendy und Jan. Die Information für S2 ist im *Anhang* auf Seite A7.

S2: Woher ist Wendy?   S1: Aus den USA.
    Wo arbeitet sie?   …

	SABINE	WENDY	OSMAN	JAN
Woher ist _____?		Aus den USA.		Aus den Niederlanden.
Wo arbeitet sie/er?		Bei einer Computerfirma.		Bei einem Gärtner.
Seit wann arbeitet sie/er dort?		Seit drei Jahren.		Seit einem Dreivierteljahr.
Wie kommt sie/er zur Arbeit?		Mit ihrem neuen BMW.		Mit der S-Bahn.
Wohin geht sie/er im nächsten Urlaub?		Zu ihren Eltern nach New York.		Zu seiner Freundin nach Amsterdam.
Woher weißt du das alles?		Von ihrem Freund.		Von seinem Chef.

7-30 **Erzähl mir etwas von deinen Eltern!** Stellen Sie einander die ersten fünf Fragen aus **7–29**.

S1: Woher ist deine   S2: Aus …
    Mutter/dein Vater?
    Wo arbeitet sie/er?   Bei …
    …

7-31 **Ein Brief aus Hamburg.** Ergänzen Sie **aus, außer, bei, mit** oder **nach.**

Hamburg, den 24. Dezember 2011
Liebe Eltern und lieber Opa,
herzliche Grüße _____ der Hansestadt Hamburg. Claudias Eltern
wollten, dass ich an Weihnachten _____ Hamburg komme, damit ich
mal sehe, wie man _____ ihnen Weihnachten feiert. Die ganze Familie
ist hier _____ Claudias Schwester Maria. Sie studiert in Berkeley und

spends

verbringt° Weihnachten _____ Freunden in San Francisco. Heute Abend
gibt es _____ Bergers wie _____ den meisten deutschen Familien nur

simple

ein ganz einfaches° Essen, und _____ dem Essen ist dann gleich die
Bescherung. Ich schenke Claudias Eltern einen Kalender _____ vielen
schönen Farbfotos von Amerika. Ich habe euch _____ München ein
Paket _____ ein paar Geschenken geschickt. Für Opa sind übrigens
auch ein paar Münchener Zeitungen im Paket.

Euch allen einen guten Rutsch ins neue Jahr!

Stephanie

7-32 **Meine Winterferien.** Stellen Sie einander die folgenden Fragen.

S1: Bei wem verbringst du die Winterferien?

S1: Was machst du da?

S2: Bei wem …

S2: Bei …

S2: Ich …

S3: Bei …

Contractions

7-21 to 7-24

The following contractions of dative prepositions and definite articles are commonly used.

bei + dem	=	**beim**	Brigitte ist heute Vormittag **beim** Zahnarzt.
von + dem	=	**vom**	Dieses Brot ist **vom** Öko-Bäcker.
zu + dem	=	**zum**	Fährt dieser Bus **zum** Bahnhof?
zu + der	=	**zur**	Seit wann fährst du denn mit dem Fahrrad **zur** Uni?

7-33 **Wo? Woher? Wohin?** Ergänzen Sie die Antworten mit **beim, vom, zum** oder **zur.**

► Wo ist Brigitte?

S1: Wo ist Brigitte?   **S2:** Beim Friseur.

1. Wohin gehst du?

3. Wohin fährst du?

5. Wohin rennst du?

7. Wohin gehst du?

2. Woher kommst du?

4. Wo ist Silke?

6. Woher kommt ihr?

8. Wo sind Bernd und Sabine?

Lerntipp: Nouns ending in **-ei**, like **die Bäckerei** and **Fleischerei** are always feminine and always stressed on the last syllable.

Zahnarzt (m)	Supermarkt (m)	Arzt (m)	Bäckerei (f)
Fleischerei (f)	Bus (m)	Baden (n)	Mittagessen (n)

Da-compounds

7-25 to 7-26

In *Kapitel 5* you were introduced to **da–**compounds with the accusative prepositions **für** and **gegen: dafür** *(for it)* and **dagegen** *(against it).* The **da–**compounds with dative prepositions are **daraus, dabei, damit, danach, davon,** and **dazu.** Note that an **r** is added to **da** if the preposition begins with a vowel: **daraus. Da–**compounds are only used to refer to things or ideas, not to people.

Was weißt du **von deutschen Festen und Feiertagen?**	*What do you know **about German celebrations and holidays?***
Jetzt weiß ich sehr viel **davon.**	*Now I know a lot **about them.***

7-34 *Da*-**Formen.** Ergänzen Sie **daraus, dabei, damit, danach,** oder **davon.**

1. Warst du bei Sabines Geburtstagsfeier?

   Nein, dieses Jahr war ich nicht _____.

2. Was soll ich aus den Äpfeln machen?

   Mach doch einen guten Nachtisch _____.

3. Was habt ihr nach dem Abendessen gemacht?

   Wir sind gleich _____ heimgegangen.

4. Hat Anna ein neues Fahrrad?

   Ja, sie fährt jetzt jeden Tag _____ zur Uni.

5. Maria hatte gestern Geburtstag.

   Warum hast du mir denn nichts _____ gesagt?

6. Kannst du mir helfen? Ich muss für meine Chemie-Prüfung lernen.

   Chemie? Ich weiß leider selber nicht viel _____.

Nach versus *zu*

7-27 to 7-28

When **nach** and **zu** indicate a point of destination, they both mean *to.* Which one you use depends on the type of destination.

nach		zu	
to a city	nach Leipzig	*to a building*	zum Bahnhof
to a state	nach Sachsen	*to an institution*	zur Uni
to a country	nach Luxemburg	*to a place of business*	zum Supermarkt
to a continent	nach Europa	*to someone's residence*	zu Zieglers

7-35 **Kleine Gespräche.** Ergänzen Sie **nach, zu, zum** oder **zur.**

1. HERR BERG: Wie weit ist es von hier _____ Ihrem Ferienhaus bei Salzburg?

   FRAU KOCH: Von hier _____ Salzburg sind es etwa 500 Kilometer und von dort _____ Ferienhaus fährt man eine halbe Stunde.

2. FRAU ROTH: Was soll ich denn tun, Frau Klein? Ich habe solche Zahnschmerzen und unser Zahnarzt ist über Weihnachten _____ Spanien geflogen.

   FRAU KLEIN: Gehen Sie doch _____ unserem Zahnarzt.

3. FRAU WOLF: Warum fliegt Herr Meyer denn _____ Detroit?

   FRAU KUNZ: Ich glaube, er geht dort _____ Internationalen Auto-Show (f).

4. CLAUDIA: Fährst du in den Semesterferien wieder _____ Köln _____ deinem Onkel?

   STEPHANIE: Nein, diesmal fahre ich mit Peter _____ Berlin.

Aus versus *von*

7-27 to 7-28

When **aus** and **von** indicate a point of origin, they both mean *from*.

aus		von	
from a city	aus Leipzig	from a building	vom Bahnhof
from a state	aus Sachsen	from an institution	von der Uni
from a country	aus Luxemburg	from a person	von meinem Freund
from a continent	aus Europa	from a point of departure	von Berlin nach Potsdam

7-36 Kleine Gespräche. Ergänzen Sie **aus** oder **von**.

1. SEBASTIAN: Weißt du vielleicht, wie lang der Bus _____ New York nach San Francisco braucht?

   PETER: Frag doch Stephanie. Sie ist _____ den USA und weiß es bestimmt.

2. CLAUDIA: Hier ist ein Brief _____ Chicago, Stephanie.

   STEPHANIE: _____ meinen Eltern?

   CLAUDIA: Nein, ich glaube, er ist _____ deiner Uni.

3. ANNETTE: _____ wem hast du diese Armbanduhr?

   CHRISTINE: _____ meinem Freund. Er hat sie mir _____ der Schweiz mitgebracht.

7-37 Von wem hast du das? Schauen Sie, welche von Ihren Mitstudenten etwas besonders Schönes haben, und fragen Sie, von wem sie es haben.

S1: Von wem hast du den interessanten Ring, Andrea?

S2: Von … / Ich habe ihn selbst gekauft.

S2: Von wem hast du …?

S3: …

das schöne Armband
das tolle Notebook
die tollen Ohrringe
die coole Jeansjacke
…

7-38 Eine Platzreservierung. Herr und Frau Baumeister haben für eine Reise mit dem ICE zwei Sitzplätze reserviert. Beantworten Sie mit Ihrer Partnerin/Ihrem Partner die Fragen zu dieser Reservierung.

1. Wohin reisen Baumeisters?
2. Von welchem Bahnhof fahren sie ab?
3. Wann fährt der ICE von Berlin ab und wann kommt er in Stuttgart an? (Datum und Uhrzeit)
4. Welche Zugnummer hat der ICE?
5. In welchem Wagen sind die reservierten Plätze? Finden Sie die Wagennummer!
6. Welche beiden Sitzplätze sind für Baumeisters reserviert?
7. Wie viel haben Baumeisters für diese Reservierung bezahlt?
8. Wann haben Baumeisters diese Reservierung beim Reisebüro Südstern gekauft? (Datum und Uhrzeit)
9. Was dürfen Baumeisters in diesem Wagen nicht tun?

DB **CIV 80**			Reservierung InterCityExpress					2 Sitzplätze
🗓	🕐	VON		NACH		🗓	🕐	Ki/Ci
29.03	11:39	BERLIN ZOO		->STUTTGRT HBF		29.03	17:08	2
ZUG 797	ICE	Wagen	4	Sitzplätze	51	53		
Großraumwagen Nichtraucher				1 Fenster, 1 Mitte				
							PREIS	EUR ****5,20
754585860 75458586-75			800990116216 DB 99 BERLIN 536813 004 RB SUEDSTERN 04.03.11			14:42	RECHNUNG	

 ## The preposition *seit*

7-29 to 7-31

When **seit** refers to a point in time, its English equivalent is usually *since;* when it refers to a *period of time,* its English equivalent is usually *for.* Note that German uses the present tense in such contexts, whereas English uses the perfect tense.

Herr Braun lebt **seit** Anfang Mai in Kiel.

Mara lernt **seit** einem Jahr Deutsch.

*Mr. Braun has been living in Kiel **since** the beginning of May.*

*Mara has been learning German **for** a year.*

7-39 **Seit wann?**

▶ haben / du dieses tolle Fahrrad   mein__ Geburtstag (m)

S1: Seit wann hast du dieses tolle   **S2:** Seit meinem Geburtstag.
      Fahrrad?

1. sein / Sandra und Holger so gute Freunde   d__ Silvesterparty (f) bei Sylvia
2. trinken / Stephanie so gern deutsches Bier   ihr__ Jahr (n) in München
3. haben / du das neue Handy   vierzehn Tage__ (pl)
4. spielen / du Saxofon   meine__ Schulzeit (f)
5. sein / Karin und Kurt verheiratet   eine__ Woche (f)

7-40 **Seit wann hast du oder machst du das?** Stellen Sie einander die
folgenden Fragen und berichten° Sie dann, was Sie herausgefunden haben.   *report*

- Hast du einen Job? Wo? Seit wann?
- Hast du einen Hund/eine Katze? Seit wann? Wie heißt er/sie?
- Hast du ein Handy? Was für ein Handy? Seit wann hast du es?
- Hast du einen Wagen? Was für einen? Seit wann?
- Spielst du ein Instrument? Was für ein Instrument? Seit wann?
- Bist du verlobt°/verheiratet? Seit wann?   *engaged*

7-41 **Immer negativ.** Ergänzen Sie in den Fragen **aus, außer, bei, mit,
nach, seit, von** oder **zu**. Ergänzen Sie in den Antworten auch die Dativendungen.

S1:

1. Fährt dieser Zug _____ Bremen?
2. Ist Stephanie _____ Kanada?
3. _____ wem hast du diese schönen
   Ohrringe? _____ deinem Freund?
4. Wo verbringst du diesmal die
   Feiertage? _____ deinen Eltern?
5. _____ wem gehst du heute Abend ins
   Kino? _____ deinem Bruder?
6. _____ wann hast du dieses schöne
   Fahrrad? _____ deinem Geburtstag?
7. _____ welchem Zahnarzt gehst du?
   _____ Dr. Haag?
8. Sind _____ David alle hier?

S2:

Nein, er fährt _____ Hamburg.
Nein, sie ist _____ d___ USA.
Nein, _____ mein___ Eltern.

Nein, _____ mein___ Großeltern.

Nein, _____ ein paar Freunde___.

Nein, schon _____ ein___ Jahr.

Nein, ich gehe _____ Dr. Meyer.

Nein, alle _____ David und Florian!

3 Describing people, places, and things

Dative endings of preceded adjectives

Adjectives that are preceded by a der-word or an ein-word in the dative case always take the ending -en.

Wer ist der Typ mit dem goldenen Ohrring und den langen Haaren?

Who's the guy with the gold earring and the long hair?

	masculine	neuter	feminine	plural
DATIVE	dem einem jungen Mann	dem einem kleinen Kind	der einer jungen Frau	den meinen kleinen Kindern

 7-42 Wer ist auf diesem Familienbild? Ergänzen Sie die passenden Endungen.

▶ die Frau mit dem grün____ Kleid und den braun____ Haaren

Das ist …

S1: Wer ist die Frau mit dem grünen Kleid und den braunen Haaren?

S2: Das ist meine Mutter.

1. der Mann mit der blau____ Jacke und der rot____ Krawatte
2. der Junge mit den braun____ Haaren und dem rot____ Hemd
3. die Frau mit der weiß____ Hose und der rosarot____ Bluse
4. der Mann mit der schwarz____ Brille und dem blau_____ Pullover
5. das Mädchen mit dem rosarot____ Kleid und den weiß____ Schuhen
6. die Frau mit dem grau____ Hut und dem gelb____ Kleid

7-43 **Wer ist das?** Folgen Sie dem Beispiel. Stellen Sie ähnliche° Fragen über *similar*
Ihre Mitstudenten. Die anderen raten°, wer das ist. *guess*

S: Wer ist die Person mit der kleinen Brille und dem schwarzen T-Shirt?

Dative endings of unpreceded adjectives

7-32 to 7-34

You will remember that adjectives not preceded by a **der**-word or an **ein**-word
show the gender, number, and case of the noun by taking the appropriate **der**-
word ending. This also holds true for the dative case.

Zu französisch**em** Camembert trinkt   *With French camembert Uncle Alfred*
   Onkel Alfred immer kanadischen   *   always drinks Canadian ice wine.*
   Eiswein.

	masculine	neuter	feminine	plural
DATIVE	gut**em** Kaffee	gut**em** Bier	gut**er** Salami	gut**en** Äpfeln

7-44 **Ein Gourmet.** Onkel Alfred isst gern international.

1. Zu französisch__ Weißbrot (n) isst er nur holländischen Käse.
2. Zu italienisch__ Lasagne (f) trinkt er nur griechischen Wein.
3. Zu polnisch__ Wurst (f) isst er nur französischen Senf°.   *mustard*
4. Zu englisch__ Cheddar (m) isst er nur neuseeländische Äpfel.
5. Zu deutsch__ Schwarzbrot (n) isst er nur irische Butter.
6. Zu italienisch__ Eis (n) trinkt er nur türkischen Kaffee.
7. Zu belgisch__ Schokolade (f) isst er nur israelische Mandarinen.
8. Zu amerikanisch__ Kartoffelchips (pl) trinkt er nur deutsches Bier.

Zusammenschau

Hören

Blumen zum Geburtstag

Stephanie hat morgen Geburtstag. Peter möchte ihr Blumen schenken und ist
deshalb im Blumengeschäft.

NEUE VOKABELN
Sie wünschen?   *May I help you?*
drei Euro das Stück   *three euros apiece*
ein·schlagen   *to wrap*

7-45 Erstes Verstehen. Hören Sie, was Peter und die Verkäuferin miteinander sprechen. Haken Sie die richtigen Antworten ab.

1. Welche Farben hören Sie?

   _____ gelb   _____ rosarot

   _____ blau   _____ rot

   _____ weiß   _____ violett

2. Welche Zahlen hören Sie?

   _____ 2   _____ 3

   _____ 15   _____ 5

   _____ 4   _____ 10

   _____ 20   _____ 30

3. Welche Imperativformen hören Sie?

   _____ Kommen Sie!   _____ Geben Sie …!

   _____ Zeigen Sie …!   _____ Schicken Sie …!

   _____ Schenken Sie …!   _____ Warten Sie!

 7-46 Detailverstehen. Hören Sie Peters Gespräch mit der Verkäuferin noch einmal und schreiben Sie Antworten zu den folgenden Fragen.

1. Warum möchte Peter seiner Freundin Blumen schenken?
2. Warum sagt die Verkäuferin, Peter soll seiner Freundin Rosen schenken?
3. Was für Rosen will Peter seiner Freundin schenken?
4. Was kosten die roten Rosen?
5. Warum schenkt Peter seiner Freundin nicht zehn oder fünfzehn Rosen?
6. Wie viele rote Rosen kauft er?
7. Warum soll die Verkäuferin Peters Freundin die Rosen nicht schicken?

Sprechen

7-47 Im Blumengeschäft. Ein Student möchte seiner Freundin zum Geburtstag Blumen schenken. Die Verkäuferin versucht, ihm zu helfen.

VARIATIONEN

seiner Freundin zum Valentinstag

seiner Mutter zum Muttertag

seiner Kusine zum Uni-Abschluss

seinen Freunden zur neuen Wohnung

seinen Freunden zum neuen Baby

…

VERKÄUFERIN	STUDENT
• Guten Tag! Sie wünschen? / Guten Tag! Darf ich Ihnen helfen?	• Guten Tag! Ich möchte meiner Freundin zum Geburtstag Blumen schenken.
• Dann schenken·Sie ihr doch …	• Was für … haben Sie? / Haben Sie vielleicht …?
• Ja, heute haben wir … / Nein, heute haben wir leider keine … Wir haben aber …	• Die sehen aber nicht sehr frisch aus.
• Wir haben auch …	• Oh, die gefallen mir! Was kosten sie denn?
• Sie kosten … Euro das Stück.	• Das ist mir zu teuer.
• Die … sind preisgünstiger und auch sehr schön.	• Gut, dann geben Sie mir mal …
• Darf ich sie Ihrer Freundin schicken?	• Ja, bitte. / Nein, ich gebe sie ihr lieber selbst.
	• Können Sie die … bitte noch schön einschlagen?
• Ja, natürlich.	• Danke schön. / Vielen Dank.

> **Die sehen…, die gefallen mir:** In colloquial German definite articles are often used as pronouns. Here **die** could translate as *they* or *those*.

Lesen

Zum besseren Verstehen

7-48 Glückwunschanzeigen. Für die großen, wichtigen Momente im Leben ist man oft so glücklich°, dass man der ganzen Welt davon erzählen will. Dafür gibt es Glückwunschanzeigen. Früher waren sie in der Zeitung und jetzt sehr oft im Internet – bunt und auch graphisch sehr kreativ.   *happy*

1. Wo haben Sie solche Anzeigen schon gesehen oder sogar selber gemacht? Was war der Anlass° für diese Anzeigen?   *occasion, reason*
2. Was denken Sie: Was macht eine Glückwunschanzeige besonders gut?

7-49 Was ist das auf Englisch?

1. Wie viele **Gäste** kommen zu deiner Party?
2. Du hast gewonnen? Gratuliere! Ich bin so **stolz auf** dich!
3. Wenn man keine Freunde oder Familie hat, kann das Leben **einsam** sein.
4. Eine **Prüfung** ist ein Test.
5. Mein Mann und ich **freuen uns über** unser neues Haus!
6. Ohne **Führerschein** darf man nicht Auto fahren.
7. Hilfst du uns bei den **Vorbereitungen** auf das Herbstfest?
8. Mario fährt so verrückt, dass er **einen Schutzengel** braucht!

a. exam
b. guardian angel
c. preparations
d. guests
e. driver's license
f. lonely
g. proud of
h. are happy about

Liebe Marie,

Für deine Erstkommunion
am Sonntag, den 9. Mai
wünschen dir Mama und Papa alles Liebe.
Wir sind stolz auf dich, bleib so wie du bist!
Vielen Dank sagen wir auch allen,
die unserer Marie bei der
Vorbereitung zur Kommunion
geholfen haben.

Familie Meyer

Hallo Welt, ich bin da!
Oskar

27. November 2011

Wir freuen uns über die Geburt unseres
Sohnes und Bruders. Die überglückliche Familie
Anna und Walter Leuschner mit Martin

Wir danken dem gesamten Team des Diakonie-Klinikums in Dissen.

FÜHRERSCHEIN BUNDESREPUBLIK DEUTSCHLAND

D

Lieber Karl!

Endich ist der Tag gekommen,
auf den Du schon so lange gewartet hast.
Herzlichen Glückwunsch zur bestandenen
Führerscheinprüfung. Wir wünschen Dir alles Gute
und einen großen Schutzengel für Deine Autofahrten!

Wir lieben Dich!

Opa und Oma

Häppi Börsdee tu juhuhu!

Liebe Julia, 18 Jahre sind nun vergangen,
seit Dein Leben angefangen.
Sport und Spaß, das ist dein Motto,
besser als ein Gewinn im Lotto!
Wir gratulieren Dir zu Deinem Feste,
auch heute sind wir wieder Deine Gäste.
Seit dem 6. Lebensjahr feiern wir dieses
Fest gemeinsam,
deshalb sind wir auch nie einsam.
Deine Clique (Susi, Mel und Jen)

Arbeit mit dem Text

7-50 **Was feiern alle?** Ergänzen Sie die Informationen unten.

	Autor der Anzeige	Anlass zum Feiern°	*Wem* gratuliert man hier?
reason for celebrating	*Anna, Walter und Martin Leuschner*	*die Geburt ihres Sohnes*	—

7-51 Geschenkideen. Was kann man diesen Leuten schenken? Denken Sie an den Anlass und alle Informationen über die Leute in jeder Anzeige. Wählen Sie ein Geschenk von der Liste aus°, oder sagen Sie Ihre Ideen!

wählen … aus
select

S: Die Leuschners feiern die Geburt ihres Babys. Deshalb schenke ich ihnen ein schönes kleines Stofftier.

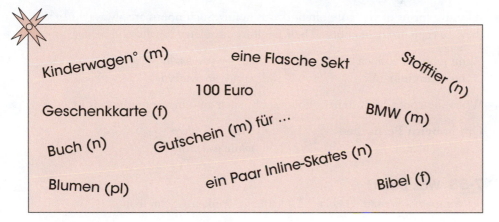

Kinderwagen° (m) eine Flasche Sekt Stofftier (n)

100 Euro

Geschenkkarte (f) BMW (m)

Buch (n) Gutschein (m) für …

Blumen (pl) ein Paar Inline-Skates (n) Bibel (f)

baby carriage

Schreiben

7-52 Die besten Glückwünsche. Schreiben Sie eine Glückwunschanzeige oder eine Karte für eine Freundin, einen Freund oder für jemand aus Ihrer Familie. Nehmen Sie als Modell die Anzeigen, die Sie gelesen haben, und die Glückwünsche im **Sprachnotiz.** Weitere Beispiele finden Sie im Internet, wenn Sie **„Glückwunschanzeigen"** oder **„Glückwunschkarten"** googeln.

Sprachnotiz | Expressing congratulations, best wishes, or toasts with *zu*

When congratulating someone or wishing someone the best for a special occasion, you can use **zu** or its contractions **zum** or **zur** to mention the occasion.

Alles Gute **zum Uni-Abschluss°!**
Alles Liebe **zum Valentinstag!**
Ich gratuliere dir **zum neuen Job!**
Zu deiner Bar-Mizwa wünsche ich dir alles Gute.
Die besten Glückwünsche **zur goldenen Hochzeit°!**

To express *Cheers!* or *To your health!* when raising or clinking glasses, you can say **Zum Wohl!**

graduation

wedding anniversary

Wort, Sinn und Klang

Wörter unter der Lupe

Predicting gender

Infinitive forms of verbs are often used as nouns. Such nouns are always *neuter* and they are capitalized, of course. Their English equivalents usually end in *-ing*.

Wann gibst du endlich
   das Rauchen auf?

When are you finally going
   *to give up **smoking?***

When the contraction **beim** is followed by such a noun, it often means *while*.

Opa ist **beim Fernsehen**
eingeschlafen.

Grandpa fell asleep
   while watching TV.

7-53 Was passt?

Schwimmen / Wissen / Leben / Einkaufen / Trinken / Schreiben

1. _____ ist sehr gesund.
2. Gestern haben wir beim _____ fast zweihundert Euro ausgegeben.
3. Fang doch endlich mit deinem Referat an! Vielleicht fällt dir beim _____ etwas ein.
4. Das viele _____ hat diesen Mann krank gemacht.
5. Helga ist gestern Abend ohne Günters _____ mit Holger ausgegangen.
6. Dieses faule° _____ gefällt mir.

lazy

Translate these two signs into English, using what you just learned here.

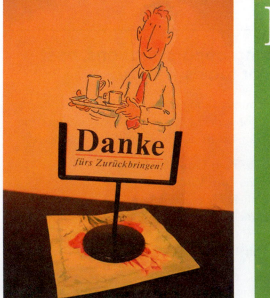

Giving language color

In *Kapitel 6* you saw how the names of body parts can be used metaphorically. As the expressions here show, the names of common food items can also be used in this way. The expressions with an asterisk are quite informal and should only be used with family or friends.

Es ist alles in Butter.★	*Everything's going smoothly.*
Das ist mir wurst.★	*I couldn't care less.*
Er will immer eine Extrawurst.★	*He always wants special treatment.*
Das ist doch alles Käse.★	*That's all bunk!*
Der Apfel fällt nicht weit vom Stamm.	*Like father, like son.*
Er gleicht seinem Bruder wie ein Ei dem anderen.	*He and his brother are as alike as two peas in a pod.*

7-54 Was passt zusammen?

1. Wie sieht Claudias Schwester aus?
2. Hast du immer noch Probleme mit deinem Freund?
3. Deine neue Jacke gefällt mir gar nicht.
4. Günter sagt, dass du ihn liebst.
5. Alle anderen kommen zu Fuß, aber Lisa sollen wir mit dem Auto abholen.
6. Ralf ist wie sein Vater. Er fängt alles an und macht nichts fertig.

a. Das ist doch alles Käse, was er sagt.
b. Das ist mir wurst.
c. Sie will doch immer eine Extrawurst.
d. Der Apfel fällt nicht weit vom Stamm.
e. Sie gleicht ihr wie ein Ei dem anderen.
f. Nein, jetzt ist alles wieder in Butter.

Zur Aussprache

7-39 to 7-40

German *r*

Good pronunciation of the German **r** will go a long way toward making you sound like a native speaker. Don't let the tip of the tongue curl upward and backward as it does when pronouncing an English *r*, but keep it down behind the lower teeth. When followed by a vowel, the German **r** is much like the sound of **ch** in **auch**. When it is not followed by a vowel, the German **r** takes on a vowel-like quality.

7-55 Hören Sie gut zu und wiederholen Sie!

1. **R**ita und **R**ichard sitzen imme**r** im Zimme**r**.
   Rita und **R**ichard sehen ge**r**n fe**r**n.

2. **R**obert und **R**osi spielen Ka**r**ten im Ga**r**ten.
   Robert und **R**osi t**r**inken Bie**r** fü**r** vie**r**.

3. Geste**r**n wa**r** **R**alf hie**r** und do**r**t,
   mo**r**gen fäh**r**t e**r** wiede**r** fo**r**t.

4. Horst ist hie**r**,
   Horst will Wu**r**st,
   Horst will Bie**r**
   fü**r** seinen Du**r**st.

Bier und Wurst für Horst.

Nomen

die Fete, –n	party
der Gast, ¨e	guest
die Kerze, –n	candle
das Mitbringsel, –	small gift (for a host)
die Süßigkeiten (pl)	sweets; candy
der Handschuh, –e	glove
der Hausschuh, –e	slipper
der Hut, ¨e	hat
die Krawatte, –n	tie
der Schmuck	jewelry
der Hockeyschläger, –	hockey stick
der Tennisschläger, –	tennis racquet
das Stofftier, –e	stuffed animal
das Tier, –e	animal
der Briefträger, – die Briefträgerin, –nen }	letter carrier
der Kugelschreiber, –	ballpoint pen
das Paket, –e	package, parcel
der Zahnarzt, ¨e die Zahnärztin, –nen }	dentist
Zahnschmerzen (pl)	toothache
die Anzeige, –n	announcement; ad
der Führerschein, –e	driver's license
die Hilfe	help
die Sache, –n	thing
der Typ, –en	guy

Verben

antworten (+ dat)	to answer
danken (+ dat)	to thank
gehören (+ dat)	to belong to
gratulieren (+ dat)	to congratulate
helfen (hilft), geholfen (+ dat)	to help
berichten	to report
leihen, geliehen	to lend
wünschen	to wish
verbringen, verbracht	to spend (time)
zeigen	to show

Andere Wörter

einfach	simple; simply
einmal	once
noch einmal, noch mal	once more; (over) again
etwa	approximately
verschieden	different
witzig	witty; funny
wohl	probably; perhaps

Ausdrücke

eine Frage stellen	to ask a question

zum Geburtstag
   gratulieren
	to wish a Happy
	   Birthday

Zum Wohl! Prost! }	Cheers! To your health!
Das ist mir egal.	I don't care.
Diese Jacke gefällt mir.	I like this jacket.
Diese Jacke steht dir.	This jacket looks good on you.
Es tut mir leid.	I'm sorry.
Mir fällt nichts ein.	I can't think of anything.
Sie wünschen?	May I help you?

Das Gegenteil

faul ≠ fleißig	lazy ≠ hard–working
glücklich ≠ unglücklich	happy ≠ unhappy
höflich ≠ unhöflich	polite ≠ impolite

Leicht zu verstehen

die Bäckerei, –en
die Kartoffelchips
der Muttertag, –e
der Valentinstag, –e
das Parfüm, –s
die Party, –s
der Ring, –e
die Rose, –n
der Supermarkt, ¨e
der Titel, –

Wörter im Kontext

7-56 Was schenkst du diesen Leuten? Antworten Sie mit „Ich schenke ihr/ihm …"

1. Maria hat immer kalte Hände.
2. Stefan hat jetzt seinen Führerschein.
3. Mein Opa schreibt viele Briefe.
4. Paul trägt immer nur Anzüge.
5. Laura hat nur sehr wenig Schmuck.
6. Kurt macht viel Sport.
7. Meine Nichte Anna wird morgen ein Jahr alt.
8. Meine Oma hat immer kalte Füße.

a. eine schicke Krawatte
b. ein Paar warme Hausschuhe
c. ein goldenes Armband
d. ein süßes Stofftier
e. einen guten Kuli
f. ein Paar warme Handschuhe
g. meinen sehr alten Wagen
h. einen Tennisschläger und einen Hockeyschläger

> **Kugelschreiber:** This word is often shortened to **Kuli.**

> **Tennisschläger, Hockeyschläger:** These nouns are derived from the verb **schlagen** *to hit.*

7-57 Was ich für Leah alles tue.

1. Wenn Leah Geburtstag hat,
2. Wenn Leah zu viel zu tun hat,
3. Wenn Leah etwas für mich getan hat,
4. Wenn Leah Zahnschmerzen hat,
5. Wenn Leah bankrott ist,
6. Wenn ich bei Leah eingeladen bin,

a. schicke ich sie zum Zahnarzt.
b. leihe ich ihr Geld.
c. kaufe ich als Mitbringsel immer Blumen.
d. helfe ich ihr.
e. danke ich ihr.
f. gratuliere ich ihr.

> **–schmerzen** can be added to other body parts to indicate pain felt there: **Kopfschmerzen, Bauchschmerzen, Rückenschmerzen.**

7-58 Mit anderen Worten. Welche Sätze° bedeuten etwa dasselbe°?

sentences / the same thing

1. Diese Jacke gefällt mir.
2. Diese Jacke steht mir.
3. Sie wünschen?
4. Diese Jacke gehört mir nicht.
5. Sind Sie immer so faul?
6. Um wie viel Uhr beginnt eure Fete?

a. Wann ist eure Party?
b. Das ist nicht meine Jacke.
c. Ich finde diese Jacke schön.
d. Tun Sie immer so wenig?
e. In dieser Jacke sehe ich gut aus.
f. Was kann ich für Sie tun?

Sprachnotiz **Derselbe, dasselbe, dieselbe**

The English equivalent of **derselbe, dasselbe,** and **dieselbe** is *the same.*
Note that both parts of this German compound word take case endings.

Sag doch nicht immer **dasselbe!**
Hat Karin immer noch **denselben** Freund?

*Don't always say **the same** thing!*
*Does Karin still have **the same** boyfriend?*

KAPITEL 8

Wohnen

Ein Studentenheim in Nürnberg

Kommunikationsziele

Talking about . . .
- how and where you live
- destination and location
- possessions and relationships

Finding a roommate

Finding a place to live

Discussing the pros and cons of where you live

Describing people, places, and things

Strukturen

Two-case prepositions

Stellen/stehen; legen/liegen; hängen

More on **da**-compounds

Word order: Infinitive phrases

The genitive case

Kultur

Student housing

Green living: **Recyceln**

Green living: **Regenerative Energien**

Video-Treff: Mein Zuhause

Lesen: Das Bauhaus

Vorschau

Mitbewohner gesucht!

Wenn man ein Zimmer sucht, dann liest man so eine selbstgemachte Anzeige. Da findet man viele Informationen zu dem Zimmer, der Wohnung, den Mitbewohnern und so weiter.

Andrea   Ben   Mia   ?

Richtig glücklich sind wir nur zu viert!

WG in Kreuzberg hat schönes 20m² großes Zimmer frei
- vollständig möbliert (Bett, Schreibtisch, usw.)
- zentrale Lage - ca. 10 Min. zur Mitte
- großes, helles Wohnzimmer, Bad + zusätzliches Klo, Küche (mit Spülmaschine), Waschmaschine
- auch süße Hauskatze 🐱

Miete: nur 240 Euro kalt   Nebenk.: 30 Euro

Wir suchen einen supernetten, humorvollen, sauberen, nicht megalauten Mitbewohner. Bitte nur Nichtraucher!

8-1 Abkürzungen. Finden Sie die Abkürzungen in der Anzeige. Dann wählen Sie die passende Bedeutung auf Englisch.

WORT	ABKÜRZUNG	BEDEUTUNG	AUF ENGLISCH
Minuten	*Min.*	e	a. shared housing
Nebenkosten			b. toilet
und so weiter			c. square meters
Wohngemeinschaft			d. etc.
Quadratmeter			e. minutes
Wasserklosett			f. about
circa			g. additional costs

8-2 Was ist das auf Deutsch? Jetzt finden Sie in der Anzeige die deutschen Äquivalente für die folgenden Wörter und Ausdrücke: *rent, dishwasher, location, furnished*

8-3 Ist das Zimmer für mich?

JA   NEIN

☐   ☐   Ich kann nicht mehr als 250 im Monat bezahlen.
☐   ☐   Ich spiele Trompete und muss jeden Tag zwei Stunden üben.
☐   ☐   Ich rauche gern.
☐   ☐   Ich habe keine Möbel.
☐   ☐   Ich bin allergisch gegen alle Haustiere.
☐   ☐   Ich bin Studentin, bin sehr nett und habe einen guten Humor.

Zimmersuche

Stephanie findet es im Studentenheim oft zu laut zum Lernen und sucht fürs Sommersemester ein Zimmer in einem Privathaus. Sie hat in der Zeitung ein Zimmer gefunden und hat gleich angerufen. Sie ist dann in die Ebersbergerstraße gefahren und spricht jetzt mit der Vermieterin. Hören Sie, was Stephanie und Frau Kuhn miteinander sprechen.

Großes helles Zimmer mit Balkon

STEPHANIE:	Guten Tag. Ich bin Stephanie Braun.
FRAU KUHN:	Ach ja, Sie haben gerade angerufen. Kommen Sie doch herein und gehen Sie gleich die Treppe hinauf. Dort, die erste Tür rechts, da ist das Zimmer.
STEPHANIE:	Oh, so schön groß und hell! Und sogar ein Balkon! Das ist ja wunderbar! Darf ich auch die Küche benutzen?
FRAU KUHN:	Nein, das möchte ich lieber nicht. Aber für Kaffee oder Tee haben Sie ja die Mikrowelle hier in Ihrem Zimmer. – Das Bad ist übrigens hier gegenüber. Ich benutze nur die Badewanne. Die Dusche ist ganz für Sie.
STEPHANIE:	Toll. – Darf ich fragen, was das Zimmer kostet?
FRAU KUHN:	Zweihundertfünfzig Euro im Monat.
STEPHANIE:	Zweihundertfünfzig Euro, das ist ein bisschen viel für mich. – Ist es hier auch wirklich ruhig? Ich muss sehr viel lernen.
FRAU KUHN:	In meinem Haus stört Sie niemand. Ich wohne hier ganz allein, wissen Sie.
STEPHANIE:	Das Zimmer gefällt mir sehr, aber …
FRAU KUHN:	Sie brauchen nicht gleich ja zu sagen. Ich halte das Zimmer gern bis heute Abend für Sie frei. Aber lassen Sie mich bitte heute noch wissen, ob Sie es nehmen oder nicht.
STEPHANIE:	Das mache ich gern, Frau Kuhn.

 8-4 Richtig oder falsch? Sie hören das Gespräch zwischen Stephanie und Frau Kuhn und nach diesem Gespräch ein paar Aussagen. Sind die Aussagen **richtig** oder **falsch?**

	RICHTIG	FALSCH		RICHTIG	FALSCH
1.	_____	_____	4.	_____	_____
2.	_____	_____	5.	_____	_____
3.	_____	_____	6.	_____	_____

8-5 Was ist die richtige Antwort?

1. Wo wohnt Frau Kuhn?   In der Ebersbergerstraße. / Im Studentenheim.

2. Wohin ist Stephanie heute gefahren?   In die Ebersbergerstraße. / In die Berge.

3. Wo steht die Mikrowelle?   In der Küche. / In dem Zimmer.

4. Wohin soll Stephanie gehen, wenn sie eine Tasse Tee machen möchte?   In die Küche. / In das Zimmer.

5. Wo ist die Badewanne?   In dem Bad. / In dem Zimmer.

6. Wohin geht Frau Kuhn, wenn sie ein Bad nehmen möchte?   In das Bad. / In das Zimmer.

8-6 **Wo und wie wohnen diese Studenten?** Die Information für S2 ist
im *Anhang* auf Seite A8.

S1: Wo wohnt Magda?   **S2:** Sie wohnt im Studentenheim.
   Wie gefällt es ihr dort?   …

	MAGDA	CINDY	PIETRO	KEVIN
Wo wohnt _____?		Sie wohnt in einer WG.		Er hat ein Zimmer in einem Privathaus.
Wie gefällt es ihr/ihm dort?		Es gefällt ihr sehr gut.		Nicht so besonders.
Warum gefällt es ihr/ihm dort (nicht)?		Weil dort alle so nett sind.		Weil er die Küche nicht benutzen darf.
Wie kommt sie/er zur Uni?		Mit dem Bus.		Zu Fuß oder mit dem Fahrrad.

8-7 **Wo und wie wohnst du?** Stellen Sie einander die folgenden Fragen und
berichten Sie, was Sie herausgefunden haben.

S1:   **S2:**

Wo wohnst du?   Ich wohne
- ☐ im Studentenheim.
- ☐ noch zu Hause.
- ☐ mit ein paar anderen Studenten zusammen in einem Haus/einer WG.

Ich habe
- ☐ ein Zimmer in einem Privathaus.
- ☐ (mit einer Freundin/einem Freund zusammen) eine kleine Wohnung.

Gefällt es dir dort?   Ja, weil
- ☐ meine Mitbewohner sehr nett sind.
- ☐ es dort sehr ruhig ist.
- ☐ das Zimmer (die Wohnung) groß und hell ist.
- ☐ ich dort kochen (backen, grillen) kann.
- ☐ …

Nein, weil
- ☐ meine Mitbewohner so unordentlich sind.
- ☐ es mir dort zu laut ist.
- ☐ ich keine Freunde einladen darf.
- ☐ ich keine laute Musik spielen darf.
- ☐ …

Wie kommst du zur Uni?   Ich
- ☐ gehe zu Fuß.
- ☐ fahre mit
  - ☐ dem Fahrrad.
  - ☐ dem Wagen.
  - ☐ dem Bus.
  - ☐ …

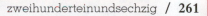

Kultur / Student housing

Finding a place to live in a **Universitätsstadt** in the German-speaking countries is often a challenge. Very few universities are situated on a campus. University buildings are scattered all over town, and the **Studentenwohnheime** that do exist do not come close to meeting the demand for student housing.

Ein typisches Zimmer im Studentenheim

The most common living situation in dorms is a single room (with no **Mitbewohner)**, typically furnished with a bed, shelves, a desk, and a sink. Residents on a hall usually share bathrooms as well as a kitchen. Kitchens are supplied with necessities like pots, pans, and dishes, and in some dorms, residents pay a small fee each semester to keep the kitchen stocked with items that everyone can use, such as salt, pepper, oil, spices, coffee, etc.

Everyone takes turns doing general chores, like taking out the recycling. A **Hausmeister** is available to handle problems like lock-outs, broken toilets, and security issues. Dorms offer amenities such as a **Partykeller, Volleyballplatz,** and **Musikräume,** and events like a **Grillabend, Filme,** and organized **Radtouren.**

Some students choose to live at home or rent a room in a **Privathaus,** with or without **Küchenbenutzung** *(kitchen privileges)*. But one of the most popular and economical living arrangements for students is the **Wohngemeinschaft,** a group of students renting an apartment together and sharing responsibility for meals and household chores. Although they serve the practical purpose of providing a cheap place to live, **WGs** are seen as a way to connect with a smaller **Gemeinschaft** *(community),* particularly in larger cities. For this reason, ads for rooms in **WGs** often reflect the personalities of those looking for a new roommate.

Beim Chillen in einer WG

8-8 **Studentenhaus Salzburg.** Schauen Sie die Webseite an und vergleichen° *compare*
Sie ein paar Aspekte dieses Studentenheims mit einem typischen Studentenheim
an Ihrer Uni.

The terms **Studentenwohnheim** and **Studentenheim** are interchangeable.

Studentenhaus Salzburg

English   Deutsch

Über uns / Zimmer / Virtuelle Tour / Uni Links / Kontakt   Suche

Online Reservierung
Familienname:
Vorname:
E-Mail:
Anfrage senden

Zimmerangebot: Einzelzimmer und Doppelzimmer, pro Person monatlich € 217,– bis € 288,–

Lage: Zentrumsnähe, 15 Gehminuten zum Bahnhof, sehr gute Einkaufsmöglichkeiten.

Ausstattung: Alle Zimmer mit WC, Dusche, Telefon, u. Internet- Anschlüssen. Auch Zimmer mit Balkon.

Sonstiges: TV-Räume mit Satelliten-TV, Studierraum, Musikzimmer, Clubraum, Sauna, Tischtennis, Tischfußball, großer Garten, Fahrradabstellplatz, Garagen. Abends Studentenkneipe.

Gefällt mir   +1

	STUDENTENHAUS SALZBURG	EIN STUDENTENHEIM AN MEINER UNI
Preis		
Lage		
Ausstattung		
Sonstiges		

Nomen

die Lage	location	das Esszimmer, -	dining room
die Miete	rent	die Küche, –n	kitchen
die Nebenkosten (pl)	additional costs	der Herd, –e	stove
der Vermieter, -	landlord	der Kühlschrank, ⁻e	refrigerator
die Vermieterin, –nen	landlady	die Mikrowelle, –n	microwave
die Wohngemeinschaft, –en	shared housing	das Spülbecken, -	sink
die WG, –s		die Spülmaschine, –n	dishwasher
		der Stuhl, ⁻e	chair
der Flur, –e	hall	der Tisch, –e	table
die Garderobe, –n	front hall closet		
die Möbel (pl)	furniture	das Schlafzimmer, -	bedroom
die Treppe, –n	staircase	das Bett, –en	bed
die Tür, –en	door	die Kommode, –n	dresser
		der Nachttisch, –e	night table
das Bad, ⁻er	bath; bathroom	der Schrank, ⁻e	wardrobe
das Badezimmer, -	bathroom	der Teppich, –e	carpet, rug
die Badewanne, –n	bathtub		
die Dusche, –n	shower	das Wohnzimmer, -	living room
das Klo, –s	toilet	das Bücherregal, –e	bookcase
die Toilette, –n	bathroom, restroom		
das Waschbecken, -	(bathroom) sink		

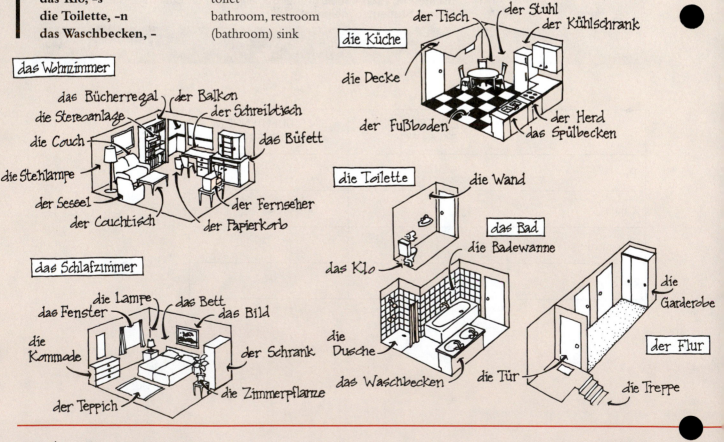

das Wohnzimmer
- das Bücherregal
- der Balkon
- die Stereoanlage
- der Schreibtisch
- die Couch
- das Büfett
- die Stehlampe
- der Sessel
- der Fernseher
- der Couchtisch
- der Papierkorb

das Schlafzimmer
- das Fenster
- die Lampe
- das Bett
- das Bild
- die Kommode
- der Schrank
- der Teppich
- die Zimmerpflanze

die Küche
- der Tisch
- der Stuhl
- der Kühlschrank
- die Decke
- der Fußboden
- der Herd
- das Spülbecken

die Toilette
- das Klo
- die Wand

das Bad
- die Badewanne
- die Dusche
- das Waschbecken
- die Tür

der Flur
- die Garderobe
- die Treppe

der Couchtisch, -e	coffee table
der Fernseher, –	television set
der Papierkorb, ⸚e	wastepaper basket
der Schreibtisch, -e	desk
der Sessel, –	armchair
die Stehlampe, -n	floor lamp
die Stereoanlage, -n	stereo

die Decke, -n	ceiling
der Fußboden, ⸚	floor
das Fenster, –	window
die Wand, ⸚e	wall

Verben

benutzen	to use
stören	to disturb
vergleichen	to compare

Andere Wörter

gegenüber	across *(the hall, the street, etc.)*
möbliert	furnished
wirklich	really
zusätzlich	additional

Ausdrücke

usw. (und so weiter)	etc. (et cetera, and so on)
zu viert	in a group of four

Das Gegenteil

mieten ≠ vermieten	to rent ≠ to rent (out)
ruhig ≠ laut	quiet ≠ loud
sauber ≠ schmutzig	clean ≠ dirty

Leicht zu verstehen

der Balkon, -e	grillen
die Couch, -es	zentral
die Lampe, -n	

Wörter im Kontext

Badezimmer, Toilette: In many homes in the German-speaking countries the tub, shower, and sink are in one room (**das Badezimmer**) and the toilet (with a very small sink) is in another (**die Toilette**).

8-9 Wie heißen diese Räume?

1. Hier duscht und badet man.
2. Hier kocht und bäckt man.
3. Hier sitzt man am Abend und sieht fern.
4. Hier schläft man.
5. Von hier geht man in alle Zimmer.
6. Hier isst man, wenn man Besuch hat.

8-10 Was passt in jeder Gruppe zusammen?

1. die Küche
2. die Toilette
3. der Flur
4. das Schlafzimmer

a. die Garderobe
b. die Kommode
c. der Herd
d. das Klo

5. der Stuhl
6. das Bett
7. der Herd
8. die Zimmerpflanze

e. gießen
f. kochen
g. liegen
h. sitzen

9. der Fußboden
10. die Wand
11. die Badewanne
12. die Garderobe

i. das Bild
j. der Teppich
k. Jacken und Mäntel
l. das Wasser

13. die Stereoanlage
14. die Lampe
15. der Kühlschrank
16. die Mikrowelle

m. schnell
n. kalt
o. laut
p. hell

8-11 Was passt wo?

Spülbecken / möblierte / ruhig / Nachttisch / Stört / Dusche / Spülmaschine

1. _____ es euch, wenn ich jetzt laute Musik spiele?
2. Eine Wohnung mit Möbeln ist eine _____ Wohnung.
3. Wenn man eine _____ hat, muss man den Abwasch nicht am _____ machen.
4. Neben meinem Bett steht ein _____.
5. Unsere neuen Nachbarn sind sehr nett und sehr _____.
6. Nach dem Joggen gehe ich gleich unter die _____.

Kommunikation und Formen

1 Talking about destination and location

Wohin and *wo*: a review

8-1

In *Kapitel 1* you learned that the English question word *where* has three equivalents in German: **wohin** *(to what place)*, **wo** *(in what place)*, and **woher** *(from what place)*. Since **wohin** and **wo** will play an important role in this chapter, you will need to fine-tune your feeling for the difference between them.

The use of **wohin** or **wo** is obvious in the following questions.

Wohin gehst du?	***Where*** *are you going?* (***to** what place?*)
Wo ist mein Mantel?	***Where*** *is my coat?* (***in** what place?*)

For speakers of English it is less obvious whether to use **wohin** or **wo** in the following example.

Where should I hang my jacket?   (*to* what place? or *in* what place?)

Here speakers of German think in terms of moving the coat from point A to point B and would therefore use **wohin.**

Wohin soll ich meine Jacke hängen?   ***Where*** *(to what place) should I hang my jacket?*

8-12 *Wohin oder wo?*

1. _____ gehst du?
2. _____ wohnst du?
3. _____ fährt dieser Bus?
4. _____ soll ich die E-Mail schicken?
5. _____ hast du dieses schöne Sweatshirt gekauft?
6. _____ fliegt ihr diesen Sommer?
7. _____ arbeitet Tina?
8. _____ soll ich meinen Mantel hängen?

Wohin geht es nach rechts, nach links und geradeaus?

Two-case prepositions

8-2 to 8-4

You have already learned that there are prepositions followed by the accusative and prepositions followed by the dative.

A third group of prepositions may be followed by either the accusative case or the dative case:

Take a moment to review accusative prepositions (Chapter 5, p. 166) and dative prepositions (Chapter 7, p. 241).

- When one of these two-case prepositions is used with a verb signaling *movement toward a destination,* the preposition answers the question **wohin?** and is followed by the accusative case.
- When a two-case preposition is used with a verb signaling a *fixed location,* the preposition answers the question **wo?** and is followed by the dative case.

		wohin?	**wo?**
		TOWARD A DESTINATION PREPOSITION + ACCUSATIVE	FIXED LOCATION PREPOSITION + DATIVE
an	on *(a vertical surface)*	Lisa hängt das Bild **an die** Wand.	Das Bild hängt **an der** Wand.
	to	Kurt geht **an die** Tür.	
	at		Kurt steht **an der** Tür.
auf	on *(a horizontal surface)*	Lisa legt das Buch **auf den** Tisch.	Das Buch liegt **auf dem** Tisch.
	to	Kurt geht **auf den** Markt.	
	at		Kurt ist **auf dem** Markt.
hinter	behind	Die Kinder laufen **hinter das** Haus.	Die Kinder sind **hinter dem** Haus.
in	in, into, to	Kurt geht **in die** Küche.	Kurt ist **in der** Küche.
neben	beside	Kurt stellt den Sessel **neben die** Couch.	Der Sessel steht **neben der** Couch.
über	over, above	Kurt hängt die Lampe **über den** Tisch.	Die Lampe hängt **über dem** Tisch.
unter	under, below	Lisa stellt die Hausschuhe **unter das** Bett.	Die Hausschuhe stehen **unter dem** Bett.
vor	in front of	Kurt stellt den Wagen **vor die** Garage.	Der Wagen steht **vor der** Garage.
zwischen	between	Lisa stellt die Stehlampe **zwischen die** Couch und **den** Sessel.	Die Stehlampe steht **zwischen der** Couch und **dem** Sessel.

8-13 **In der neuen Wohnung.** Ergänzen Sie die Präpositionen **an, auf, hinter, in, neben, über, unter, vor** und **zwischen.**

1. Der Picasso hängt _____ der Couch.
2. Uli hängt das Landschaftsbild _____ den Schreibtisch.
3. Der Kalender hängt jetzt _____ dem Landschaftsbild und dem Picasso.
4. Der Ball liegt _____ dem Schreibtisch.
5. Das Baby will den Ball und krabbelt° _____ den Schreibtisch.
6. Helga stellt den Papierkorb _____ den Schreibtisch.
7. Kurt legt den Teppich _____ die Couch.
8. Das Radio und die Zimmerpflanze stehen _____ dem Bücherregal.
9. Thomas stellt die Vase _____ das Radio und die Zimmerpflanze.
10. Die offene Tür geht _____ die Küche.
11. Antje hängt das Poster _____ die Küchentür.
12. Der Herd steht _____ der Küche.
13. Der Karton mit den Büchern steht _____ dem Bücherregal.
14. Die Stehlampe steht _____ dem Sessel.
15. Die Katze springt _____ die Couch.
16. Die Maus läuft _____ die Couch.

crawls (margin note next to item 5)

The verbs *stellen, legen,* and *hängen*

8-5 to 8-6

In English the verb *to put* can mean *to put something in a vertical, horizontal,* or *hanging position.*

> *Put* the wine glasses on the table.
> *Put* your coats on the bed.
> *Put* your jacket in the closet.

German uses three different verbs to describe the different actions conveyed by the English *to put.* Because these verbs signal movement toward a destination *(to what place?)*, a two-case preposition used with these verbs is followed by the *accusative case.*

stellen	*to put in an upright position*	**Stell** die Weingläser auf **den** Tisch!
legen	*to put in a horizontal position*	**Legt** eure Mäntel auf **das** Bett!
hängen	*to hang (up)*	**Häng** deine Jacke in **die** Garderobe!

8-14 **Wohin soll ich diese Sachen** *stellen, legen* **oder** *hängen?*

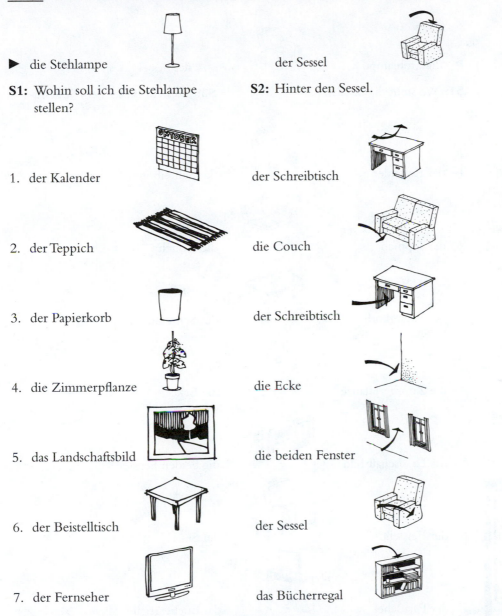

▶ die Stehlampe   der Sessel

S1: Wohin soll ich die Stehlampe
stellen?

S2: Hinter den Sessel.

1. der Kalender   der Schreibtisch

2. der Teppich   die Couch

3. der Papierkorb   der Schreibtisch

4. die Zimmerpflanze   die Ecke

5. das Landschaftsbild   die beiden Fenster

6. der Beistelltisch   der Sessel

7. der Fernseher   das Bücherregal

The verbs *stehen, liegen,* and *hängen*

German also tends to be more exact than English when describing the location
of things.

stehen	*to be standing*	Die Weingläser **stehen** auf **dem** Tisch.
liegen	*to be lying*	Eure Mäntel **liegen** auf **dem** Bett.
hängen	*to be hanging*	Deine Jacke **hängt** in **der** Garderobe.

Since these verbs are describing location *(in what place?)*, a two-case preposition
used with these verbs must be in the *dative case.*

8-15 Wo *stehen, liegen* oder *hängen* diese Sachen?

► die Stehlampe   der Sessel

S1: Wo steht die Stehlampe?   **S2:** Sie steht hinter dem Sessel.

> Note that **hängen** can be used to mean *to put into a hanging position* (with accusative) or *to be hanging* (with dative).

1. der Kalender   der Schreibtisch

2. der Teppich   die Couch

3. der Papierkorb   der Schreibtisch

4. die Zimmerpflanze   die Ecke

5. das Landschaftsbild   die beiden Fenster

6. der Beistelltisch   der Sessel

7. der Fernseher   das Bücherregal

Ein Trottel ist ein Dummkopf.

More *da*-compounds

Da-compounds with two-case prepositions are useful for describing the location of objects in relation to each other. Remember that **da-**compounds are used for things or ideas; personal pronouns are used when the objects of prepositions are people.

Moritz sitzt auf der Couch und **neben ihm** sitzt sein Freund Max.
Das ist mein Notebook und der Drucker **daneben** gehört meiner Mitbewohnerin.

*Moritz is sitting on the couch and his friend Max is sitting **beside him.***
*That's my laptop and the printer **beside it** belongs to my roommate.*

8-16 Sven beschreibt sein möbliertes Zimmer. Ergänzen Sie die passende **da**-Form.

Remember that an **r** is added to **da** if the preposition begins with a vowel.

davor / darauf / daneben / dahinter / darüber / darunter

1. Wenn man in mein Zimmer kommt, steht gleich links mein Bett und _____ ein Nachttisch mit einer Nachttischlampe _____.
2. Mitten im Zimmer hängt eine Lampe. Ich habe den Tisch direkt _____ gestellt, weil ich gutes Licht brauche, wenn ich abends meine Hausaufgaben mache.
3. An der rechten Wand steht eine Couch mit einem altmodischen Bild _____ und einem Couchtisch _____.
4. In einer Ecke steht noch ein alter Sessel mit einer hässlichen° Stehlampe _____.   *ugly*
   Hoffentlich finde ich bald ein schöneres Zimmer!

8-17 Mein Zimmer. Zeichnen Sie einen Plan von Ihrem Zimmer mit allen Möbeln, Türen und Fenstern. Beschreiben Sie das Zimmer dann in Worten. Die Ausdrücke in Übung **8-16** und die folgenden Sätze könnten Ihnen dabei helfen.

- Mein Zimmer ist ziemlich groß (klein, dunkel, hell) …
- Die Möbel sind modern (alt, neu, von der Heilsarmee°, vom Flohmarkt°) …   *Salvation Army / flea market*
- An der Nordwand (der Südwand, der Ostwand, der Westwand) steht (hängt) …
- Links neben … steht …
- Rechts daneben steht …
- Zwischen … und … steht …

Was gibt Ihrem Zimmer eine persönliche Note? Haben Sie ein Lieblingsposter, ein Lieblingsbild …?

Infobox

Green Living: Recyceln

Maintaining an environmentally healthy lifestyle is a high priority in the German-speaking countries. It includes daily habits such as buying **Bio-Produkte** (*organic foods*), using **öffentliche Verkehrsmittel** (*public transportation*), and **Recycling**.

Germany, Austria, and Switzerland are consistently ranked among the countries that recycle the most. Households, businesses, and even factories recycle about half of their waste. Recycling is taken so seriously that private citizens can be fined by the **Abfallüberwachung** (*waste monitoring department*) for not complying with recycling regulations.

German *an, auf, in,* and English *to*

In *Kapitel 7* you learned that both **zu** and **nach** can mean *to*. The prepositions **an**, **auf**, and **in** can also mean *to* if they answer the question **wohin**.

> When used to mean *to*, these prepositions can contract with the article **das** (*ans, ins, aufs*).

- **An** indicates that your point of destination is *next to* something, such as a door, a telephone, or a body of water (**an die Tür, ans Telefon, ans Meer**).

- **In** is generally used if your point of destination is *within* a place, such as a room, a theater, or even a mountain range (**ins Zimmer, ins Theater, in die Alpen**).

- **In** is used instead of **nach** to express that you are going to a country if the name of the country is masculine, feminine, or plural (**in den Libanon, in die Schweiz, in die USA**).

> Other expressions where **auf** means *to*: **auf eine Party, auf die Toilette**.

- **Auf** can be used instead of **zu** to express that you are going to a building or an institution, like the bank, the post office, or city hall, especially to do business (**auf die Bank, auf die Post, aufs Rathaus**).

use **8-18 Was passt in jeder Gruppe zusammen?** Verwenden° Sie **ans**, **auf**, **in** oder **ins** in den Antworten.

▶ Man will Schwyzerdütsch hören.   die Schweiz

S1: Wohin geht man, wenn man Schwyzerdütsch hören will?   **S2:** Man geht in die Schweiz.

1. Man braucht Geld.
2. Man möchte schlafen.
3. Man will eine Sinfonie hören.
4. Man braucht Briefmarken.
5. Man schwimmt gern in Salzwasser.

  a. das Meer
  b. das Konzert
  c. die Bank
  d. das Bett
  e. die Post

6. Man will *Hamlet* sehen.
7. Man möchte *Carmen* sehen.
8. Man kocht nicht gern.
9. Man isst gern frisches Obst.
10. Man möchte Ski laufen.

  f. das Gasthaus
  g. der Wochenmarkt
  h. die Oper
  i. die Alpen
  j. das Theater

8-19 Eine Umfrage. Stellen Sie einander die folgenden Fragen. Machen Sie Notizen und berichten Sie dann, was Sie herausgefunden haben.

☐ Gehst du oft ins Theater (ins Konzert, in die Oper, ins Kino, ins Kunstmuseum, ins Gasthaus)?

☐ Was ist dein Lieblingstheaterstück (deine Lieblingsmusik, deine Lieblingsoper, dein Lieblingsfilm, dein Lieblingsbild, dein Lieblingsessen)?

☐ Fährst du lieber in die Berge, ans Meer oder an einen See? Warum?

8-9 to 8-11

Video-Treff

Mein Zuhause

Christoph und Christina Brieger, Ursula, Karen, André, Maiga, und Stefan Kuhlmann sprechen darüber, wo und wie sie wohnen. Machen Sie die erste Aufgabe, **Was ist das auf Englisch?,** bevor Sie das Video anschauen.

8-20 Was ist das auf Englisch?

1. Wir wohnen in einem sehr schönen **Wohnviertel.**
2. Wir **wohnen** hier **zur Miete.**
3. Es gibt viele Geschäfte in den **umliegenden** Straßen.
4. Wir wohnen hier **zu fünft.**
5. Ich **fühle mich sehr wohl** hier.
6. Ich muss immer **Kohlen** in den 4. Stock tragen.
7. Ich habe keine **Wanne.**
8. Ich finde es sehr gut, wie die Wohnung **aufgeteilt** ist.
9. Man braucht eine große Couch, **falls** Freunde zu Besuch kommen.

   a. surrounding
   b. in case
   c. coal
   d. really feel at home
   e. tub
   f. rent
   g. residential area
   h. in a group of five
   i. divided up

8-21 Unser Zuhause. Ergänzen Sie die Aussagen über Christoph und Christina Brieger, Ursula und Karen.

1. Briegers wohnen in der Herderstraße 10 in _____.
   ☐ einem Einfamilienhaus   ☐ einer Wohnung
2. Christoph und Christina wohnen _____ von Wiesbaden.
   ☐ in der Nähe   ☐ praktisch im Zentrum
3. Von ihrer Wohnung ist es auch gar nicht weit zum _____.
   ☐ Bahnhof   ☐ Flughafen
4. Nicht weit von ihnen kann man gut _____.
   ☐ einkaufen gehen   ☐ schwimmen gehen
5. Außer dem Schlafzimmer, Wohnzimmer und Kinderzimmer haben Briegers _____.
   ☐ ein Esszimmer   ☐ ein Arbeitszimmer
6. Ursula wohnt in einer großen _____ in Berlin-Schöneberg.
   ☐ Wohngemeinschaft   ☐ Wohnung
7. Außer dem Wohnzimmer, Schlafzimmer und Arbeitszimmer hat Ursula in ihrer Wohnung _____.
   ☐ ein Gästezimmer   ☐ ein Kinderzimmer
8. Wenn Ursula abends Gäste hat, sind sie meistens _____.
   ☐ im Wohnzimmer   ☐ in der Küche
9. In ihrer Wohnung kann Karen _____.
   ☐ kein Bad nehmen   ☐ nur ein kaltes Bad nehmen
10. Karen findet ihre Wohnung _____.
    ☐ gar nicht schön   ☐ sehr schön

8-22 Richtig oder falsch? Lesen Sie die Aussagen über André, Maiga und Stefan Kuhlmann. Sind diese Aussagen richtig oder falsch? Wenn eine Aussage falsch ist, korrigieren Sie sie.

	RICHTIG	FALSCH
1. André wohnt allein in seiner Wohnung.	☐	☐
2. Auf dem Regal in Andrés Wohnzimmer stehen Bücher, CDs und Videos.	☐	☐
3. Außer der Küche und dem Badezimmer gibt es in seiner Wohnung drei weitere Zimmer.	☐	☐
4. Ihm gefällt an der Wohnung, dass die Zimmer nicht zu groß sind.	☐	☐
5. Maiga wohnt mit fünf anderen Leuten in einer Wohngemeinschaft.	☐	☐
6. In ihrer Wohngemeinschaft muss man das Bad und die Küche teilen.	☐	☐
7. Maiga hat das größte Zimmer in der WG.	☐	☐
8. Maigas Zimmer ist manchmal nicht so sauber.	☐	☐
9. Stefan Kuhlmann wohnt mit seiner Freundin zusammen.	☐	☐
10. In seiner Wohnung hat Stefan einen großen Fernseher, eine Couch, ein großes Bett und eine Waschmaschine.	☐	☐

> Note that in time expressions, **an** and **in** can contract with the article **dem** *(am, im)*. These contractions can also be used for location expressions: *am* **Fenster**, *im* **Schlafzimmer**.

2 Saying when something occurs

8-12 to 8-15

The two-case prepositions *an, in, vor,* and *zwischen* in time phrases

Phrases with the prepositions **an, in, vor,** and **zwischen** are often used to answer the question **wann.** In such time expressions, the objects of the prepositions are always in the dative case.

Ich bin **am** zehnten September in Salzburg angekommen.

*I arrived in Salzburg **on** the tenth of September.*

Das Wintersemester beginnt **im** Oktober.

*The winter semester begins **in** October.*

Vor dem Mittagessen gehe ich aufs Auslandsamt.

***Before** lunch I'll go to the foreign students' office.*

Vor drei Jahren war ich zum ersten Mal in Deutschland.

*Three years **ago** I was in Germany for the first time.*

Meine Eltern kommen **zwischen dem** ersten und **dem** zehnten Dezember zu Besuch.

*My parents are coming to visit **between** the first and the tenth of December.*

8-23 Wann ...?

▶ Wann fliegst du nach Europa?   In d__ Sommerferien (pl).

S1: Wann fliegst du nach Europa?   **S2:** In den Sommerferien.

1. Wann beginnt das Sommersemester in Deutschland?   I__ April (m).

2. Wann besuchst du deine Eltern?   A__ Wochenende (n).

3. Wann gehst du in die Bibliothek?   Zwischen d__ Mathevorlesung (f) und d__ Mittagessen (n).

4. Wann gehst du auf den Markt?   Vor mein__ ersten Vorlesung (f).

5. Wann hast du die Mikrowelle gekauft?   Vor ein__ Woche (f).

> Remember that in time expressions, **vor** can mean *before* or *ago*.

8-24 Detektiv spielen. Verhören° Sie Ihre Partnerin/Ihren Partner.

interrogate

- Wo waren Sie vor dieser Deutschstunde?
- Wo waren Sie gestern in der Mittagspause?
- Was haben Sie gestern zwischen dem Mittagessen und dem Abendessen gemacht?
- Wo waren Sie heute vor einer Woche?
- Was haben Sie am vergangenen° Wochenende gemacht?

past

3 Word order

Infinitive phrases

8-16 to 8-17

Infinitive phrases are phrases that contain an infinitive preceded by **zu.** Here are some verbs or expressions that may be followed by an infinitive phrase.

vergessen	**versuchen**	**Lust haben**	**Zeit haben**
versprechen	**vorhaben**	**Spaß machen**	

Ich habe versprochen, **Tim zum Flughafen** *zu fahren.*

*I promised **to drive** Tim to the airport.*

Vergiss aber diesmal nicht, **einen Parkschein** *zu lösen.*

*But don't forget **to buy** a parking pass this time.*

- In German, **zu** and the infinitive stand at the end of the phrase.
- The German infinitive phrase is often set off with a comma.

With separable-prefix verbs, **zu** is inserted between the prefix and the verb.

Hast du wirklich vor, **bald** *umzuziehen?*

*Are you really planning **to move** soon?*

If a phrase ends with more than one infinitive, **zu** precedes the last one.

Hast du Zeit, **dieses Wochenende mit uns** *campen zu gehen?*

*Do you have time **to go camping** with us this weekend?*

Some infinitive phrases are best translated into English using the *-ing* form of the verb.

Hast du Lust, **einen Kuchen** *zu backen?*

*Do you feel like **baking a cake?***

8-25 **Kleine Gespräche.** Ergänzen Sie passende **zu**–Infinitive.

bleiben / joggen

1. JUTTA: Macht es dir Spaß, jeden Morgen drei Kilometer _____?
    SYLVIA: Nicht immer, aber es hilft mir, fit _____.

kaufen / fahren

2. LAURA: Hast du wirklich vor, einen Wagen _____?
    MARKUS: Klar! Ich habe keine Lust, immer mit dem Bus _____.

anrufen / sprechen

3. JENS: Hast du vergessen, Günter _____?
    JULIA: Nein, ich hatte heute keine Zeit, mit ihm _____.

tanzen gehen / gehen / anschauen

4. LUKAS: Habt ihr Lust, heute Abend mit uns _____?
    BERND: Nein, wir haben vor, einen guten Film _____ und danach noch in die Kneipe _____.

 8-26 **Ein paar persönliche Fragen.** Stellen Sie einander die folgenden Fragen. Berichten Sie, was Sie herausgefunden haben.

S1: Was hast du heute Abend vor?
Was hast du am Wochenende vor?
Was macht dir am meisten Spaß?
Hast du mal vergessen, etwas Wichtiges zu tun?

S2: Heute Abend habe ich vor, …
Am Wochenende habe ich vor, …
Am meisten Spaß macht mir, …
Ich habe mal vergessen, …

Infinitive phrases introduced by *um*

To express the purpose of an action, you can use an infinitive phrase intoduced with **um.** The English equivalent of **um … zu** is *in order to.* English often uses only *to* instead of *in order to.* In German the word **um** is rarely omitted.

Morgen früh kommt Pietro, **um** mir beim Umziehen **zu helfen.**	*Tomorrow morning Pietro is coming* **(in order) to help** *me move.*
Ich brauche ein paar Nägel, **um** meine Bilder **aufzuhängen.**	*I need a few nails* **(in order) to hang up** *my pictures.*

8-27 **In der WG.** Sie wohnen in einer WG und fragen einander, was Ihre Mitbewohner mit diesen Geräten° machen wollen. Die Information für **S2** ist im *Anhang* auf Seite A8.

appliances

S1: Wozu° braucht Benedikt den Staubsauger?

S2: Um sein Zimmer zu putzen.

what … for

		BENEDIKT	SABRINA
	der Staubsauger	sein Zimmer putzen	
	der Dosenöffner		ihr Fahrrad reparieren
	das Bügeleisen		Quesadillas machen
	die Kaffeemaschine	für seine Freunde Kaffee kochen	
	der Korkenzieher		ihren Ring aus dem Klo holen
	die Waschmaschine		ihre alten Jeans rot färben

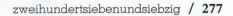

Infobox

Green Living: Regenerative Energien

Regenerative or **erneuerbare Energien** *(renewable energies)* are a main focal point of environmental policy, as Germany, Austria and Switzerland shift away from coal and nuclear power, and towards eco-friendly energy sources. **Windkraftanlagen** *(wind farms)*, for example, provide seven percent of Germany's total electricity consumption. **Sonnenenergie** *(solar power)* is another increasingly popular energy source. Solar panels are frequently installed directly onto the **Dach** of an individual's home. Excess energy can be fed back into the **Stromnetz** *(power grid)*.

4 Indicating possession or relationships

8-20 to 8-21

The genitive case

The genitive case is used to express the idea of possession or belonging together. You are already familiar with the **–s** genitive, which is used in German only with proper names. The ending **–s** is not preceded by an apostrophe.

Claudia**s** Schreibtisch   *Claudia's desk*

For nouns other than proper names you must use a different form of the genitive. Note that this form of the genitive follows the noun it modifies.

das Büro **des** Professor**s**   *the professor's office*
das Zimmer mein**er** Schwester   *my sister's room*
der Teddybär dies**es** Kind**es**   *this child's teddy bear*
die Wohnung unser**er** Eltern   *our parents' apartment*

In German this form of the genitive is used for persons, animals, and things. In English the possessive *'s* is generally used for persons and animals, while the preposition *of* is used to show that *things* belong together.

das Dach dies**es** Haus**es**   *the roof **of** this house*
die Wände unser**er** Wohnung   *the walls **of** our apartment*

	masculine		neuter		feminine		plural	
GENITIVE	des meines	Vaters	des meines	Kind**es**	der meiner	Mutter	der meiner	Kinder

- Most one-syllable masculine and neuter nouns add **-es** in the genitive singular **(Kindes),** while masculine and neuter nouns with more than one syllable add **-s** in the genitive singular **(Vaters).**
- Feminine nouns and the plural forms of all nouns have no genitive ending.

The interrogative pronoun *wessen*

The genitive form of the interrogative pronoun is **wessen**.

Wessen Jacke ist das?   *Whose* jacket is that?

	nominative	accusative	dative	genitive
for people	wer	wen	wem	**wessen**
for things or ideas	was	was	—	—

8-28 Wessen Sachen sind das?

▶

Handschuhe (pl)   mein__ Schwester

S1: Wessen Handschuhe sind das?   S2: Das sind die Handschuhe meiner Schwester.

Frau María Moser
Mariahilferstr. 52
1. A- 1070 Wien   mein__ Tante in Österreich

2.   Manfred__

3.   mein__ Bruder__

4.   unser__ Professor__

5.   Brigitte__

6.   mein__ Eltern

Bücher (pl)	Adresse (f)	Schal (m)
Fahrrad (n)	Wagen (m)	Brille (f)

8-29 **Genitiv im Alltag.** Identifizieren Sie die Genitiv-Phrasen auf den Schildern und sagen Sie, was sie auf Englisch bedeuten.

Tante Emmas
Bier - und Cafehaus

- großes Frühstücksangebot
- gute Altdeutsche Küche
- Kaffee und Kuchen
- gepflegte Biersorten

SOMMERKINO im KINOPLEX.DE
Die besten Filme des letzten Jahres 7. Juli bis 3. August
3,50 Mo–Do
4,50 Fr–So

Hamburg – Stadt der Musicals

Cocktail des Abends

SUB des TAGES 2,49 €
Von Mo. bis So. jeden Tag ein anderes frisches Sandwich für nur 2,49 €.

4. Fest der Kulturen

HAUS DER FRÖHLICHEN KINDER "VILLA KUNTERBUNT"

Volkssolidarität e.V. Kreisverband Parchim

Lange Nacht der Museen 2010

Erfurt
Freitag, 28. Mai 2010
Programm

Welt der Handarbeit

5 Describing people, places, and things

Genitive endings of preceded adjectives

8-22 to 8-24

Adjectives that are preceded by a **der**-word or an **ein**-word in the genitive case always take the ending **–en.**

		masculine		neuter		feminine		plural
GENITIVE	des eines	jung**en** Mannes	des eines	klein**en** Kindes	der einer	jung**en** Frau	der meiner	klein**en** Kinder

8-30 **Nicht alle Maler sind berühmt.** Ergänzen Sie die Genitivendungen in dieser Erzählung eines nicht so berühmten Malers.

Ich bin diese Woche in der Wohnung einer prominent__ Familie unserer Stadt, um dort die Fenster frisch zu streichen. Die Wohnung liegt direkt im Zentrum des historisch__, alt__ Teil__° der Stadt im fünften Stock° eines wunderschön__, alt__ Haus__. Die Fenster der hinter__° Zimmer gehen auf einen Park mit vielen Bäumen.   *part / floor*
back

An einer Wand des riesig__° Wohnzimmer__ hängt über der teuren Couch ein   *enormous*
Bild des berühmt__ französisch__ Maler__ Renoir. Ich kann fast nicht glauben, dass der Renoir echt ist, denn wer hat schon das Geld, um ein Original dieses groß__ Künstler__° zu kaufen?   *artist*

Mit dem Lohn° eines klein__ Maler__, wie ich einer bin, kann man die Bilder   *wages*
der berühmt__ Maler normalerweise nur im Museum anschauen.

Sprachnotiz   **Using *von* + dative instead of the genitive**

In colloquial German the idea of possession or of belonging together is often expressed by **von** with a dative object instead of the genitive case.

Ist das der neue Wagen
  von dein**em** Bruder?   =   Ist das der neue Wagen
                                    dein**es** Bruder**s**?

Herr Koch ist ein Freund
  von mein**em** Vater.   =   Herr Koch ist ein Freund
                                    mein**es** Vater**s**.

Das ist die Wohnung von einer Freundin von meinen Eltern.

Zusammenschau

Hören

Privathaus oder WG?

Im ersten Semester hatten Stephanie und Claudia im Studentenheim viele Feten und nie genug Zeit zum Lernen. Sie sind deshalb beide auf Zimmersuche und sie finden auch beide etwas, was ihnen gefällt. Hören Sie, was Stephanie und Claudia miteinander sprechen.

NEUE VOKABELN

Was ist denn los?	*What's up?*	**sicher**	*sure*
aufgeregt	*excited*	**wenigstens**	*at least*
eigen	*own*		

 8-31 **Erstes Verstehen.** In welcher Reihenfolge hören Sie das?

_____ Hast du wenigstens Küchenbenutzung?

_____ Nur drei. Na, das geht ja noch.

_____ Aber wir haben da jede unser eigenes Zimmer.

_____ Du bist ja ganz aufgeregt.

_____ Da kommst du doch lieber zu uns.

_____ Aber vielleicht nehme ich doch lieber das Zimmer bei Frau Kuhn.

 8-32 **Detailverstehen.** Hören Sie das Gespräch zwischen Claudia und Stephanie noch einmal und beantworten Sie die folgenden Fragen.

1. Warum ist Claudia so aufgeregt?
2. Was hat Stephanie gegen WGs?
3. Wo können die Studenten in dieser WG ihre Wäsche waschen?
4. Was kostet ein Zimmer in der WG und was kostet das Zimmer bei Frau Kuhn?
5. Was kann Stephanie nicht riskieren?
6. Warum soll Stephanie lieber in Claudias WG kommen?

Schreiben und Sprechen

8-33 **Vorteile und Nachteile meiner Wohnsituation.** Beschreiben Sie, wo und wie Sie wohnen und was Sie dort gut oder nicht so gut finden. Die folgenden Wörter und Ausdrücke könnten Ihnen dabei helfen.

VORTEILE ☺	NACHTEILE ☹
in der Nähe der Uni (wie nah?)	weit weg von der Uni (wie weit?)
billig / groß / hell / ruhig	teuer / klein / dunkel / laut
kann dort selbst kochen	kann dort nicht kochen
die Möbel sind schön	die Möbel sind alt und hässlich
kann dort tolle Feten geben	darf dort keine Feten geben
…	…

Schreibtipp: Pro and con lists can help you sort out your ideas when you write. In this assignment your introductory paragraph could be a description of the type and location of your accommodations, how long you have lived there, etc. The next paragraphs would then address the advantages and disadvantages (**Vorteile** and **Nachteile**). A concluding paragraph could express whether you like or dislike your living arrangements.

8-34 **Verschiedene Wohnsituationen.** Diskutieren Sie in kleinen Gruppen die Vorteile und Nachteile der folgenden Wohnsituationen.

	STUDENTENHEIM	WG	WOHNUNG	ZIMMER	ZU HAUSE
VORTEILE	_____	_____	_____	_____	_____
NACHTEILE	_____	_____	_____	_____	_____

Lesen

Zum besseren Verstehen

<u>8-35</u> Gebäude° und Architekten.

buildings

1. Welches Gebäude auf Ihrem Campus oder in Ihrer Stadt gefällt Ihnen am besten? Warum?
2. Gefallen Ihnen das Bauhaus in Dessau und das Gropius House in Lincoln, Massachusetts (siehe Fotos)? Warum oder warum nicht?
3. Kennen Sie den Namen eines berühmten Architekten/einer berühmten Architektin? Was hat er/sie gebaut und was wissen Sie sonst° von ihm/ihr?

else

Das Gropius House in Lincoln, Massachusetts

> **Gropius House:** Walter Gropius built this house as his family home when he came to teach at Harvard, and he lived there until his death. It is now a National Historic Landmark.

<u>8-36</u> Was ist das auf Englisch?

1. Der Architekt Walter Gropius **gründet** 1919 in Weimar das Bauhaus.
2. Ein **Lehrplan** beschreibt, was die Schüler lernen sollen.
3. Auf einer **Ausstellung** zeigt man Bilder, Skulpturen, Fotografien usw.
4. Gropius hat das Schulgebäude in Dessau selbst **entworfen.**
5. Die Ideen des Bauhauses hatten einen enormen **Einfluss** auf nordamerikanische Architekten und Designer.
6. Nach 1933 **verlassen** Gropius und viele andere Bauhauslehrer und -schüler das nationalsozialistische Deutschland.
7. Die meisten Bauhauslehrer finden in den USA eine neue **Heimat.**

a. leave
b. influence
c. founds
d. home
e. curriculum
f. exhibition
g. designed

Das Bauhaus

Der Beginn des Bauhauses

Im Jahr 1919 gründet der Architekt Walter Gropius in Weimar das Bauhaus, eine Schule, wo Künstler, Architekten, Handwerker und Studenten zusammen leben und lernen und zusammen versuchen, für eine industrialisierte Welt neue Formen zu finden. Auf dem Lehrplan stehen Malerei, Skulptur, Architektur, Theater, Fotografie und das Design von Handwerks- und Industrieprodukten.

Klare geometrische Linien

Typisch für die neuen Formen – von der Teekanne bis zum größten Gebäude – sind klare geometrische Linien. Auf der großen Bauhaus-Ausstellung von 1923 charakterisiert Gropius den Bauhausstil mit den folgenden Worten: Kunst und Technik – eine neue Einheit.[1]

Kaffee- und Teeservice, Bauhaus Metallwerkstatt 1924

Bauhaus zieht nach Dessau

1925 zieht das Bauhaus von Weimar nach Dessau. Das Schulgebäude, das berühmte Dessauer Bauhaus, hat Walter Gropius selbst entworfen und seine Stahl- und Glasfassade wird zur Ikone der Architektur des 20. Jahrhunderts.

Das Bauhaus in Dessau

[1] *art and technology—a new unity*

Das Ende des Bauhauses

Aber schon 1933 kommt mit Adolf Hitler das Ende des Bauhauses, denn Gropius' Ideen sind für die Nazis „undeutsch" und zu international. 1934 geht Gropius nach England und arbeitet dort als Architekt und Designer. 1937 emigriert er dann in die USA und wird dort an der Harvard-Universität *Chairman* des *Department of Architecture.* Seine größten Projekte in den USA sind das Harvard Graduate Center, das Pan Am Building (MetLife Building) in New York und das John F. Kennedy Federal Building in Boston.

Der Einfluss des Bauhauses

Der enorme Einfluss des Bauhauses auf nordamerikanische Architekten und Designer geht aber nicht nur auf Walter Gropius zurück, denn auch viele andere Bauhauslehrer und -schüler verlassen damals[2] Hitler-Deutschland und finden in den USA eine neue Heimat: László Moholy-Nagy gründet 1937 das *New Bauhaus* in Chicago, Josef Albers lehrt am Black Mountain College in North Carolina und später an der Yale-Universität, und Ludwig Mies van der Rohe lehrt am Illinois Institute of Technology in Chicago.

Den Einfluss des Bauhauses sieht man heute noch

[2] *at that time*

Arbeit mit dem Text

8-37 **Wann war das?** Finden Sie im Text die richtigen Jahreszahlen.

_____ Der Bauhauslehrer László Moholy-Nagy gründet in Chicago das *New Bauhaus.*

_____ Auf einer großen Ausstellung präsentiert das Weimarer Bauhaus seine Ideen und seine Produkte.

_____ Walter Gropius geht nach England und arbeitet dort als Architekt und Designer.

_____ Man gründet in Weimar eine Schule für Architektur, Kunst und Handwerk und nennt sie Bauhaus.

_____ Ende des Dessauer Bauhauses, weil die Nazis die Bauhausideen undeutsch und zu international finden.

_____ Das Bauhaus zieht von Weimar in das neue Schulgebäude in Dessau.

Wort, Sinn und Klang

Wörter unter der Lupe

Compound nouns

A compound noun can be a combination of:

- two or more nouns (**der Nachttisch, die Nachttischlampe**).
- an adjective and a noun (**der Kühlschrank**).
- a verb and a noun (**der Schreibtisch**).
- a preposition and a noun (**der Nachtisch**).

In German these combinations are almost always written as one word. The last element of a compound noun is the base word and determines the gender of the compound noun. All preceding elements are modifiers that define the base word more closely.

die Stadt + **der** Plan = **der** Stadtplan
der Fuß + der Ball + **das** Spiel = **das** Fußballspiel

8-38 **Was passt zusammen?** Ergänzen Sie auch die bestimmten Artikel.

1. _das_ Wochenendhaus _c_   a. family doctor
2. _____ Hausschuh ___   b. househusband
3. _____ Krankenhaus ___   c. cottage
4. _____ Haustier ___   d. single-family dwelling
5. _____ Hochhaus ___   e. pet
6. _____ Hausarzt ___   f. department store
7. _____ Reformhaus ___   g. hospital
8. _____ Hausmann ___   h. slipper
9. _____ Einfamilienhaus ___   i. high-rise
10. _____ Kaufhaus ___   j. health food store

Im Reformhaus kauft man gesundes Essen

Giving language color

In this chapter you have learned vocabulary that deals with housing and furnishings. This vocabulary is a source of many idiomatic expressions. The expressions marked with an asterisk are very informal and should only be used with family and friends.

Lena ist ganz aus dem Häuschen.	*Lena is all excited.*
Er hat wohl nicht alle Tassen im Schrank!★	*He must be crazy!*
Setz ihm doch den Stuhl vor die Tür!	*Throw him out!*
Mal den Teufel nicht an die Wand!	*Don't tempt fate!*
Lukas hat vom Chef eins aufs Dach gekriegt.★	*Lukas was bawled out by his boss.*
Auf Robert kannst du Häuser bauen.	*Robert is absolutely dependable.*

8-39 Was passt zusammen?

1. Unser Sohn will einfach keine Arbeit suchen.
2. Hat Anne eine Reise nach Hawaii gewonnen?
3. Gott sei Dank° hatten wir diesen Winter noch keinen Eisregen.
4. Warum ist Kurt denn plötzlich so fleißig?
5. Ist Sven ein guter Babysitter?
6. Ich habe mir gestern einen Porsche gekauft.

a. Ich glaube, er hat vom Chef eins aufs Dach gekriegt.
b. Aber natürlich. Auf ihn können Sie Häuser bauen.
c. Dann setzen Sie ihm doch den Stuhl vor die Tür!
d. Du hast wohl nicht alle Tassen im Schrank!
e. Ja, sie ist ganz aus dem Häuschen.
f. Mal bitte den Teufel nicht an die Wand!

Thank God!

Zur Aussprache

8-34 to 8-35

German s-sounds: *st* and *sp*

At the beginning of a word or word stem, **s** in the combinations **st** and **sp** is pronounced like English *sh*. Otherwise it is pronounced like English *s* in *list* and *lisp*.

8-40 Hören Sie gut zu und wiederholen Sie!

1. **St**efan ist **St**udent.
   Stefan **st**udiert in **St**uttgart.
   Stefan findet das **St**udentenleben **st**ressig.
2. Ha**st** du Lu**st** auf eine Wur**st**
   und auf Mo**st**° für deinen Dur**st**?
3. Herr **Sp**ielberg **sp**richt gut **Sp**anisch.
4. Worauf° **sp**art Frau **Sp**ohn?
   Auf einen **Sp**ortwagen.
   Die **sp**innt° ja!
5. Unser Ka**sp**ar li**sp**elt ein bisschen.

cider

what . . . for

is crazy

♕ **Hier ist die Königin der Würste !**			
Bockwurst	1,80 €	Schaschlik	3,20 €
Bratwurst	2,30 €	Frikadelle 200g	1,80 €
Curry–Bratwurst	2,40 €	Pommes Frites	1,30 €
Schinkenwurst	2,30 €	Hamburger	2,50 €
Riesen–Hot Dog	3,70 €	La Flûte	3,40 €

Nomen

das Dach, ¨er	roof
die Fußgängerzone, -n	pedestrian zone
das Gebäude, -	building
das Hochhaus, ¨er	high-rise
der Keller, -	basement; cellar
die Küchenbenutzung	kitchen; privileges
die Post	post office; mail
das Rathaus, ¨er	town hall; city hall
der Stadtplan, ¨e	map of the city/town
der Teil, -e	part
der Wochenmarkt, ¨e	open air market

und auf dem Mexikoplatz ist Wochenmarkt...

immer samstags
von 9 bis 15 Uhr

das Bügeleisen, -	iron
die Dose, -n	can
der Dosenöffner, -	can opener
das Gerät, -e	appliance; utensil
der Korkenzieher, -	corkscrew
der Staubsauger, -	vacuum cleaner
die Ausstellung, -en	exhibition; exhibit
der Künstler, -	} artist
die Künstlerin, -nen	
die Heimat	home (country)
die Mittagspause, -n	lunch break

Verben

auf·machen	to open
bügeln	to iron
legen	to lay (down); to put (in a horizontal position)
stellen	to put (in an upright position)
um·ziehen, ist umgezogen	to move (change residence)
versuchen	to try
wiederholen	to repeat

Andere Wörter

aufgeregt	excited
eigen	own
sicher	sure
wenigstens	at least
wozu	what . . . for

Ausdrücke

Es macht mir Spaß, . . .	I enjoy . . .
Ich habe (keine) Lust, . . .	I (don't) feel like . . .
in der Nähe der Uni	near the university
Was ist denn los?	What's up?
zu Besuch kommen	to visit

Das Gegenteil

der Vorteil, -e ≠ der Nachteil, -e	advantage ≠ disadvantage
in der Nähe ≠ weit weg	close by ≠ far away
zum ersten Mal ≠ zum letzten Mal	for the first time ≠ for the last time

Leicht zu verstehen

der Architekt, -en	das Poster, -
die Architektin, -nen	die Skulptur, -en
der Designer, -	die Technik
die Designerin, -nen	enorm
die Energie	recyceln

Was recycelst du?

Wörter im Kontext

8-41 Was passt in jeder Gruppe zusammen?

1. die Post
2. die WG
3. der Keller
4. die Künstlerin

a. die Mitbewohner
b. der Brief
c. die Skulptur
d. der Wein

5. der Staubsauger
6. alte Zeitungen
7. die Tür
8. der Wochenmarkt

e. aufmachen
f. einkaufen
g. putzen
h. recyceln

8-42 Was ist die richtige Antwort?

1. Warum bist du denn so aufgeregt?
2. Warum verkaufst du dein Auto?
3. Warum suchst du ein Zimmer mit Küchenbenutzung?
4. Warum gehst du heute Abend nicht mit uns tanzen?
5. Warum gehst du auf die Post?

a. Weil ich Briefmarken brauche.
b. Weil ich keine Lust mehr habe, immer in der Mensa zu essen.
c. Weil ich jetzt ein Zimmer in der Nähe der Uni habe.
d. Weil ich ein Zimmer in einer ganz tollen WG gefunden habe.
e. Weil es mir keinen Spaß macht, in die Disco zu gehen.

8-43 Wozu brauchst du das alles?

1. Wozu brauchst du einen Staubsauger?
2. Wozu brauchst du ein Poster?
3. Wozu brauchst du einen Korkenzieher?
4. Wozu brauchst du einen Dosenöffner?
5. Wozu brauchst du ein Bügeleisen?
6. Wozu brauchst du denn einen Stadtplan?

a. Um diese Weinflasche aufzumachen.
b. Um mein Kleid zu bügeln.
c. Um mein Zimmer sauber zu machen.
d. Um meine neue WG zu finden.
e. Um meine weiße Wand interessanter zu machen.
f. Um diese Sardinen essen zu können.

8-44 Was passt am besten zusammen?

1. Ich habe Lust, in ein Gasthaus zu gehen.
2. Frau Berg hat eine große Wohnung in einem Hochhaus.
3. Die Schweiz ist meine Heimat.
4. Im Keller von unserem Haus machen wir oft laute Musik.
5. Ich schaue gern Bilder und Skulpturen an.
6. Stefan gefällt es sehr gut in seiner WG.
7. Frau Otto ist Stadtarchitektin in Leipzig.

a. Meine Muttersprache ist Deutsch.
b. Ein Nachteil ist aber, dass seine Mitbewohner oft sehr laut sind.
c. So ein Glück, dass ich bald Mittagspause habe!
d. Ich gehe deshalb oft auf Kunstausstellungen.
e. Ihr Büro ist im Rathaus.
f. Sie vermietet zwei von ihren Zimmern an Studenten.
g. Ein großer Vorteil ist, dass wir dort niemand stören.

Das Rathaus in Leipzig

Andere Länder, andere Sitten

Vor diesem Restaurant kann man die Speisekarte in einem Kasten lesen.

Kommunikationsziele

Talking about …
- cultural differences
- personal grooming

Ordering a meal in a restaurant

Describing people, places, and things

Strukturen

Reflexive pronouns and reflexive verbs

Relative clauses and relative pronouns

Kultur

Im Gasthaus

Beim Schnellimbiss

Einkaufsgewohnheiten

Video-Treff: **Was ich gern esse und trinke**

Lesen: Robert Kalina und der Euro

Vorschau

Vor dem Restaurant

Die Anzeige, die Sie hier sehen, hängt in einem kleinen Kasten an einem Gasthaus in Königsbach. Königsbach liegt in Baden-Württemberg in der Nähe von Karlsruhe. Das gemütliche Gasthaus heißt „Schützenhaus" und hat auch einen Biergarten.

9-1 **Ein leckeres Essen im Schützenhaus.** Schauen Sie das Foto und den Text in der Anzeige genau an und beantworten Sie die folgenden Fragen.

1. Welche Farben haben diese Teile des Gerichts?

Gänsebraten	_____ rot	_____ gelb	_____ braun
Apfelrotkohl	_____ rot	_____ gelb	_____ braun
Kartoffelknödel	_____ rot	_____ gelb	_____ braun

2. Was ist der größte und wichtigste Teil des Gerichts?
3. Wie heißen die beiden kleineren Teile (man nennt sie auch „Beilagen"), die auch zu diesem Gericht gehören?
4. In welchem Monat kann man den Gänsebraten im „Schützenhaus" essen? Sagen Sie, wo Sie diese Information in der Anzeige gefunden haben.

9-2 **Mit anderen Worten.** Was passt hier zusammen?

1. auf Vorbestellung
2. hausgemacht
3. der Braten
4. auf Wunsch
5. rechtzeitig
6. wir freuen uns
7. Lokal
8. Anschrift

a. Adresse
b. Gasthaus
c. ein Stück Fleisch, das man lange im Ofen lassen muss
d. in diesem Restaurant gemacht
e. vorher anrufen und etwas bestellen
f. wenn Sie möchten
g. früh genug
h. wir sind glücklich

Im Gasthaus

Shauna ist Austauschschülerin aus den USA und wohnt bei Zieglers. Shauna und Nina stehen vor einem Gasthaus und schauen sich die Speisekarte an, die außen in einem kleinen Kasten hängt.

SHAUNA: Ich habe Lust auf etwas typisch Deutsches. Hier, Sauerbraten mit Rotkohl und Kartoffelknödeln. Das bestelle ich.

NINA: Gut, dann gehen wir hinein.

SHAUNA: Du, das ist ja ganz voll. Da ist kein einziger Tisch mehr frei.

NINA: Bei dem Ehepaar dort mit dem kleinen Jungen und dem Hund sind noch zwei freie Plätze.

SHAUNA: Kennst du die Leute?

NINA: Nein, aber das macht doch nichts. Komm, sonst setzt sich jemand anders dorthin. – Entschuldigung, sind diese beiden Plätze noch frei?

HERR: Ja, bitte, setzen Sie sich nur zu uns. Unser Hund tut Ihnen nichts.

FRAU: Hier ist auch gleich die Speisekarte. Dann können Sie sich schon etwas Gutes aussuchen, bis der Kellner kommt.

 9-3 **Richtig oder falsch?** Sie hören das Gespräch *Im Gasthaus* und nach dem Gespräch ein paar Aussagen. Sind diese Aussagen **richtig** oder **falsch?**

	RICHTIG	FALSCH
1.	_____	_____
2.	_____	_____
3.	_____	_____
4.	_____	_____

9-4 Im Gasthaus. Lesen Sie die folgenden Sätze in der richtigen Reihenfolge.

_____ Aber Nina sieht zwei freie Plätze und fragt, ob sie sich da hinsetzen dürfen.

_____ Weil Shauna Lust auf etwas typisch Deutsches hat und weil es hier Sauerbraten gibt, gehen sie hinein.

_____ Bevor Nina und Shauna in das Gasthaus gehen, schauen sie sich die Speisekarte an, die außen in einem kleinen Kasten hängt.

_____ Weil kein einziger Tisch mehr frei ist, will Shauna gleich wieder gehen.

9-5 Andere Länder, andere Sitten. Finden Sie heraus, wer von Ihren Mitstudenten aus einem anderen Land (einem anderen Staat, einer anderen Provinz) kommt, oder wer schon mal eine Reise in ein anderes Land (einen anderen Staat, eine andere Provinz) gemacht hat. Stellen Sie dann passende Fragen.

STUDENTEN, DIE NICHT VON HIER SIND

- Woher bist du?
- Seit wann bist du hier?
- Was ist hier anders als zu Hause?
- Was gefällt dir hier besonders gut (nicht so gut)?
- Was hat dir zu Hause besser gefallen?

STUDENTEN, DIE EINE REISE GEMACHT HABEN

- Wo warst du?
- Wann war das?
- Wie lange warst du dort?
- Was war dort anders als hier?
- Was hat dir dort besonders gut (nicht so gut) gefallen?

Ein Gasthaus in Schwerin.

Kultur / Im Gasthaus

Was ist „deutsches" Essen?

In den deutschsprachigen Ländern ist die Gastronomie oft sehr regional. In Nordamerika kennt man Spätzle (aus Süddeutschland und den Alpenländern) und einige Wurstsorten wie Bratwurst, Knackwurst oder Leberwurst. Bei den Würsten, wie auch bei den Knödeln, gibt es sehr viele regionale Sorten. Die regionalen Küchen[1] sind oft mit den Nachbarländern verbunden[2]. Wer in Südwestdeutschland in ein Gasthaus geht, kann zum Beispiel Flammkuchen[3] und Riesling aus dem französischen Elsass[4] finden. In Nordostdeutschland kann man in vielen Restaurants Soljanka bestellen, eine säuerlich-scharfe[5] Suppe aus Osteuropa. In Österreich sieht man auf den Speisekarten oft Gulasch, das ursprünglich[6] aus Ungarn kommt.

Die internationale Gastronomie

Es gibt in den deutschsprachigen Ländern auch eine große internationale Präsenz. Viele Restaurants und Gasthäuser gehören Italienern, Griechen, Türken, Franzosen oder Spaniern. Amerikanische und asiatische Restaurants sind auch beliebt. Viele dieser internationalen Köche kombinieren die Spezialitäten aus ihren Ländern auch mit deutschen Küchentraditionen, um den deutschen Geschmack zu treffen[7].

Schnellrestaurants

Diese Restaurants sind auch unter dem Namen Fast-Food-Restaurants bekannt und sind in den deutschsprachigen Ländern sehr erfolgreich. Neben den großen amerikanischen Ketten wie Starbucks, Burger King oder Subway sind auch mehrere[8] andere Ketten etabliert, wie zum Beispiel die deutschen Ketten Nordsee (Fischspezialitäten) und Tank @ Rast (Autobahnrestaurants) oder die schweizerische Kette Mövenpick Marché (frisches, lokales Essen). McDonald's ist das größte Gastronomieunternehmen[9] in Deutschland.

Deutsche Sitten im Gasthaus

Eiswasser bekommt man im Gasthaus fast nie und auch Softdrinks trinkt man fast nie mit Eis. Wenn man Wasser trinken will, bestellt man Mineralwasser und bezahlt etwa € 1,80 für ein Glas oder ein kleines Fläschchen. Auch Brötchen und Butter muss man oft extra bestellen und bezahlen. Eine Tasse Kaffee kostet etwa € 2,00 und wenn sie leer ist, füllt der Kellner sie nicht nach[10]. Wenn man mehr als nur eine Tasse Kaffee trinken will, bestellt man für etwa € 3,80 ein Kännchen (das sind zwei bis zweieinhalb Tassen). Die Preise sind alle inklusive Bedienungsgeld[11]. Wenn man die Rechnung[12] bezahlt, gibt man aber trotzdem noch etwa 10 Prozent Trinkgeld[13].

---

[1]*cuisines*   [2]*tied to*   [3]*tarte flambee (a kind of pizza)*   [4]*Alsace*   [5]*sour and spicy*   [6]*originally*   [7]**den Geschmack treffen:** *to appeal to the taste*   [8]*several*   [9]**Unternehmen:** *company*   [10]**füllt nach:** *refills*   [11]*service charge*   [12]*bill*   [13]*tip*

Wie man isst

Bevor man in den deutschsprachigen Ländern zu essen beginnt, sagt man meistens „Guten Appetit!" oder manchmal auch „Mahlzeit!" Beim Essen hat man das Messer immer in der rechten und die Gabel in der linken Hand und es gilt[14] als unkultiviert, das Messer auf den Tisch und eine Hand in den Schoß[15] zu legen. Wenn man gerade nicht isst, bleiben die Arme, aber nicht die Ellbogen, auf dem Tisch.

The photos show how people in the German-speaking countries hold silverware when eating. Between bites the lower arms (just above the wrist) rest on the table.

So hält man in Deutschland Messer und Gabel.

Der Arm bleibt auf dem Tisch.

[14]*is considered*   [15]*lap*

9-6 Aus dem Kochbuch. Lesen Sie das Rezept für die Apfelringe in Bierteig. Das nächste Mal, wenn Sie Gäste einladen, können Sie ihnen diese Apfelringe servieren.

Versuchen Sie, die englischen Äquivalente für die folgenden Wörter und Ausdrücke zu erraten°.   *guess*

EL (Esslöffel)   _____
TL (Teelöffel)   _____
Zucker und Zimt   _____
Mehl   _____
mit Zucker bestreuen   _____
mit Rum beträufeln   _____
Eiweiß steif schlagen   _____
in den Teig eintauchen   _____

(200 Gramm = ca. 1¹/₃ cups; ¼ Liter = ca. 1 cup)

Apfelringe in Bierteig

5 bis 6 Äpfel	Teig:	200 g Mehl
ein bisschen Zucker		3 EL Zucker
3 EL Rum		¼ l helles Bier
		2 TL Öl
3 EL Zucker und Zimt		2 Eiweiß

   Die Äpfel in dicke Ringe schneiden. Die Ringe mit Zucker bestreuen und mit Rum beträufeln.
   Aus Mehl, Zucker, Bier und Öl einen dünnen Teig machen. Eiweiß steif schlagen und in den Teig geben.
   Die Apfelringe in den Teig eintauchen und in sehr heißem Fett auf beiden Seiten hellgelb backen. Mit Zucker und Zimt bestreuen und mit Vanillesoße oder Vanilleeis servieren.

🔊 Wortschatz 1

Nomen

die Bedienung (sing)	server, waiter, waitress
das Gasthaus, ̈er	restaurant
der Kasten, ̈en	box
der Kellner, -	server, waiter
die Kellnerin, -nen	server, waitress
die Rechnung, -en	bill
die Speisekarte, -n	menu
das Trinkgeld, -er	Tip
das Geschirr (sing)	dishes
das Glas, ̈er	glass
die Kaffeekanne, -n	coffeepot
die Pfanne, -n	pan
die Schüssel, -n	bowl
die Tasse, -n	cup
die Untertasse, -n	saucer
die Teekanne, -n	teapot
der Teller, -	plate
der Topf, ̈e	pot
das Besteck	cutlery, silverware
die Gabel, -n	fork
der Löffel, -	spoon
der Esslöffel, -	tablespoon
der Teelöffel, -	teaspoon
die Serviette, -n	napkin, serviette
die Beilage, -n	side dish
der Braten, -	roast
die Gans, ̈e	goose
der Knödel, -	dumpling

> The form **Speisenkarte** is also very common.

das Mehl	flour
das Rezept, -e	recipe
der Rotkohl (sing)	red cabbage
die Soße, -n	sauce
der Teig	dough; batter
der Austauschschüler, -	
die Austauschschülerin, -nen	exchange student *(high school)*
das Ehepaar, -e	married couple
der Platz, ̈e	place; seat
der Wunsch, ̈e	wish

> Can you guess the English cognate for **Mehl?** Hint: You can use it to complete the following words: *corn____; ____ y potatoes.*

Verben

aus·suchen	to choose; to pick out
bedienen	to serve *(guests in a restaurant)*
bestellen	to order

> **bedienen:** Note the difference between **bedienen** *to serve guests in a restaurant* and **servieren** *to s... a dish.*

Andere Wörter

beliebt	popular
deutschsprachig	German-speaking
einzig	single; only
knusprig	crispy
rechtzeitig	on time; early enough
steif	stiff

> Parents often admonish small children with the saying **Messer, Gabel, Schere** *(scissors),* **Licht** *(i.e., matches),* **sind für kleine Kinder nicht**.

Ausdrücke

jemand anders	someone else
Das macht doch nichts.	That doesn't matter.
eine Frage beantworten	to answer a question
Er tut dir nichts.	He won't hurt you.
Guten Appetit!	Enjoy your meal!

Leicht zu verstehen

die Gastronomie	der Rum
das Gramm	der Softdrink, –s
der Liter, –	servieren
	international

> **füllen, bestellen:** For these verbs the prefix **nach** is the equivalent of the English prefix *re-:* **nachbestellen** *to reorder,* **nachfüllen** *to refill.*

Das Gegenteil

füllen ≠ leeren	to fill ≠ to empty
außen ≠ innen	outside ≠ inside

Wörter im Kontext

9-7 Was brauche ich? Beginnen Sie alle Antworten mit „Ich brauche …"

1. Ich bin im Gasthaus und möchte etwas zu essen bestellen.
2. Ich möchte die Suppe essen, die der Kellner mir gebracht hat.
3. Ich möchte wissen, wie man Apfelringe in Bierteig macht.
4. Ich will die Apfelringe jetzt backen.
5. Ich möchte die Knödel, die ich gekocht habe, nicht im Topf auf den Tisch stellen.
6. Ich möchte mein Steak essen.

> **Kellner:** Originally, each **Wirtshaus** had its own **Weinkeller.** Among his other duties, the **Kellner** had to go to the **Keller** to get wine for his guests. Hence his name.

eine Schüssel	eine Speisekarte
eine Pfanne	ein Messer und eine Gabel
ein Rezept	einen Löffel

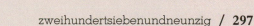

9-8 Was passt in jeder Gruppe zusammen?

1. der Softdrink   a. der Kellner
2. die Pfanne   b. das Trinkgeld
3. das Gasthaus   c. das Glas
4. die Rechnung   d. das Steak

5. das Geschirr   e. servieren
6. das Essen   f. waschen
7. die Gäste   g. füllen
8. die Gläser   h. bedienen

> Other words for **Gasthaus** are **die Gaststätte, der Gasthof, das Wirtshaus, das Restaurant, die Raststätte** (on the **Autobahn**).

9-9 Was ist hier identisch? Welche zwei Sätze in jeder Gruppe bedeuten etwa dasselbe?

1. Knödel sind hier sehr beliebt.
   Ich bestelle oft Knödel.
   Die Leute hier essen sehr gern Knödel.

2. Der Hund tut dir nichts.
   Der Hund tut mir leid.
   Der Hund beißt nicht.

3. Diese Jacke gehört mir.
   Diese Jacke gehört jemand anders.
   Diese Jacke gehört mir nicht.

4. Kein einziger von meinen Freunden war da.
   Keiner von meinen Freunden war da.
   Nur ein einziger von meinen Freunden war da.

Kommunikation und Formen

1 Talking about actions one does to or for oneself

Reflexive pronouns

To express the idea that one does an action *to oneself* or *for oneself*, English and German use reflexive pronouns. In German the reflexive pronoun can be in the accusative or the dative case, depending on its function.

ACCUSATIVE:	Ich habe **mich** geschnitten.	*I cut **myself**.*
DATIVE:	Ich hole **mir** ein Pflaster.	*I'm getting **myself** a bandage.*

When a sentence starts with the subject, the reflexive pronoun is placed right after the verb, as in the examples above. When an element other than the subject stands at the beginning of the sentence, the reflexive pronoun usually follows the subject, which is placed after the verb, as in the examples below.

ACCUSATIVE:	Gerade habe ich **mich** geschnitten.	*I just cut **myself**.*
DATIVE:	Jetzt hole ich **mir** ein Pflaster.	*Now I'm getting **myself** a bandage.*

9-1 to 9-3

Reflexive pronouns in the accusative case

Ich wasche **mich**.	*I am washing **myself**.*
Tina kämmt **sich**.	*Tina is combing **her** hair.*
Wann ziehen **Sie sich** um?	*When are **you** changing **(your clothes)**?*

The accusative reflexive pronoun differs from the accusative personal pronoun only in the 3rd person singular and plural and in the **Sie–**form, where it is **sich.** Note that in the **Sie–**form **sich** is not capitalized.

personal pronouns		reflexive pronouns
NOMINATIVE	ACCUSATIVE	ACCUSATIVE
ich	mich	**mich**
du	dich	**dich**
er	ihn	
es	es	*sich*
sie	sie	
wir	uns	**uns**
ihr	euch	**euch**
sie	sie	*sich*
Sie	Sie	*sich*

Reflexive pronouns are used much more frequently in German than in English, as for example with the following verbs.

sich waschen	*to wash*
sich baden	*to take a bath*
sich duschen	*to take a shower*
sich kämmen	*to comb one's hair*
sich rasieren	*to shave*
sich schminken	*to put on makeup*
sich anziehen	*to get dressed*
sich ausziehen	*to get undressed*
sich umziehen	*to change (one's clothes)*

9-10 **Was macht Otilia um sieben Uhr zehn?** Die Information für **S2** ist im *Anhang* auf Seite A9.

S1: Was macht Otilia um sieben Uhr zehn?   **S2:** Sie schminkt sich.

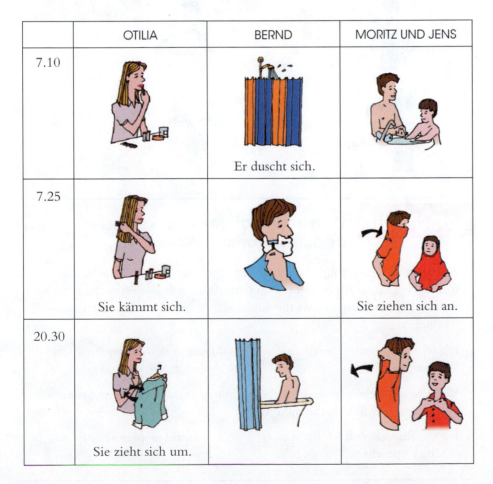

9-11 Morgens vor der Uni.

▶

S1: Was machst du morgens
vor der Uni?

S2: Zuerst dusche ich mich.   Und dann rasiere ich mich.

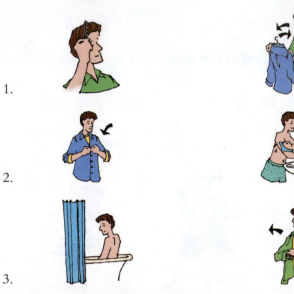

1.

2.

3.

Sprachnotiz **Using modal verbs in reflexive constructions**

As you know, when you use a modal verb, the main verb is in the infinitive form and comes at the end of the sentence. With reflexive verbs, the reflexive pronoun immediately follows the modal verb, when the sentence begins with the subject.

Ich **will** mich heute Abend vor dem
Konzert **rasieren.**

*I **want to shave** before the concert
tonight.*

When another element stands at the beginning of the sentence, the reflexive pronoun usually follows the subject.

Für das Konzert **will** ich mich auch
schick **anziehen.**

*I also **want to dress** nicely for the
concert.*

9-12 Wir machen das gleich!

MUTTER: Kinder, duscht ihr euch bald? KINDER: Wir duschen uns gleich, Mama!

 1.

 2.

 3.

 4.

5.

6.

9-13 Was ich alles mache, bevor ich zur Uni gehe. Schreiben Sie ein paar Sätze und verwenden° Sie so viele reflexive Verben wie möglich.

°*use*

Ich stehe meistens um _____ auf. Vor dem Frühstück … Nach dem Frühstück …

joggen gehen
sich duschen/baden
sich anziehen
frühstücken
CNN anschauen
schnell meine Hausaufgaben
    machen
meine Facebook-Seite checken

sich rasieren
sich schminken
sich kämmen
Radio hören
mein Bett machen
meine Freundin/
    meinen Freund anrufen
…

 9-14 Bevor ich zur Uni gehe, … Erzählen Sie Ihren Mitstudenten, was Sie alles machen, bevor Sie zur Uni gehen.

Reflexive pronouns in the dative case

9-4 to 9-10

In the examples below, the reflexive pronouns are indirect objects and are therefore in the dative case.

Ich kaufe **mir** ein neues Snowboard   *I'm buying **myself** a new snowboard*
    zum Geburtstag.   *for my birthday.*

Note the difference in the way German and English refer to actions that involve one's own body.

Oliver wäscht **sich** jeden Tag **die** Haare.   ***Oliver** washes **his** hair every day.*

dreihunderteins / **301**

Where English uses the possessive adjective (***his*** *hair*), German uses the dative reflexive pronoun and the definite article (***sich die*** **Haare**).

The dative reflexive pronoun differs from the dative personal pronoun only in the 3rd person singular and plural and in the **Sie**-form, where it is **sich**.

personal pronouns		reflexive pronouns
NOMINATIVE	DATIVE	DATIVE
ich	mir	**mir**
du	dir	**dir**
er	ihm	
es	ihm	*sich*
sie	ihr	
wir	uns	**uns**
ihr	euch	**euch**
sie	ihnen	*sich*
Sie	Ihnen	*sich*

9-15 Was machen diese Leute?

▶ Anita  sich die Haare bürsten

Anita bürstet sich die Haare.

1. Peter

2. Stephanie

3. ich

4. wir

5. ich

6. Martin und Claudia

sich einen Film anschauen	sich eine Tasse Kaffee machen	sich ein Stück Kuchen nehmen
sich die Haare waschen	sich die Hände waschen	sich die Zähne putzen

9-16 Eine Umfrage°: Wie oft machst du das? Stellen Sie Ihren   *poll*
Mitstudenten Fragen mit den folgenden reflexiven Verben. Benutzen Sie das
passende Pronomen im Akkusativ oder im Dativ. Markieren Sie die dann die
Antworten in der Tabelle.

S1: Wie oft putzt du dir   **S2:** Ich putze mir zweimal am Tag die
die Zähne?   Zähne.

WIE OFT?	NIE	SELTEN	JEDEN TAG	ZWEIMAL AM TAG	ZWEIMAL DIE WOCHE	EINMAL IM MONAT
sich die Haare waschen						
sich die Hände waschen						
sich die Zähne putzen						
sich rasieren						
sich schminken						
sich die Haare färben						
sich die Haare stylen						

9-17 Was kaufst du dir mit diesem Geld? Sie haben 500 Dollar
gewonnen und sollen sich damit drei Dinge kaufen. Fragen Sie einander, wie Sie
das Geld ausgeben wollen. Berichten Sie, was Sie herausgefunden haben.

S1: Was kaufst du dir?   **S2:** Ich kaufe mir für etwa _____
                                      Dollar …
Was kaufst du dir dann?   Dann kaufe ich mir für …
Und was kaufst du dir   Ich kaufe mir noch für …
noch°?   *else*

S1: Lisa/David kauft sich für etwa _____ Dollar …

Reflexive pronouns used to express *each other*

9-11 to 9-12

In German you can use the plural reflexive pronoun as a reciprocal pronoun meaning *each other*. Note that the pronoun is not always expressed in English.

Wie habt ihr **euch** kennen gelernt?   *How did you get to know **each other?***
Wo sollen wir **uns** treffen?   *Where should we meet?*

9-18 Was passt zusammen? Ergänzen Sie die Reflexivpronomen in den Fragen und beantworten Sie die Fragen. Ein paar Antworten passen mehr als einmal.

S1:

1. Seit wann kennen Claudia und Martin _____?
2. Wie haben sie _____ kennen gelernt?
3. Wie oft rufen _____ die beiden an?
4. Wann trefft ihr _____ heute Abend?
5. Wo sollen wir _____ morgen Abend treffen?
6. Wann sehen wir _____ wieder?
7. Wie oft schreibt ihr _____?
8. Seit wann grüßen Müllers und Maiers _____ nicht mehr?

S2:

Durch Freunde.
Hoffentlich sehr bald.
Um acht.
Am besten wieder bei mir.
Seit einem halben Jahr.
Fast jeden Tag.

9-19 Freundschaften. Stellen Sie einander die folgenden Fragen.

Hast du eine gute Freundin / einen guten Freund?
Seit wann kennt ihr euch?
Wo und wie habt ihr euch kennen gelernt?
Wo trefft ihr euch am liebsten?
Warum versteht ihr euch so gut?

Reflexive verbs

9-13 to 9-16

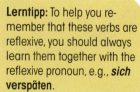

Lerntipp: To help you remember that these verbs are reflexive, you should always learn them together with the reflexive pronoun, e.g., *sich verspäten*.

Many German verbs are always or almost always accompanied by a reflexive pronoun even though their English equivalents are rarely reflexive. Here are some important ones. The reflexive pronoun for these verbs is in the accusative case.

sich verspäten	*to be late*
sich beeilen	*to hurry (up)*
sich auf·regen	*to get worked up; to get upset*
sich benehmen	*to behave*
sich entschuldigen	*to apologize*
sich erkälten	*to catch a cold*
sich wohl fühlen	*to feel well*
sich setzen	*to sit down*

9-20 Was passt in die Sprechblasen°?

speech bubbles

1.   2.   3.   4.

Ich habe mich erkältet.	Reg dich doch nicht so auf!
Sie haben sich verspätet.	Beeil dich doch ein bisschen!

5.   6.   7.   8.

Komm, setz dich zu mir!	Du benimmst dich schlecht.
Ich fühle mich nicht wohl.	Können Sie sich nicht wenigstens entschuldigen?

9-21 Was passt? Finden Sie zu jeder Situation die passende Reaktion aus dem Kasten.

Situationen

1. Frau Gürlük ist Kellnerin und liest in der Zeitung, dass das Hotel „Vier Jahreszeiten" Kellnerinnen sucht. Als sie in die Personalabteilung kommt, sagt die Personalchefin:
2. Patrick ist gestern schwimmen gegangen, obwohl das Wasser noch eiskalt war. Heute Morgen fühlt er sich gar nicht wohl und denkt:
3. Holger ist mit Anna auf einer Party. Er isst und trinkt zu viel, steht dann plötzlich auf und will gehen. Anna fragt, warum er denn schon gehen will. Holger antwortet:
4. Günter ist mit Tina auf einer Party. Er trinkt zu viel und fängt an, ziemlich laut zu werden. Tina sagt:

Benimm dich doch nicht so schlecht!	Ich glaube, ich habe mich gestern erkältet!
Guten Tag! Bitte setzen Sie sich!	Ich fühle mich gar nicht wohl.

9-22 Persönliche Fragen. Stellen Sie einander die folgenden Fragen.

- Was machst du, wenn du dich erkältet hast?   Wenn ich mich erkältet habe, …
- In was für Situationen regst du dich auf?   Ich rege mich auf, wenn …
- Verspätest du dich manchmal? Warum?   Ich verspäte mich manchmal, weil …
- Wann fühlst du dich wohl/schlecht?   Ich fühle mich wohl/schlecht, wenn …

Video-Treff

Was ich gern esse und trinke

Anja Szustak, Maiga, Thomas, Karen, Stefan Meister, Stefan Kuhlmann, Ursula und Öcsi erzählen, was sie gern essen und trinken. Machen Sie die erste Aufgabe **Was ist das auf Englisch?**, bevor Sie das Video ansehen.

Zum besseren Verstehen

9-23 Was ist das auf Englisch?

1. Mein Lieblingsgericht sind **Dampfnudeln.**
2. Am liebsten esse ich Salate mit **Putenfleisch.**
3. Ich esse lieber im Restaurant, weil ich da **bedient werde.**
4. Das ist eine **Frage des Geldes.**
5. Mir gefällt die italienische **Küche** so gut, weil sie so einfach ist.
6. Jetzt **schäle** ich die Karotten.
7. Ich werde das Gericht dann scharf **würzen.**

a. peel
b. turkey
c. dumplings
d. cuisine
e. get waited on
f. season
g. question of money

9-24 Richtig oder falsch? Lesen Sie die Aussagen über Anja, Maiga, Thomas und Karen. Sind diese Aussagen richtig oder falsch? Wenn eine Aussage falsch ist, korrigieren Sie sie.

	RICHTIG	FALSCH
1. Anja mag sehr gern Sachen wie Kuchen, Torten und Schokolade.	☐	☐
2. Anja kauft oft eine Waffel, weil sie nur drei Euro kostet.	☐	☐
3. Statt zu Hause zu kochen, geht Maiga meistens ins Restaurant.	☐	☐
4. Maigas Lieblingsgericht ist Dampfnudeln mit Vanillesoße.	☐	☐
5. Thomas geht gern in „Die rote Harfe", ein Café und Restaurant in Kreuzberg.	☐	☐
6. „Die rote Harfe" ist nur im Herbst und Winter geöffnet.	☐	☐
7. Dort isst er am liebsten vegetarische Gerichte.	☐	☐
8. Karen geht nicht oft ins Restaurant, und sie kocht auch nicht so oft.	☐	☐
9. Am liebsten isst Karen eine Stulle°.	☐	☐ *sandwich*
10. Karen trinkt abends am liebsten Tee.	☐	☐

9-25 Essen und Trinken. Welche der folgenden Aussagen passt zu den Aussagen, die Stefan Meister, Stefan Kuhlmann, Ursula oder Öcsi in dem Video machen?

	Stefan Meister	Stefan Kuhlmann	Ursula	Öcsi
1. Mein Lieblingsgericht ist ein sehr großer Hamburger.	☐	☐	☐	☐
2. Ich esse am liebsten alle Pastasorten.	☐	☐	☐	☐
3. Ich koche am liebsten für Freunde zu Hause.	☐	☐	☐	☐
4. Ich mag italienisches Essen, weil es nicht kompliziert ist.	☐	☐	☐	☐
5. Ich koche noch nicht sehr lange und deshalb brauche ich ein Kochbuch.	☐	☐	☐	☐
6. Was ich gern trinke, ist ein Bier aus Deutschland.	☐	☐	☐	☐
7. Mein Lieblingsrestaurant ist eine Rockkneipe.	☐	☐	☐	☐
8. Am liebsten esse ich Gerichte mit viel Gemüse drin.	☐	☐	☐	☐
9. Ich denke, ein Big Mäc ist nicht so gesund.	☐	☐	☐	☐
10. Ich habe einen neuen Wok.	☐	☐	☐	☐

Infobox

Beim Schnellimbiss

Ein Berliner Schnellimbiss

Für Leute, die wenig Zeit haben, gibt es verschiedene Möglichkeiten, schnell im Stehen etwas zu essen:

- Würstchenstände verkaufen Bockwurst, Knackwurst oder Currywurst mit Senf[1] und Brötchen.
- Beim Schnellimbiss gibt es außer Wurst mit Brötchen auch noch Hamburger und heiße Gulaschsuppe.
- Beim Kebabstand kaufen nicht nur türkische Mitbürger[2] ihren Döner Kebab, sondern auch viele Deutsche. Für Vegetarier gibt es hier auch oft Falafel oder türkische Pizza.

Natürlich kann man bei den Schnellrestaurants auch aus dem Auto etwas bestellen. Bei McDonald's oder Burger King fährt man dazu durch den „Drive-in".

[1]*mustard* [2]*fellow citizens*

2 Describing people, places, and things

Relative clauses and relative pronouns

9-17 to 9-23

Like adjectives, relative clauses are used to describe people, places, and things.

	ADJECTIVE	**NOUN**	
This	*expensive*	wine	is not very good.

	NOUN	**RELATIVE CLAUSE**	
The	wine	*that cost you so much*	is not very good.

Relative clauses are introduced by relative pronouns. A relative pronoun refers back to a noun, which is called its *antecedent*.

	RELATIVE CLAUSE		
ANTECEDENT	**RELATIVE PRONOUN**		
The wine	*that*	*you bought*	is not very good.
The friend	*to whom*	*you want to give it*	is a wine connoisseur.

Relative clauses and relative pronouns in German

	RELATIVE CLAUSE		
ANTECEDENT	**REL. PRON.**		
Der Wein,	**der**	**so viel gekostet hat,**	ist nicht sehr gut.
Der Wein,	**den**	**du gekauft hast,**	ist nicht sehr gut.
Der Freund,	**dem**	**du den Wein schenkst,**	ist ein Weinkenner.
Die Freunde,	**die**	**uns eingeladen haben,**	sind Weinkenner.

The relative pronoun has the same *gender* (masculine, neuter, or feminine) and *number* (singular or plural) as its antecedent. Its *case* (nominative, accusative, or dative) is determined by its function within the relative clause.

Der Wein, **den** du gekauft hast, ist nicht sehr gut.

*The wine **that** you bought is not very good.*

The relative pronoun **den,** like its antecedent **Wein,** is masculine and singular. It is in the accusative case because it is the direct object of the verb within the relative clause.

Note:

- Relative clauses are dependent clauses. They are marked off by a comma, and the conjugated verb appears at the end of the clause.
- In contrast to English, the German relative pronoun can never be omitted.

Der Wein, **den** du gekauft hast, ist nicht sehr gut.

The wine you bought is not very good.

Lerntipp: The graphic below may help you remember how to determine the gender, number, and case of a relative pronoun.

antecedent   rel. clause

m., n., or f.   nom., acc., or dat.

rel. pron.

sing. or pl.

forms of the relative pronoun				
	MASCULINE	NEUTER	FEMININE	PLURAL
NOMINATIVE	der	das	die	die
ACCUSATIVE	den	das	die	die
DATIVE	dem	dem	der	**denen**

Note that except for **denen,** the forms in the chart are identical to those of the definite article.

Die Freunde, **denen** ich den Wein schenken will, sind Weinkenner.	*The friends **to whom** I want to give the wine are wine connoisseurs.*

9-26 Der erste Tag. Heute ist Ihr erster Tag als Kellnerin/Kellner und Sie sind oft noch ein bisschen verwirrt°. Ergänzen Sie die Relativpronomen …   *confused*

… im Nominativ:
1. Wo ist denn der Mann, d__ dieses Bier bestellt hat?
2. Wo ist denn das Ehepaar, d__ dieses Gulasch bestellt hat?
3. Wo ist denn die Frau, d__ diese Tasse Kaffee bestellt hat?
4. Wo sind denn die Leute, d__ diese Suppe bestellt haben?

… im Akkusativ:
5. Wo ist denn der Mann, d__ ich so schnell bedienen soll?
6. Wo ist denn das Ehepaar, d__ ich so schnell bedienen soll?
7. Wo ist denn die Frau, d__ ich so schnell bedienen soll?
8. Wo sind denn die Leute, d__ ich so schnell bedienen soll?

… im Dativ:
9. Wo ist denn der Mann, d__ ich dieses Schnitzel bringen soll?
10. Wo ist denn das Ehepaar, d__ ich diesen Rotwein bringen soll?
11. Wo ist denn die Frau, d__ ich die Speisekarte bringen soll?
12. Wo sind denn die Leute, d__ ich diesen Nachtisch bringen soll?

9-27 Wer ist das? Was für Leute gehören zu den Namensschildern° an diesem Mietshaus°? Die Information für **S2** ist im *Anhang* auf Seite A9.

name plates
apartment building

S2: Wer sind Paul und Lisa Borg?	**S1:** Das sind die Leute, die fast jeden Tag ins Gasthaus gehen.
S1: Wer ist Ergül Ertem?	**S2:** Das ist der Mann, …

If **Mittel** are *resources* or *means,* what is the literal meaning of **Lebensmittel?**

Ergül Ertem 🔔	
Paul u. Lisa Borg 🔔	die fast jeden Tag ins Gasthaus gehen
Maria Schulz 🔔	
Manuel Lima 🔔	der immer die tollen Partys gibt

Monika Strzinska 🔔	der der große, weiße Hund gehört
Hans Maier 🔔	
Karl u. Anna Weiler 🔔	denen das Lebensmittel- geschäft° um die Ecke gehört
Teresa Venitelli 🔔	

grocery store

9-28 Definitionen.

▶ Eine Ärztin ist eine Frau, …

die kranke Menschen wieder gesund macht.

Eine Ärztin ist eine Frau, die kranke Menschen wieder gesund macht.

1. Ein Kellner ist ein Mann, …

3. Ein Automechaniker ist ein Handwerker, …

2. Ein Psychiater ist ein Arzt, …

4. Eine Marktfrau ist eine Frau, …

den man braucht, wenn das Auto kaputt ist.	die auf dem Wochenmarkt Obst und Gemüse verkauft.
der im Gasthaus das Essen serviert.	dem man alles erzählen kann.

bird 5. Eine Fleischerei ist ein Geschäft, …

7. Ein Huhn ist ein Vogel° (m), …

6. Eine Schnecke ist ein Tier (n), …

8. Eine Kaffeemaschine ist eine Maschine, …

den wir für Eier und für Fleisch brauchen.	die man braucht, um Kaffee zu machen.
das Fleisch und Wurst verkauft.	das man in Frankreich gern isst.

9-29 **Weißt du das?** S1 stellt die Fragen und ergänzt die Relativpronomen. S2 beginnt die Antworten mit „Er/Es/Sie heißt …" oder mit „Sie heißen …".

1. Wie heißt das große Technikmuseum, d__ man in München besuchen kann?
2. Wie heißt die berühmte Kunsthochschule, d__ Walter Gropius 1919 gegründet hat?
3. Wie heißt eine europäische Hauptstadt, d__ an der Donau liegt?
4. Wie heißen die Berge, d__ in der Schweiz liegen?
5. Wie heißt die Brücke°, d__ der Ingenieur Johann August Röbling   *bridge* entworfen hat?
6. Wie heißt das berühmteste Schloss, d__ König Ludwig II. gebaut hat?
7. Wie heißt der österreichische Immigrant, d__ 2003 in Kalifornien Gouverneur geworden ist?
8. Wie heißt der schweizerische Tennisspieler, d__ zwei olympische Medaillen gehören?
9. Wie heißt der Komponist, d__ man in Salzburg liebt?

9-30 **Kettenreaktion: Wie heißt …?** Schreiben Sie zwei Fragen über eine Mitstudentin oder einen Mitstudenten. Eine Person beginnt dann eine Kettenreaktion und stellt der Klasse die erste Frage. Die Person, die korrekt antwortet, stellt dann die nächste Frage, und immer so weiter. Folgen Sie dem Beispiel.

▶ **S1:** Wie heißt der Student, der heute ein schickes, rotes T-Shirt trägt?

Maximilian

S2: Das ist Maximilian!

▶ **S2:** Wie heißt die Studentin, die schon viele Reisen gemacht hat?

Anna

S3: Das ist Anna!

…

Nur für Kunden

Kostenlose Parkmünzen <u>NUR</u> bei Einkauf !!

  **3 N-Nouns**

9-24 to 9-25

N-nouns are a group of masculine nouns that take the ending **–n** or **–en** in all cases except the nominative singular. **Der Kunde** *(customer)* and **der Student** are two examples. In the paragraph below, note that only the nominative form **(der Student)** does not have an **–n** or **–en** ending.

> Ich habe gestern **einen Studenten** aus dem Soziologieseminar im Parkhaus getroffen. Das Parkhaus ist nur **für Kunden. Der Student** hat mir erzählt, dass **die Kunden** hier kostenlos parken dürfen, wenn sie etwas im Kaufhaus kaufen.

Most German dictionaries, as well as the *Wortschatz* sections in *Treffpunkt Deutsch*, show the nominative singular of a noun followed by any changes that occur in the genitive singular and in the plural. This convention clearly identifies **n-**nouns: If the genitive singular ending is **–en** or **–n,** the noun is an **n-**noun. Some additional common **n-**nouns:

der Athlet, –en, –en	der Mensch, –en, –en	der Präsident, –en, –en
der Herr, –n, –en	der Nachbar, –n, –n	der Tourist, –en, –en
der Junge, –n –n	der Patient, –en, –en	
der Kollege, –n, –n	der Polizist, –en, –en	

Infobox

Einkaufsgewohnheiten[1]

Öko? – Logisch!

Kontrolliert ökologische Landwirtschaft

In den deutschsprachigen Ländern gibt es in jeder Stadt viele Bäcker und Fleischer, obwohl man Brot, Brötchen, Fleisch und Wurst auch im Supermarkt kaufen kann. Viele Leute kaufen ihr Brot und ihre Wurst aber immer noch bei ihrem Lieblingsbäcker oder -fleischer, weil sie glauben, dass kein anderer Bäcker oder Fleischer so gut ist wie ihrer. Um frische Sachen aus der Region zu bekommen, gehen viele Leute auf den Wochenmarkt.

Bio-Läden[2] und Reformhäuser[3] gibt es in den deutschsprachigen Ländern schon viel länger als in Nordamerika. Dort kann man chemiefreie, nicht genetisch manipulierte Lebensmittel aus ökologisch kontrolliertem Anbau[4] kaufen, und auch Vitamine und viele andere Dinge, die besonders gesund sein sollen. Viele Supermärkte haben jetzt auch eine Abteilung für Bio-Lebensmittel.

Eine Drogerie ist nicht ganz dasselbe wie ein nordamerikanischer *drugstore,* denn rezeptpflichtige[5] Medikamente und sogar[6] rezeptfreie Medikamente wie Aspirin kann man in den deutschsprachigen Ländern nur in der Apotheke kaufen.

---

[1]*shopping habits* [2]*organic food stores* [3]*health food stores* [4]*certified organic farming* [5]*prescription* [6]*even*

SCHILDHORN APOTHEKE

Zusammenschau

🔊 ## Hören

Wandern macht hungrig

Martin und Peter sind übers Wochenende in die Alpen gefahren, sind seit dem frühen Morgen gewandert und sitzen jetzt im Gasthof Fraundorfer in Garmisch-Partenkirchen. Hören Sie, was Peter, Martin und der Kellner miteinander sprechen.

NEUE VOKABELN

Kassler	*smoked pork chop*	**Die Kartoffeln sind nicht gar.**	*The potatoes are not done.*
Alles in Ordnung?	*Is everything OK?*	**getrennt**	*separate*
		Schon gut.	*It's all right.*

More on restaurant etiquette: In the German-speaking countries, customers often pay the server directly at the table, especially in a pub when only drinks are ordered. The server carries a special purse from which to give change. Leaving money on the table for the bill or a tip is not a common practice.

9-31 Erstes Verstehen. In welcher Reihenfolge hören Sie das?

_____ Alles in Ordnung, meine Herren?
_____ Sollen wir etwas sagen?
_____ Die Speisekarte, bitte.
_____ Möchten Sie vielleicht ein paar Knödel?
_____ Machen Sie's sechsundzwanzig Euro.
_____ Du, was machen wir denn nach dem Essen?
_____ Und zu trinken?

9-32 Detailverstehen. Hören Sie das Gespräch noch einmal und schreiben Sie Antworten zu den folgenden Fragen.

1. Warum essen Martin und Peter beide Kassler?
2. Was trinken die beiden?
3. Was machen Martin und Peter nach dem Essen?
4. Was ist mit den Kartoffeln, die der Kellner gebracht hat, nicht in Ordnung?
5. Warum will Peter nichts sagen?
6. Wie viel kostet alles zusammen und auf wie viel rundet Peter auf?

dreihundertdreizehn / **313**

Sprechen und Schreiben

9-33 Ein Abendessen im Gasthof Fraundorfer. Heute Abend gehen Sie mit ein paar Freunden in den Gasthof Fraundorfer. Sehen Sie sich die Speisekarte an, die die Kellerin Ihnen bringt, und sprechen Sie mit Ihrem Partner / Ihrer Partnerin über Ihr Essen.

- Welches Menü oder welches Gericht nehmen Sie? Warum finden Sie dieses Gericht so lecker?
  Weil ich gern scharfe / süße / saure Sachen esse. Weil ich gern Gemüse / Fleisch / Pasta esse. Weil die Beilagen mir gefallen.
- Was bestellen Sie sich zu trinken dazu? Warum?
  Weil es gut zu meinem Essen passt. Weil ich das noch nie getrunken habe.
- Schreiben Sie Ihre eigene Rechnung für das Abendessen. Wie viel hat es gekostet? Wie viel Trinkgeld geben Sie der freundlichen Bedienung?

Tagesmenü: Note that **Menü** and *menu* are not equivalents. How would you translate **Tagesmenü?**

In restaurants beverages are served in glasses with a line and number **(der Eichstrich)** showing how much liquid is in the glass (0,2 l; 0,25 l; 0,33 l). In a glass of beer, the foam starts at this line.

SPEISEKARTE

TAGESMENÜ I Tagessuppe Wiener Schnitzel mit Kartoffelsalat Vanilleeis	€ 12,20
TAGESMENÜ II Tagessuppe Sauerbraten mit Kartoffelpüree und Salat Vanilleeis	€ 12,70
SUPPEN	
Tagessuppe	€ 2,00
Nudelsuppe	€ 2,60
HAUPTGERICHTE	
1. Bratwurst mit Sauerkraut und Bratkartoffeln	€ 8,50
2. Ungarisches Gulasch, Eiernudeln und gemischter Salat	€ 9,00
3. Schweinebraten mit Rotkraut und Salzkartoffeln	€ 9,50
4. Hühnchen mit Weinsoße, Reis und Tomatensalat	€ 10,00
5. Filetsteak gegrillt mit Champignons, Pommes frites und Gurkensalat	€ 14,60
ZUM NACHTISCH	
Schokoladenpudding	€ 1,50
Fruchtsalat mit frischen Früchten	€ 3,00
Apfelstrudel	€ 4,00
Schwarzwälder Kirschtorte	€ 4,00
GETRÄNKE	
Cola (0,2 l)	€ 1,60
Apfelsaft (0,2 l)	€ 1,80
Kaffee, Tasse	€ 1,80
Kaffee, Kännchen	€ 3,50
Tee, Kännchen	€ 3,00
Bier, vom Fass (0,33 l)	€ 2,00
Weißwein, Mosel (0,2 l)	€ 3,50
Rotwein, Lemberger (0,2 l)	€ 3,50

9-34 Wie war's? Schreiben Sie eine Bewertung *(review)* des Gasthofs Fraundorfer für eine Webseite. Wie hat es Ihnen geschmeckt (Tagessuppe, Tagesmenü, Hauptgericht, Nachtisch, Getränke)? Wie war die Bedienung? Wie waren die Preise? Wie viele Sterne geben Sie dem Gasthof Fraundorfer?

★★★★★
★★★★
★★★
★★
★

Lesen

Zum besseren Verstehen

9-35 Geldscheine°.

banknotes, bills

1. Kennen Sie Geldscheine von anderen Ländern? Wenn ja, von welchen?
2. Was gefällt Ihnen an diesen Geldscheinen nicht so gut wie oder besser als an den Geldscheinen Ihres Landes?

9-36 Was ist das auf Englisch?

1. Geldscheine sind aus Papier und **Münzen** sind aus Metall.
2. **Vorderseite** ist das Gegenteil von Rückseite.
3. Durch einen **Wettbewerb** findet man heraus, wer etwas am besten kann.
4. Felix studiert Musik und **nimmt** oft **an** Wettbewerben **teil.**
5. Mit dem Computer hat ein neues **Zeitalter** begonnen.
6. In seinem Charakter hat Daniel große **Ähnlichkeit** mit seinem Vater.
7. Ein Banknoten-Designer **entwirft** Banknoten.
8. Was ein Designer entwirft, ist ein **Entwurf.**
9. Über eine **Brücke** kommt man von einer Seite eines Flusses auf die andere.
10. Geldscheine und Münzen sind **Bargeld.**

a. design
b. epoch
c. cash
d. similarity
e. front
f. takes part in
g. competition
h. bridge
i. coins
j. designs

At present, the euro is the official currency in 17 of the 27 EU member states: Austria, Belgium, Cyprus, Estonia, Finland, France, Germany, Greece, Ireland, Italy, Luxembourg, Malta, the Netherlands, Portugal, Slovakia, Slovenia, and Spain. Take a look at the map at the back of the book to locate the 10 EU member states that are currently using their national currencies.

Robert Kalina und der Euro

Der Euro: Europäisch und national

Seit dem 1. Januar 2002 bezahlen die Europäer ihre Einkäufe nicht mehr mit
Mark, Schilling, Franken, Lire, Peseten, Gulden, Drachmen usw., sondern mit
Euros. Die Euromünzen haben eine „europäische" Vorderseite – sie ist das Werk
des belgischen Münzen-Designers Luc Luycx – und eine „nationale" Rückseite,
die in jedem Land anders aussieht. Bei den Euroscheinen sind aber beide Seiten
„europäisch" und alle sieben Scheine (5, 10, 20, 50, 100, 200 und 500 Euro) sind
das Werk des österreichischen Banknoten-Designers Robert Kalina.

Das Design des Euro

Robert Kalina ist Banknoten-Designer bei der Österreichischen
Nationalbank. Als die EZB (Europäische Zentralbank) im Februar 1996 zu ei-
nem Wettbewerb für das Design des Euro einlädt, nimmt auch Robert Kalina
daran teil und wählt[1] das Thema „Zeitalter und Stile Europas". Mögliche
Motive sind Porträts und Architektur, aber ohne Ähnlichkeit mit wirklichen
Personen oder realen Gebäuden. Porträts von imaginären Europäern, denkt
Robert Kalina, machen wenig Sinn[2]. Er entwirft deshalb imaginäre Gebäude
in den Baustilen verschiedener europäischer Epochen: von der griechisch-

römischen Antike auf dem 5-Euro-Schein bis
zum Ende des zwanzigsten Jahrhunderts auf dem
500-Euro-Schein. Auf der Vorderseite zeigen
Kalinas Scheine Tore[3] und Fenster und auf der
Rückseite Brücken, alles Symbole für den Weg[4]
der europäischen Staaten zueinander. Die verschiedenen Größen und Farben der Scheine sind
übrigens von der EZB vorgegeben[5]. Man soll
daran sofort erkennen, welchen Schein man in
der Hand hält.

Die Entscheidung für Kalinas Design

Im September 1996 wählt eine Experten-Jury die fünf
besten Entwürfe und Robert Kalinas Entwurf ist einer
davon. Danach prüft[6] die EZB die Akzeptanz dieser
Entwürfe durch eine Gallup-Umfrage unter 2000
Europäern, die viel mit Bargeld zu tun haben, wie zum
Beispiel Taxifahrer, Verkäufer und Kassierer[7]. Robert
Kalinas Designs gefallen diesen Leuten am besten und
im Juli 1999 beginnt in zwölf europäischen Ländern die
Produktion von 16 Milliarden[8] Scheinen.

[1]selects [2]sense [3]gates [4]path [5]set [6]tests [7]cashiers [8]billion

Arbeit mit dem Text

9-37 **Richtig oder falsch?**

1. ____ Bei den Euromünzen ist nur eine Seite „europäisch".
2. ____ Die Euroscheine haben eine „nationale" Rückseite.
3. ____ Imaginäre europäische Personen und Gebäude sind mögliche Motive für das Design der Euroscheine.
4. ____ Für den 5-Euro-Schein wählt Robert Kalina den Baustil der griechisch-römischen Antike.
5. ____ Fenster, Tore und Brücken sollen symbolisieren, dass die europäischen Staaten einander immer näher kommen.
6. ____ Robert Kalina wählt für seine Scheine verschiedene Größen und Farben.
7. ____ Die Jury will durch eine Umfrage herausfinden, welches Design der EZB am besten gefällt.

Das Hauptquartier der Europäischen Zentralbank in Frankfurt.

The European Central Bank administers the monetary policy of the 17 member states that have adopted the euro as their common currency. The ECB was established in 1998 and is headquartered in Frankfurt/Main. The tall building to the left of the ECB is the headquarters of Commerzbank, Germany's second-largest bank after Deutsche Bank. The Commerzbank Tower, which opened in 1997, is considered Europe's first "green" skyscraper.

Wort, Sinn und Klang

Wörter unter der Lupe

Predicting gender

In German and in English the suffix **–er** is used to form *agent nouns,* i.e., nouns that show who or what does the action described by a given verb. Agent nouns with the suffix **–er** are always masculine and can refer to things as well as people. Some of these nouns take an umlaut.

kaufen	*to buy*	**der** Käuf**er,** –	*buyer*
wecken	*to wake (someone) up*	**der** Weck**er,** –	*alarm clock*

If an agent noun refers to a female, the suffix **–in** is added to the masculine suffix **–er.**

der Käuf**er**	*(male) buyer*	**die** Käuf**erin, –nen**	*(female) buyer*

9-38 **Was passt wo?** Choosing appropriate infinitives, create German equivalents of the English nouns listed below. The articles indicate whether the nouns are to refer to a male or a thing **(der)** or to a female **(die).** Note that there are three compound nouns.

vermieten / einwandern / verkaufen / kennen / übersetzen / Korken + ziehen / anfangen (Umlaut!) / besuchen / Arbeit + geben / Anruf + beantworten

1. beginner   der _____
2. translator   die _____
3. corkscrew   der _____
4. immigrant   der _____
5. answering   der _____
   machine
6. visitor   die _____
7. sales clerk   der _____
8. employer   der _____
9. landlady   die _____
10. connoisseur   der _____

Giving language color

There are so many expressions based on the names of the parts of the body that another sampling is in order!

Mir raucht der Kopf.	*I can't think straight anymore.*
Sie findet immer ein Haar in der Suppe.	*She finds fault with everything.*
Ich muss mit dir unter vier Augen sprechen.	*I have to talk to you in private.*
Sie tanzen ihr auf der Nase herum.	*They walk all over her.*
hit **Er hat mich übers Ohr gehauen°.**	*He pulled a fast one on me.*
Wir haben uns die Beine in den Bauch gestanden.	*We stood until we were ready to drop.*
Ich drücke dir die Daumen.	*I'll keep my fingers crossed for you.*

9-39 Was passt zusammen?

1. Warum hörst du denn schon auf, zu lernen?
2. Warum soll ich denn nicht Lehrerin werden?
3. Warum soll ich weggehen, wenn Günter kommt?
4. Warum kaufst du Ulis Wagen nicht?
5. Warum willst du mich dein Referat nicht lesen lassen?
6. Warum soll *ich* denn die Karten für das Fußballspiel kaufen?
7. Warum hast du in dieser Klausur nur eine Drei bekommen?

a. Weil ich mit ihm unter vier Augen sprechen muss.
b. Weil du immer ein Haar in der Suppe findest.
c. Weil mir der Kopf raucht.
d. Weil du dir auch mal die Beine in den Bauch stehen kannst.
e. Weil dir die Schüler bestimmt alle auf der Nase herumtanzen.
f. Weil du mir die Daumen nicht gedrückt hast.
g. Weil ich Angst habe°, dass er mich übers Ohr haut.

Angst habe: *am afraid*

9-34 to 9-35

Zur Aussprache

German *s*-sounds: voiced *s* and voiceless *s*

Before vowels the sound represented by the letter **s** is *voiced,* i.e., it is pronounced like English *z* in **z**ip.

1. Wohin rei**s**en **S**u**s**e und **S**abine? – Auf eine **s**onnige **S**üd**s**eein**s**el.
2. **S**o ein **S**auwetter! **S**eit **S**onntag keine **S**onne!

Before consonants and at the end of a word, the sound represented by the letter **s** is *voiceless,* i.e., it is pronounced like English *s* in *sip.* The sounds represented by **ss** and **ß (Eszett)** are also *voiceless.*

1. Der Mensch i**s**t, wa**s** er i**ss**t.
2. I**s**t da**s** alle**s**, wa**s** du wei**ß**t?
3. Wo i**s**t hier da**s** be**s**te Gasthau**s**?

The sound represented by the letter **z** is pronounced like English *ts* in *hits.*

1. Der **Z**ug nach **Z**ürich fährt um **z**ehn.
2. Wann kommt Hein**z** aus Gra**z** **z**urück?
3. **Z**ahnär**z**te **z**iehen **Z**ähne.

Contrasting German *s*-sounds

so	**Z**oo	Gra**s**	Gra**z**	
seit	**Z**eit	Schwei**ß**°	Schwei**z**	*sweat*
Saal	**Z**ahl	Kur**s**	kur**z**	
selten	**z**elten	hei**ß**en	hei**z**en°	*to heat*
Sieh!	**Z**ieh!	bei**ß**en	bei**z**en°	*to stain (wood)*

Remember that at the beginning of a word or word stem, **s** in the combinations **st** and **sp** is pronounced like English *sh.*

Liechten**s**tein	Österreich	**Sp**eisekarte	A**s**pik	
Stadt	Ga**s**t	**Sp**ende°	We**s**pe°	*donation / wasp*
Student	A**ss**istent	Au**ss**prache	A**s**pirin	
Be**s**teck	Fe**s**t	**sp**ielen	li**s**peln	
Lippen**s**tift°	Li**s**te	ver**sp**rechen	ve**s**pern°	*lipstick / to have a snack*

Schloss Eggenberg in Graz, Österreich

🔊 Wortschatz 2

Nomen

der Föhn, -e	blow-dryer
die Haarbürste, -n	hairbrush
das Handtuch, ¨er	towel
der Kamm, ¨e	comb
der Lippenstift, -e	lipstick
der Rasierapparat, -e	shaver, electric razor
das Rasierwasser	aftershave
die Seife, -n	soap
der Spiegel, -	mirror
der Waschlappen, -	washcloth
die Zahnbürste, -n	toothbrush
die Zahnpasta	toothpaste
die Apotheke, -n	pharmacy
die Drogerie, -n	drugstore
das Reformhaus, ¨er	health food store
das Bargeld	cash
die Brücke, -n	bridge
der Geldschein, -e	} banknote, bill *(money)*
der Schein, -e	
die Münze, -n	coin
die Vorspeise, -n	hors d'oeuvre
das Gericht, -e	dish *(food)*
das Hauptgericht, -e	main course
der Essig	vinegar
das Öl	oil
der Pfeffer	pepper
das Salz	salt
der Senf	mustard
die Stulle, -n	sandwich
der Herr, -n, -en	gentleman; Mr.
der Kollege, -n, -n	} colleague
die Kollegin, -nen	
der Kunde, -n, -n	} customer
die Kundin, -nen	
der Mitbürger, -	} fellow citizen
die Mitbürgerin, -nen	
der Polizist, -en, -en	} police officer
die Polizistin, -nen	

die Drogerie: Remember that most nouns that end in **-ie** are feminine.

Verben

sich an·ziehen, angezogen	to dress, to get dressed
sich aus·ziehen, ausgezogen	to undress, to get undressed
sich um·ziehen, umgezogen	to change one's clothes
sich baden	to take a bath
sich duschen	to take a shower
sich die Haare föhnen/ trocknen	to blow-dry/dry one's hair
sich kämmen	to comb one's hair
sich rasieren	to shave
sich schminken	to put on make-up
sich auf·regen	to get worked up; to get upset
sich beeilen	to hurry
sich benehmen (benimmt), benommen	to behave
sich entschuldigen	to apologize
sich erkälten	to catch a cold
sich setzen	to sit down
sich verspäten	to be late
sich wohl fühlen	to feel well

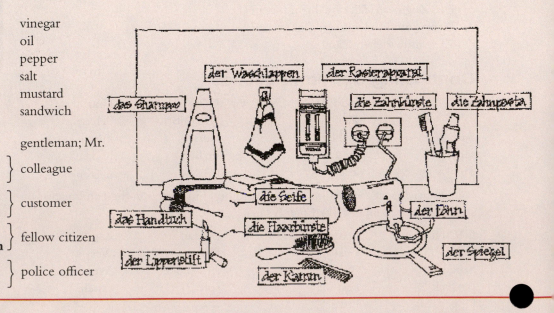

der Waschlappen · der Rasierapparat · die Zahnbürste · die Zahnpasta · das Shampoo · die Seife · der Zahn · das Handtuch · die Haarbürste · der Föhn · der Lippenstift · der Kamm · der Spiegel

entwerfen (entwirft), entworfen	to design		
fühlen	to feel		
verwenden	to use		
wählen	to choose, to select		
treffen (trifft), getroffen	to meet		

Ausdrücke

Alles in Ordnung?	Is everything okay?
Angst haben	to be afraid

Andere Wörter

ähnlich	similar
sogar	even

Das Gegenteil

bevor ≠ nachdem	before ≠ after (conj)

Leicht zu verstehen

der Athlet, -en, -en	der Vegetarier, -
die Athletin, -nen	die Vegetarierin, -nen
der Patient, -en, -en	vegetarisch
die Patientin, -nen	

Wörter im Kontext

9-40 Was passt zusammen? Beginnen Sie mit **Was brauche ich,** …

1. um mir die Haare zu waschen?
2. um mir die Haare zu trocknen?
3. um mir die Zähne zu putzen?
4. um mir die Hände zu waschen?
5. um mich zu kämmen?
6. um mich zu schminken?
7. um mich zu rasieren?

a. Einen Lippenstift.
b. Einen Kamm und einen Spiegel.
c. Einen Rasierapparat.
d. Wasser und Seife.
e. Ein Handtuch und einen Föhn.
f. Wasser und Shampoo.
g. Eine Zahnbürste und Zahnpasta.

9-41 Was passt?

sich umziehen / sich anziehen / sich ausziehen / sich beeilen
sich erkälten / sich wohl fühlen / sich entschuldigen

1. Bevor man sich duscht oder sich badet, _____ man _____ _____.
2. Nachdem man sich geduscht oder sich gebadet hat, _____ man _____ wieder _____.
3. Bevor man in die Oper geht, _____ man _____ _____.
4. Viele Menschen _____ _____ im Winter.
5. Wenn man morgens zu spät aufgestanden ist, sollte man _____ _____.
6. Wenn man sich verspätet hat oder wenn man sich schlecht benommen hat, sollte man _____ _____.
7. Wenn man _____ nicht _____ _____, sollte man zu Hause bleiben.

9-42 Was ist hier identisch? Welche zwei Sätze in jeder Gruppe bedeuten etwa dasselbe?

1. Ich habe den Gänsebraten mit Rotkohl gewählt.
   Ich habe für uns Gänsebraten mit Rotkohl gemacht.
   Ich habe den Gänsebraten mit Rotkohl genommen.

2. Bitte sei freundlich zu den anderen Gästen.
   Bitte bestell dir ein vegetarisches Gericht.
   Bitte benimm dich!

3. Ich fühle mich nicht wohl.
   Es tut mir leid.
   Mir geht es nicht gut.

4. Kommt ja rechtzeitig!
   Verspätet euch nicht!
   Regt euch nicht auf!

Lust auf Lesen

Büchermarkt in Freiburg

Kommunikationsziele

Telling stories

Talking about . . .
  • history
  • your own past experiences

Describing people, places, and things

Strukturen

Simple past tense

Wann, als, wenn

More on relative pronouns

Summary of adjective endings

Kultur

Vom Buch zum E-Buch

Zeitungen und Zeitschriften

Die Brüder Grimm

Video-Treff: **Meine Lieblingslektüre**

Lesen: **Der Hase und der Igel**

Der schlaue Student vom Paradies

nach Hans Sachs

Im sechzehnten Jahrhundert studierte einmal ein deutscher Student in Paris.
Im Juli war das Sommersemester zu Ende und der Student wollte zu seinen
Eltern nach Deutschland zurück. Weil er aber sehr arm war, konnte er kein
Pferd kaufen, sondern musste zu Fuß nach Deutschland wandern. (Busse
5 und Züge gab es damals natürlich noch nicht.)

Als der Student nach einer Woche zum ersten deutschen Dorf kam, war es
gerade Mittag, und weil er heute noch nichts gegessen hatte, war er sehr
hungrig. Er blieb deshalb bei einer Bäuerin stehen, die vor ihrem Haus im
Garten arbeitete, und sagte: „Guten Tag, liebe Frau. Haben Sie vielleicht
10 etwas zu essen für mich? Ich bin heute schon weit gewandert und habe
noch nicht mal gefrühstückt."

Die Bäuerin schaute von ihrer Arbeit auf und fragte: „Wer sind Sie denn
und woher kommen Sie?"

„Ich bin ein armer Student", antwortete er, „und ich komme von Paris."

15 Nun war die gute Frau zwar sehr fromm, aber nicht sehr intelligent. Sie
ging jeden Sonntag in die Kirche und sie hörte dort viel vom Paradies, aber
von Paris hatte sie noch nie etwas gehört. Und so verstand sie nicht *Paris,*
sondern *Paradies* und rief: „Was, Sie kommen vom Paradies?! Ja, dann
kennen Sie doch sicher meinen ersten Mann. Er war gut und fromm und ist
20 jetzt bestimmt im Paradies."

„Wie heißt er denn?" fragte der schlaue Student.

„Hans", antwortete die Bäuerin, „Hans Krüger."

„Oh, der Hans!" rief der Student. „Aber natürlich kenne ich ihn. Er
ist sogar ein guter Freund von mir und ich habe kürzlich mit ihm
25 gesprochen."

„Wie geht es ihm im Paradies?" fragte die Frau.

„Leider nicht sehr gut", antwortete der Student. „Hans ist sehr arm. Er hat
kein Geld, ist in Lumpen gekleidet und hat oft nicht mal genug zu essen."

„Oh, du mein armer Hans", weinte da die gute Frau, „du hast kein Geld
30 und keine Kleider und musst oft hungern und frieren. Aber vielleicht kann
ich dir helfen. Mein zweiter Mann ist reich und gut." Dann fragte sie den
Studenten: „Wann gehen Sie wieder ins Paradies zurück, junger Mann?"

Da rief der Bauer: „Oh, Frau!"

„Meine Ferien sind fast zu Ende", antwortete er, „und ich gehe schon übermorgen wieder zurück."

„Könnten Sie vielleicht für meinen armen Hans ein bisschen Geld und ein paar gute Kleider mitnehmen?"
40 fragte die Frau.

„Aber natürlich", sagte der Student, „das mache ich gern. Holen Sie nur das Geld und die Kleider, dann muss Ihr Hans bald nicht mehr hungern und frieren."

Da war die gute Frau sehr glücklich. Sie lief ins Haus und bald kam sie mit einem Bündel Kleider, mit zehn Goldstücken und mit einem großen Stück Brot wieder zurück. Das Brot gab sie dem Studenten und die
45 Goldstücke steckte sie in das Bündel. „Bitte, geben Sie meinem Hans dieses Bündel", sagte sie, „und grüßen Sie ihn von mir. Ich habe zwar wieder geheiratet, aber meinen Hans vergesse ich nie."

Der Student dankte der Bäuerin für das Brot, nahm das Bündel und wanderte so schnell wie möglich weiter.

Nach einer halben Stunde kam der Bauer vom Feld und die glückliche Frau erzählte ihm alles. Da rief er: „Oh, Frau!", lief schnell in den Stall, sattelte sein Pferd und galoppierte dem Studenten nach.

50 Der Student war mit seinem Bündel schon weit gewandert. Als er plötzlich ein Pferd galoppieren hörte, nahm er das Bündel schnell vom Rücken und versteckte es in einem Busch.

Der Bauer kam, hielt sein Pferd an und fragte: „Haben Sie vielleicht einen Studenten mit einem Bündel auf dem Rücken gesehen?"

„Ja", log der schlaue Student, „das ist sicher der Mann, mit dem ich gerade gewandert bin. Als er Ihr Pferd hörte,
55 hat er Angst gekriegt und ist schnell in den Wald gerannt."

„Halten Sie doch bitte mein Pferd!" rief da der Bauer. „Ich muss diesen Studenten fangen." Er stieg schnell vom Pferd und lief in den Wald. Der Student aber holte das Bündel aus dem Busch, stieg auf das Pferd und ritt schnell weg.

Der Bauer fand niemand im Wald, und als er wieder zurückkam, fand er auch den Studenten und das Pferd nicht
60 mehr. Da wurde ihm alles klar und er ging langsam zu Fuß nach Hause zurück.

Zu Hause fragte ihn seine Frau: „Warum kommst du zu Fuß zurück? Wo ist denn dein Pferd?"

„Ich habe es dem Studenten gegeben", antwortete der Bauer. „Mit dem Pferd kommt er schneller ins Paradies."

Sprachnotiz The past perfect tense

Like the English past perfect, the German past perfect is used to refer to an event that precedes another event in the past. It is formed with the simple past of the auxiliaries **haben** or **sein** and the past participle.

Der Student war sehr hungrig, denn er **war** weit **gewandert** und **hatte** noch nichts **gegessen**.

*The student was very hungry, because he **had walked** a long way and **had** not eaten anything yet.*

10-1 Wahrheit oder Lüge°? Sie hören *Der schlaue Student vom Paradies* und   *lie*
dann acht Aussagen. Markieren Sie nach jeder Aussage:

a. wer das sagt (der Student, die Bäuerin, der Bauer)
b. ob diese Leute glauben, was sie sagen (Wahrheit), oder ob sie lügen (Lüge).

A. DER STUDENT	DIE BÄUERIN	DER BAUER	B. WAHRHEIT	LÜGE
1. _____	_____	_____	_____	_____
2. _____	_____	_____	_____	_____
3. _____	_____	_____	_____	_____
4. _____	_____	_____	_____	_____
5. _____	_____	_____	_____	_____
6. _____	_____	_____	_____	_____
7. _____	_____	_____	_____	_____
8. _____	_____	_____	_____	_____

10-2 Was passt wo?

arbeitete / kam / sah

1. Als der Student durch das erste deutsche Dorf _____, _____ er dort eine
    Bäuerin, die vor ihrem Haus im Garten _____.

hatte / fragte / war / sagte

2. Weil es gerade Mittag _____ und weil er Hunger _____, _____ er „Guten
    Tag!" und _____: „Haben Sie vielleicht etwas zu essen für mich?"

hörte / fragte / verstand / antwortete

3. Die Frau _____: „Woher kommen Sie?" und der Student _____: „Von Paris."
    Weil die Frau aber jeden Sonntag vom Paradies _____, _____ sie nicht Paris,
    sondern Paradies.

hörte / holte / zurückging / war

4. Als die Frau _____, dass der Student übermorgen wieder ins Paradies _____,
    _____ sie ganz glücklich und _____ Geld, Kleider und ein Stück Brot.

galoppierte / sattelte / erzählte / lief

5. Als die Frau dem Bauern später von dem Studenten und dem Bündel _____,
    _____ er schnell in den Stall, _____ sein Pferd und _____ dem Studenten nach.

fragte / hörte / schickte / versteckte

6. Als der Student ein Pferd galoppieren _____, _____ er das Bündel schnell in
    einem Busch. Als der Bauer ihn nach° dem Studenten _____, _____ er ihn in   *about*
    den Wald.

stieg / fand / ritt / holte

7. Der Bauer _____ natürlich niemand. Der Student aber _____ das Bündel aus
    dem Busch, _____ auf das Pferd und _____ schnell weg.

Der Beginn des Informationszeitalters

Wenn wir heute vom Informationszeitalter[1] sprechen, denken wir an Computer, Internet und Satelliten, und wir vergessen, dass dieses Zeitalter eigentlich vor etwa 550 Jahren mit Johannes Gutenberg, dem Erfinder[2] des Buchdrucks,[3] begonnen hat. Vor Gutenberg brauchte ein Schreiber zwei volle Jahre, um eine einzige Bibel zu kopieren. Nach Gutenberg gab es bald Tausende von Druckereien in Europa, die Millionen von Büchern und anderen Texte produzierten.

Eine Sprache, die alle verstehen

Genauso wichtig wie die Erfindung des Buchdrucks war für die deutschsprachigen Länder Martin Luthers Bibelübersetzung. Die deutschen Dialekte waren so verschieden, dass die Menschen aus dem Norden ihre Nachbarn im Süden oft nicht verstanden. Die wenigen Gebildeten[4] schrieben und sprachen damals Latein. Luther übersetzte nun die Bibel in ein Deutsch, das auch einfache Menschen in allen deutschsprachigen Ländern verstehen konnten. Seine Übersetzungstechnik beschreibt er so: „… man muss die Mutter im Haus, die Kinder auf der Straße und den gemeinen[5] Mann auf dem Markt fragen und ihnen auf den Mund sehen, wie sie reden …"

Mehr Leute lesen und schreiben

Durch Gutenbergs Erfindung des Buchdrucks und Luthers Bibelübersetzung konnten immer mehr Menschen die Bibel und viele andere Texte lesen, und manche[6] von ihnen begannen sogar, selbst zu schreiben. So schrieb der Schuhmacher Hans Sachs aus Nürnberg (1494–1576) (Autor von *Der schlaue Student vom Paradies*) in seiner Freizeit Tausende Werke. Nicht viel später (1605) kam die erste Zeitung der Welt in Deutsch heraus. Bis in die erste Hälfte des 20. Jahrhunderts blieb die gedruckte Zeitung die wichtigste Informationsquelle[7].

[1]*information age*   [2]*inventor*   [3]*printing*   [4]*educated people*   [5]*common*   [6]*some*
[7]*source of information*

Weitere deutsche Erfindungen in der Kommunikationstechnologie

- 1861 erfand Philipp Reis ein Telefongerät
- 1941 baute Konrad Zuse den ersten programmierbaren Computer
- 1963 erfand Rudolf Hell den ersten Scanner
- 1995 entwickelte ein Team des Fraunhofer-Instituts die Audiokompression MP3

Neue Medien

Ähnlich wie Gutenbergs Erfindung vor 550 Jahren gibt uns heutzutage das Internet leichteren Zugang[8] zu Texten und Information — und papierlos dazu. Gutenbergs Konzept lebt also weiter: Webseiten wie *Project Gutenberg* bieten[9] digitalisierte E-Bücher und Audiobücher kostenlos zum Downloaden auch für elektronische Mobilgeräte.

[8]*access*   [9]*offer*

10-3 **Der durchschnittliche° Medienkonsum.** Was stimmt?   *average*

Die Grafik zeigt, …

____ wie die Situation im Jahr 2010 war.

____ was für Medien die Deutschen täglich nutzen.

____ wie viele Tage im Jahr man diese Medien nutzt.

____ welche Zeitschriften° die Deutschen gern lesen.   *magazines*

____ dass man mehr Radio hört als DVDs anschaut.

____ dass man mehr Zeit mit Büchern als mit Videos verbringt.

Nomen

der Erfinder, –	} inventor
die Erfinderin, –nen	
die Erfindung, –en	invention
das Informationszeitalter	information age
die Medien (pl)	media
die Quelle, –n	source
die Übersetzung, –en	translation
der Zugang	access

der Bauer, –n, –n	} farmer
die Bäuerin, –nen	
das Pferd, –e	horse
der Stall, ̈e	stable

die Angst	fear
das Glück	luck
das Jahrhundert, –e	century
die Kirche, –n	church

Verben

drucken	to print
erfinden, erfand, erfunden	to invent
fangen (fängt), fing, gefangen	to catch
frieren, fror, gefroren	to be cold
grüßen	to greet; to say hello
holen	to get; to fetch
lügen, log, gelogen	to lie
reiten, ritt, ist geritten	to ride (a horse)
rufen, rief, gerufen	to call
stecken	to stick (put); to be
stehen bleiben, blieb stehen, ist stehen geblieben	to stop (walking)
steigen, stieg, ist gestiegen	to climb
verstecken	to hide
weinen	to cry

Starting in this chapter, irregular verbs are listed with their principal parts. See p. 335 for more about principal parts.

Andere Wörter

als	when (conj)
damals	back then; at that time
durchschnittlich	average
einfach	simple; ordinary
fromm	pious
gekleidet	dressed
kürzlich	a short time ago, recently
manche	some
schlau	crafty, clever

Ausdrücke

Angst kriegen	to get scared
Viel Glück!	Good luck!

Das Gegenteil

die Lüge, –n ≠ die Wahrheit	lie ≠ truth
einfach ≠ kompliziert	simple ≠ complicated
hungrig ≠ satt	hungry ≠ full, sated

Leicht zu verstehen

die Bibel, –n	die Kommunikation
das Bündel, –	das Konzept, –e
der Busch, ̈e	das Paradies
der Dialekt, –e	das Team, –s
die Technologie, –n	kopieren
der Satellit, –en, –en	satteln
galoppieren	papierlos

Wörter im Kontext

10-4 Was passt?

1. Leute, _____, grüßen einander.
2. Katzen, _____, fangen keine Mäuse.
3. Ein Mann, _____, ist ein Bauer.
4. Ein Mensch, _____, ist ein Lügner.
5. Eine Firma, _____, ist papierlos.
6. Ein Mensch, _____, ist fromm.
7. Ein Mensch, _____, ist ein Erfinder.

a. der im Stall und auf dem Feld arbeitet
b. der sehr religiös ist
c. der nicht die Wahrheit sagt
d. die nicht hungrig sind
e. der sich etwas ganz Neues ausdenkt
f. die sich kennen
g. die keine gedruckten Dokumente benutzt

10-5 Mit anderen Worten. Welche zwei Sätze in jeder Gruppe bedeuten etwa dasselbe?

1. Mir ist kalt.
   Ich friere.
   Heute ist es kalt.

2. Warum stecken Sie die Fotos nicht ins Album?
   Warum stecken die Fotos nicht im Album?
   Warum sind die Fotos nicht im Album?

3. Ich habe genug gegessen.
   Ich bin satt.
   Ich habe Hunger.

4. Warum bleibst du stehen?
   Warum bleibst du nicht stehen?
   Warum gehst du nicht weiter?

5. Er sagt immer die Wahrheit.
   Er sagt nie die Wahrheit.
   Er lügt immer.

6. Das ist gar nicht kompliziert.
   Das ist ganz einfach.
   Das ist sehr schlau.

10-6 Was passt in jeder Gruppe zusammen?

1. die Kirche
2. die Technologie
3. das Jahrhundert
4. das Pferd

a. der Reiter
b. die Bibel
c. die Zeit
d. der Satellit

9. der Stall
10. die Erfindung
11. der Bauer
12. der Dialekt

i. das Konzept
j. die Sprache
k. das Pferd
l. das Feld

5. fangen
6. reiten
7. frieren
8. drucken

e. der Winter
f. der Ball
g. das Buch
h. das Pferd

10-7 Assoziationen. Was passt wo?

der Christ: ____, ____, ____, ____   das Pferd: ____, ____, ____, ____

der Satellit: ____, ____, ____, ____

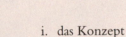

a. der Stall
b. die Information
c. reiten
d. papierlos
e. die Medien
f. die Kommunikation

g. fromm
h. galoppieren
i. die Bibel
j. die Kirche
k. das Paradies
l. satteln

Kommunikation und Formen

1 Narrating past events

The simple past tense

The simple past tense is used mainly in written German to narrate a series of connected events in the past. Sometimes called the narrative past, it is usually found in texts that tell a story, like biographies, histories, police and news reports, and literature. You will see that there are some similarities in the way the simple past is formed in German and English.

NEWS REPORT:

Als das Flugzeug **landete, kam**
der Präsident zum Flughafen
und **grüßte** die Soldaten.

*When the plane **landed,** the president
came to the airport and **greeted** the
soldiers.*

10-1 to 10-2

The simple past of regular verbs

Lerntipp: Regular verbs in the simple past tense use the same endings as **hatte.**

The simple past of regular verbs is formed by adding a past-tense marker to the verb stem (**–t–** in German and **–ed** in English). The **–t–** is inserted between the verb stem and the personal endings.

singular		plural	
ich	lernte	wir	lernten
du	lerntest	ihr	lerntet
er/es/sie	lernte	sie	lernten
		Sie lernten	

The German simple past has more than one English equivalent.

ich lernte	*I learned*
	I did learn
	I was learning

Verb stems that end in **–d, –t** (**land–en, arbeit–en**), or certain consonant combinations (**regn–en**) add an **e** before the past tense marker **–t–.**

singular		plural	
ich	land**e**te	wir	land**e**ten
du	land**e**test	ihr	land**e**tet
er/es/sie	land**e**te	sie	land**e**ten
		Sie land**e**ten	

10-8 Die Geschichte einer deutschen Burg. Ergänzen Sie die passenden Verben im Präteritum°.

simple past tense

baute / erzählten / besuchten

Im Jahr 1067 _____ man die Burg im Nordwesten des Thüringer Waldes. Zwischen 1190 und 1220 _____ oft berühmte Dichter° die Burg und im Sängersaal _____ sie ihre Geschichten.

writers; poets

spielte / hängte / protestierte

Die Burg _____ auch eine Rolle in der Reformation der katholischen Kirche in Deutschland. 1517 _____ Martin Luther gegen kirchliche Korruption, als er 95 Thesen an die Tür der Schlosskirche in Wittenberg _____.

übersetzte / versteckte / lebte

Drei Jahre später _____ sich Luther auf der Wartburg. Dort _____ er inkognito als „Junker Jörg" und in nur elf Wochen _____ er das Neue Testament aus dem Griechischen ins Deutsche.

restaurierte / feierte

1983 _____ man die Burg und _____ im selben Jahr die Neueröffnung der Burg zum 500. Geburtstag Luthers.

Hier lebte Luther inkognito als Junker Jörg.

10-3 to 10-8

The simple past of irregular verbs

Just as in English, the simple past of irregular verbs in German is signaled by a stem change.

German	English
sehen: ich s**a**h	to see: I s**aw**
gehen: ich g**ing**	to go: I **went**
schlafen: ich schl**ief**	to sleep: I sl**ept**

Lerntipp: Irregular verbs in the simple past tense use the same endings as **war.**

The simple past of German irregular verbs has no ending in the 1st and 3rd person singular.

singular	plural
ich trank	wir tranken
du trankst	ihr trankt
er/es/sie trank	sie tranken
	Sie tranken

10-9 Aus dem Polizeibericht.

ging / gab / starb / rief

deer

Kollision: Am Samstag _____ es kurz vor 21 Uhr auf der Waldstraße eine Kollision zwischen einem Auto und einem Reh°, das über die Straße _____. Die 27-jährige Fahrerin _____ die Polizei sofort an. Das Tier_____.

versprach / gab / fuhr / kam

gas theft

collateral

Tankbetrug°: Ein 21-jähriger Marburger _____ am Freitag, 11. Mai, gegen 17 Uhr mit seinem blauen Renault an die Tankstelle in der Uferstraße und tankte Benzin im Wert von 40 Euro. Da er kein Geld hatte, _____ er noch am gleichen Abend wieder zu kommen, und _____ sogar seinen Pass als Pfand°. Der Mann _____ trotzdem bis zum 30. Mai nicht wieder.

Sprachnotiz   The simple past of separable-prefix verbs

In the simple past, the prefix of separable-prefix verbs functions just as it does in the present tense.

Der Bauer sattelte sein Pferd und **galoppierte** dem Studenten **nach.**
Als der Bauer wieder **heimkam,** hatte er kein Pferd mehr.

10-10 **Gedenktafeln°.** Lesen Sie die Gedenktafeln und erklären Sie auf Englisch, was hier stattfand°.

commemorative plaques
took place

BERLINER GEDENKTAFEL

In diesem Hause lebten von 1934 bis zu ihrem Tode
HANNING SCHRÖDER
4. 7. 1896 – 16. 10. 1987
Komponist
CORNELIA SCHRÖDER-AUERBACH
24. 8. 1900 – 21. 10. 1997
Musikwissenschaftlerin

Von Anfang 1944 bis zum März 1945 versteckten sie
hier ein jüdisches Ehepaar
und halfen ihm so die »Shoa« zu überleben

Hier wohnte
Thüringens erste
Bäckermeisterin
Luzie Unruh
1917   2007

HIER STAND DAS HAUS IN DEM
JOHANN SEBASTIAN BACH
VON 1708–1717 WOHNTE

HIER WURDE GEBOREN
FRIEDEMANN BACH
AM 17. NOVEMBER 1710
PHILIPP EMANUEL BACH
AM 8. MÄRZ 1714

BERLINER GEDENKTAFEL

In diesem Hause wohnte und arbeitete
von 1893 bis 1894
RUDOLF DIESEL
18. 3. 1858 – 29. 9. 1913
Ingenieur und Erfinder des
Diesel-Motors

The simple past of mixed verbs

10-9 to 10-13

In the simple past, mixed verbs have the stem change of the irregular verbs, but the past-tense marker **–t–** and personal endings of the regular verbs.

bringen	**brachte**	nennen	**nannte**
denken	**dachte**	rennen	**rannte**
kennen	**kannte**	wissen	**wusste**

The verb **werden** has characteristics of a mixed verb: it has a stem change and the same personal endings as mixed verbs, but no **–t–** is added:

Tom **wird** morgen 21. ➜ Tom **wurde** gestern 21.

10-11 Mein erstes Semester. Ergänzen Sie die passenden Verben im Präteritum.

kannte / brachte

Anfang September _____ mein Vater mich zu meiner Uni. Obwohl ich dort keinen Menschen _____, hatte ich bald viele Freunde.

rannten / dachten

Wir _____ von einer Party zur anderen, hatten viel Spaß, aber _____ nur selten *of* an° unser Studium.

nannten / wurden / wusste

Natürlich _____ meine Zensuren immer schlechter. Mein Eltern _____ mich *good-for-nothing* einen richtigen Nichtsnutz°. Im zweiten Semester _____ ich, dass ich viel mehr lernen musste!

10-12 Manchmal sollte man gar nicht erst aufstehen. Suchen Sie die passenden Sätze zu diesen Bildern und lesen Sie dann die Geschichte laut vor.

__1__	Als Martin gestern aufwachte, schien ihm die Sonne ins Gesicht.

neither / nor _____ Da blieb zu nichts Zeit, weder° zum Duschen noch° zum Frühstück.

_____ Es war schon halb zehn und um zehn hatte er eine wichtige Klausur!

hardly _____ Und als er auf seinen Wecker schaute, konnte er kaum° glauben, was er da sah.

_____ Er sprang aus dem Bett und zog schnell Hemd und Hose an.

_____ Aber er kam zu spät: der Bus fuhr gerade um die Ecke.

bus stop _____ Wie verrückt rannte er zur Bushaltestelle°.

finally _____ Schließlich° stoppte er ein Taxi.

_____ „Was jetzt?" dachte Martin.

_____ Er versuchte, ein Auto anzuhalten, aber niemand hielt.

_____ Punkt zehn hielt das Taxi vor der Uni und der Fahrer sagte: „Fünf Euro, bitte."

_____ „Schnell zur Uni, bitte!" rief er, als er in das Taxi stieg.

_____ „Verflixt!° Sie steckt zu Hause in meiner anderen Jacke!"   *Darn it!*

_____ Aber da sah Martin auch schon die Lösung seines Problems: das war doch
        Claudia dort vor der Eingangstür!

_____ Und als das Taxi dann zur Uni raste°, wollte Martin seine Geldtasche aus   *raced*
        der Jacke holen.

_____ Und Gott sei Dank hörte sie ihn und hatte auch fünf Euro bei sich.

_____ Aber obwohl es schon fünf nach zehn war, war der Hörsaal leer!

_____ Schnell steckte er den Kopf durchs Fenster und rief: „Claudia!"

_____ Und an der Tafel stand: Impressionismus–Klausur auf nächste Woche
        verschoben°.   *postponed*

_____ Dann rannten sie zusammen die Treppe zum Hörsaal hinauf.

Principal parts of irregular
and mixed verbs can be
found on pp. A28–A30.

Sprachnotiz   Principal parts of verbs

Most verbs are *regular* verbs and their tenses derive from the stem of the
infinitive. Their forms are completely predictable in German, just as in English.

*lern*en	er *lern*t	er *lern*te	er hat ge*lern*t
to **learn**	he **learn**s	he **learn**ed	he has **learn**ed

In both German and English, all tenses of *irregular* and *mixed* verbs are
derived from a set of *principal parts*: the infinitive, the simple past, and the
past participle. If you know the principal parts of a verb, you can figure out
any form of that verb.

Principal parts: **singen, sang, gesungen**   *to sing, sang, sung*
                  schreiben, schrieb, geschrieben *to write, wrote, written*
                  bringen, brachte, gebracht   *to bring, brought, brought*

German verbs that are irregular in the present tense have an additional
principal part that reflects this irregularity, e.g., **geben,** *gibt,* **gab, gegeben.**

2 Expressing *when* in German

Wann, als, and *wenn*

Although **wann, als,** and **wenn** all correspond to English *when,* they are not interchangeable.

Wann introduces direct and indirect questions.

> Note that the verb in an **als**-clause is often in the simple past tense, even in conversation.

Wann kriegt Nina ihren Führerschein?
Ich weiß nicht, **wann** Nina ihren Führerschein kriegt.

When *is Nina getting her driver's license?*
I don't know **when** *Nina is getting her driver's license.*

Als introduces dependent clauses referring to a single event in the past or a block of time in the past.

Als ich ankam, klingelte das Telefon.
Als wir in Bremen lebten, war ich sieben.

When *I arrived, the phone rang.*
When *we lived in Bremen, I was seven.*

Wenn introduces dependent clauses referring to events in the present or future or to *repeated* events in any time frame.

Ruf mich bitte gleich an, **wenn** du in Frankfurt ankommst.
Wenn Oma uns besuchte, brachte sie immer einen Kuchen mit.

Please call me right away **when** *you arrive in Frankfurt.*
When *(whenever) grandma visited us, she always brought a cake.*

wann?	als	wenn
• questions	• single event in the past • block of time in the past	• events in the present or future • repeated events (all time frames)

10-13 **Fragen und Antworten.** Ergänzen Sie **als** oder **wenn.**

1. Wann hat Stephanie Peter kennen gelernt?

   _____ sie nach München kam, um dort ein Jahr lang zu studieren.

2. Wann macht Stephanie ihre tollen Pancakes?

   Immer _____ Peter zum Frühstück kommt.

3. Wann fährt Stephanie mit Peter zu seinen Eltern nach Berlin?

   _____ das Wintersemester zu Ende ist.

4. Wann fliegt Stephanie wieder nach Amerika zurück?

   _____ das Sommersemester zu Ende ist.

10-14 **Ein toller Reiter.** Ergänzen Sie **als** oder **wenn.**

_____ ich zwölf war, lebten wir in Berlin. Im Sommer 2005 besuchten wir meinen Großvater in Schleswig-Holstein. Er war Bauer und hatte ein wunderschönes Pferd. Jeden Morgen, _____ wir im Stall fertig waren, durfte ich auf diesem Pferd reiten.

Mein kleiner Bruder hatte Angst vor° Pferden. Jedes Mal _____ Großvater das Pferd aus dem Stall holte, rannte er ins Haus. Aber _____ wir wieder in Berlin waren, sagte er zu seinen Freunden: „_____ ich bei meinem Opa in Schleswig-Holstein war, habe ich sogar reiten gelernt."

hatte Angst vor:
was afraid of

10-15 Wann war das? Beginnen Sie jede Antwort mit *Als ich …* und verwenden Sie das Präteritum.

- Wann hast du Rad fahren gelernt? *Als ich …*
- Wann hast du schwimmen gelernt?
- Wann hast du deinen Führerschein gekriegt?
- Wann bist du zum ersten Mal zum Rockkonzert gegangen?
- Wann hast du zum ersten Mal Deutsch gesprochen?
- Wann bist du zum ersten Mal geflogen?

10-16 Eine Erinnerung°. Wählen Sie eine Frage von **10-15** und schreiben Sie kurz im Präteritum über diese Erinnerung: Wo war das? Mit wem waren Sie? War das eine schöne oder schlechte Zeit für Sie? usw.

memory

Infobox

Zeitungen und Zeitschriften

Viele Deutsche lesen täglich die Zeitung — entweder im Internet oder in gedruckter Version. Das Boulevardblatt[1] *Bild* ist Deutschlands meistgelesene Zeitung. Weniger gelesen, aber mit enormem Einfluss[2] sind überregionale Tageszeitungen wie die *Frankfurter Allgemeine (FAZ)* und die *Süddeutsche Zeitung* und die Wochenzeitung *Die Zeit*.

Die Zeitschriften *Der Spiegel*, *Focus* und *Stern* erscheinen[3] wie *Time*, *Newsweek* und das kanadische *Maclean's* wöchentlich. *Der Spiegel* hat übrigens auch eine englischsprachige Online-Version.

In Österreich ist *Die Presse* die größte Tageszeitung. Die *Wiener Zeitung,* die älteste Zeitung der Welt, gibt es seit dem 8. August 1703.

Die größte Tageszeitung der Schweiz, die *Neue Zürcher Zeitung,* erschien am 12. Januar 1780 zum ersten Mal und gehört zu den international angesehensten[4] deutschsprachigen Zeitungen.

Die größte luxemburgische Tageszeitung ist das dreisprachige *d'Wort*. 82 Prozent sind darin auf Deutsch geschrieben, 16 Prozent auf Französisch und 2 Prozent auf Lëtzebuergesch.

[1]*tabloid*   [2]*influence*   [3]*appear*   [4]*most respected*

Meine Lieblingslektüre

Kristina, Anja Szustak, André, Stefan Meister, Maiga, Thomas und Stefan Kuhlmann erzählen, was sie gern lesen. Machen Sie die erste Aufgabe, **Was ist das auf Englisch?,** bevor Sie das Video anschauen.

10-17 Was ist das auf Englisch?

1. Ich lese englische Bücher, damit mein Englisch **am Leben bleibt.**
2. Das ist ein Mensch, der immer noch **auf der Suche** ist.
3. Ich lese Bücher, die mich **fesseln.**
4. Ich muss ja leider viel für die Uni lesen, und **das reicht mir.**
5. Hier geht es **größtenteils** um lokale Nachrichten.
6. Wenn ich **nicht gerade** Bücher lese, lese ich Zeitschriften.
7. Diese Zeitschrift gibt es **seit den 80er Jahren.**

a. searching
b. largely
c. grab
d. not at the moment
e. since the eighties
f. stays alive
g. that's enough for me

10-18 Richtig oder falsch? Lesen Sie die Aussagen über Kristina, Anja, André und Stefan Meister. Sind diese Aussagen richtig oder falsch? Wenn eine Aussage falsch ist, korrigieren Sie sie.

	RICHTIG	FALSCH
1. Kristina kauft sich jeden Monat eine Sportzeitschrift.	☐	☐
2. In der Zeitschrift gefallen ihr besonders die Informationen über Sport, Gesundheit und so weiter.	☐	☐
3. Anja isst kein Fleisch und kauft deshalb die Zeitschrift *Vegetarisch Fit*.	☐	☐
4. Sie kauft *Vegetarisch Fit*, weil sie die Leserbriefe so interessant findet.	☐	☐
5. André liest gern Krimis, Autobiografien und Fantasiegeschichten.	☐	☐
6. Er liest jetzt eine Autobiografie.	☐	☐
7. Das Buch, das André im Moment liest, ist sehr gut aber nicht sehr lang.	☐	☐
8. Stefan Meister mag Bücher mit Geschichten, mit denen er sich identifizieren kann.	☐	☐
9. Stefan liest manchmal Bücher auf Englisch.	☐	☐
10. Stefans Lieblingsbuch ist von einem deutschen Autor.	☐	☐

10-19 **Was ich gern lese.** Ergänzen Sie die Aussagen über Maiga, Thomas und Stefan Kuhlmann.

1. Maiga liest am liebsten Bücher _____.
   ☐ im Urlaub ☐ für die Uni

2. Maiga liest gern _____, die sie fesseln.
   ☐ Bücher ☐ Zeitschriften

3. Thomas sagt, die *Berliner Zeitung* ist eine _____.
   ☐ Wochenzeitung ☐ Tageszeitung

4. Im _____ der *Berliner Zeitung* liest Thomas zum Beispiel Berichte über die Berliner Oper.
   ☐ Wirtschaftsteil ☐ Feuilleton

5. In der *Berliner Zeitung* gibt es einen Teil über Berlin, in dem man sich gut über _____ Nachrichten informieren kann.
   ☐ lokale ☐ nationale

6. Stefan Kuhlmann sagt, _____ ist die beste Filmzeitschrift in Deutschland.
   ☐ *Empire* ☐ *Cinema*

7. Stefan meint, der deutsche *Rolling Stone* ist _____ der amerikanische *Rolling Stone*.
   ☐ sehr viel besser als ☐ nicht so gut wie

8. Stefan sagt, der *Musikexpress* existiert seit _____.
   ☐ den 60er Jahren ☐ den 90er Jahren

9. Die Zeitschrift, die ihm am wichtigsten ist, hat Information über _____.
   ☐ Fernsehprogramme ☐ Rockmusiker

10. Stefan Kuhlmann liest _____ Bücher.
    ☐ nie ☐ auch

Was war dein Lieblingsbuch, als du klein warst?

3 Giving information about people, places, and things

The relative pronoun as object of a preposition

10-17 to 10-21

In *Kapitel 9* you learned that except for the dative plural **(denen),** the forms of the relative pronoun and the definite article are identical.

Das Haus, in dem man gut kauft.

forms of the relative pronoun				
	MASCULINE	NEUTER	FEMININE	PLURAL
NOMINATIVE	der	das	die	die
ACCUSATIVE	den	das	die	die
DATIVE	dem	dem	der	denen

You also learned that the relative pronoun has the same gender and number as its antecedent, but that its case is determined by its function within the relative clause.

	ANTECEDENT	RELATIVE CLAUSE	
		REL. PRON.	
Ist das	**der Computer,**	**den**	du gekauft hast?
Is that	**the computer**	**that**	*you bought?*

When a relative pronoun is the object of a preposition, the gender and number of the relative pronoun are still determined by the antecedent, but the case is determined by the preposition.

	ANTECEDENT	RELATIVE CLAUSE		
		PREP.	REL. PRON.	
Das ist	**der Computer,**	**für**	**den**	ich nur 800 Euro bezahlt habe.
This is	**the computer**	**for**	**which**	*I paid only 800 euros.*
Kennst du	**den Typ,**	**mit**	**dem**	Eva so oft chattet?
Do you know	**the guy**	**with**	**whom**	*Eva chats so often?*

The English translation could also read *This is the computer (that) I paid only 800 Euros for.* But in German, the preposition always *precedes* the relative pronoun and the relative pronoun can't be omitted.

10-20 Definitionen. Ergänzen Sie die Relativsätze.

▶ Was ist eine Säge?

Eine Säge ist ein Werkzeug, … mit dem man Bäume fällen kann.

S1: Was ist eine Säge?

S2: Eine Säge ist ein Werkzeug, mit dem man Bäume fällen kann.

1. Was ist ein Lkw?

Ein Lkw ist ein Fahrzeug, …

3. Was sind Bienen?

Bienen sind Insekten, …

2. Was ist ein Bücherregal?

Ein Bücherregal ist ein Möbelstück, …

4. Was ist ein Spiegel?

Ein Spiegel ist ein Stück Glas, …

in das man seine Bücher stellt.	in dem man sich selbst sehen kann.
von denen wir Honig bekommen.	mit dem man schwere Sachen transportiert.

10-21 Weißt du das? S1 stellt die Fragen und ergänzt die Relativpronomen. S2 beginnt die Antworten mit „Er/Es/Sie heißt …"

1. Wie heißt die Stadt, in d__ das Oktoberfest stattfindet?
2. Wie heißt der Ozean, über d__ man von Amerika nach Europa fliegt?
3. Wie heißt das deutschsprachige Land, in d__ auch Italienisch eine offizielle Sprache ist?
4. Wie heißt das Land, aus d__ der Euro-Banknoten-Designer kommt?
5. Wie heißt die Stadt, in d__ man beim KaDeWe einkaufen kann?
6. Wie heißt der Fluss, an d__ Wien liegt?
7. Wie heißt die Stadt, in d__ Walter Gropius das Bauhaus gründete?
8. Wie heißt die Burg, auf d__ Martin Luther inkognito lebte?

die Wartburg	die Schweiz	Weimar
Berlin	München	
der Atlantik	Österreich	die Donau

10-22 Ein paar Fragen über dein Leben an der Uni. Stellen Sie einander die folgenden Fragen.

- Wie heißt die Vorlesung, für die du am meisten lernen musst?
- Wie heißt die Vorlesung, in der du am öftesten einschläfst?
- Wie heißt der Professor, mit dem du die meisten Vorlesungen gehabt hast?
- Wie heißt das Campus-Gebäude, in dem du den größten Teil° deiner Zeit verbringst?

…

den größten Teil: *the greatest amount*

4 A review of adjective endings

10-22

Adjectives preceded by *der*-words

Lerntipp: To help remember the endings, think of the five places the adjective ending **-e** as forming the shape of a frying pan. All other adjective endings are **-en**.

Adjectives preceded by **der-words** take one of two endings: **–e** or **–en.**

	masculine	neuter	feminine	plural
NOMINATIVE	der jung**e** Mann	das klein**e** Kind	die jung**e** Frau	die klein**en** Kinder
ACCUSATIVE	den jung**en** Mann	das klein**e** Kind	die jung**e** Frau	die klein**en** Kinder
DATIVE	dem jung**en** Mann	dem klein**en** Kind	der jung**en** Frau	den klein**en** Kindern
GENITIVE	des jung**en** Mannes	des klein**en** Kindes	der jung**en** Frau	der klein**en** Kinder

10-23 Die reichen Müllers. Ergänzen Sie die Adjektivendungen.

1. Dieser reich__, alt__ Mann heißt Müller.

3. Das ist die einzig__ Tochter dieses reich__, alt__ Mannes.

showy

2. Dieses groß__, protzig__° Haus gehört dem reich__, alt__ Müller.

4. Diese beid__ weiß__ Pudel gehören der einzig__ Tochter des reich__, alt__ Müller.

10-24 Was?! Du kennst die reichen Müllers nicht? Ergänzen Sie die Adjektivendungen.

1. JENS: Kennst du den alt__ Mann dort?
   ANN: Welchen alt__ Mann?
   JENS: Den alt__ Mann mit der groß__ Nase und der dick__ Zigarre.
   ANN: Ja klar, das ist doch der reich__, alt__ Müller.

2. JENS: Wem gehört denn das groß__ Haus dort?
   ANN: Welches groß__ Haus?
   JENS: Das groß__ Haus mit der protzig__ Fassade.
   ANN: Das gehört dem reich__, alt__ Müller.

3. JENS: Wer ist denn die jung__ Frau dort?
   ANN: Welche jung__ Frau?
   JENS: Die jung__ Frau mit der lang__ Nase und den kurz__ Haaren.
   ANN: Das ist die einzig__ Tochter des reich__, alt__ Müller.

4. JENS: Wem gehören denn die beid__ Pudel dort?
   ANN: Welche beid__ Pudel?
   JENS: Die beid__ weiß__ Pudel vor dem groß__, protzig__ Haus.
   ANN: Das sind die beid__ Pudel der einzig__ Tochter des reich__, alt__ Müller.

Adjectives preceded by *ein*-words

10-23 to 10-24

Adjectives preceded by **ein**-words take endings identical to those after **der**-words, except in the three instances where the **ein**-word has no ending.

Lerntipp: Again, it may help you to picture the five places where the adjective endings are *not* **-en** as having the shape of a frying pan.

	masculine	neuter	feminine	plural
NOM.	ein jung**er** Mann	ein klein**es** Kind	eine junge Frau	meine klein**en** Kinder
ACC.	einen jung**en** Mann	ein klein**es** Kind	eine junge Frau	meine klein**en** Kinder
DAT.	einem jung**en** Mann	einem klein**en** Kind	einer jung**en** Frau	meinen klein**en** Kindern
GEN.	eines jung**en** Mannes	eines klein**en** Kindes	einer jung**en** Frau	meiner klein**en** Kinder

10-25 Lieschen Maiers Hund. Ergänzen Sie!

Lieschen Maier hatte einmal einen klein__, weiß__ Hund. Er war ein sehr schön__, weiß__ Hund und Lieschen liebte ihn sehr. Jeden Morgen gab sie ihm eine klein__ Dose Hundefutter und ging dann in die Schule. Wenn Lieschen nach der Schule mit ihrem klein__, weiß__ Hund im Park spazieren ging, hatte sie ihn immer an einer lang__ Leine. Und in Lieschens Schlafzimmer stand neben ihrem eigen__ Bett das Bettchen ihres klein__, weiß__ Hundes.

10-26 Fritzchen Müllers Katze.

Fritzchen Müller hatte einmal eine groß__, schwarz__ Katze. Sie war eine sehr schön__, schwarz__ Katze und Fritzchen liebte sie sehr. Jeden Morgen gab er ihr eine groß__ Dose Katzenfutter und ging dann in die Schule. Wenn Fritzchen nach der Schule mit seiner groß__, schwarz__ Katze im Park spazieren ging, hatte er sie immer an einer lang__ Leine. Und in Fritzchens Schlafzimmer stand neben seinem eigen__ Bett das Bettchen seiner groß__, schwarz__ Katze.

huge

10-27 Unser Krokodil.

Wir hatten einmal ein riesig__°, grün__ Krokodil. Es war ein sehr schön__, grün__ Krokodil und wir liebten es sehr. Jeden Morgen gaben wir ihm eine riesig__ Dose Krokodilfutter und gingen dann in die Schule. Wenn wir nach der Schule mit unserem riesig__, grün__ Krokodil im Park spazieren gingen, hatten wir es immer an einer lang__ Leine. Und in unserem Schlafzimmer stand neben unserem eigen__ Bett das Bettchen unseres riesig__, grün__ Krokodils.

10-28 Worauf hast du Lust?°

Beschreiben Sie mit passenden Adjektiven, worauf Sie Lust haben.

S1: Worauf hast du Lust?　　**S2:** Ich habe Lust auf einen großen, saftigen° Apfel. Und du?

groß / riesig / eiskalt / heiß / saftig / lecker …

What do you feel like (having)?

juicy

ZUM TRINKEN	ZUM ESSEN
ein _____ Glas Orangensaft	ein _____ Steak
eine _____ Cola	einen _____ Hamburger
ein _____ Bier	einen _____ Becher Eis
eine _____ Tasse Kaffee / Tee	ein _____ Stück Apfelkuchen
…	…

Lust auf ein großes Glas?

10-25 to 10-27

Unpreceded adjectives

When an adjective is not preceded by a **der-**word or an **ein-**word, the adjective shows the gender, number, and case of the noun by taking the appropriate **der-**word ending. The genitive forms are not listed here, because they are less common.

	masculine	neuter	feminine	plural
NOMINATIVE	gut**er** Kaffee	gut**es** Bier	gut**e** Salami	gut**e** Äpfel
ACCUSATIVE	gut**en** Kaffee	gut**es** Bier	gut**e** Salami	gut**e** Äpfel
DATIVE	gut**em** Kaffee	gut**em** Bier	gut**er** Salami	gut**en** Äpfeln

Was ist Rindfleisch?

10-29 **Essen und Trinken.** Ohne **der–**Wörter oder **ein–**Wörter, bitte!

▶ **Dieser** französische Käse ist sehr gut.

S: Französischer Käse ist sehr gut.

1. Mögen Sie **dieses** deutsche Bier?
2. Mit **einem** echten italienischen Mozzarella schmeckt die Pizza viel besser.
3. So **eine** gute Leberwurst habe ich noch nie gegessen.
4. Möchten Sie **den** kalifornischen Wein oder **den** italienischen?
5. Mit **einem** trockenen Wein schmeckt **dieser** französische Camembert besonders gut.
6. **Diese** spanischen Mandarinen sind sehr süß.

foreign

10-30 **Internationaler Geschmack.** Erzählen Sie einander, was für ausländische° Produkte Sie besonders gern haben.

- Ich trinke gern …   amerikanisch   Bier (n), Wein (m) …
- Ich esse gern …   deutsch   Käse (m), Brot (n) …
- Ich lese gern …   mexikanisch   Literatur (f), Comics (pl) …
- Ich fahre gern …   französisch   Autos (pl) …
- Ich sehe gern …   japanisch   Filme (pl) …
- …   …   …

Zusammenschau

Hören

Trying to please everybody

Es allen recht machen°

nach einer Fabel von Äsop

Fables often contain a moral and frequently use animals as main characters. Many fables were attributed to Aesop. Legend has it that he lived in Greece in the 6th century BCE.

tailor

Die Personen in dieser Fabel sind ein Vater und sein Sohn mit ihrem Esel, ein Bäcker, ein Fleischer, ein Schneider° und ein Bauer. Die neun Bildchen illustrieren die Fabel.

NEUE VOKABELN

sie trafen	*they met*	**sie banden**	*they tied*
kurz danach	*shortly afterwards*	**der Stock**	*stick*

10-31 **Erstes Verstehen.** Schauen Sie die Bildchen an und ergänzen Sie die folgende Tabelle. Erst danach sollten Sie die Fabel zum ersten Mal anhören.

	WER REITET?	WER GEHT ZU FUSS?		WER SPRICHT?
Bild 1:	*Der Vater.*		Bild 2:	
Bild 3:			Bild 4:	
Bild 5:			Bild 6:	
Bild 7:			Bild 8:	

10-32 **Detailverstehen.** Hören Sie die Fabel ein zweites Mal und schreiben Sie, wie Vater und Sohn auf die Kritik der vier Männer aus ihrem Dorf reagierten.

1. Der Bäcker sagte: „Ich finde es nicht recht, dass du reitest und dass dein kleiner Sohn zu Fuß geht. Du bist doch viel stärker als er."
   Da stieg …
2. Der Fleischer sagte: „Was, Junge, du reitest und lässt deinen Vater zu Fuß gehen? Das ist nicht recht!"
   Da stieg …
3. Der Schneider sagte: „Zwei Menschen auf einem kleinen Esel! Das ist nicht recht!"
   Da stiegen …
4. Der Bauer sagte: „Warum reitet denn nicht einer von euch?"
   Weil nun aber nur der Esel noch nicht reiten durfte, banden …

Schreiben und Sprechen

10-33 **Ein neues Ende.** Schreiben Sie ein neues Ende zur Fabel *Es allen recht machen.* Beginnen Sie nach Bild 8 so: *Als der Vater und der Sohn dann fast zu Hause waren, …*

10-34 **Wir erzählen eine neue Fabel.** Lesen Sie Ihr neues Ende zur Fabel vor. Wenn Sie den neuen Versionen Ihrer Mitstudenten zuhören, versuchen Sie, die neue Moral zu identifizieren.

Lesen

Zum besseren Verstehen

10-35 Geschichten für Kinder.

1. Welche Geschichten haben Sie als Kind gehört oder gelesen?
2. In welchen von diesen Geschichten haben Tiere eine Rolle gespielt? Was für Tiere waren das?
3. Die Illustration zeigt einen kleinen, dicken Igel und einen langen, dünnen Hasen. In Nordamerika gibt es den Igel nur im Zoo oder manchmal als Haustier. Wie nennt man ihn auf Englisch?

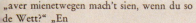

„aver mienetwegen mach't sien, wenn du so
de Wett?" „En
ranwien", seggt
pröök de Haas,
os gahn." „Nä,
n de Swinegel,
erst will ick to
stücken; inner
'n Platz."
denn de Haas
ges dachte de
verlett sick up

10-36 Was ist das auf Englisch?

1. Ein Igel ist ein Tier, das kurze, **krumme** Beine hat.	a. run a race
2. Dass der Hase über seine kurzen, krummen Beine lachte, **ärgerte** den Igel.	b. happily
	c. crooked
3. Er wollte deshalb mit dem Hasen **einen Wettlauf machen.**	d. made angry
	e. beside himself
4. Ich **wette,** der Hase kann schneller laufen als der Igel.	f. upper
5. Sie wollten vom **oberen** bis zum unteren Ende eines Feldes laufen.	g. bet
	h. lost
6. Jeder lief in einer **Furche** im Feld.	i. clever
7. Der Hase war **außer sich,** als der Igel vor ihm am unteren Ende des Feldes war.	j. furrow
8. Wer hat die Wette **verloren**?	
9. Der Igel gewann die Wette und ging **vergnügt** nach Hause.	
10. Der Igel war sehr **klug.**	

Der Hase und der Igel
nach einem Märchen der Brüder Grimm

Es war an einem Sonntagmorgen zur Sommerzeit. Die Sonne schien hell vom blauen Himmel, der Morgenwind ging warm über die Felder und die Leute gingen in ihren Sonntagskleidern zur Kirche.

Der Igel aber stand vor seiner Tür und schaute in den schönen Morgen hinaus. Als
5 er so stand, dachte er: „Warum gehe ich nicht schnell aufs Feld und schaue meine Rüben an, solange meine Frau die Kinder anzieht und das Frühstück macht."

Als der Igel zum Rübenfeld kam, traf er dort seinen Nachbarn, den Hasen, der auch einen Spaziergang machte. Der Igel sagte freundlich: „Guten Morgen!" Aber der Hase grüßte nicht zurück, sondern sagte: „Wie kommt es denn, dass
10 du hier am frühen Morgen auf dem Feld herumläufst?" „Ich gehe spazieren", sagte der Igel. „Spazieren?" lachte der Hase, „Du, mit deinen kurzen, krummen Beinen?"

Diese Antwort ärgerte den Igel sehr, denn für einen Igel hatte er sehr schöne Beine, obwohl sie von Natur kurz und krumm waren. „Denkst du vielleicht",
15 sagte er zum Hasen, „dass du mit deinen langen, dünnen Beinen schneller laufen kannst als ich?" „Das denke ich wohl", lachte der Hase, „willst du wetten?" „Ja, ein Goldstück und eine Flasche Schnaps", antwortete der Igel. „Gut", rief der Hase, „fangen wir an!" „Nein, so große Eile hat es nicht", sagte der Igel, „ich will erst noch nach Hause gehen und ein bisschen frühstücken.
20 In einer halben Stunde bin ich wieder zurück."

Auf dem Heimweg dachte der Igel: „Diese Wette hast du verloren, lieber Hase, denn du hast zwar die langen Beine, aber ich habe den klugen Kopf." Als er zu Hause ankam, sagte er zu seiner Frau: „Frau, zieh schnell eine von meinen Hosen an, du musst mit mir aufs Feld."

25 „Eine von deinen Hosen? Ja, was ist denn los?" fragte seine Frau. „Ich habe mit dem Hasen um ein Goldstück und eine Flasche Schnaps gewettet. Ich will mit ihm einen Wettlauf machen und da brauche ich dich." „Oh, Mann", rief da die Frau ganz aufgeregt, „bist du nicht ganz recht im Kopf? Wie kannst du mit dem Hasen um die Wette laufen?" „Lass das mal meine Sache sein", sagte
30 der Igel. „Zieh jetzt die Hose an und komm mit."

Unterwegs sagte der Igel zu seiner Frau. „Nun pass mal auf, was ich dir sage. Siehst du, auf dem langen Feld dort wollen wir unseren Wettlauf machen. Der Hase läuft in der einen Furche und ich in der anderen, und dort oben fangen wir an. Du aber sitzt hier unten in meiner Furche, und wenn der Hase hier
35 ankommt, springst du auf und rufst: ‚Ich bin schon da.'"

Als der Igel am oberen Ende des Feldes ankam, wartete der Hase dort schon. „Können wir endlich anfangen?" fragte er. „Oder willst du nicht mehr?" „Doch", sagte der Igel. Dann ging jeder zu seiner Furche. Der Hase zählte:

„Eins, zwei, drei" und rannte wie ein Sturmwind über das Feld. Der Igel aber
40 blieb ruhig auf seinem Platz.

Als der Hase am unteren Ende des Feldes ankam, sprang die Frau des Igels auf
und rief: „Ich bin schon da!" Der Hase konnte es kaum glauben. Aber weil die
Frau des Igels genauso aussah wie ihr Mann, rief er: „Einmal ist nicht genug!"
Und zurück raste er, dass ihm die Ohren am Kopf flogen. Die Frau des Igels
45 aber blieb ruhig auf ihrem Platz. Als der Hase am oberen Ende des Feldes
ankam, sprang der Igel auf und rief: „Ich bin schon da!" Der Hase war ganz
außer sich und schrie „Noch einmal!" „Sooft du Lust hast", lachte der Igel. So
lief der Hase noch dreiundsiebzigmal, und jedes Mal, wenn er oben oder unten
ankam, riefen der Igel oder seine Frau: „Ich bin schon da!"

50 Das letzte Mal aber kam der Hase nicht mehr bis zum Ende, sondern stürzte
mitten auf dem Feld tot zur Erde. Der Igel aber nahm das Goldstück und die
Schnapsflasche, rief seine Frau, und beide gingen vergnügt nach Hause. Und
wenn sie nicht gestorben sind, so leben sie noch heute.

Arbeit mit dem Text

 10-37 **Wer war das?** Sie hören zwölf Fragen zu *Der Hase und der Igel*.
Markieren Sie nach jeder Frage die richtige „Person" oder „Personen".

	1.	2.	3.	4.	5.	6.	7.	8.	9.	10.	11.	12.
IGEL	____	____	____	____	____	____	____	____	____	____	____	____
FRAU IGEL	____	____	____	____	____	____	____	____	____	____	____	____
IGEL UND FRAU	____	____	____	____	____	____	____	____	____	____	____	____
HASE	____	____	____	____	____	____	____	____	____	____	____	____
HASE UND IGEL	____	____	____	____	____	____	____	____	____	____	____	____

Sprachnotiz Contradicting negative statements or questions

You can use **doch** to contradict a negative statement or question. In this
usage, **doch** has no direct English equivalent.

SAM: Hast du dieses Märchen noch
        nicht gelesen?

EMILY: Doch, schon zweimal.

Haven't you read this fairy
    tale yet?

Yes, I have, twice already.

Infobox

Die Brüder Grimm

Im Jahr 1807 begannen die Brüder Jacob und Wilhelm Grimm, die uralten[1] Geschichten zu sammeln, die einfache Leute einander erzählten. Ihr Ziel[2] war, diese Geschichten aufzuschreiben, bevor sie für immer verloren gingen. Die beliebten *Kinder- und Hausmärchen* der Brüder Grimm gibt es heute in über 160 Sprachen.

Die Grimms waren auch Linguisten: Ihr zweites großes Projekt war das *Deutsche Wörterbuch,* das sich auf die Geschichte der Wörter konzentrierte. Das war so viel Arbeit, dass sie erst zum Buchstaben "F" gekommen waren, als sie starben.

[1]*ancient*   [2]*goal*

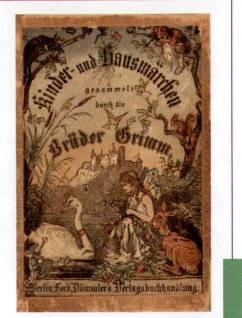

It took generations of linguists to complete the monumental 32-volume dictionary, which was finally finished in 1960.

Wort, Sinn und Klang

Wörter unter der Lupe

Words as chameleons: *als*

You have learned that **als** has a variety of meanings. Here is a summary.

as	in expressions like **als Kind**	**Als** Kind konnte ich sehr schnell laufen.
than	after the comparative form of an adjective or adverb	Mit meinen langen Beinen konnte ich schneller laufen **als** alle meine Freunde.
when	as a conjunction	**Als** ich mit meinen Freunden mal einen Wettlauf machen wollte, hatten sie keine Lust.
but	after **nichts**	Ich hatte auch später nichts **als** Probleme mit meinen langen Beinen.

10-38 Was bedeutet *als* hier? *Than, when, as,* or *but?*

1. Als Mensch ist Professor Huber sehr nett.
2. Professor Huber ist viel netter, als ich dachte.
3. Gestern habe ich den ganzen Tag nichts als gelesen.
4. Als Maria nach Hause kam, hatte ich das Buch gerade fertig gelesen.
5. Kathrin war schon als kleines Mädchen sehr sportlich.
6. In Hamburg hatten wir leider nichts als miserables Regenwetter.
7. Als wir in Hamburg waren, regnete es fast jeden Tag.
8. Diesen Juni hat es in Hamburg mehr geregnet als letztes Jahr im ganzen Sommer.

Giving language color

Hundreds of colorful expressions make use of the names of animals. Here is a small sampling.

Da hast du Schwein gehabt!	*You were lucky!*
Ich habe einen Bärenhunger.	*I'm hungry as a bear.*
Es ist alles für die Katz.	*It's all for nothing.*
Da bringen mich keine zehn Pferde hin!	*Wild horses couldn't drag me there!*
Du musst dir Eselsbrücken bauen.	*You'll have to find some tricks to help you remember.*
Mein Name ist Hase, ich weiß von nichts.	*Don't ask me. I don't know anything about it.*
Da lachen ja die Hühner!	*What a joke!*

10-39 Was passt zusammen?

1. Gehst du mit zum Fußballspiel?
2. Günter denkt, er kriegt eine Eins in dieser Klausur.
3. Warum hörst du denn schon auf, zu lernen?
4. Wer hat denn die ganzen Bierflaschen ausgetrunken?
5. Wie soll ich denn alle diese Wörter lernen?
6. Sollen wir essen gehen?
7. Ich habe eine Eins in Physik!

a. Du musst dir Eselsbrücken bauen.
b. Mein Name ist Hase. Ich weiß von nichts.
c. Da hast du aber Schwein gehabt!
d. Der eine Eins?! Da lachen ja die Hühner!
e. Klar! Ich habe einen Bärenhunger.
f. Es ist ja doch alles für die Katz!
g. Bei dem Wetter bringen mich da keine zehn Pferde hin!

Zur Aussprache

German *f, v,* and *w*

In German the sound represented by the letter **f** is pronounced like English *f* and the sound represented by the letter **v** is generally also pronounced like English *f.*

10-40 Hören Sie gut zu und wiederholen Sie!

für	**v**ier
Form	**v**or
folgen	**V**olk

Familie **F**eldmann **f**ährt in den **F**erien nach **F**innland.
Volkmars **V**orlesung ist um **V**iertel **v**or **v**ier **v**orbei°.   *over*
Volker ist **V**erkäufer **f**ür **F**arb**f**ernseher.

When the letter **v** appears in a word of foreign origin, it is pronounced like English *v:* **V**ase, **V**ideo, **V**ariation.

In German the sound represented by the letter **w** is always pronounced like English *v:* **w**ann, **w**ie, **w**o.

10-41 Hören Sie gut zu und wiederholen Sie!

Wolfgang und **V**eronika **w**ohnen in einer **V**illa am **W**annsee.
Walter und Da**v**id **w**aren im No**v**ember in **V**enedig.
Oli**v**er ist **V**egetarier und **w**ill keine **W**urst.

In the following word pairs, distinguish clearly between German **f** and **w** sounds.

Vetter	**W**etter	**F**arm	**w**arm
vier	**w**ir	**f**ein	**W**ein
viel	**w**ill	**F**est	**W**est
voll	**W**olle	**F**elder	**W**älder

Felder und Wälder

Nomen

die Bushaltestelle, –n	bus stop
der Lkw, –s (Lastkraftwagen) / der Lastwagen, –	truck
der Bericht, –e	report
der Einfluss, ¨-e	influence
die Erde	earth; ground
der Krimi, –s	mystery; crime thriller
die Nachrichten (pl)	news
der Wettlauf	race (contest)
das Werkzeug, –e	tool
das Ziel, –e	goal; aim

Verben

ärgern	to make angry; annoy
schreien, schrie, geschrien	to scream; to shout
statt·finden, fand statt, stattgefunden	to take place
verschieben, verschob, verschoben	to postpone
wetten	to bet

Andere Wörter

kaum	scarcely; hardly
komisch	strange; funny
krumm	crooked
saftig	juicy
unterwegs	on the way
weder … noch	neither . . . nor

Ausdrücke

Angst haben vor (+ dat)	to be afraid of
das letzte Mal	the last time
einen Wettlauf machen	to run a race

Gott sei Dank!	Thank God!
Ich habe Lust (auf) …	I feel like (having or doing something) . . .

Das reicht (mir).	That's enough (for me).
Sie war außer sich.	She was beside herself.
Verflixt!	Darn it!

Das Gegenteil

gewinnen, gewann, gewonnen ≠ verlieren, verlor, verloren	to win ≠ to lose
lokal ≠ national	local ≠ national
oben ≠ unten	above ≠ below
riesig ≠ winzig	huge ≠ tiny

Leicht zu verstehen

die Autobiografie, –n	die Tabelle, –n
das Insekt, –en	das Thema, Themen
das Produkt, –e	

Synonyme

kriegen	=	bekommen		
klug	=	intelligent	=	schlau
miserabel	=	schlecht		
schließlich	=	endlich		

Wörter im Kontext

10-42 Was passt zusammen?

1. Ein Lkw ist ein Fahrzeug,
2. Eine Autobiografie ist eine Geschichte,
3. Ein Krimi ist ein Buch,
4. Die Erde ist der Planet,
5. Ein Hammer ist ein Werkzeug,
6. Ein Marathonlauf ist ein Wettlauf,

a. auf dem wir leben.
b. mit dem man Nägel schlagen kann.
c. in der man von seinem Leben erzählt.
d. mit dem man schwere Sachen transportiert.
e. für den man lang trainieren muss.
f. in dem oft ein Detektiv eine wichtige Rolle spielt.

10-43 Was ist hier identisch? Welche zwei Sätze in jeder Gruppe bedeuten in etwa dasselbe?

1. Stefan ist sehr klug.
   Stefan hat sich sehr aufgeregt.
   Stefan war außer sich.

2. Ann ist nicht hier, sondern in ihrem Zimmer.
   Ann ist weder hier noch in ihrem Zimmer.
   Ann ist nicht hier, und in ihrem Zimmer ist sie auch nicht.

3. Das Meeting findet jetzt später statt.
   Wir müssen das Treffen verschieben.
   Wir können uns gar nicht treffen.

4. Ich bekomme bald einen neuen Computer.
   Bald kriege ich einen neuen Computer.
   Ich brauche bald einen neuen Computer.

5. Ich habe verloren.
   Ich will nicht mehr.
   Das reicht mir.

6. Habt ihr nicht gewonnen?
   Habt ihr nicht gewettet?
   Habt ihr verloren?

10-44 Was passt wo?

riesiges / winziges / kluger / nationaler / miserable

1. Ein Feiertag, den das ganze Land feiert, ist ein _____ Feiertag.
2. Eine Note, die sehr schlecht ist, ist eine _____ Note.
3. Ein Insekt, das sehr klein ist, ist ein _____ Insekt.
4. Ein Mensch, der sehr intelligent ist, ist ein _____ Mensch.
5. Ein Gebäude, das so groß wie ein Berg ist, ist ein _____ Gebäude.

Geschichte und Gegenwart

Die Weltzeituhr, Berlin
Alexanderplatz

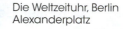

The famous **Weltzeituhr** symbolizes the connectedness of today's Germany to the rest of the world. It is located in the largest open marketplace of the former East Berlin, **Alexanderplatz**. In the years of totalitarian rule, the clock was an equally good symbol of the irony that pervaded life in the GDR, since the citizens of East Germany were not permitted to travel to many of the cities depicted.

Kommunikationsziele

Talking about recent German history and current events

Making resolutions

Describing people, places, and things

Expressing feelings and emotions

Strukturen

The passive voice

Participles used as adjectives

Verb-preposition combinations

Wo-compounds

Kultur

Die Berliner Mauer

Kleine deutsche Chronik: 1918 bis heute

Video-Treff: So war's in der DDR

Lesen: Go West!

Vorschau

Extrablatt: Berliner Morgenpost

11-1 13. August 1961.

Extrablatt: Before the Internet and widespread TV, late-breaking news was often communicated via a one-page **Extrablatt** of the local newspaper.

1. Lesen Sie die größte Schlagzeile. Was ist an diesem Tag passiert? Markieren Sie die richtige Antwort.

    ☐ Der Zweite Weltkrieg ist zu Ende.
    ☐ Man hat Deutschland in vier Zonen geteilt.
    ☐ Die Volksarmee hat Ost-Berlin blockiert.
    ☐ Ostdeutsche Soldaten haben eine Mauer durch Berlin gebaut.

Ostdeutsche Soldaten und Stacheldraht

2. Lesen Sie die vier Schlagzeilen des Artikels. Schreiben Sie zu jedem Satz die passende Schlagzeile.

    Ostdeutsche Soldaten stehen um West-Berlin herum.

    _____

    Zwischen Ost- und West-Berlin gibt es Stacheldraht und Straßensperren.

    _____

    Der östliche Teil Berlins ist blockiert.

    _____

    Die U- und S-Bahn-Linien fahren nicht mehr zwischen Ost und West.

    _____

The verb **flüchten** *(to flee)* is related to the noun **Flüchtling** *(refugee)* and **Flucht** *(the flight* itself). The verb **fliehen** can be used synonymously with **flüchten**.

11-2 Flüchtlingszahlen.

Welche Informationen finden Sie in der Tabelle?

1. Wie viele Menschen flüchteten im Juni und Juli 1961 aus der DDR nach West-Berlin?
2. Wie viele DDR–Bürger flüchteten im August des Jahres?
3. Warum sind im September und Oktober nicht so viele Menschen geflüchtet?

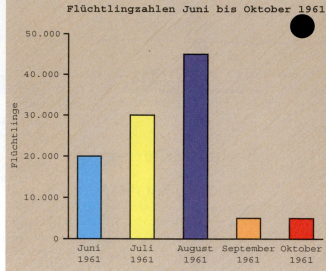

Flüchtlingzahlen Juni bis Oktober 1961

Between September 1949 and August 1961, more than 2.5 million people out of a population of approximately 17 million fled from the GDR to West Germany. The resulting hemorrhage of skilled workers became a significant threat to the East German government. In August 1961 it responded by building a wall to stop the "brain drain."

take apart

11-3 Wortschatz zum Thema: Nachkriegszeit und Wiedervereinigung.

Viele lange deutsche Wörter können Sie leicht auseinandernehmen° und sie dadurch besser verstehen. Was bedeuten die folgenden Wörter? Suchen Sie die passenden Definitionen auf der rechten Seite. Dann suchen Sie mit einem Partner weitere solche Wörter in der Infobox.

Wiedervereinigung: This word is easier to understand if you take it apart. You know the meaning of **wieder**. Now think of the German name for the United States.

1. die Nachkriegszeit
2. die Flüchtlingszahlen
3. die Weltzeituhr
4. die Wiedervereinigung
5. die Grenzpolizisten
6. …
7. …

a. eine Uhr, die die Zeiten in verschiedenen Städte der Welt zeigt
b. Deutschland wurde wieder zu einem Land. Ost und West waren eins!
c. die Jahre direkt nach dem zweiten Weltkrieg; die Zeit ab 1945
d. die Anzahl von Menschen, die von Ost nach West flüchteten
e. ostdeutsche Polizisten, die an der Grenze zwischen Ost– und West arbeiteten

---

Sprachnotiz   Using *eigentlich* and *überhaupt* to intensify expressions

The German adverbs *eigentlich* and *überhaupt* intensify the meaning of the word or phrase directly following these words. Note how the bolded phrases below are best understood as a single unit. Each word of such phrases is stressed in spoken German.

Die Berliner Mauer war **eigentlich viel mehr** als nur eine Mauer.

*The Berlin Wall was **actually much more** than just a wall.*

Ich kenne Berlin **überhaupt nicht**.

*I do **not** know Berlin **at all**.*

Infobox

Die Berliner Mauer

Von 1949 bis 1990 lag West-Berlin mitten in der DDR. Bis 1961 flohen 1,6 Millionen Ostdeutsche über West-Berlin in die BRD. Um diesen letzten Fluchtweg zu schließen[1], baute die DDR 1961 die Mauer. Der Teil der Mauer, der mitten durch Berlin ging, war 43 km lang. Die restlichen 112 km trennten[2] West-Berlin von der DDR.

Die Mauer begann als eine einfache Sperre aus Stacheldraht. Sie wurde aber bald durch eine Mauer aus Betonklötzen[3] ersetzt und immer weiter ausgebaut. Im Jahre 1975 gab es schon eine Mauer, die viel mehr als nur eine Mauer war. Man nannte sie deshalb den „Todesstreifen"[4]. An der Mauer zwischen Ost und West haben über 160 Menschen ihr Leben verloren.

Das Schaubild zeigt, warum nur wenige Ostdeutsche über West-Berlin in die BRD fliehen konnten. An der Mauer bestand Schießbefehl. Das hieß, die Grenzpolizisten mussten auf jeden schießen[5], der versuchte, durch die Mauer zu fliehen. Die meisten bezahlten mit dem Leben.

Lerntipp: As you read through the description of the wall, find each of the numbers in the diagram. The pictures will help you understand most of the new vocabulary.

1. Kontaktzaun
2. Signalgerät
3. Beobachtungsturm
4. Beleuchtungsanlage
5. Führungsdraht der Hundelaufanlage
6. Kfz-Graben
7. Kontrollstreifen
8. Betonplattenwand
9. Metallgitterzaun

- Zuerst musste der Flüchtling durch den **Kontaktzaun** (#1) kommen.
- Der Kontaktzaun aktivierte **Signalgeräte** (#2).
- Die Signalgeräte alarmierten die Grenzpolizisten in den **Beobachtungstürmen** (#3). Es war aber ein stiller Alarm, den der Flüchtling nicht hören konnte.
- Es gab eine **Beleuchtungsanlage** (#4), so dass die Grenzpolizisten bei Nacht alles genau sehen konnten.
- Unter den Beobachtungstürmen waren **Hunde** in **Laufanlagen** angeleint (#5).
- Der **Kfz-Graben** (#6) stoppte Fahrzeuge, die versuchten, durch die Mauer zu kommen.
- Zwischen dem Kfz-Graben und der eigentlichen Mauer gab es einen weiteren **Kontrollstreifen** (#7). Die Grenzpolizisten kontrollierten diesen Streifen Tag und Nacht.
- Nur wenn man durch diese vielen Hindernisse kommen konnte, erreichte man die **Betonplattenwand** (#8) oder den **Metallgitterzaun** (#9) der eigentlichen Mauer.
- Auf der anderen Seite dieser Mauer, die vier Meter hoch war, lag West-Berlin.

[1]close the escape route [2]separated [3]concrete blocks [4]death strip [5]shoot

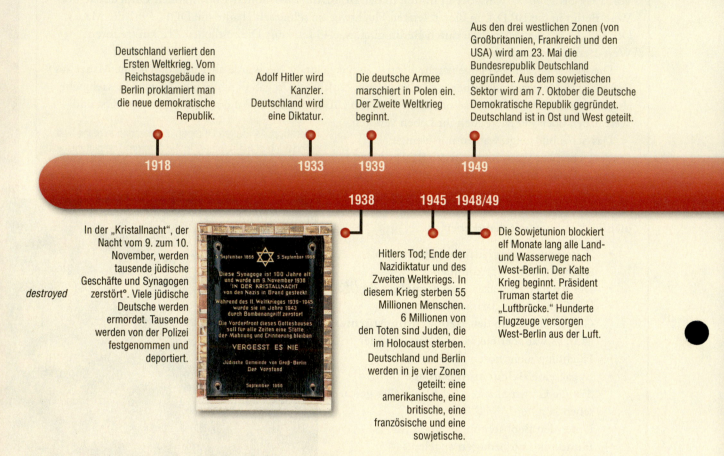

Deutschland verliert den Ersten Weltkrieg. Vom Reichstagsgebäude in Berlin proklamiert man die neue demokratische Republik.

Adolf Hitler wird Kanzler. Deutschland wird eine Diktatur.

Die deutsche Armee marschiert in Polen ein. Der Zweite Weltkrieg beginnt.

Aus den drei westlichen Zonen (von Großbritannien, Frankreich und den USA) wird am 23. Mai die Bundesrepublik Deutschland gegründet. Aus dem sowjetischen Sektor wird am 7. Oktober die Deutsche Demokratische Republik gegründet. Deutschland ist in Ost und West geteilt.

1918   **1933**   **1939**   **1949**

1938   **1945**   **1948/49**

destroyed

In der „Kristallnacht", der Nacht vom 9. zum 10. November, werden tausende jüdische Geschäfte und Synagogen zerstört°. Viele jüdische Deutsche werden ermordet. Tausende werden von der Polizei festgenommen und deportiert.

5 September 1856   5 September 1956
Diese Synagoge ist 100 Jahre alt und wurde am 9.November 1938 ‚IN DER KRISTALLNACHT' von den Nazis in Brand gesteckt.
Während des II. Weltkrieges 1939-1945 wurde sie im Jahre 1943 durch Bombenangriff zerstört
Die Vorderfront dieses Gotteshauses soll für alle Zeiten eine Stätte der Mahnung und Erinnerung bleiben
VERGESST ES NIE
Jüdische Gemeinde von Groß-Berlin Der Vorstand
September 1956

Hitlers Tod; Ende der Nazidiktatur und des Zweiten Weltkriegs. In diesem Krieg sterben 55 Millionen Menschen. 6 Millionen von den Toten sind Juden, die im Holocaust sterben. Deutschland und Berlin werden in je vier Zonen geteilt: eine amerikanische, eine britische, eine französische und eine sowjetische.

Die Sowjetunion blockiert elf Monate lang alle Land- und Wasserwege nach West-Berlin. Der Kalte Krieg beginnt. Präsident Truman startet die „Luftbrücke." Hunderte Flugzeuge versorgen West-Berlin aus der Luft.

11-4 Stationen der deutschen Geschichte. Lesen Sie die Informationen auf diesen zwei Seiten. Wann passierte das?

1. die „Reichskristallnacht"   a. 1948–1949
2. die Wiedervereinigung   b. 1989
3. die Öffnung der Mauer   c. 1990
4. die Gründung der DDR und der BRD   d. 1938
5. die Blockade Berlins und die Luftbrücke   e. 1949

Die Luftbrücke: Was war das eigentlich?

Beginning shortly after 1945, the Soviets tried to gain control of the entire city of Berlin, including the three western parts administered by the occupation forces of Great Britain, France, and the US. In June 1948, the Berlin conflict reached a climax. The Soviets blockaded all roads, rail lines, and waterways from West Germany to Berlin in an attempt to starve out the population of West Berlin and take control of the western sectors.

The American response was immediate. Just 24 hours after the blockade began, American transport planes began landing in West Berlin, and the largest air transport operation of all time, the Berlin Airlift **(Berliner Luftbrücke)** or "Operation Vittles" had begun. Like clockwork, planes took off and landed every 10 minutes, utilizing air corridors which were the city's only open connection to the West. The Soviets finally reopened ground transit routes to Berlin in May 1949.

John F. Kennedy besucht West-Berlin. Er beendet seine Rede vor dem Rathaus mit den berühmten Worten: „Ich bin ein Berliner."

Deutschland feiert ein Jubiläum: 20 Jahre nach dem Fall der Mauer!

Ost- und Westdeutschland werden wieder ein Land.

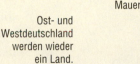

1963

1990

2009

1961

1989

Tausende fliehen aus der DDR in den Westen. Die Volksarmee baut eine Mauer, um die Abwanderung Ostdeutschen in die BRD zu stoppen.

Im Januar proklamiert Erich Honecker, der Staatschef der DDR, dass die Mauer in hundert Jahren noch steht. Aber am 9. November öffnet die DDR die Berliner Mauer und die Grenze zur BRD.

Das Reichstagsgebäude

The German **Reichstagsgebäude**, completed in 1894, took the spotlight when the **Weimarer Republik** was declared from its balcony in 1918. The building was heavily damaged during World War II, then rebuilt. It served as a museum before and after the **Wende**. Today, the German parliament meets in the **Reichstag**.

🔊 Wortschatz 1

Nomen

die Alliierten (pl)	the Allies
der Bürger, –	
die Bürgerin, –nen	citizen
das Extrablatt, ⸚er	special edition
der Flüchtling, –e	refugee
die Grenze, –n	border
der Kalte Krieg	Cold War
die Luftbrücke, –n	airlift (*literally: air bridge*)
die Mauer, –n	wall
die Nachkriegszeit	post-war period
die Rede, –n	speech; talk
das Reichstagsgebäude	German parliament building (Berlin)
die Schlagzeile, –n	headline
der Soldat, –en, –en	soldier
der Stacheldraht	barbed wire
der Weg, –e	path, way
der Weltkrieg, –e	world war
die Wiedervereinigung	reunification

Verben

ermorden	to murder
fliehen, floh, ist geflohen	to flee
flüchten, ist geflüchtet	to flee; to seek refuge
schießen, schoss, geschossen	to shoot
schließen, schloss, geschlossen	to close
teilen	to divide
trennen	to separate

> Note that the principal parts of **fliehen**, **schießen**, and **schließen** show the same stem vowel changes (**ie-o-o**).

Andere Wörter

eigentlich	actually
überhaupt	at all

Das Gegenteil

die Demokratie ≠ die Diktatur	democracy ≠ dictatorship
der Krieg, –e ≠ der Frieden	war ≠ peace
schrecklich ≠ wunderbar	terrible ≠ wonderful

Synonyme

das Schaubild, –er	=	die Grafik, –en
öffnen	=	auf·machen
zerstören	=	kaputt·machen

Leicht zu verstehen

die Blockade, –n	alarmieren
die Republik, –en	blockieren
der Staat, –en	

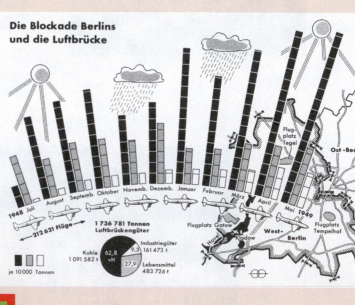

The future tense

You can use the present tense to express that something is going to happen in the future, as long as the context refers to future time.

Nächstes Jahr **schreibe** ich ein Buch über mein Leben nach der Wende.

Next year I'm going to write a book about my life after the fall of the Wall.

You can also use the future tense to express the same idea. The future tense consists of the auxiliary verb **werden** and an infinitive. The position of the auxiliary and infinitive follows the patterns you already know.

Nächstes Jahr **werde** ich ein Buch über meine Kindheit in der DDR **schreiben.**

Next year I'm going to write a book about my childhood in the GDR.

Wörter im Kontext

11-5 Was passt wo?

geteiltes / schießen / zerstört / Diktatur / flohen / blockierten / Demokratie / ermordet / geschlossen / schreckliche / Alliierten / Wiedervereinigung / Mauer

1. In der Kristallnacht wurden in Deutschland viele jüdische Deutsche _____ und fast alle Synagogen _____.
2. Von 1949 bis zur _____ im Jahr 1990 war Deutschland ein _____ Land.
3. 1948 _____ die Sowjets alle Land- und Wasserwege nach West-Berlin.
4. Die _____ brachten deshalb fast ein Jahr lang alle lebenswichtigen Güter über eine Luftbrücke nach Berlin.
5. Bis 1961 _____ 1,6 Millionen Ostdeutsche über West-Berlin in die BRD.
6. 1961 baute die DDR um ganz West-Berlin eine _____. Damit war die Grenze zwischen der DDR und West-Berlin _____.
7. Die Grenzpolizisten mussten auf Menschen _____, die durch die Mauer nach West-Berlin flüchten wollten.
8. Die DDR war keine _____, sondern eine _____.
9. So begann eine _____ Zeit für viele, die in Ostdeutschland lebten.

11-6 Zusammengesetzte Nomen. Kombinieren Sie in jeder der zwei Gruppen die passenden Nomen.

Remember that the gender of a compound noun is determined by the last element.

▶ die Luft + der Krieg = der Luftkrieg

1. die Schau	a. die Freiheit	4. die Luft	d. der Hafen
2. die Rede	b. das Bild	5. die Mauer	e. die Brücke
3. die Welt	c. der Krieg	6. der Flug	f. der Fall

Kommunikation und Formen

1 Focusing on the receiver of an action

The passive voice

In grammatical terms, the doer of an action is usually the subject of the sentence. Such a sentence is said to be in the *active voice*.

Peter holt mich um sieben ab.	**Peter** *is picking me up at seven.*

However, when you find it unnecessary or unimportant to mention the doer of the action, you can make the *receiver* of the action the subject of the sentence. Such a sentence is said to be in the *passive voice*.

Ich *werde* um sieben **abgeholt**.	**I'm being picked up** at seven.

Note that in the passive voice

- the receiver of the action appears in the nominative case.
- the verb appears as a past participle with a form of **werden** as auxiliary.

The most commonly used tenses in the passive voice are the present and the simple past. The tense is indicated by the auxiliary **werden**.

PRESENT	ich **werde** abgeholt	*I'm being picked up*
SIMPLE PAST	ich **wurde** abgeholt	*I was picked up*

Use of the passive voice

In the passive voice, attention is focused on the receiver of the action and on the action itself. You may have been taught to avoid the passive in English, but in German it is used fairly frequently. In the examples below, the active sentences give unnecessary or unimportant information. This is particularly obvious in the second example. For the police, arresting people is routine; for Mr. Müller, being arrested is momentous. Here the passive voice is the more natural mode of expression, because what happens to the receiver of the action is more important than who does it.

passive	active
Mein Wagen **wird repariert**. *My car **is being repaired**.*	Der Automechaniker **repariert** meinen Wagen. *The car mechanic **is repairing** my car.*
Herr Müller **wurde verhaftet**. *Mr. Müller **was arrested**.*	Die Polizei **hat** Herrn Müller **verhaftet**. *The police **arrested** Mr. Müller.*

In diesem Bereich werden die Getränke serviert!
Speisen – Selbstbedienung! vom Grill und Buffet

11-1 to 11-11

11-7 Was wird hier gemacht?

ein Haus / gebaut

S1: Was wird hier gemacht?   **S2:** Hier wird ein Haus gebaut.

1.   2.   3.

4.   5.   6.

| Blumen / gegossen | Kleider / anprobiert | Eis / verkauft |
| ein Rasen / gemäht | ein Auto / repariert | Bier / getrunken |

11-8 Was weißt du von Mario und Ann? Die Information für S2 ist im *Anhang* auf Seite A10.

S1: Warum ist Mario   **S2:** Er wird nie nach seiner Meinung°   *opinion*
denn so sauer°?   gefragt.   *annoyed*

MARIO		ANN	
Warum ist Mario denn so sauer?		Warum arbeitet Ann schon so lange bei IBM?	
	Seine Wohnung wird renoviert.		Ein neuer Teppich wird dort gelegt.
	Damit sein Mercedes nicht gestohlen wird.	Warum ist Ann heute mit dem Bus gekommen?	
Warum ist Mario so wenig zu Hause?			Sie wird gleich abgeholt.

11-9 Was wurde hier gemacht?

ein Zaun / gestrichen

S1: Was wurde hier gemacht?

S2: Hier wurde ein Zaun gestrichen.

1.

3.

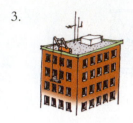

2.

4.

Äpfel / gepflückt	Schnee / geschaufelt
Fenster (pl) / geputzt	Bier / getrunken

5.

7.

6.

8.

wood

ein Baum / gefällt	Brot / gebacken
ein Feld / gepflügt	Holz° / gespalten

11-10 Gute Vorsätze. Sie sind auf einer Neujahrsparty und es ist kurz vor Mitternacht. Schreiben Sie drei gute Vorsätze für das neue Jahr. Lesen Sie Ihre Vorsätze dann vor.

SINGULAR

Von heute ab wird	jeden Tag Sport	
	viel mehr Gemüse	
	viel weniger Schokolade	gelernt.
	viel weniger Bier	ausgegeben.
	viel weniger Kaffee	gemacht.
	einmal täglich der Abwasch	erzählt.
	nicht mehr so viel Geld	gegessen.
	keine einzige Zigarette mehr	angeschaut.
		getrunken.

PLURAL

Von heute ab werden	keine blöden Witze° mehr	geraucht.	*jokes*
	keine doofen Seifenopern mehr	…	
	jeden Tag ein paar deutsche Vokabeln		
	…		

> It's typical to make resolutions (**Vorsätze**) using the passive voice. Practice this carefully by focusing first on resolutions with singular subjects, and then on plural ones.

Mentioning the agent in a passive sentence

11-12 to 11-13

In most passive sentences, the agent (the doer of the action) is omitted. However, if the agent is mentioned, it appears in the dative case after the preposition **von.**

| 1923 wurde Adolf Hitlers Münchner Putschversuch **von Regierungs-truppen** niedergeschlagen. | *In 1923 Adolf Hitler's coup attempt in Munich was put down **by government forces.*** |

Dieses Parkhaus wird vom ADAC empfohlen
ADAC

11-11 Ein bisschen deutsche Geschichte. Ergänzen Sie das Agens.

▶ Am 30. Januar 1933 wurde Adolf Hitler _____ zum Kanzler ernannt. (der Reichspräsident)
Am 30. Januar 1933 wurde Adolf Hitler vom Reichspräsidenten zum Kanzler ernannt.

1. In der Nacht vom 9. zum 10. November 1938 wurden _____ fast alle deutschen Synagogen zerstört. (die Nazis)
2. Am 1. September 1939 wurde Polen _____ überfallen°. (deutsche Truppen)   *invaded*
3. In den folgenden vier Jahren wurden fast ganz Europa und große Teile der Sowjetunion _____ besetzt°. (Nazideutschland)   *occupied*
4. Im Frühjahr 1945 wurde Berlin _____ erobert°. (die Rote Armee)   *conquered*
5. Im Juni 1945 wurden Deutschland und Berlin _____ in je vier Besatzungszonen geteilt. (die Alliierten)
6. Von Juni 1948 bis Mai 1949 wurden alle Land- und Wasserwege nach West-Berlin _____ blockiert. (die Sowjetunion)
7. Elf Monate lang wurde die Millionenstadt _____ mit Lebensmitteln und Kohle versorgt°. (amerikanische und britische Transportflugzeuge)   *supplied*
8. 1961 wurde _____ der Bau der Berliner Mauer angeordnet°. (die Regierung° der DDR)   *ordered*   *government*
9. Am 9. November 1989 wurde die Mauer _____ geöffnet. (die Grenzpolizei der DDR)

> Historical events like those described in these sentences are often expressed in the passive, even though the agent is mentioned. English does this also, e.g., *He was rejected by the Senate Judicial Committee.*

2 Describing people, places, and things

📖 The past participle used as an adjective

In your reading you have frequently seen past participles used as adjectives. Before a noun, the past participle takes the same endings as other adjectives.

Er ist ein gut **bezahlter** Architekt.   *He is a well-**paid** architect.*

11-12 Was ist das?

▶

eine elegant _____ Dame
gekleidet

Das ist eine elegant gekleidete Dame.

1. frisch _____ Hemden

2. ein frisch _____ Brot (n)

3. ein schlecht _____ Mann

4. ein _____ Pferd (n)

5. ein _____ Brief (m)

6. eine _____ Jacke

7. ein gut _____ junger Mann

8. frisch _____ Äpfel

9. zwei _____ Koffer

gebaut	gesattelt	gebacken	gepackt	rasiert
gewaschen	vergessen	angefangen	gepflückt	

👥 11-13 Modenschau im Deutschkurs. Beschreiben Sie, was Ihre Mitstudentinnen und Mitstudenten tragen.

S: Lisa trägt einen langen, geschlitzten Rock.
David trägt ein sportliches, blau und weiß gestreiftes Polohemd.

interessant	braun	geblümt (flowered)	einen Pullover
cool	blau	gestreift (striped)	ein T-Shirt
sportlich	gelb	handgestrickt (hand-knit)	ein Sweatshirt
praktisch	grün	kariert (plaid, checked)	Jeans
toll	rot	geschlitzt (slit)	eine Jacke
. . .	. . .	. . .	. . .

Video-Treff

So war's in der DDR

Thomas, Ines und Susann erzählen von ihrem Leben in der DDR.

11-14 Was ist das auf Englisch?

1. Wo wir jetzt stehen war früher **Niemandsland.**
2. Die Mauer sieht erst seit **Anfang der 90er-Jahre** so aus.
3. Früher war die Mauer nicht **bemalt.**
4. Auf der Mauer sind Bilder **zum Thema** Ost- und West-Berlin und zur Trennung der Stadt.
5. Für mich wurde die Mauer erst real nach **der Wende,** also Anfang der 90er-Jahre.
6. Man konnte dann die Mauer **anfassen** und kleine Steine aus der Mauer nehmen.
7. Wir haben beide **Erinnerungen an** die DDR.
8. Meine Eltern haben dort **im Gefängnis** gesessen.
9. Sie **haben** die Meinung des DDR-Regimes **nicht vertreten.**

a. touch
b. in prison
c. painted
d. did not agree with
e. no man's land
f. on the topic of
g. memories of
h. the turning point (i.e., the fall of the Wall)
i. the beginning of the nineties

Die East Side Gallery

Die Mauer spricht! In the days of the Berlin Wall, colorful graffiti created in protest completely covered the west side of the wall. As you saw earlier in this chapter, the east side of the Berlin wall was blank, because it was located within the **Todesstreifen** itself. After the Wall came down in 1989, artists from all over the world created the **East Side Gallery**, a huge outdoor gallery and memorial with over 100 paintings on a portion of its formerly inaccessible and untouchable east side. Although some of the paintings have deteriorated with time, it is the longest remaining section of the Wall.

11-15 **Richtig oder falsch?**

DIE EAST SIDE GALLERY	RICHTIG	FALSCH
1. Früher sah diese Seite der Mauer ganz anders aus: sie war nämlich nicht bemalt.	☐	☐
2. Die East Side Gallery ist ein Gebäude, in dem es Stücke der Berliner Mauer gibt.	☐	☐
3. Die Gallery ist jetzt ein Magnet für Touristen, die Fotos von der Mauer machen wollen	☐	☐
4. Bei der East Side Gallery werden Andenken wie Fotos, Postkarten oder kleine Mauerstücke verkauft.	☐	☐

FAMILIENGESCHICHTEN		
5. Wenn Ines in der DDR unter Freunden war, konnte sie endlich sagen, was sie denkt.	☐	☐
6. Susann hat länger in der DDR gelebt als Ines.	☐	☐
7. Susann ist mit ihren Eltern in den Westen geflohen.	☐	☐
8. Wenn Susann und Ines an die DDR denken, denken beide an Unfreiheit.	☐	☐

11-16 **Das Leben in der DDR.** Wer sagt was?

	Thomas	Ines	Susann
1. Ich habe 20 Jahre meines Lebens in der DDR verbracht.	☐	☐	☐
2. Ich habe 8 Jahre in der DDR gelebt.	☐	☐	☐
3. Ich habe mein Abitur in der DDR gemacht.	☐	☐	☐
4. Anfang der 90er Jahre habe ich verstanden, was die Mauer für uns bedeutete.	☐	☐	☐
5. Meine Eltern sind aus der DDR in den Westen geflohen.	☐	☐	☐
6. Meine Eltern haben in der DDR im Gefängnis gesessen.	☐	☐	☐
7. In der DDR hatte ich immer das Gefühl, ich konnte nie sagen, was ich denke.	☐	☐	☐
8. Für mich wurde die Mauer erst dann real, als ich sie anfassen konnte.	☐	☐	☐

3 Expanding the meaning of some verbs

 ## Special verb-preposition combinations

11-19 to 11-22 Many English and German verbs are used in combination with prepositions. In the examples below, the prepositions used in both languages have some parallels to English, but not all are direct equivalents.

Barbara Harper studiert ein Semester **an** der Humboldt-Universität in Berlin.
Sie arbeitet gerade **an** einem Referat über Berlin.

*Barbara Harper is studying for a semester **at** the Humboldt University in Berlin.*
*She's currently working **on** a report about Berlin.*

In most instances, however, the prepositions used in German verb-preposition combinations do not correspond to those used in English.

Barbara interessiert sich **für** europäische Politik.

Sie wartet **auf** die Gelegenheit, ein Praktikum beim deutschen Bundestag zu machen.

Barbara is interested in European politics.

She's waiting for the opportunity to do an internship at the German Bundestag.

Below are two groups of commonly used verb-preposition combinations. Note that for the two-case prepositions, the test of **wohin/wo** does not apply, and the correct case is therefore given in parentheses.

arbeiten an *(+ dative)*	*to work on*
denken an *(+ accusative)*	*to think of, about*
erzählen von	*to tell about*
wissen von	*to know about*
warten auf *(+ accusative)*	*to wait for*
Angst haben vor *(+ dative)*	*to be afraid of*

11-17 Was passt zusammen? Ergänzen Sie die passenden Präpositionen. S2 gibt eine sinnvolle Antwort.

S1:

1. Was weißt du _____ der ehemaligen° DDR?
2. Wann erzählst du uns _____ deiner Reise durch die neuen Bundesländer?
3. Wie lange hast du _____ diesem Referat gearbeitet?
4. Ich habe Angst _____ dieser Klausur.
5. Wo soll ich _____ dich warten, Peter?
6. _____ wen denkst du, Martin?

S2:

a. An Claudia.   *former*
b. Ich auch.
c. Morgen Abend.
d. Eine ganze Woche.
e. Eine ganze Menge°.   *a lot*
f. Vor der Bibliothek.

11-18 Was machen diese Leute? Ergänzen Sie die Präpositionen und die passenden Objekte.

1. Tanja hat Angst _____ _____.

2. Kevin wartet im Büro _____ _____ von seiner Freundin.

3. Frau Kemp denkt oft _____ _____.

4. Bob weiß noch nichts _____ _____.

5. Nicole arbeitet _____ _____.

6. Holger erzählt _____ _____.

ihrem Referat	Mäusen	seiner Geburtstagsparty
seinem Autounfall°	ihren alten Vater	einen Anruf

accident

Verbs that occur in verb–preposition combinations are often reflexive.

sich ärgern über (+ *accusative*)   *to be annoyed with, about*
sich auf·regen über (+ *accusative*)   *to get upset about; to get worked up about*
sich freuen über (+ *accusative*)   *to be happy about; to be pleased with*
sich freuen auf (+ *accusative*)   *to look forward to*
sich interessieren für   *to be interested in*
sich verlieben in (+ *accusative*)   *to fall in love with*

11-19 Was passt zusammen? Ergänzen Sie die passenden Präpositionen.
S2 gibt eine sinnvolle Antwort.

S1:

1. Warum interessiert sich Sabine so _____ die Geschichte der DDR?
2. Warum hat sich Herr Merz _____ den Fall der Mauer so gefreut?
3. Warum haben sich die DDR-Bürger so sehr _____ ihren Staat aufgeregt?
4. Warum freust du dich denn nicht _____ die Semesterferien?
5. Warum ärgerst du dich denn so _____ Müllers Hund?
6. Warum hat sich Maria denn _____ so einen komischen Typ verliebt?

S2:

a. Weil er jetzt auch in westliche Länder reisen konnte.
b. Weil sie nicht reisen und keine eigene Meinung sagen durften.
c. Weil ihre Familie aus der DDR kommt.
d. Weil er die ganze Nacht bellt.
e. Weil sie ihn nett findet.
f. Weil ich arbeiten und Geld verdienen muss.

11-20 Was machen diese Leute? Ergänzen Sie die Präpositionen und die passenden Objekte.

1. Anna freut sich _____ _____.

2. Frau Klein ärgert sich _____ _____.

3. Maria freut sich _____ _____.

4. Heike regt sich _____ _____ auf.

5. Claudia interessiert sich _____ _____.

6. Peter hat sich _____ _____ verliebt.

stubborn

| ihren dickköpfigen° Sohn | ihre Eins in Geschichte | historische Maschinen |
| ihre Reise nach Italien | Stephanie | Toms doofen Haarschnitt |

4 Asking questions about people or things

11-23 to 11-27

Wo-compounds

The question words **wem** and **wen** refer to persons. If a preposition is involved, it precedes the question word.

Vor wem hast du Angst?   **Who** are you afraid **of**?
An wen denkst du?   **Who** are you thinking **of**?

The question word **was** refers to things or ideas. If a preposition is involved, a **wo**-compound is used.

Wovor hast du Angst?   **What** are you afraid **of**?
Woran denkst du?   **What** are you thinking **of**?

Note that an **r** is added to **wo** if the preposition begins with a vowel: **woran, worauf, worüber,** etc.

WIR STEHEN FÜR MODERNE FAMILIENPOLITIK.

SPD
Vertrauen in Deutschland.

ABER WOFÜR STEHEN DIE ANDEREN?

11-21 Was für Leute sind Karin und Bernd? Die
Information für **S2** ist im *Anhang* auf Seite A10.

S1: Wofür interessiert sich Karin am meisten?   **S2:** Für Politik und Geschichte.

	KARIN	BERND
Wofür interessiert sich Karin/Bernd am meisten?		Für Computer und das Internet.
Woran arbeitet sie/er gerade so intensiv?		An einer Website für die Firma seines Vaters.
Worüber hat sie/er sich gestern so aufgeregt?		Über einen defekten Scanner.
Worauf wartet sie/er denn so sehr?		Auf eine längere E-Mail von seiner Freundin.
Worüber freut sie/er sich am meisten?		Über tolle, neue Software.
Wovor hat sie/er manchmal Angst?		Vor einem besonders cleveren Virus.

11-22 Ein paar persönliche Fragen.

- An wen oder woran denkst du im Moment?
- Wofür interessierst du dich ganz besonders?
- Hast du manchmal Angst? Wovor?
- Ärgerst du dich manchmal? Worüber oder über wen? Warum?
- Worauf freust du dich im Moment am meisten? Warum?

Zusammenschau

Since reunification, the term **die neuen Bundesländer** is frequently used for the states that were formerly **DDR** territory.

Hören

Eine Radtour in den neuen Bundesländern

Es ist Mitte Juli, und Stephanie, Claudia, Martin und Peter sitzen bei einem Glas Bier im Englischen Garten. Hören Sie was die vier Freunde miteinander sprechen.

NEUE VOKABELN

überhaupt nicht	*not at all*	**der Schlafsack, ⸚e**	*sleeping bag*
die Gegend	*area*	**sich um·schauen nach**	*to look around for*
nördlich von	*north of*	**der Radwanderführer**	*cycling tour*
jederzeit	*anytime*		*guidebook*

11-23 Erstes Verstehen. Wer sagt das? Schreiben Sie C (Claudia), S (Stephanie), M (Martin) oder P (Peter).

_____ Ja, und ich kenne außer München, Berlin, Hamburg und Köln immer noch sehr wenig von Deutschland.

_____ Brandenburg und Mecklenburg-Vorpommern sind für eine Radtour absolut ideal.

_____ Wenn's uns da mal zu heiß wird, können wir jederzeit baden gehen.

_____ Sie möchten Stephanie sowieso noch mal sehen.

_____ Aber planen müssen wir gleich jetzt.

_____ Und dann setzen wir uns zusammen und schauen, was es dort oben alles zu tun und zu sehen gibt.

11-24 Detailverstehen.

1. Wie lange ist Stephanie noch in Deutschland?
2. Welchen Teil von Deutschland kennt Stephanie überhaupt nicht?
3. Warum findet Claudia Brandenburg und Mecklenburg-Vorpommern so ideal für eine Radtour?
4. Was war auf den schönen Bildern, die Stephanie gesehen hat?
5. Wer bekommt die folgenden Aufgaben?
   a. Im Internet nach einer preisgünstigen Gruppenreise schauen.
   b. Einen Radwanderführer und eine gute Karte von Nordostdeutschland kaufen.
   c. Sich nach Zelten umschauen.
   d. In Berlin anrufen.

Cycling is very popular in the German-speaking countries, and there are **Radwanderführer** for every region in Germany, Austria, and Switzerland. It's typical for cycling trips to last a week or more.

Schreiben und Sprechen

Ferienerlebnisse: You have learned a different term for *experience* in the compound noun **Arbeitserfahrung** in *Chapter 6*. **Erlebnis** is used for an exciting or unforgettable experience, such as a trip.

11-25 Ferienerlebnisse. Beschreiben Sie in drei kurzen Absätzen° …   *paragraphs*

- wann, wo und mit wem Sie mal schöne Ferienerlebnisse gemacht haben.
- was Sie alles gesehen und erlebt° haben.   *experienced*
- was Sie besonders schön, interessant oder aufregend° fanden.   *exciting*

11-26 Besuch in Berlin, der Hauptstadt Deutschlands. Planen Sie nun in einer Kleingruppe ein Wochenende in Berlin. Was möchten Sie alles sehen? In welche Museen gehen Sie?

Das Brandenburger Tor

1. Entscheiden Sie zuerst wie viele Personen mitfahren.
   - wie die Gruppe nach Berlin kommt.
   - ob man zwei oder drei Nächte in Berlin bleibt.

2. Diskutieren Sie auch darüber, was die Gruppe in Berlin alles machen will. Hier sind einige Touristen-Tipps für Sie:

> der Reichstag   die Museumsinsel   das Theater am Ku-damm
>
> das DDR-Museum   das Stasimuseum
>
> das Mauermuseum
>
> das Ägyptische Museum   das Schloß Charlottenburg
>
> das Kaufhaus des Westens (KaDeWe)   das Brandenburger Tor

Beispiele:

- Ich möchte unbedingt° das Brandenburger Tor sehen.   *really*
- Ich interessiere mich für Geschichte. Ich möchte ins Deutsche Historische Museum gehen.
- Zuerst will ich den Reichstag besuchen.
- Ich interessiere mich für die Stasi in der DDR. Ich gehe ins Stasimuseum.

3. Machen Sie gemeinsam Pläne für das Wochenende.

   ▶ Wir können zuerst in das Mauermuseum gehen. Dann können wir … sehen. Am letzten Tag können wir … besuchen.

Besucherterrasse des Reichstagsgebäudes

This playful glass and metal **Kuppel** was added to the historic Reichstagsgebäude in the 1990s. From the **Dachterrasse** here, tourists have an impressive 360-degree view of the entire city.

Infobox

Mosques: Germany has approximately 2500 mosques and prayer rooms.

Ethnische Gruppen und Nationalitäten in Deutschland

In den 50er und 60er Jahren, einer Zeit rapider wirtschaftlicher Expansion, gab es in der Bundesrepublik Deutschland viele neue Arbeitsplätze, aber nicht genug Arbeiter. Deshalb rekrutierte die Bundesregierung Arbeiter aus anderen Ländern. Diese so genannten „Gastarbeiter" kamen aus Italien, Spanien, Griechenland, aus der Türkei, Marokko, Portugal, Tunesien und Jugoslawien. Die meisten Gastarbeiter in der DDR kamen aus Vietnam, aber auch aus Kuba, Mosambik, Polen und Angola. Nach dem Fall der Berliner Mauer und dem Zusammenbruch des kommunistischen Blocks immigrierten viele Menschen aus politischen und wirtschaftlichen Gründen nach Deutschland. Außerdem nahm die Bundesrepublik in den letzten 20 Jahren viele Flüchtlinge aus Regionen auf, in denen es Krieg und Verfolgung gab, wie zum Beispiel aus den ehemaligen jugoslawischen Ländern, dem Irak, dem Iran, der Türkei, Afghanistan, Syrien, Pakistan und Somalia. Heute leben zwischen 7 und 8 Millionen Menschen mit Migrationshintergrund in Deutschland.

Die Sehitlik-Moschee in Berlin

Seit dem 1. Januar 2000 ist es für Ausländer leichter geworden, deutsche Bürger zu werden, wenn sie schon 8 Jahre in Deutschland gelebt haben, finanziell gesichert sind und Deutsch können. Kinder, die ausländische Eltern haben aber in Deutschland geboren sind, haben automatisch die die doppelte Staatsbürgerschaft bis zum Alter von 23. Dann müssen sie eine Nationalität wählen.

Die Integration von Migranten ist nicht immer einfach gewesen. Diskriminierung und auch Gewalttaten° passieren immer noch, aber die meisten Deutschen erkennen, dass Einwanderer das Land kulturell und wirtschaftlich bereichern.

°*acts of violence*

Earlier terms for immigrants (**Ausländer, Gastarbeiter: Ausländische Mitbewohner**) came to sometimes have negative connotations. Today, **Menschen mit Migrationshintergrund** is a more neutral term to refer to people whose family background has involved migration.

Lesen

Jana Hensel wurde 1976 in der DDR geboren und war 13, als die Mauer fiel und aus Ost- und Westdeutschland wieder ein Land wurde. Als sie 26 war, schrieb sie in Zonenkinder über ihre Kindheit, über die Wende und den Kulturschock nach der Wiedervereinigung und über die Jahre der Anpassung an die neue Freiheit. In der zweiten Hälfte ihres Lebens wandeln sich ihre Gefühle vom „Sometimes you're better off dead" zum „we will start life new" aus den Liedern „West End Girls" und „Go West" der Pet Shop Boys.

Jana Hensel sieht sich jetzt als eine der „ersten Wessis aus Ostdeutschland", d. h. als eine der jungen Ostdeutschen, die ihre Zukunft nicht mehr dem Staat überlassen, sondern sie in die eigene Hand nehmen wollen. Hensels Buch wurde ins Englische übersetzt und erschien mit dem Titel After the Wall.

Zum besseren Verstehen

11-27 **Synonyme und Kurzdefinitionen.** Unten sind einige wichtige Wörter aus dem Text. Besprechen Sie sie mit einem Partner, bevor Sie den Text lesen.

1. eine **Hälfte** + eine **Hälfte** = 100%
2. **sich wandeln** = anders werden
3. die **Zukunft** = das, was noch nicht passiert ist, sondern vor uns steht
4. **ebenfalls** = auch
5. die **Herkunft** = wo man herkommt
6. **erschrecken** = schocken
7. **behaupten** = sagen
8. **jedoch** = aber
9. **daher** = deshalb
10. **meinen** = sagen, oder auch denken
11. **einst** = damals

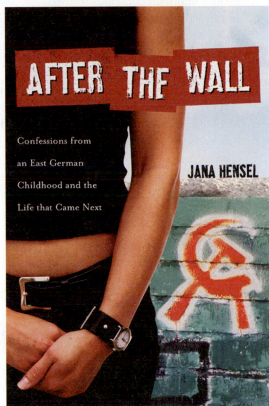

Die englische Ausgabe von *Zonenkinder*

11-28 Was ist das auf Englisch?

1. Für viele Ostdeutsche brachte die **Wende** nicht nur Positives.
2. Aber für Jana Hensel waren die ersten zehn Jahre in der Freiheit sehr **ereignisreich.**
3. Sie musste von ihrer Kindheit in der DDR **Abschied nehmen.**
4. Ihre **Anpassung an** das Leben in der Freiheit war erfolgreich.
5. Sie sah ihre Kindheit und die DDR wie im **Rückspiegel** eines Autos immer kleiner und märchenhafter werden.
6. In Ostdeutschland gab es nach der Wiedervereinigung den **Aufkleber** „Die DDR ist tot, es lebe die DDR".
7. Jana Hensel hat diesen Aufkleber von ihrem **Armaturenbrett** weggemacht.
8. Kürzlich fand sie unter dem **Beifahrersitz** ein altes Tape.
9. Ihr Freund Jonathan hatte es ihr vor ein paar Jahren in die Hand **gedrückt.**
10. Auf diesem Tape waren **Lieder** der Pet Shop Boys.
11. Das Lied „Go West" läuft jetzt **unaufhörlich,** wenn sie in Berlin unterwegs ist.
12. Seit kurzem läuft das Lied unaufhörlich, **d. h.** heute ist das Lied sehr populär. Man hört es immer wieder.
13. Sie **wundert sich,** dass sie dieses Lied früher nicht verstanden hat.
14. Sie meint, ihre Generation ist **erwachsen** geworden.

a. front passenger seat
b. eventful
c. constantly
d. adjustment to
e. dashboard
f. is surprised
g. sticker
h. rearview mirror
i. turning point (i.e., the fall of the Wall)
j. pressed
k. songs
l. bid farewell
m. that is to say
n. grown up

Go West!
aus Zonenkinder *von Jana Hensel*

… Die ersten zehn Jahre in der Freiheit waren sehr ereignisreich. Viele Abschiede. Neue Bekannte. Die nächsten zehn Jahre werden ruhiger werden. Wir sind die ersten Wessis aus Ostdeutschland, und an Sprache, Verhalten und Aussehen ist unsere Herkunft nicht mehr zu erkennen. Unsere Anpas-
5 sung verlief erfolgreich, und wir wünschten, wir könnten dies ebenfalls von unseren Eltern und Familien behaupten. Es erschreckt uns, bemerken wir, dass wir in unserer Heimat nur kurz zu Gast gewesen sind. Die paar Jahre vor dem Fall der Mauer, die wir dort gelebt haben, machen zurzeit noch die Hälfte unseres Lebens aus. Von nun an werden sie jedoch zahlenmäßig
10 in die Minderheit geraten und die DDR wird für uns, als schauten wir in den Rückspiegel eines Autos, noch ferner, kleiner und immer märchen-hafter werden.
Die Hand am Steuer des eigenen Wagens, heißt es daher, Abschied von unserem Heimatland zu nehmen. Wir sind erwachsen geworden, und auf
15 dem Armaturenbrett klebt kein Aufkleber „Die DDR ist tot, es lebe die DDR" mehr. Stattdessen habe ich kürzlich unter dem Beifahrersitz ein altes Tape von Jonathan wiedergefunden. Zu Beginn unserer Freundschaft in Leipzig hatte er es mir mit einem Augenzwinkern in die Hand gedrückt und gemeint, hier würde ich viel lernen. Ich habe die Kassette damals nicht

20 oft gehört und obendrein nie verstanden, was er mit dem Versprechen der Pet
Shop Boys „Go West, Life is peaceful there" sagen wollte. Das Lied über die
„West End Girls" und „East End Boys" mochte ich viel lieber.

   Seit kurzem jedoch läuft sie unaufhörlich, wenn ich in Berlin unterwegs
bin. Ich muss lachen, singen mir die beiden Engländer „we will fly so high, tell
25 all our friends goodbye, we will start life new" ins Ohr, und wundere mich:
Was es wohl daran einst nicht zu verstehen gab? …

11-29 **Anders gesagt.** Markieren Sie in Jana Hensels Text die Sätze oder
Satzteile, die etwa dasselbe bedeuten.

1. Im ersten Jahrzehnt nach der Wende ist sehr viel passiert.
2. Wir sind die ersten Ostdeutschen, die nicht mehr so sprechen, sich nicht
   mehr so benehmen und nicht mehr so aussehen, wie „typische Ossis".
3. … und es tut uns leid, dass wir dies nicht auch von unseren Vätern und
   Müttern und anderen Verwandten sagen können.
4. Wenn wir daran denken, dass wir nur wenige Jahre Bürger der DDR waren,
   sind wir geschockt.
5. Von jetzt ab wird die Zahl der Jahre vor dem Fall der Mauer immer kleiner
   als die Zahl der Jahre danach …
6. Unser Leben selbst in die Hand nehmen bedeutet, dass wir nicht mehr so
   leben wollen wie in der DDR.
7. Wir sind keine Kinder mehr und wünschen uns ein Leben wie in der DDR
   nicht zurück.
8. Bald nachdem ich meinen Freund kennen gelernt hatte, gab er mir eine Kassette
   und sagte: „Was auf diesem Tape zu hören ist, ist bestimmt sehr interessant für dich."
9. Jetzt höre ich die Kassette mit dem Lied „Go West" aber die ganze Zeit, wenn …
10. … und ich bin überrascht, dass ich damals nicht verstanden habe, was mir
    dieses Lied sagen sollte.

11-30 **1949–1990: Das geteilte Deutschland.** Schauen Sie die Landkarte
der deutschen Bundesländer am Anfang des Buches an. Wie viele Bundesländer
kennen Sie schon gut? Zeichnen Sie auf der Karte den „Eisernen Vorhang"°
zwischen der BRD und der DDR ein.

> **Mecklenburg-Vorpommern,
> Brandenburg, Sachsen-
> Anhalt, Thüringen,** and
> **Sachsen** were the German
> Democratic Republic (GDR)
> from 1949–1990. The capital
> of the GDR was officially
> called **Berlin** in East Germany,
> but actually referred to
> **Ost-Berlin,** the part of the
> city officially controlled by
> the Soviets in the post-war
> division of Berlin.

Iron Curtain

Wort, Sinn und Klang

Wörter unter der Lupe

Words as chameleons: *gleich*

As an adjective, **gleich** means *same*.

Monika und ich wurden im **gleichen** Jahr geboren.

Monika and I were born in the **same** year.

As an adverb, **gleich** has three meanings:

a. Expressing the idea of sameness, **gleich** means *equally*.

Monika und ich sind beide **gleich** intelligent.

Monika and I are both **equally** intelligent.

b. Expressing time, **gleich** means *right (away)*, *immediately*.

Ich komme **gleich** nach dem Mittagessen.

I'm coming **right** after lunch.

Ich komme **gleich**.

I'm coming **right away (immediately)**. I'll be **right** there.

c. Expressing location, **gleich** means *right, directly*.

Die Bank ist **gleich** neben dem Postamt.

The bank is **right** beside the post office.

11-31 **Was bedeutet gleich?** *Same, equally, right (right away)*, or *right (directly)*?

1. Der Tennisplatz ist gleich hinter dem Studentenheim.
2. Die Jeans waren so billig, dass ich gleich zwei Paar gekauft habe.
3. Du hast ja genau das gleiche Kleid an wie ich!
4. Ich wohne gleich neben der Bäckerei Biehlmaier.
5. Steh gleich auf, Holger! Es ist schon zehn nach zehn.
6. Meine Schwester und ich spielen gleich gut Klavier.
7. Meine Freundin hat für den gleichen Pulli fünfzehn Euro mehr bezahlt als ich.
8. Möchtest du die fünfzig Euro gleich jetzt?
9. Sind die beiden Hotels gleich teuer?

mistakes 10. Mach doch nicht immer die gleichen Fehler°!

Predicting gender

All nouns with the suffixes **–heit** and **–keit** are *feminine* and most are derived from adjectives. The plural forms always end in **–en**. The suffix **–keit** is used whenever an adjective ends in **–lich** or **–ig.** Both suffixes frequently correspond to the English suffix *-ness*.

krank	*ill, sick*	**die** Krank**heit**	*illness, sickness*
freundlich	*friendly*	**die** Freundlich**keit**	*friendliness*
richtig	*right, correct*	**die** Richtig**keit**	*rightness, correctness*

Note that the German suffixes **–heit** and **–keit** do not always correspond to the English suffix -*ness*.

wichtig	*important*	**die** Wichtig**keit**	*importance*
schön	*beautiful*	**die** Schön**heit**	*beauty*

Some adjectives are extended with **–ig** before the suffix **–keit** is added.

arbeitslos	*unemployed*	**die** Arbeitslos**igkeit**	*unemployment*

11-32 **Was ist das?** Form nouns from the following adjectives and give their English meanings. Adjectives marked with an asterisk must be extended with **–ig** before adding the suffix **–keit.**

1. dunkel
2. hell★
3. gesund
4. klar
5. frei

6. klug
7. dumm
8. schnell★
9. wirklich
10. genau★

Zur Aussprache

11-31 to 11-33

The consonant clusters *pf* and *kn*

In the German consonant clusters **pf** and **kn,** both consonants are pronounced.

Was für ein süßer Zopf

11-33 **Hören Sie gut zu und wiederholen Sie.**

Pfanne	A**pf**el	Dam**pf**	
Pfennig	im**pf**en°	Ko**pf**	*to vaccinate*
Pfeffer	klo**pf**en	To**pf**	
Pflaume	tro**pf**en°	Zo**pf**°	*to drip / braid*
Pfund	Schnu**pf**en°	Strum**pf**°	*sniffles / stocking*

Nimm diese Tro**pf**en für deinen Schnu**pf**en.
A**pf**el**pf**annkuchen mit **Pf**efferminztee? **Pf**ui!

Knast°	**kn**abbern°	**Kn**äckebrot°	*jail / to nibble / crisp bread*
Kneipe	**kn**ipsen°	**Kn**oblauch°	*to snap a photo / garlic*
Knödel	**kn**utschen°	**Kn**ackwurst	*to smooch*

Herr **Kn**opf sitzt im **Kn**ast und **kn**abbert **Kn**äckebrot.
Knusper, **kn**usper **kn**äuschen. Wer **kn**uspert an meinem Häuschen?

Knusper, knusper, knäuschen: This rhyming phrase is said by the witch in the fairy tale *Hänsel und Gretel* when she finds the children nibbling on her house. Do you remember what she says in the English version?

zum Bäcker Lang lohnt jeder Gang

Nomen

das Erlebnis, -se	experience
der Fehler, -	mistake; error
das Gefühl, -e	feeling
die Gegend, -en	area
die Meinung, -en	opinion
der Schlafsack, ⸚e	sleeping bag
der Witz, -e	joke
der Beifahrersitz, -e	front passenger seat (in a car)
der Rückspiegel, -	rearview mirror
das Steuer(rad)	steering wheel
der Aufkleber, -	sticker
der Eiserne Vorhang	Iron Curtain
die Hälfte, -n	half
die Wende	turning point (i.e., fall of the Berlin Wall)
die Zukunft	future

Verben

arbeiten an (+ dat)	to work on
sich ärgern über (+ acc)	to be annoyed with, about
sich auf·regen über (+ acc)	to get upset about; to get worked up about
begreifen, begriff, begriffen	to understand, to grasp
behaupten	to claim
denken an (+ acc)	to think of, about
sich freuen auf (+ acc)	to look forward to
sich freuen über (+ acc)	to be happy about; to be pleased with
sich interessieren für	to be interested in
meinen	to mean; to think, to be of or voice an opinion
studieren an (+ dat)	to study at

sich verlieben in (+ acc)	to fall in love with
warten auf (+ acc)	to wait for
wissen von	to know about
verhaften	to arrest
sich wundern	to be surprised

Andere Wörter

aufregend	exciting
dickköpfig	stubborn
ehemalig	former
erwachsen	grown up
jederzeit	(at) any time

Ausdrücke

d. h. (= das heißt)	that is, that is to say
etwas in die eigene Hand nehmen	to take something into one's own hands

Das Gegenteil

fern ≠ nah	far ≠ near
die Freiheit ≠ die Unfreiheit	freedom ≠ absence of freedom
Positives ≠ Negatives	positive things ≠ negative things

Synonyme

ebenfalls	=	auch
jedoch	=	aber
unaufhörlich	=	nonstop
eine Menge	=	viel
seit kurzem	=	seit kurzer Zeit
zu Beginn	=	am Anfang

Leicht zu verstehen

die Attraktion, -en	clever
der Kulturschock	kommunistisch
die Mitternacht	

Wörter im Kontext

11-34 Was passt zusammen?

1. Wenn man lustig ist,
2. Wenn man immer nur das macht, was man selbst will,
3. Wenn man schöne Erlebnisse im Ausland hat,
4. Wenn man in einer Klausur eine Menge dumme Fehler gemacht hat,

   a. ärgert man sich.
   b. ist das Leben aufregend.
   c. erzählt man manchmal Witze.
   d. ist man dickköpfig.

11-35 Optimist. Was passt zusammen?

1. Für meinen Deutschkurs
2. Vor den Klausuren in diesem Kurs
3. Über die lieben Mails von zu Hause
4. In meinen deutschen Freund
5. Auf seinen Besuch im Sommer

a. habe ich eigentlich nie Angst.
b. freue ich mich immer sehr.
c. interessiere ich mich sehr.
d. freue ich mich schon jetzt.
e. habe ich mich beim Chatten im Internet verliebt.

11-36 Pessimist. Was passt zusammen?

1. Meine Probleme mit dem Leben im Studentenheim
2. Über die laute Musik im Nachbarzimmer
3. Oft muss ich bis nach Mitternacht
4. Und auf das Geld von meinen Eltern

a. an einem blöden Referat arbeiten.
b. begreifen meine Eltern überhaupt nicht.
c. ärgere ich mich manchmal sehr.
d. muss ich auch oft viel zu lang warten.

11-37 Zusammengesetzte Nomen. Kombinieren Sie in jeder der zwei Gruppen die passenden Nomen.

▶ die Luft + die Brücke = die Luftbrücke

1. die Rede
2. der Beifahrer
3. die Touristen
4. die Kultur
5. die Heimat
6. das Fahrrad

a. die Freiheit
b. die Attraktion
c. der Sitz
d. das Land
e. der Schock
f. die Route

Zwei Touristenattraktionen in Berlin: Fernsehturm am Alexanderplatz und Hackesche Höfe am Hackeschen Markt

KAPITEL 12

So ist das Leben

Kommunikationsziele

Talking about …
- relationships
- equal rights for women and men
- careers and family obligations
- your dreams for the future

Expressing feelings

Expressing wishes, regrets, and polite requests and questions

Asking for and giving advice

Strukturen

Present-time subjunctive

The subjunctive in wishes and polite requests

Past-time subjunctive

Genitive prepositions

Kultur

Frauen im 21. Jahrhundert

Video-Treff: Wenn ich im Lotto gewinnen würde, …

Lesen: Meine Zukunft

Vorschau

Annett Louisan wurde 1977 in Havelberg im Bundesland Sachsen-Anhalt geboren. „Eve" ist ein Lied von ihrem zweiten, sehr erfolgreichen Album Unausgesprochen *(2005).*

EVE
von Annett Louisan

meine Freundin Eve ist aktiv,
denkt immer positiv
kennt kein Stimmungstief
ihr Freund Steve
5 ist sportiv.

sie ist porentief rein und attraktiv
sie ist kreativ, dekorativ, sensitiv
sie lebt intensiv
für die Art wie mich das ankotzt gibt's kein Adjektiv
10 seh' ich Eve, sag' ich: „Na, Eve …"
treff' ich Eve, sag' ich: „Na, Eve …"

doch bei Eve geht nie 'was schief
sie ist sehr kommunikativ
überzeugt argumentativ
15 instinktiv
meistert Eve
spielend den Beruf
und den Alltagsmief

sie ist progressiv, alternativ
20 innovativ, sehr impulsiv
geschickt und effektiv
ich hasse sie abgrundtief
seh' ich Eve, sag' ich: „Na, Eve …"
treff' ich Eve, sag' ich: „Na, Eve …"

25 wär' ich Eve, hätt' ich Steve.
mein Leben wär' erfüllt
und nicht so primitiv
wäre, würde, rein fiktiv
was wär' wenn's für mich besser lief'
30 vollkommen bin ich leider nur
im Konjunktiv

seh' ich Eve, macht mich das aggressiv
treff' ich Eve, wechsle ich die Straßenseite
und zwar demonstrativ

12-1 Was ist das auf Englisch?

1. Eve ist sehr kommunikativ und **überzeugt** mich mit guten Argumenten.
2. Wenn ich Eve treffe, **wechsle** ich die Straßenseite.
3. Ich **hasse** sie, weil sie so schön ist.
4. Bei Eve **geht** nie was **schief.**
5. **Wenn ich** schön **wäre,** hätte ich auch einen tollen Freund.
6. Es **kotzt mich an,** dass sie in allem so talentiert ist!
7. Sie **ist porentief rein** und attraktiv.
8. **Na?** Wie geht's dir?

a. hate
b. makes me puke
c. has immaculate skin
d. what's up?
e. persuades
f. goes wrong
g. if I were
h. switch

12-2 Anders gesagt. Markieren Sie in Annett Louisans Lied die Aussagen, die etwa dasselbe bedeuten.

1. Eve ist Optimistin und nie schlechter Laune°. *mood*
2. Eve navigiert ohne Probleme durch alle Schwierigkeiten° bei der Arbeit oder zu Hause. *difficulties*
3. Ich kann nicht beschreiben, wie sehr ich sie hasse.
4. Weil sie so gut spricht, bringt Eve andere auf ihre Seite.
5. Ich werde total wütend°, wenn ich Eve sehe. *furious*
6. Ich zeige Eve, dass ich sie nicht mag, wenn ich sie in der Stadt sehe.
7. Eves Freund macht viel Sport.
8. So perfekt wie Eve bin ich nur in meiner Imagination.

12-3 Warum ist die Frau so neidisch° auf Eve? Markieren Sie die passenden Antworten. *envious*

	Weil Eve immer gut angezogen ist.		Weil Eve und Steve einen schnellen Sportwagen haben.
	Weil Eve einen attraktiven Freund hat.		Weil die Frau auch gern ein Fotomodell wäre.
	Weil Eves Eltern ihr immer Geld schicken.		Weil das Leben der Frau nicht erfüllt ist.
	Weil Eve charismatisch ist.		Weil Eve ständig° erzählt, wie gut ihr Freund küssen kann.
	Weil die Frau sich auch in Steve verliebt hat.		Weil Eve in allem, was sie tut, Erfolg hat.

constantly

12-4 Bist du manchmal neidisch? Wenn wir ehrlich° sind, müssen wir zugeben°, dass wir alle manchmal auf andere Leute neidisch sind. Erzählen Sie einander, auf wen Sie manchmal neidisch sind und warum.

honest
admit

S1: Auf wen bist du manchmal neidisch? Warum?

S2: Auf meine Schwester. Weil sie so einen tollen Sportwagen hat.

S2: Auf wen …?

S3: Auf …

meinen Bruder	spielt so gut Gitarre
meine Kusine	(Fußball, Tennis usw.)
meinen Vetter	hat so eine tolle Figur
meine Freundin	bekommt immer eine Eins
meinen Freund	für ihre/seine Referate
meine Mitbewohnerin	verdient eine Menge Geld
meinen Mitbewohner	hat so einen interessanten Job
…	…

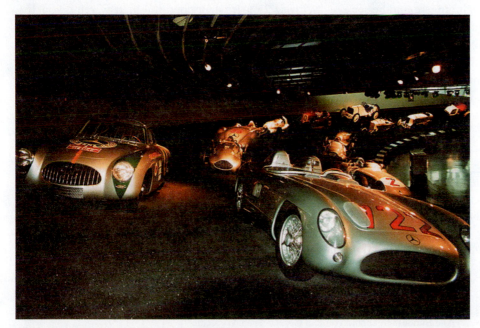

Tolle Sportwagen im Mercedes-Benz-Museum in Stuttgart.

Kultur / Frauen im 21. Jahrhundert

In den Verfassungen[1] der deutschsprachigen Länder steht, dass Frauen und Männer gleichberechtigt[2] sind und dass Frauen deshalb auch den gleichen Lohn[3] für gleichwertige Arbeit bekommen sollen. Die Statistik zeigt aber immer noch einen ziemlichen Unterschied[4] in der Bezahlung von Männern und Frauen. Ein Grund[5] dafür ist, dass viele ältere Frauen keine so gute Ausbildung[6] haben und für besser bezahlte Berufe nicht qualifiziert sind. Aber auch jüngere und besser ausgebildete Frauen haben selten höhere Positionen. Wenn sie dann auch noch Mütter werden, wird ihre Karriere unterbrochen[7], und danach beginnen sie meist dort, wo sie aufgehört haben. Sie haben in den stressigen Jahren, in denen sie für Familie und Kinder sorgten[8], vieles gelernt, was in höheren Positionen oft wichtig ist, aber viele Arbeitgeber[9] haben das noch nicht begriffen[10].

Angela Merkel, Deutschlands erste Bundeskanzlerin.

Viele Frauen möchten beides, Beruf und Familie, aber solange sie die meisten Aufgaben in Haushalt und Familie übernehmen[11], bleibt Gleichberechtigung im Beruf Utopie.

Zum Glück[12] spielen Frauen in der Politik eine immer größere Rolle. Anfang 2009 waren in Deutschland 32,8% der Abgeordneten[13] im Parlament Frauen, in Österreich 28,5% und in der Schweiz 25%. Im deutschen Kabinett waren 6 von 16 Mitgliedern Frauen, im österreichischen 6 von 19 und in der Schweiz 4 von 7. Im November 2005 wurde Angela Merkel Deutschlands erste Bundeskanzlerin und sie wurde 4 Jahre später wiedergewählt.

[1]*constitutions* [2]**sind … gleichberechtigt:** *have equal rights* [3]*pay* [4]*difference* [5]*reason* [6]*education* [7]*interrupted* [8]*cared* [9]*employers* [10]*grasped* [11]*take on* [12]*fortunately* [13]*representatives*

Grundgesetz der Bundesrepublik Deutschland, Artikel 3

(1) Alle Menschen sind vor dem Gesetz gleich.

(2) Männer und Frauen sind gleichberechtigt. Der Staat fördert[1] die tatsächliche[2] Durchsetzung[3] der Gleichberechtigung von Frauen und Männern und wirkt[4] auf die Beseitigung[5] bestehender[6] Nachteile hin.

[1]*promotes* [2]*actual* [3]*implementation* [4]**wirkt hin auf:** *works towards* [5]*removal* [6]*existing*

Grundgesetz (Basic Law): The constitution of West Germany was drawn up in 1949, four years after the end of World War II. **Grundgesetz** was chosen as a provisional title, which was to serve until the two Germanies were reunited. It was generally thought that this would be achieved in a very short time. When reunification finally took place 41 years later, changes were made to the document itself, but the title remained the same.

Verfassung der Republik Österreich, Artikel 7

(1) Alle Bundesbürger sind vor dem Gesetz gleich. Vorrechte[1] der Geburt, des Geschlechtes[2], des Standes[3], der Klasse und des Bekenntnisses[4] sind ausgeschlossen[5]…

[1]*privileges* [2]*gender* [3]*social status* [4]*religious affiliation* [5]*precluded*

Bundesverfassung der Schweiz, Artikel 8

(3) Mann und Frau sind gleichberechtigt. Das Gesetz sorgt für ihre rechtliche[1] und tatsächliche Gleichstellung[2], vor allem in Familie, Ausbildung und Arbeit. Mann und Frau haben Anspruch auf gleichen Lohn für gleichwertige Arbeit.

[1]*legal* [2]*equality*

12-5 **Was ist wichtig für junge Frauen?** Dieses Schaubild zeigt, wie Männer und Frauen diese Frage beantworten. Man kann sehen, wie unterschiedlich die Meinungen der beiden Geschlechter sind.

NEUE VOKABELN

nach Meinung der Männer / der Frauen	*in the opinion of men/women*	**die Markenkleidung**	*brand name clothing*
für eine Sache eintreten	*to advocate for something*	**der Übergang, ⸚e**	*transition*
Verantwortung übernehmen	*to take on responsibility*	**die Beziehung, –en**	*relationship*

WAS IST WICHTIG FÜR JUNGE FRAUEN?

● Nach Meinung der Männer   ● Nach Meinung der Frauen

Angaben in Prozent   0   20   40   60   80   100

Viel Geld verdienen — Beruf
Karriere machen
Für eine Sache eintreten
Auf eigenen Beinen stehen
Verantwortung übernehmen
Gut ausgebildet sein
Kinder bekommen — Familie und Heiratsmarkt
Gut aussehen
Markenkleidung tragen
Heiraten
Dünn sein
Guten Sex haben

1. Ergänzen Sie: Dieses Schaubild zeigt, was für _____ _____ wichtig ist. Zwölf mögliche Lebensziele auf der _____ Seite sind in die zwei Kategorien „_____" und „_____ und _____ _____" auf der _____ Seite gruppiert. In dem Schaubild zeigt die _____ Linie die Meinung der Männer. Die _____ Linie zeigt die Meinung der Frauen.
2. Was ist nach Meinung der Männer das wichtigste Lebensziel für junge Frauen? Was ist nach Meinung der Frauen das wichtigste Lebensziel für junge Frauen?
3. Was ist nach Meinung der Männer das unwichtigste Lebensziel für junge Frauen? Was ist nach Meinung der Frauen das unwichtigste Lebensziel für junge Frauen?
4. Bei welchen Lebenszielen für junge Frauen ist die Diskrepanz zwischen den Meinungen am größten? Am kleinsten?
5. Was passiert in der Mitte des Schaubildes, am Übergang von der Kategorie „Beruf" zu der Kategorie „Familie und Heiratsmarkt"?
6. **Meiner Meinung nach …** Sprechen Sie mit Ihren Nachbarn. Welche Lebensziele für junge Frauen sind Ihrer Meinung nach am wichtigsten? Welche finden Sie nicht so wichtig? Haben Männer und Frauen in Ihrer Klasse unterschiedliche Meinungen zu diesen Fragen? Was müssen junge Frauen in Ihrem Land tun, um Karriere zu machen *und* eine Familie oder Beziehung zu haben?

Nomen

der Arbeitgeber, -	} employer
die Arbeitgeberin, -nen	
der Arbeitnehmer,-	} employee
die Arbeitnehmerin, -nen	
die Aufgabe, -n	assignment; task
die Ausbildung	education; job training
die Beziehung, -en	relationship
die Figur, -en	figure, physique
das Geschlecht, -er	gender
das Gesetz, -e	law
die Gleichberechtigung	equal rights; equality
der Grund, ¨e	reason
der Haushalt, -e	household
die Markenkleidung	brand name clothing
die Sache, -n	cause
der Übergang	transition
der Unterschied, -e	difference
die Verantwortung, -en	responsibility
die Verfassung, -en	constitution

> What are the literal meanings of **Arbeitgeber** and **Arbeitnehmer?**

> You learned **Sache** in the sense of *thing* or *object* in *Kapitel 7*.

Verben

begreifen, begriff, begriffen	to grasp; to comprehend
ein·treten für (tritt ein), trat ein, ist eingetreten	to advocate for
sorgen für	to care for
übernehmen (übernimmt), übernahm, übernommen	to take on (a duty)
überzeugen	to persuade
unterbrechen (unterbricht), unterbrach, unterbrochen	to interrupt
zu·geben (gibt zu), gab zu, zugegeben	to admit

> When **über-** and **unter-** are prefixed to verbs, they are usually inseparable.

Andere Wörter

ständig	constant(ly)
tatsächlich	actual(ly)
solange	as long as

Ausdrücke

auf (seinen) eigenen Beinen stehen	to stand on (one's) own feet
meiner Meinung nach	in my opinion
neidisch auf (+ acc)	envious of
gleichberechtigt sein	to have equal rights
gut ausgebildet sein	to be well educated, to be well trained
Karriere machen	to get ahead in one's career
zum Glück	fortunately, luckily
wütend auf (+ acc)	furious at

Das Gegenteil

ehrlich ≠ unehrlich	honest ≠ dishonest
unterschiedlich ≠ gleich	different ≠ same; equal(ly)

Synonyme

der Lohn, ¨e = das Gehalt, ¨er = die Bezahlung

Leicht zu verstehen

aggressiv	die Pore, -n
die Diskrepanz, -en	die Position, -en
impulsiv	positiv
instinktiv	das Prozent, -e
das Kabinett, -e	qualifiziert
die Karriere, -n	die Statistik, -en
das Parlament, -e	die Utopie, -n

20 JAHRE FRAUENSTIMMRECHT
2004: ANTEIL FRAUEN IM LANDTAG:

2001:	12%	
1997:	4%	
1993:	8%	
1993:	4%	
1989:	4%	
1986:	6,7%	

12%

> Ein Plakat *(placard)* aus Liechtenstein: There are 25 Members of Parliament in Liechtenstein. In 1997, there was one woman in the Parliament, which constituted 4% of the total. How many female members were there in 2004? In 2009, there were six female members. What percentage is that?

Wörter im Kontext

12-6 Mit anderen Worten. Ergänzen Sie die Sätze in der rechten Spalte° so, *column*
dass sie etwa dasselbe bedeuten wie die Sätze in der linken Spalte.

Aufgabe / gleichberechtigt / Karriere / unterbrichst / qualifiziert / eigenen / ständig

1. Warum lässt du mich denn nie fertig reden?   Warum _____ du mich denn immer?

2. Mach doch mal was ohne meine Hilfe!   Steh doch mal auf deinen _____ Beinen!

3. Was soll ich tun?   Was ist meine _____?

4. Gina hat eine sehr gute Ausbildung.   Gina ist hoch _____.

5. Gina bekommt sicher mal eine hohe Position.   Gina macht bestimmt mal _____.

6. Im Grundgesetz steht, dass Frauen und Männer dieselben Rechte haben.   Im Grundgesetz steht, dass Frauen und Männer _____ sind.

7. Sag doch nicht immer dasselbe!   Sag doch nicht _____ dasselbe!

12-7 Was passt zusammen?

1. Wenn Eves Freund eine bessere Bezahlung als Eve für die gleiche Arbeit bekommt,
2. Wenn Eve nicht ins Kino gehen möchte,
3. Wenn Eve einen Fehler gemacht hat,
4. Wenn Eve ihre neue Position bei BMW anfängt,
5. Wenn Eves Mutter krank wird,
6. Wenn Eve Geld für das Kinderkrankenhaus spendet,
7. Wenn Eve immer teure Markenkleidung tragen möchte,

a. muss Steve sie überzeugen.
b. muss sie viel Geld verdienen.
c. ist Eve nicht gleichberechtigt.
d. tritt sie für eine gute Sache ein.
e. übernimmt sie die Verantwortung für ein wichtiges Projekt.
f. gibt sie es zu.
g. muss sie für sie sorgen.

Photo: Schrittgeschwindigkeit = *walking speed*

12-8 Mit anderen Worten. Ergänzen Sie die Sätze in der rechten Spalte so, dass sie etwa dasselbe bedeuten wie die Sätze in der linken Spalte.

unehrlich / Haushalt / Diskrepanz / unterschiedlich / Arbeitgeber / ausgebildet

1. Robert war auf einer sehr guten Uni.   Robert ist gut _____.
2. Ihre Gehälter sind nicht gleich.   Es gibt eine _____ zwischen ihren Gehältern.
3. Eve und Steve sind nicht einer Meinung.   Ihre Meinungen sind _____.
4. Paul sagt nicht immer die Wahrheit.   Paul ist manchmal _____.
5. Laura arbeitet bei BMW.   BMW ist Lauras _____.
6. Wer kocht und putzt bei euch?   Wer macht bei euch den _____?

Kommunikation und Formen

1 Talking about contrary-to-fact situations (1)

12-1 to 12-5

Present-time subjunctive

In English, when you talk about something that is contrary to the facts, you often use a different verb form than you do for factual statements.

FACT	CONTRARY-TO-FACT
I **have** only fifty dollars.	If only I **had** a million dollars!

The form *had* in the contrary-to-fact example is not the simple past and does not refer to past time. It is a subjunctive form of the verb *to have* and it refers to the present. By using subjunctive forms you indicate that what you are saying is contrary-to-fact.

I **don't have** a car.	If only I **had** a car!
David **isn't** here.	If only David **were** here!
David **has to** work and **can't** pick me up.	If David **didn't have to** work, he **could** pick me up.
I **don't know** where the nearest bus stop is.	If only I **knew** where the nearest bus stop was.

In German, you also use subjunctive forms to talk about contrary-to-fact situations. As in English, these subjunctive forms are very similar in form to the simple past, but they refer to present time.

Ich **habe** keinen Wagen.	Wenn ich nur einen Wagen **hätte!**
David **ist** nicht hier.	Wenn David nur hier **wäre!**
David **muss** arbeiten und **kann** mich nicht abholen.	Wenn David nicht arbeiten **müsste, könnte** er mich abholen.
Ich **weiß** nicht, wo die nächste Bushaltestelle ist.	Wenn ich nur **wüsste,** wo die nächste Bushaltestelle ist!

überlegen = *think about*

Man muss gut überlegen, was man sich wünscht. Es könnte passieren, dass man es bekommt

The forms of the present-time subjunctive are derived from the simple past. Below are the subjunctive forms of **haben, sein, werden, wissen,** and the modals. Except for **sollte** and **wollte,** these forms are all umlauted.

infinitive	simple past	subjunctive
haben	hatte	**hätte**
sein	war	**wäre**
werden	wurde	**würde**
wissen	wusste	**wüsste**
dürfen	durfte	**dürfte**
können	konnte	**könnte**
mögen	mochte	**möchte**
müssen	musste	**müsste**
sollen	sollte	**sollte**
wollen	wollte	**wollte**

Fahr vorsichtig
Es könnte auch Dein Kind sein

In the subjunctive, all verbs have the following set of personal endings.

singular		plural	
ich	hätt**e**	wir	hätt**en**
du	hätt**est**	ihr	hätt**et**
er/es/sie	hätt**e**	sie	hätt**en**
	Sie hätt**en**		

English equivalents for these forms often include the auxiliary verb *would*.

Wenn du nicht so eifersüchtig **wärst,**
   hätten wir eine bessere Beziehung.
Du **könntest** doch versuchen, nicht
   immer so eifersüchtig zu sein.

*If you **were**n't so jealous, we **would**
   have a better relationship.
You **could** really try not to be so
   jealous all the time.*

> For **sein,** the **e** in **du wär**e**st** and **ihr wär**e**t** is often omitted: **du wärst, ihr wärt.**

<u>12-9</u> Was passt zusammen?

1. Wenn ich besser qualifiziert wäre,

2. Wenn Frau Kuhn keine so wichtige Position hätte,

3. Wenn ich krank würde,

4. Wenn du kein so hohes Fieber hättest,

5. Wenn ich Pauls E-Mail-Adresse wüsste,

6. Wenn Beate kein Baby hätte,

7. Wenn Moritz nicht so unhöflich wäre,

a. müsste ich die Klausur nicht schreiben.

b. hätte er bestimmt mehr Freunde.

c. könnte ich viel schneller Karriere machen.

d. könnte ich ihm schreiben.

e. wollte sie gern noch mehr Kinder.

f. dürftest du aufstehen.

g. müsste sie ihre Karriere nicht unterbrechen.

12-10 Wenn das Leben nur nicht so kompliziert wäre! Ergänzen Sie Konjunktivformen.

1. Holger **hat** kein Fahrrad und **will** deshalb immer mein Fahrrad leihen. Ich mag das gar nicht, aber ich **kann** nicht nein sagen.

   Wenn Holger nur ein Fahrrad _____!
   Wenn Holger nur nicht immer mein Fahrrad leihen _____!
   Wenn ich nur nein sagen _____!

2. Es ist Winter und es **wird** schon um fünf dunkel. Ich **habe** bis halb sechs Vorlesungen und **muss** zu Fuß nach Hause.

   Wenn es nur nicht so früh dunkel _____!
   Wenn ich nur nicht bis halb sechs Vorlesungen _____!
   Wenn ich nur nicht zu Fuß nach Hause _____!

3. Es **ist** sehr heiß, aber weil ich erkältet **bin, darf** ich nicht schwimmen gehen.

   Wenn es nur nicht so heiß _____!
   Wenn ich nur nicht erkältet _____!
   Wenn ich nur schwimmen gehen _____!

was … ist: *what's the matter with me*

4. Ich **werde** immer so schnell müde. Ich möchte gern **wissen,** was mit mir los ist,° aber ich **habe** keine Zeit, zum Arzt zu gehen.

   Wenn ich nur nicht immer so schnell müde _____!
   Wenn ich nur _____, was mit mir los ist!
   Wenn ich nur Zeit _____, zum Arzt zu gehen!

12-11 Unglückliche Liebe! Ergänzen Sie Konjunktivformen.

too bad

1. TILMANN DENKT: Schade°, dass ich Nicoles Telefonnummer nicht weiß!

   Wenn ich ihre Nummer _____, _____ ich sie anrufen. (wissen / können)
   Wenn sie viel Hausaufgaben _____, _____ ich ihr helfen. (haben / können)
   Wenn wir die Hausaufgaben dann fertig _____, _____ wir zusammen fernsehen und eine Pizza essen. (haben / können)

2. NICOLE DENKT: Gut, dass Tilmann meine Telefonnummer nicht weiß!

   Wenn er meine Nummer _____, _____ er mich anrufen. (wissen / können)
   Wenn er dann kommen _____, _____ ich lügen und sagen, ich _____ zu viel Hausaufgaben. (wollen / müssen / haben)
   Und was _____ ich sagen, wenn er mir bei den Hausaufgaben helfen _____? (können / wollen)

Würde + infinitive

12-6 to 12-10

To talk about a contrary-to-fact situation, you use the subjunctive forms for **haben, sein, werden, wissen,** and the modals. For all other verbs you usually use a construction that is parallel to English *would + infinitive:* **würde** + *infinitive.*

Was **würdest** du **tun,** wenn dein Freund ständig eifersüchtig wäre?

*What **would** you **do** if your boyfriend were constantly jealous?*

Ich **würde** mir einen anderen Freund **suchen.**

*I **would look for** another boyfriend.*

singular		plural	
ich **würde** suchen		wir **würden** suchen	
du **würdest** suchen		ihr **würdet** suchen	
er/es/sie **würde** suchen		sie **würden** suchen	
	Sie **würden** suchen		

12-12 **Wenn es nur wahr wäre!** Die Information für **S2** ist im *Anhang* auf Seite A11.

S1: Was würde Claudia tun, wenn sie eine Million Euro gewinnen würde?

S2: Sie würde ihr Studium unterbrechen und eine Weltreise machen.

Claudia	
Martin	Er würde sich einen Porsche kaufen.
Stephanie und Peter	Sie würden heiraten und sich ein schönes Haus kaufen.
Herr und Frau Ziegler	
Robert	

12-13 **Was würdest du mit all dem Geld tun?**

S1: Was würdest du tun, wenn du eine Million Dollar gewinnen würdest?

S2: Ich würde …

12-14 **Um Rat° fragen.**

advice

▶ Ich bin immer so müde.   zum Arzt gehen

S1: Ich bin immer so müde. Was würdest du tun?

S2: Ich würde zum Arzt gehen.

1. Ich kann nachts nicht schlafen.
2. Ich weiß, dass meine Schwester magersüchtig° ist.   *anorexic*
3. Ich habe kein Geld mehr.
4. Ich will nicht auf Davids Party gehen.

mir einen Job suchen	eine Schlaftablette nehmen
ihr raten°, sofort eine Therapie zu machen	ihm sagen, dass ich ein Referat fertig schreiben muss

advise

5. Ich darf in meinem Zimmer keine laute Musik spielen.
6. Ich bin immer so nervös.
7. Ich kann kein Zimmer finden.
8. Ich habe Halsschmerzen.

mit Salzwasser gurgeln	eine Anzeige in die Zeitung setzen
weniger Kaffee trinken	mir gute Kopfhörer kaufen

12-15 Was würdest du tun, wenn …? Stellen Sie Ihren Mitstudenten diese oder ähnliche Fragen.

Was würdest du tun, wenn jemand …

dir … gehen: *get on your nerves*

- in der Vorlesung texten würde?
- dich ständig unterbrechen würde?
- nie zugeben könnte, dass sie/er nicht recht hat?

- dir ständig auf die Nerven gehen° würde?
- immer dumme Witze machen würde?
- ständig betrunken Auto fahren würde?

2 Expressing wishes, polite requests, and polite questions

 ## The subjunctive in wishes and polite requests

12-11 to 12-12 In *Kapitel 4* you learned that **ich möchte** expresses wishes or requests more politely than **ich will,** and you have since used the **möchte-**forms without necessarily realizing that they are subjunctive forms.

Ich **will** ein Glas Bier.	*I **want** a glass of beer.*
Ich **möchte** ein Glas Bier.	*I **would like** a glass of beer.*

You can also express wishes or requests by using phrases like **hätte gern, wäre gern,** or **wüsste gern**.

Ich **hätte gern** ein Glas Bier.	*I **would like to have** a glass of beer.*
Ich **wäre** jetzt **gern** in Hawaii.	*I **would like to be** in Hawaii now.*
Wir **wüssten gern,** was wir für dieses Quiz lernen müssen.	*We **would like to know** what we have to study for this quiz.*

wishes **12-16 Wünsche°.** Die Information für **S2** ist im *Anhang* auf Seite A11.

S1: Was hätte Laura gern?

S2: Sie hätte gern so eine gute Position wie ihre Freundin Mia.

	WAS HÄTTE … GERN?	WO WÄRE … JETZT GERN?	WAS WÜSSTE … GERN?
Laura			
Lisa	einen Freund, der auch mal etwas im Haushalt macht	auf einer sonnigen Südseeinsel	wie viel die männlichen Kollegen in der Firma verdienen
Paul	so einen tollen Körper wie sein Freund	mit Frau und Kindern in der Karibik	warum sein Vater ihn ständig kritisiert
Thomas			

 12-17 Was sind deine Wünsche?

S1: Was hättest du gern?
Wo wärst du jetzt gern?
Was wüsstest du gern?
Was möchtest du später beruflich machen?

S2: Ich hätte gern …
Ich wäre jetzt gern …
Ich wüsste gern, …
Ich möchte später …

The subjunctive in polite questions

You can also formulate questions more politely by using **haben, sein, werden, wissen,** and the modal verbs in present-time subjunctive.

Könnten Sie mir bitte sagen, wo die Apotheke ist?

Could you please tell me where the pharmacy is?

12-18 Höfliche Fragen. In jeder der folgenden sechs Gruppen sind zwei Fragen und zwei Antworten. **S1** drückt die beiden Fragen höflicher aus. **S2** antwortet. Wechseln Sie die Rollen nach den ersten drei Kurzdialogen.

S1:

1. Weißt du vielleicht, ob es hier ein Fitnessstudio für Frauen gibt? Und wo ist das?

2. Darf ich Ihnen noch ein Stück Kuchen anbieten°? Kann ich dann wenigstens Ihr Glas noch mal füllen?

3. Haben Sie vielleicht ein gutes Buch über Berlin? Kann ich es mir ein bisschen genauer anschauen?

4. Darf ich fragen, wie viel Zinsen° ich auf dem Sparkonto° bekomme? Und was muss ich tun, um ein bisschen mehr zu bekommen?

5. Hast du Lust, am Sonntag mit uns nach Schwerin zu fahren? Du musst dann aber schon um halb sieben bei uns sein.

6. Können Sie mir sagen, wo das Büro von Frau Dr. Berger ist? Hat Dr. Berger vielleicht Zeit für ein kurzes Gespräch?

S2:

Ja, hier gibt es sogar ein ganz tolles.

Gleich um die nächste Ecke, in der Schillerstraße.

Danke, nein. Ich kann wirklich nichts mehr essen.

Ja, bitte. Dieser Wein ist wirklich sehr gut.

Ja, dieses hier kann ich Ihnen besonders empfehlen.

Aber sicher, lassen Sie sich nur Zeit.°

Normalerweise bekommen Sie zwei Prozent.

Sie dürften nie weniger als 5000 Euro auf dem Konto haben.

Klar! Da fahre ich gern mit.

Kein Problem. Ich bin sowieso Frühaufsteher.

Ja, ihr Büro ist gleich hier rechts, die Nummer 418.

Ja, das müsste gehen. Sie ist zum Glück heute da.

offer

lassen Sie sich Zeit: *take your time*

interest
savings account

Sprachnotiz   *Kommen and gehen in present-time subjunctive*

Instead of **würde** + infinitive you will also commonly read and hear present-time subjunctive forms of verbs other than **haben, sein, werden, wissen,** and the modals. The most frequent are:

ich **käme** = ich würde kommen   ich **ginge** = ich würde gehen

„Wie würden Sie sich fühlen, wenn Sie jung und knackig in die Mülltonne kämen?"

Video-Treff

Wenn ich im Lotto gewinnen würde, ...

Anja Szustak und Kristina, Anja Peter, Öcsi, Stefan Meister und Stefan Kuhlmann erzählen, was sie mit ihrem Lottogewinn tun würden. Machen Sie die erste Aufgabe **Anders gesagt**, bevor Sie das Video anschauen.

12-19 Anders gesagt.

1. Ich würde meinen Eltern einen Urlaub **spendieren.**
2. Ich würde einfach so **Kleinigkeiten** kaufen.
3. Ich würde einkaufen gehen, ohne aufs Geld zu **gucken.**
4. Ich würde 'n Job suchen, den ich **unbedingt** machen möchte.
5. Ich würde von den Zinsen leben, wenn es **richtig** viel Geld ist.
6. Dann würde ich beim nächsten Flug ins All **mitmachen.**

a. mitfliegen
b. sehen
c. absolut
d. bezahlen
e. kleine Sachen
f. sehr

12-20 Was passt? Ergänzen Sie die Aussagen mit der Information, die Sie im Video hören.

1. Mit so viel Geld würde Anja Szustak nach Australien oder _____ fliegen.

   ☐ Nordamerika   ☐ Asien

2. Wenn Sie im Lotto gewinnen würde, würde Kristina sich _____ kaufen.

   ☐ einen teuren Mantel   ☐ ein teures Motorrad

3. Wenn sie reich wäre, würde Anja Peter _____ einen neuen Wagen kaufen.

   ☐ ihrem Bruder   ☐ ihren Eltern

4. Mit 10 Millionen Euro würde Öcsi wahrscheinlich _____ kaufen.

   ☐ Land   ☐ ein Haus

5. Öcsi möchte _____ in Dänemark verbringen.

   ☐ den Sommer   ☐ den Winter

6. Wenn er so viel Geld hätte, würde Stefan Meister _____.

   ☐ nie wieder arbeiten   ☐ einen interessanten Job finden

7. Stefan Kuhlmann möchte eine Wohnung in _____ verschiedenen Städten.

   ☐ drei   ☐ zwei

12-21 Richtig oder falsch? Lesen Sie die Aussagen über Kristina, Anja Szustak, Anja Peter, Öcsi, Stefan Kuhlmann und Stefan Meister und ihre Pläne. Sind diese Aussagen richtig oder falsch? Wenn eine Aussage falsch ist, korrigieren Sie sie.

	RICHTIG	FALSCH
1. Hätte Kristina viel Geld, dann würde sie mit Freunden eine Reise machen.	☐	☐
2. Wenn Anja Szustak im Lotto gewinnen würde, dann würde sie sofort ins Reisebüro gehen.	☐	☐
3. Auch wenn sie im Lotto gewinnen würde, würde Anja Peter weiterstudieren.	☐	☐
4. Anja Peter würde auch eine Reise machen.	☐	☐
5. Öcsi hat sehr viele Ideen, wie er so viel Geld ausgeben könnte.	☐	☐
6. Wenn er richtig viel Geld hätte, würde Stefan Meister von den Zinsen leben.	☐	☐
7. Stefan Meister möchte mit dem Geld eine lange Reise machen.	☐	☐
8. Stefan Kuhlmann würde absolut nichts sparen.	☐	☐
9. Mit 10 Millionen Euro würde Stefan Kuhlmann als Allererstes überall hinreisen.	☐	☐
10. Stefan Kuhlmann hat schon seit langem den Traum, ins All zu fliegen.	☐	☐

3 Talking about contrary-to-fact situations (2)

Past-time subjunctive

12-15 to 12-20

To talk about past-time contrary-to-fact situations, you use the past participle of the verb with the appropriate auxiliary in the subjunctive (i.e., a form of **wäre** or **hätte**).

FACT	CONTRARY-TO-FACT
Ich **bin** zu schnell **gefahren.**	Wenn ich nur nicht zu schnell **gefahren wäre!**
I was driving too fast.	*If only I hadn't been driving too fast!*
Ich **habe** einen Strafzettel **bekommen.**	Wenn ich nur keinen Strafzettel **bekommen hätte!**
I got a ticket.	*If only I hadn't gotten a ticket!*

Note that in past-time subjunctive, German never uses **würde**.

Meine Eltern **wären** nicht zu schnell **gefahren.**	*My parents wouldn't have driven too fast.*
Und sie **hätten** keinen Strafzettel **bekommen.**	*And they wouldn't have gotten a ticket.*

12-22 Wenn wir nur nicht so dumm gewesen wären! Ergänzen Sie die passenden Partizipien und **hätte(n)** oder **wäre(n)**.

1. Gestern **sind** wir nicht in unsere Vorlesungen **gegangen,** sondern **haben** Günter **angerufen** und **haben** den ganzen Tag mit ihm Karten **gespielt.**

   Wenn wir nur in unsere Vorlesungen _____ _____!
   Wenn wir nur Günter nicht _____ _____!
   Wenn wir nur nicht den ganzen Tag mit Günter Karten _____ _____!

2. Gestern Abend **bin** ich mit Stefan **ausgegangen, habe** die halbe Nacht mit ihm Billard **gespielt,** aber meine Hausaufgaben **habe** ich nicht **gemacht.**

   Wenn ich nur nicht mit Stefan _____ _____!
   Wenn ich nur nicht die halbe Nacht Billard _____ _____!
   Wenn ich nur meine Hausaufgaben _____ _____!

3. Gestern **sind** wir nicht um sieben **aufgestanden,** sondern **sind** bis zehn im Bett **geblieben.** Wir **sind** deshalb leider nicht joggen **gegangen.**

   Wenn wir nur um sieben _____ _____!
   Wenn wir nur nicht bis zehn im Bett _____ _____!
   Wenn wir nur joggen _____ _____!

4. Gestern Nachmittag **habe** ich mich auf die Couch **gelegt** und **bin** gleich **eingeschlafen.** Deshalb **habe** ich mein Referat nicht fertig **geschrieben.**

   Wenn ich mich nur nicht auf die Couch _____ _____!
   Wenn ich nur nicht _____ _____!
   Wenn ich nur mein Referat fertig _____ _____!

regrets

12-23 Wenn ich das nur getan oder nicht getan hätte! Jeder Mensch tut manchmal Dinge, die er später bereut°. Erzählen Sie Ihren Mitstudenten ein paar Dinge, die Sie bereuen.

S1: Wenn ich nur meine Hausaufgaben gemacht hätte!
S2: Wenn ich nur gestern Nacht nicht so lange aufgeblieben wäre!
S3: …

12-24 Was hättest du getan, wenn …?

▶ Jemand hat meinen Wagen gestohlen.

… sofort zur Polizei gegangen.

S1: Was hättest du getan, wenn jemand deinen Wagen gestohlen hätte?

S2: Ich wäre sofort zur Polizei gegangen.

1. Ich habe eine Geldtasche mit 300 Dollar gefunden.
2. Meine Professorin hat mir verboten, in die Kneipe zu gehen.
3. Die Verkäuferin hat mir zehn Dollar zu viel herausgegeben.
4. Mir ist in Europa das Geld ausgegangen.
5. Ich habe in Europa meinen Pass verloren.

… mit ihr darüber gesprochen.	… meine Eltern angerufen.
… sofort zum nächsten Konsulat gegangen.	… ihr das Geld sofort zurückgegeben.
	… damit zur Polizei gegangen.

Wenn ich nur nicht so lange Beachvolleyball gespielt hätte! Dann hätte ich jetzt keinen Sonnenbrand!

Haben and *sein* in past-time subjunctive

12-15 to 12-20
In *Kapitel 5* you learned that most speakers of German use the simple past of **haben** and **sein** instead of the perfect tense to refer to past events.

Weil ich heute eine Klausur **hatte,** **war** ich gestern nicht auf Lauras Fete.	*Because I **had** a test today, I **wasn't** at Laura's party yesterday.*

However, when **haben** and **sein** are the main verbs in past-time contrary-to-fact situations, you need to use the past participles of these verbs.

Wenn ich heute keine Klausur **gehabt hätte, wäre** ich gestern auf Lauras Fete **gewesen.**	*If I **hadn't had** a test today, I **would have been** at Laura's party yesterday.*

12-25 Was hättest du gemacht, wenn …? Ergänzen Sie **wäre, hätte** oder **hättest**.

▶ …, wenn es gestern nicht so heiß gewesen _____?

Ich _____ Tennis gespielt.

S1: Was hättest du gemacht, wenn es gestern nicht so heiß gewesen wäre?

S2: Ich hätte Tennis gespielt.

1. …, wenn wir letzten Winter mehr Schnee gehabt _____?

2. …, wenn du letztes Wochenende mehr Geld gehabt _____?

3. …, wenn es letzten Sonntag nicht so kalt gewesen _____?

flat tire

4. …, wenn dein Drucker gestern Nacht plötzlich nicht mehr genug Toner gehabt _____?

5. …, wenn das Konzert gestern Abend nicht gut gewesen _____?

6. …, wenn dein Fahrrad heute früh einen Platten° gehabt _____?

Ich _____ in einem teuren Restaurant gegessen.	Ich _____ den Bus genommen.
Ich _____ mein Referat von Hand fertig geschrieben.	Ich _____ Skilaufen gegangen.
Ich _____ aufgestanden und rausgegangen.	Ich _____ baden gegangen.

4 Expressing cause, opposition, alternatives, and simultaneity

Genitive prepositions

12-21 to 12-22 The following prepositions require an object in the genitive case.

wegen	*because of*	**Wegen des Schneesturms** waren gestern keine Vorlesungen.
trotz	*in spite of*	Eve ist **trotz des Schneesturms** in die Bibliothek gegangen.
statt	*instead of*	Sie hat aber **statt einer Jacke** einen dicken Wintermantel angezogen.
während	*during*	Eve war **während des ganzen Sturms** in der Bibliothek.

Photo: Note that **wegen** sometimes follows its object.

12-26 *Wegen, trotz, statt* oder *während?*

1. Warum gehen wir nicht zu Bernd zum Kaffee trinken?

   Weil er _____ des Tages nicht zu Hause ist.

2. Warum war Sarah heute nicht in der Vorlesung?

   Weil sie _____ einer schweren Erkältung° im Bett bleiben musste.   *cold*

3. Warum fühlt Laura sich denn nicht wohl?

   Weil sie _____ ihrer Erkältung tanzen gegangen ist.

4. Fährt Ralf immer noch seinen alten VW?

   Nein, er hat jetzt ein Motorrad _____ eines Wagens.

5. Warum spielst du dienstags nie mit uns Tennis?

   Weil ich _____ der Woche zu viel zu tun habe.

6. Isst du oft Fertiggerichte°?

   Nein, ich esse lieber Selbstgekochtes _____ Fertiggerichte.   *convenience foods*

7. Warum kaufst du deine Milch in Flaschen statt in Kartons?

   _____ der Umwelt.°   *environment*

8. Warum seid ihr denn so nass?

   Weil wir _____ des Regens zu Fuß zur Uni gegangen sind.

Wann darf man hier parken?

You know that in German the interrogative pronoun *whose* is **wessen**.

Wessen Fahrrad ist das?   *Whose* bicycle is this?

Whose can also be a relative pronoun. In this function it has two German equivalents: **dessen** if the antecedent is masculine or neuter, and **deren** if it is feminine or plural.

Der Student, **dessen** Wagen ich kaufe, zieht in die USA.   *The student **whose** car I'm buying is moving to the U.S.*

Die Studentin, **deren** Wagen ich kaufe, zieht in die USA.   *The student **whose** car I'm buying is moving to the U.S.*

Infobox

Luxemburg

Die Altstadt von Luxemburg

Das Großherzogtum[1] Luxemburg ist ein kleines Land, das zweitkleinste innerhalb der Europäischen Union (nach Malta). Von den 502 000 Einwohnern sind etwa 215 300 Ausländer, d. h.[2] etwa 43 Prozent der Gesamtbevölkerung[3]. Damit hält Luxemburg den absoluten Rekord unter den Ländern der EU. Dazu kommen noch etwa 138 000 Pendler[4], die täglich aus den Nachbarländern Deutschland, Frankreich und Belgien nach Luxemburg zur Arbeit kommen. Es ist deshalb kein Wunder, dass in dieser multikulturellen Gesellschaft[5] Sprachkompetenz eine enorme Rolle spielt. Luxemburgs offizielle Sprachen sind Luxemburgisch, Deutsch und Französisch. Schon in der Grundschule[6] lernen die Kinder alle drei offiziellen Sprachen und alle Grundschullehrer müssen dreisprachig sein. Anders als in der Schweiz sprechen deshalb in Luxemburg viele Menschen nicht nur eine, sondern alle offiziellen Sprachen.

Luxemburg ist ein hoch industrialisiertes Land, doch der dynamischste Sektor der Luxemburger Wirtschaft[7] sind die Banken. In Luxemburg sind auch drei Institutionen der EU mit über 7000 „Eurokraten" aus allen Ländern der EU. In der Hauptstadt – auch sie heißt Luxemburg – kontrastieren die modernen Gebäude der Banken und der EU mit der historischen Altstadt, die seit 1994 zum Weltkulturerbe[8] der UNESCO gehört.

Dass Luxemburgisch dem Deutschen sehr ähnlich ist, können Sie an den folgenden Beispielen sehen. Finden Sie die deutschen Äquivalente.

1. Kënne mir eis?
2. Mir schwätze Lëtzebuergesch.
3. Mir léiere Lëtzebuergesch.
4. Wéivill Auer ass et?
5. Wéivill kascht dat?
6. Wéi geet et Iech?
7. Et geet mir gutt.

a. Wie viel Uhr ist es?
b. Wie geht es Ihnen?
c. Wie viel kostet das?
d. Es geht mir gut.
e. Wir lernen Luxemburgisch.
f. Kennen wir uns?
g. Wir sprechen Luxemburgisch.

[1]grand duchy   [2]i.e.   [3]total population   [4]commuters   [5]society   [6]elementary school   [7]economy   [8]world cultural heritage

Zusammenschau

Lesen

Zum besseren Verstehen

12-27 Meine Zukunft. Wie könnte Ihr Leben in zehn Jahren aussehen? Was wären Sie dann gern von Beruf und was hätten Sie gern alles?

12-28 Versicherungen°. Was passt wo?

insurances

Lebensversicherung / Rentenversicherung / Vollkaskoversicherung / Zusatz°-Krankenversicherung

supplementary

1. Wenn ich Geld haben will, um im Krankenhaus für ein Privatzimmer bezahlen zu können, brauche ich eine _____.
2. Wenn ich will, dass meine Familie genug Geld hat, wenn ich sterbe, brauche ich eine _____.
3. Wenn ich will, dass mein Auto auch dann voll versichert ist, wenn ich es selbst kaputt fahre, brauche ich eine _____.
4. Wenn ich als Rentner° genug Geld haben will, brauche ich eine _____.

pensioner

Meine Zukunft
von Nina Achminow

Ein Schulabschluss[1]
ein paar wilde Jahre
ein Haufen[2] Idealismus
ein Beruf
5 eine Hochzeit[3]
eine Wohnung
ein paar Jahre weiterarbeiten
eine Wohnzimmergarnitur[4]
ein Kind
10 eine wunderbare komfortable Einbauküche
noch 'n Kind
ein Mittelklassewagen[5]
ein Bausparvertrag[6]
ein Farbfernseher
15 noch 'n Kind
ein eigenes Haus
eine Lebensversicherung
eine Rentenversicherung
eine Zusatz-Krankenversicherung

[1]*z. B. das Abitur* [2]*eine Menge* [3]*Heirat* [4]*Wohnzimmermöbel* [5]*mittelgroßer Wagen*
[6]*home savings plan*

20 ein Zweitwagen mit Vollkaskoversicherung
und so weiter …
und so weiter …
Hoffentlich bin ich stark genug,
meiner Zukunft zu entgehen[7]!

[7]*escape*

Arbeit mit dem Text

line   **12-29 Anders gesagt.** Welche Zeile° oder Zeilen in Nina Achminows Gedicht *Meine Zukunft* sagen etwa dasselbe?

<u>8, 10, 14</u>   Man macht es sich schön in der Wohnung.

_____   Man heiratet und mietet eine Wohnung.

_____   Man will die Welt verbessern.

_____   Man macht das Abitur.

_____   Man ist rebellisch.

old age   _____   Man beginnt, ans Alter° zu denken.

_____   Man hat Kinder.

_____   Man findet einen Job.

_____   Man beginnt, an ein eigenes Haus zu denken.

_____   Man kauft einen Wagen, in dem auch die ersten beiden Kinder Platz haben.

_____   Man kauft noch einen Wagen und versichert ihn so gut wie möglich.

_____   Man möchte im Krankenhaus ein Privatzimmer haben.

_____   Man baut oder kauft ein Einfamilienhaus.

12-30 Zur Interpretation und Diskussion.

1. Wie gibt Nina Achminow dem Gedicht *Meine Zukunft* die Struktur einer Liste?
2. Warum verwendet Nina Achminow diese Struktur? Was will sie vielleicht damit ausdrücken?
3. Finden Sie die Zukunft, die Nina Achminow beschreibt, auch so negativ wie die Autorin selbst? Warum oder warum nicht?

Schreiben

12-31 Meine Zukunft. Wie sehen Sie Ihre Zukunft? Schreiben Sie dazu ein Gedicht im Stil des Gedichts von Nina Achminow.

Schreibtipp: When writing a poem in a particular style, it helps to study the style and imitate it carefully while infusing it with your own personal meaning through the words you choose. Before you begin writing, look at Achminow's poem again. Note its structure and patterns (such as repeating words or lines), and use them as a model when composing your poem.

Hören

Karrieren

Julia und Dieter leben in Köln. Julia hat eine gute Stelle bei einer Exportfirma und Dieter ist Motorenkonstrukteur bei Ford. Sein Traum ist aber, bei Porsche zu arbeiten. Weil Dieter heute vor Julia zu Hause ist, kocht er gerade das Abendessen.

NEUE VOKABELN

die Stelle	*job; position*	**an·bieten**	*to offer*
der Traum	*dream*	**träumen von**	*to dream about*
riechen	*to smell*	**die Abteilungsleiterin**	*department*
Champignons	*mushrooms*		*manager*

12-32 Erstes Verstehen. Markieren Sie die richtigen Antworten.

	JULIA	DIETER
1. Wer hat nächste Woche Geburtstag?	_____	_____
2. Wer hat gut verkauft?	_____	_____
3. Wer hat Kerzen auf den Tisch gestellt?	_____	_____

	IN KÖLN	IN STUTTGART
4. Wo möchte Dieter arbeiten?	_____	_____
5. Wo könnte Julia bald Abteilungsleiterin werden?	_____	_____
6. Wo müsste Julia wieder von unten anfangen?	_____	_____

12-33 Detailverstehen.

1. Warum würde ein Glas Wein Julia so gut tun?
2. Wann hat Julia Geburtstag?
3. Was findet Julia so romantisch?
4. Warum bietet Porsche Dieter eine Stelle an?
5. Warum will Julia nicht nach Stuttgart?
6. Warum will Dieter jetzt nicht mehr weiterdiskutieren?

Sprechen

12-34 **Traumberufe der deutschen Jugend.** Studieren Sie das Schaubild auf der nächsten Seite und beantworten Sie die Fragen. Schreiben Sie die Antworten zu Fragen eins bis vier in die Tabelle.

NEUE VOKABELN

die Flugbegleiterin, -nen	*flight attendant*
die Bürokauffrau, -en	*office administrator*
die Bankkauffrau, -en	*office administrator at a bank*
die Rechtsanwältin, -nen	*lawyer*
der Softwareentwickler, -	*software developer*
der Informatiker, -	*computer specialist*
der EDV-Fachmann,	*data processing specialist*
die EDV-Fachleute	
der Kfz-Mechaniker, -	*car mechanic*
der Maschinenbaumechaniker, -	*machinist*

1. Wie viele der Traumberufe der Mädchen sind technisch orientiert?
2. Wie viele der Traumberufe der Jungen sind technisch orientiert?
3. Bei wie vielen der Traumberufe der Mädchen spielen menschliche Kontakte eine besonders wichtige Rolle?
4. Bei wie vielen der Traumberufe der Jungen spielen menschliche Kontakte eine besonders wichtige Rolle?
5. Welche von den Berufen in diesem Schaubild sind Ihrer Meinung nach besonders kreativ?
6. Welche von diesen besonders kreativen Berufen sind Ihrer Meinung nach mehr künstlerisch kreativ und welche sind mehr mathematisch-technisch kreativ?

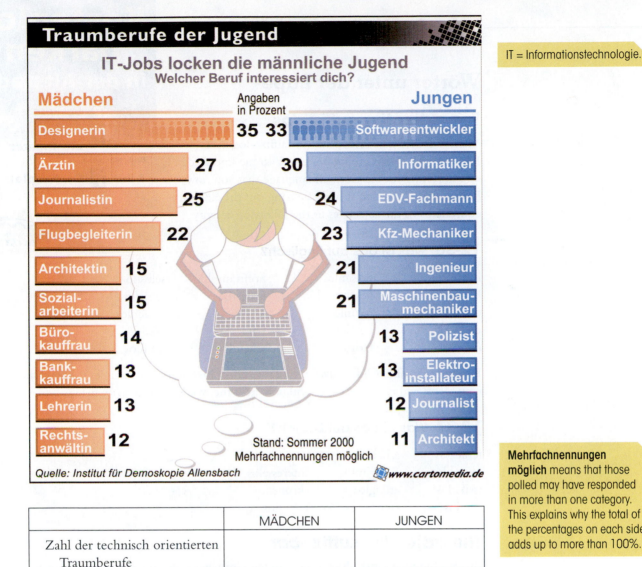

Traumberufe der Jugend

IT-Jobs locken die männliche Jugend
Welcher Beruf interessiert dich?

Mädchen	Angaben in Prozent	Jungen
Designerin	35 · 33	Softwareentwickler
Ärztin	27 · 30	Informatiker
Journalistin	25 · 24	EDV-Fachmann
Flugbegleiterin	22 · 23	Kfz-Mechaniker
Architektin	15 · 21	Ingenieur
Sozialarbeiterin	15 · 21	Maschinenbaumechaniker
Bürokauffrau	14 · 13	Polizist
Bankkauffrau	13 · 13	Elektroinstallateur
Lehrerin	13 · 12	Journalist
Rechtsanwältin	12 · 11	Architekt

Stand: Sommer 2000
Mehrfachnennungen möglich

Quelle: Institut für Demoskopie Allensbach

www.cartomedia.de

IT = Informationstechnologie.

Mehrfachnennungen möglich means that those polled may have responded in more than one category. This explains why the total of the percentages on each side adds up to more than 100%.

	MÄDCHEN	JUNGEN
Zahl der technisch orientierten Traumberufe		
Zahl der kontaktorientierten Traumberufe		

12-35 Unsere Traumberufe. Finden Sie die Traumberufe Ihrer Mitstudenten heraus und zeichnen Sie ein ähnliches Schaubild.

Viele junge deutsche Frauen möchten Bankkauffrau werden.

Wort, Sinn und Klang

Wörter unter der Lupe

The adjective suffix *-los*

Many German adjectives with the suffix **–los** have English equivalents ending in *-less*. With the knowledge of and feeling for the German language that you now have, you will have no trouble figuring out the English equivalents of the adjectives in the following activity.

12-36 **Was ist das auf Englisch?**

baumlos	fleischlos	hoffnungslos	selbstlos
bedeutungslos	geschmacklos	klassenlos	schlaflos
danklos	harmlos	leblos	sprachlos
endlos	herzlos	kinderlos	taktlos
farblos	hilflos	schamlos	zahnlos

However, not all English equivalents of the suffix **–los** are *-less*. Sometimes the English equivalents end in *-free* or begin with *un-*, as in the words in the activity below.

12-37 **Was ist das auf English?**

fehlerlos	arbeitslos	gefühllos
kostenlos	disziplinlos	interesselos
risikolos	erfolglos	skrupellos
sorglos	fantasielos	talentlos

The adjective suffix *-bar*

By attaching the suffix **–bar** to verb stems, German creates hundreds of adjectives. The English equivalents of **–bar** are often *-able* and *-ible*. These suffixes usually convey the idea that the action expressed by the verb can be done.

machen	**machbar**	*to do*	*doable*

In contrast to German, English sometimes attaches the suffix not to the Germanic verb stem, but to its Latin-based counterpart.

hören	**hörbar**	*to hear*	*audible*

To show that the action expressed by the verb can *not* be done, German attaches the prefix **un–** to the adjective. The English equivalents of this prefix are *un-* or *in-*.

bewohnen	**unbewohnbar**	*to inhabit*	*uninhabitable*

12-38 Man kann es oder man kann es nicht. Write the German adjectives and their English equivalents.

	DEUTSCH	ENGLISCH
1. Man kann es trinken.	_____	_____
2. Man kann es essen.	_____	_____
3. Man kann es erklären.	_____	_____
4. Man kann es verwenden.	_____	_____
5. Man kann es waschen.	_____	_____
6. Man kann es nicht denken.	_____	_____
7. Man kann es nicht definieren.	_____	_____
8. Man kann es nicht kontrollieren.	_____	_____
9. Man kann es nicht übersetzen.	_____	_____

12-29 to 12-30

Zur Aussprache

The glottal stop

In order to distinguish *an ice boat* from *a nice boat* in pronunciation, you use a glottal stop, i.e., you momentarily stop and then restart the flow of air to your voice box before saying the word *ice*. The glottal stop is much more frequent in German than in English. It occurs before words and syllables that begin with a vowel.

12-39 Hören Sie gut zu und wiederholen Sie!

1. Onkel __Alfred __ist __ein __alter __Esel!
2. Tante __Emma will __uns __alle __ent__erben°!   **enterben:** *disinherit*
3. Be__eilt __euch! __Esst __euer __Eis __auf!
4. Lebt __ihr __in __Ober__ammergau __oder __in __Unter__ammergau?

🔊 Wortschatz 2

Nomen

die Erkältung, –en	cold
das Gedicht, –e	poem
der Strafzettel, –	(traffic) ticket
die Umwelt	environment
die Versicherung, –en	insurance
der Traum, ¨e	dream
der Wunsch, ¨e	wish
das Sparkonto, Sparkonten	savings account
die Zinsen (pl)	(bank) interest

Verben

an·bieten, bot an, angeboten	to offer
bereuen	to regret
raten, (rät), riet, geraten (+ dat)	to advise
riechen, roch, gerochen	to smell
träumen	to dream

Andere Wörter

magersüchtig	anorexic
stark	strong
statt (+ gen)	instead of
trotz (+ gen)	in spite of
während (+ gen)	during
wegen (+ gen)	because of

Ausdrücke

eifersüchtig auf (+ acc)	jealous of
einen Platten haben	to have a flat tire
eine schwere Erkältung	a bad cold
erkältet sein	to have a cold
Lassen Sie sich Zeit.	Take your time.
Schade!	Too bad!
Was ist denn los mit dir?	What's the matter with you?

Synonyme

ein Haufen	= eine Menge	= viel	
die Heirat, –en	= die Hochzeit, –en		
die Rente, –n	= die Pension, –en		
die Stelle, –n	= die Position, –en	= der Job, –s	

> What is the literal meaning of **Hochzeit**?

Leicht zu verstehen

der Idealismus	der Sturm, ¨e
das Konsulat, –e	die Tablette, –n
der Kontakt, –e	die Therapie, –n
die Polizei	wild

> **riechen:** Can you guess the English cognate?

> **magersüchtig, eifersüchtig:** The suffixes **–sucht** (*addiction*) and **–süchtig** (*addicted*) are added to many words. Try to guess the English equivalents of **Drogensucht, Kaufsucht, Arbeitssucht, nikotinsüchtig.**

ab **4,35** % jetzt **30 jahre** zinsen sichern

NÄHERE INFORMATIONEN ERHALTEN SIE IN JEDER FILIALE

Wörter im Kontext

12-40 Was passt wo?

Stelle / magersüchtig / Strafzettel / Zinsen / Rente

1. Wenn man zu schnell fährt, bekommt man einen _____.
2. Wenn man Geld auf dem Sparkonto hat, bekommt man _____.
3. Wenn man ständig zu wenig isst, könnte man _____ werden.
4. Wenn man eine gute Ausbildung hat, bekommt man hoffentlich auch eine gute _____.
5. Wenn man ein Leben lang gearbeitet hat, bekommt man eine _____.

12-41 Was sind die richtigen Antworten?

1. Wie bist du so guter Laune?
2. Warum gehst du denn zum Arzt?
3. Warum bist du mit dem Bus gekommen?
4. Was ist denn los mit dir?
5. Wann gehst du einkaufen?
6. Warum warst du gestern nicht in der Vorlesung?

a. Gar nichts. Ich habe nur einen Haufen Arbeit und weiß nicht, wo ich anfangen soll.
b. Wegen des Schneesturms.
c. Während der Mittagspause.
d. Weil mein Fahrrad einen Platten hat.
e. Weil BMW mir eine Stelle angeboten hat.
f. Weil ich so erkältet bin.

12-42 Was sind die richtigen Antworten?

1. Hätten Sie lieber Tee statt Kaffee?
2. Warum lernt Doris jedes Wochenende, statt mit uns mal auszugehen?
3. Was riecht denn hier so gut?
4. Bist du wieder so oft aufgewacht?
5. Warum kaufst du keinen Wagen?
6. Ich kann leider nicht zu deiner Fete kommen.

a. Das ist sicher Omas Rhabarberkuchen.
b. Schade.
c. Weil die Versicherung so teuer ist.
d. Weil ihre Lieblingsprofessorin ihr das geraten hat.
e. Ja, trotz der Schlaftabletten.
f. Ja, aber bitte keinen so starken.

12-43 Was ist hier identisch? Welche zwei Sätze in jeder Gruppe bedeuten etwa dasselbe?

1. Wie viel Zinsen bezahlen Sie?
   Wie hoch ist Ihr Lohn?
   Wie viel verdienen Sie?

2. Sie müssen sich nicht beeilen.
   Lassen Sie sich Zeit.
   Sie sind sehr eifersüchtig.

3. Wann war eure Hochzeit?
   Seit wann seid ihr verheiratet?
   Wann heiratet ihr?

4. Es tut ihm leid.
   Er bereut es.
   Er tut es leider nicht.

Anhang ///////////////////////////

Information Gap Activities   A1

Expressions for the Classroom   A12

German Grammatical Terms   A13

Useful Word Sets   A14

- Studienfächer A14
- Jobs und Berufe A14
- Hobbys und Sport A15
- Musikinstrumente A16
- Kleidungsstücke A16
- Accessoires A17
- Essen und Trinken A17
- Länder und Sprachen A18
- Persönliche Merkmale A19
- Höfliche Ausdrücke A20

Grammatical Tables   A21

Principal Parts of Irregular and Mixed Verbs   A28

German-English Vocabulary   A32

English-German Vocabulary   A68

Index   A91

Information Gap Activities

Erste Kontakte

E-14 **Telefonnummer.** You **(S2)** and a friend **(S1)** are students in Heidelberg and are updating your phone contacts. Your information is on this page.

S1: Was ist Daniels Telefonnummer?   **S2:** Daniels Nummer ist 2 10 72.

NAME	TELEFON
Daniel	2 10 72
Justin	
Heather	53 90 99
Lilli	

KAPITEL 1

1-32 **Wie ist die Uni?** You and your partner know different things about a university you've visited. Find out what your partner knows, and tell what you know.

S1: Ist die Uni gut?   **S2:** Ja, sie ist sehr gut.
S2: Sind die Computer up to date?   **S1:** Nein, sie sind nicht alle up to date.
  …   …

	Ja, _____ ist sehr gut.
Sind die Computer up to date?	
	Nein, _____ ist nicht sehr groß, aber _____ ist sehr schön.
	Ja, _____ sind fast alle sehr interessant.
Ist das Sportprogramm gut?	
Ist das Footballteam gut?	
	Ja, _____ sind fast alle sehr fair.
	Nein, _____ ist nicht sehr populär, aber _____ ist sehr gut.
Sind die Studenten intelligent?	
	Nein, _____ ist nicht sehr groß, aber _____ ist sehr gut.
Sind die Studentenheime modern?	
	Ja, _____ ist sehr gut.

KAPITEL 2

2-15 Was machen diese Leute gern?

S1: Was für Sport macht Anna gern? S2: Sie geht gern schwimmen.
S2: Was für Musik hört Anna gern? S1: Sie hört gern …
S1: Was für Spiele spielt Anna gern? S2: Sie spielt gern …

… …

	SPORT	MUSIK	SPIELE
Anna	schwimmen		Scrabble
Peter	Fußball	klassische Musik	
Maria			Billard
Moritz		Rock	

2-22 Günters Stundenplan. With a partner, complete Günter's schedule. Take turns asking your questions.

S1: Was hat Günter montags von acht bis zehn? S2: Da hat er Zoologie.
S2: Was hat Günter montags von fünfzehn bis siebzehn Uhr? S1: …

> Note that the indefinite article **eine** will only be used when the response contains the word **-übung** *(lab)*:
> **Da hat er *eine* Matheübung.**

2. Was hat Günter montags von fünfzehn bis siebzehn Uhr?
4. Was hat Günter mittwochs von neun bis elf?
6. Was hat Günter donnerstags von acht bis zehn?
8. Was hat Günter freitags von acht bis elf?
10. Was macht Günter freitags von vierzehn bis sechzehn Uhr?
12. Was macht Günter samstags?
14. Wie viele Freundinnen hat Günter?

	Mo	Di	Mi	Do	Fr	Sa	So
8.00	Zoologie						
9.00							
10.00		Botanik					
11.00			Mit Helga Tennis				bei Tina
12.00					Mathe		
13.00			Matheübung				
14.00							
15.00							
16.00				Botanikübung			
17.00							
18.00							

2-38 Wir spielen Trivial Pursuit. In each response, use the appropriate form of the indefinite article.

S1: Wer ist Johnny Depp?

S2: Johnny Depp ist ein amerikanischer Filmstar.

…

…

LEUTE (WER?)		GETRÄNKE (WAS?)		GEOGRAPHIE (WAS?)	
Johnny Depp	amerikanischer Filmstar	Löwenbräu		Angola	
Margaret Atwood	kanadische Autorin	Chianti	italienischer Rotwein	Linz	österreichische Stadt
David Cameron		Fanta	deutscher Softdrink	die Wolga	
Maria Callas	griechische Opernsängerin	Budweiser		Brandenburg	deutsches Bundesland
Felix Mendelssohn		Benedictine	französischer Likör	der Vesuv	

KAPITEL 03

3-39 Was machen diese Leute gern?

S2: Was isst Maria gern?

S1: Sie isst gern Spaghetti.

S1: Was isst Thomas gern?

S2: Er isst sehr gern Nudeln.

S2: Was essen Tina und Lisa gern?

S1: Sie essen gern Pizza.

	MARIA	THOMAS	TINA UND LISA
ESSEN		Nudeln	
LESEN	Comics		Sciencefiction
SEHEN	Horrorfilme		
SPRECHEN		Deutsch	
FAHREN	Rad		Inlineskates
TRAGEN		Pullover	Bermudashorts

KAPITEL 04

4-27 **Verkehrszeichen.** Ask each other what these German traffic signs mean.

S1: Was bedeutet Verkehrszeichen Nummer 1?

S2: Hier kommt gleich eine scharfe Rechtskurve.

1 Hier kommt gleich eine scharfe Rechtskurve.	2	3 Diese Straße hört bald auf.
4 Hier darf man nicht unter 60 fahren.	5	6
7 Hier hört die Autobahn auf.	8	9 Hier darf man nicht über 60 fahren.
10	11	12 Hier muss man langsam fahren, denn hier spielen oft Kinder.

4-43 Fragen, Fragen, Fragen. You and your partner are sharing information about Kathrin, Florian, and Frau Özal. Begin the responses to your partner's requests for information with the conjunctions provided.

S1: Warum geht Florian nicht ins Kino?

S2: Weil er ein Referat schreiben muss.

S2: Warum geht Kathrin nicht ins Kino?

S1: Weil sie...

		KATHRIN	FLORIAN	FRAU ÖZAL
Warum geht ... nicht ins Kino?	weil		Er muss ein Referat schreiben.	
Geht ... heute schwimmen?	wenn	Es regnet nicht.		Sie muss nicht arbeiten.
Wann geht ... nach Hause?	wenn			Sie hat ihre Arbeit fertig.
Wann sieht ... gern fern?	bevor		Er isst zu Abend.	Sie geht ins Bett.
Warum arbeitet ...?	weil			Ihre Familie braucht genug Geld.

KAPITEL 05

5-17 Weißt du das? You and your partner are sharing general knowledge. Use the comparative forms for the adjectives given.

S1: Ist der Rhein länger als die Donau?

S2: Nein, der Rhein ist kürzer als die Donau.

FRAGEN	ANTWORTEN
	kurz: Nein, der Rhein ist _____ als die Donau.
kalt: Ist es in Island _____ als in Grönland?	
	hoch: Ja, der Mount McKinley ist _____ als der Mount Fudschi.
	viel: Nein, in Deutschland leben _____ Menschen als in Kalifornien.
groß: Ist Deutschland _____ als Kalifornien?	
teuer: Ist der Audi A4 _____ als der Volkswagen Golf?	

KAPITEL 06

6-5 **Was steht in Lauras Pass?** You want to know what Thomas and Bettina look like and your partner wants information about Laura and Philipp.

S1: Ist Laura groß oder klein?
Was für eine Form hat ihr Gesicht?
Was für Augen hat sie?
Was für Haar hat sie?

S2: Sie ist …
Sie hat ein ___es Gesicht.
Sie hat ___e Augen.
Sie hat ___es, ___es Haar.

	LAURA	THOMAS	BETTINA	PHILIPP
Größe	mittelgroß			nicht sehr groß
Gesichtsform	oval			oval
Augen	graugrün			schwarz
Haar	lang, rotbraun			schwarz, glatt

6-11 **Was haben Yusuf, Maria und Jennifer gestern gemacht?**

S1: Was hat Yusuf gestern Vormittag gemacht?

S2: Gestern Vormittag hat er seinen Wagen repariert.

	MARIA	YUSUF	JENNIFER
gestern Vormittag		seinen Wagen repariert	
gestern Nachmittag	ihren Stammbaum gezeichnet	stundenlang gebloggt	
gestern Abend			Reisebroschüren studiert

6-14 **Was haben Julia, Moritz und Lisa gestern gemacht?**

S1: Was hat Julia gestern Vormittag gemacht?

S2: Gestern Vormittag hat sie eine Torte gebacken.

	JULIA	MORITZ	LISA
gestern Vormittag	eine Torte gebacken	bis zwölf im Bett gelegen und geschlafen	
gestern Nachmittag			mit Professor Weber gesprochen
gestern Abend	stundenlang vor dem Fernseher gesessen	seine Wäsche gewaschen	

KAPITEL 07

7-13 Geschenke.

S1: Was schenkt Florian seinen Eltern?

S2: Florian schenkt seinen Eltern Weingläser.

	DAVID	FLORIAN
seinen Eltern	eine neue Kaffeemaschine	
seiner Schwester	einen neuen Hammer	
seinem Bruder		das neueste Album von Lady Gaga
seiner Freundin		ein teures Parfüm

7-16 Geschenke.

S1: Weißt du, was Sophia Onkel Thomas und Tante Barbara schenkt?

S2: Ich glaube, sie schenkt ihnen eine Safari in Südafrika.

	DANIEL	SOPHIA
Onkel Thomas und Tante Barbara	ihnen einen neuen Mülleimer	
Silvia		ihr 5 000 Euro
Frank	ihm einen ganz lauten Wecker	

7-29 **Was weißt du von diesen Leuten?** **S1** stellt Fragen° über Sabine und Osman, und **S2** möchte Information über Wendy und Jan.   **stellen Fragen:** *ask questions*

S1: Woher ist Wendy?   **S2:** Aus den USA.
Wo arbeitet sie?   …

	SABINE	WENDY	OSMAN	JAN
Woher ist _____?	Aus der Schweiz.		Aus der Türkei.	
Wo arbeitet sie/er?	Bei der Bank.		Bei der Post.	
Seit wann arbeitet sie/er dort?	Seit einem Jahr.		Seit einem halben Jahr.	
Wie kommt sie/er zur Arbeit?	Mit dem Fahrrad.		Mit dem Bus.	
Wohin geht sie/er im nächsten Urlaub?	Zu ihrem Freund nach Zürich.		Zu seiner Familie nach Ankara.	
Woher weißt du das alles?	Von ihr selbst.		Von seinem Bruder.	

KAPITEL 08

 8-6 **Wo und wie wohnen diese Studenten?**

S2: Wo wohnt Magda?
Wie gefällt es ihr dort?

S1: Sie wohnt im Studentenheim
…

	MAGDA	CINDY	PIETRO	KEVIN
Wo wohnt ___?	Sie wohnt im Studentenheim.		Er wohnt noch zu Hause.	
Wie gefällt es ihr/ihm dort?	Sie findet es ganz toll.		Es gefällt ihm gar nicht gut.	
Warum gefällt es ihr/ihm dort (nicht)?	Weil es da viele Partys gibt.		Weil er zu viel helfen muss.	
Wie kommt sie/er zur Uni?	Sie geht zu Fuß.		Er hat einen Wagen.	

8-27 **In der WG.** Sie wohnen in einer WG und fragen einander, was Ihre Mitbewohner mit diesen Geräten machen wollen.

what . . . for **S1:** Wozu° braucht Benedikt den Staubsauger?

S2: Um sein Zimmer zu putzen.

		BENEDIKT	SABRINA
	der Staubsauger		ein großes Insekt in ihrem Zimmer töten
	der Dosenöffner	eine Dose Suppe aufmachen	
	das Bügeleisen	seine Hemden bügeln	
	die Kaffeemaschine		ein paar chemische Experimente machen
	der Korkenzieher	eine Flasche Sherry aufmachen	
	die Waschmaschine	seine T-Shirts waschen	

KAPITEL 09

9-10 Was macht Otilia um sieben Uhr zehn?

S1: Was macht Otilia um sieben Uhr zehn?

S2: Sie schminkt sich.

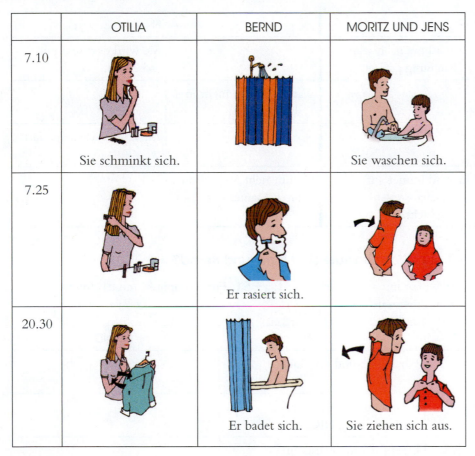

	OTILIA	BERND	MORITZ UND JENS
7.10	Sie schminkt sich.		Sie waschen sich.
7.25		Er rasiert sich.	
20.30		Er badet sich.	Sie ziehen sich aus.

9-27 Wer ist das? Was für Leute gehören zu den Namensschildern° an diesem Mietshaus°?

name plates
apartment building

S2: Wer sind Paul und Lisa Borg?

S1: Das sind die Leute, die fast jeden Tag ins Gasthaus gehen.

S1: Wer ist Ergül Ertem?

S2: Das ist der Mann, …

Ergül Ertem	dem der Schnellimbiss beim Bahnhof gehört	Monika Strsinska	
Paul u. Lisa Borg		Hans Maier	den wir immer beim Einkaufen sehen
Maria Schulz	die im Café Mozart als Kellnerin arbeitet	Karl u. Anna Weiler	
Manuel Lima		Teresa Venitelli	die mit einem Polizisten zusammen ist

KAPITEL 11

 11-8 **Was weißt du von Mario und Ann?**

opinion
annoyed

S1: Warum ist Mario denn so sauer°?

S2: Er wird nie nach seiner Meinung° gefragt.

MARIO		ANN	
	Er wird nie nach seiner Meinung gefragt.		Sie wird dort sehr gut bezahlt.
Warum wohnt Mario wieder zu Hause?		Warum ist Ann nicht in ihrem Büro?	
Wozu braucht Mario eine Alarmanlage?			Ihr Wagen wird repariert.
	Er wird immer auf Geschäftsreisen geschickt.	Warum zieht Ann schon ihren Mantel an?	

 11-21 **Was für Leute sind Karin und Bernd?**

S2: Wofür interessiert sich Bernd am meisten?

S1: Für Computer und das Internet.

	KARIN	BERND
Wofür interessiert sich Karin/Bernd am meisten?	Für Politik und Geschichte.	
Woran arbeitet sie/er gerade so intensiv?	An einem Projekt über die ehemalige DDR.	
Worüber hat sie/er sich gestern so aufgeregt?	Über die laute Musik im Nachbarzimmer.	
Worauf wartet sie/er denn so sehr?	Auf einen Scheck von ihren Eltern.	
Worüber freut sie/er sich am meisten?	Über gute Zensuren.	
Wovor hat sie/er manchmal Angst?	Vor der Zeit nach dem Studium.	

KAPITEL 12

12-12 Wenn es nur wahr wäre!

S1: Was würde Claudia tun, wenn sie eine Million Euro gewinnen würde?

S2: Sie würde ihr Studium unterbrechen und eine Weltreise machen.

Claudia	Sie würde ihr Studium unterbrechen und eine Weltreise machen.
Martin	
Stephanie und Peter	
Herr und Frau Ziegler	Sie würden erst mal ihre Schulden bezahlen.
Robert	Er würde seinen Eltern eine Villa am Bodensee kaufen.

12-16 Wünsche°.

wishes

S1: Was hätte Laura gern?

S2: Sie hätte gern so eine gute Position wie ihre Freundin Mia.

	WAS HÄTTE … GERN?	WO WÄRE … JETZT GERN?	WAS WÜSSTE … GERN?
Laura	so eine gute Position wie ihre Freundin Mia	beim Skilaufen in den Alpen	was für eine Zensur sie für ihr Referat bekommt
Lisa			
Paul			
Thomas	eine höhere Position und mehr Lohn	zu Hause vor seinem Computer	warum Paul neidisch auf ihn ist

Expressions for the Classroom

As you progress in this course, you will want to ask your instructor questions in German and understand and respond to your instructor's German instructions. The following expressions will help you.

What you might say or ask

I have a question. **Ich habe eine Frage.**
I don't understand that. **Ich verstehe das nicht.**
I don't know. **Ich weiß nicht.**
Pardon me? **Wie bitte?**
Could you speak more slowly, please? **Könnten Sie bitte langsamer sprechen?**
Could you please repeat that? **Könnten Sie das bitte wiederholen?**
What does . . . mean? **Was bedeutet . . .?**
How do you write (spell) . . .? **Wie schreibt (buchstabiert) man . . .?**
Is that correct? **Ist das richtig?**
What is . . . in German (in English)? **Was ist . . . auf Deutsch (auf Englisch)?**
What page is that on? **Auf welcher Seite ist das?**
Do we have to do that in writing? **Müssen wir das schriftlich machen?**
What homework do we have today? **Was haben wir heute für Hausaufgaben?**
When do we have to hand this in? **Wann müssen wir das abgeben?**
Will this be graded? **Wird das benotet?**
When are your office hours? **Wann sind Ihre Sprechstunden?**

What your instructor might say or ask

Auf Deutsch, bitte. In German, please.
Hören Sie bitte gut zu. Please listen carefully.
Wiederholen Sie das, bitte. Please repeat that.
Sprechen Sie das bitte nach. Please repeat after me.
Alle zusammen. All together.
Versuchen Sie es bitte noch einmal. Please try again.
Ausgezeichnet! Excellent!
Sprechen Sie bitte ein bisschen lauter (deutlicher). Please speak a bit louder (more clearly).

Schauen Sie bitte an die Tafel. Please look at the board.
Gehen Sie bitte an die Tafel. Please go to the board.
Bilden Sie bitte Zweiergruppen (Dreiergruppen, einen Kreis). Please form groups of two (groups of three, a circle).
Erzählen Sie einander (Ihren Mitstudenten), . . . Tell each other (your classmates) . . .
Fragen Sie einander, . . . Ask each other . . .
Stellen Sie einander die Fragen. Ask each other the questions.
Beschreiben Sie . . . Describe . . .
Berichten Sie . . . Report . . .
Machen Sie das bitte schriftlich (mündlich). Please do that in writing (orally).
Fangen Sie bitte an. Please begin.
Sind Sie fertig? Are you finished?
Schlagen Sie Ihre Bücher bitte auf Seite . . . auf. Please open your books to page . . .
Machen Sie Ihre Bücher bitte zu. Please close your books.
Finden Sie im Text . . . Find . . . in the text.
Wo steht das? Where does it say that?
Was fehlt hier? What is missing here?
Ergänzen Sie bitte die Endungen. Please supply the endings.
Ergänzen Sie bitte die Tabelle. Please complete the table.
Unterstreichen Sie bitte . . . Please underline . . .
Wer weiß die Antwort? Who knows the answer?
Lesen Sie den Satz vor. Read the sentence aloud.
Lesen Sie das bitte bis morgen. Please read that for tomorrow.
Legen Sie Ihre Hausaufgaben bitte auf meinen Schreibtisch. Please put your homework on my desk.
Wir schreiben (morgen) ein Quiz (eine Klausur). (Tomorrow) we're having a quiz (a test).
Hat jemand noch Fragen? Does anyone have any questions?

German Grammatical Terms

article	der Artikel, -
definite article	der bestimmte Artikel
indefinite article	der unbestimmte Artikel
der-word	das der-Wort, ¨er
ein-word	das ein-Wort, ¨er
noun	das Nomen, -
gender	das Genus, Genera
masculine, feminine,	maskulin, feminin,
neuter	neutrum
singular	der Singular
plural	der Plural
case	der Fall, ¨e; der Kasus, -
nominative	der Nominativ
accusative	der Akkusativ
dative	der Dativ
genitive	der Genitiv
subject	das Subjekt, -e
subject completion	der Prädikatsnominativ
object	das Objekt, -e
direct object	das direkte Objekt
indirect object	das indirekte Objekt
object of the	das Objekt der
preposition	Präposition
pronoun	das Pronomen, -
personal pronoun	das Personalpronomen
interrogative pronoun	das Fragepronomen
reflexive pronoun	das Reflexivpronomen
relative pronoun	das Relativpronomen
possessive adjective	das Possessivpronomen
verb	das Verb, -en
infinitive	der Infinitiv, -e
principal part	die Grundform, -en
regular verb	das regelmäßige Verb
irregular verb	das unregelmäßige Verb
mixed verb	das gemischte Verb
prefix	das Präfix, -e
separable-prefix verb	das trennbare Verb
inseparable-prefix verb	das untrennbare Verb
reflexive verb	das reflexive Verb
modal verb	das Modalverb
tense	die Zeitform, -en; das Tempus, Tempora
present tense	das Präsens
simple past tense	das Präteritum
perfect tense	das Perfekt
past perfect tense	das Plusquamperfekt
future tense	das Futur
auxiliary verb	das Hilfsverb, -en
past participle	das Partizip Perfekt
imperative	der Imperativ
passive voice	das Passiv
doer of the action	das Agens
receiver of the action	das Patiens
subjunctive	der Konjunktiv
subjunctive form	die Konjunktivform, -en
adjective	das Adjektiv, -e
adjective ending	die Adjektivendung, -en
comparative	der Komparativ
superlative	der Superlativ
adverb	das Adverb, -ien
preposition	die Präposition, -en
accusative preposition	die Akkusativpräposition
dative preposition	die Dativpräposition
two-case preposition	die Akkusativ-Dativ Präposition
genitive preposition	die Genitivpräposition
contraction	die Kontraktion, -en
da-compound	die da-Form, -en
wo-compound	die wo-Form, -en
sentence	der Satz, ¨e
independent clause	der Hauptsatz
dependent clause	der Nebensatz
object clause	der Objektsatz
infinitive phrase	der Infinitivsatz
relative clause	der Relativsatz
conjunction	die Konjunktion, -en
coordinating	die koordinierende
conjunction	Konjunktion
subordinating	die subordinierende
conjunction	Konjunktion
flavoring particle	die Modalpartikel, -n
word order	die Wortstellung
verb in (second)	Verb (zweites) Element
position	
time / manner /	Zeit / Art und Weise /
place	Ort

Useful Word Sets

These word sets provide convenient groupings of active vocabulary from the **Wortschatz** sections of each chapter as well as supplementary vocabulary relating to each topic.

Studienfächer

accounting	**Buchhaltung**
African studies	**Afrikanistik**
American studies	**Amerikanistik**
anthropology	**Anthropologie**
archaeology	**Archäologie**
architecture	**Architektur**
art	**Kunst**
art history	**Kunstgeschichte**
astronomy	**Astronomie**
biochemistry	**Biochemie**
biology	**Biologie**
botany	**Botanik**
business	**Betriebswirtschaftslehre (BWL)**
chemical engineering	**Chemotechnik**
chemistry	**Chemie**
Chinese language and literature	**Sinologie**
communications	**Kommunikationswissenschaft**
comparative literature	**Komparatistik**
computer science	**Informatik**
criminal justice	**Kriminologie**
East Asian Studies	**Ostasienwissenschaften**
ecology	**Ökologie**
economics	**Volkswirtschaft**
education	**Erziehungswissenschaften**
electrical engineering	**Elektrotechnik**
English language and literature	**Anglistik**
exercise science	**Sportwissenschaft**
film studies	**Filmwissenschaft**
finance	**Finanzwirtschaft**
forestry	**Forstwissenschaft**
gender studies	**Geschlechterforschung**
genetics	**Genetik**
geography	**Geographie**
geology	**Geologie**
German language and literature	**Germanistik**
graphic design	**Graphikdesign**
history	**Geschichtswissenschaft**
humanities	**Geisteswissenschaften**
interior design	**Innenarchitektur**
international affairs	**Internationale Beziehungen**
journalism	**Publizistik**
Latin American studies	**Lateinamerikanistik**
law	**Jura**
linguistics	**Linguistik**
marketing	**Marketing**
mathematics	**Mathematik**
mechanical engineering	**Maschinenbau**
media studies	**Medienkunde**
medicine	**Medizin**
microbiology	**Mikrobiologie**
Middle Eastern Studies	**Mittelost-Studien**
music	**Musik**
nursing	**Krankenpflege**
nutritional science	**Ernährungswissenschaft**
philosophy	**Philosophie**
physical education	**Sport**
physics	**Physik**
political science	**Politikwissenschaft**
psychology	**Psychologie**
public health	**Gesundheitswesen**
religious studies	**Religionswissenschaft**
Romance languages and literatures	**Romanistik**
Slavic studies	**Slawistik**
sociology	**Soziologie**
theater	**Theaterwissenschaft**
women's studies	**Frauenstudien**
zoology	**Zoologie**

Jobs und Berufe

accountant	**Wirtschaftsprüfer/in**
actor	**Schauspieler/in**
archaeologist	**Archäologe/Archäologin**
architect	**Architekt/in**
artist	**Künstler/in**
athlete	**Athlet/in**
babysitter	**Babysitter/in**

baker	**Bäcker/in**
banker	**Bankkaufmann/ Bankkauffrau**
barber; hairdresser	**Friseur/in**
bookkeeper	**Buchhalter/in**
bus driver	**Busfahrer/in**
businessman/ businesswoman	**Kaufmann/Kauffrau**
butcher	**Fleischer/in; Metzger/in**
chemist	**Chemiker/in**
computer programmer	**Programmierer/in**
computer specialist	**Informatiker/in**
construction worker	**Bauarbeiter/in**
cook; chef	**Koch/Köchin**
consultant	**Berater/in**
dancer	**Tänzer/in**
dentist	**Zahnarzt/Zahnärztin**
designer	**Designer/in**
detective	**Detektiv/in**
diplomat	**Diplomat/in**
DJ	**DJ**
doctor	**Arzt/Ärztin**
editor	**Lektor/Lektorin**
electrician	**Elektriker/in**
engineer	**Ingenieur/in**
event technician	**Veranstaltungs- techniker/in**
factory worker	**Fabrikarbeiter/in**
farmer	**Bauer/Bäuerin**
fashion designer	**Modedesigner/in**
flight attendant	**Flugbegleiter/in**
gardener	**Gärtner/in**
housewife/ househusband	**Hausfrau/Hausmann**
interpreter	**Dolmetscher/in**
journalist	**Journalist/in**
lawyer	**Rechtsanwalt/ Rechtsanwältin**
letter carrier	**Briefträger/in**
librarian	**Bibliothekar/in**
lifeguard	**Rettungsschwimmer/in**
manager	**Manager/in**
mechanic	**Mechaniker/in**
model	**Dressman/das Model**
musician	**Musiker/in**
nurse	**Krankenpfleger/in**
occupational therapist	**Ergotherapeut/in**
office worker	**Büroarbeiter/in**
painter	**Maler/in**
pediatrician	**Kinderarzt/Kinderärztin**
pharmacist	**Apotheker/in**

physical therapist	**Physiotherapeut/in**
plumber	**Klempner/in**
police officer	**Polizist/in**
politician	**Politiker/in**
professor	**Professor/in**
psychiatrist	**Psychiater/in**
psychologist	**Psychologe/Psychologin**
real estate agent	**Immobilienmakler/in**
salesperson	**Verkäufer/in**
server *(in a restaurant)*	**Kellner/in**
scientist	**Wissenschaftler/in**
secretary	**Sekretär/in**
social worker	**Sozialarbeiter/in**
software developer	**Softwareentwickler/in**
stockbroker	**Börsenmakler/in**
tax consultant	**Steuerberater/in**
teacher	**Lehrer/in**
tour guide	**Fremdenführer/in**
translator	**Übersetzer/in**
trucker *(long distance)*	**Fernfahrer/in**
veterinarian	**Tierarzt/Tierärztin**
waiter/waitress	**Kellner/in**
writer	**Schriftsteller/in**

Hobbys und Sport

to bake	**backen**
to blog	**bloggen**
to collect stamps (old comics, beer bottles)	**Briefmarken (alte Comics, Bierflaschen) sammeln**
to cook	**kochen**
to draw or sketch	**zeichnen**
to garden	**im Garten arbeiten**
to go out with friends	**mit Freunden ausgehen**
to go shopping	**einkaufen gehen**
to go to concerts	**ins Konzert gehen**
to go to museums	**ins Museum gehen**
to go to (the) movies	**ins Kino gehen**
to go to the theater	**ins Theater gehen**
to hang out	**rumhängen**
to knit	**stricken**
to listen to music	**Musik hören**
to make videos	**Videos machen**
to paint	**malen**
to play cards	**Karten spielen**
to play chess	**Schach spielen**
to play Scrabble	**Scrabble spielen**
to play computer games	**Computerspiele spielen**
to play video games	**Videospiele spielen**
to read	**lesen**

to sing	singen
to sew	nähen
to surf the Web	im Internet surfen
to take photos	fotografieren
to travel	reisen
to watch TV	fernsehen
to watch videos	Videos anschauen
to write (poetry, stories)	(Gedichte, Geschichten) schreiben

to do aerobics	Aerobics machen
to do bodybuilding	Bodybuilding machen
to do gymnastics	turnen
to do weight lifting	Gewichtheben machen
to do weight training	Krafttraining machen
to work out	Fitnesstraining machen

to go biking	Rad fahren
to go bowling	kegeln gehen
to go camping	campen gehen
to go canoeing	Kanu fahren
to go dancing	tanzen gehen
to go fishing	angeln gehen
to go hang gliding	Drachenfliegen gehen
to go hiking	wandern gehen
to go hunting	jagen gehen
to go ice skating	Schlittschuhlaufen gehen
to go in-line skating	inlineskaten gehen
to go jogging	joggen gehen
to go kayaking	Kajak fahren
to go mountain biking	mountainbiken gehen
to go rowing	rudern gehen
to go sailing	segeln gehen
to go skateboarding	skateboarden gehen
to go skiing	Skilaufen gehen
to go cross-country skiing	Skilanglauf machen
to go downhill skiing	Abfahrtslauf machen
to go snowboarding	snowboarden gehen
to go surfing	surfen gehen
to go swimming	schwimmen gehen
to go windsurfing	windsurfen gehen

to play badminton	Federball spielen
to play baseball	Baseball spielen
to play basketball	Basketball spielen
to play football	Football spielen
to play golf	Golf spielen
to play hockey	Eishockey spielen
to play pool	Billard spielen
to play racquetball	Racquetball spielen

to play soccer	Fußball spielen
to play softball	Softball spielen
to play squash	Squash spielen
to play table tennis (Ping-Pong)	Tischtennis spielen
to play tennis	Tennis spielen
to play volleyball	Volleyball spielen

Musikinstrumente

I play ...	Ich spiele ...
accordion	Akkordeon
(double) bass	Bass, Kontrabass
bassoon	Fagott
cello	Cello
clarinet	Klarinette
drums, percussion	Schlagzeug
flute	Querflöte
guitar	Gitarre
harmonica	Mundharmonika
harp	Harfe
keyboard	Keyboard
oboe	Oboe
organ	Orgel
piano	Klavier
recorder	Blockflöte
saxophone	Saxofon
the trombone	Posaune
trumpet	Trompete
viola	Bratsche
violin	Geige, Violine

Kleidungsstücke

I'm wearing ...	Ich trage ...
a baseball cap	eine Baseballkappe
a belt	einen Gürtel
a blazer	einen Blazer
a blouse	eine Bluse
boots	Stiefel
hiking boots	Wanderstiefel
clothes	Kleider; Klamotten (colloq.)
a coat	einen Mantel
a dress	ein Kleid
gloves	Handschuhe
a hat	einen Hut
a jacket	eine Jacke
a down jacket	eine Daunenjacke
a jeans jacket	eine Jeansjacke
a leather jacket	eine Lederjacke
jeans	Jeans
pants	eine Hose

a polo shirt	ein Polohemd
sandals	Sandalen
a scarf	einen Schal
a shirt	ein Hemd
shorts	Shorts
shoes	Schuhe
tennis shoes	Tennisschuhe
sneakers or running shoes	Turnschuhe
a skirt	einen Rock
slippers	Hausschuhe
socks	Socken
pantyhose	eine Strumpfhose
a suit *(men's)*	einen Anzug
a sweater	einen Pullover
a light sweater	einen Pulli
sweatpants	eine Jogginghose
a sweatshirt	ein Sweatshirt
a sweatsuit	einen Jogginganzug
a tie	eine Krawatte, einen Schlips
tights	Leggings
a T-shirt	ein T-Shirt
a tuxedo	einen Smoking

Accessoires

I'm wearing . . .	Ich trage . . .
a bracelet	ein Armband
contact lenses	Kontaktlinsen
earrings	Ohrringe
an ear stud	einen Ohrstecker
glasses	eine Brille *(sing)*
sunglasses	eine Sonnenbrille *(sing)*
a nose stud	einen Nasenstecker
a necklace	eine Halskette
a ring	einen Ring
a wristwatch	eine Armbanduhr
I have . . .	Ich habe . . .
a beard	einen Bart
a mustache	einen Schnurrbart
a tattoo	eine Tätowierung

Essen und Trinken

I eat . . .	Ich esse . . .
for breakfast	zum Frühstück
bacon	Speck
bacon and eggs	Eier mit Speck
a bagel	einen Bagel
with cream cheese	mit Frischkäse

(a bowl of) cornflakes	(eine Schüssel) Cornflakes
an egg	ein Ei
eggs, sunny-side up	Spiegeleier
scrambled eggs	Rührei
granola, muesli	Müsli
a granola bar	einen Müsliriegel
a muffin	einen Muffin
(a slice of) bread	(eine Scheibe) Brot
(a slice of) toast	(eine Scheibe) Toast
with butter	mit Butter
with honey	mit Honig
with jam	mit Marmelade
with peanut butter	mit Erdnussbutter
(a container of) yogurt	(einen Becher)
with fruit	Fruchtjoghurt
a smoothie	einen Smoothie
for lunch	zum Mittagessen
for supper	zum Abendessen
a bowl of soup	einen Teller Suppe
bread	Brot
a burrito	einen Burrito
chicken	Huhn
chicken salad	Geflügelsalat
French fries	Pommes frites, Pommes
fish	Fisch
a hamburger	einen Hamburger
a hotdog	ein Hotdog
with ketchup	mit Ketchup
with mustard	mit Senf
with onions	mit Zwiebeln
with relish	mit Relish
meat	Fleisch
noodles	Nudeln
pickles	Essiggurken
a pizza	eine Pizza
porkchops	Schweineschnitzel
potatoes	Kartoffeln
potato salad	Kartoffelsalat
rice	Reis
rolls	Brötchen
a sandwich	ein belegtes Brot
a cheese sandwich	ein Käsebrot
a ham sandwich	ein Schinkenbrot
a sausage	eine Wurst
a steak	ein Steak
sushi	Sushi
a taco	einen Taco
tuna	Thunfisch
turkey	Pute

vegetables	Gemüse
asparagus	Spargel
beans	Bohnen
bell peppers	Paprika
broccoli	Brokkoli
carrots	Karotten
cauliflower	Blumenkohl
coleslaw	Krautsalat
cucumbers	Gurken
corn	Zuckermais
mushrooms	Champignons
peas	Erbsen
red cabbage	Rotkohl
salad	Salat
sauerkraut	Sauerkraut
spinach	Spinat
tomatoes	Tomaten

snacks	Snacks
nuts	Nüsse
potato chips	Kartoffelchips
popcorn	Popcorn
pretzels	Brezeln
tortilla chips	Tortillachips

for dessert	zum Nachtisch
(a piece of) cake	(ein Stück) Kuchen
(a piece of) layer cake	(ein Stück) Torte
with whipped cream	mit Schlagsahne
a chocolate bar	eine Tafel Schokolade
cookies	Kekse
(a dish of) ice cream	(einen Becher) Eis

fruit	Obst
an apple	einen Apfel
a banana	eine Banane
blackberries	Brombeeren
blueberries	Heidelbeeren
cherries	Kirschen
a grapefruit	eine Grapefruit
grapes	Trauben
melon	Melone
an orange	eine Orange
a peach	einen Pfirsich
a pear	eine Birne
pineapple	Ananas
a plum	eine Pflaume
raspberries	Himbeeren
strawberries	Erdbeeren

I drink . . .	Ich trinke …
(a bottle of) beer	(eine Flasche) Bier
(a can of) cola	(eine Dose) Cola
(a cup of) coffee	(eine Tasse) Kaffee
(a cup of) tea	(eine Tasse) Tee
(a cup of) cocoa	(eine Tasse) Kakao
(a glass of) milk	(ein Glas) Milch
(a glass of) sparkling wine	(ein Glas) Sekt
(a glass of) water	(ein Glas) Wasser
(a glass of) wine	(ein Glas) Wein
(a glass of) juice	(ein Glas) Saft
apple juice	Apfelsaft
grapefruit juice	Grapefruitsaft
orange juice	Orangensaft
tomato juice	Tomatensaft
a hot chocolate	eine heiße Schokolade
a soft drink	einen Softdrink

Länder und Sprachen

The names of most countries are neuter and are not preceded by an article. However, when the name of a country is masculine, feminine, or plural, the article must be used.

Afghanistan	Kanada
Ägypten	Kolumbien
Algerien	Korea
Argentinien	Kroatien
Australien	Kuba
Belgien	Lettland
Brasilien	der Libanon
Bulgarien	Liechtenstein
Chile	Litauen
China	Luxemburg
Dänemark	Malta
Deutschland	Mexiko
England	Neuseeland
Estland	die Niederlande (pl)
Finnland	Nigeria
Frankreich	Nordirland
Griechenland	Norwegen
Indien	Österreich
der Irak	Pakistan
der Iran	Peru
Irland	Polen
Israel	Portugal
Italien	Rumänien
Japan	Russland

Schottland	Französisch	envious	**neidisch**
Schweden	Griechisch	exotic	**exotisch**
die Schweiz	Hebräisch	extravagant	**extravagant**
Serbien	Hindi	fabulous	**fabelhaft**
die Slowakei	Holländisch	fair	**fair**
Slowenien	Italienisch	famous	**berühmt**
Spanien	Japanisch	fantastic	**fantastisch**
Südafrika	Koreanisch	fashionably dressed	**modisch gekleidet**
Tschechien	Kroatisch	fit	**fit**
die Türkei	Lettisch	fun, funny	**lustig**
die Ukraine	Litauisch	friendly	**freundlich**
Ungarn	Norwegisch	furious	**wütend**
Venezuela	Polnisch	generous	**großzügig**
die Vereinigten	Portugiesisch	great	**spitze**
Staaten, die USA *(pl)*	Rumänisch	happy	**glücklich; froh**
Vietnam	Russisch	hard-working	**fleißig**
Wales	Schwedisch	healthy	**gesund**
Zypern	Serbisch	helpful	**hilfsbereit**
	Slowakisch	honest	**ehrlich**
Sie/Er spricht ...	Spanisch	humorous; having	**humorvoll**
Arabisch	Tschechisch	a sense of humor	
Chinesisch	Türkisch	idealistic	**idealistisch**
Dänisch	Ukrainisch	imaginative	**fantasievoll**
Deutsch	**Ungarisch**	impulsive	**impulsiv**
Englisch	Urdu	informed	**informiert**
Estnisch	**Vietnamesisch**	in love	**verliebt**
Finnisch		innovative	**innovativ**
		intelligent	**intelligent; klug**
		interesting	**interessant**

Persönliche Merkmale

		jealous	**eifersüchtig**
ambitious	**ehrgeizig**	lazy	**faul**
angry	**böse; verärgert**	liberal	**liberal**
arrogant	**arrogant**	messy	**unordentlich**
artistic	**künstlerisch begabt**	modern	**modern**
athletic	**sportlich**	mood: (always) in a	**(immer) guter Laune**
attractive	**attraktiv**	good mood	
(of) average height	**mittelgroß**	moody	**launisch**
beautiful	**schön**	musical	**musikalisch**
bilingual	**zweisprachig**	nice	**nett**
blond	**blond**	natural	**natürlich**
brilliant	**genial**	nervous	**nervös**
brunette	**brünett**	optimistic	**optimistisch**
calm	**ruhig**	outgoing	**aufgeschlossen**
chic	**schick**	pessimistic	**pessimistisch**
conservative	**konservativ**	plump	**mollig**
cool	**cool**	polite	**höflich**
crazy	**verrückt**	popular	**populär; beliebt**
creative	**kreativ**	practical	**praktisch**
critical	**kritisch**	pretty	**hübsch**
elegant	**elegant**	private	**introvertiert**
enchanting	**bezaubernd**	punctual	**pünktlich**

respectful	respektvoll
religious	fromm
romantic	romantisch
selfless	selbstlos
sentimental	sentimental
serious	ernst
short	klein
silly	albern
slim	schlank
smart	klug
spontaneous	spontan
strong	stark
stubborn	dickköpfig
successful	erfolgreich
sweet	süß
tactful	taktvoll
tall	groß
thrifty	sparsam
tidy	ordentlich
tired	müde
tolerant	tolerant
witty	witzig

Höfliche Ausdrücke

All the best!	Alles Gute!
Bless you!	Gesundheit!
Get well soon!	Gute Besserung!
Good luck!	Viel Glück!
Thanks a lot!	Vielen Dank!
Thanks a million!	Tausend Dank!
You're welcome.	Bitte schön.
Don't mention it.	Nichts zu danken.
No problem.	Kein Problem.
That's too bad.	Schade.
Excuse me; I'm sorry.	Entschuldigung;
	Es tut mir leid.
Have fun!	Viel Spaß!
Have a good weekend!	Schönes Wochenende!
Have a nice day!	Schönen Tag noch!
Same to you!	Gleichfalls!

Grammatical Tables

1. *Der-words*

Common **der-**words are **der, das, die** *(the)*; **dieser** *(this)*; **jeder** *(each, every)*; and **welcher** *(which)*.

	masculine	neuter	feminine	plural
NOMINATIVE	der	das	die	die
	dieser	dieses	diese	diese
ACCUSATIVE	den	das	die	die
	diesen	dieses	diese	diese
DATIVE	dem	dem	der	den
	diesem	diesem	dieser	diesen
GENITIVE	des	des	der	der
	dieses	dieses	dieser	dieser

2. *Ein-words*

The **ein-**words are **ein** *(a, an)*, **kein** *(not a, not any, no)*, and the possessive adjectives **mein** *(my)*, **dein** *(your)*, **sein** *(his, its)*, **ihr** *(her, its)*, **unser** *(our)*, **euer** *(your)*, **ihr** *(their)*, **Ihr** *(your)*.

	masculine	neuter	feminine	plural
NOMINATIVE	ein	ein	eine	—
	mein	mein	meine	meine
ACCUSATIVE	einen	ein	eine	—
	meinen	mein	meine	meine
DATIVE	einem	einem	einer	—
	meinem	meinem	meiner	meinen
GENITIVE	eines	eines	einer	—
	meines	meines	meiner	meiner

3. Pronouns

a. Personal pronouns

nom.	subj.	acc.	dir. obj.	dat.	ind. obj.
ich	*I*	mich	*me*	mir	*me*
du	*you*	dich	*you*	dir	*you*
er	*he, it*	ihn	*him, it*	ihm	*him, it*
es	*it*	es	*it*	ihm	*it*
sie	*she, it*	sie	*her, it*	ihr	*her, it*
wir	*we*	uns	*us*	uns	*us*
ihr	*you*	euch	*you*	euch	*you*
sie	*they*	sie	*them*	ihnen	*them*
Sie	*you*	Sie	*you*	Ihnen	*you*

b. Reflexive pronouns

	accusative	dative	direct or indirect object
(ich)	mich	mir	*myself*
(du)	dich	dir	*yourself*
(er)	sich	sich	*himself, itself*
(es)	sich	sich	*itself*
(sie)	sich	sich	*herself, itself*
(wir)	uns	uns	*ourselves*
(ihr)	euch	euch	*yourselves*
(sie)	sich	sich	*themselves*
(Sie)	sich	sich	*yourself*
			yourselves

c. Interrogative pronouns

	for persons	for things
NOMINATIVE	wer	was
ACCUSATIVE	wen	was
DATIVE	wem	—
GENITIVE	wessen	—

d. Relative pronouns

	masculine	neuter	feminine	plural
NOMINATIVE	der	das	die	die
ACCUSATIVE	den	das	die	die
DATIVE	dem	dem	der	denen
GENITIVE	dessen	dessen	deren	deren

4. Adjective endings

a. After *der*-words

	masculine	neuter	feminine	plural
NOM.	der jung**e** Mann	das lieb**e** Kind	die jung**e** Frau	die lieb**en** Kinder
ACC.	den jung**en** Mann	das lieb**e** Kind	die jung**e** Frau	die lieb**en** Kinder
DAT.	dem jung**en** Mann	dem lieb**en** Kind	der jung**en** Frau	den lieb**en** Kindern
GEN.	des jung**en** Mannes	des lieb**en** Kindes	der jung**en** Frau	der lieb**en** Kinder

b. After *ein*-words

	masculine	neuter	feminine	plural
NOM.	ein jung**er** Mann	ein lieb**es** Kind	eine jung**e** Frau	keine lieb**en** Kinder
ACC.	einen jung**en** Mann	ein lieb**es** Kind	eine jung**e** Frau	keine lieb**en** Kinder
DAT.	einem jung**en** Mann	einem lieb**en** Kind	einer jung**en** Frau	keinen lieb**en** Kindern
GEN.	eines jung**en** Mannes	eines lieb**en** Kindes	einer jung**en** Frau	keiner lieb**en** Kinder

c. For unpreceded adjectives

	masculine	neuter	feminine	plural
NOM.	gut**er** Käse	gut**es** Brot	gut**e** Wurst	gut**e** Äpfel
ACC.	gut**en** Käse	gut**es** Brot	gut**e** Wurst	gut**e** Äpfel
DAT.	gut**em** Käse	gut**em** Brot	gut**er** Wurst	gut**en** Äpfeln

5. *N*-nouns

All **n**-nouns are masculine. They are listed in dictionaries as follows:
der Student, **–en**, **–en**.

	singular	plural
NOMINATIVE	der Student	die Studenten
ACCUSATIVE	den Studenten	die Studenten
DATIVE	dem Studenten	den Studenten
GENITIVE	des Studenten	der Studenten

6. Prepositions

accusative	dative	accusative or dative	genitive
durch	aus	an	statt
für	außer	auf	trotz
gegen	bei	hinter	während
ohne	mit	in	wegen
um	nach	neben	
	seit	über	
	von	unter	
	zu	vor	
		zwischen	

7. Irregular comparatives and superlatives

BASE FORM	gern	gut	groß	hoch	nah	viel
COMPARATIVE	lieber	besser	größer	höher	näher	mehr
SUPERLATIVE	liebst-	best-	größt-	höchst-	nächst-	meist-

8. Verbs

a. Indicative (to express facts)
Present tense

	lernen[1]	arbeiten[2]	reisen[3]	geben[4]	tragen[5]	laufen[6]	weg-gehen[7]
ich	lerne	arbeite	reise	gebe	trage	laufe	gehe … weg
du	lernst	arbeitest	reist	gibst	trägst	läufst	gehst … weg
er/es/sie	lernt	arbeitet	reist	gibt	trägt	läuft	geht … weg
wir	lernen	arbeiten	reisen	geben	tragen	laufen	gehen … weg
ihr	lernt	arbeitet	reist	gebt	tragt	lauft	geht … weg
sie	lernen	arbeiten	reisen	geben	tragen	laufen	gehen … weg
Sie	lernen	arbeiten	reisen	geben	tragen	laufen	gehen … weg

[1] Regular verbs
[2] Verbs with expanded endings (e.g., **arbeiten, finden, regnen, öffnen**)
[3] Verbs with contracted endings (e.g., **reisen, heißen, sitzen**)
[4] Irregular verbs with stem-vowel change **e** to **i (ie)**
[5] Irregular verbs with stem-vowel change **a** to **ä**
[6] Irregular verbs with stem-vowel change **au** to **äu**
[7] Separable-prefix verbs

Present tense of the auxiliaries *haben, sein, werden*

	haben	sein	werden
ich	habe	bin	werde
du	hast	bist	wirst
er/es/sie	hat	ist	wird
wir	haben	sind	werden
ihr	habt	seid	werdet
sie	haben	sind	werden
Sie	haben	sind	werden

Present tense of the modal verbs

	dürfen	können	mögen	(möcht-)	müssen	sollen	wollen
ich	darf	kann	mag	(möchte)	muss	soll	will
du	darfst	kannst	magst	(möchtest)	musst	sollst	willst
er/es/sie	darf	kann	mag	(möchte)	muss	soll	will
wir	dürfen	können	mögen	(möchten)	müssen	sollen	wollen
ihr	dürft	könnt	mögt	(möchtet)	müsst	sollt	wollt
sie	dürfen	können	mögen	(möchten)	müssen	sollen	wollen
Sie	dürfen	können	mögen	(möchten)	müssen	sollen	wollen

Simple past tense

	regular verbs		irregular verbs
ich	lernte	landete	ging
du	lerntest	landetest	gingst
er/es/sie	lernte	landete	ging
wir	lernten	landeten	gingen
ihr	lerntet	landetet	gingt
sie	lernten	landeten	gingen
Sie	lernten	landeten	gingen

You will find the principal parts of the irregular verbs used in this text on pp. A28–A30.

Simple past tense of the auxiliaries *haben, sein, werden*

	haben	sein	werden
ich	hatte	war	wurde
du	hattest	warst	wurdest
er/es/sie	hatte	war	wurde
wir	hatten	waren	wurden
ihr	hattet	wart	wurdet
sie	hatten	waren	wurden
Sie	hatten	waren	wurden

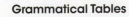

Simple past tense of mixed verbs

	bringen	denken	kennen	nennen	rennen	wissen
ich	brachte	dachte	kannte	nannte	rannte	wusste
du	brachtest	dachtest	kanntest	nanntest	ranntest	wusstest
er/es/sie	brachte	dachte	kannte	nannte	rannte	wusste
wir	brachten	dachten	kannten	nannten	rannten	wussten
ihr	brachtet	dachtet	kanntet	nanntet	ranntet	wusstet
sie	brachten	dachten	kannten	nannten	rannten	wussten
Sie	brachten	dachten	kannten	nannten	rannten	wussten

Simple past tense of the modal verbs

	dürfen	können	mögen	müssen	sollen	wollen
ich	durfte	konnte	mochte	musste	sollte	wollte
du	durftest	konntest	mochtest	musstest	solltest	wolltest
er/es/sie	durfte	konnte	mochte	musste	sollte	wollte
wir	durften	konnten	mochten	mussten	sollten	wollten
ihr	durftet	konntet	mochtet	musstet	solltet	wolltet
sie	durften	konnten	mochten	mussten	sollten	wollten
Sie	durften	konnten	mochten	mussten	sollten	wollten

Perfect tense

	regular verbs				irregular verbs			
ich	habe	gelernt	bin	gereist	habe	gesungen	bin	gegangen
du	hast	gelernt	bist	gereist	hast	gesungen	bist	gegangen
er/es/sie	hat	gelernt	ist	gereist	hat	gesungen	ist	gegangen
wir	haben	gelernt	sind	gereist	haben	gesungen	sind	gegangen
ihr	habt	gelernt	seid	gereist	habt	gesungen	seid	gegangen
sie	haben	gelernt	sind	gereist	haben	gesungen	sind	gegangen
Sie	haben	gelernt	sind	gereist	haben	gesungen	sind	gegangen

You will find the principal parts of the irregular verbs used in this text on pp. A28–A30.

b. Imperative (to express commands or requests)

FAMILIAR SINGULAR	Lern(e)!	Gib!	Sei!
FAMILIAR PLURAL	Lernt!	Gebt!	Seid!
FORMAL	Lernen Sie!	Geben Sie!	Seien Sie!

c. Subjunctive (to express contrary-to-fact situations)
Present-time subjunctive

	haben	sein	können	wissen
ich	hätte	wäre	könnte	wüsste
du	hättest	wär(e)st	könntest	wüsstest
er/es/sie	hätte	wäre	könnte	wüsste
wir	hätten	wären	könnten	wüssten
ihr	hättet	wär(e)t	könntet	wüsstet
sie	hätten	wären	könnten	wüssten
Sie	hätten	wären	könnten	wüssten

For verbs other than **haben**, **sein**, **werden**, **wissen**, and the modals, use **würde** + infinitive.

	würde	
ich	würde	lernen
du	würdest	lernen
er/es/sie	würde	lernen
wir	würden	lernen
ihr	würdet	lernen
sie	würden	lernen
Sie	würden	lernen

Past-time subjunctive

ich	hätte	gelernt	wäre	gegangen
du	hättest	gelernt	wär(e)st	gegangen
er/es/sie	hätte	gelernt	wäre	gegangen
wir	hätten	gelernt	wären	gegangen
ihr	hättet	gelernt	wär(e)t	gegangen
sie	hätten	gelernt	wären	gegangen
Sie	hätten	gelernt	wären	gegangen

d. Passive voice

	present tense		simple past tense	
ich	werde	abgeholt	wurde	abgeholt
du	wirst	abgeholt	wurdest	abgeholt
er/es/sie	wird	abgeholt	wurde	abgeholt
wir	werden	abgeholt	wurden	abgeholt
ihr	werdet	abgeholt	wurdet	abgeholt
sie	werden	abgeholt	wurden	abgeholt
Sie	werden	abgeholt	wurden	abgeholt

Principal Parts of Irregular and Mixed Verbs

The following list contains the principal parts of the irregular and mixed verbs in *Treffpunkt Deutsch*. With a few exceptions, the separable- and inseparable-prefix verbs are not included since the stem changes are the same as for the basic verb (e.g., **ausgeben–geben, mitbringen–bringen**).

INFINITIVE	IRR. PRESENT	SIMPLE PAST	PAST PARTICIPLE	
anfangen	(fängt an)	fing an		angefangen	*to begin*
backen	(bäckt)	backte		gebacken	*to bake*
beißen		biss		gebissen	*to bite*
beginnen		begann		begonnen	*to begin*
begreifen		begriff		begriffen	*to grasp; to comprehend*
bekommen		bekam		bekommen	*to get; to receive*
beweisen		bewies		bewiesen	*to prove*
bieten		bot		geboten	*to offer*
bitten		bat		gebeten	*to ask*
bleiben		blieb	ist	geblieben	*to stay; to remain*
bringen		brachte		gebracht	*to bring*
denken		dachte		gedacht	*to think*
einladen	(lädt ein)	lud ein		eingeladen	*to invite*
empfangen	(empfängt)	empfing		empfangen	*to welcome*
empfehlen	(empfiehlt)	empfahl		empfohlen	*to recommend*
entscheiden		entschied		entschieden	*to decide*
entwerfen	(entwirft)	entwarf		entworfen	*to design*
essen	(isst)	aß		gegessen	*to eat*
fahren	(fährt)	fuhr	ist	gefahren	*to drive*
fallen	(fällt)	fiel	ist	gefallen	*to fall*
fangen	(fängt)	fing		gefangen	*to catch*
finden		fand		gefunden	*to find*
fliegen		flog	ist	geflogen	*to fly*
fliehen		floh	ist	geflohen	*to flee*
fließen		floss	ist	geflossen	*to flow*
fressen	(frisst)	fraß		gefressen	*to eat (of animals)*
frieren		fror		gefroren	*to be cold*
geben	(gibt)	gab		gegeben	*to give*
gehen		ging	ist	gegangen	*to go*
gelten	(gilt)	galt		gegolten	*to be considered*
geschehen	(geschieht)	geschah	ist	geschehen	*to happen*
gewinnen		gewann		gewonnen	*to win*
gießen		goss		gegossen	*to water*
haben	(hat)	hatte		gehabt	*to have*
halten	(hält)	hielt		gehalten	*to hold; to keep; to stop*
hängen		hing		gehangen	*to be hanging*
heißen		hieß		geheißen	*to be called*

INFINITIVE	IRR. PRESENT	SIMPLE PAST	PAST PARTICIPLE	
helfen	(hilft)	half	geholfen	to help
kennen		kannte	gekannt	to know (be acquainted with)
kommen		kam	ist gekommen	to come
laden	(lädt)	lud	geladen	to load
lassen	(lässt)	ließ	gelassen	to let; to leave
laufen	(läuft)	lief	ist gelaufen	to run
leihen		lieh	geliehen	to lend
lesen	(liest)	las	gelesen	to read
liegen		lag	gelegen	to lie; to be situated
lügen		log	gelogen	to tell a lie
nehmen	(nimmt)	nahm	genommen	to take
nennen		nannte	genannt	to call; to name
raten	(rät)	riet	geraten	to guess; to advise
reiten		ritt	ist geritten	to ride
rennen		rannte	ist gerannt	to run
riechen		roch	gerochen	to smell
rufen		rief	gerufen	to call
scheinen		schien	geschienen	to shine; to seem
schieben		schob	geschoben	to push
schlafen	(schläft)	schlief	geschlafen	to sleep
schließen		schloss	geschlossen	to close
schneiden		schnitt	geschnitten	to cut
schreiben		schrieb	geschrieben	to write
schreien		schrie	geschrien	to shout
schwimmen		schwamm	ist geschwommen	to swim
sehen	(sieht)	sah	gesehen	to see
sein	(ist)	war	ist gewesen	to be
singen		sang	gesungen	to sing
sinken		sank	ist gesunken	to sink
sitzen		saß	gesessen	to sit
spinnen		spann	gesponnen	to spin; to be crazy
sprechen	(spricht)	sprach	gesprochen	to speak
springen		sprang	ist gesprungen	to jump
stehen		stand	gestanden	to stand
stehlen	(stiehlt)	stahl	gestohlen	to steal
steigen		stieg	ist gestiegen	to climb
sterben	(stirbt)	starb	ist gestorben	to die
stinken		stank	gestunken	to stink
streichen		strich	gestrichen	to paint
tragen	(trägt)	trug	getragen	to carry; to wear
treffen	(trifft)	traf	getroffen	to meet
trinken		trank	getrunken	to drink
tun		tat	getan	to do
verbieten		verbot	verboten	to forbid
verbinden		verband	verbunden	to connect
vergessen	(vergisst)	vergaß	vergessen	to forget

INFINITIVE	IRR. PRESENT	SIMPLE PAST	PAST PARTICIPLE	
vergleichen		verglich	verglichen	*to compare*
verlieren		verlor	verloren	*to lose*
vermeiden		vermied	vermieden	*to avoid*
verstehen		verstand	verstanden	*to understand*
vorschlagen	(schlägt vor)	schlug vor	vorgeschlagen	*to suggest*
waschen	(wäscht)	wusch	gewaschen	*to wash*
werden	(wird)	wurde	ist geworden	*to become*
wissen	(weiß)	wusste	gewusst	*to know (a fact)*
ziehen		zog	gezogen	*to pull*

Modal verbs

dürfen	(darf)	durfte	gedurft	*to be allowed to*
können	(kann)	konnte	gekonnt	*to be able to*
mögen	(mag)	mochte	gemocht	*to like*
müssen	(muss)	musste	gemusst	*to have to*
sollen	(soll)	sollte	gesollt	*to be supposed to*
wollen	(will)	wollte	gewollt	*to want to*

German-English Vocabulary

This German–English vocabulary includes all the words and expressions used in *Treffpunkt Deutsch* except numbers and names of countries. The latter are listed in the *Useful Word Sets* on page A14. Each item is followed by the number of the chapter (and E for *Erste Kontakte)* in which it first occurs. Chapter numbers followed by –1 or –2 (e.g., 1-1 or 1-2) refer to items listed in the first or second vocabulary list in each chapter *(Wortschatz 1 or Wortschatz 2)*.

Nouns are listed with their plural forms: **die Studentin, –nen.** If no plural entry is given, the plural is rarely used or nonexistent. When two entries follow a noun, the first one indicates the genitive and the second the plural: **der Student, –en, –en.**

Irregular, mixed, and modal verbs are listed with their principal parts. Vowel changes in the present tense are noted in parentheses: **lesen (liest), las, gelesen.** Auxiliary verbs are given only for verbs conjugated with **sein: kommen, kam, ist gekommen; reisen, reiste, ist gereist.** Separable prefixes are indicated by a raised dot between the prefix and the verb stem: **an·fangen.**

The following abbreviations are used:

acc	accusative	*gen*	genitive
adj	adjective	*indef*	indefinite
adv	adverb	*neg*	negative
art	article	*pl*	plural
conj	conjunction	*prep*	preposition
coord	coordinating	*sing*	singular
dat	dative	*sub*	subordinating

A

ab: ab morgen from tomorrow on (7)

der Abend, –e evening (E)
  Guten Abend! 'n Abend! Good evening! (E-1)
  heute Abend this evening, tonight (1)
  zu Abend essen to have supper (4-1)

das Abendbrot evening meal of bread and cold cuts (4)

das Abendessen supper; evening meal (4-1)
  zum Abendessen for supper; for dinner (4-1)

abends in the evening (2)

aber *(coord conj)* but (1-2)

ab·fahren (fährt ab), fuhr ab, ist abgefahren to leave, to depart (4-2)

der/die Abgeordnete, –n representative (12)

abgrundtief profound(ly)
  Ich hasse sie abgrundtief. I hate her with a passion. (12)

ab·haken to check off (7)

ab·holen to pick up (5-2)

das Abitur high school diploma (1)

die Abkürzung, –en abbreviation (E)

ab·reisen to leave, to depart (6)

der Abschied, –e farewell (11)
  Abschied nehmen (nimmt), nahm, genommen to bid farewell (11)

die Abteilung, –en department (7-1)

der Abteilungsleiter, –/die Abteilungsleiterin, –nen department manager (12)

die Abwanderung moving away; migration (11)

der Abwasch dirty dishes (7)
  den Abwasch machen to do the dishes (7-1)

ADAC (Allgemeiner Deutscher Automobil-Club) German automobile club (E)

die Adresse, –n address (E)

der Adventskalender, – Advent calendar (7)

der Affe, –n, –n ape; monkey (2)

der Agent, –en, –en/die Agentin, –nen agent (5)

aggressiv aggressive (12-1)

ähnlich similar (7, 9-2)

die Ähnlichkeit, –en similarity (9)

die Akzeptanz *(sing)* acceptance (9)

alarmieren to alarm (11)

das Album, Alben album (6-2)

der Alkohol alcohol (4-2)

das All outer space (12)

alle all (the) (1); everybody (7)

allein alone (8)

allergisch (gegen) allergic (to) (8)
alles everything; all (3-2)
   Alles in Ordnung? Is everything okay? (9-2)
   Es ist alles für die Katz. It's all for nothing. (10)
   vor allem above all (4)
die **Alliierten** *(pl)* the Allies (11-1)
das **Alltagsleben** everyday life (4)
der **Alltagsmief** stale routine (12)
die **Alltagsszene, -n** everyday scene (4)
die **Alpen** *(pl)* Alps (1)
als from (2); as (2); than (2); when *(conj)* (9, 10-1); but (10)
   als Kind as a child (5-2)
   anders als different from (2)
   nichts als Ärger nothing but trouble (10)
also so, thus (4)
alt old (1, 3-2)
die **Alte Pinakothek** *art gallery in Munich* (5)
das **Alter** age (4); old age (12)
altmodisch old-fashioned (5-2)
die **Altstadt, ⸚e** old city center (12)
(das) **Amerika** America (6)
der **Amerikaner, -/**die **Amerikanerin, -nen** American *(person)* (1-1)
amerikanisch *(adj)* American (2)
das **Amt, ⸚er** office, department (8)
an *(prep + acc/dat)* at; to; on *(a vertical surface)* (2)
der **Anbau** farming (9)
an·bieten, bot an, angeboten to offer (7, 12-2)
das **Andenken, -** souvenir (11)
ander different, other (1)
ändern to change (4)
anders different(ly) (2)
   anders als different from (2)
   jemand anders somebody else (9-1)
der **Anfang, ⸚e** beginning (4-2)
   am Anfang at the beginning (11-2)
   Anfang Juli (at) the beginning of July (5-1)

an·fangen (fängt an), fing an, angefangen to begin; to start (4-1)
an·fassen to touch (11)
an·funkeln to light into (11)
das **Angebot, -e** offering, choice (8)
angeln to fish (5-1)
angesehen respected (10)
der **Angler, -/**die **Anglerin, -nen** fisher (5-1)
die **Angst, ⸚e** fear (10-1)
   Angst haben to be afraid (9-2)
   Angst haben vor *(+ dat)* to be afraid of (10-2)
   Angst kriegen to get scared (10-1)
   Keine Angst! Don't worry! (6)
an·halten (hält an), hielt an, angehalten to stop (4-2, 10-1)
der **Anhang, ⸚e** appendix
an·hören to listen to (4-2)
an·kommen, kam an, ist angekommen to arrive (4-2)
an·kotzen: es kotzt mich an it makes me puke (12)
der **Anlass** occasion (7)
die **Anmeldung, -en** registration (2)
an·ordnen to order (11)
die **Anpassung an** *(+ acc)* adjustment to (11)
an·probieren to try on (4-2)
an·rufen, rief an, angerufen to call *(on the telephone)* (4-2)
an·schauen to look at (5-2); to watch (9)
   sich etwas an·schauen to look at something; to watch something (9)
die **Anschrift** address (9)
die **Anstalt des öffentlichen Rechts** public institution (6)
die **Antike** antiquity (9)
die **Antwort, -en** answer (1-2)
antworten *(+ dat)* to answer (7-2)
die **Anzeige, -n** ad; announcement (7-2)
sich an·ziehen, zog an, angezogen to dress, to get dressed (9-2)
der **Anzug, ⸚e** *(men's)* suit (2-2)
der **Apfel, ⸚** apple (1)
   Der Apfel fällt nicht weit vom Stamm. Like father, like son. (7)

der **Apfelkuchen, -** apple pie (4)
der **Apfelsaft** *(sing)* apple juice (4)
die **Apotheke, -n** pharmacy (9-2)
der **Apparat, -e** apparatus, appliance (9)
der **Appetit** appetite (9)
   Guten Appetit! Enjoy your meal! (9-1)
der **April** April (1-2)
die **Arbeit** work (2-2)
arbeiten to work (1-2)
   arbeiten an *(+ dat)* to work on (11-2)
der **Arbeiter, -/**die **Arbeiterin, -nen** worker (5)
der **Arbeitgeber, -/**die **Arbeitgeberin, -nen** employer (12-1)
der **Arbeitnehmer, -/** die **Arbeitnehmerin, -nen** employee (12-1)
die **Arbeitserfahrung, -en** work experience (6-2)
der **Arbeitskollege, -n, -n/**die **Arbeitskollegin, -nen** colleague from work (2)
arbeitslos unemployed (6-1)
die **Arbeitslosigkeit** unemployment (11)
der **Arbeitsplatz** place of work (7)
der **Arbeitsraum, ⸚e** study (8)
der **Architekt, -en, -en/**die **Architektin, -nen** architect (8-2)
die **Architektur** architecture (1)
der **Ärger** annoyance, trouble (10)
   nichts als Ärger nothing but trouble (10)
ärgern to make angry; annoy (10-2)
sich ärgern über *(+ acc)* to be annoyed with, about (11-2)
das **Argument, -e** argument (5-2)
arm poor (5-2)
der **Arm, -e** arm (1, 6-1)
das **Armaturenbrett** dashboard (11)
das **Armband, ⸚er** bracelet (3, 5-2)
die **Armbanduhr, -en** wristwatch (7-1)
die **Armee, -n** army (4)
arrogant arrogant (5-2)
die **Art, -en** way; method (12)
der **Artikel, -** article (4)

der **Arzt, ⸚e**/die **Ärztin, -nen** physician (1, 5-2)

der **Assistent, -en, -en**/die **Assistentin, -nen** assistant (5)

der **Athlet, -en, -en**/die **Athletin, -nen** athlete (9-2)

die **ATM Karte, -n** ATM card (5-2)

die **Attraktion, -en** attraction (5, 11-2)

auch also (E, 1-1)

  Claudia kommt auch nicht. Claudia isn't coming either. (1-2)

der **Audi, -s** Audi *(car)* (4)

auf *(prep + acc/dat)* up (4); on, onto (6); to; on *(a horizontal surface)* (8)

  auf sein to be up (4)

der **Aufenthalt, -e** stay (5-1)

auf·essen (isst auf), aß auf, aufgegessen to eat up (11)

die **Aufgabe, -n** assignment; task (7, 12-1)

aufgeregt excited (8-2)

aufgeschlossen outgoing (8)

auf·hören to end; to stop (4-1)

der **Aufkleber, -** sticker (11-2)

auf·legen to hang up *(the receiver)* (8)

auf·listen to list (10)

auf·machen to open (8-2)

auf·passen to pay attention (4-2)

auf·räumen to clean up (4-2)

sich **auf·regen** to get worked up; to get upset (9-2)

sich **auf·regen über** *(+ acc)* to get upset about; to get worked up about (9-2, 11-2)

aufregend exciting (11-2)

auf·setzen to put on *(one's head)* (11)

auf·stehen, stand auf, ist aufgestanden to get up; to stand up (4-1)

auf·wachen to wake up (4-2)

der **Aufzug** costume, get-up (11)

das **Auge, -n** eye (2, 6-1)

  kein Auge zu tun to not sleep a wink (6)

  unter vier Augen in private (9)

der **August** August (1-2)

aus *(prep + dat)* from, out of (E-1); over (4)

die **Ausbildung, -en** job training; education (12-1)

der **Ausdruck, ⸚e** expression (1)

aus·drücken to express (12)

auseinander·nehmen (11) to take apart

die **Ausgabe, -n** edition (2)

aus·geben (gibt aus), gab aus, ausgegeben to spend *(money)* (5-2)

ausgebildet: gut ausgebildet sein to be well educated; to be well trained (12-1)

aus·gehen, ging aus, ist ausgegangen to go out (4-2)

ausgestattet equipped (8)

ausgezeichnet excellent (3-2)

aus·höhlen to hollow out (7)

das **Ausland** foreign countries

  ins Ausland abroad (4)

der **Ausländer, -**/die **Ausländerin, -nen** foreigner (12)

ausländisch foreign (10)

das **Auslandsamt** foreign students office (1-1)

aus·machen to represent, to constitute (11)

aus·packen to unpack (6-2)

aus·probieren to try out (4-2)

die **Aussage, -n** statement (7-1)

das **Aussehen** *(sing)* looks, appearance (11)

aus·sehen (sieht aus), sah aus, ausgesehen (wie) to look like, to appear (7-1); to look (8)

außen outside (9-1)

außer *(prep + dat)* except for (7)

  Sie war außer sich. She was beside herself. (10-2)

außerdem besides; in addition (7-1)

außerhalb von *(+ dat)* outside of (3)

die **Aussicht, -en** view (11)

aus·spannen to relax (5-1)

die **Aussprache** pronunciation (E)

die **Ausstattung** facilities (8)

aus·steigen, stieg aus, ist ausgestiegen to get off *(a train, bus, etc.)* (4-2)

aus·stellen to exhibit (6)

die **Ausstellung, -en** exhibition, exhibit (6, 8-2)

aus·suchen to choose; to pick out (9-1)

sich etwas **aus·suchen** to pick something out (9)

der **Austauschschüler, -**/die **Austauschschülerin, -nen** exchange student *(high school)* (9-1)

der **Austauschstudent, -en, -en**/die **Austauschstudentin, -nen** exchange student *(college)* (11)

aus·wählen to select (7)

die **Auswahl** selection, choice (10)

der **Auswanderer, -**/die **Auswanderin, -nen** emigrant (6-1)

aus·wandern, wanderte aus, ist ausgewandert to emigrate (6-1)

sich **aus·ziehen, zog aus, hat ausgezogen** to undress, to get undressed (9-2)

das **Auto, -s** car (1, 3-1)

Auto fahren (fährt Auto), fuhr Auto, ist Auto gefahren to drive (4)

die **Autobahn, -en** freeway, expressway (4-2)

die **Autobiografie, -n** (10-2)

der **Automechaniker, -**/die **Automechanikerin, -nen** *(car)* mechanic (1)

der **Autor, -en**/die **Autorin, -nen** author (2)

die **Autorität, -en** authority (11)

der **Autounfall, ⸚e** car accident (11)

B

das **Baby, -s** baby (1)

der **Babysitter, -**/die **Babysitterin, -nen** babysitter (4)

backen (bäckt), backte, gebacken to bake (3)

der **Bäcker, -** /die **Bäckerin, -nen** baker (E)

die **Bäckerei, -en** bakery (7-2)

das **Bad, ⸚er** bath; bathroom (2, 8-1)

der **Badeanzug, ⸚e** bathing suit (4)

die **Bademöglichkeit, -en** *(place to go)* swimming; swimming facility (5-1)

baden to swim; to bathe (5-1)

(sich) **baden** to bathe, to take a bath (9-2)

die **Badewanne, -n** bathtub (8-1)

das **Badezimmer, -** bathroom (3, 8-1)

der **Bagel, -s** bagel (4-1)

die **Bahn** *(sing)* railway (4)

die **Bahnfahrt, -en** train trip (6)

der **Bahnhof, ⁻e** train station (4-2)

bald soon (1, 2-2)

so bald wie möglich as soon as possible (4)

der **Balkon, -e** balcony (8-1)

der **Ball, ⁻e** ball (1)

der **Balletttänzer, -**/die **Balletttänzerin, -nen** ballet dancer (2)

die **Banane, -n** banana (1, 4-1)

die **Band, -s** band (2)

die **Bank, -en** bank (3)

der **Bankkaufmann, Bankkaufleute**/die **Bankkauffrau, -en** office administrator at a bank (12)

die **Banknote, -n** banknote (9)

bankrott bankrupt (7)

der **Bär, -en, -en** bear (7)

einen Bärenhunger haben to be famished (10)

das **Bargeld** cash (9-2)

die **Bar-Mizwa** *(sing)* Bar Mitzvah (7)

das **Barometer, -** barometer (1)

der **Bart, ⁻e** beard (5-2)

die **Baseballkappe, -n** baseball cap (5-2)

der **Basketball, ⁻e** basketball (2-1)

der **Bastelladen, ⁻** crafts store (2)

basteln to do crafts (2)

das **Basteln** *(sing)* crafts (4)

der **Bau** construction (10)

der **Bauch, ⁻e** stomach; belly (6-1)

sich *(dat)* die **Beine in den Bauch stehen** to stand until one is ready to drop (9)

die **Bauchschmerzen** *(pl)* stomachache (6)

bauen to build (5, 8-1)

Auf ihn kannst du Häuser bauen. He's absolutely dependable. (8)

der **Bauer, -n, -n**/die **Bäuerin, -nen** farmer (10-1)

der **Baum, ⁻e** tree (5-1)

baumlos treeless (12)

der **Bausparvertrag, ⁻e** home savings plan (12)

der **Baustil, -e** building style (9)

bayerisch *(adj)* Bavarian (5)

(das) **Bayern** Bavaria (5)

beantworten to answer (7)

eine Frage beantworten to answer a question (7)

der **Becher, -** cup; container (4-1)

ein Becher Joghurt a container of yogurt (4-1)

bedeckt cloudy (1)

bedeuten to mean (2-2)

die **Bedeutung, -en** meaning (8)

bedeutungslos meaningless (12)

bedienen to serve *(guests in a restaurant)* (9-1)

die **Bedienung** *(sing)* waiter/ waitress, server *(in a restaurant)* (9-1)

das **Bedienungsgeld** service charge (9)

sich **beeilen** to hurry (9-2)

beeindrucken to impress (12-2)

befragen to ask (12)

der **Beginn** beginning (1)

zu Beginn at the beginning (11-2)

beginnen, begann, begonnen to begin (1-1)

begreifen, begriff, begriffen to understand, to grasp, to comprehend (12-1)

behaupten to claim (11-2)

beherrschen to know (5)

bei *(prep + dat)* at (E); for; near (7)

bei uns, bei Zieglers at our house, at the Zieglers (2-1)

beide both; two (2-2)

der **Beifahrersitz,** front passenger seat *(in a car)* (11-2)

die **Beilage, -n** side dish (9-1)

das **Bein, -e** leg (6-1)

Hals- und Beinbruch! Break a leg! Good luck! (6-2)

auf (seinen) eigenen Beinen stehen to stand on (one's) own feet (12-1)

sich *(dat)* die **Beine in den Bauch stehen** to stand until one is ready to drop (9)

das **Beisel, -n** *(Austrian)* pub (2)

das **Beispiel, -e** example (6-2)

zum Beispiel (z.B.) for example (e.g.) (4, 6-2)

beißen, biss, gebissen to bite (7)

der **Beistelltisch, -e** end table (8)

beizen to stain wood (9)

bekannt well-known (4-2)

der/die **Bekannte, -n** acquaintance (8)

bekommen, bekam, bekommen to get; to receive (3-2)

beladen loaded (11)

die **Beleuchtungsanlage, -n** illumination system (11)

belgisch *(adj)* Belgian (7)

beliebt popular, well-loved (9-1)

bellen to bark (11)

bemalt painted (11)

bemerken to notice (11)

sich **benehmen (benimmt), benahm, benommen** to behave (9-2)

benutzen to use (8-1)

der **Beobachtungsturm, ⁻e** watch tower *(for guards)* (11)

beraten to advise (5)

bereuen to regret (12-2)

der **Berg, -e** mountain (5-1)

die **Bergwelt** alpine world (5)

der **Bericht** report (10-2)

berichten to report (7-2)

die **Bermudashorts** *(pl)* Bermuda shorts (3)

der **Beruf, -e** profession, occupation (1)

Er ist Koch von Beruf. He's a cook by trade. (3)

Was sind Sie von Beruf? What's your occupation? (3-2)

berühmt famous (3, 5-2)

die **Besatzungszone, -n** occupation zone (7)

beschämt shamefacedly (7)

die **Bescherung** gift-giving *(at Christmas)* (7)

die **Beschränkung, -en** restriction (11)

beschreiben, beschrieb, beschrieben to describe (6)

die **Beschreibung, -en** description (3)

besetzen to occupy (11)

besondere(r, s) special

  besondere Kennzeichen distinguishing marks (6)

besonders particularly, especially (1-2)

besprechen to discuss (11)

besser better (1)

  besser als better than (5)

best best (2)

das **Besteck, -e** silverware, cutlery (9-1)

bestellen to order (6, 9-1)

bestens very well (10)

bestimmt definite(ly); for sure (4, 5-1)

bestreuen to sprinkle (9)

der **Besuch, -e** visit (3)

  zu Besuch kommen to come to visit (8-2)

besuchen to visit (2-2)

der **Besucher, -** visitor (4)

der **Beton** concrete (11)

der **Betonklotz, ⸚e** concrete block (11)

Betonplattenwand, ⸚e wall made from concrete slabs (11)

beträufeln to drizzle (9)

das **Bett, -en** bed (1, 8-1)

  ins Bett to bed (1-2)

betteln (um) to beg (for) (10)

das **Bettzeug** *(sing)* bedding, sheets, bedclothes (3)

die **Bevölkerung** population (11)

bevor before *(sub conj)* (4-2)

bewölkt cloudy (1)

bewundern to admire (8)

bezahlen to pay (3-2)

die **Bezahlung** pay; wages (6-2)

die **Beziehung, -en** relationship (12-1)

der **Beziehungsstatus** relationship status (2)

die **Bibel, -n** bible (10-1)

die **Bibliothek, -en** library (1)

  in die Bibliothek to the library (1-2)

die **Biene, -n** bee (10)

das **Bier** beer (1, 2-1)

  Das ist nicht mein Bier! That's not my problem!

der **Bierbauch, ⸚e** beer belly (5)

der **Biergarten, ⸚** beer garden (5)

das **Bierglas, ⸚er** beer glass (1)

bieten, bot, geboten to offer (4)

das **Bild, -er** picture; painting (1, 5-2)

das **Billard** *(sing)* billiards (2)

billig cheap (2-2)

bin: Ich bin's. It's me. (5-2)

die **Biochemie** biochemistry (2)

biografisch biographical (3)

der **Bio-Laden, ⸚** organic food store (9)

die **Biologie** biology (1)

die **Birne, -n** pear (4)

bis until *(prep + acc)* (2-1); *(sub conj)* (6)

  Bis später! See you later! (1-1)

  von ... bis from . . . to (1-2)

bisschen: ein bisschen a bit (1-2)

bitte please (E, 1-1)

  Wie bitte? Pardon? (E-1)

  Bitte schön! You're welcome! (6-2)

blau blue (1-1); drunk (3)

  in Blau in blue (3)

der **Blazer, -** blazer (2)

bleiben, blieb, ist geblieben to stay, to remain (3, 4-2)

der **Blick, -e** look (6)

blitzen: es blitzt it's lightning (1)

die **Blockade, -n** blockade (11-1)

blockieren to block (11-1)

blöd stupid; dumb (2-1)

bloggen to blog (2-1)

blond blond (1, 3-2)

blühen to blossom; to flourish (5-1)

die **Blume, -n** flower (1, 6-2)

das **Blumengeschäft, -e** flower shop (6)

die **Blumenzwiebel, -n** (flower) bulb (7)

die **Bluse, -n** blouse (1, 2-2)

das **Blut** blood (1)

die **Blüte, -n** blossom (5)

die **Bockwurst, ⸚e** smoked sausage (9)

der **Bodensee** Lake Constance (4)

das **Boot, -e** boat (1)

Bord: an Bord on board (6-2)

die **Botanik** botany (2)

das **Boulevardblatt, ⸚er** tabloid (10)

der **Braten, -** roast (9-1)

die **Bratkartoffeln** *(pl)* fried potatoes (4-1)

brauchen to need (3-2); to take *(of time)* (4)

die **Brauerei, -en** brewery (7)

braun brown (1-1)

das **Brett, -er** board

  das Schwarze Brett bulletin board (8)

der **Brief, -e** letter (E)

der **Briefkasten, ⸚** mailbox (5)

die **Briefmarke, -n** stamp (2-1)

der **Briefträger, -/die Briefträgerin, -nen** letter carrier (7-2)

die **Brille, -n** (eye)glasses (5-2)

bringen, brachte, gebracht to bring (5, 6-2)

der **Brokkoli** broccoli (4-1)

die **Broschüre, -n** brochure (5-1)

das **Brot, -e** bread; sandwich (1, 4-1)

das **Brötchen, -** roll (4-1)

  ein belegtes Brötchen sandwich (2)

die **Brücke, -n** bridge (9-2)

der **Bruder, ⸚** brother (1, 3-1)

brünett brunette (3-2)

die **Brust, ⸚e** breast; chest (6-1)

das **Buch, ⸚er** book (1-1)

der **Buchdruck** printing (10)

die **Buche, -n** beech tree (11)

buchen to book (5-2)

die **Bücherei, -en** library (7)

das **Bücherregal, -e** bookcase (8-1)

der **Buchhalter, –**/die
Buchhalterin, -nen
bookkeeper (1)
sich **buchstabieren: Das
buchstabiert sich …** That's
spelled . . . (1)
das **Bügeleisen, –** iron *(for clothes)*
(8-2)
bügeln to iron (8-2)
der **Bulle, -n** bull (1)
das **Bündel, –** bundle (10-1)
der **Bundeskanzler, –**/die
Bundeskanzlerin, -nen federal
chancellor (12)
das **Bundesland, ̈er** German state
(6)
die **Bundesliga, Bundesligen**
premier league *(of sports)* (5)
das **Bundesministerium,
Bundesministerien** federal
ministry (3)
die **Bundesrepublik Deutschland
(die BRD)** the Federal
Republic of Germany (the
FRG) (1-1)
der **Bundestag** German parliament
(7)
die **Burg, -en** castle (10)
der **Bürger, –**/die **Bürgerin, -nen**
citizen (11-1)
das **Büro, -s** office (E)
der **Bürokaufmann,
Bürokaufleute**/die
Bürokauffrau, -en office
administrator (12)
bürsten to brush (9)
der **Bus, -se** bus (E, 3-1)
der **Busch, ̈e** bush (10-1)
buschig bushy (2)
die **Bushaltestelle, -n** bus stop
(10-2)
die **Buslinie, -n** bus route (5)
die **Butter** butter (1, 4-1)
Es ist alles in Butter. Everything's
going smoothly. (7)

C

der **Camembert** Camembert
(cheese) (10)
campen to camp (5-1)

campen gehen to go camping (1)
das **Campen** camping (5-1)
der **Campingplatz, ̈e**
campground; campsite (5-1)
der **Campus, –** campus (1)
der **Cappuccino, -s** cappuccino (10)
die **CD, -s** compact disc, CD (3-2)
der **CD-Spieler, –** CD player (3-2)
der **Cent, –** cent (6)
der **Champagner** champagne (7)
der **Champignon, -s** mushroom
(12)
(die) **Chanukka** Hanukkah (7)
der **Charakter, -e** character (9)
charakterisieren to characterize (8)
der **Cheddar** cheddar (cheese) (7)
der **Chef, -s**/die **Chefin, -nen** boss
(5-2)
chemiefrei chemical-free (9)
chinesisch *(adj)* Chinese (4)
der **Chor, ̈e** choir (6)
die **Chronik** chronicle (11)
Ciao! Bye! (E-1)
clever smart, clever (11-2)
die **Cola, -s** cola (2-1)
das **College, -s** college (7)
die **Comics** comics (3)
der **Computer, –** computer (2-1)
das **Computerspiel, -e** computer
game (4, 7-1)
cool cool *(excellent)* (2-2)
die **Couch, -es** couch (8-1)
der **Couchtisch, -e** coffee table
(8-1)
die **Currywurst** curry sausage (9)

D

d.h., das heißt i.e., that is (11-2)
da then (1)
das **Dach, ̈er** roof (8-2)
eins aufs Dach kriegen to be
bawled out (8)
dafür for it (5-2)
dagegen against it (5-2)
damalig at the time, former (7)
damals back then; at that time
(6, 10-1)
die **Dame, -n** lady (10)
die **Damenabteilung, -en**
women's department (7-1)

damit so that *(sub conj)* (4)
der **Dampf, ̈e** steam (11)
die **Dampfnudel, -n** dumpling (9)
danach accordingly (10)
dänisch *(adj)* Danish (2)
der **Dank** thanks
Gott sei Dank! Thank God!
(10-2)
Vielen Dank! Many thanks! (6-2)
danke thank you (E-1)
Danke, gut. Fine, thanks. (E-1)
Danke schön! Thank you! (6-2)
danken *(+ dat)* to thank (2, 7-2)
danklos thankless (12)
dann then (E, 1-1)
das this; that (1)
dass that *(sub conj)* (5)
dasselbe the same (7, 9-2)
das **Datum, Daten** date; *(pl)* data (5)
dauern to last (4-1)
dauernd constantly (8)
der **Daumen, –** thumb (6-1)
Ich drücke dir die Daumen.
I'll keep my fingers crossed for
you. (9)
die **Decke, -n** ceiling (8-1)
decken: den Tisch decken to set
the table (7-1)
dein, dein, deine your (2)
die **Demokratie, -n** democracy
(1, 11-1)
denken, dachte, gedacht to think
(2-2)
denken an *(+ acc)* to think of,
about (11-2)
denkste that's what you think (5)
denn because, for *(coord conj)* (1-2)
derselbe, dasselbe, dieselbe the
same (7, 9-2)
deshalb therefore; that's why (4-2)
der **Designer, –**/die **Designerin,
-nen** designer (8-2)
detailliert in detail (10)
der **Detektiv, -e** detective (8)
deutsch *(adj)* German (1)
das **Deutsch** German *(language)* (1)
auf Deutsch in German (4-1)
der/die **Deutsche, -n** German
(person) (1-1)
der **Deutschkurs, -e** German
course; German class (4)

(das) **Deutschland** Germany (1)

deutschsprachig German-speaking (2, 9-1)

der **Dezember** December (1-2)

der **Dialekt, -e** dialect (10-1)

der **Dialog, -e** dialogue (4)

der **Dichter, -/**die **Dichterin, -nen** writer; poet

dick thick; fat (2-2)

dickköpfig stubborn (11-2)

der **Dienstag** Tuesday (1-2)

  am Dienstagabend on Tuesday evening (2)

  am Dienstagmorgen on Tuesday morning (2)

  am Dienstagnachmittag on Tuesday afternoon (2)

dienstags Tuesdays, on Tuesdays (2)

dieselbe the same (7, 9-2)

dieser, dieses, diese this (2)

diesmal this time (5)

die **Diktatur, -en** dictatorship (5, 11-1)

das **Ding, -e** thing (2, 3-1)

das **Diplom** diploma (1)

  das Diplom machen to do or take one's diploma (1)

direkt directly (6)

die **Disco, -s** disco (1)

  in die Disco to the disco (1-2)

die **Diskette, -n** disk (1)

die **Diskrepanz, -en** discrepancy (12-1)

diskutieren to discuss (8)

die **Diva, -s** diva (12)

disziplinlos undisciplined (12)

der **DJ, -s** DJ (2)

doch but; anyway (4); *used to contradict negative statement or question* (10)

das **Dokument, -e** document (5)

der **Dokumentarfilm, -e** documentary film (3)

der **Dollar, -s** dollar (6)

  fünfundzwanzig Dollar twenty-five dollars (6)

die **Donau** Danube *(river)* (1)

der **Donner** thunder (2)

donnern: es donnert it's thundering (1)

der **Donnerstag** Thursday (1-2) *(see also **Dienstag**)*

doof stupid; dumb (2-1)

doppelt double (3)

das **Doppelzimmer, -** double room (8)

das **Dorf, -̈er** village (2, 5-1)

dort there (1-2)

die **Dose, -n** can (8-2)

der **Dosenöffner, -** can opener (7, 8-2)

downloaden to download (2-1)

die **Drachme, -n** drachma *(former Greek currency)* (9)

draußen outside (4)

die **Dreiergruppe, -n** group of three (10)

dreisprachig trilingual (9)

das **Dreivierteljahr** nine months (7)

der **Dressman, Dressmen** male model (2)

die **Drogensucht** drug addiction (12)

die **Drogerie, -n** drugstore (9-2)

drucken to print (10-1)

drücken to press (9)

  Ich drücke dir die Daumen. I'll keep my fingers crossed for you. (9)

der **Drucker, -** printer (3)

die **Druckerei** print shop (10)

dumm stupid; dumb (2-1)

dunkel dark (1-2)

dünn thin; skinny (2-2)

durch *(prep + acc)* through (2)

durch·lesen (liest durch), las durch, durchgelesen to read through (4-2)

durch·machen to go through (11)

die **Durchsage, -n** announcement (10)

der **Durchschnitt, -e** average (10)

  durchschnittlich average; on average (4, 10-1)

dürfen (darf), durfte, gedurft to be allowed to, be permitted to, may (4)

der **Durst** thirst (5)

  Ich habe Durst. I'm thirsty. (5-2)

die **Dusche, -n** shower (4, 8-1)

  unter die Dusche gehen to have a shower (4)

sich **duschen** to take a shower (9-2)

der **DVD-Spieler, -** DVD player (9)

E

eben: So bin ich eben. That's just the way I am. (4-1)

ebenfalls also (11-2)

echt real, really (2)

  echt spitze really great (2-2)

die **Ecke, -n** corner (5-2)

EDV = Elektronische Datenverarbeitung data processing (12)

der **EDV-Fachmann, EDV-Fachleute/**die **EDV-Fachfrau, -en** data processing specialist (12)

egal no matter, regardless (11)

  Das ist mir egal. I don't care. (7-2)

die **Ehefrau** wife (6)

ehemalig former (11-2)

das **Ehepaar, -e** married couple (9-1)

ehrenamtlich on a voluntary basis (7)

ehrlich honest (4, 12-1)

das **Ei, -er** egg (4-1)

  Er gleicht seinem Bruder wie ein Ei dem anderen. He and his brother are as alike as two peas in a pod. (7)

eifersüchtig auf *(+ acc)* jealous of (12-2)

eigen own (8-2)

  etwas in die eigene Hand nehmen to take something into one's own hands (11-2)

eigentlich actually (11-1)

die **Eile** hurry (10)

  Es hat keine Eile. There's no rush. (10)

ein, ein, eine a; an; one (1)

einander each other, one another (E)

die **Einbauküche, -n** built-in kitchen (12)

eineinhalb one and a half (4)

einfach simple, simply (7-2); ordinary (10-1)

ein·fallen (fällt ein), fiel ein, ist eingefallen (7)

Mir fällt nichts ein. I can't think of anything. (7-2)

der **Einfluss, -̈e** influence (10-2)

der **Eingang, -̈e** entrance (10)

die **Einheit, -en** unity, whole (7)

einheitlich common (11)

das **Einhorn, -̈er** unicorn (1)

die **Einkäufe** *(pl)* shopping, purchases (9)

ein·kaufen to shop, to go shopping (5-2)

das **Einkaufen** shopping (4)

die **Einkaufsgewohnheit, -en** shopping habit (9)

die **Einkaufsmöglichkeit, -en** shopping facility (5)

ein·laden (lädt ein), lud ein, eingeladen to invite (4-2)

einmal once (7-2)

  noch (ein)mal once more; (over) again (7-2)

ein·marschieren to invade (11)

ein·packen to pack (4)

einsam lonely (7)

ein·schlafen (schläft ein), schlief ein, ist eingeschlafen to fall asleep (4-2)

ein·schlagen (schlägt ein), schlug ein, eingeschlagen to wrap (7)

ein·steigen, stieg ein, ist eingestiegen to board, get on *(a train, bus, etc.)* (4-2)

ein·tauchen to dip (9)

ein·treten für to advocate for (12-1)

der **Eintritt** admission (2)

der **Einwanderer, -/**die **Einwanderin, -nen** immigrant (6-1)

ein·wandern, wanderte ein, ist eingewandert to immigrate (6-1)

der **Einwohner, -/**die **Einwohnerin, -nen** inhabitant (2)

das **Einzelkind, -er** only child (3-1)

das **Einzelzimmer, -** single room (8)

einzig single; only (9-1)

das **Eis** ice; ice cream (4-1)

der **Eiserne Vorhang** Iron Curtain (11-2)

(das) **Eishockey** (ice)hockey (1, 2-1)

eisig icy (2)

elegant elegant (2-2)

der **Elektroinstallateur, -e/**die **Elektroinstallateurin, -nen** electrician (12)

das **Elektronikgeschäft, -e** electronics store (3)

das **Element, -e** element (5)

der **Ellbogen, -** elbow (1)

die **Eltern** *(pl)* parents (2, 3-1)

die **Elternzeit** parental leave (3)

die **E-Mail, -s** e-mail (2-1)

die **E-Mail-Adresse, -n** e-mail address (2)

emailen to e-mail (2-1)

der **Emigrant, -en, -en/**die **Emigrantin, -nen** emigrant (6-1)

emigrieren to emigrate (8)

die **Empfehlung, -en** recommendation (6)

das **Ende, -n** end (1, 4-2)

  Ende Juli (at) the end of July (1-2)

  zu Ende sein to be over (2-2)

enden to end (11)

endlich finally, at last (4-2)

die **Energie, -n** energy (3, 8-2)

englisch *(adj)* English (7)

das **Englisch** English *(language)* (1)

  auf Englisch in English (1)

englischsprachig English-speaking (5)

der **Enkel, -** grandson, grandchild (3-1)

die **Enkelin, -nen** granddaughter (3-1)

enorm enormous (8-2)

enterben to disinherit (12)

die **Entfernung, -en** distance (5)

entgehen, entging, ist entgangen to escape (12)

entlang along (11)

die **Entscheidung, -en** decision (5)

sich **entschuldigen** to apologize (9-2)

Entschuldigung! Excuse me! (E-1)

entweder ... oder either . . . or (4)

entwerfen (entwirft), entwarf, entworfen to design (6, 9-2)

entwickeln to develop (4)

der **Entwurf, -̈e** design (9)

die **Epoche, -n** epoch (9)

die **Erde** earth; ground (4, 10-2)

ereignisreich eventful (11)

erfahren (erfährt), erfuhr, erfahren to find out (11)

die **Erfahrung, -en** experience (6)

erfinden, erfand, erfunden to invent (10-1)

der **Erfinder, -/**die **Erfinderin, -nen** inventor (10-1)

die **Erfindung, -en** invention (10-1)

der **Erfolg, -e** success (7)

erfolglos unsuccessful(ly) (12)

erfolgreich successful(ly) (4-2)

erfrieren, erfror, ist erfroren to freeze to death (11)

erfüllt fulfilled (12)

ergänzen to complete (1); to supply (7)

erhältlich available (3)

die **Erinnerung, -en** memory (11)

sich **erkälten** to catch a cold (9-2)

erkältet sein to have a cold (12-2)

die **Erkältung, -en** cold (12-2)

  eine schwere Erkältung a bad cold (12-2)

erkennen, erkannte, erkannt to recognize (3-2)

erklärbar explicable (12)

erklären to explain; to declare (5, 6-2)

erleben to experience (11)

das **Erlebnis, -se** experience (11-2)

ermöglichen to make possible (4)

ermorden to murder (11-1)

erneuerbar renewable (8)

ernst serious (8)

eröffnen to open up *(shop)* (4)

erraten (errät), erriet, erraten to guess (9)

erscheinen, erschien, ist erschienen to appear (10)

erschießen, erschoss, erschossen to shoot dead (11)

erschrecken to frighten, to shock (11)

ersetzen (durch) to replace (with) (11)

erst *(adv)* not until (1-1)

erst- first (1, 3-2)

   zum ersten Mal for the first time (8-2)

erstklassig first-class (3)

die **Erstkommunion** (sing) First Communion (7)

ertrinken, ertrank, ist ertrunken to drown (6)

erwachsen werden (wird), wurde, ist geworden to grow up (become adult) (11-2)

erzählen to tell (a story) (2-2, 6-1)

   erzählen von to tell about (11)

die **Erzählung, -en** story, narrative (6)

der **Erzbischof, ⸚e** archbishop (3)

der **Erziehungsurlaub** child-rearing leave (3)

der **Esel, -** donkey (3)

die **Eselsbrücke, -n** mnemonic device (10)

essbar edible (12)

essen (isst), aß, gegessen to eat (3-2)

   zu Mittag essen to have lunch (4-1)

   zu Abend essen to have supper (4-1)

das **Essen** meal, food (7)

der **Essig** vinegar (9-2)

der **Esslöffel, -** tablespoon (9-1)

das **Esszimmer, -** dining room (8-1)

die **Etage, -n** floor, story (7)

etwa approximately (E, 7-2)

etwas something (5-2)

euer, euer, eure your (2)

der **Euro, -s** euro (common European currency) (1, 2-2)

   drei Euro das Stück three euros apiece (7)

(das) **Europa** Europe (1)

der **Europäer, -**/die **Europäerin, -nen** European (person) (9)

europäisch (adj) European (9)

   die **Europäische Union (die EU)** the European Union (the EU) (3)

der **Euroschein, -e** euro bill (9)

evangelisch protestant (3)

das **Experiment, -e** experiment (5-2)

der **Experte, -n, -n**/die **Expertin, -nen** expert (9)

der **Export, -e** export (4)

exportieren to export (4)

das **Extrablatt, ⸚er** special edition (11)

extravagant extravagant (5)

die **Extrawurst: eine Extrawurst wollen** to want special treatment (7)

F

die **Fabel, -n** fable (10)

fabelhaft fabulous (5)

das **Fach, ⸚er** field of study, subject (2-2)

die **Fahne, -n** flag (7)

fahren (fährt), fuhr, ist gefahren to drive, to go (3-2)

der **Fahrer, -**/die **Fahrerin, -nen** driver (5)

der **Fahrplan, ⸚e** train or bus schedule (4-2)

das **Fahrrad, ⸚er** bicycle (3-1)

der **Fahrradabstellplatz, ⸚e** bicycle parking area (8)

der **Fahrradhelm, -e** bicycle helmet (7-1)

der **Fahrradverleih, -e** bike rental (5-1)

die **Fahrt, -en** ride (6)

das **Fahrzeug, -e** vehicle (3-1)

fair fair (1)

der **Fall, ⸚e** fall (11)

fallen (fällt), fiel, ist gefallen to fall (6)

   Der Apfel fällt nicht weit vom Stamm. Like father, like son. (7)

   Er ist nicht auf den Kopf gefallen. He's no fool. (6)

   Mir fällt nichts ein. I can't think of anything. (7-2)

fällen to fell (6)

falls in case (8)

falsch wrong, incorrect, false (E, 1-1)

die **Familie, -n** family (E, 3-1)

das **Familienbrunch** family brunch (7)

der **Familienname, -ns, -n** last name (E, 3-2)

die **Familienpolitik** family policy (3)

der **Fan, -s** fan (2)

fangen (fängt), fing, gefangen to catch (10-1)

die **Fantasie** imagination (3-1)

fantasielos unimaginative(ly) (12)

fantastisch fantastic (5-2)

die **Farbe, -n** color (1)

   Welche Farbe hat Lisas Bluse? What color is Lisa's blouse? (1)

färben to color, to dye (8)

der **Farbfernseher, -** color TV (10)

das **Farbfoto, -s** color photo (7)

die **Farm, -en** farm (6)

der **Farmer, -** farmer (6)

die **Fassade** façade (10)

fast almost (1-1)

faul lazy (7-2)

der **Februar** February (1-2)

die **Feder, -n** feather (2)

der **Federball** badminton; badminton birdie (1)

   Federball spielen to play badminton (1)

fehlen to be missing (8)

der **Fehler, -** mistake; error (11-2)

fehlerlos error-free (12)

feiern to celebrate (4, 7-1)

der **Feiertag, -e** holiday (7-1)

das **Feinkostgeschäft, -e** gourmet foods store (2)

das **Feld, -er** field (5-1)

das **Fenster, -** window (1, 8-1)

die **Ferien** (pl) vacation (generally of students) (5-1)

   Ferien machen to go on vacation (5-1)

das **Ferienhaus, ⸚er** vacation home (8)

der **Ferienjob, -s** summer job (6-2)

die **Ferienzeit** holiday time (5)

fern far (away) (11-2)

fern·sehen (sieht fern), sah fern, ferngesehen to watch TV (4-2)

das **Fernsehen** TV (7)

der **Fernseher, –** television set (4-2)

  vor dem Fernseher in front of the TV (4-2)

das **Fernsehprogramm, –e** TV show (3)

fertig ready; finished (4-1); *(with verbs)* finish (4)

fertig lesen (liest fertig), las fertig, fertig gelesen to finish reading (7)

fertig schreiben, schrieb fertig, fertig geschrieben to finish writing (4)

fesseln to captivate, to grab (10)

das **Fest, –e** celebration; festival (2, 7-1)

die **Fete, –n** party (7-2)

das **Fett** fat (9)

fettig fatty (2)

fett gedruckt in boldface (10)

die **Figur** *(sing)* figure; physique (12-1)

der **Film, –e** film (1, 2-2)

der **Filmstar, –s** filmstar *(male or female)* (1)

die **Finanzen** *(pl)* finances (5)

der **Finanzier, –s** financier (5)

finanzieren to finance (5-2)

die **Finanzwirtschaft** finance (1)

finden, fand, gefunden to find (1-2)

der **Finger, –** finger (1, 6-1)

der **Fingernagel, ¨** fingernail (1)

die **Firma, Firmen** business, company (4-2)

der **Fisch, –e** fish (1, 4-1)

fischen to fish (2)

fit fit (4)

das **Fitnesscenter, –** fitness center (5-1)

das **Fitnessstudio, –s** fitness studio (12)

Fitnesstraining machen to work out (2-1)

der **Flammkuchen** tarte flambée (9)

die **Flasche, –n** bottle (5-1)

das **Fleisch** *(sing)* meat (2, 4-1)

der **Fleischer, –/die Fleischerin, –nen** butcher (9)

die **Fleischerei, –en** butcher shop (7)

fleischlos meatless (12)

fleißig hard-working (7-2)

fliegen, flog, ist geflogen to fly (1-2)

fliehen, floh, ist geflohen to flee (11-1)

fließen, floss, ist geflossen to flow (5-1)

der **Flohmarkt, ¨e** flea market (8)

die **Flucht** flight *(as in to flee)* (11)

flüchten, ist geflüchtet to flee; to seek refuge (11-1)

der **Flüchtling, –e** refugee (11-1)

der **Fluchtweg, –e** escape route (11)

der **Flug, ¨e** flight (3-2)

der **Flugbegleiter, –/die Flugbegleiterin, –nen** flight attendant (12)

der **Flügel, –** wing (3-1)

der **Flughafen, ¨** airport (3-2)

die **Flugnummer, –n** flight number (3-2)

der **Flugplatz, ¨e** airport (11)

das **Flugzeug, –e** airplane (3-1)

der **Flur, –e** hall (8-1)

der **Fluss, ¨e** river (2, 5-1)

folgen, folgte, ist gefolgt *(+ dat)* to follow (7)

folgend following (6)

der **Föhn, –e** blow-dryer (9-2)

föhnen: sich *(dat)* **die Haare föhnen** to blow-dry one's hair (9-2)

das **Footballteam, –s** football team (1)

die **Form, –en** shape; form (6-1)

die **Formel, –n** formula (12-1)

fort away (7)

das **Foto, –s** photo (1, 4-2)

das **Fotoalbum, –alben** (2)

das **Fotogeschäft, –e** photo store (2)

die **Fotografie, –n** photograph (8)

fotografieren to photograph, take a picture (2-1)

das **Fotomodell, –e** model (2)

der **Foxterrier, –** fox terrier (3)

die **Frage, –n** question (1-2)

  eine Frage beantworten to answer a question (9-1)

  eine Frage stellen to ask a question (7-2)

  Das kommt nicht in Frage! That's out of the question! (9-2)

fragen to ask (1-2)

  fragen nach to ask about (10)

der **Franken, –** franc *(former French currency)* (9)

französisch *(adj)* French (7)

Frau Mrs., Ms. (E-1)

die **Frau, –en** woman; wife (1, 2-2)

das **Frauenstimmrecht** women's right to vote (12)

(das) **Fräulein, –** Miss (5)

frei free *(of time)* (2, 5-1)

die **Freiheit** *(sing)* freedom (11-2)

das **Freilandei, –er** free-range egg (7)

der **Freitag** Friday (1-2) *(see also* **Dienstag***)*

die **Freizeit** free time; leisure time (5-1)

fressen (frisst), fraß, gefressen to eat *(of animals)* (2)

die **Freude, –n** joy, happiness (11)

sich **freuen auf** *(+ acc)* to look forward to (11-2)

sich **freuen über** *(+ acc)* to be happy about; to be pleased with (7, 11-2)

der **Freund, –e** *(male)* friend, boyfriend (1-2)

der **Freundeskreis** circle of friends (7)

die **Freundin, –nen** *(female)* friend, girlfriend (1-2)

freundlich friendly (2, 3-1)

die **Freundlichkeit** friendliness (11)

die **Freundschaft, –en** friendship (2-2)

der **Frieden** peace (11-1)

frieren, fror, gefroren to be cold (10-1)

frisch fresh (1)

der **Frischkäse** *(sing)* cream cheese (4)

die **Frisur, –en** hairdo; hair style (5-2)
froh happy (7)
fromm pious (10-1)
früh early (4-1)
  morgen früh tomorrow morning (2)
das **Frühjahr** spring (7)
der **Frühling** spring (1-2)
das **Frühstück** breakfast (1, 4-1)
  zum Frühstück for breakfast (4-1)
frühstücken to have breakfast (4-1)
die **Frühstücksgewohnheit, –en** breakfast habit (4)
der **Fuchs, ⸚e** fox (1)
fühlen to feel (9-2)
  sich **wohl fühlen** to feel well; to feel at home (9-2)
der **Führerschein, –e** driver's license (7-2)
füllen to fill (9-1)
für *(prep + acc)* for (1)
die **Furche, –n** furrow (10)
der **Fuß, ⸚e** foot (1, 6-1)
  Hand und Fuß haben to make sense (6)
  zu Fuß gehen to go on foot, to walk (4-2)
der **Fußball, ⸚e** soccer; soccer ball (1)
  Fußball spielen to play soccer (1)
das **Fußballspiel, –e** soccer game (5)
das **Fußballstadion, -stadien** soccer stadium (5)
die **Fußballweltmeisterschaft, –en** soccer World Cup (5)
der **Fußboden, ⸚** floor (8-1)
die **Fußgängerzone, –n** pedestrian zone (8-2)
füttern to feed (6-2)

G

die **Gabel, –n** fork (9-1)
gähnen to yawn (4)
galoppieren to gallop (10-1)
die **Gans, ⸚e** goose (7, 9-1)
der **Gänsebraten** roast goose (9)
ganz quite; very; all; whole (3); absolutely; completely (10)

die **ganze Familie** the whole family (3-2)
  ganz kurz very short (3-2)
gar tender *(in cooking)* (9)
gar nicht not at all (1-1)
gar nichts nothing at all (7)
der **Garantieschein, –e** warranty (7)
die **Garderobe, –n** front hall closet (8-1)
der **Garten, ⸚** garden (1, 5-1)
die **Gartenterrasse, –n** garden terrace, patio (8)
der **Gärtner, –/die Gärtnerin, –nen** gardener (E)
die **Gärtnerei, –en** nursery (7)
der **Gast, ⸚e** guest; customer *(in a restaurant)* (3, 7-2)
das **Gästezimmer, –** guest room (8)
das **Gasthaus, ⸚er** restaurant (8, 9-1)
die **Gaststätte, –n** restaurant (9)
die **Gastronomie** gastronomy (9-1)
das **Gebäude, –** building (8-2)
geben (gibt), gab, gegeben to give (3-2)
  es gibt *(+ acc)* there is, there are (3-2)
das **Gebirge** mountain range (5-1)
geblümt flowered (11)
geboren born (1)
  Wann bist du geboren? When were you born? (6-1)
der **Geburtsort, –e** birthplace (6-1)
der **Geburtstag, –e** birthday (6-2)
  Herzliche Glückwünsche zum Geburtstag! Happy Birthday! (7-1)
  zum Geburtstag for one's birthday (6, 7-1)
  zum Geburtstag gratulieren to wish a Happy Birthday (7-2)
das **Geburtstagsgeschenk, –e** birthday present (7)
die **Geburtstagskarte, –n** birthday card (7)
die **Gedenktafel, –n** commemorative plaque (10)
das **Gedicht, –e** poem (10, 12-2)
gefallen (gefällt), gefiel, gefallen *(+ dat)* to like (7)

gefallen an *(+ dat)* to like about (7)
  Diese Jacke gefällt mir. I like this jacket. (7-2)
das **Gefängnis, –se** prison (11)
das **Gefühl, –e** feeling (11-2)
gefühllos unfeeling(ly) (12)
gegen *(prep + acc)* against; around *(time)* (5)
die **Gegend, –en** area (3, 11-2)
das **Gegenteil, –e** opposite (1)
gegenüber across *(the hall, the street, etc.)* (8-1)
das **Gehalt, ⸚er** pay, wages (12-1)
gehen, ging, ist gegangen to go (1-1)
  Wie geht es Ihnen?/Wie geht's? How are you? (E-1)
  zu Fuß gehen to go on foot, to walk (4-2)
gehören *(+ dat)* to belong to (7-2)
gekleidet dressed (10-1)
gelb yellow (1-1)
das **Geld** money (1, 2-2)
  Mir ist das Geld ausgegangen. I ran out of money. (12)
der **Geldschein, –e** banknote, (money) bill (9-2)
die **Geldtasche, –n** wallet (7-1)
die **Gelegenheit, –en** opportunity (11)
geliebt beloved (5)
gelten (gilt), galt, gegolten to be considered (9)
gemein common (10); together (11)
gemeinsam common (2-2)
die **Gemeinschaft, –en** community (8)
das **Gemüse** *(sing)* vegetables (4-1)
gemütlich cozy; comfortable (5-1)
genau exact(ly); careful(ly) (4-1)
der **General, ⸚e** general (10)
die **Generation, –en** generation (7)
die **Genetik** genetics (2)
genial brilliant (3)
genug enough (4-2)
der **Genuss, ⸚e** *(culinary)* delight (10)
die **Geographie** geography (1)
geometrisch geometric (8)
gepflegt: gepflegte Biersorten excellent choice of beers (8)

gerade just, just now (7-1); currently (10)

die **Geranie, -n** geranium (8)

das **Gerät, -e** utensil; appliance (8-2)

das **Gericht, -e** dish *(food)* (4, 9-2)

die **Germanistik** *(sing)* German Studies (1)

gern (lieber, am liebsten) gladly (2)

   jemand *(acc)* **gern haben** to like somebody (2)

   Ich koche gern. I like to cook. (2-1)

die **Gesamtbevölkerung** total population (12)

das **Geschäft, -e** business; store (2, 3-2)

der **Geschäftsmann**, die **Geschäftsleute** businessman (3-2)

der **Geschäftspartner, -**/die **Geschäftspartnerin, -nen** business partner (4)

das **Geschenk, -e** present, gift (7-1)

die **Geschenkkarte, -n** gift card (7-1)

die **Geschichte, -n** history; story (6-1)

geschickt clever; coordinated (12)

geschieden divorced (3-1)

das **Geschirr** *(sing)* dishes (9-1)

die **Geschirrspülmaschine, -n** dishwasher (8)

das **Geschlecht, -er** gender (12-1)

geschlitzt slit (11)

der **Geschmack** *(sing)* taste (9)

   den Geschmack treffen to appeal to the taste (9)

geschmacklos tasteless (5-2)

geschmackvoll tasteful (5-2)

die **Geschwister** *(pl)* sisters and brothers, siblings (3-1)

die **Geselligkeit** camaraderie (4)

die **Gesellschaft, -en** company (5); society (12)

das **Gesetz, -e** law (12-1)

das **Gesicht, -er** face (6-1)

das **Gespräch, -e** conversation (1)

die **Gestalt** stature, build (6)

gestern yesterday (3-2)

   gestern Nacht last night (2)

gestreift striped (11)

gesund healthy (3-2)

das **Getränk, -e** beverage, drink (2-1)

getrennt separate(ly); separated (2)

   getrennt leben to be separated (3)

das **Getue** carrying on (12)

gewinnen, gewann, gewonnen to win (7, 10-2)

die **Gewohnheit, -en** (4) habit

gießen, goss, gegossen to water (6-2)

die **Gitarre, -n** guitar (2-1)

das **Glas, ⸚er** glass (1, 4-1)

   die Nase zu tief ins Glas stecken to drink too much (6)

   ein Glas Orangensaft a glass of orange juice (4-1)

   zwei Glas Milch two glasses of milk (4)

glatt straight *(of hair)*; smooth (3-2)

glauben to believe, to think (1-2)

gleich right away (4-2); same; right, directly; equal(ly) (11, 12-1)

   gleich um die Ecke right around the corner (5)

gleichberechtigt sein to have equal rights (12-1)

die **Gleichberechtigung** equal rights; equality (12-1)

gleichwertig of equal value (12)

glitzern to glitter (3)

das **Glück** luck (10-1)

   Viel Glück! Good luck!, Lots of luck! (10-1)

   zum Glück fortunately, luckily (12-1)

glücklich happy (7-2)

der **Glückwunsch, ⸚e** congratulations, best wishes *(pl)* (7)

   Herzliche Glückwünsche zum Geburtstag! Happy Birthday! (7-1)

die **Glückwunschanzeige, -n** congratulatory announcement (7)

die **Glückwunschkarte, -n** (congratulatory) card (10)

das **Gold** gold (2)

golden gold (3)

der **Goldschmied, -e**/ die **Goldschmiedin, -nen** goldsmith (6)

(das) **Golf** golf (2-1)

(der) **Gott** God (10)

   Gott sei Dank! Thank God! (8, 10-2)

der **Gourmet, -s** gourmet (7)

der **Gouverneur, -e**/die **Gouverneurin, -nen** governor (6)

das **Grab, ⸚er** grave (2)

der **Graben, ⸚** trench (11)

der **Grabstein, -e** gravestone, tombstone (10)

der **Grad, -e** degree (E)

die **Grafik, -en** graphic (11-1)

das **Gramm** gram (9-1)

die **Grapefruit, -s** grapefruit (4-1)

der **Grapefruitsaft** *(sing)* grapefruit juice (4)

das **Gras, ⸚er** grass (1)

gratulieren *(+ dat)* to congratulate (7-2)

   zum Geburtstag gratulieren to wish a Happy Birthday (7-2)

grau gray (1-1)

das **Grauen** horror (7)

die **Grenze, -n** border (11-1)

grenzen an *(+ acc)* to border on (11)

der **Grieche, -n, -n**/die **Griechin, -nen** Greek *(person)* (9)

griechisch *(adj)* Greek (7)

grillen to grill (8-1)

groß big, tall (1, 2-1)

die **Größe, -n** height; size (6-1)

die **Großeltern** *(pl)* grandparents (3-1)

das **Großherzogtum** grand duchy (12)

die **Großmutter, ⸚** grandmother (3-1)

größtenteils for the most part, largely (10)

der **Großvater, ⸚** grandfather (3-1)

Grüezi! Hello! *(Swiss dialect)* (E)

grün green (E, 1-1)

der **Grund, ⸚e** reason (4, 12-1)

gründen to found (4)

das **Grundgesetz** Basic Law *(constitution of Germany)* (12)

die **Grundschule, -n** elementary school; primary school (12)

die **Gründung,** -en founding (11)

grunzen to grunt (3)

die **Gruppe, -n** group (2)

der **Gruß,** ⸚e greeting (7)

  Herzliche Grüße Kind regards *(closing in a letter)* (7)

grüßen to greet; to say hello (10-1)

  Grüß dich! Hello! Hi! (E-1)

  Grüß Gott! Hello! *(in Southern Germany and Austria)* (E)

die **Grußformel, -n** greeting (E)

gucken to look (12)

die **Gulaschsuppe** goulash soup (9)

der **Gulden, -** guilder *(former Dutch currency)* (9)

gurgeln to gargle (12)

der **Gürtel, -** belt (2-2)

gut good, well (E, 1-2)

  Guten Appetit! Enjoy your meal! (9-1)

  Guten Tag! Hello! Hi! (E-1)

  Mach's gut! Take care! (1-2)

  Schon gut. It's all right. (9)

der **Gutschein, -e** voucher (7-1)

das **Gymnasium, Gymnasien** *(academic)* high school (1, 6-2)

H

das **Haar, -e** hair (1, 6-1)

  ein Haar in der Suppe finden to find fault with something (9)

die **Haarbürste, -n** hairbrush (9-2)

haarig hairy (2)

der **Haarschnitt, -e** haircut (5-2)

haben (hat), hatte, gehabt to have (1, 2-1)

  jemand *(acc)* **gern haben** to like somebody (2)

der **Hafen,** ⸚ harbor (11)

der **Hahn,** ⸚e rooster (4)

der **Hai, -e** shark (10)

halb half (2)

  halb zwei half past one (2)

die **Halbgeschwister** *(pl)* half sisters and brothers (2)

die **Hälfte, -n** half (11-2)

die **Halle, -n** hall (1)

Hallo! Hello! Hi! (E-1)

(das) **Halloween** *(sing)* Halloween (6)

der **Hals,** ⸚e neck; throat (6-1)

  Hals- und Beinbruch! Break a leg! Good luck! (6-2)

die **Halskette, -n** necklace (5-2)

die **Halsschmerzen** *(pl)* sore throat (6)

halten (hält), hielt, gehalten to hold; to stop; to keep (3-2)

der **Hammer,** ⸚ hammer (1)

der **Hamster, -** hamster (10)

die **Hand,** ⸚e hand (1, 6-1)

  etwas in die eigene Hand nehmen to take something into one's own hands (11-2)

  Hand und Fuß haben to make sense (6)

der **Händler, -** dealer (4)

handgestrickt hand-knit (11)

der **Handschuh, -e** glove (7-2)

das **Handtuch,** ⸚er towel (9-2)

der **Handwerker, -/ die Handwerkerin, -nen** craftsperson, tradesperson (8)

das **Handy, -s** cell phone (E, 2-1)

hängen to hang *(put in a hanging position)* (8)

hängen, hing, gehangen to hang *(be in a hanging position)* (8)

  Es hängt mir zum Hals heraus! I'm totally sick of it! (11-2)

die **Harfe, -n** harp (2)

harmlos harmless (12)

hart hard (1)

der **Harz** Harz Mountains *(pl)* (1)

der **Hase, -n, -n** hare (10)

  Mein Name ist Hase, ich weiß von nichts. Don't ask me. I don't know anything about it. (10)

hassen to hate (3)

hässlich ugly (8)

hauen to hit (9)

  jemand *(acc)* **übers Ohr hauen** to cheat someone (9)

der **Haufen, -** pile; a lot of (12-2)

häufig often (2)

der **Hauptbahnhof,** ⸚e main railway station (5)

das **Hauptfach,** ⸚er major (field of study) (5)

das **Hauptgericht** main course (4, 9-2)

die **Hauptreisezeit, -en** peak time for travel (5)

die **Hauptstadt,** ⸚e capital city (1, 5-2)

die **Hauptstraße, -n** main street (4)

das **Haus,** ⸚er house (1, 2-2)

  Auf ihn kannst du Häuser bauen. He's absolutely dependable. (8)

  nach Hause gehen to go home (4-1)

  zu Hause sein to be at home (2, 4-1)

der **Hausarzt,** ⸚e/die **Hausärztin, -nen** family doctor (8)

die **Hausaufgabe, -n** homework (assignment) (4-2)

Häuschen: aus dem Häuschen sein to be all excited (8)

die **Hausfrau, -en** housewife (3-2)

hausgemacht homemade (9)

der **Haushalt, -e** household; housekeeping; budget (12-1)

  den Haushalt machen to do household chores (12)

der **Hausmann,** ⸚er househusband (3-2)

der **Hausmeister, -** janitor; building caretaker (8)

die **Hausnummer, -n** house number (1)

der **Hausschuh, -e** slipper (7-2)

das **Haustier, -e** pet (3-1)

die **Hecke, -n** hedge (6-2)

  die Hecke schneiden to clip the hedge (6)

der **Heilige Abend** Christmas Eve (7)

die **Heilsarmee** *(sing)* Salvation Army (8)

die **Heimat, -en** home (country) (8-2)

das **Heimatland,** ⸚er homeland (11)

heim·kommen, kam heim, ist heimgekommen to come home (4-2)

der **Heimtrainer, –** exercise bike (7-1)

der **Heimweg, –e** way home (10)

die **Heirat, –en** marriage (12-2)

heiraten to marry (3-2)

der **Heiratsmarkt, ⸚e** marriage market (12)

heiß hot (1-1)

heißen, hieß, geheißen to be called (E); to mean (11)

  das heißt (d.h.) that is (i.e.) (11)

  Ich heiße ... My name is . . . (E-1)

  Wie heißen Sie?/Wie heißt du? What's your name? (E-1)

heiter: es ist heiter it's sunny with some clouds (1)

heizen to heat (9)

helfen (hilft), half, geholfen *(+ dat)* to help (2, 7-2)

  helfen bei to help with (7)

hell light; bright (1-2)

das **Hemd, –en** shirt (2-2)

herauf·ziehen, zog herauf, heraufgezogen to pull up (6)

heraus·finden, fand heraus, herausgefunden to find out (7)

heraus·geben (gibt heraus), gab heraus, herausgegeben to give *(change)* (12)

heraus·kommen, kam heraus, ist herausgekommen to come out (6)

heraus·ziehen, zog heraus, herausgezogen to pull out (4)

der **Herbst** fall, autumn (1-2)

der **Herd, –e** stove (8-1)

Herein! Come in! (6)

herein·kommen, kam herein, ist hereingekommen to come in (6)

her·fahren (fährt her), fuhr her, ist hergefahren to come here, to get here; to drive here (6)

die **Herkunft, ⸚e** origin (11)

Herr Mr. (E-1)

der **Herr, –n, –en** gentleman (9-2)

herrlich wonderful (11)

her·stellen to make, produce (7)

die **Herstellung** *(sing)* production (7)

herüber·springen, sprang herüber, ist herübergesprungen to jump across (6)

herum·sitzen, saß herum, herumgesessen to sit around (10)

herum·tanzen: jemand *(dat)* **auf der Nase herumtanzen:** to walk all over someone (9)

herunter down (4)

herunter·fallen (fällt herunter), fiel herunter, ist heruntergefallen to fall down (6)

herzlich warm, hearty (11)

  Herzliche Glückwünsche zum Geburtstag! Happy Birthday! (7-1)

herzlos heartless (12)

heute today (1-1)

  heute Abend tonight (1)

  heute Morgen this morning (2)

  heute Nachmittag this afternoon (1-1)

heutzutage nowadays (7-1)

hier here (E, 1-2)

die **Hilfe** help (6, 7-2)

hilflos helpless (7)

der **Himmel** sky; heaven (1-1)

  Himmel und Hölle hopscotch (10)

hinaus·gehen, ging hinaus, ist hinausgegangen to go out (6)

das **Hindernis, –se** barrier (11)

hinein·fahren (fährt hinein), fuhr hinein, ist hineingefahren to drive in (4)

hinein·gehen, ging hinein, ist hineingegangen to go in (6)

sich **hinsetzen** to sit down (9)

hinter *(prep + acc/dat)* behind; *(as adj)* back (8)

der **Hintergrund** background (11)

der **Hinterhof, ⸚e** courtyard (E)

hinüber·springen, sprang hinüber, ist hinübergesprungen to jump across (6)

hinunter·fallen (fällt hinunter), fiel hinunter, ist hinuntergefallen to fall down (6)

hinunter·schauen to look down (8)

hip hip (2-2)

historisch historical (5)

die **Hitze** heat (3)

das **Hobby, –s** hobby (2-1)

hoch (hoh-) high (5-2)

das **Hochhaus, ⸚er** high-rise (8-2)

die **Hochschule, –n** university (2)

der **Hochschulsport** university sports (2)

die **Hochzeit, –en** wedding (3-2,12-2)

  die **goldene Hochzeit** golden wedding anniversary (7)

der **Hockeyschläger, –** hockey stick (7-2)

hoffen to hope (2, 5-2)

hoffentlich hopefully, I hope (so) (6-2)

hoffnungslos hopeless (12)

höflich polite (7-2)

holen to get; to fetch (5, 10-1); to summon (5)

holländisch *(adj)* Dutch (7)

höllisch hellish (2)

der **Holocaust** holocaust (11)

das **Holz** wood (11)

der **Holzfäller, –** lumberjack (6)

die **Homepage, –s** home page (2-1)

der **Honig** honey (4-1)

hörbar audible (12)

hören to hear (2-2); to listen to (1)

der **Horrorfilm, –e** horror film (3)

der **Hörsaal, Hörsäle** lecture hall (E)

die **Hose, –n** pants (2-2)

das **Hotdog, –s** hotdog (3)

das **Hotel, –s** hotel (1, 5-1)

hübsch pretty (2-2)

das **Huhn, ⸚er** hen (4)

  Da lachen ja die Hühner! What a joke! (10)

human humane (7)

der **Humor** humor (3-1)

humorlos humorless (5)

humorvoll humorous (5)

der **Hund, –e** dog (3-1)

das **Hundefutter** dog food (6)

das **Hundewetter** rotten weather (1)

der **Hunger** hunger (5)

  Ich habe Hunger. I'm hungry. (4, 5-2)

hungern to go hungry (10)
hungrig hungry (10-1)
der **Hut, ¨e** hat (7-2)

I

der **ICE** InterCity Express (4)
ich: Ich bin's. It's me. (5-2)
ideal ideal (5-1)
der **Idealismus** (12-2)
die **Idee, -n** idea (E, 7-1)
identisch identical (9)
der **Igel, -** hedgehog (10)
ihr, ihr, ihre her (1), their (2)
Ihr, Ihr, Ihre your (2)
die **Ikone, -n** icon (8)
die **Illustration, -en** illustration (6)
imaginär imaginary (9)
die **Imitation, -en** imitation (4)
immer always (2-1)
   immer mehr more and more (3-2)
   immer noch still (3)
der **Immigrant, -en, -en**/die
   Immigrantin, -nen immigrant
   (6-1)
der **Immobilienmakler, -**/die
   Immobilienmaklerin, -nen
   real estate agent (3)
impfen to vaccinate (11)
der **Import, -e** import (7)
impulsiv impulsive (12-1)
in (prep + acc/dat) in (E, 8), into;
   to (1, 8)
der **Individualist, -en, -en**/
   die **Individualistin, -nen**
   individualist (8)
industrialisiert industrialized (12)
die **Industrie, -n** industry (3)
industriell industrial (4)
die **Infobox, -en** infobox (E)
der **Informatiker, -**/die
   Informatikerin, -nen
   computer specialist (12)
die **Information, -en** information (7)
das **Informationszeitalter**
   information age (10-1)
sich **informieren über** (+ acc) to
   inform oneself about (10)
informiert informed (10)
der **Ingenieur, -e**/die **Ingenieurin,**
   -nen engineer (4)

inklusive inclusive of (9)
die **Inlineskates** in-line skates (3)
innen inside (9-1)
innerhalb within (12)
die **Innovation, -en** innovation
   (4-2)
innovativ innovative (4-2)
das **Insekt, -en** insect (2, 10-2)
die **Insel, -n** island (5-1)
instinktiv instinctive (12-1)
das **Instrument, -e** instrument (2)
intelligent intelligent, smart (1, 2-1)
interessant interesting (1-2)
das **Interesse, -n** interest (2)
interesselos uninterested (12)
interessieren to interest (6)
sich **interessieren für** to be
   interested in (11-2)
interkulturell intercultural (2)
international international(ly) (9-1)
das **Internet** Internet (2-1)
   im Internet surfen to surf the
   Internet (6)
das **Interview, -s** interview (3-2)
investieren to invest (1)
der **iPod, -s** iPod (3)
irgendwann sometime or other (8)
irisch (adj) Irish (2)
israelisch (adj) Israeli (7)
der **Italiener, -**/die **Italienerin,**
   -nen Italian (person) (9)
italienisch (adj) Italian (3)

J

ja yes (E-1)
die **Jacke, -n** jacket (1, 2-2)
das **Jahr, -e** year (1-2)
   auf ein Jahr for a year (8)
   die 80er-Jahre the eighties (10)
   Ein gutes Neues Jahr! Happy
   New Year! (7-1)
   letztes Jahr last year (5)
jahraus, jahrein year in, year out (1)
die **Jahreszeit, -en** season (1-2)
das **Jahrhundert, -e** century
   (3, 10-1)
jährlich yearly, annual(ly) (2)
das **Jahrzehnt, -e** decade (11)
der **Januar** January (1-2)
   im Januar in January (1-2)

der **Japaner, -**/die **Japanerin, -nen**
   Japanese (person) (4)
die **Jeans, -** (pl) jeans (2-2)
jedenfalls at any rate (11)
jeder, jedes, jede each, every (2)
jederzeit (at) any time (11-2)
jedoch but (11-2)
jemand somebody, someone
   (3-2)
   jemand anders somebody else
   (9-1)
jetzig present (4)
jetzt now (E, 1-1)
   von jetzt ab from now on (6)
der **Job, -s** job (2-2)
jobben to work (part-time or during
   vacation) (1)
der **Jockey, -s** jockey (2)
joggen to jog (2, 4-2)
   joggen gehen to go jogging (2-1)
der **Jogginganzug, ¨e** jogging
   suit (3)
die **Jogginghose, -n** jogging pants
   (3)
der **Joghurt** yogurt (4-1)
das **Jonglieren** (sing) juggling (4)
der **Journalist, -en, -en**/die
   Journalistin, -nen journalist (4)
das **Jubiläum, Jubiläen** anniversary
   (4)
der **Jude, -n, -n**/die **Jüdin, -nen**
   Jew (11)
jüdisch Jewish (11)
die **Jugend** (sing) youth (3, 5-2)
die **Jugendherberge, -n** youth
   hostel (E, 5-1)
jugendlich youthful (4)
der **Jugendstil** art nouveau (3)
der **Juli** July (1-2)
jung young (1, 5-1)
der **Junge, -n, -n** boy (5-2)
der **Juni** June (1-2)
das **Junkfood** junk food (4)
die **Jury, -s** jury (9)

K

das **Kabinett, -e** cabinet (12-1)
der **Kaffee** coffee (1, 2-1)
die **Kaffeekanne, -n** coffeepot
   (1, 9-1)

die **Kaffeemaschine, -n** coffee maker (3-2)

der **Käfig, -e** cage (10)

der **Kaiser, -/**die **Kaiserin, -nen** emperor/empress (3)

der **Kajak, -s** kayak (5)

der **Kajaker, -/**die **Kajakerin, -nen** kayaker (5)

das **Kalb, -̈er** calf (2)

der **Kalender, -** calendar (5-2)

(das) **Kalifornien** California (5)

kalt cold (1-1); not including heat *(of rent)* (8)

der **Kalte Krieg** Cold War (11-1)

die **Kamera, -s** camera (3-2)

der **Kamm, -̈e** comb (9-2)

sich **kämmen** to comb one's hair (9-2)

(das) **Kanada** Canada (1-1)

der **Kanadier, -/**die **Kanadierin, -nen** Canadian *(person)* (1-1)

kanadisch *(adj)* Canadian (3)

der **Kanal, -̈e** channel (6); canal (10)

das **Känguru, -s** kangaroo (10)

das **Kännchen, -** little pot (9)

die **Kantate, -n** cantata (3)

die **Kantine, -n** cafeteria *(at a workplace)* (4)

der **Kanzler, -/**die **Kanzlerin, -nen** chancellor (11)

kaputt broken (7-1)

kaputt fahren (fährt kaputt), fuhr kaputt, kaputt gefahren to drive into the ground (12)

kaputt machen to break; to ruin (7-1)

der **Karfreitag** Good Friday (7)

kariert plaid (11)

die **Karikatur, -en** caricature (7)

der **Karneval** Mardi Gras (1)

die **Karotte, -n** carrot (1)

die **Karriere, -n** career (3, 12-1)

Karriere machen to get ahead in one's career (12-1)

die **Karte, -n** card *(also* playing card); postcard; map (1-1); ticket (2)

die **Kartoffel, -n** potato (4-1)

der **Kartoffelknödel, -** potato dumpling (9)

die **Kartoffelchips** potato chips (7-2)

der **Karton, -s** box, carton (8)

der **Käse,** cheese (E, 4-1)

Das ist alles Käse. That's all baloney. (7)

der **Käsekuchen, -** cheesecake (4)

die **Kassette, -n** cassette (11)

das **Kassler Rippchen, -** *(das* **Kassler)** smoked pork chop (9)

der **Kasten, -̈** box (9-1)

katholisch Catholic (3)

die **Katze, -n** cat (1, 3-1)

Es ist alles für die Katz. It's all for nothing. (10)

das **Katzenfutter** cat food (6)

kaufen to buy (1-1)

der **Käufer, -/**die **Käuferin, -nen** buyer (9)

das **Kaufhaus, -̈er** department store (3-2)

die **Kaufsucht** shopping addiction (12)

kaum scarcely; hardly (10-2)

der **Kaviar** caviar (3)

kein, kein, keine not a, not any, no (1)

der **Keller, -** cellar, basement (7, 8-2)

der **Kellner, -/**die **Kellnerin, -nen** server, waiter/waitress (3, 9-1)

kellnern to work as a waiter/waitress (6)

kennen, kannte, gekannt to know; to be acquainted with (2, 3-1)

kennen lernen to get to know (E, 4-2)

das **Kennzeichen, -** characteristic (6)

der **Kerl, -e** guy (6)

die **Kerze, -n** candle (7-2)

der **Kessel, -** kettle (3)

die **Kette, -n** chain *(also of businesses)* (9)

das **Keyboard, -s** keyboard *(musical instrument)* (3)

das **Kfz, -s (Kraftfahrzeug)** motor vehicle (11)

der **Kfz-Mechaniker, -/**die **Kfz-Mechanikerin, -nen** car mechanic (12)

der **Kilometer, -** kilometer (1)

das **Kind, -er** child (1, 3-1)

als Kind as a child (5-2)

die **Kinderabteilung, -en** children's department (10)

der **Kindergarten, -̈** kindergarten; nursery school (1)

kinderlos childless (12)

die **Kindheit** *(sing)* childhood (11)

kindisch childish (2)

kindlich childlike (2)

das **Kinn, -e** chin (6-1)

das **Kino, -s** movies (1)

ins Kino to the movies (1-2)

die **Kirche, -n** church (10-1)

die **Klamotten** *(pl)* clothes (3-2)

der **Klang, -̈e** sound (1)

Klar! Of course! (1-1)

die **Klarinette, -n** clarinet (3)

die **Klasse, -n** class (3-2)

klassenlos classless (12)

klassisch classical (2)

die **Klausur, -en** test (5-2)

eine Klausur schreiben to take a test; to have a test (5)

das **Klavier** piano (2)

Klavier spielen to play the piano (2-1)

das **Klavierkonzert, -e** piano concerto (3)

der **Klavierlehrer, -/**die **Klavierlehrerin, -nen** piano teacher (7)

das **Kleid, -er** dress; *(pl)* clothes (2-2)

kleiden to dress (10)

das **Kleidergeschäft, -e** clothing store (3-2)

das **Kleidungsstück, -e** article of clothing (2-2)

klein little, small; short (1, 2-1)

klicken to click (2)

klingeln to ring (10)

das **Klischee, -s** cliché (1)

das **Klo, -s** toilet (8-1)

klopfen to knock (11)

der **Klub, -s** club (10)

klug smart, intelligent (10-2)

knabbern to nibble (11)

das **Knäckebrot** crispbread (11)

die **Knackwurst, -̈e** knockwurst (9)

die **Kneipe, -n** pub (1)

in die Kneipe to a pub (1-2)

das **Knie, -** knee (1, 6-1)

knipsen to snap a photo (11)

der **Knödel, -** dumpling (9-1)

knusprig crispy (9-1)

der **Koch, ̈e**/die **Köchin, -nen** cook; chef (3)

das **Kochbuch, ̈er** cookbook (7-1)

kochen to cook (2-1)

die **Kocherei** *(constant)* cooking (5)

der **Kochkurs, -e** cooking lessons (5)

die **Kochmöglichkeit, -en** cooking facilities (5)

das **Koffein** caffeine (2)

der **Koffer, -** suitcase (2, 6-2)

der **Kofferraum** trunk *(of a car)* (4)

der **Kognak** cognac (7)

die **Kohle, -n** coal (1)

der **Kollege, -en, -en/**die **Kollegin, -nen** colleague (2, 9-2)

(das) **Köln** Cologne (12)

kombinieren to combine (4)

komfortabel comfortable (4, 5-1)

komisch funny; strange (10-2)

kommen, kam, ist gekommen to come (E, 1-1)

  Ich komme aus ... I'm from . . . (E-1)

  kommend coming (8)

  Woher kommen Sie/kommst du? Where are you from? (E-1)

  zu Besuch kommen to visit (8-2)

die **Kommode, -n** dresser (8-1)

die **Kommunikation, -en** communication (1, 10-1)

kommunistisch communist (11-2)

die **Komödie, -n** comedy (3)

das **Kompliment, -e** compliment (5-2)

kompliziert complicated (9, 10-1)

der **Komponist, -en, -en/**die **Komponistin, -nen** composer (2, 3-2)

die **Komposition, -en** composition (3)

die **Konditorei, -en** shop selling cakes and pastries (7)

der **König, -e** king (1)

die **Konjunktion, -en** conjunction (4)

können (kann), konnte, gekonnt to be able to, can (4)

konservativ conservative (2, 5-2)

das **Konsulat, -e** consulate (12-2)

der **Konsum** consumption (10)

der **Kontakt, -e** contact (E, 12-2)

die **Kontaktlinse, -n** contact lens (5-2)

kontaktorientiert contact-oriented (12)

der **Kontext, -e** context (1)

der **Kontinent, -e** continent (2)

kontrollieren to monitor (11)

der **Kontrollstreifen, -** patrolled strip of land *(part of the Berlin Wall)* (11)

sich **konzentrieren auf** *(+ acc)* to concentrate on (10)

das **Konzept, -e** concept (4, 10-1)

das **Konzert, -e** concert (1, 2-2); concerto (3)

  ins Konzert to a concert, to concerts (1-2)

der **Kopf, ̈e** head (6-1)

  den Kopf schütteln to shake one's head (10)

  Er ist nicht auf den Kopf gefallen. He's no fool. (6)

  Mir raucht der Kopf. I can't think straight anymore. (9)

die **Kopfhörer** *(pl)* headphones (12)

die **Kopfschmerzen** *(pl)* headache (6)

kopieren to copy (10-1)

der **Korken, -** cork (9)

der **Korkenzieher, -** corkscrew (8-2)

der **Körper, -** body (6-1)

kosten to cost (1-2)

krabbeln to crawl (8)

der **Krampf, ̈e** cramp (3)

krank sick (3-2)

das **Krankenhaus, ̈er** hospital (6-2)

die **Krankenversicherung, -en** health insurance (12)

die **Krankheit, -en** illness, sickness (11)

die **Krawatte, -n** tie (7-2)

kreativ creative (2-1)

der **Kredit, -e** credit; loan (5)

die **Kreditkarte, -n** credit card (5-2)

der **Kreis, -e** circle (11)

das **Kreuz, -e** cross (1, 4)

der **Krieg, -e** war (7, 11-1)

  der **Kalte Krieg** Cold War (11-1)

kriegen to get, to receive (8, 10-2)

  Angst kriegen to get scared (10-1)

  eins aufs Dach kriegen to be bawled out (8)

der **Krimi, -s** detective story (3, 10-2)

die **Kritik** *(sing)* criticism (10)

der **Kritiker, -/**die **Kritikerin, -nen** critic (10)

kritisch critical (5)

kritisieren to criticize (3-2)

die **Krone, -n** crown (1)

krumm crooked, bent (10-2)

die **Küche, -n** kitchen (8-1); cuisine (9)

der **Kuchen, -** cake (3, 4-1)

  ein Stück Kuchen a piece of cake (3)

die **Küchenbenutzung** *(sing)* kitchen privileges (8-2)

die **Kuckucksuhr, -en** cuckoo clock (2)

die **Kugel, -n** ball (3)

der **Kugelschreiber, -** ballpoint pen (7-2)

die **Kuh, ̈e** cow (1)

kühl cool *(of weather)* (5-2)

der **Kühlschrank, ̈e** refrigerator (7, 8-1)

der **Kuli, -s** ballpoint pen (7)

die **Kultur, -en** culture (1)

der **Kulturschock** culture shock (11-2)

der **Kunde, -n, -n/**die **Kundin, -nen** customer (9-2)

die **Kunst, ̈e** art (5-2)

der **Künstler, -/**die **Künstlerin, -nen** artist (8-2)

künstlerisch artistic(ally) (12)

der **Kürbis, -se** pumpkin (4)

das **Kürbisschnitzen** *(sing)* pumpkin carving (4)

der **Kurs, -e** course; class (5-2)
kurz short (2-2)
  seit kurzem recently (11-2)
  seit kurzer Zeit recently (11-2)
kürzlich a short time ago, recently
  (10-1)
kuschelig cuddly (7)
die **Kusine, -n** *(female)* cousin (3-1)
die **Küste, -n** coast (11)

L

lachen to laugh (3-1)
  Da lachen ja die Hühner!
    What a joke! (10)
der **Lachs** salmon, lox (3)
der **Laden, ⁻** store (3)
laden (lädt), lud, geladen to load
  (6)
die **Lage, -n** location (8-1)
lahm lame (2)
das **Lama, -s** llama (2)
das **Lamm, ⁻er** lamb (1)
die **Lampe, -n** lamp (1, 8-1)
das **Land, ⁻er** country (E, 2-2); state
  (6-1)
landen, landete, ist gelandet to
  land *(of airplanes)* (6-2)
die **Landschaft, -en** landscape (5-1)
das **Landschaftsbild, -er** landscape
  painting (8)
die **Landung, -en** landing (6)
lang long (1, 2-2)
  eine Stunde lang for an hour (4)
langsam slow(ly) (3-1)
langweilig boring (3-1)
die **Lasagne** lasagna (4)
lassen (lässt), ließ, gelassen to let;
  to leave (3-2); to have (something)
  done (11)
  Lass mich in Ruhe! Stop
    bothering me! (4-2)
  Lassen Sie sich Zeit. Take your
    time. (12-2)
der **Lastkraftwagen, -** truck (10-2)
der **Lastwagen, -** truck (10-2)
(das) **Latein** Latin *(language)* (6)
die **Laufanlage, -n** run *(e.g., for*
  dogs) (11)
laufen (läuft), lief, ist gelaufen to
  run (2, 3-2)

die **Laune, -n** mood (12)
die **Laus, ⁻e** louse (1)
lausig lousy (2)
laut loud (1, 3-2)
der **Lautsprecher, -** loudspeaker (5)
leben to live *(in a country or a city)*
  (1, 2-2)
das **Leben, -** life (3-1)
lebendig alive (11)
das **Lebensjahr** year of *(one's)* life (3)
die **Lebensmittel** *(pl)* food;
  groceries (9)
das **Lebensmittelgeschäft, -e**
  grocery store (9)
der **Lebensstil, -e** lifestyle (4, 5-2)
die **Lebensversicherung, -en** life
  insurance (12)
lebenswichtig essential (11)
die **Leberwurst, ⁻e** liver sausage (10)
leblos lifeless (12)
lecker delicious (5-2)
das **Leder** leather (2)
ledig single (3-1)
leer empty (7-1)
leeren to empty (9-1)
legen to lay *(down)*, to put *(in a*
  horizontal position) (8-2)
lehren to teach (11)
der **Lehrer, -/**die **Lehrerin, -nen**
  teacher, instructor (1-2)
der **Lehrplan** curriculum (8)
leicht easy; light (5, 6-2)
leid: Es tut mir leid. I'm sorry.
  (7-2)
leiden, litt, gelitten to suffer (11)
leider unfortunately (5-2)
leihen, lieh, geliehen to lend (7-2)
die **Leine, -n** leash (10)
leiten to lead (4)
die **Lektüre** *(sing)* reading
  material (10)
lernen to learn; to study *(e.g. for a*
  test) (1-2)
lesen (liest), las, gelesen to read
  (3-2)
letzt last (3-2)
  das letzte Mal the last time
    (10-2)
  in letzter Zeit recently (6-2)
  zum letzten Mal for the last
    time (8-2)

die **Leute** *(pl)* people (2-2)
das **Licht, -er** light (8)
lieb dear (6)
die **Liebe** love (2)
lieben to love (2, 5-2)
lieber rather (2)
liebevoll loving (5)
der **Liebling, -e** darling; favorite (3-1)
das **Lieblingsbuch, ⁻er** favorite
  book (3-1)
die **Lieblingsfarbe** favorite color
  (3)
der **Lieblingsfilm, -e** favorite film
  (2)
das **Lieblingsgericht, -e** favorite
  dish (9)
der **Lieblingsonkel, -** favorite
  uncle (3)
das **Lieblingsprogramm, -e**
  favorite program (5)
der **Lieblingssport** favorite
  sport (5)
die **Lieblingstante, -n** favorite
  aunt (3)
lieblos loveless (5)
liebst: Wo machst du am
  liebsten Ferien? Where's your
  favorite vacation spot? (5-1)
das **Lied, -er** song (6-2)
liegen, lag, gelegen to lie, to be
  situated (6-2)
  es liegt daran the reason is (11)
der **Likör, -e** liqueur (2)
die **Lilie, -n** lily (1)
die **Linie, -n** line (8)
links left; to the left (4-2)
die **Lippe, -n** lip (1)
der **Lippenstift, -e** lipstick (3, 9-2)
die **Lira, Lire** lira *(former Italian*
  currency) (9)
lispeln to lisp (8)
die **Liste, -n** list (7)
der **Liter, -** liter (9-1)
die **Literatur, -en** literature (5-2)
der **Lkw, -s (Lastkraftwagen)**
  truck (10-2)
lockig curly (3-2)
der **Löffel, -** spoon (9-1)
der **Lohn, ⁻e** wages, pay (8, 12-1)
das **Lokal, -e** pub; restaurant (9)
lokal local (9, 10-2)

los

> **Was ist denn los?** What's up? (8-2)

> **Was ist denn los mit dir?** What's the matter with you? (12-2)

löschen to delete; to extinguish (10)

lösen to solve (4); to pay (8)

die **Lösung, -en** solution (5-1)

der **Lottogewinn, -e** lottery winnings (12)

die **Luft** air (4)

die **Luftbrücke, -n** airlift (literally: air bridge) (11-1)

die **Luftbrückengüter** (pl) goods transported by airlift (11)

die **Lüge, -n** lie (10-1)

lügen, log, gelogen to lie (tell an untruth) (10-1)

der **Lumpen, -** rag (10)

die **Lüneburger Heide** Lüneburg Heath (1)

die **Lupe, -n** magnifying glass (1)

die **Lust** enjoyment (8)

> **Ich habe (keine) Lust ...** I (don't) feel like ... (8-2)

> **Ich habe Lust (auf) ...** I feel like (having or doing something) . . . (10-2)

lustig funny, humorous; happy (7-1)

der **Luxus** luxury (7)

M

machbar doable (12)

machen to make; to do (1-1)

> **Das macht doch nichts.** That doesn't matter. (9-1)

> **Sport machen** to do sports, to be active in sports (1-2)

das **Mädchen, -** girl (5-2)

das **Magazin, -e** magazine (2-2)

magersüchtig anorexic (12-2)

mähen to mow (6-2)

der **Mai** May (1-2)

die **Mail, -s** e-mail (3-1)

die **Makkaroni** (pl) macaroni (3)

das **Mal, -e** (occurrence) time (7)

> **das letzte Mal** the last time (10-2)

> **jedes Mal** every time (10)

mit einem Mal suddenly (11)

> **zum ersten Mal** for the first time (8-2)

> **zum letzten Mal** for the last time (8-2)

mal, einmal once; for a change (3)

> **nicht mal** not even (10)

> **noch mal** once more; (over) again (7-2)

malen to paint (a picture) (6-2)

das **Malen** (sing) drawing, painting (as an activity) (4)

der **Maler, -**/die **Malerin, -nen** painter; artist (6-2)

die **Malerei** painting (as an activity) (8)

man one, you (E, 4-1)

> **Wie sagt man das?** How does one say that? How do you say that? (4-1)

manche (pl) some (10-1)

manchmal sometimes (4-1)

die **Mandarine, -n** mandarin (orange) (1)

der **Mann, ⁼er** man; husband (1, 2-2)

der **Mantel, ⁼** coat (2-2)

das **Märchen, -** fairy tale (4, 5-2)

märchenhaft fairy-tale (adj), fantastic (5-2)

der **Märchenkönig, -e** fairy-tale king (5)

die **Märchensammlung, -en** collection of fairy tales (10)

die **Märchenstadt, ⁼e** fairy-tale city (5)

die **Märchenwelt** wonderland (5)

die **Markenkleidung** brand name clothing (12-1)

der **Markt, ⁼e** market (4)

die **Marktforschung** market research (9)

marktwirtschaftlich (adj) free enterprise (11)

die **Marmelade, -n** jam (4-1)

marschieren to march (5)

der **März** March (1-2)

die **Maschine, -n** machine (5-2)

der **Maschinenbaumechaniker, -**/ die **Maschinenbaumechanikerin, -nen** machinist (12)

das **Massenprodukt, -e** mass-produced product (4)

massiv heavy; solid (5)

die **Mathe** math (2)

die **Mathematik** mathematics (E)

die **Mauer, -n** wall (7, 11-1)

die **Maus, ⁼e** mouse (1, 2-1)

die **Medien** (pl) media (10-1)

das **Medikament, -e** medicine (9)

das **Meer, -e** ocean, sea (5)

das **Mehl** flour (9-1)

mehr more (3-2)

> **immer mehr** more and more (3-2)

> **nicht mehr** no longer, not any more (3)

mehrere several (9)

die **Mehrzahl** majority (6)

mein, mein, meine my (E)

meinen to mean; to think, to be of or voice an opinion (3, 11-2)

die **Meinung, -en** opinion (11-2)

> **meiner Meinung nach** in my opinion (12-1)

meist most (5)

meistens most of the time, usually (4-1)

meistern to master (12)

sich **melden** to apply (3); to register (8)

die **Menge, -n** lot, great deal (11-2)

> **eine Menge** a lot; viel (11-2)

die **Mensa** university cafeteria (E, 1-1)

> **in die Mensa** to the cafeteria (1-2)

der **Mensch, -en, -en** human being; person; (pl) people (5-2)

menschlich human (12)

der **Mercedes** Mercedes (3)

das **Merkmal, -e** characteristic; trait (2)

die **Messe, -n** trade fair (1)

> **auf die Messe** to the trade fair (1)

das **Messer, -** knife (4-2)

der **Messerschmied, -e**/die **Messerschmiedin, -nen** knifesmith (4)

die **Messerwerkstatt, ⁼en** knifesmith's shop (4)

das **Metall, -e** metal (9)

der **Meter, -** meter (1)

der **Mief** (*sing*) smell; stench (12)
die **Miete, –n** rent (2, 8-1)
mieten to rent (6-2, 8-1)
der **Mieter, –**/die **Mieterin, –nen** renter (10)
das **Mietshaus, ̈er** apartment building (2)
der **Mietwagen, –** rental car (5)
die **Mikrobiologie** microbiology (2)
das **Mikroskop, –e** microscope (1)
die **Mikrowelle, –n** microwave (oven) (8-1)
die **Milch** milk (1, 2-1)
die **Milliarde, –n** billion (9)
die **Million, –en** million (4)
das **Mineralwasser** mineral water (3-2)
der **Minister, –**/ die **Ministerin, –nen** minister (*in government*) (5)
der **Ministerpräsident, –en, –en**/ die **Ministerpräsidentin, –nen** prime minister (10)
die **Minute, –n** minute (1, 2-1)
miserabel miserable (10-2)
der **Mist** manure (6)
mit (*prep + dat*) with (1); (*as verb prefix*) along (4)
der **Mitarbeiter, –**/die **Mitarbeiterin, –nen** (fellow) employee (4)
der **Mitbewohner, –**/die **Mitbewohnerin, –nen** housemate; roommate (1-2)
der **Mitbürger, –**/die **Mitbürgerin, –nen** fellow citizen (9-2)
mit·bringen, brachte mit, mitgebracht to bring along (4)
das **Mitbringsel, –** small gift (*for a host*) (7-2)
der **Mitbürger, –**/die **Mitbürgerin, –nen** fellow citizen (9-2)
miteinander with each other; together (2-1)
mit·gehen, ging mit, ist mitgegangen to go along (4)
das **Mitglied, –er** member (12)
mit·kommen, kam mit, ist mitgekommen to come along (4-2)
mit·lesen (liest mit), las mit, mitgelesen to read along (4)

mit·machen to take part in (12)
mit·nehmen (nimmt mit), nahm mit, mitgenommen to take along (4)
mit·schreiben, schrieb mit, mitgeschrieben to make notes
mit·singen, sang mit, mitgesungen to sing along (4)
der **Mitstudent, –en, –en**/die **Mitstudentin, –nen** classmate; fellow student (7)
der **Mittag** noon; midday (2)
  zu Mittag essen to have lunch (4-1)
das **Mittagessen** lunch; noon meal (4-1)
  zum Mittagessen for lunch (4-1)
die **Mittagspause, –n** lunch break (8-2)
die **Mitte, –n** middle (2)
  Mitte Juli (in) mid-July (5-1)
mittel average; medium
  mittelgroß of average height (6)
der **Mittelklassewagen, –** midsized car (12)
das **Mittelmeer** (*sing*) Mediterranean Sea (5)
mitten: mitten im Winter in the middle of winter (3)
(die) **Mitternacht** midnight (2, 11-2)
  nach Mitternacht after midnight (4-2)
der **Mittwoch** Wednesday (1-2) (*see also* **Dienstag**)
die **Möbel** (*pl*) furniture (8-1)
das **Möbelstück, –e** piece of furniture (8)
das **Mobilgerät, –e** mobile device (10)
möbliert furnished (8-1)
das **Modell, –e** model (4)
die **Modenschau** fashion show (11)
modern modern (1, 2-1)
mögen (mag), mochte, gemocht to like (4)
  ich möchte I would like (3)
möglich possible (4-2)
  so bald wie möglich as soon as possible (4)
  so schnell wie möglich as quickly as possible (10)

  so viel wie möglich as much as possible (9)
die **Möglichkeit, –en** possibility (5)
möglichst viel as much as possible (11)
mollig plump (2-1)
der **Moment, –e** moment (7)
  im Moment at the moment (11)
die **Monarchie, –n** monarchy (11)
der **Monat, –e** month (1-2)
monatlich monthly (2)
der **Mond** moon (1)
der **Montag** Monday (1-2) (*see also* **Dienstag**)
  am Montag on Monday (1-2)
morgen tomorrow (1-1)
  morgen früh tomorrow morning (2)
  morgen Nachmittag tomorrow afternoon (2)
der **Morgen, –** morning (E)
  Guten Morgen! Morgen! Good morning! (E-1)
  heute Morgen this morning (1-2)
morgens in the morning (1)
der **Moskito, –s** mosquito (2)
der **Most** cider (8)
das **Motiv, –e** motif (9)
der **Motor, –en** motor (3)
das **Motorboot, –e** motorboat (4)
der **Motorenkonstrukteur, –e** engine designer (12)
das **Motorrad, ̈er** motorcycle (2, 3-1)
das **Mountainbike, –s** mountain bike (3-2)
der **Mozzarella** mozzarella (*cheese*) (10)
mucksmäuschenstill quiet as a mouse (8)
müde tired (6-2)
der **Muffin, –s** muffin (4-1)
der **Mülleimer, –** garbage can (7-1)
multikulturell multicultural (12)
(das) **München** Munich (5)
der **Mund, ̈er** mouth (6-1)
  den Mund voll nehmen to talk big (6)
die **Münze, –n** coin (9-2)
das **Museum, Museen** museum (2-2)
die **Musik** music (1)

musikalisch musical (2-1)

der **Musiker, -**/die **Musikerin, -nen** musician (3)

das **Müsli** *(sing)* muesli *(cold, whole-grain cereal with nuts and fruit)* (4-1)

  eine Schüssel Müsli a bowl of muesli (4-1)

muslimisch *(adj)* Muslim

der **Müsliriegel, -** granola bar (4-1)

müssen (muss), musste, gemusst to have to, must (4)

die **Mutter, ̈** mother (E, 3-1)

mütterlich motherly (2)

mütterlicherseits maternal (6-1)

der **Muttertag, -e** Mother's Day (7-2)

die **Mutti** mom (5)

mysteriös mysterious (5)

N

na well (E)

nach *(prep + dat)* after; to (1); according to (10)

  meiner Meinung nach in my opinion (12-2)

  nach Claudias Vorlesung after Claudia's lecture (1-2)

  nach Florida to Florida (1-2)

  nach Hause gehen to go home (1, 4-1)

der **Nachbar, -n, -n**/die **Nachbarin, -nen** neighbor (2-2)

nach·bestellen to reorder (9)

nachdem after *(sub conj)* (9-2)

nach·füllen to refill (9)

nach·galoppieren to gallop after (10)

nachher after; afterwards *(adv)* (6-1)

die **Nachkriegszeit** post-war period (11-1)

der **Nachmittag, -e** afternoon (1)

  heute Nachmittag this afternoon (1)

  morgen Nachmittag tomorrow afternoon (2)

nachmittags in the afternoon (2)

der **Nachmittagskaffee** afternoon coffee (4-1)

zum Nachmittagskaffee for afternoon coffee (4-1)

die **Nachrichten** *(pl)* news (10-2)

nächst next (1)

  nächstes Jahr next year (1, 3-2)

die **Nacht, ̈e** night (2)

  bei Nacht at night (2)

  gestern Nacht last night (2)

  Gute Nacht! Good night! (E)

der **Nachteil, -e** disadvantage (8-2)

der **Nachtisch, -e** dessert (3, 4-1)

  zum Nachtisch for dessert (3, 4-1)

der **Nachtmensch, -en, -en** night person (4)

nachts at night (2)

der **Nachttisch, -e** night table (8-1)

die **Nachttischlampe, -n** bedside lamp (8)

nah near (5-1)

die **Nähe** vicinity (8)

  in der Nähe close by (8-2)

    in der Nähe der Uni near the university (8-2)

der **Name, -ns, -n** name (E-1)

das **Namensschild, -er** name plate (9)

nämlich you see (5)

die **Narzisse, -n** daffodil (5)

die **Nase, -n** nose (6-1)

  die Nase zu tief ins Glas stecken to drink too much (6)

  jemand *(dat)* **auf der Nase herumtanzen** to walk all over someone (9)

der **Nasenstecker, -** nose stud (5-2)

nass wet (5-1)

national national (4, 10-2)

der **Nationalfeiertag, -e** national holiday (7)

die **Nationalität, -en** nationality (1)

die **Natur** nature (10)

  von Natur by nature (10)

natürlich of course (5-2); natural (2)

neben *(prep + acc/dat)* in addition to; beside, next to (8)

die **Nebenkosten** *(pl)* additional costs (8-1)

neblig foggy (1)

der **Neffe, -n, -n** nephew (3-1)

negativ negative (1)

  Negatives negative things (11-2)

nehmen (nimmt), nahm, genommen to take (3-2)

neidisch jealous, envious (12)

  neidisch auf *(+ acc)* envious of (12-1)

nein no (E-1)

die **Nelke, -n** carnation (6)

nennen, nannte, genannt to call, to name (4)

der **Nerv, -en** nerve (12)

  Er/sie geht mir auf die Nerven. He/she gets on my nerves. (12)

nerven to get on one's nerves (4, 8-2)

nervös nervous, on edge (4-2)

nett nice; pleasant (2-1)

das **Netz, -e** net (3)

das **Netzwerken** networking (2)

  soziales Netzwerken social networking (2)

neu new (3-2)

  Ein gutes neues Jahr! Happy New Year! (7-1)

die **Neue Nationalgalerie** *art gallery in Berlin* (6)

die **Neue Pinakothek** *art gallery in Munich* (5)

die **Neueröffnung** reopening (10)

(das) Neujahr New Year (6)

neuseeländisch *(adj)* New Zealand (7)

nicht not (1-1)

  gar nicht not at all (1-1)

  nicht mal not even (10)

  nicht mehr no longer, not any more (3-2)

  noch nicht not yet (E)

  überhaupt nicht not at all (11)

die **Nichte, -n** niece (3-1)

der **Nichtraucher, -** nonsmoker (8)

nichts nothing (1-2)

  Das macht doch nichts. That doesn't matter. (9-1)

  Er tut dir nichts. He won't hurt you. (9-1)

gar nichts nothing at all (7)

überhaupt nichts nothing at all (11)

der **Nichtsnutz, -e** good-for-nothing (10)

nie never (2-2)

niemand nobody, no one (3-2)

das **Niemandsland**, no man's land (11)

nieseln: es nieselt it's drizzling (1)

nikotinsüchtig addicted to nicotine (12)

noch still (1-1)

immer noch still (3)

noch einmal (over) again, once more (7-2)

noch mal (over) again, once more (2, 7-2)

noch nicht not yet (E, 1-1)

das **Nomen, -** noun (1)

nonstop nonstop (11-2)

(das) **Nordamerika** North America (3)

nordamerikanisch *(adj)* North American (8)

(das) **Norddeutschland** Northern Germany (3)

der **Norden** north (6)

nördlich (von) north (of) (11)

der **Nordpol** North Pole (1)

die **Nordsee** North Sea (1)

normalerweise usually, normally (2, 4-1)

das **Notebook, -s** notebook *(computer)* (2)

die **Notiz, -en** note (E)

der **November** November (1-2)

die **Nudel, -n** noodle (2, 4-1)

die **Nummer, -n** number (E)

nun now (8)

nur only (1-1)

die **Nuss, ⸚e** nut (3)

die **Nutzung** use (5)

O

ob whether *(sub conj)* (5)

oben above (10-2)

ober upper (10)

das **Obst** *(sing)* fruit (4-1)

obwohl although, even though *(sub conj)* (4-2)

der **Ochse, -n, -n** ox (1)

die **Ode, -n** ode (11)

oder *(coord conj)* or (1-2)

der **Ofen, ⸚** oven (9)

offen open (2, 3-2)

öffentlich public (1)

öffentliche Verkehrsmittel public transportation (8)

der **Offizier, -e** officer (4)

öffnen to open (5, 11-1)

oft often (1-1)

ohne *(prep + acc)* without (E, 5-2)

das **Ohr, -en** ear (6-1)

jemand *(acc)* **übers Ohr hauen** to pull a fast one on someone (9)

die **Ohrenschmerzen** *(pl)* earache (6)

der **Ohrring, -e** earring (5-2)

der **Oktober** October (1-2)

das **Oktoberfest** Octoberfest (1)

das **Öl, -e** oil (9-2)

der **Oldtimer, -** vintage car (2)

die **Olive, -n** olive (2-2)

das **Olivenöl** olive oil (2-2)

die **Oma, -s** grandma (3-1)

der **Onkel, -** uncle (3-1)

der **Opa, -s** grandpa (3-1)

die **Oper, -n** opera (2-2)

optimistisch optimistic (2, 3-1)

die **Orange, -n** orange (1, 4-1)

der **Orangensaft** *(sing)* orange juice (4-1)

das **Orchester, -** orchestra (2, 3-2)

ordentlich decent (2); neat, tidy (4-2)

die **Ordnung** order (9)

Alles in Ordnung? Is everything okay? (9-2)

in Ordnung bringen, brachte, gebracht to tidy up (4)

orientiert oriented (12)

das **Ornament, -e** ornament (5)

der **Ort, -e** place (1)

vor Ort on site (1)

der **Ossi, -s** citizen of former East Germany (11)

der/die **Ostdeutsche, -n** citizen of East Germany (11)

(das) **Ostdeutschland** East Germany (11)

der **Osten** east (1)

der **Osterhase, -n, -n** Easter bunny (7)

der **Ostermontag** Easter Monday (7)

Ostern Easter (7-1)

(das) **Österreich** Austria (1-1)

der **Österreicher, -/** die **Österreicherin, -nen** Austrian *(person)* (1-1)

österreichisch *(adj)* Austrian (9)

der **Ostersonntag** Easter Sunday (7)

osteuropäisch *(adj)* Eastern European (11)

östlich (von) east (of) (11)

die **Ostsee** Baltic Sea (1)

der **Ozean, -e** ocean (10)

P

das **Paar, -e** pair, couple (6)

paar: ein paar a couple of, a few (1-1)

packen to pack (4, 6-2)

die **Packung, -en** package (5)

der **Pädagoge, -n, -n**/die **Pädagogin, -nen** educator (6)

das **Paket, -e** package, parcel (7-2); package deal (5)

das **Papier, -e** paper (9)

der **Papierkorb, ⸚e** wastepaper basket (8-1)

papierlos paperless (10-1)

das **Paradies** paradise (10-1)

der **Paragraph, -en, -en** paragraph (11)

das **Parfüm, -s** perfume (7-2)

der **Park, -s** park (1)

die **Parkmöglichkeit, -en** parking facility (5)

der **Parkschein, -e** parking pass (8)

das **Parlament, -e** parliament (11, 12-1)

die **Partei, -en** *(political)* party (E); party *(to an agreement)* (8)

der **Partner, -/**die **Partnerin, -nen** partner (2, 3-1)

die **Party, -s** party (7-2)

der **Pass, ⸚e** passport (5-2)

passen to fit (E)

passend appropriate (7)

passieren, passierte, ist passiert to happen (6-2)

passioniert ardent (5-1)

der **Patient, -en, -en**/die **Patientin, -nen** patient (5, 9-2)

die **Pause, -n** break (12)

der **Pendler, -**/die **Pendlerin, -nen** commuter (12)

die **Pension, -en** pension (12-2)

die **Person, -en** person, individual (2, 3-2)

die **Personalabteilung, -en** personnel department (9)

der **Personalchef, -s**/ die **Personalchefin, -nen** personnel manager (6-1)

das **Personalpronomen, -** personal pronoun (7)

die **Personenbeschreibung, -en** description of a person (3)

persönlich personal(ly) (5)

die **Peseta, Peseten** peseta *(former Spanish currency)* (9)

pessimistisch pessimistic (3-1)

der **Pfad, -e** path (3)

die **Pfanne, -n** pan (3, 9-1)

der **Pfeffer** pepper (1, 9-2)

die **Pfeife, -n** pipe (3)

der **Pfennig, -e** penny (3)

das **Pferd, -e** horse (10-1)

Da bringen mich keine zehn Pferde hin. Wild horses couldn't drag me there. (10)

(das) **Pfingsten, -** Pentecost (7)

die **Pflanze, -n** plant (3)

das **Pflaster, -** Band-Aid (9)

die **Pflaume, -n** plum (11)

pflücken to pick (11)

pflügen to plough (11)

der **Pfosten, -** post (3)

das **Pfund, -e** pound (3)

Pfui! Yuck! (11)

die **Philharmonie** philharmonic orchestra (1)

die **Philosophie, -n** philosophy (3)

die **Physik** physics (1)

der **Physiotherapeut, -en, -en**/ die **Physiotherapeutin, -nen** physical therapist (3)

der **Pianist, -en, -en**/die **Pianistin, -nen** pianist (3)

das **Picknick, -s** picnic (4)

die **Pistazie, -n** pistachio (2)

die **Pistole, -n** pistol (7)

die **Pizza, -s** pizza (3)

der **Pkw, -s (Personenkraftwagen)** car (10)

der **Plan, ⸚e** plan (1, 5-1)

planen to plan (7)

Platte: einen Platten haben to have a flat tire (12-2)

der **Platz, ⸚e** place; space; room; seat (4, 5-1); city square (5)

die **Platzreservierung, -en** seat reservation (7)

plötzlich suddenly, all of a sudden (6-2)

poetisch poetic (10)

die **Politik** politics (5)

der **Politiker, -**/die **Politikerin, -nen** politician (2)

politisch political(ly) (2)

die **Polizei** police (4, 12-2)

der **Polizeibericht, -e** police report (10)

der **Polizist, -en, -en**/die **Polizistin, -nen** police officer (2, 9-2)

polnisch *(adj)* Polish (2)

das **Polohemd, -en** polo shirt (3)

die **Pommes**/die **Pommes frites** *(pl)* French fries (4-1)

populär popular (1, 10-2)

die **Pore, -n** pore (12-1)

das **Porträt, -s** portrait (9)

die **Position, -en** position (12-1)

positiv positive (12-1)

Positives positive things (11-2)

die **Post** post office; mail (8-2)

das **Postamt, ⸚er** post office (10)

das **Poster, -** poster (8-2)

die **Postleitzahl, -en** zip code, postal code (E)

praktisch practical (2-1)

die **Präsenz** presence (9)

der **Präsident, -en, -en**/die **Präsidentin, -nen** president (1)

das **Präteritum** simple past tense (10)

der **Preis, -e** price (3-2)

preisgünstig inexpensive (3-2)

primitiv primitive (5-1)

privat private (11)

das **Privathaus, ⸚er** private home (8)

das **Problem, -e** problem (3-1)

das **Produkt, -e** product (4, 10-2)

die **Produktion** production (4)

der **Professor, -en**/die **Professorin, -nen** professor (1)

der **Profi, -s** pro (4)

das **Programm, -e** (2)

der **Programmierer, -**/die **Programmiererin, -nen** programmer (1)

der **Projektor, -en** projector (5)

proklamieren to proclaim (11)

prominent prominent (8)

Prost! Prosit! Cheers! To your health! (7-2)

protzig swanky, showy (10)

das **Prozent, -e** percent (1, 12-1)

prüfen to test (9)

die **Prüfung, -en** test (7)

der **Psychiater, -**/die **Psychiaterin, -nen** psychiatrist (9)

der **Psychologe, -n, -n**/die **Psychologin, -nen** (6)

der **Pudding, -s** pudding (3, 4-1)

der **Pudel, -n** poodle (2)

der **Pulli, -s** sweater (2-2)

der **Pullover, -** sweater (1, 2-2)

der **Punkt, -e** dot; period (4)

Punkt halb zwei at one-thirty on the dot (4, 5-2)

pünktlich punctual, on time (7)

die **Puppe, -n** doll (7)

das **Putenfleisch** *(sing)* turkey *(meat)* (9)

putzen to clean (4, 6-2)

Q

der **Quadratfuß** square foot (8)

der **Quadratmeter, -** square meter (8)

qualifiziert qualified (12-1)

die **Quelle, -n** source (10-1)

das **Quiz, -** quiz (5-2)

R

das **Rad, ⸚er** bike; wheel (3-1)

Rad fahren (fährt Rad), fuhr Rad, ist Rad gefahren to ride a bike, to go cycling (4-2)

das **Radio, -s** radio (6)

der **Radiomoderator, -en, -en/ die Radiomoderatorin, -nen** radio host (1)

die **Radtour, -en** bicycle trip (2)

eine **Radtour machen** to go on a bicycle trip (5)

der **Radwanderführer, -** cycling tour guidebook (11)

die **Radwanderkarte, -n** cycling tour map (11)

rasen to race (10)

der **Rasen, -** lawn (6-2)

der **Rasierapparat, -e** shaver, electric razor (9-2)

(sich) **rasieren** to shave (9-2)

das **Rasierwasser** *(sing)* aftershave (9-2)

rasseln to rattle (3)

die **Raststätte, -n** restaurant *(on the freeway)* (9)

der **Rat** *(sing)* advice (4)

um **Rat fragen** to ask for advice (12)

raten (rät), riet, geraten *(+ dat)* to advise (12-2); to guess (7)

das **Rathaus, ⸚er** town hall; city hall (8-2)

der **Ratschlag, ⸚e** piece of advice (5)

die **Ratte, -n** rat (1)

rauchen to smoke (4-2)

Mir raucht der Kopf. I can't think straight anymore. (9)

das **Rauchen** smoking (7)

der **Raum, ⸚e** room (8)

rauskommen, kam raus, ist rausgekommen to come out (6)

reagieren (auf) to react (to) (10)

real real (9)

recherchieren to do research (6-2)

die **Rechnung, -en** bill (9-1)

recht right *(adj)*

es allen **recht machen** trying to please everybody (10)

Es ist nicht recht, dass ... It's not right that . . . (10)

recht haben to be right (12-2)

das **Recht, -e** right (12)

rechtlich legal (12)

rechts right; to the right (4-2)

der **Rechtsanwalt, ⸚e/die Rechtsanwältin, -nen** lawyer (12)

die **Rechtskurve, -n** right curve (4)

rechtzeitig on time; early enough (9-1)

recyceln to recycle (8-2)

die **Rede, -n** speech; talk (11-1)

reden to speak, to talk (4-2)

reduziert reduced (7)

das **Referat, -e** (oral) report; paper (4-2)

das **Reformhaus, ⸚er** health food store (8, 9-2)

das **Regal, -e** shelf (6)

regelmäßig regular(ly) (11)

der **Regen** rain (2, 5-1)

der **Regenschirm, -e** (5)

das **Regenwetter** rainy weather (1)

die **Regierung, -en** government (11)

die **Region, -en** region (6-1)

regnen to rain (1-1)

Es regnet. It's raining. (1)

reich rich (1, 5-2)

reichen: Das reicht (mir). That's enough (for me). (10-2)

der **Reichspräsident, -en, -en** German president *(before World War II)* (11)

reif ripe (2)

die **Reihenfolge** sequence (7)

rein pure(ly) (12)

rein·gehen, ging rein, ist reingegangen to go in (6)

der **Reis** rice (4-1)

die **Reise, -n** trip (2, 3-1)

eine **Reise machen** to go on a trip, to take a trip (5-1)

der **Reiseleiter, -/ die Reiseleiterin, -nen** travel guide (6)

die **Reisebroschüre, -n** travel brochure (5)

das **Reisebüro, -s** travel agency (5-2)

reisen, reiste, ist gereist to travel (1-2)

reiten, ritt, ist geritten to ride *(a horse)* (10-1)

der **Reiter, -** horseback rider (10)

der **Rekord, -e** record (12)

die **Relativitätstheorie** theory of relativity (6)

die **Religion, -en** religion (11)

rennen, rannte, ist gerannt to run (6-2)

renovieren to renovate (11)

die **Rente, -n** pension (12-2)

die **Rentenversicherung, -en** pension plan (12)

der **Rentner, -/die Rentnerin, -nen** pensioner (12)

reparieren to repair (4)

die **Republik, -en** republic (11-1)

das **Requiem, Requien** requiem (3)

reservieren to reserve (4)

respektlos disrespectful (5)

respektvoll respectful (5)

das **Restaurant, -s** restaurant (1)

restaurieren to restore (10)

restlich rest of the, remaining (11)

das **Rezept, -e** recipe (9-1)

rezeptfrei prescription-free *(drugs)* (9)

rezeptpflichtig prescription *(drugs)* (9)

der **Rhabarber** *(sing)* rhubarb (7)

der **Rhein** Rhine *(river)* (1)

das **Rheintal** Rhine valley (1)

richtig right; true (1-1); correct (4)

die **Richtigkeit** rightness, correctness (11)

riechen, roch, gerochen to smell (12-2)

riesig huge (8, 10-2)

der **Ring, -e** ring (1, 7-2)

der **Ringfinger, -** ring finger (6)

risikolos risk-free (12)

riskieren to risk (8)

der **Rock** *(sing)* rock music (2)

der **Rock, ⸚e** skirt (2-2)

das **Rockfest, -e** rock festival (1)

die **Rockgruppe, -n** rock group (1)

der **Rockstar, -s** rock star (2)

die **Rolle, -n** role (12)

der **Roman, -e** novel (5-2)

romantisch romantic (5-2)

rosarot pink (1-1)

die **Rose, -n** rose (1, 7-2)

rostfrei stainless (4)

rostig rusty (2)

rot red (1-1)

das **Rote Kreuz** the Red Cross (4)

der **Rotkohl** red cabbage (9-1)

der **Rotwein, -e** red wine (3)

die **Rübe, -n** turnip (4)

der **Rücken, -** back (6-1)

die **Rückenschmerzen** *(pl)* backache (6)

der **Rucksack, ̈e** backpack (7)

die **Rückseite, -n** back (9)

der **Rückspiegel, -** rearview mirror (11-2)

rufen, rief, gerufen to call (10-1)

die **Ruhe** peace and quiet (8)

  Lass mich in Ruhe! Stop bothering me! (4-2)

Ruhetag: Dienstag Ruhetag closed all day Tuesday (1)

ruhig calm, quiet (8-1)

das **Rührei** *(sing)* scrambled eggs (4-1)

der **Rum** rum (9-1)

rum·hängen, hing rum, rumgehangen to hang out (5, 6-2)

rund round (6)

  rund um around (10)

russisch *(adj)* Russian (7)

der **Rutsch: Einen guten Rutsch (ins Neue Jahr)!** Happy New Year! (7-1)

S

der **Saal, Säle** hall (9)

die **Sache, -n** thing (4, 7-2); cause (12-1)

die **Sächsische Schweiz** Saxon Switzerland (E)

säen to sow (4)

der **Saft, ̈e** juice (4)

saftig juicy (10-2)

die **Säge, -n** saw *(tool)* (10)

sagen to say, to tell (2-1)

  sag mal say, tell me (1)

Wie sagt man das auf Deutsch? How do you say that in German? (4-1)

die **Salami, -s** salami (2-2)

der **Salat, -e** salad (4-1)

das **Salz** salt (1, 9-2)

salzig salty (2)

sammeln to collect (2-1)

die **Sammlung, -en** collection (10)

der **Samstag** Saturday (1-2) *(see also* **Dienstag***)*

die **Sandale, -n** sandal (3-2)

sandig sandy (2)

der **Sandstein** sandstone (E)

der **Sänger, -/**die **Sängerin, -nen** singer (5)

der **Sankt Nikolaus** Saint Nicholas (7)

die **Sardine, -n** sardine (8)

der **Satellit, -en, -en** satellite (10-1)

satt full, satiated (10-1)

  Ich bin satt. I'm full. (10)

satteln to saddle (10-1)

der **Satz, ̈e** sentence (3)

der **Satzteil, -e** part of a sentence (11)

sauber clean (8-1)

sauer sour (1); annoyed (11)

der **Sauerbraten** marinated roast beef (9)

das **Sauerkraut** sauerkraut (4-1)

säuerlich sourish (9)

die **Sauna, -s** sauna (5-1)

das **Sauwetter** rotten weather (9)

die **S-Bahn** *commuter train* (5)

der **Scanner, -** scanner (2-1, 3)

Schade! Too bad! (12-2)

der **Schal, -e** scarf (8)

schälen to peel (9)

schamlos shameless (12)

scharf sharp (2); spicy, hot (9)

schattig shady (2)

das **Schaubild, -er** diagram; graph (11-1)

schauen (auf) to look (at) (7-1)

der **Schauspieler, -/**die **Schauspielerin, -nen** (6)

die **Scheibe, -n** slice (4-1)

  eine Scheibe Brot a slice of bread (4-1)

der **Schein, -e** certificate *(for successfully completing a university course)* (1); banknote, bill *(money)* (9-2)

scheinen, schien, geschienen to shine (1-1)

schenken to give *(a gift)* (7-1)

die **Schere, -n** scissors (9)

schick chic (2-2)

schicken to send (6-1)

schief crooked; leaning

  schief gehen to go wrong (12)

schießen, schoss, geschossen to shoot (11-1)

das **Schiff, -e** ship (2)

der **Schilling, -** shilling *(former Austrian currency)* (2)

schlafen (schläft), schlief, geschlafen to sleep (3-2)

schlaflos sleepless (12)

die **Schlafmöglichkeit, -en** place to sleep (5)

der **Schlafsack, ̈e** sleeping bag (11-2)

die **Schlaftablette, -n** sleeping pill (4)

das **Schlafzimmer, -** bedroom (8-1)

schlagen (schlägt), schlug, geschlagen to hit; to beat (9)

die **Schlagzeile, -n** headline (11-1)

schlank slim (2-1)

schlau crafty, clever (10-1)

schlecht bad (1-2)

schleimig slimy (2)

schlemmen to feast; to indulge (7)

der **Schlemmer, -** gourmand (7)

schleppen to drag (5-2)

schließen, schloss, geschlossen to close (11-1)

schließlich finally (10-2)

Schlittschuhlaufen gehen to go (ice) skating (1)

das **Schloss, ̈er** castle (5-1)

der **Schlosser, -** toolmaker (6)

schlüpfrig slippery (2)

der **Schlussverkauf, ̈e** clearance sale (7-1)

schmal slim, narrow; *(face)* thin (6)

schmecken to taste; to taste good (4-1)

der **Schmerz, -en** pain (6-2)

das **Schminken** face painting (4)

(sich) **schminken** to put on make-up (9-2)

der **Schmuck** jewelry (7-2)

schmutzig dirty (8-1)

der **Schnaps, ⸚e** schnapps; hard liquor (10)

schnarchen to snore (4)

die **Schnecke, -n** snail (9)

der **Schnee** snow (4-2)

der **Schneeregen** sleet (1)

der **Schneesturm, ⸚e** snowstorm (12)

schneeweiß snow-white (11)

schneiden, schnitt, geschnitten to cut (6-2)

schneien to snow (1, 4-2)
   Es schneit. It's snowing. (1)

schnell fast, quick (E, 3-1)

der **Schnellimbiss, -e** fast-food stand (9)

das **Schnitzel, -** cutlet (7)
   das Wiener Schnitzel breaded veal cutlet (7)

der **Schnupfen** the sniffles (11)

der **Schnurrbart, ⸚e** mustache (5-2)

der **Schock** shock (11-2)

die **Schokolade** chocolate (1, 2-2)
   eine Tafel Schokolade a chocolate bar (10)

schon already (2-2)
   schon gut it's all right (9)

schön nice; beautiful (E, 1-1)

die **Schönheit** beauty (11)

der **Schopf, ⸚e** top (*of a turnip*) (4)

der **Schoß, ⸚e** lap (9)

der **Schrank, ⸚e** closet (8-1)
   nicht alle Tassen im Schrank haben to be crazy (8)

der **Schrebergarten, ⸚** garden plot at the edge of town (8)

schrecklich awful(ly), terrible; terribly (11-1)

schreiben, schrieb, geschrieben to write (E, 1-1)

der **Schreiber, -** scribe (10)

der **Schreibtisch, -e** desk (8-1)

das **Schreibzeug, -e** writing utensil (3)

schreien, schrie, geschrien to scream; to shout (10-2)

die **Schrift, -en** writing (10)

schriftlich in writing; written (4-2)

die **Schrittgeschwindigkeit** (*sing*) walking speed (12)

der **Schuh, -e** shoe (1, 2-2)

das **Schuhgeschäft, -e** shoe store (2)

der **Schuhmacher, -/die Schuhmacherin, -nen** shoemaker (10)

der **Schulabschluss** high school graduation (12)

der **Schulbeginn** beginning of school (1)

die **Schuld, -en** debt (5)

schulden to owe (7-1)

der **Schuldschein, -e** IOU (7-1)

die **Schule, -n** school (1, 2-1)

der **Schüler, -/die Schülerin, -nen** pupil; student in a primary or secondary school (2-1)

die **Schulter, -n** shoulder (1, 6-1)

die **Schulzeit** schooldays (*pl*) (7)

die **Schüssel, -n** bowl (4-1)
   eine Schüssel Müsli a bowl of muesli (4-1)

der **Schutz** (*sing*) protection (4)

schützen to protect (4)

schwach weak (6-2)

die **Schwäche, -n** weakness (6-2)

der **Schwan, ⸚e** swan (1)

schwarz black (1-1)

das **Schwarzbrot** rye bread (7)

das **Schwarzfahren** traveling without a ticket (4)

der **Schwarzwald** Black Forest (1)

die **Schwarzwälder Kirschtorte** Black Forest cake (10)

schwedisch (*adj*) Swedish (2)

das **Schwein, -e** pig (10)
   Du hast Schwein gehabt. You were lucky. (10)

die **Schweinerei, -en** mess (7)

der **Schweiß** sweat (9)

die **Schweiz** Switzerland (1-1)

der **Schweizer, -/die Schweizerin, -nen** Swiss (*person*) (1-1)

schweizerisch (*adj*) Swiss (4)

schwer hard; heavy; difficult (5, 6-2)
   eine schwere Erkältung a bad cold (12-2)

die **Schwester, -n** sister (1, 3-1)

die **Schwierigkeit, -en** difficulty (12)

schwimmen, schwamm, ist geschwommen to swim (1, 2-1)
   schwimmen gehen to go swimming (1, 2-1)

schwül humid (1)

das **Schwyzerdütsch** Swiss German (8)

(die) **Sciencefiction** science fiction (3)

das **Scrabble** Scrabble (2)

der **See, -n** lake (5-1)

die **See, -n** sea (11)

seekrank seasick (6)

das **Segelboot, -e** sailboat (3)

segeln to sail (1)

sehen (sieht), sah, gesehen to see (3-2); to look (12-1)

sehenswert worth seeing (11)

sehr very (1-2)

die **Seife, -n** soap (9-2)

sein, sein, seine his, its (2)

sein (ist), war, ist gewesen to be (E)

Ich bin's. It's me. (5-2)

seit (*prep + dat*) since (2); for (7)
   seit kurzem recently (11-2)
   seit kurzer Zeit recently (11-1)

die **Seite, -n** page (7); side (8)

der **Sekt** sparkling wine (5-1)

die **Sekunde, -n** second (1, 2-1)

selber myself; yourself; herself; etc. (3)

selbst myself, yourself, herself, etc. (2, 4-2)
   von selbst by oneself (7)

selbstgemacht homemade (2)

selbstlos selfless (12)

der **Selbstmord, -e** suicide (11)

selten seldom, rarely (2, 3-1, 4-2)

das **Semester, -** semester (1-1)

die **Semesterferien** (*pl*) vacation (7)

das **Semesterticket, -s** low cost student pass for public transportation (E) das **Seminar, -e** seminar (4-2)

der **Senf** mustard (7, 9-2)

der **Senior, -en** senior citizen (3)

die **Sensation, -en** sensation (3-2)

sentimental sentimental (5-2)

der **September** September (1-2)

servieren to serve *(a dish)* (9-1)

die **Serviette, -n** napkin, serviette (9-1)

Servus! Hello! Hi! Good-bye! So long! *(Austrian)* (E)

der **Sessel, -** armchair (8-1)

das **Set, -s** place mat (2)

setzen to set (3)

sich **setzen** to sit down (9-2)

der **Shootingstar, -s** suddenly successful person (2)

die **Shorts** *(pl)* shorts (2-2)

die **Show, -s** show (6)

   eine Show abziehen to put on a show (12)

sicher sure, certainly; probably (8-2)

die **Signatur, -en** signature (4)

signieren to sign (7)

das **Silber** silver (4)

silbern silver (3)

(der) **Silvester** New Year's Eve (7-1)

die **Sinfonie, -n** symphony (8)

das **Sinfonieorchester, -** symphony orchestra (3)

singen, sang, gesungen to sing (1)

der **Sinn** *(sing)* meaning (1); sense (4)

die **Sinologie** Chinese Studies (4)

die **Sitte, -n** custom (9)

der **Sitz, -e** seat (3)

sitzen, saß, gesessen to sit (1-2)

der **Sitzplatz, ⸚e** seat (7)

der **Ski, -er** ski (1)

Ski laufen (läuft Ski), lief Ski, ist Ski gelaufen to ski (3)

das **Skilaufen** *(sing)* skiing (1)

Skilaufen gehen to go skiing (1)

der **Skilehrer, -/**die **Skilehrerin, -nen** ski instructor (1)

die **Skizze, -n** sketch *(drawing)* (10)

skrupellos unscrupulous (12)

die **Skulptur, -en** sculpture (8-2)

der **Smoking, -s** tuxedo (2)

die **SMS, -** text message (E)

snowboarden gehen to go snowboarding (2-1)

so so, such (1)

so ein (ein, eine) such a (2)

so lang(e) *(adv)* so long (2)

so … wie as … as (2-2)

sobald as soon as *(sub conj)* (4)

die **Socke, -n** sock (2-2)

das **Sofa, -s** sofa (3)

sofort immediately, right away; in a minute (6-2)

das **Softdrink, -s** soft drink (2-1)

das **Softeis** soft ice cream (10)

die **Software** software (11)

der **Softwareentwickler, -/**die **Softwareentwicklerin, -nen** software developer (12)

sogar even (7, 9-2)

der **Sohn, ⸚e** son (1, 3-1)

solange *(sub conj)* as long as (10, 12-1)

solcher, solches, solche such (7)

der **Soldat, -en, -en/**die **Soldatin, -nen** soldier (4, 11-1)

sollen, sollte, gesollt to be supposed to, should (4)

der **Sommer, -** summer (1-2)

die **Sommerferien** *(pl)* summer holidays, summer vacation (5)

sondern *(coord conj)* but; (but) . . . instead; but rather (3)

der **Song, -s** song (3)

die **Sonne** sun (1-1)

die **Sonnenbrille, -n** sunglasses (3-2)

die **Sonnencreme, -s** suntan lotion (4)

die **Sonnenenergie** solar energy (8)

sonnig sunny (2)

der **Sonntag, -e** Sunday (1-2) *(see also* **Dienstag***)*

sonst otherwise, or else (9)

   was … sonst what else (8)

   Sonstiges miscellaneous (8)

sooft *(sub conj)* as often as (10)

sorgen für to care for (12-1)

sorglos carefree (12)

die **Soße, -n** sauce (4, 9-1)

sowieso anyway (4, 8-1)

die **Sowjetunion** Soviet Union (11)

der **Sozialarbeiter, -/**die **Sozialarbeiterin, -nen** social worker (2)

die **Soziologie** sociology (9)

die **Spaghetti** *(pl)* spaghetti (3)

die **Spalte, -n** column (12)

spalten to split (11)

(das) **Spanisch** Spanish *(language)* (4)

spanisch *(adj)* Spanish (2)

sparen to save (6-2)

das **Sparkonto, -konten** savings account (12-2)

der **Spaß** fun, enjoyment (1)

   Es macht mir Spaß, … I enjoy . . . (8-2)

   Spaß haben to have fun (5-1)

spät late (4-1)

   Wie spät ist es? What time is it? (2-2)

später: Bis später! See you later! (1-1)

die **Spätzle** *(pl)* *traditional Southern German egg pasta* (9)

der **Spaziergang, ⸚e** walk (7)

   einen Spaziergang machen to go for a walk (7)

spazieren gehen, ging spazieren, ist spazieren gegangen to go for a walk (4-2)

der **Speck** *(sing)* bacon (4)

die **Speise(n)karte, -n** menu (9-1)

der **Speisesaal, Speisesäle** dining hall, refectory (1)

spekulieren to speculate (7)

die **Spende, -n** donation (9)

spenden to donate (4)

spendieren *(+ dat)* to buy *(for someone)* (12)

die **Sperre, -n** barrier; barricade (11)

die **Spezialität, -en** specialty (3)

der **Spiegel, -** mirror (9-2)

das **Spiegelei, -er** fried egg (sunny-side up) (4-1)

spielen to play (1-2)

das **Spielzeug** toy (3)

der **Spinat** spinach (10)

spinnen, spann, gesponnen to be crazy (8)

spitze great (2)

   echt spitze really great (2-2)

der **Sport** sport(s), athletics (1-2)

   Sport machen to do sports (1-2)

Was für Sport machst du?
What sports do you do? (1-2)

die **Sportabteilung, –en** sporting goods department (10)

das **Sportcoupé, –s** sport coupe (3)

das **Sportgeschäft, –e** sporting goods store (2)

sportlich athletic (1-2); sporty (2)

das **Sportprogramm, –e** sports program (1)

die **Sportreportage, –n** sports report (3)

die **Sprache, –n** language (3-2)

die **Sprachkompetenz** language ability (12)

die **Sprachnotiz, –en** note on language (usage) (E)

sprechen (spricht), sprach, gesprochen to speak, to talk (2, 3-2)

springen, sprang, ist gesprungen to jump (8)

das **Spülbecken, –** sink (8-1)

die **Spülmaschine, –n** dishwasher (8-1)

das **Squash** squash (sport) (2)

der **Staat, –en** state (9)

der **Staatssicherheitsdienst** (former East German) state security service) (11)

der **Stacheldraht** barbed wire (11-1)

das **Stadion, Stadien** stadium (5)

die **Stadt, ⁼e** city, town (1, 2-2)
  in die Stadt to town (3)

der **Stadtplan, ⁼e** map of the city/town (8-2)

der **Stahl** steel (4)

der **Stall, ⁼e** stable (10-1)

der **Stamm, ⁼e** tree trunk (7)
  Der Apfel fällt nicht weit vom Stamm. Like father, like son. (7)

der **Stammbaum, ⁼e** family tree (6-1)

der **Stand** (sing) social status (12)

ständig constant(ly) (12-1)

stark strong (6-2)
  stark reduziert sharply reduced (7-1)

die **Stärke, –n** strength (6-2)

der **Starnberger See** (lake south of Munich) (4)

starten, startete, hat gestartet to start (something, e.g., a motor) (6-2)

starten, startete, ist gestartet to start; to take off (of airplanes) (6-2)

die **Statistik, –en** statistic (12-1)

statt instead of (7, 8-2); (+ gen) (12-2)

statt·finden, fand statt, stattgefunden to take place (10-2)

der **Staubsauger, –** vacuum cleaner (8-2)

stecken in to put in, to stick in (10-1)
  die Nase zu tief ins Glas stecken to drink too much (6)

stehen, stand, gestanden to stand; to be standing (1-2); to say (6-2)
  auf seinen (eigenen) Beinen stehen to stand on one's (own) feet (12-1)
  Diese Jacke steht dir. This jacket looks good on you. (7-2)

stehen bleiben, blieb stehen, ist stehen geblieben to stop (walking) (10-1)

die **Stehlampe, –n** floor lamp (8-1)

stehlen (stiehlt), stahl, gestohlen to steal (11)

steif stiff (9-1)

steigen, stieg, ist gestiegen to climb (10-1)

die **Stelle, –n** job, position (12-2)

stellen to put (in an upright position) (8-2)
  eine Frage stellen to ask a question (7-2)

sterben (stirbt), starb, ist gestorben to die (4, 6-2)

die **Stereoanlage, –n** stereo (8-1)

der **Stern, –e** star (11)

das **Steuer(rad)** steering wheel (11-2)

der **Stiefel, –** boot (2-2)

die **Stiefmutter, ⁼** stepmother (3-1)

der **Stiefvater, ⁼** stepfather (3-1)

der **Stil, –e** style (8)

stillen to satisfy (hunger, thirst) (4)

die **Stimme, –n** voice; vote (12)

stimmen to be right (4)
  Das stimmt. That's right. (6-2)
  das **Stimmrecht** right to vote (12)

die **Stimmung, –en** mood (12)

das **Stimmungstief, –e** down mood (12)

stinkig stinky (2)

stinklangweilig deadly boring (3)

die **Stirn, –en** forehead (6-1)

der **Stocherkahn, ⁼e** punting boat (1)

der **Stock, ⁼e** stick (10)

der **Stock, Stockwerke** floor, story (8)

der **Stoffbär, –en, –en** stuffed bear (7)

das **Stofftier, –e** stuffed animal (7-2)

stolz proud (7)

stolz sein auf (+ acc) to be proud of (7)

stoppen to stop (6-2)

stören to disturb (8-1)

der **Strafzettel, –** (traffic) ticket (12-2)

der **Strand, ⁼e** beach (1, 5-1)

die **Straße, –n** street (E, 2-2)

das **Straßenfest, –e** street festival (7)

die **Straßenseite, –n** side of the street (12)

die **Straßensperre, –n** street barricade (11)

streichen, strich, gestrichen to paint (e.g., a fence, a house) (6-2)

der **Stress** stress (4-2)

stressig stressful (8)

strikt strict (8)

das **Stromnetz** power grid (8)

der **Strumpf, ⁼e** stocking (11)

das **Stück, –e** piece (3, 4-1)
  ein Stück Torte a piece of layer cake (3, 4-1)
  drei Stück Kuchen three pieces of cake (4)
  fünf Euro das Stück five euros apiece (7)
  Stück für Stück bit by bit (11)

der **Student, –en, –en**/die **Studentin, –nen** student (1-1)

der **Studentenausweis, –e** student ID (5-2)

der **Studentenchor, -̈e** student choir (6)

das **Studentenheim, -e** dormitory, student residence (2-2)

das **Studentenleben** student life (6)

das **Studentenwerk** student center (E, 6-2)

das **Studienfach, -̈er** field of study; subject (2-2)

studieren to study (*i.e., to attend college or university*), *to major in* (1-1)

studieren an *(+dat)* to study at a college or university (11-2)

das **Studium** *(sing)* studies (10)

der **Stuhl, -̈e** chair (2, 8-1)

  jemand *(dat)* **den Stuhl vor die Tür setzen** to throw somebody out (8)

  die **Stulle, -n** sandwich (9-2)

die **Stunde, -n** hour (2-1)

  eine Stunde lang for an hour (4)

  pro Stunde per hour (6)

stundenlang for hours (2-1)

der **Stundenplan, -̈e** schedule, timetable (2-2)

der **Sturm, -̈e** storm (12-2)

stürmisch stormy (6)

stürzen to fall; to plunge (10)

stylen to style (2)

die **Suche** search (2)

auf der Suche sein to be searching (10)

suchen to look for (2-2)

süchtig addicted (12)

süddeutsch *(adj)* Southern German (7)

der **Süden** south (8)

südlich (von) south (of) (11)

der **Südpol** South Pole (1)

die **Südseeinsel, -n** South Sea island (9)

super super (E)

der **Superlativ, -e** superlative (5)

der **Supermarkt, -̈e** supermarket (7-2)

supersüß very sweet (3)

die **Suppe, -n** soup (2)

  ein Haar in der Suppe finden to find fault with something (9)

das **Surfbrett, -er** surfboard (4)

surfen to surf (6)

  surfen gehen to go surfing (1)

süß sweet (7)

die **Süßigkeiten** *(pl)* candy; sweets (6, 7-2)

das **Sweatshirt, -s** sweatshirt (1, 2-2)

das **Symbol, -e** symbol (1)

die **Synagoge, -n** synagogue (11)

das **Synonym, -e** synonym (10)

T

die **Tabelle, -n** chart, table (10-2)

die **Tablette, -n** pill, tablet (12-2)

die **Tafel, -n** (black)board (10)

  eine Tafel Schokolade a chocolate bar (10)

der **Tag, -e** day (E, 1-2)

  Guten Tag! Tag! Hello! (E-1)

  Tag der Arbeit Labor Day (7)

  Tag der Deutschen Einheit Day of German Reunification (7)

  Tag der Fahne Flag Day (7)

  vierzehn Tage two weeks (1, 5-1)

das **Tagebuch, -̈er** diary (6-2)

der **Tagesjob, -s** job for a day (6)

das **Tagesmenü, -s** special of the day (10)

die **Tageszeitung, -en** daily newspaper (10)

täglich daily (2)

taktlos tactless (5)

taktvoll tactful (5)

das **Tal, -̈er** valley (5-1)

talentiert talented (12)

talentlos untalented (12)

die **Talkshow, -s** talk show (4)

der **Tango, -s** tango (2)

die **Tante, -n** aunt (3-1)

tanzen to dance (1-2)

der **Tänzer, -/** die **Tänzerin, -nen** dancer (2)

der **Tanzrhythmus** dance rhythm (E)

die **Tasche, -n** bag; pocket (4-2)

das **Taschenmesser, -** pocket knife (4-2)

die **Tasse, -n** cup (4-1)

  eine Tasse Kaffee a cup of coffee (4-1)

nicht alle Tassen im Schrank haben to be crazy (8)

die **Tätowierung, -en** tattoo (5)

tatsächlich actual(ly) (12-1)

tauchen to dive (5)

das **Tausend, -e** thousand (4)

das **Taxi, -s** taxi (4)

das **Team, -s** team (10-1)

die **Technik** technology (8-2)

technisch technical (12)

die **Technologie, -n** technology (10-1)

der **Teddybär, -en, -en** teddy bear (2)

der **Tee** tea (2-1)

die **Teekanne, -n** teapot (1, 9-1)

der **Teekessel, -** tea kettle (1)

der **Teelöffel, -** teaspoon (9-1)

der **Teenager, -** teenager (4)

der **Teig** batter; dough (9-1)

der **Teil, -e** part, area (8-2)

teilen to divide (11-1)

teilnehmen (nimmt teil), nahm teil, teilgenommen (an + *dat*) to take part (in) (9)

das **Telefon, -e** telephone (E)

das **Telefonbuch, -̈er** telephone book (E)

telefonieren (mit) to talk on the phone (with) (2-1)

die **Telefonnummer, -n** telephone number (E)

das **Teleskop, -e** telescope (1)

der **Teller, -** plate (5, 9-1)

die **Temperatur, -en** temperature (5)

das **Tennis** tennis (1)

  Tennis spielen to play tennis (2-1)

der **Tennisklub, -s** tennis club (10)

das **Tennismatch, -es** tennis match (10)

der **Tennisschläger, -** tennis racquet (7-2)

der **Tennisschuh, -e** tennis shoe (3)

der **Tenor, -̈e** tenor (2)

der **Teppich, -e** carpet, rug (3, 8-1)

teuer expensive (2-2)

der **Teufel, -** devil (8)

  den Teufel an die Wand malen to tempt fate (8)

der **Text, -e** text (7-1)

das **Theater, -** theater (1)
  ins Theater to the theater (1-2)
die **Theaterkarte, -n** theater
  ticket (4)
das **Theaterstück, -e** play (8)
das **Thema, Themen** topic (10-2)
die **Theorie, -n** theory (3)
die **Therapie, -n** therapy (12-2)
das **Thermometer,**
  - thermometer (1)
das **Ticket, -s** ticket (2)
das **Tief** (*sing*) low; low point (12)
tief deep; low (6)
die Nase zu tief ins Glas stecken
  to drink too much (6)
das **Tier, -e** animal (4, 7-2)
der **Tipp, -s** tip (*helpful hint*) (10)
der **Tisch, -e** table (7, 8-1)
  den Tisch decken to set the
    table (7-1)
der **Titel, -** title (7-2)
der **Toast** toast (4-1)
der **Toaster, -** toaster (7)
die **Tochter, ̈** daughter (1, 3-1)
der **Tod** death (3-2)
die **Todesanzeige, -n** death
  announcement (10)
der **Todesstreifen, -** death strip (11)
die **Toilette, -n** lavatory; bathroom;
  restroom (8-1)
tolerieren to tolerate (11)
toll fantastic, neat (1-1)
die **Tomate, -n** tomato (1)
der **Ton, ̈e** tone; sound; note (2)
der **Toner** toner (12)
der **Topf, ̈e** pot (9-1)
das **Tor, -e** gate (9)
die **Torte, -n** layer cake (4-1)
  ein Stück Torte a piece of layer
    cake (4-1)
tot dead (3-2)
total completely (1)
der **Totenschein, -e** death
  certificate (7)
der **Tourist, -en, -en**/die
  Touristin, -nen tourist (2, 5-2)
die **Touristenattraktion, -en**
  tourist attraction (5, 11)
die **Tournee, -n** tour (3-2)
tragen (trägt), trug, getragen to
  wear (3-2); to carry (8)

der **Traum, ̈e** dream (12-2)
der **Traumberuf, -e** job of one's
  dreams (12)
träumen to dream (12-2)
(sich) **treffen (trifft), traf,**
  getroffen to meet (9-2)
das **Treffen, -** meeting; gathering (7)
trennen to separate (11-1)
die **Treppe, -n** staircase (8-1)
trinkbar drinkable (12)
trinken, trank, getrunken to
  drink (2-1)
das **Trinkgeld, -er** tip (*in a*
  restaurant) (6, 9-1)
trocken dry (5-1)
sich (*dat*) **die Haare trocknen** to
  dry one's hair (9-2)
die **Trompete, -n** trumpet (2)
tropfen to drip (11)
trotz (*prep + gen*) in spite of (12-2)
trotzdem anyway; nevertheless
  (4, 5-2)
das **T-Shirt, -s** T-shirt (2-2)
Tschüss! Good-bye! So long!
  (E-1)
die **Tulpe, -n** tulip (1)
tun, tat, getan to do (1-2)
  Er tut dir nichts. He won't hurt
    you. (9-1)
  Es tut mir leid. I'm sorry. (7-2)
die **Tür, -en** door (8-1)
  jemand (*dat*) **den Stuhl vor die**
    Tür setzen to throw someone
    out (8)
der **Türke, -n, -n**/die **Türkin,**
  -nen Turk (2)
türkisch (*adj*) Turkish (2)
der **Turm, ̈e** tower (3)
das **Turnier, -e** tournament (2)
die **Tüte, -n** bag (10)
der **Typ, -en** guy (7-2)
typisch typical(ly) (4-2)

U

die **U-Bahn** subway
  die **U-Bahn-Linie, -n** subway
    line
üben to practice (6-2)
über (*prep + acc/dat*) about (2);
  across (1); over, above (6); via (6)

überfallen (überfällt), überfiel,
  überfallen to attack; to invade
  (11)
überfluten to flood (11)
der **Übergang, ̈e** crossing;
  transition (12-1)
überglücklich overjoyed (7)
überhaupt at all; anyway (11-1)
  überhaupt nicht not at all (11)
  überhaupt nichts nothing at
    all (11)
überlassen (überlässt), überließ,
  überlassen to leave to (11)
überleben to survive (10)
überlegen to think about (12)
übermorgen the day after
  tomorrow (3-2)
übernachten to spend the night; to
  stay overnight (5-2)
die **Übernachtung, -en** overnight
  accommodation (6)
übernehmen (übernimmt),
  übernahm, übernommen to
  assume (*a role*) (12); to take on (*a*
  duty) (12-1)
die **Überraschung, -en** surprise
  (7-1)
überreden to persuade (12)
überregional national, nationwide
  (10)
übersetzen to translate (6-2)
der **Übersetzer, -**/die **Übersetzerin,**
  -nen translator (9)
die **Übersetzung, -en** translation
  (10-1)
überzeugen to persuade (12-1)
übrigens by the way (2-1)
die **Übung, -en** exercise; seminar;
  lab; discussion section (2-2)
die **Uhr, -en** clock; watch (2-1)
  zehn Uhr ten o'clock (2-1)
  um zehn Uhr at ten o'clock (2-1)
  um wie viel Uhr? (at) what
    time? (2-2)
  Wie viel Uhr ist es? What time
    is it? (2-2)
die **Uhrzeit, -en** time of day (7)
um (*prep + acc*) at (2); around (5)
  um zehn at ten o'clock (2)
  um die Ecke around the corner (5)
um … zu in order to (8)

die **Umfrage, -n** survey, poll (5)

das **Umland** (sing) surrounding area (11)

umliegend surrounding (8)

sich **um·schauen (nach)** to look around (for) (10)

um·steigen, stieg um, ist umgestiegen to change trains (4-2)

die **Umwelt** environment (12-2)

um·ziehen, zog um, ist umgezogen to move (change residence) (8-2)

sich **um·ziehen, zog um, hat umgezogen** to change (one's clothes) (9-2)

unaufhörlich constantly (11-2)

unbedingt really (11)

unbewohnbar uninhabitable (12)

und (coord conj) and (E, 1-2)

undankbar ungrateful (12)

undefinierbar indefinable (12)

uneben uneven (2)

unehrlich dishonest (12-1)

der **Unfall, ⸚e** accident (11)

die **Unfreiheit** lack of freedom (11-2)

unfreundlich unfriendly (3-1)

ungesund unhealthy (4-2)

unglücklich unhappy (7-2)

unhöflich impolite (7-2)

die **Uni, -s** university (1-1)

an der Uni at the university (2-2)
  zur Uni to the university (2-2)

der **Uni-Abschluss** graduation (7)

die **Universität, -en** university (1-1)

das **Universitätsleben** (sing) university life (2-2)

die **Universitätsstadt, ⸚e** university town (8)

unkontrollierbar uncontrollable (12)

das **Unkraut** weeds (6)

unkultiviert uncultivated (9)

unmöglich impossible (4-2)

unordentlich messy, sloppy (4-2)

unregelmäßig irregular (11)

unser, unser, unsere our (1)

unten below (8, 10-2)

dort unten down there (8)

hier unten down here (10)

von unten from the bottom (12)

unter (prep + acc/dat) under, below (4); among (9)

unterbrechen (unterbricht), unterbrach, unterbrochen to interrupt (12-1)

die **Unterkunft, ⸚e** (living) accommodation (8)

das **Unternehmen, -** company (9)

der **Unternehmer, -/die Unternehmerin, -nen** entrepreneur (6)

der **Unterschied, -e** difference (12-1)

unterschiedlich different (3, 12-1)

die **Untertasse, -n** saucer (9-1)

unterwegs on the way (10-2)

unübersetzbar untranslatable (12)

unvorstellbar unimaginable (12)

up to date up-to-date (1)

uralt ancient (10)

die **Urgroßeltern** (pl) great-grandparents (6-1)

die **Urgroßmutter, ⸚** great-grandmother (6-1)

der **Urgroßvater, ⸚** great-grandfather (6-1)

der **Urlaub** vacation (generally of people in the work force) (5-1)

Urlaub machen to go on vacation (5-1)

ursprünglich originally (9)

usw. (und so weiter) etc. (et cetera, and so on) (E, 8-1)

die **Utopie, -n** utopia (12-1)

die **UV-Strahlen** (pl) UV rays (7)

V

(der) **Valentinstag** Valentine's Day (6, 7-2)

das **Vanilleeis** vanilla ice cream (9)

die **Vanillesoße** vanilla sauce (9)

die **Vase, -n** vase (1)

der **Vater, ⸚** father (E, 3-1)

väterlich fatherly (2)

väterlicherseits paternal (6-1)

der **Vati** dad (5)

der **Vegetarier, -/die Vegetarierin, -nen** vegetarian (4, 9-2)

vegetarisch vegetarian (9-2)

(das) **Venedig** Venice (10)

die **Veranstaltung, -en** event (2)

der **Veranstaltungstechniker, -/die Veranstaltungstechnikerin, -nen** event technician (2)

die **Verantwortung, -en** responsibility (12-1)

das **Verb, -en** verb (1)

der **Verband, ⸚e** association (4)

verbessern to improve; to correct (6-2)

verbinden, verband, verbunden to connect (9)

verbittert bitter, embittered (5)

verbringen, verbrachte, verbracht to spend (time) (7-2)

verdienen to earn (3-2)

die **Vereinigten Staaten (die USA)** the United States (the U.S.) (1-1)

die **Verfassung, -en** constitution (12-1)

Verflixt! Darn it! (10-2)

vergangen past (7)

vergessen (vergisst), vergaß, vergessen to forget (3, 4-2)

vergleichen, verglich, verglichen (8-1)

vergnügt happy, in a good mood (10)

verhaften to arrest (11-2)

das **Verhalten** (sing) behavior (11)

verheiratet married (3-1)

verhören to interrogate (8)

verkaufen to sell (3-2)

der **Verkäufer, -/die Verkäuferin, -nen** sales clerk, salesman/saleswoman (3-2)

die **Verkehrsmittel** (pl) transportation (8)

öffentliche Verkehrsmittel public transportation (8)

das **Verkehrszeichen, -** traffic sign (4)

verlassen (verlässt), verließ, verlassen to leave (8)

verlaufen (verläuft), verlief, ist verlaufen to happen, to run (12)

sich **verlieben in** *(+ acc)* to fall in
love with (5, 11-2)
verliebt in love (2)
verlieren, verlor, verloren to lose
(10-2)
vermieten to rent (out) (8-1)
der **Vermieter, -**/die **Vermieterin,
-nen** landlord/landlady (8-1)
verrecken to croak, to die (8)
verrückt crazy; insane (5-2)
versammeln to gather (11)
**verschieben, verschob,
verschoben** to postpone
(10-2)
verschieden different (7-2); various
(9)
verschwenderisch wasteful (5)
versichern to insure (12)
die **Versicherung, -en** insurance
(12-2)
versorgen to supply (11)
sich **verspäten** to be late (9-2)
**versprechen (verspricht),
versprach, versprochen** to
promise (3-2)
das **Verständnis** *(sing)*
understanding (4)
verstecken to hide (10-1)
(das) **Verstecken** hide-and-seek (10)
verstehen, verstand, verstanden
to understand (3-1)
das **Verstehen** understanding (1)
verstümmelt crippled (6)
versuchen to try (5, 8-2)
vertreten to represent (6)
die **Verwaltung, -en** administration
(6)
verwandt related (1)
der/die **Verwandte, -n** relative
(3-1)
die **Verwandschaft** relatives *(as a
group)* (12)
verwendbar usable (12)
verwenden to use (8, 9-2)
verwirrt confused (9)
das **Verwöhnarrangement** "Let
us spoil you" package *(e.g., at a
hotel)* (8)
verwundert astonished (6)
der **Vetter, -n** *(male)* cousin (3-1)

das **Video, -s** video (3)
die **Videokamera, -s** video camera
(10)
der **Videokassettenrecorder, -**
video cassette recorder (3)
viel much; a lot (E, 1-1)
viel zu viel far too much (3)
viel zu schnell much too fast (3-1)
viele many (1)
vielleicht perhaps (6-2)
viert: zu viert in a group of four
(8-1)
das **Viertel** quarter (2)
Viertel nach elf quarter after
eleven (2)
Viertel vor elf quarter to
eleven (2)
die **Viertelstunde** quarter hour (8)
die **Villa, Villen** villa (10)
violett purple (1-1)
der **Violinist, -en, -en**/die
Violinistin, -nen violinist (3)
der **Virus, Viren** virus (11)
das **Vitamin, -e** vitamin (4)
der **Vogel, ¨** bird (2)
die **Vokabeln** *(pl)* vocabulary (1)
voll full (1, 7-1)
den Mund voll nehmen to talk
big (6)
der **Volleyball, ¨e** volleyball (1)
die **Vollkaskoversicherung, -en**
comprehensive auto insurance
(12)
vollkommen perfect; immaculate
(12)
vollständig complete(ly) (8)
von *(prep + dat)* from (E); of (E)
von … bis from . . . to (1-2)
von jetzt ab from now on (6)
vor *(prep + acc/dat)* in front of;
before (4); ago (7)
vor dem Fernseher in front of
the TV (4-2)
vorbei sein to be over (10)
die **Vorbereitung, -en** preparation
(7)
die **Vorbestellung, -en** advance
order (9)
auf Vorbestellung by ordering in
advance (9)

die **Vorderseite, -n** front (9)
der **Vorfahr, -en, -en** ancestor
(6-1)
**vor·geben (gibt vor), gab vor,
vorgegeben** to set *(in advance)*
(9)
vorgestern the day before yesterday
(3-2)
**vor·haben (hat vor), hatte vor,
vorgehabt** to plan, to have
planned (4-2)
die **Vorhand** forehand (E)
der **Vorhang, ¨e** curtain (11)
der Eiserne Vorhang the Iron
Curtain (11)
vorher before *(adv)* (6-1)
**vor·lesen (liest vor), las vor,
vorgelesen** to read aloud (10)
die **Vorlesung, -en** lecture; class
(1-1)
in die Vorlesung to a lecture
(1-2)
der **Vormittag, -e** morning (4)
vormittags in the morning (2)
der **Vorname, -ns, -n** first name
(3-2)
das **Vorrecht, -e** privilege (12)
der **Vorsatz, ¨e** resolution (9)
die **Vorschau** preview (1)
der **Vorschlag, ¨e** suggestion (7)
Vorsicht! Careful! (10)
die **Vorspeise, -n** hors d'œuvre
(4, 9-2)
der **Vorteil, -e** advantage (8-2)
die **Vorwahl** area code (E)
der **Vulkan, -e** volcano (2)

W

wach sein to be awake (4)
das **Wachs** wax (5)
der **Wagen, -** car (3-1)
wählen to dial (5); to choose, select
(9-2)
wahr true (6-2)
wahrscheinlich probably (12)
während *(prep + gen)* during
(6, 12-2)
die **Wahrheit, -en** truth (10-1)
die **Währung, -en** currency (11)

der **Wald, ⸚er** forest; woods (5-1)

der **Walzer, -** waltz (1)

die **Wand, ⸚e** wall (8-1)

  den Teufel an die Wand malen to temp fate (8)

sich **wandeln** to change (11)

wandern, wanderte, ist gewandert to hike (2-1); to wander, to roam (5)

  wandern gehen to go hiking (2-1)

der **Wanderschuh, -e** hiking boot (5)

die **Wanderung, -en** hike (5)

wann when (1)

die **Wanne, -n** bathtub (8)

die **Ware, -n** merchandise (11)

warm warm (1-2)

warnen to warn (6-2)

die **Warnung, -en** warning (6-2)

warten to wait (6-2)

  warten auf *(+ acc)* to wait for (11-2)

warum why (1-2)

was what (E, 1-2)

  Was für ein Hundewetter! What rotten weather! (1)

  Was für Sport machst du? What sports do you do? (1-2)

  was ... sonst what else (8)

waschbar washable (12)

das **Waschbecken, -** (bathroom) sink (8-1)

die **Wäsche** wash, laundry (5, 6-2)

  die **Wäsche waschen** to do the laundry (6-2)

waschen (wäscht), wusch, gewaschen to wash (3-2)

die **Wäscherei, -en** laundry *(place of business)* (7)

der **Waschlappen, -** washcloth (9-2)

die **Waschmaschine, -n** washer (4)

der **Waschsalon, -s** laundromat (6-2)

das **Wasser** water (1, 2-1)

wässerig watery (2)

das **WC, -s** toilet (8)

die **Website, -s** Web site (2)

wechseln to switch (12)

wecken to wake *(someone)* up (9)

der **Wecker, -** alarm clock (7-1)

weder ... noch neither . . . nor (10-2)

weg away; gone (6)

der **Weg, -e** way, path (9, 11-1)

wegen *(prep + gen)* because of (12-2)

weg·fahren (fährt weg), fuhr weg, ist weggefahren to drive away (4-2)

weg·fliegen, flog weg, ist weggeflogen to fly away (8)

weg·gehen, ging weg, ist weggegangen to go away (4)

weg·laufen (läuft weg), lief weg, ist weggelaufen to run away (4)

weg·nehmen (nimmt weg), nahm weg, weggenommen to take away (4)

weg·räumen to clear away (11)

weg·rennen, rannte weg, ist weggerannt to run away (6)

weg·schwimmen, schwamm weg, ist weggeschwommen to swim away (4)

weg·sehen (sieht weg), sah weg, weggesehen to look away (4)

Weihnachten Christmas (7-1)

  Frohe Weihnachten! Merry Christmas! (7-1)

  zu Weihnachten at, for Christmas (7-1)

der **Weihnachtsbaum, ⸚e** Christmas tree (7-1)

der **Weihnachtsfeiertag** Christmas Day (7)

die **Weihnachtsferien** *(pl)* Christmas vacation (5)

die **Weihnachtsgans, ⸚e** Christmas goose (7)

das **Weihnachtsgeschenk, -e** Christmas present (7)

der **Weihnachtsmarkt, ⸚e** Christmas market (7)

weil because *(sub conj)* (4-2)

der **Wein, -e** wine (1, 2-1)

weinen to cry (10-1)

das **Weinerntefest, -e** wine harvest festival (7)

das **Weinfest, -e** wine festival (7)

das **Weinglas, ⸚er** wine glass (1)

der **Weinkeller, -** wine cellar (7)

der **Weinkenner, -** wine connoisseur (9)

die **Weinprobe, -n** wine tasting (7)

weiß white (1-1)

das **Weiße Haus** White House (4)

der **Weißwein, -e** white wine (3)

weit far (4, 5-1)

  weit weg far away (8-2)

weiter *(as verb prefix)* to continue (4)

weiter·arbeiten to keep on working (4)

weiter·essen (isst weiter), aß weiter, weitergegessen to continue eating (4)

weiter·fahren (fährt weiter), fuhr weiter, ist weitergefahren to keep on driving (4-2)

weiter·geben (gibt weiter), gab weiter, weitergegeben to pass along (10)

weiter·lesen (liest weiter), las weiter, weitergelesen to continue reading (4-2)

weiter·schlafen (schläft weiter), schlief weiter, weitergeschlafen to continue sleeping (4)

weiter·schreiben, schrieb weiter, weitergeschrieben to continue writing (4)

weiter·studieren to continue studying (4)

welcher, welches, welche which (1); *(pl)* some (7)

wellig wavy (3)

der **Wellness-Bereich** spa (5)

die **Welt, -en** world (4, 5-2)

die **Weltfirma, -en** worldwide company (7)

der **Weltkrieg, -e** world war (11-1)

das **Weltkulturerbe** world cultural heritage (12)

die **Weltreise, -n** trip around the world (4)

die **Wende** turning point *(i.e., the fall of the Berlin Wall)* (11-2)

wenig little (1-2)

wenigstens at least (8-2)

wenn when *(sub conj)*; if *(sub conj)* (4-2)

wer who (1-2)

werden (wird), wurde, ist geworden to become; to get; to be (3-2)

  Er wird Koch. He's going to be a cook. (3)

  Sie wird zwanzig. She's turning twenty. (3-2)

das **Werk, -e** work (9)

die **Werkstatt, ̈en** workshop (4)

das **Werkzeug, -e** tool (3, 10-2)

die **Wespe, -n** wasp (9)

der/die **Wessi, -s** citizen of former West Germany (11)

(das) **Westdeutschland** West Germany (11)

der **Westen** west (8)

westlich (von) west (of) (11)

der **Wettbewerb, -e** contest (9)

die **Wette, -n** bet (10)

  um die Wette laufen to run a race (with someone) (10)

wetten to bet (10-2)

das **Wetter** weather (1-1)

  Wie ist das Wetter? What's the weather like? (1)

die **Wetterkarte, -n** weather map (1)

der **Wettlauf, ̈e** race *(contest)* (10-2)

  einen Wettlauf machen to run a race (10-2)

die **WG, -s die (Wohngemeinschaft, -en)** shared housing (8-1)

wichtig important (4, 7-1)

die **Wichtigkeit** importance (11)

wie how (E, 1-2); like (3)

  so ... wie as ... as (2-2)

  Wie bitte? Pardon? (E-1)

  wie ein König like a king (3)

  Wie geht es Ihnen?/Wie geht's? How are you? (E-1)

  Wie heißen Sie?/Wie heißt du? What's your name? (E-1)

  Wie ist das Wetter? What's the weather like? (1)

  Wie ist Ihr Name und Ihre Adresse? What's your name and your address? (3)

Wie ist Ihre Wohnung? What's your apartment like? (3)

Wie spät ist es? What time is it? (2-2)

wie viel how much (E, 1-2)

  Wie viel Uhr ist es? What time is it? (2-2)

wie viele how many (1-2)

wieder again (2-2)

  immer wieder again and again (9-1)

wiederholen to repeat (E, 8-2)

Wiederhören! Auf Wiederhören! Good-bye! *(on the telephone)* (E-1)

wieder·sehen (sieht wieder), sah wieder, wiedergesehen to see again (E)

  Auf Wiedersehen! Wiedersehen! Good-bye! (E-1)

die **Wiedervereinigung** reunification (11-1)

(das) **Wien** Vienna (1)

  das **Wiener Schnitzel** breaded veal cutlet (7)

die **Wiese, -n** meadow (5)

der **Wievielte** (6)

  am Wievielten on what date (6)

  Den Wievielten haben wir heute? What's the date today? (6-2)

  Der Wievielte ist heute? What's the date today? (6-2)

wild wild (12-2)

die **Windenergie** wind power (E)

windig windy (1-1)

der **Windpark, -s** wind farm (E)

windstill windless, calm (1)

der **Winter, -** winter (1-2)

  im Winter in winter (1-2)

die **Winterjacke, -n** winter jacket (7)

der **Wintermantel, ̈** winter coat (10)

der **Winterschlussverkauf, ̈e** winter clearance sale (7)

winzig tiny (10-2)

wirklich really (8-1)

die **Wirklichkeit** reality (11)

die **Wirtschaft** economy (12)

das **Wirtschaftswunder** economic miracle (7)

das **Wirtshaus, ̈er** restaurant (9)

wissen (weiß), wusste, gewusst to know (5-1)

  wissen von to know about (11-2)

der **Witz, -e** joke (11-2)

witzig witty; funny (7-2)

wo where *(in what place)* (E, 1-2)

die **Woche, -n** week (1-2)

das **Wochenende, -n** weekend (2-2)

das **Wochenendhaus, ̈er** cottage (8)

der **Wochenmarkt, ̈e** open-air market (8-2)

der **Wochentag, -e** day of the week (1-2)

wöchentlich weekly (2)

die **Wochenzeitung, -en** weekly newspaper (10)

woher where . . . from *(from what place)* (E, 1-2)

wohin where *(to what place)* (1-2)

Wohl: zum Wohl! Cheers! To your health! (7-2)

wohl probably; perhaps (7-2)

  sich **wohl fühlen** to feel well (9-2); to feel at home (8)

der **Wohlstand** affluence (11)

  vor lauter Wohlstand for all (their) affluence (11)

wohnen to live *(in a building or on a street)* (1, 2-2)

die **Wohngemeinschaft, -en (die WG, -s)** shared housing (2, 8-1)

das **Wohnhaus, ̈er** residential building (8)

der **Wohnort, -e** place of residence (1, 6-1)

die **Wohnung, -en** apartment (2-2)

das **Wohnviertel, -** residential area (8)

das **Wohnzimmer, -** living room (8-1)

die **Wohnzimmergarnitur, -en** living room set (12)

der **Wok, -s** wok (9)

wollen (will), wollte, gewollt to want to (4)

die **Wolke, -n** cloud (5-1)

die **Wolle** wool (10)

das **Wort, –e** word *(in a meaningful context)* (6)

das **Wort, ¨er** word *(lexical item)* (1, 7-1)

das **Wörterbuch, ¨er** dictionary (7-1)

der **Wortschatz, ¨e** vocabulary (1)

wozu what . . . for (8-2)

das **Wunder, –** miracle (12)

kein Wunder no wonder (12)

wunderbar wonderful (3-2)

das **Wunderkind, –er** child prodigy (3)

sich **wundern** to be surprised (11-2)

wunderschön very beautiful (3-2)

wundervoll marvelous (5)

der **Wunsch, ¨e** wish (9-1)

   auf Wunsch by request (9)

wünschen to wish (7-2)

   Sie wünschen? May I help you? (7-2)

der **Wurm, ¨er** worm (1)

wurmig wormy (2)

die **Wurst, ¨e** sausage; cold cuts (4-1)

   Das ist mir wurst. I couldn't care less. (7)

würzen to season (9)

die **Wut** anger, rage (11)

wütend furious (12)

 wütend auf (+acc) furious at (12-1)

Z

z.B.; zum Beispiel e.g., for example (6-2)

die **Zahl, –en** number (7)

zählen to count (10)

der **Zahn, ¨e** tooth (6-1)

der **Zahnarzt, ¨e**/die **Zahnärztin, –nen** dentist (7-2)

die **Zahnbürste, –n** toothbrush (5, 9-2)

zahnlos toothless (12)

die **Zahnpasta** toothpaste (9-2)

die **Zahnschmerzen** *(pl)* toothache (6, 7-2)

der **Zaun, ¨e** fence (6-2)

die **Zehe, –n** toe (6-1)

zeichnen to draw *(a picture)*; to draft (6-1)

zeigen to show (1, 7-2)

   Das Thermometer zeigt zehn Grad. The thermometer reads ten degrees. (1-1)

die **Zeile, –n** line *(of text on a page)* (12)

die **Zeit, –en** time (2-1)

   in letzter Zeit recently (6-2)

   seit kurzer Zeit recently (11-2)

   Lassen Sie sich Zeit! Take your time! (12-2)

das **Zeitalter** age (9)

die **Zeitschrift, –en** magazine, periodical (10)

die **Zeitung, –en** newspaper (3-2)

das **Zelt, –e** tent (5-1)

zelten to camp *(in a tent)* (9)

die **Zensur, –en** grade (5-2)

zentral central(ly) (8-1)

das **Zentrum, Zentren** center (5)

zerfallen (zerfällt), zerfiel, ist zerfallen to disintegrate (11)

zerkochen to cook to a pulp (11)

zerschneiden, zerschnitt, zerschnitten to cut up (11)

zerstören to destroy (11-1)

das **Zeug** *(sing)* thing (3)

ziehen, zog, gezogen to pull (4); to move (10)

das **Ziel, –e** goal, aim; destination (10-2)

ziemlich quite; rather (5-2); considerable (12)

die **Zigarre, –n** cigar (10)

die **Zigarette, –n** cigarette (4-2)

das **Zimmer, –** room (2-2)

die **Zimmerpflanze, –n** house plant (6-2)

der **Zimmermann, Zimmerleute** carpenter (8)

der **Zimt** cinnamon (9)

die **Zinsen** *(pl)* (bank) interest (12-2)

zirka approximately (1)

die **Zone, –n** zone (11)

die **Zoologie** zoology (2)

der **Zopf, ¨e** braid (11)

zu *(prep + dat)* to; too (1); for (7)

   zu Hause (at) home (2, 4-1)

   zu viel too much (1)

   zu viert in a group of four (8-1)

der **Zucker** *(sing)* sugar (4-1)

zu·decken to cover up (4)

zuerst first (1-1)

der **Zug, ¨e** train (3-1)

der **Zugang** access (10-1)

zu·geben (gibt zu), gab zu, zugegeben to admit (12-1)

zu·hören to listen (E)

die **Zukunft** future (11-2)

zuletzt last (4-2); finally (6-1)

zum Beispiel (z.B.) for example (e.g.) (6-2)

zum Glück fortunately, luckily (12-1)

die **Zunge, –n** tongue (3)

zurück back (4)

zurück·bringen, brachte zurück, zurückgebracht to bring back (4)

zurück·fahren (fährt zurück), fuhr zurück, ist zurückgefahren to drive back (4)

zurück·geben (gibt zurück), gab zurück, zurückgegeben to give back (4)

zurück·gehen, ging zurück, ist zurückgegangen to go back (4)

zurück·kommen, kam zurück, ist zurückgekommen to come back (4-2)

zurück·nehmen (nimmt zurück), nahm zurück, zurückgenommen to take back (4)

zurück·rufen, rief zurück, zurückgerufen to call back (4)

zurück·zahlen to pay back (11)

zurzeit at the moment (7)

zusammen together (1-2)

zusammen·binden, band zusammen, zusammengebunden to tie together (10)

zusammen·passen to go together; to match (1)

zusammen·rufen, rief zusammen, zusammengerufen to call together (10)
die **Zusammenschau** summary (1)
der **Zusatz** supplement (12)
die **Zusatz-Krankenversicherung** supplementary medical insurance (12)

zusätzlich additional (8-1)
der **Zuschlag, ⸚e** surcharge (5)
zwar ... aber it's true . . . but (10)
zweieinhalb two and a half (9)
zweimal twice (5, 6-2)
der **Zweite Weltkrieg** Second World War (4)
der **Zweitwagen, –** second car (12)

der **Zwetschgenkuchen, –** plum cake (10)
zwischen (*prep + acc/dat*) between (8)
die **Zwischenprüfung, –en** exam after two years of university (1)
das **Zwischenspiel, –e** interlude (1)

English-German Vocabulary

For classroom expressions and grammatical terms, see pages A12 and A13. For vocabulary referring to fields of study, jobs and professions, hobbies and sports, musical instruments, articles of clothing, accessories, food and drink, countries and languages, personal characteristics, and courteous expressions, see the *Useful Word Sets* beginning on page A14.

A

a lot (of) viel; eine Menge; ein Haufen

able: to be able to können (kann), konnte, gekonnt

about *(prep)* über *(+ acc)*; *(approximately)* etwa

above *(prep)* über *(+ acc/dat)* ; *(adv)* oben

  above all vor allem

absolute(ly) absolut; ganz

access der Zugang

accident der Unfall, ¨-e

acquaintance der/die Bekannte, -n

acquainted: to be acquainted with kennen, kannte, gekannt

across (from) gegenüber

active(ly) aktiv

  to **be active in sports** Sport machen

actor der Schauspieler, -

actress die Schauspielerin, -nen

actually eigentlich

ad die Anzeige, -n

addition: in addition außerdem

additional zusätzlich; weiter

address die Adresse, -n, die Anschrift, -en

  What's your address? Was (Wie) ist Ihre Adresse?

to **admire** bewundern

admission der Eintritt

to **admit** zugeben (gibt zu), gab zu, zugegeben

adult der/die Erwachsene, -n

advantage der Vorteil, -e

advertisement die Reklame, -n, die Werbung, -en

advice der Rat

  to **ask for advice** um Rat fragen

to **advise** raten (rät), riet, geraten

to **advocate for** eintreten für (tritt ein), trat ein, ist eingetreten

afraid: to be afraid (of) Angst haben (vor + *dat*)

African-American der Afro-Amerikaner, -/die Afro-Amerikanerin, -nen

after *(prep)* nach *(+ dat)*; *(conj)* nachdem; *(adv)* nachher

afternoon der Nachmittag, -e

  in the afternoon nachmittags

  this afternoon heute Nachmittag

afterwards nachher

again wieder; schon wieder

  again and again immer wieder

  (over) again noch einmal; noch mal

against *(prep)* gegen *(+ acc)*

age das Alter

aggressive aggressiv

ago vor *(+ dat)*

aim das Ziel, -e

air die Luft

airplane das Flugzeug, -e

airport *(international)* der Flughafen, ¨-; *(regional)* der Flugplatz, ¨-e

to **alarm** alarmieren

alarm clock der Wecker, -

album das Album, Alben

alcohol der Alkohol

all (the) alle

  above all vor allem

  at all überhaupt

Allies die Alliierten *(pl)*

allowed: to be allowed to dürfen (darf), durfte, gedurft

almost fast

alone allein

  Leave me alone! Lass mich in Ruhe!

along *(as prefix)* mit

Alps die Alpen *(pl)*

already schon

also auch

although *(sub conj)* obwohl

always immer

America (das) Amerika

American *(adj)* amerikanisch; *(person)* der Amerikaner, -/ die Amerikanerin, -nen

among *(prep)* unter *(+ acc/dat)*

ancestor der Vorfahr, -en, -en

and *(coord conj)* und

angry wütend

  angry at wütend auf (+acc)

animal das Tier, -e

to **annoy** ärgern

annoyed sauer

  to **be (get) annoyed (with, about)** sich ärgern (über + acc)

anorexic magersüchtig

another *(different)* ander; *(in addition)* noch ein

answer die Antwort, -en

to **answer** *(someone)* antworten *(+ dat)*

  to **answer a question** eine Frage beantworten

answering machine der Anrufbeantworter, -

anyway sowieso; trotzdem; doch

apartment die Wohnung, -en

apiece: three euros apiece drei Euro das Stück

to **apologize** sich entschuldigen

to **appear** erscheinen, erschien, ist erschienen

appetite der Appetit

apple der Apfel, ¨

  apple pie der Apfelkuchen, -

appliance der Apparat, -e; das Gerät, -e

apprentice der/die Auszubildende, -n; *(abbr)* der/die Azubi, -s

approximately etwa

April der April

area das Gebiet, -e; die Gegend, -en; *(of a city)* der Stadtteil, -e

area code die Vorwahl

to **argue** argumentieren

argument das Argument, -e

arm der Arm, -e

armchair der Sessel, -

around *(place)* um, rund um (+ acc); *(time)* gegen (+ acc)

   around five o'clock gegen fünf

to **arrive** ankommen, kam an, ist angekommen

arrogant(ly) arrogant

art die Kunst, ⸚e

article der Artikel, -

   article of clothing das Kleidungsstück, -e

artist der Künstler, -/die Künstlerin, -nen

artistic(ally) künstlerisch

as

   as a child als Kind

   as . . . as so … wie

   as long as *(sub conj)* solange

   as often as *(sub conj)* sooft

   as soon as *(sub conj)* sobald

to **ask** *(a question)* fragen

   to **ask a question** eine Frage stellen

assistant der Assistent, -en, -en/die Assistentin, -nen

astonished verwundert

at *(prep)* bei (+ dat); *(time)* um (+ acc); *(a vertical surface)* an (+ acc/dat)

   at all überhaupt

   at our house bei uns

   at the Zieglers bei Zieglers

   not at all gar nicht, überhaupt nicht

athlete der Athlet, -en, -en/die Athletin, -nen

athletic sportlich

athletics der Sport

to **attend** besuchen

attraction die Attraktion, -en

August der August

aunt die Tante, -n

Australian *(adj)* australisch

Austria (das) Österreich

Austrian *(adj)* österreichisch; *(person)* der Österreicher, -/ die Österreicherin, -nen

author der Autor, -en/die Autorin, -nen

autobiography die Autobiografie, -n

autumn der Herbst

average der Durchschnitt, -e; *(adj)* durchschnittlich

   of average height mittelgroß

   on average durchschnittlich

away fort; weg

awful(ly) schrecklich

B

baby das Baby, -s

babysitter der Babysitter, -/die Babysitterin, -nen

back der Rücken, -; *(of a chair)* die Lehne, -n; *(adv)* zurück

back then damals

backache die Rückenschmerzen *(pl)*

backpack der Rucksack, ⸚e

bad(ly) schlecht

   Too bad! Schade!

badminton: to play badminton Federball spielen

bag die Tasche, -n

to **bake** backen (bäckt), backte, gebacken

baker der Bäcker, -/die Bäckerin, -nen

bakery die Bäckerei, -en

balcony der Balkon, -e

ball der Ball, ⸚e

ballpoint pen der Kugelschreiber, -

banana die Banane, -n

band die Band, -s

Band–Aid das Pflaster, -

bank die Bank, -en

bank manager der Bankdirektor, -en/die Bankdirektorin, -nen

bankrupt bankrott

Bar Mitzvah die Bar Mizwa

barbed wire der Stacheldraht

barber der Friseur, -e/die Friseurin, -nen

to **bark** bellen

barricade die Sperre, -n

barrier das Hindernis, -se

basement der Keller, -

bath das Bad, ⸚er

to **bathe,** to **have a bath** (sich) baden

bathing suit der Badeanzug, ⸚e

bathroom das Badezimmer, -; das Bad, ⸚er; das Klo, -s

bathroom sink das Waschbecken, -

bathtub die Badewanne, -n

batter der Teig

Bavaria (das) Bayern

Bavarian *(adj)* bayerisch

to **be** sein (ist), war, ist gewesen; *(become)* werden (wird), wurde, ist geworden

   He's going to be a cook. Er wird Koch.

beach der Strand, ⸚e

bean die Bohne, -n

beard der Bart, ⸚e

beautiful(ly) schön

   very beautiful wunderschön

beauty die Schönheit, -en

because *(sub conj)* weil; *(coord conj)* denn

because of *(prep)* wegen (+ gen)

to **become** werden (wird), wurde, ist geworden

bed das Bett, -en

   to **go to bed** ins Bett gehen

bedroom das Schlafzimmer, -

beer das Bier

   beer belly der Bierbauch, ⸚e

   beer garden der Biergarten, ⸚

before *(prep)* vor (+ acc/dat); *(conj)* bevor; *(adv)* vorher

to **begin** anfangen (fängt an), fing an, angefangen; beginnen, begann, begonnen

beginning der Anfang, ⸚e, der Beginn

   at the beginning zu Beginn

   (at) the beginning of Juli Anfang Juli

   beginning of school der Schulbeginn

to **behave** sich benehmen (benimmt), benahm, benommen

behind *(prep)* hinter *(+ acc/dat)*

Belgian *(adj)* belgisch

to **believe** glauben *(+ dat)*

belly der Bauch, ⸚e

to **belong to** gehören *(+ dat)*

beloved geliebt

below *(prep)* unter *(+ acc/dat)*; *(adv)* unten

belt der Gürtel, -

bent krumm

beside *(prep)* neben *(+ acc/dat)*

   She was beside herself. Sie war außer sich.

besides außerdem

best best

to **bet** wetten

better besser

   better than besser als

between *(prep)* zwischen *(+ acc/dat)*

beverage das Getränk, -e

bicycle das Fahrrad, ⸚er

   bicycle helmet der Fahrradhelm, -e

   bicycle rental der Fahrradverleih, -e

   bicycle trip die Radtour, -en

   to **go on a bicycle trip** eine Radtour machen

big groß

bike das Rad, ⸚er

bike rental der Fahrradverleih, -e

biking: to go biking Rad fahren (fährt Rad), fuhr Rad, ist Rad gefahren

bill die Rechnung, -en; *(money)* der Schein, -e

billiards (das) Billard *(sing)*

billion die Milliarde, -n

biographical biografisch

biography die Biografie, -n

bird der Vogel, ⸚

birth die Geburt, -en

birthday der Geburtstag, -e

   for one's birthday zum Geburtstag

   Happy Birthday! Herzliche Glückwünsche zum Geburtstag!

   to **wish a Happy Birthday** zum Geburtstag gratulieren

birthday card die Geburtstagskarte, -n

birthday present das Geburtstagsgeschenk, -e

birthplace der Geburtsort, -e

bit: a bit ein bisschen; einigermaßen

   bit by bit Stück für Stück

to **bite** beißen, biss, gebissen

black schwarz

   Black Forest der Schwarzwald

   Black Forest cake die Schwarzwälder Kirschtorte

blackboard die Tafel, -n, die Wandtafel, -n

to **block** blockieren

blockade die Blockade, -n

to **blog** bloggen

blonde blond

to **blossom** blühen

blouse die Bluse, -n

to **blow-dry one's hair** sich *(dat)* die Haare föhnen

blow-dryer der Föhn, -e

blue blau

   in blue in Blau

board das Brett, -er

boat das Boot, -e

body der Körper, -

book das Buch, ⸚er

to **book** buchen

bookcase das Bücherregal, -e

boot der Stiefel, -

border die Grenze, -n

to **border on** grenzen an *(+ acc)*

boring langweilig

   deadly boring stinklangweilig

born geboren

   When were you born? Wann bist du geboren?

boss der Chef, -s/die Chefin, -nen

both beide

bother: Stop bothering me! Lass mich in Ruhe!

bottle die Flasche, -n

bowl die Schüssel, -n

box der Karton, -s; der Kasten, ⸚

boy der Junge, -n, -n

   Boy! Mensch!

boyfriend der Freund, -e

bracelet das Armband, ⸚er

to **brag** angeben (gibt an), gab an, angegeben

braid der Zopf, ⸚e

brand name clothing die Markenkleidung *(sing)*

brand-new brandneu

bread das Brot, -e

   a slice of bread eine Scheibe Brot

break die Pause, -n

to **break** kaputt machen

breakfast das Frühstück

   for breakfast zum Frühstück

   to **have breakfast** frühstücken

breast die Brust, ⸚e

bridge die Brücke, -n

bright(ly) hell

brilliant(ly) genial

to **bring** bringen, brachte, gebracht

to **bring along** mitbringen, brachte mit, mitgebracht

broccoli der Brokkoli

brochure die Broschüre, -n

broken kaputt

brooch die Brosche, -n

brother der Bruder, ⸚

brothers and sisters die Geschwister *(pl)*

brown braun

brunch der Brunch, -es

brunette brünett

to **brush** bürsten

to **build** bauen

building das Gebäude, -

bulletin board das Schwarze Brett

   on the bulletin board am Schwarzen Brett

bus der Bus, -se

bus route die Buslinie, -n

bus stop die Bushaltestelle, -n

bush der Busch, ⸚e

business die Firma, Firmen; das Geschäft, -e

but *(coord conj)* aber; *(in the sense of*

   but rather, (but) . . . instead) sondern

butcher der Fleischer, -/ die Fleischerin, -nin

butcher shop die Fleischerei, -en

butter die Butter

to **buy** kaufen

by: by then bis dahin

C

cafeteria *(for full meals)* die Mensa; *(for snacks)* die Cafeteria, –s
  to the cafeteria in die Mensa
caffeine das Koffein
cake der Kuchen, –
  a piece of cake ein Stück Kuchen
  layer cake die Torte, –n
calculator der Taschenrechner, –
calendar der Kalender, –
to **call** rufen, rief, gerufen; *(on the telephone)* anrufen, rief an, angerufen; *(name)* nennen, nannte, genannt
called: to be called heißen, hieß, geheißen
calm ruhig; *(weather)* windstill
camera die Kamera, –s
to **camp** campen; *(in a tent)* zelten
campground der Campingplatz, ¨e
camping das Campen
  to go camping campen gehen
campsite der Campingplatz, ¨e
campus der Campus
can die Dose, –n
  can opener der Dosenöffner, –
can *(to be able to)* können (kann), konnte, gekonnt
Canadian *(adj)* kanadisch
Canadian *(person)* der Kanadier, –/die Kanadierin, –nen
candle die Kerze, –n
candy die Süßigkeiten *(pl)*
capital city die Hauptstadt, ¨e
cappuccino der Cappuccino, –s
car das Auto, –s; der Wagen, –; der Personenwagen, –; der Pkw, –s (Personenkraftwagen)
car accident der Autounfall, ¨e
car mechanic der Automechaniker, –/die Automechanikerin, –nen
card die Karte, –n
  ATM card die ATM-Karte, –n
  credit card die Kreditkarte, –n
care
  I don't care. Das ist mir egal.
  I couldn't care less. Das ist mir wurst.
to **care for** sorgen für

career die Karriere, –n
Careful! Vorsicht!
careful(ly) sorgfältig
carpet der Teppich, –e
carrot die Karotte, –n
to **carry** tragen (trägt), trug, getragen
carton der Karton, –s
cashier der Kassierer, –/die Kassiererin, –nen
cassette die Kassette, –n
castle das Schloss, ¨er
cat die Katze, –n
to **catch** fangen (fängt), fing, gefangen
  to catch a cold sich erkälten
cause *(political)* die Sache, –n
CD die CD, –s
CD player der CD-Spieler, –
CD-ROM drive das CD-ROM-Laufwerk, –e
ceiling die Decke, –n
to **celebrate** feiern
cell phone das Handy, –s
cellar der Keller, –
cent der Cent, –
center das Zentrum, Zentren
central zentral
century das Jahrhundert, –e
certain(ly) sicher
chair der Stuhl, ¨e
champagne der Champagner
change: for a change mal
to **change** ändern; *(one's clothes)* sich umziehen, zog um, umgezogen; *(trains)* umsteigen, stieg um, ist umgestiegen; *(a situation; one's behavior)* sich verändern
to **chat** *(online)* chatten
cheap billig
check der Scheck, –s
checkout die Kasse, –n
Cheers! Zum Wohl! Prosit!
cheese der Käse
cheesecake der Käsekuchen, –
chef der Koch, ¨e/die Köchin, –nen
chest die Brust
chic schick
child das Kind, –er
  as a child als Kind
  only child das Einzelkind, –er

childhood die Kindheit
childish kindisch
childlike kindlich
chin das Kinn, –e
china das Geschirr *(sing)*
Chinese *(adj)* chinesisch
chocolate die Schokolade
  a chocolate bar eine Tafel Schokolade
choir der Chor, ¨e
to **choose** aussuchen; wählen
Christmas (das) Weihnachten
  at Christmas an (zu) Weihnachten
  for Christmas zu Weihnachten
  Merry Christmas! Frohe Weihnachten!
  Christmas Day der erste Weihnachtsfeiertag
  Christmas Eve der Heilige Abend, Heiliger Abend
  Christmas present das Weihnachtsgeschenk, –e
  Christmas tree der Weihnachtsbaum, ¨e
church die Kirche, –n
cigarette die Zigarette, –n
circle der Kreis, –e
circle of friends der Freundeskreis, –e
citizen der Bürger, –/die Bürgerin, –nen
city die Stadt, ¨e
  city hall das Rathaus, ¨er
  part of the city der Stadtteil, –e
class die Klasse, –n; der Kurs, –e; die Stunde, –n
  German class der Deutschkurs, –e; die Deutschstunde, –n
classmate der Mitstudent, –en, –en/die Mitstudentin, –nen
clean sauber
to **clean** putzen
to **clean up** aufräumen
clever clever
to **climb** steigen, stieg, ist gestiegen
clock die Uhr, –en
to **close** zumachen; schließen, schloss, geschlossen
closet der Schrank, ¨e
  front hall closet die Garderobe, –n

clothes die Kleider *(pl)*, die Klamotten *(pl)*

clothing store das Kleidergeschäft, -e

cloud die Wolke, -n

  sunny with some clouds heiter

cloudy bedeckt; bewölkt

clue: She doesn't have a clue. Sie hat keine Ahnung.

coast die Küste, -n

coat der Mantel, ¨

coffee der Kaffee

  coffee maker die Kaffeemaschine, -n

  coffeepot die Kaffeekanne, -n

  coffee table der Couchtisch, -e

cola die Cola, -s

cold kalt; *(illness)* die Erkältung, -en; der Schnupfen, -

  a bad cold eine schwere Erkältung

  cold cuts die Wurst *(sing)*

  to **be cold** frieren, fror, gefroren

  to **catch a cold** sich erkälten

  to **have a cold** erkältet sein

colleague der Kollege, -n, -n/ die Kollegin, -nen; *(from work)* der Arbeitskollege, -n/die Arbeitskollegin, -nen

to **collect** sammeln

collection die Sammlung, -en

college das College, -s

color die Farbe, -n

  What color is Lisa's blouse? Welche Farbe hat Lisas Bluse?

to **color** färben

color photo das Farbfoto, -s

color TV der Farbfernseher, -

colorless farblos

comb der Kamm, ¨e

to **comb one's hair** sich kämmen

to **come** kommen, kam, ist gekommen

  to **come along** mitkommen

  to **come back** zurückkommen

  to **come in** hereinkommen

  to **come out** herauskommen

  to **come to visit** zu Besuch kommen

comfortable komfortabel; *(in the sense of* **cozy***)* gemütlich

comics die Comics

communication die Kommunikation

communist kommunistisch

commuter der Pendler, -/die Pendlerin, -nen

compact disc die CD, -s

company die Firma, Firmen; die Gesellschaft, -en; das Unternehmen, -

to **compare** vergleichen, verglich, verglichen

complete(ly) total; ganz; vollständig

complicated kompliziert

compliment das Kompliment, -e

composer der Komponist, -en, -en/ die Komponistin, -nen

computer der Computer, -, der Rechner, -

computer game das Computerspiel, -e

computer screen der Bildschirm, -e

concept das Konzept, -e

concert das Konzert, -e

  to a concert, to concerts ins Konzert

condominium die Eigentumswohnung, -en

conflict der Konflikt, -e

confused verwirrt

to **congratulate** gratulieren *(+ dat)*

congratulations der Glückwunsch, ¨e

  Congratulations! Herzliche Glückwünsche!

conservative konservativ

considered: to be considered gelten als (gilt), galt, gegolten

constant(ly) ständig

constitution *(political)* die Verfassung, -en

consulate das Konsulat, -e

consumption der Konsum

contact der Kontakt, -e

contact lens die Konkaktlinse, -n

container: a container of yogurt ein Becher *(m)* Joghurt

contest der Wettbewerb, -e

continue *(as verb prefix)* weiter

  to **continue studying** weiterstudieren

to **converse** sich unterhalten (unterhält) unterhielt, unterhalten

conversation das Gespräch, -e

cook der Koch, ¨e/die Köchin, -nen

to **cook** kochen

cookbook das Kochbuch, ¨er

cooking lessons der Kochkurs, -e

cool *(of weather)* kühl; *(excellent)* cool

  really cool echt cool

to **copy** kopieren

corkscrew der Korkenzieher, -

corner die Ecke, -n

correct richtig

to **correct** verbessern

to **cost** kosten

cottage das Wochenendhaus, ¨er; das Ferienhaus, ¨er

couch die Couch, -es

to **count** zählen

countless zahllos

country das Land, ¨er

couple *(pair)* das Paar, -e

  a couple of ein paar

  married couple das Ehepaar, -e

course der Kurs, -e

  main course *(of a meal)* das Hauptgericht

  Of course! Klar! Natürlich!

cousin *(female)* die Kusine, -n; *(male)* der Vetter, -n

cozy gemütlich

crafty schlau

crazy verrückt

  to **be crazy** spinnen

creative(ly) kreativ

credit card die Kreditkarte

crispy knusprig

critical(ly) kritisch

criticism die Kritik

to **criticize** kritisieren

crooked krumm; schief, kriminell

cruel grausam

to **cry** weinen

cuddly kuschelig

cuisine die Küche -n

culture die Kultur, -en

culture shock der Kulturschock

cup die Tasse, -n; der Becher, -

  a cup of coffee eine Tasse Kaffee

curly lockig

curtain der Vorhang, ‑̈e
custom die Sitte, ‑n
customer der Kunde, ‑n, ‑n/ die Kundin, ‑nen; *(in a restaurant)* der Gast, ‑̈e
to **cut** schneiden, schnitt, geschnitten
cutlery das Besteck

D

dad der Vati, ‑s; der Papa, ‑s
daily täglich
to **dance** tanzen
   to **go dancing** tanzen gehen
Danish *(adj)* dänisch
Danube *(river)* die Donau
dark dunkel
darling der Liebling, ‑e
Darn it! Verflixt!
data processing EDV (Elektronische Datenverarbeitung)
date das Datum, Daten
   on what date? am Wievielten?
   What's the date today? Den Wievielten haben wir heute? Der Wievielte ist heute?
daughter die Tochter, ‑̈
day der Tag, ‑e
   day of the week der Wochentag, ‑e
   one day eines Tages
   the day after tomorrow übermorgen
   Today I have a day off. Heute habe ich frei.
dead tot
dear lieb
death der Tod
debt die Schuld, ‑en
December der Dezember
decent ordentlich
decision die Entscheidung, ‑en
deep tief
defective defekt
definite(ly) bestimmt; unbedingt
degree der Grad, ‑e
   ten degrees Celsius zehn Grad Celsius
delicious lecker

democracy die Demokratie
to **depart** abfahren (fährt ab), fuhr ab, ist abgefahren
department die Abteilung, ‑en
department manager der Abteilungsleiter, ‑/die Abteilungsleiterin, ‑nen
department store das Kaufhaus, ‑̈er
depression die Depression, ‑en
to **describe** beschreiben, beschrieb, beschrieben
description die Beschreibung, ‑en
to **design** entwerfen (entwirft), enwarf, entworfen
designer der Designer, ‑/die Designerin, ‑nen
desk der Schreibtisch, ‑e
dessert der Nachtisch, ‑e
   for dessert zum Nachtisch
destination das Ziel, ‑e
detective story der Krimi, ‑s
to **destroy** zerstören
diagram das Schaubild, ‑er; die Grafik, ‑en
dialect der Dialekt, ‑e
dialogue der Dialog, ‑e
diary das Tagebuch, ‑̈er
dictatorship die Diktatur
dictionary das Wörterbuch, ‑̈er
to **die** sterben (stirbt), starb, ist gestorben
difference der Unterschied, ‑e
different *(adj)* ander‑; verschieden; *(adv)* anders
dining hall *(at a university)* die Mensa
dining room das Esszimmer, ‑
diploma das Diplom, ‑e
   to **do** or **take one's diploma** das Diplom machen
direct(ly) direkt
director der Direktor, ‑en/die Direktorin, ‑nen
dirty schmutzig
disadvantage der Nachteil, ‑e
disco die Disco, ‑s
   to the disco in die Disco
discrepancy die Diskrepanz, ‑en
to **discuss** diskutieren
discussion die Diskussion, ‑en
disgusting widerlich

dish *(food)* das Gericht, ‑e
dishes das Geschirr *(sing)*
   dirty dishes der Abwasch *(sing)*
   to **do the dishes** den Abwasch machen
dishonest unehrlich
dishwasher die Geschirrspülmaschine, ‑n
disk die Diskette, ‑n
dissatisfied unzufrieden
distinct(ly) deutlich
district der Stadtteil, ‑e
to **disturb** stören
to **divide** teilen
divorced geschieden
to **do** machen; tun, tat, getan
   to **do sports** Sport machen
doable machbar
doctor der Arzt, ‑̈e/die Ärztin, ‑nen
document das Dokument, ‑e
documentary film der Dokumentarfilm, ‑e
dog der Hund, ‑e
dog food das Hundefutter
doll die Puppe, ‑n
dollar der Dollar, ‑s
   twenty-five dollars fünfundzwanzig Dollar
door die Tür, ‑en
dormitory das Studentenheim, ‑e
dot: at eleven on the dot Punkt elf
double doppelt
to **download** downloaden
to **drag** schleppen
drama das Drama, Dramen
to **draw** zeichnen
drawing die Zeichnung, ‑en
dream der Traum, ‑̈e
to **dream** träumen
to **dress** sich anziehen, zog an, angezogen
dress das Kleid, ‑er
dressed gekleidet; angezogen
   to **get dressed** sich anziehen, zog an, angezogen
dresser die Kommode, ‑n
to **drink** trinken, trank, getrunken
to **drive** fahren (fährt), fuhr, ist gefahren; Auto fahren
   to **drive away** abfahren

driver der Fahrer, -/
die Fahrerin, -nen
driver's license
der Führerschein, -e
to **drizzle** (rain) nieseln
to **drown** ertrinken, ertrank, ist
ertrunken
drugstore die Drogerie, -n
dry trocken
to **dry one's hair** sich (dat) die
Haare trocknen
dumpling der Knödel, -; die
Dampfnudel, -n
during (prep) während (+ gen)
Dutch (adj) holländisch
DVD drive das DVD-Laufwerk, -e

E

each jeder, jedes, jede
each other einander
with each other miteinander
ear das Ohr, -en
ear stud der Ohrstecker, -
early früh
early enough rechtzeitig
to **earn** verdienen
earring der Ohrring, -e
earth die Erde
east der Osten
east (of) östlich (von + dat)
Easter Ostern
Easter bunny der Osterhase, -n
easy leicht
to **eat** essen (isst), aß, gegessen;
(of animals) fressen (frisst), fraß,
gefressen
to **eat up** aufessen (isst auf), aß auf,
aufgegessen
eatery das Lokal, -e
economy die Wirtschaft, -en
to **educate** ausbilden
educated ausgebildet
to **be well educated** gut
ausgebildet sein
education die Ausbildung
egg das Ei, -er
either: Claudia isn't coming
either. Claudia kommt auch
nicht.
either . . . or entweder ... oder

elbow der Ellbogen, -
to **elect** wählen
electric elektrisch
electric kettle der Wasserkocher, -
elegant elegant
elementary school die
Grundschule, -n
else
or else sonst
what else was ... sonst
e-mail die E-Mail, -s, die Mail, -s
to **e-mail** emailen
e-mail address
die E-Mail-Adresse, -n
embarrassed beschämt
embarrassing peinlich
emigrant der Auswanderer, -/
die Auswanderin, -nen; der
Emigrant, -en, -en/ die
Emigrantin, -nen
to **emigrate** auswandern;
emigrieren
employee der Arbeitnehmer, -/ die
Arbeitnehmerin, -nen
employer der Arbeitgeber, -/ die
Arbeitgeberin, -nen
empty leer
to **empty** leeren
enchanting bezaubernd
end das Ende, -n
(at) the end of January Ende
Januar
end table der Beistelltisch, -e
to **end** aufhören; enden; beenden
endless endlos
to **endure** aushalten (hält aus), hielt
aus, ausgehalten
energy die Energie
renewable energy erneuerbare
Energie
engineer der Ingenieur, -e/die
Ingenieurin, -nen
English (adj) englisch
English (language) Englisch
in English auf Englisch
enjoy
Enjoy your meal! Guten
Appetit!
I enjoy it. Es macht mir Spaß.
enjoyment der Spaß; die Lust
enormous enorm

enough genug
entrance der Eingang, ̈-e
entrepreneur der Unternehmer, -/
die Unternehmerin, -nen
envious neidisch
to **be envious of** neidisch sein
auf (+ acc)
environment die Umwelt
equal(ly) gleich
equal rights; equality die
Gleichberechtigung
to **have equal rights**
gleichberechtigt sein
error der Fehler, -
especially besonders
essay der Aufsatz, ̈-e
etc. (et cetera) usw. (und so weiter)
euro der Euro, -s
five euros fünf Euro
Europe (das) Europa
European (adj) europäisch
even sogar
even though (sub conj) obwohl
evening der Abend, -e
evening meal das Abendessen, -
Good evening! Guten Abend! 'n
Abend!
in the evening abends
this evening heute Abend
ever jemals
every jeder, jedes, jede
every time jedes Mal
everybody alle
everyday life das Alltagsleben
everything alles
exact(ly) genau
example das Beispiel, -e
for example (e.g.) zum Beispiel
(z.B.)
excellent ausgezeichnet
except for (prep) außer (+ dat)
exception die Ausnahme, -n
to **exchange** umtauschen
exchange student der
Austauschstudent, -en, -en/die
Austauschstundentin, -nen; (high
school) der Austauschschüler, -/
die Austauschschülerin, -nen
excited aufgeregt
to **get excited (about)** sich
aufregen (über + acc)

excuse die Ausrede, –n
    Excuse me! Entschuldigung!
exercise die Übung, –en
exercise bike der Heimtrainer, –
exhibition die Ausstellung, –en
to **exist** existieren
exotic exotisch
expensive teuer
experience die Erfahrung, –en;
    das Erlebnis, –se; *(knowledge)* die
    Kenntnisse *(pl)*
to **experience** erleben
experiment das Experiment, –e
to **explain** erklären
to **express** ausdrücken
expressway die Autobahn, –en
eye das Auge, –n
eyeglasses die Brille, –n

F

fabulous fabelhaft
face das Gesicht, –er
factory die Fabrik, –en
fair fair
fairy tale das Märchen, –
fall *(season)* der Herbst
    in the fall im Herbst
to **fall** fallen (fällt), fiel, ist gefallen
to **fall asleep** einschlafen (schläft
    ein), schlief ein, ist eingeschlafen
to **fall down** hinunterfallen (fällt
    hinunter), fiel hinunter, ist
    hinuntergefallen
to **fall in love with** sich verlieben
    in *(+ acc)*
family die Familie, –n
family doctor der Hausarzt, ̈e/die
    Hausärztin, –nen
family tree der Stammbaum, ̈e
famished: to be famished einen
    Bärenhunger haben
famous berühmt
fantastic toll, fantastisch
    That's really fantastic. Das ist
    echt toll.
far weit
    far too much viel zu viel
farm die Farm, –en
farmer der Bauer, –n, –n/die
    Bäuerin, –nen; der Farmer, –

fashion show die Modenschau
fashionable modisch
fast schnell
fast-food stand der Schnellimbiss, –e
fat dick
father der Vater, ̈
fatty fettig
fault *(blame)* die Schuld
favorite der Liebling, –e
    favorite CD die Lieblings-CD, –s
    favorite color
      die Lieblingsfarbe, –n
    favorite program das
      Lieblingsprogramm, –e
    favorite sport der Lieblingssport
fax das Fax, –e
fear die Angst, ̈e
February der Februar
to **feed** füttern
to **feel** spüren, fühlen
    I don't feel like it. Ich habe
    keine Lust.
    **I feel like having a chocolate
    bar.** Ich habe Lust auf eine
    Tafel Schokolade.
    I feel like playing tennis. Ich
    habe Lust auf Tennis.
to **feel well** sich wohl fühlen
fellow citizen der Mitbürger, –/
    die Mitbürgerin, –nen
fellow student der Mitstudent, –en, –en/
    die Mitstudentin, –nen
fence der Zaun, ̈e
festival das Fest, –e
fever das Fieber
feverishly fieberhaft
few ein paar
field das Feld, –er
field of study das Fach, ̈er, das
    Studienfach, ̈er
figure die Figur *(sing)*
to **fill** füllen
film der Film, –e
finally endlich; schließlich; zuletzt
to **finance** finanzieren
finances die Finanzen *(pl)*
financial finanziell
to **find** finden, fand, gefunden
to **find out** herausfinden, fand
    heraus, herausgefunden; erfahren
    (erfährt), erfuhr, erfahren

fine: Fine, thanks. Danke, gut.
finger der Finger, –
fingernail der Fingernagel, ̈
to **finish reading** fertig lesen (liest
    fertig), las fertig, fertig gelesen
to **finish writing** fertig schreiben,
    schrieb fertig, fertig geschrieben
finished fertig
first *(adj)* erst; *(adv)* zuerst
    for the first time zum ersten
    Mal
first name der Vorname, –ns, –n
fish der Fisch, –e
to **fish** angeln; fischen
fit fit
to **fit** passen
    That coat doesn't fit you. Der
    Mantel passt dir nicht.
fitness center das Fitnesscenter, –
flag die Fahne, –n; die Flagge, –n
flat tire der Platte, –n, –n
    to **have a flat tire** einen Platten
    haben
to **flee** fliehen, floh, ist geflohen;
    flüchten
flight der Flug, ̈e
flight number die Flugnummer, –n
floor der Fußboden, ̈; *(story)* der
    Stock, Stockwerke; die Etage, –n
    first (ground) floor das Erdgeschoss
    on the first floor im
      Erdgeschoss
    on the second floor im ersten
      Stock
floor lamp die Stehlampe, –n
flour das Mehl
to **flow** fließen, floss, ist geflossen
flower die Blume, –n
flower shop das Blumengeschäft, –e
flowered geblümt
to **fly** fliegen, flog, ist geflogen
foggy neblig
to **follow** folgen *(+ dat)*
food das Essen; die Lebensmittel *(pl)*
foot der Fuß, ̈e
    to **go on foot** zu Fuß gehen
football team das Footballteam, –s
for *(prep)* für *(+ acc)*; *(prep)* seit
    (+ dat); *(coord conj)* denn
    I've known him for years. Ich
    kenne ihn seit Jahren.

to **forbid** verbieten, verbot,
    verboten
forehead die Stirn, -en
foreign ausländisch
foreign students office das
    Auslandsamt
foreigner der Ausländer, -/ die
    Ausländerin, -nen
forest der Wald, ¨-er
forever ewig
to **forget** vergessen (vergisst),
    vergaß, vergessen
fork die Gabel, -n
form die Form, -en
to **form** bilden
former ehemalig
fortunately zum Glück
free frei
freedom die Freiheit
freeway die Autobahn, -en
French *(adj)* französisch
French fries die Pommes frites *(pl)*
fresh frisch
Friday der Freitag, -e
    Fridays, on Fridays freitags
    on Friday afternoon am
        Freitagnachmittag
    on Friday evening am
        Freitagabend
    on Friday morning am
        Freitagmorgen
friend der Freund, -e/
    die Freundin, -nen
friendliness die Freundlichkeit
friendly freundlich
friendship die Freundschaft, -en
from *(prep) (a city, country)* aus *(+
    dat)*; *(an institution)* von *(+ dat)*
    from now on von jetzt ab
    from . . . to von ... bis
front: in front of vor *(+ acc/dat)*
fruit das Obst *(sing)*
full voll
fun der Spaß
    That's fun. Das macht Spaß.
    to have fun Spaß haben
funny lustig; komisch; witzig
furious wütend
furnished möbliert
furniture die Möbel *(pl)*
future die Zukunft

G

to **gallop** galoppieren
garage die Garage, -n
garbage bin die Mülltonne, -n
garbage can der Mülleimer, -
garden der Garten, ¨-
garden terrace
    die Gartenterrasse, -n
gas das Benzin
gate das Tor, -e
generation die Generation, -en
generous großzügig
gentleman der Herr, -n, -en
German *(adj)* deutsch
German *(language)* Deutsch
    in German auf Deutsch
German class die Deutschstunde, -n,
    der Deutschkurs, -e
German parliament der
    Bundestag
German-speaking deutschsprachig
German state das Bundesland, ¨-er
Germany *(das)* Deutschland
to **get** *(fetch)* holen; *(receive)*
    bekommen, bekam, bekommen;
    kriegen
to **get dressed** sich anziehen, zog
    an, angezogen
to **get to know** kennen lernen
to **get undressed** sich ausziehen,
    zog aus, ausgezogen
to **get up** aufstehen, stand auf, ist
    aufgestanden
gift das Geschenk, -e
gift card die Geschenkkarte, -n
gift-giving *(at Christmas)* die
    Bescherung
girl das Mädchen, -
girlfriend die Freundin, -nen
to **give** geben (gibt), gab, gegeben;
    (a gift) schenken; *(change)*
    herausgeben (gibt heraus), gab
    heraus, herausgegeben
to **give back** zurückgeben
    (gibt zurück), gab zurück,
    zurückgegeben
gladly gern (lieber, am liebsten)
glass das Glas, ¨-er
    a glass of orange juice ein Glas
        Orangensaft

two glasses of milk zwei Glas
    Milch
glasses *(eye)* die Brille, -n
glove der Handschuh, -e
to **go** gehen, ging, ist gegangen; *(by
    car, bus, train)* fahren (fährt), fuhr,
    ist gefahren
    She's going to be twenty-one.
        Sie wird einundzwanzig.
to **go along** mitgehen, ging mit, ist
    mitgegangen; mitfahren (fährt
    mit), fuhr mit, ist mitgefahren
to **go away** weggehen, ging weg, ist
    weggegangen
to **go off the deep end** ausrasten
to **go out** ausgehen, ging aus, ist
    ausgegangen; hinausgehen
to **go wrong** schief gehen, ging
    schief, ist schief gegangen
goal das Ziel, -e
God *(der)* Gott
    Thank God! Gott sei Dank!
gone weg
good gut
    Good evening! Guten Abend!
        'n Abend!
    Good morning! Guten Morgen!
        Morgen!
    Good night! Gute Nacht!
Good-bye! Auf Wiedersehen!
    Wiedersehen! Tschüss!; *(on the
    telephone)* Auf Wiederhören!
good-for-nothing
    der Nichtsnutz, -e
to **google** googeln
goose die Gans, ¨-e
gossip der Klatsch
grade die Zensur, -en
graduation der Uni-Abschluss
gram das Gramm
grandchild der Enkel, -
granddaughter die Enkelin, -nen
grandfather der Großvater, ¨-
grandma die Oma, -s
grandmother die Großmutter, ¨-
grandpa der Opa, -s
grandparents die Großeltern *(pl)*
grandson der Enkel, -
graph das Schaubild, -er
to **grasp** begreifen, begriff, begriffen
grass das Gras, ¨-er

gray grau

great spitze; toll

  really great echt spitze

great-grandfather der Urgroßvater, ‥

great-grandmother die Urgroßmutter, ‥

Greek *(adj)* griechisch

green grün

to **greet** grüßen

greeting der Gruß, ‥e

to **grill** grillen

groceries die Lebensmittel *(pl)*

ground die Erde

group die Gruppe, -n

group of three die Dreiergruppe, -n

to **grow** wachsen (wächst), wuchs, ist gewachsen

to **grow up** aufwachsen (wächst auf), wuchs auf, ist aufgewachsen; *(become an adult)* erwachsen werden

grown up erwachsen

gruesome grausam

to **guess** erraten (errät), erriet, erraten

guest der Gast, ‥e

guide dog der Blindenhund, -e

guitarist der Gitarrist, -en, -en/die Gitarristin, -nen

guy der Typ, -en; der Kerl, -e

H

habit die Gewohnheit, -en

hair das Haar, -e

hair style die Frisur, -en

hairbrush die Haarbürste, -n

haircut der Haarschnitt, -e

hairdo die Frisur, -en

hairdresser der Friseur, -e/die Friseurin, -nen

half halb

  half past one halb zwei

hall, hallway der Flur, -e

Halloween (das) Halloween

hamburger der Hamburger, -

hamster der Hamster, -

hand die Hand, ‥e

  on the other hand dagegen

handicapped behindert

hand-knit handgestrickt

handwriting die Handschrift, -en

to **hang** *(be in a hanging position)* hängen, hing, gehangen; *(put in a hanging position)* hängen

to **hang out** rumhängen, hing rum, rumgehangen

to **hang up** *(the receiver)* auflegen

Hanukkah (die) Chanukka

to **happen** passieren, passierte, ist passiert

  What's happening? Was ist los?

happy glücklich; froh; vergnügt

  to **be happy (about)** sich freuen (über + acc)

  Happy Birthday! Herzliche Glückwünsche zum Geburtstag!

  Happy New Year! Einen guten Rutsch ins Neue Jahr!

hard hart; *(difficult)* schwer

hard disk die Festplatte, -n

hardly kaum

hard-working fleißig

harmless harmlos

hat der Hut, ‥e

to **hate** hassen

to **have** haben (hat), hatte, gehabt; *(something done)* etwas machen lassen

to **have to** müssen (muss), musste, gemusst

head der Kopf, ‥e

head lettuce der Kopfsalat, -e

headache die Kopfschmerzen *(pl)*

headline die Schlagzeile, -n

headphone der Kopfhörer, -

health food store das Reformhaus, ‥er

healthy gesund

to **hear** hören

hearty herzlich

heat die Hitze

heavy schwer

height die Größe, -n

  of average height mittelgroß

Hello! Hallo! Grüß dich! Guten Tag! Tag!

help die Hilfe

to **help** helfen (hilft), half, geholfen (+ dat)

  May I help you? *(to a customer)* Sie wünschen?

her ihr, ihr, ihre

here hier

  down here hier unten

Hi! Grüß dich! Hallo! Guten Tag! Tag!

to **hide** verstecken

  hide-and-seek (das) Verstecken

high hoch (hoh-)

high-rise das Hochhaus, ‥er

high school *(college track)* das Gymnasium, Gymnasien

high school diploma das Abitur

hike die Wanderung, -en

to **hike** wandern; wandern gehen

hiking boot die Wanderstiefel, -; der Wanderschuh, -e

his sein, sein, seine

historical historisch

history die Geschichte

to **hit** hauen; schlagen (schlägt), schlug, geschlagen

hobby das Hobby, -s

hockey das Eishockey

hockey stick der Hockeyschläger, -

to **hold** halten (hält), hielt, gehalten

hole das Loch, ‥er

holiday der Feiertag, -e; das Fest, -e

home *(country)* die Heimat, -en

  at home zu Hause

  to **come home** nach Hause kommen; heimkommen

  to **go home** nach Hause gehen; heimgehen

home page die Homepage, -s

homework assignment die Hausaufgabe, -n

honest ehrlich

honey der Honig

hope die Hoffnung

to **hope** hoffen

  I hope hoffentlich

hopefully hoffentlich

hopeless hoffnungslos

hopscotch Himmel und Hölle

hors d'oeuvre die Vorspeise, -n

horse das Pferd, -e

hospital das Krankenhaus, ‥er

hot heiß; *(taste)* scharf

hotdog das Hotdog, -s

hotel das Hotel, -s

hour die Stunde, –n
   for an hour eine Stunde lang
   for hours stundenlang
house das Haus, ¨er
   at our house bei uns
house number die Hausnummer, –n
house plant die Zimmerpflanze, –n
household der Haushalt, –e
   to do household chores den
     Haushalt machen
househusband der Hausmann, ¨er
housemate der Mitbewohner, –/die
   Mitbewohnerin, –nen
housewife die Hausfrau, –en
how wie
   How are you? Wie geht's?/
     Wie geht es Ihnen?
   how many wie viele
   how much wie viel
huge riesig
human being der Mensch, –en, –en
humid schwül
humor der Humor
humorous lustig; humorvoll
hunger der Hunger
hungry hungrig
   I'm hungry. Ich habe Hunger.
to hurry sich beeilen
hurt: He won't hurt you. Er tut
   dir nichts.
husband der Mann, ¨er
hymn die Hymne, –n

I

i.e., that is d.h., das heißt
ice das Eis
ice cream das Eis
icy eisig
idea die Idee, –n
   I have no idea. Ich habe keine
     Ahnung.
ideal ideal
idealism der Idealismus
if *(sub conj)* wenn; *(whether) (sub conj)*
   ob
illness die Krankheit, –en
illustration die Illustration, –en
imagination die Fantasie
to imagine (something) sich
   (etwas) vorstellen

immediately gleich; sofort
immigrant der Einwanderer, –/
   die Einwanderin, –nen; der
   Immigrant, –en, –en/die
   Immigrantin, –nen
to immigrate einwandern
impolite unhöflich
importance die Wichtigkeit
important wichtig
impossible unmöglich
to impress beeindrucken
to improve verbessern
in, into *(prep)* in (+ *dat or acc*)
income das Einkommen
incorrect(ly) falsch
independent unabhängig
individual der Mensch, –en, –en;
   die Person, –en
inexpensive billig; preisgünstig
influence der Einfluss, ¨e
information die Information, –en;
   die Infos *(pl)*
information age das
   Informationszeitalter
informed informiert
inhabitant der Einwohner, –/die
   Einwohnerin, –nen
in-line skates die Inlineskates
innovation die Innovation, –en
innovative innovativ
insect das Insekt, –en
inside innen
instead of *(prep)* anstatt, statt
   (+ *gen*)
instructor der Lehrer, –/die
   Lehrerin, –nen
instrument das Instrument, –e
insurance die Versicherung, –en
intelligent intelligent, klug
interest *(bank)* die Zinsen *(pl)*
to interest interessieren
interested: to be interested in
   sich interessieren für (+ *acc*)
interesting interessant
international international
Internet das Internet
to interrupt unterbrechen
   (unterbricht), unterbrach,
   unterbrochen
interview das Interview, –s
invention die Erfindung, –en

inventor der Erfinder, –/ die
   Erfinderin, –nen
to invest investieren
to invite einladen (lädt ein), lud ein,
   eingeladen
iPod der iPod, –s
Irish *(adj)* irisch
iron *(for clothes)* das Bügeleisen, -
to iron bügeln
irregular unregelmäßig
island die Insel, –n
Israeli *(adj)* israelisch
Italian *(adj)* italienisch
its sein, sein, seine; ihr, ihr, ihre

J

jacket die Jacke, –n
jam die Marmelade, –n
January der Januar
jazz der Jazz
jealous eifersüchtig
jealousy die Eifersucht
jeans die Jeans, – *(pl)*
jewelry der Schmuck
Jewish *(adj)* jüdisch
job die Stelle, –n; der Job, –s
   job for a day der Tagesjob, –s
to jog joggen
jogging pants die Jogginghose, –n
jogging suit der Jogginganzug, ¨e
joke der Witz, –e
journalist der Journalist, –en, –en/
   die Journalistin, –nen
joy die Freude, –n
juice der Saft, ¨e
juicy saftig
July der Juli
to jump springen, sprang, ist
   gesprungen
June der Juni
junk food das Junkfood
just nur; bloß; *(time)* gerade
   just as good (well) genauso gut
   just now gerade

K

keyboard *(instrument)* das Keyboard, –s;
   (computer) die Tastatur, –en
kilometer der Kilometer, -

kind: What kind of music do you like to listen to? Was für Musik hörst du gern?
kindergarten der Kindergarten, ¨
king der König, -e
kitchen die Küche, -n
kitchen privileges die Küchenbenutzung *(sing)*
knee das Knie, -
knife das Messer, -
to **knock** klopfen
to **know** *(a fact)* wissen (weiß), wusste, gewusst; *(be acquainted with)* kennen, kannte, gekannt
to **know about** wissen von *(+ dat)*

L

lab die Übung, -en
lady die Dame, -n
lake der See, -n
Lake Constance der Bodensee
lamp die Lampe, -n
to **land** landen
landlord/landlady der Vermieter, -/ die Vermieterin, -nen
landscape die Landschaft, -en
language die Sprache, -n
lap der Schoss, ¨e
laptop das Notebook, -s
lasagna die Lasagne
to **last** *(take time)* dauern
last letzt; zuletzt
 at last endlich
late spät
 to **be late** sich verspäten
to **laugh** lachen
laundromat der Waschsalon, -s
laundry die Wäsche
lavatory die Toilette, -n
lawn der Rasen, -
to **lay** *(down)* legen
lazy faul
LCD projector der Beamer, -
to **learn** lernen
least: at least wenigstens
to **leave** *(depart)* abfahren (fährt ab), fuhr ab, ist abgefahren; *(let)* lassen (lässt), ließ, gelassen

lecture die Vorlesung, -en
 to a lecture, to lectures in die Vorlesung
lecture hall der Hörsaal, Hörsäle
left; to the left links
leg das Bein, -e
 Break a leg! Hals- und Beinbruch!
leisure time die Freizeit
to **lend** leihen, lieh, geliehen
to **let** lassen (lässt), ließ, gelassen
letter der Brief, -e
letter carrier der Briefträger, -/ die Briefträgerin, -nen
library die Bibliothek, -en
 to the library in die Bibliothek
lie die Lüge, -n
to **lie** *(tell a lie)* lügen, log, gelogen; *(be situated)* liegen, lag, gelegen
life das Leben, -
lifestyle der Lebensstil, -e
light das Licht, -er
light hell; *(weight)* leicht
lightning der Blitz, -e
 it's lightning es blitzt
 with lightning speed blitzartig
like wie
 like a king wie ein König
 What's your apartment like? Wie ist Ihre Wohnung?
to **like** mögen (mag), mochte, gemocht; gefallen (gefällt), gefiel, gefallen *(+ dat)*
 to **like about** gefallen an *(+ dat)*
 to **like somebody** jemand *(acc)* gern haben
 I like this jacket. Diese Jacke gefällt mir.
 I like to cook. Ich koche gern.
 I would like . . . Ich möchte ...
lip die Lippe, -n
lipstick der Lippenstift, -e
list die Liste, -n
to **listen** zuhören
to **listen to** hören; anhören
liter der Liter, -
literature die Literatur, -en
little *(size)* klein; *(amount)* wenig
to **live** *(in a country or a city)* leben; *(in a street or building)* wohnen

living: What do you do for a living? Was sind Sie von Beruf?
living accommodation die Unterkunft, ¨e
living expenses der Lebensunterhalt
living room das Wohnzimmer, -
to **load** laden (lädt), lud, geladen
location die Lage, -n
lonely einsam
long lang
to **look** schauen; *(appear)* aussehen (sieht aus), sah aus, ausgesehen
to **look at** anschauen; schauen auf *(+ acc)*
to **look for** suchen
to **look forward to** sich freuen auf *(+ acc)*
to **lose** verlieren, verlor, verloren
lot die Menge, -n
 a lot viel; eine Menge
loud laut
loudspeaker der Lautsprecher, -
love die Liebe; *(as closing of a letter)* Herzliche Grüße, Liebe Grüße
 to **fall in love with** sich verlieben in *(+ acc)*
 in love verliebt
to **love** lieben
lox der Lachs, -
luck das Glück
 Good luck! Hals- und Beinbruch!; Viel Glück!
lunch das Mittagessen
 for lunch zum Mittagessen
 to **have lunch** zu Mittag essen
 lunch break die Mittagspause, -n
luxury der Luxus

M

macaroni die Makkaroni *(pl)*
machine die Maschine, -n
magazine das Magazin, -e; die Zeitschrift, -en
mail die Post
main course das Hauptgericht, -e
majority die Mehrzahl
to **make** machen
make-up: to put on make-up (sich) schminken

man der Mann, ¨er
many viele
map die Karte, –n
  map of the city der Stadtplan, ¨e
March der März
mark *(grade)* die Zensur, –en
market der Markt, ¨e; der
  Wochenmarkt, ¨e
marriage die Ehe, –n;
  die Heirat, –en
married verheiratet
to **marry** heiraten
maternal mütterlicherseits
math die Mathe
matter
  no matter egal
  That doesn't matter! Das
    macht doch nichts!
  What's the matter with you?
    Was ist los mit dir?
May der Mai
may: to be allowed to dürfen
  (darf), durfte, gedurft
  May I help you? *(to a customer)*
    Sie wünschen?
meal das Essen
  Enjoy your meal! Guten
    Appetit!
to **mean** meinen; bedeuten; heißen,
  hieß, geheißen
meaning die Bedeutung, –en; der
  Sinn *(sing)*
meantime: in the meantime
  inzwischen
meat das Fleisch
media die Medien *(pl)*
medicine das Medikament, –e
Mediterranean Sea das
  Mittelmeer
to **meet** (sich) treffen (trifft), traf,
  getroffen
member das Mitglied, –er
to **memorize** auswendig lernen
memory die Erinnerung, –en
to **mend** flicken
menu die Speisekarte, –n
messy unordentlich
meter der Meter, –
microwave (oven) die Mikrowelle,
  –n
middle die Mitte, –n

in the middle of mitten in
(in) the middle of July Mitte
  Juli
midnight (die) Mitternacht
milk die Milch
mineral water das Mineralwasser
minute die Minute, –n
  in a minute gleich; sofort
mirror der Spiegel, –
miserable miserabel
mistake der Fehler, –
model *(photographer's)* das
  Fotomodell, –e
modern modern
modest bescheiden
mom die Mutti, –s, die Mama, –s
moment der Moment, –e
Monday der Montag, –e *(see also*
  Friday)
money das Geld
monitor *(computer, TV)* der
  Bildschirm, –e
month der Monat, –e
monthly monatlich
mood die Laune, –n
  in a bad mood schlechter
    Laune
  in a good mood guter Laune;
    vergnügt
moon der Mond, –e
more mehr
  more and more immer mehr
  not any more nicht mehr
  once more noch einmal; noch
    mal
morning der Morgen, –; der
  Vormittag, –e
  Good morning! Guten Morgen!
    Morgen!
  in the morning morgens;
    vormittags
  this morning heute Morgen
  tomorrow morning morgen
    früh
mosquito der Moskito, –s
most meist
mostly meistens
mother die Mutter, ¨
  on one's mother's side
    mütterlicherseits
  Mother's Day der Muttertag, –e

motherly mütterlich
motor der Motor, –en
motorboat das Motorboot, –e
motorcycle das Motorrad, ¨er
mountain der Berg, –e
mountain bike
  das Mountainbike, –s
mountain biking: to
  go mountain biking
  Mountainbiking gehen
mountain range das Gebirge, –
mouse *(also computer)* die Maus, ¨e
mustache der Schnurrbart, ¨e
mouth der Mund, ¨er
to **move** *(change residence)* umziehen,
  zog um, ist umgezogen
to **move in** einziehen, zog ein, ist
  eingezogen
to **move out** ausziehen, zog aus, ist
  ausgezogen
movies das Kino, –s
  to the movies ins Kino
to **mow** mähen
Mr. Herr
Mrs., Ms. Frau
much viel
  far too much viel zu viel
  too much zu viel
muesli das Müsli
  a bowl of muesli eine Schüssel
    Müsli
Munich (das) München
to **murder** ermorden
museum das Museum, Museen
mushroom der Champignon, –s
music die Musik
musical musikalisch
must: to have to müssen (muss),
  musste, gemusst
mustard der Senf, –e
my mein, mein, meine
myself, yourself, herself, etc.
  selbst

N

name der Name, –ns, –n
  first name der Vorname, –ns, –n
  last name
    der Familienname, –ns, –n
  My name is . . . Ich heiße . . .

What's your name? Wie heißen Sie?/Wie heißt du? Wie ist Ihr Name?

to **name** nennen, nannte, genannt

napkin die Serviette, -n

narrator der Erzähler, -/die Erzählerin, -nen

narrow schmal

nationality die Nationalität, -en

natural(ly) natürlich

nature die Natur

  by nature von Natur

near bei; nah

  near the university in der Nähe der Uni

neat *(tidy)* ordentlich; *(excellent)* cool; toll

neck der Hals, ⸚e

necklace die Halskette, -n

to **need** brauchen

negative negativ

neighbor der Nachbar, -n, -n/die Nachbarin, -nen

neither . . . nor weder ... noch

nephew der Neffe, -n, -n

nerves: She gets on my nerves. Sie geht mir auf die Nerven. Sie nervt mich.

nervous nervös

never nie; niemals

nevertheless trotzdem

new neu

New Year das Neujahr

  Happy New Year! Einen guten Rutsch ins Neue Jahr!

New Year's Eve der Silvesterabend, -e, (der) Silvester

news die Nachrichten *(pl)*

newspaper die Zeitung, -en

newspaper ad die Anzeige, -n

next nächst

  next to neben (+ *acc/dat*)

  next year nächstes Jahr

nice *(pleasant)* nett; *(beautiful)* schön

niece die Nichte, -n

night die Nacht, ⸚e

  at night bei Nacht; nachts

  Good night! Gute Nacht!

  last night gestern Nacht

night table der Nachttisch, -e

no nein; *(neg indef art)* kein, kein, keine

  no longer nicht mehr

no one niemand

nobody niemand

Nonsense! Quatsch!

noodle die Nudel, -n

noon der Mittag

normally normalerweise

north der Norden

  north (of) nördlich (von + *dat*)

North America (das) Nordamerika

North American *(adj)* nordamerikanisch

nose die Nase, -n

not nicht

  not any more nicht mehr

  not at all gar nicht; überhaupt nicht

  not even nicht mal

  not until erst

  not yet noch nicht

not a, not any, no kein, kein, keine

note die Notiz, -en

notebook *(computer)* das Notebook, -s

nothing nichts

  nothing at all gar nichts; überhaupt nichts

  nothing but trouble nichts als Ärger

to **notice** merken

novel der Roman, -e

November der November

now jetzt

  from now on von jetzt ab

nowadays heutzutage

number die Nummer, -n; die Zahl, -en

nut die Nuss, ⸚e

O

ocean das Meer, -e; der Ozean, -e

occasion der Anlass, ⸚e

occupation der Beruf, -e

  What's your occupation? Was sind Sie von Beruf?

o'clock: at one o'clock um ein Uhr; um eins

October der Oktober

of *(prep)* von (+ *dat*)

  Of course! Natürlich! Klar!

offer das Angebot, -e

to **offer** anbieten, bot an, angeboten

office das Büro, -s

office help die Bürohilfe

often oft

oil das Öl, -e

OK in Ordnung

old alt

old age das Alter

old-fashioned altmodisch

olive die Olive, -n

on, onto *(prep) (a vertical surface)* an (+ *acc/dat*); *(a horizontal surface)* auf (+ *acc/dat*)

once einmal

  once more noch einmal, noch mal

one *(you)* man

  one and a half eineinhalb

  one another einander

only bloß; nur; erst; *(single)* einzig

only child das Einzelkind, -er

to **open** aufmachen; öffnen

opera die Oper, -n

opinion die Meinung, -en

  in my opinion meiner Meinung nach

optimistic optimistisch

or *(coord conj)* oder

  or else sonst

orange die Orange, -n

orange juice der Orangensaft

orchestra das Orchester, -

order die Ordnung

  in order to um ... zu

to **order** bestellen

ordinary einfach

organic food store der Bio-Laden, ⸚en

organic foods die Bio-Produkte *(pl)*

originally ursprünglich

other ander-

otherwise sonst

our unser, unser, unsere

out of *(prep)* aus (+ *dat*)

outfit das Outfit, -s

outside außen

over über (+ acc/dat)
  to be over zu Ende sein; vorbei
    sein
overnight
  overnight accommodation die
    Übernachtung, -en
  to stay overnight übernachten
to owe schulden
own eigen

P

to pack packen; einpacken
package die Packung, -en
page die Seite, -n
pain der Schmerz, -en
to paint (a picture) malen; (a house)
  streichen, strich, gestrichen
painter der Maler, -/
  die Malerin, -nen
pair das Paar, -e
a pair of shoes ein Paar Schuhe
pan die Pfanne, -n
pants die Hose, -n
paper das Papier, -e; (report) das
  Referat, -e
  paperless papierlos
  piece of paper der Zettel, -
paragraph der Absatz, -̈e; der
  Paragraph, -en, -en
parcel das Paket, -e
Pardon? I beg your pardon? Wie
  bitte?
parents die Eltern (pl)
park der Park, -s
to park parken
parking lot der Parkplatz, -̈e
parking space der Parkplatz, -̈e
part der Teil, -e
partially teilweise
particularly besonders
partner der Partner, -/die Partnerin,
  -nen
party die Party, -s; die Fete, -n;
  (political) die Partei, -en
passport der Pass, -̈e
paternal väterlicherseits
path der Weg, -e
patio die Terrasse, -n
pay die Bezahlung; der Lohn, -̈e
to pay bezahlen

to pay attention aufpassen
peace der Frieden; die Ruhe
  in peace and quiet in aller Ruhe
pedestrian area die
  Fußgängerzone, -n
to peek gucken
to peel schälen
penny der Pfennig, -e
people die Leute (pl); die Menschen
  (pl)
pepper der Pfeffer
percent das Prozent, -e
perfume das Parfüm, -s
perhaps vielleicht; wohl
permission die Erlaubnis
permitted: to be permitted
  dürfen (darf), durfte, gedurft
person der Mensch, -en, -en; die
  Person, -en
personal persönlich
personnel manager der
  Personalchef, -s/die
  Personalchefin, -nen
to persuade überreden; überzeugen
pessimistic pessimistisch
pet das Haustier, -e
pharmacy die Apotheke, -n
photo das Foto, -s; die Fotografie, -n
photo store das Fotogeschäft, -e
to photograph fotografieren
physique die Figur
to pick out something sich (dat)
  etwas aussuchen
to pick up abholen
picnic das Picknick, -s
picture das Bild, -er
piece das Stück, -e
  a piece of cake ein Stück Kuchen
  piece of furniture das
    Möbelstück
pig das Schwein, -e
pile der Haufen, -
pill die Tablette, -n
pink rosarot
pizza die Pizza, -s
pizzeria die Pizzeria, -s
place der Ort, -e; der Platz, -̈e
  place of residence
    der Wohnort, -e
  place of work der Arbeitsplatz, -̈e
plaid kariert

plan der Plan, -̈e
to plan planen
to plan, to have planned vorhaben
  (hat vor), hatte vor, vorgehabt
plant die Pflanze, -n
plastic das Plastik
plate der Teller, -
play das Theaterstück, -e
to play spielen
pleasant nett
please bitte
pleased: to be pleased (with) sich
  freuen (über + acc)
plump mollig
pocket die Tasche, -n
pocket knife das Taschenmesser, -
poem das Gedicht, -e
police die Polizei (sing)
police station die Polizeiwache, -n
Polish (adj) polnisch
polite höflich
political politisch
politics die Politik
poll die Umfrage, -n
poor arm
popular beliebt; populär
population die Bevölkerung
position die Position, -en
possibility die Möglichkeit, -en
possible möglich
  as much (quickly, soon) as
    possible so viel (schnell, bald)
    wie möglich
post office die Post; das Postamt, -̈er
postal code die Postleitzahl, -en
postcard die Postkarte, -n
poster das Poster, -
to postpone verschieben, verschob,
  verschoben
postwar period die Nachkriegszeit
pot der Topf, -̈e
potato die Kartoffel, -n
potato chips die Kartoffelchips (pl)
pound das Pfund, -e
practical praktisch
to practice üben
preparation die Vorbereitung, -en
prescription only rezeptpflichtig
present das Geschenk, -e
president der Präsident, -en, -en/
  die Präsidentin, -nen

pretty hübsch
pretzel die Brezel, –n
price der Preis, –e
primitive primitiv
to **print** drucken
printer der Drucker, –
prison das Gefängnis, –se
private privat
private home das Privathaus, ¨er
pro der Profi, –s
probably wohl; sicher
problem das Problem, –e
to **produce** produzieren
product das Produkt, –e
profession der Beruf, –e
professionally beruflich
project das Projekt, –e
to **promise** versprechen (verspricht), versprach, versprochen
pronunciation die Aussprache
proud: to **be proud of** stolz sein auf *(+ acc)*
province die Provinz, –en
psychologist der Psychologe, –n/ die Psychologin, –nen
pub die Kneipe, –n; *(Austria)* das Beisel, –
  to a pub in die Kneipe
public transportation öffentliche Verkehrsmittel *(pl)*
pudding der Pudding, –s
to **pull** ziehen, zog, gezogen
punctual pünktlich
punk der Punk, –s
pure(ly) rein
purple violett
to **put** *(in an upright position)* stellen; *(stick)* stecken; *(in a horizontal position)* legen
to **put on** anziehen, zog an, angezogen; *(one's head)* aufsetzen
to **put on make-up** sich schminken

Q

qualified qualifiziert
quarter das Viertel, –
  quarter after eleven Viertel nach elf
  quarter to eleven Viertel vor elf

queen die Königin, –nen
question die Frage, –n
  to **ask (answer) a question** eine Frage stellen (beantworten)
quick(ly) schnell
quiet ruhig
quite ganz; ziemlich

R

to **race** rasen
radio das Radio, –s
rag der Lumpen, –
rage die Wut
railway die Bahn
rain der Regen
to **rain** regnen
rainy weather das Regenwetter
rare selten
rate: at any rate jedenfalls
rather ziemlich
to **reach** erreichen
to **react (to)** reagieren (auf + *acc*)
to **read** lesen (liest), las, gelesen
  The thermometer reads ten degrees. Das Thermometer zeigt zehn Grad.
to **read aloud** vorlesen (liest vor), las vor, vorgelesen
to **read through** durchlesen (liest durch), las durch, durchgelesen
ready fertig
real echt
reality die Wirklichkeit
to **realize** merken
really wirklich; echt
  That's really fantastic. Das ist echt toll.
to **rearrange** umstellen
reason der Grund, ¨e
reasonable *(price)* preisgünstig
to **receive** bekommen, bekam, bekommen; kriegen
receiver *(of a telephone)* der Hörer, –
recently in letzter Zeit
recipe das Rezept, –e
to **recognize** erkennen, erkannte, erkannt
to **recommend** empfehlen (empfiehlt), empfahl, empfohlen

recommendation die Empfehlung, –en
to **recycle** recyceln
recycling das Recycling
red rot
red cabbage der Rotkohl *(sing)*
red wine der Rotwein, –e
reduced reduziert
  sharply reduced stark reduziert
to **refill** nachfüllen
refrigerator der Kühlschrank, ¨e
refugee der Flüchtling, –e
regardless egal
registration die Anmeldung
to **regret** bereuen
regular(ly) regelmäßig
related verwandt
relationship die Beziehung, –en
relative der/die Verwandte, –en; **relatives** *(as a group)* die Verwandschaft
to **relax** ausspannen
to **renovate** renovieren
rent die Miete, –n
to **rent** mieten
to **rent out** vermieten
rental car der Mietwagen, –
to **repair** reparieren
to **repeat** wiederholen
to **replace (with)** ersetzen (durch + *acc*)
report *(for a class)* das Referat, –e; *(an account)* der Bericht, –e
to **report** berichten
representative *(political)* der Abgeordnete/die Abgeordnete, –n
republic die Republik, –en
to **reserve** reservieren
residence *(place of)* der Wohnort, –e; *(student)* das Studentenheim, –e
resolution der Vorsatz, ¨e
responsibility die Verantwortung *(sing)*
rest stop die Raststätte, –n
restaurant das Gasthaus, ¨er; das Restaurant, –s
reunification die Wiedervereinigung
Rhine *(river)* der Rhein
rhubarb der Rhabarber
rice der Reis

rich reich
ride die Fahrt, -en
to **ride** *(a bike)* Rad fahren (fährt
Rad), fuhr Rad, ist Rad gefahren
to **ride** *(a horse)* reiten, ritt, ist geritten
right richtig; das Recht, -e
 It's not right that . . . Es ist
 nicht recht, dass ...
 right around the corner gleich
 um die Ecke
 right away gleich; sofort
 That's right. Das stimmt.
 to **be right** stimmen; *(of a person)*
 recht haben
 You're right. Du hast recht.
right, to the right rechts
ring der Ring, -e
to **ring** klingeln
ripe reif
to **risk** riskieren
river der Fluss, ¨e
roast der Braten, -
rock festival das Rockfest, -e
rock group die Rockgruppe, -n
rock music der Rock
rock star der Rockstar, -s
rocking chair der Schaukelstuhl, ¨e
role die Rolle, -n
roll das Brötchen, -
romantic romantisch
roof das Dach, ¨er
room das Zimmer, -
roommate der Mitbewohner, -/die
 Mitbewohnerin, -nen
rose die Rose, -n
round rund
rug der Teppich, -e
to **ruin** kaputtmachen
to **run** rennen, rannte, ist gerannt;
 laufen (läuft), lief, ist gelaufen
 I ran out of money. Mir ist das
 Geld ausgegangen.
rush: There's no rush. Es hat
 keine Eile.
Russian *(adj)* russisch
rye bread das Schwarzbrot

S

to **saddle** satteln
to **sail** segeln

sailboat das Segelboot, -e
salad der Salat, -e
salami die Salami, -s
salesperson der Verkäufer, -/die
 Verkäuferin, -nen
salt das Salz
salty salzig
 too salty versalzen
same gleich; derselbe, dasselbe,
 dieselbe
sandal die Sandale, -n
sandwich das Brot, -e; die Stulle, -n
satisfied zufrieden
Saturday der Samstag, -e *(see also*
 Friday)
sauce die Soße, -n
saucer die Untertasse, -n
sauerkraut das Sauerkraut
sauna die Sauna, -s
sausage die Wurst, ¨e
to **save** sparen
to **say** sagen
 Say . . . Sag mal ...
scanner der Scanner, -
scarcely kaum
scared
 to **be scared (of)** Angst haben
 (vor + *dat*)
 to **get scared** Angst kriegen
scarf der Schal, -e
scene die Szene, -n
schedule *(train or bus)*
 der Fahrplan, ¨e
school die Schule, -n
schooldays die Schulzeit
science fiction die Sciencefiction
Scrabble das Scrabble
to **scream** schreien, schrie,
 geschrien
scoop *(ice cream)* die Kugel, -n
sea das Meer, -e; die See, -n
seasick seekrank
season die Jahreszeit, -en
to **season** würzen
seat der Sitz, -e; der (Sitz)platz, ¨e
second die Sekunde, -n; *(ordinal)*
 zweit
secretary der Sekretär, -e/die
 Sekretärin, -nen
to **see** sehen (sieht), sah, gesehen
 See you later! Bis später!

to **see again** wiedersehen
 (sieht wieder), sah wieder,
 wiedergesehen
seldom selten
to **select** wählen
selection die Auswahl
to **sell** verkaufen
semester das Semester, -
seminar das Seminar, -e; die
 Übung, -en
to **send** schicken
senior citizens' home das
 Seniorenheim, -e
sense der Sinn
sentence der Satz, ¨e
sentimental sentimental
separate getrennt
to **separate** trennen
September der September
serious ernst
to **serve** servieren; *(guests in a
 restaurant)* bedienen
server der Kellner, -/
 die Kellnerin, -nen;
 die Bedienung *(sing)*
service der Service
serviette die Serviette, -n
to **set** setzen
to **set the table** den Tisch decken
several mehrere
sewing machine
 die Nähmaschine, -n
to **shake** schütteln
 to **shake one's head** den Kopf
 schütteln
shape die Form, -en
shared housing die
 Wohngemeinschaft, -en;
 die WG, -s
sharp scharf
to **shave** (sich) rasieren
shaver der Rasierapparat, -e
to **shine** scheinen, schien, geschienen
ship das Schiff, -e
shirt das Hemd, -en
shock der Schock
to **shock** schockieren
shoe der Schuh, -e
shoe store das Schuhgeschäft, -e
to **shoot** schießen, schoss,
 geschossen

shopping das Einkaufen
    to go shopping einkaufen gehen
short kurz; *(stature)* klein
shorts die Shorts *(pl)*
should *(to be supposed to)* sollen,
    sollte, gesollt
shoulder die Schulter, –n
to shout schreien, schrie,
    geschrien
to show zeigen
shower die Dusche, –n
to shower sich duschen
showy protzig
siblings die Geschwister *(pl)*
sick krank
    I'm sick of it. Ich habe es satt.
    I'm totally sick of it! Das hängt
        mir zum Hals heraus!
sickness die Krankheit, –en
side die Seite, –n
side dish die Beilage, –n
silver das Silber
silverware das Besteck *(sing)*
similar ähnlich
simple einfach
since *(prep)* seit *(+ dat)*
    since then seither
to sing singen, sang, gesungen
singer der Sänger, –/
    die Sängerin, –nen
single einzig; *(unmarried)* ledig
    single-family dwelling das
        Einfamilienhaus, ¨er
sink das Spülbecken, –; *(bathroom)*
    das Waschbecken, –
to sink sinken, sank, ist gesunken
sister die Schwester, –n
sisters and brothers die
    Geschwister *(pl)*
to sit sitzen, saß, gesessen
to sit down sich setzen; sich
    hinsetzen
size die Größe, –n
skate (ice) der Schlittschuh, –e
    to go (ice) skating
        Schlittschuhlaufen gehen
ski der Ski, –er
    to go skiing Skilaufen gehen
skirt der Rock, ¨e
skit der Sketch, –es
sky der Himmel

to sleep schlafen (schläft), schlief,
    geschlafen
sleeping bag der Schlafsack, ¨e
sleeping pill die Schlaftablette, –n
sleeve der Ärmel, –
slice die Scheibe, –n
    a slice of bread eine Scheibe
        Brot
slim schlank; schmal
slipper der Hausschuh, –e
slit *(adj)* geschlitzt
slow(ly) langsam
small klein
smart klug; intelligent; clever
to smell riechen, roch, gerochen
to smoke rauchen
smooth(ly) glatt
to snore schnarchen
snow der Schnee
to snow schneien
snowstorm der Schneesturm, ¨e
so so
    So long! Auf Wiedersehen!
        Tschüss!
    so that *(sub conj)* damit
    so-called so genannt
soap die Seife, –n
soccer: to play soccer Fußball
    spielen
soccer ball der Fußball, ¨e
soccer game das Fußballspiel, –e
soccer stadium das Fußballstadion,
    –stadien
social networking soziales
    Netzwerken
society die Gesellschaft, –en
sock die Socke, –n
soft drink der Softdrink, –s
soft ice cream das Softeis
software die Software
solar energy die Sonnenenergie
soldier der Soldat, –en, –en/die
    Soldatin, –nen
solution die Lösung, –en
to solve lösen
some manche
    some . . . or other irgendein,
        irgendein, irgendeine
somebody, someone jemand
    somebody else jemand anders
something etwas

sometimes manchmal
somewhat einigermaßen
son der Sohn, ¨e
song das Lied, –er; der Song, –s
soon bald
    as soon as possible so bald wie
        möglich
sore throat die Halsschmerzen *(pl)*
sorry: I'm sorry. Es tut mir leid.
soup die Suppe, –n
sour sauer
source die Quelle, –n
south der Süden
    south (of) südlich (von + *dat*)
space der Platz
spaghetti die Spaghetti *(pl)*
Spanish *(adj)* spanisch
sparkling wine der Sekt
to speak sprechen (spricht), sprach,
    gesprochen; reden
special
    special day das Fest, –e
    special of the day das
        Tagesmenü, –s
speech die Rede, –n
    to give a speech eine Rede
        halten
to spell buchstabieren
to spend *(money)* ausgeben (gibt
    aus), gab aus, ausgegeben; *(time)*
    verbringen, verbrachte, verbracht;
    (the night) übernachten
spicy scharf
spinach der Spinat
spite: in spite of *(prep)* trotz *(+ gen)*
spoon der Löffel, –
sport coupe das Sportcoupé, –s
sport(s) der Sport
    What sport(s) do you do? Was
        für Sport machst du?
sporting goods store das
    Sportgeschäft, –e
sports program das
    Sportprogramm, –e
spring der Frühling; das Frühjahr
    in spring im Frühling (Frühjahr)
square foot der Quadratfuß
    ten square feet zehn Quadratfuß
squash *(sport)* das Squash
stable der Stall, ¨e
stadium das Stadion, Stadien

staircase die Treppe, –n

stamp die Briefmarke, –n

to **stand** stehen, stand, gestanden; *(put in an upright position)* stellen; *(endure)* aushalten (hält aus), hielt aus, ausgehalten

to **stand up** aufstehen, stand auf, ist aufgestanden

star der Stern, –e

to **start** anfangen (fängt an), fing an, angefangen; beginnen, begann, begonnen; starten

state der Staat, –en; das Land, ⸚er

statement die Aussage, –n

statistic die Statistik, –en

stay der Aufenthalt, –e

to **stay** bleiben, blieb, ist geblieben

to **stay overnight** übernachten

steak das Steak, –s

to **steal** stehlen (stiehlt), stahl, gestohlen

stepfather der Stiefvater, ⸚

stepmother die Stiefmutter, ⸚

stereo die Stereoanlage, –n

to **stick** stecken

stiff steif

still noch; immer noch

stocking der Strumpf, ⸚e

stomach der Bauch, ⸚e

stomachache die Bauchschmerzen *(pl)*

stool der Hocker, –

to **stop** halten (hält), hielt, gehalten; anhalten (hält an), hielt an, angehalten; stoppen; *(doing something)* aufhören; *(walking)* stehen bleiben, blieb stehen, ist stehen geblieben

Stop bothering me! Lass mich in Ruhe!

store das Geschäft, –e

clothing store das Kleidergeschäft, –e

department store das Kaufhaus, ⸚er

electronics store das Elektronikgeschäft, –e

gourmet foods store das Feinkostgeschäft, –e

storm der Sturm, ⸚e

stormy stürmisch

story die Geschichte, –n; die Erzählung, –en; *(in a building)* der Stock, Stockwerke; die Etage, –n

stove der Herd, –e

straight *(of hair)* glatt

street die Straße, –n

stress der Stress

to **stress** betonen

stressful stressig

striped gestreift

strong(ly) stark

stubborn dickköpfig

student *(university)* der Student, –en, –en/die Studentin, –nen; *(elem. or high school)* der Schüler, –/ die Schülerin, –nen

student choir der Studentenchor, ⸚e

student center das Studentenwerk

student ID der Studentenausweis, –e

student residence das Studentenheim, –e

studies das Studium *(sing)*

to **study** *(i.e., to attend college or university)* studieren; *(to spend time studying)* lernen

stuffed toy animal das Stofftier, –e

stupid dumm; doof; blöd; bescheuert

stylish flott

subject *(of study)* das Fach, ⸚er, das Studienfach, ⸚er

subway die U-Bahn

subway line die U-Bahn-Linie, –n

success der Erfolg, –e

such solcher, solches, solche

such a so ein

suddenly plötzlich; mit einem Mal; auf einmal

sugar der Zucker

suit *(men's)* der Anzug, ⸚e

jogging suit der Jogginganzug, ⸚e

to **suit** passen; stehen

That doesn't suit me at all. Das passt mir gar nicht.

suitable geeignet; passend

something suitable etwas Passendes

suitcase der Koffer, –

summer der Sommer, –

in summer im Sommer

summer cottage das Ferienhaus, ⸚er

summer holidays, summer vacation die Sommerferien *(pl)*

summer job der Ferienjob, –s

summer sale der Sommerschlussverkauf, ⸚e

sun die Sonne

Sunday der Sonntag, –e *(see also Friday)*

sunglasses die Sonnenbrille, –n

sunny sonnig

sunny with some clouds heiter

suntan lotion die Sonnencreme, –s

super super

supermarket der Supermarkt, ⸚e

supper das Abendessen, –

for supper zum Abendessen

to **have supper** zu Abend essen

supposed: to be supposed to sollen, sollte, gesollt

surcharge der Zuschlag, ⸚e

sure, surely sicher

for sure bestimmt

surfboard das Surfbrett, –er

surfing: to go surfing surfen gehen

surprise die Überraschung, –en

survey die Umfrage, –n

swanky protzig

sweater der Pulli, –s; der Pullover, –

sweatshirt das Sweatshirt, –s

sweet *(adj)* süß; *(candy)* die Süßigkeit, –en

to **swim** schwimmen, schwamm, ist geschwommen

swimming: to go swimming baden gehen; schwimmen gehen

swimming weather (das) Badewetter

Swiss *(adj)* schweizerisch

to **switch** wechseln

Switzerland die Schweiz

symphony die Sinfonie, –n

synagogue die Synagoge, –n

T

T-shirt das T-Shirt, –s

table der Tisch, –e

to **set the table** den Tisch decken

tablet die Tablette, –n
tablespoon der Esslöffel, –
tactless taktlos
to **take** nehmen (nimmt), nahm, genommen; *(time)* dauern, brauchen
  Take care! Mach's gut!
to **take along** mitnehmen (nimmt mit), nahm mit, mitgenommen
to **take off** *(airplane)* starten
to **take on** *(a duty)* übernehmen (übernimmt), übernahm, übernommen
to **take part (in)** teilnehmen (nimmt teil), nahm teil, teilgenommen (an + *dat*)
to **take place** stattfinden, fand statt, stattgefunden
talent das Talent, –e
talk die Rede, –n
  talk show die Talkshow, –s
to **talk** sprechen (spricht), sprach, gesprochen; reden; *(converse)* sich unterhalten (unterhält), unterhielt, unterhalten
  to **talk on the phone (with)** telefonieren (mit)
tall groß
tango der Tango, –s
task die Aufgabe, –n
taste der Geschmack
to **taste,** to **taste good** schmecken
tasteful geschmackvoll
tasteless geschmacklos
taxi das Taxi, –s
tea der Tee
  tea kettle der Teekessel, –; der Wasserkocher, –
to **teach** lehren; unterrichten
teacher der Lehrer, –/ die Lehrerin, –nen
team das Team, –s
teapot die Teekanne, –n
teaspoon der Teelöffel, –
technology die Technologie
teddy bear der Teddybär, –en, –en
teenager der Teenager, –
telephone das Telefon, –e
telephone number die Telefonnummer, –n

television der Fernseher, –; *(TV broadcasting)* das Fernsehen
to **watch television** fernsehen (sieht fern), sah fern, ferngesehen
television set der Fernseher, –
to **tell** sagen; *(a story)* erzählen
  Tell me . . . Sag mal …
  to **tell about** erzählen von
tender *(cooking)* gar
tennis: to play Tennis Tennis spielen
tennis court der Tennisplatz, ¨-e
tennis racquet der Tennisschläger, –
tent das Zelt, –e
terrible schrecklich
test die Klausur, –en; die Prüfung, –en
to **test** prüfen
text message die SMS
to **text** eine SMS schicken
textbook das Unterrichtsbuch, ¨-er; das Lehrbuch, ¨-er
than als
  better than besser als
to **thank** danken (+ *dat*)
  Thank God! Gott sei Dank!
  thank you danke; danke schön
thanks der Dank *(sing)*
  Fine, thanks. Danke, gut.
that *(sub conj)* dass
that is (i.e.) das heißt (d.h.)
theater das Theater, –
  to the theater ins Theater
their ihr, ihr, ihre
then dann; da; *(at that time)* damals
  since then seither
therapy die Therapie, –n
there dort; da
  down there dort unten
  over there dort drüben
there is, there are es gibt *(+ acc)*
therefore deshalb
thermometer das Thermometer, –
  The thermometer reads ten degrees. Das Thermometer zeigt zehn Grad.
thick dick
thin dünn; *(face)* schmal
thing das Ding, –e; die Sache, –n
to **think** denken, dachte, gedacht; glauben; meinen

I can't think of anything. Mir fällt nichts ein.
that's what you think denkste
to **think of (about)** denken (an + *acc*)
thirst der Durst
  I'm thirsty. Ich habe Durst.
this dieser, dieses, diese
  this afternoon (evening, morning) heute Nachmittag (Abend, Morgen)
thrifty sparsam
through *(prep)* durch *(+ acc)*
to **throw** werfen (wirft), warf, geworfen
thumb der Daumen, –
thunder der Donner
to **thunder** donnern
Thursday der Donnerstag, –e *(see also* **Friday***)*
ticket die Karte, –n; *(traffic)* der Strafzettel, –
tie die Krawatte, –n
tied to verbunden mit *(+ dat)*
time die Zeit, –en; *(occurrence)* das Mal, –e
  (at) any time jederzeit
  at that time damals
  (at) what time um wie viel Uhr
  every time jedes Mal
  for the first time zum ersten Mal
  on time rechtzeitig; pünktlich
  the last time das letzte Mal
  this time diesmal
  What time is it? Wie spät ist es? Wie viel Uhr ist es?
time of day die Uhrzeit
timetable der Stundenplan, ¨-e
tiny winzig
tip das Trinkgeld, –er
tired müde
title der Titel, –
to **to** zu; *(a city or country)* nach; *(an institution)* auf *(+ acc/dat)*; *(a vertical surface)* an *(+ acc/dat)*; in *(+ acc/dat)*
toast der Toast
toaster der Toaster, –
today heute
toe die Zehe, –n

together zusammen

    to **go together** *(match)* zusammenpassen

toilet das Klo, -s; das WC, -s

tomato die Tomate, -n

tomorrow morgen

    the day after tomorrow übermorgen

    tomorrow afternoon morgen Nachmittag

    tomorrow morning morgen früh

toner der Toner

tongue die Zunge, -n

tonight heute Abend

too *(also)* auch; zu

tool das Werkzeug, -e

tooth der Zahn, ¨e

toothache die Zahnschmerzen *(pl)*

toothbrush die Zahnbürste, -n

toothpaste die Zahnpasta

topic das Thema, Themen

to **touch** anfassen

tour die Tournee, -n

tourist der Tourist, -en, -en/die Touristin, -nen

tournament das Turnier, -e

towel das Handtuch, ¨er

town die Stadt, ¨e

    to town in die Stadt

trade: He's a cook by trade. Er ist Koch von Beruf.

train der Zug, ¨e

    train trip die Bahnfahrt, -en

    train station der Bahnhof, ¨e

to **train** ausbilden

training die Ausbildung

transition der Übergang, ¨e

to **translate** übersetzen

translation die Übersetzung, -en

transportation: public transportation öffentliche Verkehrsmittel *(pl)*

to **travel** reisen

travel agency das Reisebüro, -s

travel brochure die Reisebroschüre, -n

tree der Baum, ¨e

trip die Reise, -n

    to **go on a trip** eine Reise machen

trouble der Ärger

    nothing but trouble nichts als Ärger

truck der Lastwagen, -; der Lastkraftwagen, -; der Lkw, -s

true wahr; richtig

trunk *(of a car)* der Kofferraum

truth die Wahrheit, -en

to **try** versuchen

to **try on** anprobieren

to **try out** ausprobieren

T-shirt das T-Shirt, -s

Tuesday der Dienstag, -e *(see also* **Friday***)*

turkey meat das Putenfleisch *(sing)*

Turkish *(adj)* türkisch

turn: Now it's your turn. Jetzt bist du dran.

TV der Fernseher, -; *(TV broadcasting)* das Fernsehen

    to **watch TV** fernsehen (sieht fern), sah fern, ferngesehen

TV screen der Bildschirm, -e

TV set der Fernseher, -

TV show das Fernsehprogramm, -e

twice zweimal

two zwei; beide

typical(ly) typisch

U

ugly hässlich

umbrella der Regenschirm, -e

uncle der Onkel, -

under *(prep)* unter *(+ acc/dat)*

to **underline** unterstreichen, unterstrich, unterstrichen

to **understand** verstehen, verstand, verstanden; begreifen, begriff, begriffen; kapieren

to **undress** sich ausziehen, zog sich aus, sich ausgezogen

unemployed arbeitslos

unemployment die Arbeitslosigkeit

unfortunately leider

unhappy unglücklich

unhealthy ungesund

university die Universität, -en; die Uni, -s; die Hochschule, -n

    to the university zur Uni

university dining hall die Mensa

university town die Universitätsstadt, ¨e

to **unpack** auspacken

until *(prep)* bis *(+ acc)*

    not until erst

up

    to **be up** auf sein

    What's up? Was ist denn los?

upset: to get upset (about) sich aufregen *(über + acc)*

up-to-date up to date

use die Nutzung, -en

to **use** benutzen; verwenden

used: to get used to sich gewöhnen an *(+ acc)*

usually meistens; normalerweise

V

vacation *(generally of students)* die Ferien *(pl)*; die Semesterferien *(pl)*; *(generally of people in the work force)* der Urlaub

    to **go on vacation** Ferien (Urlaub) machen

vacuum cleaner der Staubsauger, -

Valentine's Day der Valentinstag

valid: to be valid gelten (gilt), galt, gegolten

valley das Tal, ¨er

vase die Vase, -n

vegetables das Gemüse *(sing)*

vegetarian der Vegetarier, -/ die Vegetarierin, -nen; *(adj)* vegetarisch

vehicle das Fahrzeug, -e

very sehr

    very short ganz kurz

via *(prep)* über *(+ dat/acc)*

vicinity die Nähe

    in the vicinity of in der Nähe von *(+ dat)*

video das Video, -s

video camera die Videokamera, -s

video game das Videospiel, -e

Vienna *(das)* Wien

view die Aussicht, -en

village das Dorf, ¨er

vinegar der Essig

violinist der Violinist, -en, -en/die Violinistin, -nen

visit der Besuch, –e
    to **come to visit** zu Besuch kommen
to **visit** besuchen
visitor der Besucher, –
vitamin das Vitamin, –e
vocabulary die Vokabeln (pl); der Wortschatz, ꞓe
voice die Stimme, –n
volleyball der Volleyball, ꞓe
vote die Stimme, –n
voucher der Gutschein, –e

W

wages die Bezahlung; der Lohn, ꞓe; der Verdienst, –e
to **wait (for)** warten (auf + acc)
to **wait tables** kellnern
waiter der Kellner, –
waitress die Kellnerin, –nen
to **wake up** aufwachen
to **wake up** (someone) wecken
walk der Spaziergang, ꞓe
    to **go for a walk** spazieren gehen, ging spazieren, ist spazieren gegangen; einen Spaziergang machen
to **walk** gehen, ging, ist gegangen; zu Fuß gehen
wall die Mauer, –n; (of a room) die Wand, ꞓe
wallet die Geldtasche, –n
to **want to** wollen (will), wollte, gewollt
war der Krieg, –e
    Cold War der Kalte Krieg
    world war der Weltkrieg, –e
warm warm; herzlich
to **warn** warnen
warning die Warnung, –en
wash die Wäsche
to **wash** waschen (wäscht), wusch, gewaschen
washcloth der Waschlappen, –
washer die Waschmaschine, –n
wastepaper basket der Papierkorb, ꞓe
watch die Armbanduhr, –en; die Uhr, –en

to **watch TV** fernsehen (sieht fern), sah fern, ferngesehen
water das Wasser
to **water** gießen, goss, gegossen
way der Weg, –e
    by the way übrigens
    in this way auf diese Weise
    on the way unterwegs
    That's just the way I am. So bin ich eben.
weak schwach
to **wear** tragen (trägt), trug, getragen; (put on) anziehen, zog an, angezogen
weather das Wetter
    What rotten weather! Was für ein Hundewetter!
    What's the weather like? Wie ist das Wetter?
weather map die Wetterkarte, –n
Web site die Website, –s
wedding die Hochzeit, –en
Wednesday der Mittwoch, –e (see also **Friday**)
weeds das Unkraut (sing)
week die Woche, –n
    day of the week der Wochentag, –e
    two weeks vierzehn Tage
weekday der Wochentag, –e
weekend das Wochenende, –n
weekly wöchentlich
weekly newspaper die Wochenzeitung, –en
Welcome! Willkommen!
    You're welcome. Bitte schön!
well gut
    to **feel well** sich wohl fühlen
well-known bekannt
well-loved beliebt
west der Westen
    west (of) westlich (von + dat)
wet nass
what was
    what . . . for wozu
    what else was ... sonst
wheel das Rad, ꞓer
wheelchair der Rollstuhl, ꞓe
when (sub conj) wenn; (sub conj) als; (question word) wann

where (to what place) wohin; (in what place) wo
    where . . . from woher
whether (sub conj) ob
which welcher, welches, welche
while (sub conj; prep + gen) während
white weiß
white wine der Weißwein, –e
who wer
whole ganz
why warum
    that's why deshalb
wife die Frau, –en
wild wild
to **win** gewinnen, gewann, gewonnen
wind der Wind, –e
    wind power die Windenergie
windless windstill
window das Fenster, –
windsurfing: to go windsurfing windsurfen gehen
windy windig
wine der Wein, –e
wine glass das Weinglas, ꞓer
wing der Flügel, –
winter der Winter, –
    in winter im Winter
winter jacket die Winterjacke, –n
winter sale der Winterschlussverkauf, ꞓe
wish der Wunsch, ꞓe
to **wish** wünschen
    to **wish a Happy Birthday** zum Geburtstag gratulieren
with (prep) mit (+ dat)
without (prep) ohne (+ acc)
witty witzig
woman die Frau, –en
women's advocate die Frauenbeauftragte, –n
women's department die Damenabteilung, –en
wonderful wunderbar; herrlich
wood das Holz
woods der Wald, ꞓer
wool die Wolle
word (in a meaningful context) das Wort, –e; (individual vocabulary item) das Wort, ꞓer
work die Arbeit

work experience die Arbeitserfahrung, –en

to **work** arbeiten; *(part-time or during vacation)* jobben

to **work as a waiter/waitress** kellnern

to **work on** arbeiten an *(+ dat)*

worked up aufgeregt

to get worked up (about) sich aufregen (über + *acc*)

worker der Arbeiter, –/die Arbeiterin, –nen

world die Welt, –en

World Cup die Weltmeisterschaft, –en

worry: Don't worry! Keine Angst!

Wow! Mensch!

wristwatch die Armbanduhr, –en

to **write** schreiben, schrieb, geschrieben

writing die Schrift, –en

in writing schriftlich

wrong falsch

Y

to **yawn** gähnen

year das Jahr, –e

for a year auf ein Jahr

last year letztes Jahr

year in, year out jahraus, jahrein

yearly jährlich

to **yell** brüllen

yellow gelb

yes ja

yesterday gestern

yesterday night gestern Nacht

the day before yesterday vorgestern

yet: not yet noch nicht

yogurt der Joghurt

you *(one, people)* man

young jung

your dein, dein, deine; Ihr, Ihr, Ihre; euer, euer, eure

youth die Jugend

youth hostel die Jugendherberge, –n

youthful jugendlich

Yuck! Pfui!

Z

zip code die Postleitzahl, –en

Index

A

Abendessen, 146
abends, 65
aber, 31, 144
die Abitur, 27
accusative case
  adjective endings in, 101–102, 104
  and dative object, 236
  der and **ein** in, 94–95
  der- and **ein-**words in, 97, 98
  personal pronouns in, 162
  possessive adjectives in, 98
  prepositions taking, 164
  reflexive pronouns in, 298–299
  in time expressions, 98
Achminow, Nina, 403–404
adjective(s)
  accusative endings of, when preceded by **der-**words, 101
  accusative endings of, when preceded by **ein-**words, 102
  accusative endings of unpreceded, 104
  comparative of, 167, 168
  dative case with, 237
  dative endings of, when preceded by **der-** and **ein-**words, 248
  dative endings of unpreceded, 249
  der words, preceded by, 342
  ein words, preceded by, 343
  genitive endings of, when preceded by **der-** and **ein-**words, 281
  nominative endings of, when preceded by **der-**words, 73
  nominative endings of, when preceded by **ein-**words, 74
  nominative endings of unpreceded, 75
  past participle as, 366
  possessive, 71–72, 98
  superlative of, 170
  unpreceded, 344

adverbs
  comparative of, 167
  superlative of, 170
After the Wall (Jana Hensel), 375
agent (passive voice), 365
Alexanderplatz (Berlin), 354
Die Alpen, 20, 125
alphabet, 8
als, 336, 349
am ____sten, 170
an, 267, 272, 274
Angles, 48
art and architecture, Austrian, 90
au (diphthong), 116
auf, 267, 272
aus, 241
  von vs., 245
außer, 241
Austria, 88–90
Autostadt Wolfsburg, 6
auxiliary verb
  position of, in past participle, 198, 199
  sein as, in perfect tense, 204

B

Die Bahn, 137
-bar (suffix), 408
Bauhaus, 284–285
bei, 241
Berlin, 377
Berliner Luftbrücke, 358
Die Berliner Mauer, 357, 367
beverages, 58
birthday parties, 236
bitte, 141
Bitte schön!, 216
body parts, 196
  in idiomatic expressions, 220, 318
books, 326–327
Brötchenservice, 122
Bundesrepublik Deutschland (BRD), 229, 358–359

C

Campingplätze, 158
capitalization of nouns, 3
Carl Schurz Society, 194
Celsius scale, 9
ch, pronunciation of, 12–13, 187
-chen (suffix), 186
clothing, articles of, 82
Cocoon Club (Frankfurt), 6
cognates, 48, 79, 115
colloquial German
  accusative prepositions, 164
  away from and *toward* in, 215
  flavoring particles, 156
  telling time, 62, 65
colors, 22
comparative, 167, 168
compound nouns, 286
congratulations, expressing, 253
conjunctions, 31
  coordinating, 144
contractions, 243
  accusative prepositions in, 164
  dative prepositions in, 243
coordinating conjunctions, 144
country names, 23

D

da-compounds, 244, 270
dafür, 166
dagegen, 166
Danke, Danke schön, 216
dann, denn vs., 150
das, 24
  accusative of, 95
dass, object clauses introduced by, 174
dates, 213
dative case, 232–234, 236–238
  with adjectives, 237
  in idiomatic expressions, 238
  with indirect object, 232
  interrogative pronoun in, 233
  personal pronouns in, 234

prepositions taking, 241, 243
    reflexive pronouns in, 301–302
    verbs taking, 237
    and word order, 236
days of the week, 51, 65
definite article
    in accusative case, 94–95
    gender of, 24
    plural forms, 25–26, 95
denn, 31
    dann vs., 150
dependent clause(s)
    position of auxiliary verb and past
        participle in, 199
    verb position in, 144, 145
der, 24. *See also* **das; die**
    accusative of, 94–95
    as relative pronoun, 308
deren, 402
derselbe, dasselbe, dieselbe, 257
der-words
    in accusative case, 97
    accusative endings of adjectives
        preceded by, 101
    adjectives preceded by, 342
    dative endings of adjectives
        preceded by, 248
    genitive endings of adjectives
        preceded by, 281
    in nominative case, 70
    nominative endings of adjectives
        preceded by, 73
dessen, 402
**Deutsche Demokratische
    Republik (DDR),** 192, 228,
    358–359, 375, 377
die
    accusative of, 95
    as feminine definite article, 24
    as plural definite article, 25–26
dieser, dieses, diese, 70, 97
diminutives, 186
diphthongs, 116
direction, indicating, 214, 266, 267
direct object, 94
doch, 141, 156, 348
die Donau, 20
Dresden, 192
du, 3, 38
du-imperative, 142
durch, 164

dürfen
    present tense of, 129
    subjunctive of, 391

E

each other, 304
ei
    as diphthong, 116
    ie vs., 49
eigentlich, 356
ein, eine, 27
    accusative of, 94–95
Einkaufsgewohnheiten, 312
ein-words
    in accusative case, 98
    accusative endings of adjectives
        preceded by, 102
    adjectives preceded by, 343
    dative endings of adjectives
        preceded by, 248
    genitive endings of adjectives
        preceded by, 281
    in nominative case, 71
    nominative endings of adjectives
        preceded by, 74
Elsener, Carl, 149
Elsener, Karl, 148
Elterngeld, 110
Elternzeit, 110
English
    German words used in, 13
    loan words in German, 57
    similarities between German and,
        48, 79, 115
    verb forms in German vs., 31
Englisher Garten (München), 176
-ent (suffix), 186
er (pronoun), 38
-er (suffix), 167, 186, 318
erneuerbare Energien, 278
es gibt, 106
Eszett (ß), 3, 12
"Ethnische Gruppen und
    Nationalitäten in Deutschland,"
    374
eu (diphthong), 116
euer, 98
Euro, 89, 316
Europäische Union (EU), 89
"Eve" (Annett Louisan), 383

F

f, pronunciation of, 351
Fahrenheit scale, 9
Die Fälscher (film), 90
family members, 92
die Farben, 22
farewells, 5
Fasching, 228
fast food restaurants, 294
Fastnacht, 228
favorite, 87
Federal Republic of Germany. *See*
    **Bundesrepublik Deutschland
    (BRD)**
Federer, Roger, 6
Feiertage, 172, 228–229
Fernsehturm (Berlin), 354
festivals, 228–229
film, Austrian, 90
flavoring particles, 141, 156
food and drink, 58, 126, 127,
    294–295, 320
"Frauen im 21. Jahrhundert," 386
Freiburg, 20
Frühstück, 121–123
für, 164
furniture, 264–265
Fußball, 166
Fußball-Weltmeisterschaft, 6
future tense, 361

G

das Gasthaus, 294–295
gegen, 164
gehen, in present-time subjunctive,
    395
gender
    and definite articles, 24
    grammatical, 38
    and noun suffixes, 186
    predicting, 220, 254, 318,
        378–379
genitive case, 278
    of interrogative pronoun **wer,**
        279
    of preceded adjectives, 281
    prepositions taking, 401
    relative pronoun in, 402
    von + dative as alternative to, 281

German Democratic Republic. *See*
Deutsche Demokratische Republik (DDR)
German language
  English loan words in, 57
  in North America, 206
  similarities with English, 48, 79, 115
  written German, 3
Germany
  ethnic groups and nationalities in, 374–375
  historical timeline (1918–present), 358–359
gern, 61
gern haben, 62
gleich, 378
glottal stop, 409
"Go West!" (Jana Hensel), 376–377
grading system, 27
grammatical gender, 38
greetings, 5, 14
Grimm, die Brüder, 347–349
grooming, 320
Gropius, Walter, 284, 285
Der Grundgesetz, 386
Gutenberg, Johannes, 326, 327
das Gymnasium, 27

H

haben
  in past perfect tense, 324
  in past-time subjunctive, 399
  perfect tense of, 205
  perfect tense with, 198
  present tense of, 60
  simple past tense of, 178, 180
  subjunctive of, 391
hängen, 268, 269
die Hansa, 165
die Harz, 20
"Der Hase und der Igel" (Brüder Grimm), 347–348
-heit (suffix), 378–379
Hensel, Jana, 375–377
her, 214
herein-, 215
herunter-, 215
hin, 214
hinauf-, 215
hinaus-, 215

hinter, 267
hobbies, 58
holidays, 228–230
house, rooms of a, 264–265

I

ich, 38
idiomatic expressions
  animals in, 350
  body parts in, 220, 318
  dative case in, 238
  food items in, 255
  housing/furnishing words in, 287
ie, ei vs., 49
-ig (suffix), 187
Ihr, 71
ihr, 3, 38
ihr-imperative, 142
imperatives, 140–142
in (preposition), 267, 272, 274
-in (suffix), 186
indefinite article, 27
  in accusative case, 94–95
  omission of, 100
independent clauses, verb position in, 144, 145
indirect object, dative case with, 232
infinitive phrases
  um, introduced by, 277
  and word order, 275–276
infinitive(s), 41
  with **-n** ending, 42
  as nouns, 254
  omission of, after modal verbs, 131
information questions
  as object clauses, 175
  verb position in, 29
inseparable-prefix verbs, past participle of, 211
Internationales Rotes Kreuz, 125
interrogative pronouns, 68
  in dative case, 233
  wen, 96
  wessen, 279
invitations, 236
irregular verbs, 105–107
  du-imperative with, 142
  past participle of, 201
  principle parts of, 335

simple past of, 332
-ium (suffix), 186

J

ja, 31
jeder, jedes, jede, 70, 97
jewelry, 188
Jugendherbergen, 158
Jugendstil, 90

K

KaDeWe, 226
Kaffee und Kuchen, 146, 236
Kalina, Robert, 316
Kalter Krieg, 358–359
Karneval, 228
kein, keine, 27
-keit (suffix), 378–379
kennen, wissen vs., 178
Kinderbetreuungsgeld, 110
kitchen utensils, 296
Die Klavierspielerin (film), 90
kn (consonant cluster), 379
kommen, present-time subjunctive of, 395
können
  present tense of, 128
  subjunctive of, 391
Kristallnacht, 358
Kuckucksuhr, 64

L

l, pronunciation of, 221
legen, 268
Lehnwörter, 57
-lein (suffix), 186
Leipzig, 192
letters, addressing of, 10
lieber, 62
Lieblings-, 87
Liechtenstein, 71
liegen, 269
likes, expressing, 61, 62
Linz, 20
literature, Austrian, 90
-los (suffix), 408
Louisan, Annett, 383
Ludwig II. von Bayern, 184

Lüneberger Heide, 20
Luther, Martin, 326
Luxemburg, 402

M

magazines, 337
mal, 141, 156
man, 122
meals, 126
"Meine Zukunft" (Nina
    Achminow), 403–404
die Mensa, 2
–ment (suffix), 186
Merkel, Angela, 386
mit, 241
Mittagessen, 146
mixed verbs
    past participle of, 211
    principle parts of, 335
    simple past of, 333
möchte, 130
modal verbs (modals), 128–131
    meaning and position of, 128
    omission of infinitive after, 131
    position of nicht in sentences
        with, 131
    position of separable-prefix verbs
        with, 134
    in reflexive constructions, 300
    simple past tense of, 178, 180
mögen
    möchte vs., 130
    present tense of, 129
    subjunctive of, 391
money, 320
months, 51
die Mosel, 20
Mozart, Wolfgang Amadeus, 113–114
München, 176
music, Austrian, 90
müssen
    present tense of, 128
    subjunctive of, 391

N

nach, 241
    zu vs., 244
nachmittags, 65
nachts, 65

narrative past. See simple past tense
nationalities, 23
neben, 267
nein, 31
Neue Bundesländer, 192
newspapers, 337
nicht ... sondern, 144
nicht, position of, 34
    and direct object, 104
    in perfect tense, 200
    in sentences with modals, 131
    with separable-prefix verbs, 134
n-nouns, 312
nominative case, 68
    adjective endings in, 73–75
    der-words in, 70
    ein-words in, 71
die Nordsee, 20
North America
    German cultural roots in, 194–195
    German language in, 206
noun(s)
    adjective in comparative before
        a, 168
    adjective in superlative before a, 170
    capitalization of, 3
    compound, 286
    predicting gender of, 186, 220,
        254, 318, 378–379
numbers
    cardinal, 9
    ordinal, 212

O

object clauses
    dass, introduced by, 174
    information questions as, 175
oder, 31
ohne, 164
Oktoberfest, 176, 229
–or (suffix), 186
ordinal numbers, 212
Ostern, 228
Österreich, 88–90
die Ostsee, 20

P

parties, 236
Passau, 20

passive voice, 362, 365
past participle
    as adjective, 366
    in dependent clause, 199
    of inseparable-prefix verbs, 211
    of irregular verbs, 201
    of mixed verbs, 211
    position of, in perfect tense, 198,
        199
    of regular verbs, 199
    of separable-prefix verbs, 209
past perfect tense, 324
past-time subjunctive
    construction of, 397
    haben and sein in, 399
perfect tense, 198–201. See also past
        participle
    formation of, 198
    with haben, 198
    position of nicht in, 200
    of sein and haben, 205
    sein as auxiliary in, 204
    word order in, 198–200
personal pronouns, 38
    in accusative case, 162
    in dative case, 234
pf (consonant cluster), 379
phone numbers, 10
place, word order with expressions
        of, 33
plural forms
    of definite articles and nouns,
        25–26, 95
    of personal pronouns, 38
polite questions, subjunctive in, 395
polite requests, subjunctive in, 394
possession, indicating, 278–279, 281
possessive adjectives
    in accusative case, 98
    in nominative case, 71–72
die Postleitzahl, 10
predicate, 67
preferences, expressing, 61
prefixes
    directional, 214
    separable. See separable-prefix verbs
preposition(s)
    accusative, 164
    dative, 241, 243
    genitive, 401
    relative pronoun as object of, 340

two-case, 267, 270, 274
  verb-preposition combinations, 368–369
present tense, 31, 41, 42
  to express future time, 43
  verbs with stem-vowel changes in, 105–107
present-time subjunctive, 390–395
  construction of, 390–391
  kommen and **gehen in,** 395
  in polite questions, 395
  in wishes and polite requests, 394
  würde + infinitive, 392–393
pronouns. *See also* personal pronouns
  interrogative, 68, 96, 233
  reflexive, 298–302, 304
  relative, 308–309
pronunciation, 12–13
  of alphabet, 8
  of **ch,** 187
  of **f, v,** and **w,** 351
  of **–ig,** 187
  of **l,** 221
  of long vs. short vowels, 80
  of **pf** and **kn,** 379
  of **r,** 255
  of **st** and **sp,** 287
  of umlauted vowels, 151
  of voiced and voiceless **s,** 319

Q

questions
  contradicting negative, 348
  object clauses, information questions as, 175
  subjunctive in polite, 395
  verb position in information questions, 29
  wo–compounds in, 371
question words, 50

R

r, pronunciation of, 255
Recyceln, 271
reflexive pronouns, 298–302
  in accusative case, 298–299
  in dative case, 301–302
  to express *each other,* 304
  with modals, 300

reflexive verbs, 304
regenerative Energien, 278
Regensburg, 20
regular verbs
  past participle of, 199
  simple past of, 330
Das Reichtagsgebäude, 374
relative clauses, 308–309
relative pronoun(s), 308–309
  in genitive case, 402
  as object of preposition, 340
renewable energy, 278
der Rhein, 20
das Rheintal, 20
rooms of a house, 264–265

S

s, voiced vs. voiceless, 319
Sachs, Hans, 323–324, 326
Sachsen, 192
Sächsische Schweiz, 6
Salzburger Festspiele, 90
Saxons, 48
Scheine, 27
"Der schlaue Student vom Paradies" (Hans Sachs), 323–324
"Schneien" (Robert Walser), 125
Schnellimbiss, 307
Schnellrestaurants, 294, 307
Schurz, Carl, 194
der Schwarzwald, 20, 64
die Schweiz, 124–125
Schweizer Alpen, 125
sein
  as auxiliary verb in perfect tense, 204
  in past perfect tense, 324
  in past-time subjunctive, 399
  perfect tense of, 205
  present tense, 40
  Sie–imperative form of, 140
  simple past tense of, 178
  subjunctive of, 391
seit, 241, 246
der Semester, 34
Semesterticket, 1, 2
separable-prefix verbs, 132–134
  meaning of, 132
  past participle of, 209
  position of, with modals, 134

  position of **nicht** with, 134
  position of prefix in, 133
  simple past of, 332
  verb-noun and verb-verb combinations behaving like, 136
shopping, 312
sich, 298
Sie, 3, 38
sie, 38
Sie–imperative, 140
silverware, 296
Silvester, 228
simple past tense, 330, 332–333
  of **haben,** 178, 180
  of irregular verbs, 332
  of mixed verbs, 333
  of modals, 178, 180
  of regular verbs, 330
  of **sein,** 178
  of separable-prefix verbs, 332
sollen
  present tense of, 129
  subjunctive of, 391
sondern, 144
sp (consonant cluster), 287
sports, 58, 166
st (consonant cluster), 287
–st (suffix), 170
Stasi, 374
statements, verb position in, 30
statt, 401
stehen, 269
Steiermark, 6, 155
stellen, 268
Studentenwohnheime, 262
student housing, 262
Studienbuch, 27
subject, grammatical, 67
subject completion, 74
subjunctive
  past-time, 397, 399
  in polite questions, 395
  present-time, 390–395
  in wishes and polite requests, 394
Südtirol, 181
suffixes. *See also specific suffixes, e.g.:* **–keit**
  directional, 214
  and gender of nouns, 186
superlative, 170
Switzerland, 124–125

T

Tag der deutschen Einheit, 229
time, telling, 58, 62, 63, 65
time expressions
    accusative case in, 98
    with present tense, 43
    referring to parts of the day, 65
    two-case prepositions in, 274
    wann, als, and **wenn,** 336
    word order with, 33
time/manner/place, 240
Tirol, 89
to, 244, 272
toasts, 253
transportation, 92
travel, affordable, 158
trotz, 401
24-hour clock, 63

U

über, 267
überhaupt, 356
um, 164
    infinitive phrases introduced
      by, 277
-um (suffix), 186
Umlaut, 3, 12, 151
und, 31
-ung (suffix), 220
die Universität, 27
Universitätsstadt, 262
universities, 1, 2, 27, 34, 82, 262
unpreceded adjectives, 344
unter, 267
-ur (suffix), 186
Urlaubstage, 172

V

v, pronunciation of, 12–13, 351
verb(s). *See also specific headings, e.g.:*
    modal verbs; present tense
    endings of, 3
    imperative form of, 140–142
    infinitive of, 41
    inseparable-prefix, 211
    irregular, 105–107
    mixed, 211

    position of, in independent and
      dependent clauses, 144, 145
    position of, in information
      questions, 29
    position of, in statements, 30
    principle parts of, 335
    reflexive, 304
    separable-prefix, 132–134, 136, 209
    with stem-vowel changes in
      present tense, 105–107
    taking dative case, 237
    verb-preposition combinations,
      368–369
Victorinox (Firma), 148–149
Vielen Dank, 216
von, 241
    aus vs., 245
    + dative (instead of genitive), 281
vor, 267, 274
vormittags, 65
die Vorwahl, 10
vowels
    pronunciation of, 80, 151
    umlauted, 12, 151

W

w, pronunciation of, 12–13, 351
Wagner, Richard, 184
während, 401
Walser, Robert, 125
wann, 29, 274, 336
warum, 29
was, as interrogative pronoun, 29, 68
wegen, 401
Weihnachten, 228
Das weiße Band (film), 90
welcher, welches, welche, 70, 97
Weltzeituhr (Berlin), 354
wen, 96
wenn, 336
wer, 29, 68
werden
    in future tense, 361
    as mixed verb, 333
    in passive voice, 362
    subjunctive of, 391
wessen, 279, 402
when, expressing, 336
wie, 29, 115

Wien, 20, 88
wie viel?, wie viele?, 29
Windenergie, 6
wir, 38
Wirtschaftswunder, 226
wishes, subjunctive in, 394
wissen
    conjugation of, 177
    kennen vs., 178
    subjunctive of, 391
wo, 29, 214, 266, 267
wo-compounds, 371
woher, 29, 266
wohin, 29, 266, 267
Wohngemeinschaft, 262
Wolfsburg, 6
wollen
    present tense of, 128
    subjunctive of, 391
word order
    expressions of time and place, 33
    independent and dependent
      clauses, 144, 145
    with infinitive phrases, 275–276
    with **nicht,** 34, 104, 131, 134
    object clauses, 174, 175
    objects, sequence of, 236
    separable-prefix verbs, 133, 134
    of subject, 67
    time/manner/place, 240
written German, distinctive
    features of, 3
würde + infinitive, 392–393

Y

yes/no questions, as object clauses, 175
you, 3
youth hostels, 158

Z

z, pronunciation of, 12–13
Zeitungen und Zeitschriften, 337
zu, 241
    expressing congratulations
      with, 253
    with infinitive phrases, 275–276
    nach vs., 244
zwischen, 267, 274
Zwischenprüfungen, 27

Credits

Text Material

p. 125: "Schneien", aus: Robert Walser, Sämtliche Werke in Einzelausgaben. Herausgegeben von Jochen Greven. Band 5: Der Spaziergang, S. 159. © Robert Walser-Zentrum, Bern. Alle Rechte bei und vorbehalten durch Suhrkamp Verlag Zürich 1978 und 1985. **p. 375:** Jana Hensel, "Zonenkinder". Copyright © 2002 by Rowohlt Verlag GmbH, Reinbek bei Hamburg. **p. 383:** "Eve" by Annett Louisan, Frank Ramond, and Matthias Hass. Copyright 2005 by Peermusic Germany GmbH and Dexter Music Publishing. Administered by Songs of Peer, Ltd. In the United States. Used by Permission. All Rights Reserved. **p. 403:** "Meine Zukunft" by Nina Achminow. In Morgen beginnt heute. Jugendliche schreiben uber die Zukunft, ed. Biedermann/Boseke/Burkert, Beltz Verlag, Weinheim und Basel 1981.

Photos and Realia

Photos are by Fritz and Rosemarie Widmaier except for the following:
p. 1: Courtesy of Andrew Dexter. **p. 2:** Courtesy of Andrew Dexter. **p. 6** (tl): Frank Richter/www. saechsische-schweiz.de. **p. 6** (tr): Tauernwind – Austria 8762 Oberzeiring. **p. 6** (b): Courtesy Cornelius Partsch. **p. 7** (tl): Autostadt GmbH. **p. 7** (r): 3deluxe/system modern gmbh, Wiesbaden. **p. 7** (bl): © Bernick | Dreamstime.com. **p. 16:** Baden-Württemberg, Tourismus Marketing GmbH. **p. 17:** Courtesy Deutsche Welle. **p. 19:** Courtesy Margaret Gonglewski. **p. 20** (t): Andrea Kaster/German National Tourist Board. **p. 20** (b): Baden-Württemberg, Tourismus Marketing GmbH. **p. 21** (r): Courtesy German National Tourist Board. **p. 21** (tl): Courtesy Austrian Tourist Office. **p. 21** (bl): Switzerland Tourism/swiss-image.ch, Christ of Sonderegger. **p. 22:** Courtesy Margaret Gonglewski. **p. 31:** Courtesy Margaret Gonglewski. **p. 34** (t): Courtesy Margaret Gonglewski. **p. 47:** © Rick Strange. **p. 54:** Courtesy Margaret Gonglewski. **p. 55:** Gottfried Wilhelm, Leibniz Universitat Hannover. **p. 57** (l, m, mr, tmr, tr): Courtesy Margaret Gonglewski. **p. 61** (tr): Courtesy Margaret Gonglewski. **p. 64** (b): Brunner Welt der Tausend Uhren Titisee. **p. 69** (bl, bm, br): Jane Pittman. **p. 71** (l): LGT Group. **p. 71** (r): LCT Group. **p. 76:** Courtesy Cornelius Partsch. **p. 78:** Courtesy StudiVZ. **p. 80:** Courtesy Margaret Gonglewski. **p. 84:** Courtesy Jürgen Zudrell. **p. 85:** Mercedes-AMB GmbH. **p. 88:** UN Multimedia. **p. 89** (t): © Dontsov Evgeny Victorovich/Shutterstock. **p. 89** (b): Courtesy Jürgen Zudrell. **p. 90** (b): © PAUL BUCK/EPA/Newscom. **p. 91:** Austrian National Tourist Office. **p. 101** (l, m, r): Jane Pittman. **p. 114:** Della Croce, Johann Nepomuk. The Mozart Family: at the piano, Wolfgang and his sister "Nannerl"; father Leopold Mozart with violin; mother Anna Maria, dead by the time the painting was made, present in her portrait. (1780-1781). Oil on canvas. 140 x 168 cm. Mozart House, Salzburg, Austria. Erich Lessing/Art Resource, NY. **p. 121** (t, b): Ferrero Deutschland GmbH. **p. 122:** Courtesy of Margaret Gonglewski. **p. 124** (b): PHOTOPRESS. **p. 125** (t): Courtesy Switzerland Tourism. **p. 125** (b): Switzerland Tourism. **p. 137** (t): Deutsche Bahn. **p. 138:** Deutsche Bahn. **p. 149** (t, bm, br): PHOTOPRESS. **p. 153:** PHOTOPRESS. **p. 155:** Courtesy Margaret Gonglewski. **p. 158** (t): Gerd Hermann. **p. 158** (b): Courtesy Margaret Gonglewski. **p. 159:** Regionaler Fremdenverkehrsverband Erzgebirge e.V. **p. 165** (r): Fußballclub Hansa Rostock. **p. 165** (l): Erster Fußballsportverein Mainz 05. **p. 166** (t): © John Cress/Corbis. **p. 172:** Courtesy Margaret Gonglewski. **p. 174** (l, r): Jane Pittman. **p. 176:** Tourismusamt der Landeshauptstadt München, Film- und Fotoservice. **p. 184** (b): Courtesy Deutsche Zentrale für Tourismus (German National Tourist Board). **p. 187** (l): Courtesy of Margaret Gonglewski. **p. 187** (r): Courtesy of Cornelius Partsch. **p. 190:** © Bettmann/CORBIS. **p. 194** (ml): Courtesy of Deutsche Post AG. **p. 194** (b): © gors4730/Fotolia. **p. 206** (b): Courtesy Margaret Gonglewski. **p. 208** (bl, br): Jane Pittman. **p. 212:** Lang. **p. 217:** Courtesy of Cornelius Partsch. **p. 220:** Courtesy of Cornelius Partsch.

EUROPA 2012

Mitglieder der Europäischen Union (EU-27)

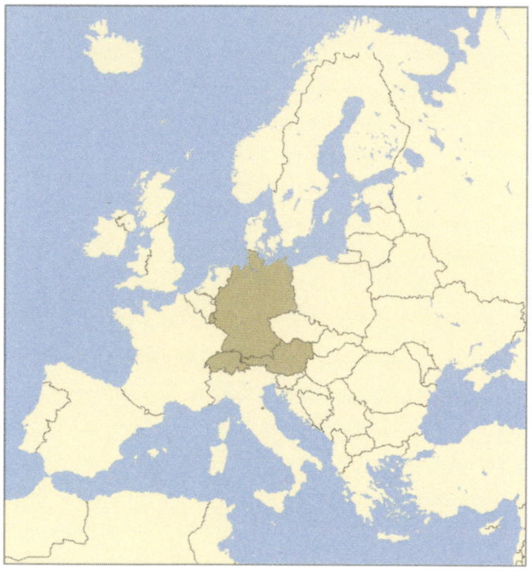

Deutschsprachige Länder

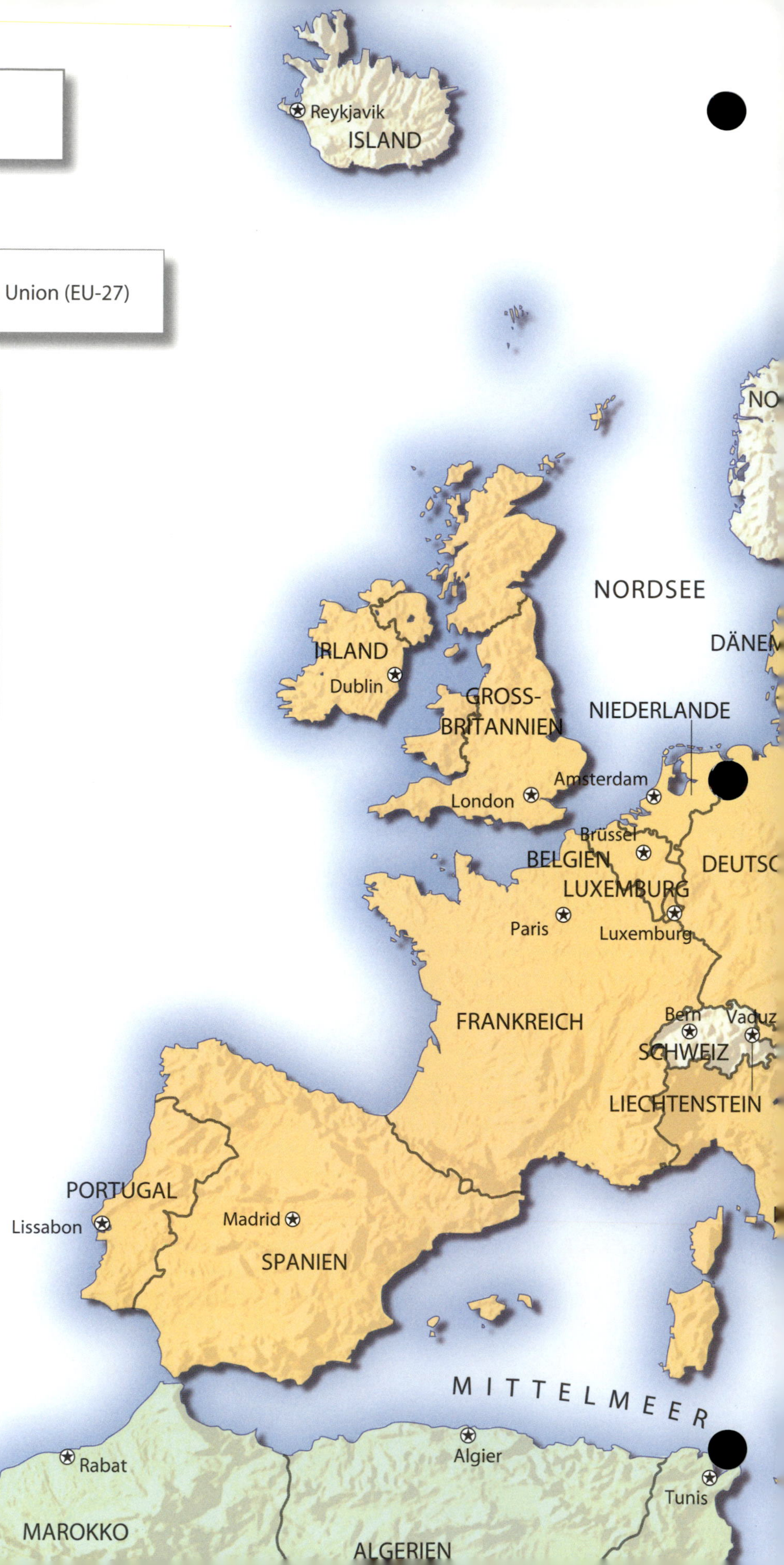
Reykjavik
ISLAND
NORDSEE
DÄNEM
NO
IRLAND
Dublin
GROSS-
BRITANNIEN
NIEDERLANDE
Amsterdam
London
Brüssel
BELGIEN
DEUTSC
LUXEMBURG
Paris
Luxemburg
ATLANTISCHER
OZEAN
FRANKREICH
Bern
Vaduz
SCHWEIZ
LIECHTENSTEIN
N
500 Kilometer
500 Meilen
PORTUGAL
Lissabon
Madrid
SPANIEN
MITTELMEER
Rabat
Algier
Tunis
MAROKKO
ALGERIEN